A Reader in

International Corporate Finance

Volume Two

A Reader in

International Corporate Finance

Edited by
Stijn Claessens and Luc Laeven

Volume Two

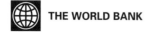 **THE WORLD BANK**

©2006 The International Bank for Reconstruction and Development / The World Bank
1818 H Street NW
Washington DC 20433
Telephone: 202-473-1000
Internet: www.worldbank.org
E-mail: feedback@worldbank.org

1 2 3 4 5 09 08 07 06

This volume is a product of the staff of the International Bank for Reconstruction and Development / The World Bank. The findings, interpretations, and conclusions expressed in this volume do not necessarily reflect the views of the Executive Directors of The World Bank or the governments they represent.

The World Bank does not guarantee the accuracy of the data included in this work. The boundaries, colors, denominations, and other information shown on any map in this work do not imply any judgement on the part of The World Bank concerning the legal status of any territory or the endorsement or acceptance of such boundaries.

ISBN-10:   0-8213-6700-5
ISBN-13:   978-0-8213-6700-1
eISBN: 0-8213-6701-3
eISBN-13:   978-0-8213-6701-8
DOI: 10.1596/978-0-8213-6700-1

Library of Congress Cataloging-in-Publication data has been applied for.

Contents

v

VOLUME II. PART III. POLITICAL ECONOMY OF FINANCE

Book Title:

Foreword

Y20

This two-volume set reprints more than twenty of what we think are the most influential articles on international corporate finance published over the course of the past six years. The book covers a range of topics covering the following six areas: law and finance, corporate governance, banking, capital markets, capital structure and financing constraints, and political economy of finance. All papers have appeared in top academic journals and have been widely cited in other work.

The purpose of the book is to make available to researchers and students, in an easy way and at an affordable price, a collection of articles offering a review of the present thinking on topics in international corporate finance. The book is ideally suited as an accompaniment to existing textbooks for courses on corporate finance and emerging market finance at the graduate economics, law, and MBA levels.

The articles selected reflect two major trends in the corporate finance literature that are significant departures from prior work: One is the increased interest in international aspects of corporate finance, particularly topics specific to emerging markets. The other is the increased awareness of the importance of institutions in explaining differences in corporate finance patterns—at the country and firm levels—around the world. The latter has culminated in a new literature known as the "law and finance literature," which focuses on the legal underpinnings of finance. It has also been accompanied by a greater understanding of the importance of political economy factors in countries' economic development and has led to the increased application of a political economy framework to the study of corporate finance.

This collection offers an overview of the present thinking on topics in international corporate finance. We hope that the papers in this book will serve the role of gathering in one place the background reading most often used for an advanced course in corporate finance. We also think that researchers will appreciate the benefit of having all these articles in one place, and we hope that the book will stimulate new research and thinking in this exciting new field. We trust the students and their instructors will deepen their understanding of international corporate finance by reading the papers. Of course, any of the remaining errors in the papers included in this book are entirely those of the authors and not of the editors.

Acknowledgments

The editors wish to thank the following authors and publishers who have kindly given permission for the use of copyright material.

Blackwell Publishing for the following articles:
Stijn Claessens and Luc Laeven (2003), "Financial Development, Property Rights, and Growth," *Journal of Finance*, Vol. 58 (6), pp. 2401–36; Stijn Claessens, Simeon Djankov, Joseph Fan, and Larry Lang (2002), "Disentangling the Incentive and Entrenchment Effects of Large Shareholdings," *Journal of Finance*, Vol. 57 (6), pp. 2741–71; Alexander Dyck and Luigi Zingales (2004), "Private Benefits of Control: An International Comparison," *Journal of Finance*, Vol. 59 (2), pp. 537–600; Maria Soledad Martinez Peria and Sergio L. Schmukler (2001), "Do Depositors Punish Banks for Bad Behavior? Market Discipline, Deposit Insurance, and Banking Crises," *Journal of Finance*, Vol. 56 (3), pp. 1029–51; Peter Blair Henry (2000), "Stock Market Liberalization, Economic Reform, and Emerging Market Equity Prices," *Journal of Finance*, Vol. 55 (2), pp. 529–64; Utpal Bhattacharya and Hazem Daouk (2002), "The World Price of Insider Trading," *Journal of Finance*, Vol. 57 (1), pp. 75–108; Rafael La Porta, Florencio Lopez-de-Silanes, and Andrei Shleifer (2006), "What Works in Securities Laws?" *Journal of Finance*, Vol. 61 (1), pp. 1–32; Art Durnev, Randall Morck, and Bernard Yeung (2004), "Value-Enhancing Capital Budgeting and Firm-Specific Stock Return Variation," *Journal of Finance*, Vol. 59 (1), pp. 65–105; Laurence Booth, Varouj Aivazian, Asli Demirgüç-Kunt, and Vojislav Maksimovic (2001), "Capital Structures in Developing Countries," *Journal of Finance*, Vol. 56 (1), pp. 87–130; Mihir Desai, Fritz Foley, and James Hines (2004), "A Multinational Perspective on Capital Structure Choice and Internal Capital Markets," *Journal of Finance*, Vol. 59 (6), pp. 2451–87; Thorsten Beck, Asli Demirgüç-Kunt, and Vojislav Maksimovic (2005), "Financial and Legal Constraints to Growth: Does Firm Size Matter?" *Journal of Finance*, Vol. 60 (1), pp. 137–77.

Elsevier for the following articles:
Thorsten Beck, Asli Demirgüç-Kunt, and Ross Levine (2003), "Law, Endowments, and Finance," *Journal of Financial Economics*, Vol. 70 (2), pp. 137–81; Stefano Rossi and Paolo F. Volpin (2004), "Cross-Country Determinants of Mergers and Acquisitions," *Journal of Financial Economics*, Vol. 74 (2), pp. 277–304; Paola Sapienza (2004), "The Effects of Government Ownership on Bank Lending," *Journal of Financial Economics*, Vol. 72 (2), pp. 357–84; Kee-Hong Bae, Jun-Koo Kang, and Chan-Woo Lim (2002), "The Value of Durable Bank Relationships: Evidence from Korean Banking Shocks," *Journal of Financial Economics*, Vol. 64 (2), pp.

147–80; Geert Bekaert, Campbell R. Harvey, and Christian Lundblad (2005), "Does Financial Liberalization Spur Growth?" *Journal of Financial Economics*, Vol. 77 (1), pp. 3–55; Raghuram G. Rajan and Luigi Zingales (2003), "The Great Reversals: The Politics of Financial Development in the 20th Century," *Journal of Financial Economics*, Vol. 69 (1), pp. 5–50; Simon Johnson and Todd Mitton (2003), "Cronyism and Capital Controls: Evidence from Malaysia," *Journal of Financial Economics*, Vol. 67 (2), pp. 351–82.

Oxford University Press for the following article:
Inessa Love (2003), "Financial Development and Financing Constraints: International Evidence from the Structural Investment Model," *Review of Financial Studies*, Vol. 16 (3), pp. 765–91.

American Economic Association for the following article:
Raymond Fisman (2001), "Estimating the Value of Political Connections," *American Economic Review*, Vol. 91 (4), pp. 1095–1102.

MIT Press for the following articles:
Josh Lerner and Antoinette Schoar (2005), "Does Legal Enforcement Affect Financial Transactions? The Contractual Channel in Private Equity," *Quarterly Journal of Economics*, Vol. 120 (1), pp. 223–46; Marianne Bertrand, Paras Mehta, and Sendhil Mullainathan (2002), "Ferreting Out Tunneling: An Application to Indian Business Groups," *Quarterly Journal of Economics*, Vol. 117 (1), pp. 121–48; Rafael La Porta, Florencio Lopez-de-Silanes, and Guillermo Zamarripa (2003), "Related Lending," *Quarterly Journal of Economics*, Vol. 118 (1), pp. 231–68.

We would like to thank Rose Vo for her assistance in obtaining the copyrights of the articles from the authors and publishers, Joaquin Lopez for his technical assistance in reproducing the papers, Stephen McGroarty of the Office of the Publisher of the World Bank for his assistance and guidance in publishing the book, and the World Bank for financial support.

The views presented in these published papers are those of the authors and should not be attributed to, or reported as reflecting, the position of the World Bank, the International Monetary Fund, the executive directors of both organizations, or any other organization mentioned therein. The book was largely completed when the second editor was at the World Bank.

Book Title:
Introduction
y20

Volume I. Part I. Law and Finance

Volume I begins with an examination of the legal and financial aspects of international capital markets. In recent years, there has been an increased interest in international aspects of corporate finance. There are stark differences in financial structures and financing patterns of corporations around the world, particularly as they relate to emerging markets. Recent work has suggested that most of these differences can be explained by differences in laws and institutions of countries and in countries' economic and other endowments. These relationships have been the focus of a new literature on law and finance. La Porta et al. (1997, 1998) were the first to show that the legal traditions of a country determine to a large extent the financial development of a country. They started a large literature investigating the determinants and effects of legal systems across countries.

In chapter 1, "Law, Endowments, and Finance," Thorsten Beck, Asli Demirguc-Kunt, and Ross Levine contribute to this literature by assessing the importance of both legal traditions and property rights institutions. The law and finance theory suggests that legal traditions brought by colonizers differ in protecting the rights of private investors in relation to the state, with important implications for financial markets. The endowments theory argues that initial conditions—as proxied by natural endowments, including the disease environment—influence the formation of long-lasting property rights institutions that shape financial development, even decades or centuries later. Using information on the origin of the law and on the disease environment encountered by colonizers centuries ago, the authors extract the independent effects of both law and endowments on financial development. They find evidence supporting both theories, although the initial endowments theory explains more of the cross-country variation in financial development than the legal traditions theory does. This suggests that there are economic and other forces at play that make certain initial conditions translate into the institutional environments of today.

In chapter 2, "Financial Development, Property Rights, and Growth," Stijn Claessens and Luc Laeven add to this literature by showing that better legal and property rights institutions affect economic growth through two equally important channels: one is improved access to finance resulting from greater financial development, the channel already highlighted in the law and finance literature; the other is improved investment allocation resulting from more secure property rights, as firms and other investors allocate resources raised in a more efficient manner. Quantitatively, the effects of these two channels on economic growth are similar. This suggests that the legal system is important not only for financial sector development but also for an efficient operation of the real sectors. Better property rights, for example, can stimulate investment in sectors that are more intangibles-intensive or that heavily depend on intellectual property rights, such as the services, software, and telecommunications industries. As these industries have become drivers of growth in many countries, the second channel has become more important.

In chapter 3, "Does Legal Enforcement Affect Financial Transactions? The Contractual Channel in Private Equity," Josh Lerner and Antoinette Schoar show that legal tradition and law enforcement have direct implications for how financial contracts are shaped. Taking a much more micro approach and using data on private equity investments in developing countries, they show that investments in high-enforcement and common law nations often use convertible preferred stock with covenants, while investments in low-enforcement and civil law nations tend to use common stock and debt and rely on equity and board control. While relying on ownership rather than contractual provisions may help to alleviate legal enforcement problems, there appears to be a real cost to operating in a low-enforcement environment because transactions in low-enforcement countries have lower valuations and returns. In other words, the low-enforcement environments force investors to use less-than-optimal contracts to assure their ownership and control rights, which in turn makes the operations of the businesses less efficient.

Volume I. Part II. Corporate Governance

Corporate governance is another field that has gained increased interest from academics and policy makers around the world in the past decade, spurred by major corporate scandals and governance problems in a host of countries, including the corporate scandals of Enron in the United States and Parmalat in Italy and the expropriation of minority shareholders in the East Asian crisis countries and other emerging countries. Governance problems are particularly pronounced in many emerging countries where family control is the predominant form of corporate ownership and where minority shareholder rights are often not enforced.

In chapter 4, "Disentangling the Incentive and Entrenchment Effects of Large Shareholdings," Stijn Claessens, Simeon Djankov, Joseph Fan, and Larry Lang show that ownership of firms in East Asian countries is highly concentrated and that there is often a large difference between the control rights and the cash-flow rights of the principal shareholder of the firm. They argue that the larger the cash-flow rights of the shareholder, the more his or her incentives are aligned with those of the minority shareholder because the investor has his or her own money at stake. On the other hand, control rights give the principal owner the ability to direct the firm's resources. The larger the difference between control and cash-flow rights, the more likely that the principal shareholder is entrenched and that the minority shareholders are expropriated as the controlling owner directs resources to his or her own advantages. Using data on a large number of listed companies in eight East Asian countries, the authors find that firm value increases with the cash-flow rights of the largest shareholder, consistent with a positive incentive effect; however, firm value falls when the control rights of the largest shareholder exceed its cash-flow ownership, consistent with an entrenchment effect. This suggests expropriation, which may have further economic costs as resources are poorly invested.

The private benefits of control for the controlling shareholder are often substantial, particularly in environments where shareholder rights are low. This explains why concentrated ownership is the predominant form of ownership around the world, particularly in developing economies, but also in continental Europe, where property rights are weaker and often poorly enforced. In chapter 5, "Private Benefits of Control: An International Comparison," Alexander Dyck and Luigi Zingales propose a method that estimates the private benefits of control. For a sample of 39 countries and using individual transactions, they find that private benefits of control vary widely across countries, from a low of −4 percent to a high of +65 percent. Across countries, higher private benefits of control are associated with less developed capital markets, more concentrated ownership, and more privately negotiated privatizations. Legal institutions plus enforcement and pressure by the media appear to be important factors in curbing private benefits of control. Because private benefits are associated with inefficient investment, their findings confirm the importance of establishing strong property rights and enforcing these to increase growth.

Controlling shareholders often devise complex ownership structures of firms (for example, through pyramidal structures) to create a gap between voting rights and cash-flow rights and to be able to direct resources through internal markets to affiliated firms. This is particularly the case for business groups in emerging markets. Owners of such business groups are often accused of expropriating minority shareholders by tunneling resources from firms where they have low cash-flow rights—with little costs of taking away money—to firms where they have high cash-flow rights—with large gains of bringing in money. In chapter 6, "Ferreting Out Tunneling: An Application to Indian Business Groups," Marianne Bertrand, Paras Mehta, and Sendhil Mullainathan propose a methodology to measure the extent of tunneling activities in business groups. This methodology rests on isolating and then testing the distinctive implications of the tunneling hypothesis for the propagation of earnings shocks across firms within a group. Using data on Indian business groups, the authors find a significant amount of tunneling, much of it occurring via nonoperating components of profit. This suggests a cost-of-business group that may have to be mitigated by some other measures, such as better property rights, increased disclosure, and specific restrictions (such as preventing or limiting intragroup ownership structures).

The threat of takeover can play a potentially important disciplining role for poorly governed firms because management risks being removed; however, in practice, the market for corporate control is generally inactive in countries where it is most needed: where shareholder protection is weak. The rules limiting takeovers are often more restricted in these environments, making domestic takeovers more difficult. Still, there is evidence that foreign takeovers can have important positive implications for the governance of local target firms, particularly in countries with poor investor protection. This is the theme of chapter 7, "Cross-Country Determinants of Mergers and Acquisitions," by Stefano Rossi and Paolo Volpin. They study the determinants of mergers and acquisitions (M&As) around the world by focusing on differences in laws and regulations across countries. They find that M&A activity is significantly larger in countries with better accounting standards and stronger shareholder protection. In cross-border deals, targets are typically from countries with poorer investor protection than their acquirers' countries, suggesting that cross-border transactions play a governance role by improving the degree of investor protection within target firms. As such, globalization and internationalization of financial services can help countries improve their corporate governance arrangements.

Volume I. Part III. Banking

Another common feature of developing countries is the predominance of state banks. State banks also played an important role in many industrial countries, at least until recently, but many governments have privatized in the past decade. In 1995, government ownership of banks around the world averaged around 42 percent (La Porta et al. 2002). In chapter 8, "The Effects of Government Ownership on Bank Lending," Paola Sapienza uses information on individual loan contracts in Italy, where lending by state-owned banks represents more than half of total lending, to study the effects of government ownership on bank lending behavior. She finds that lending by state banks is inefficient. State-owned banks charge lower interest rates than do privately owned banks to similar or identical firms, even if firms are able to borrow more from privately owned banks. State-owned banks also favor large firms and firms located in depressed areas, again in contrast to the choices of private banks. Finally, the lending behavior of state-owned banks is affected by the electoral results of the party affiliated with the bank: the stronger the political party in the area where the firm is borrowing, the lower the interest rates charged. This suggests that the political forces affect the lending behavior of state-owned banks in an adverse manner and offers an argument for the privatization of state-owned banks.

Private banks can, however, also have problems when not properly governed and monitored. When banks are privately owned in emerging economies, they are often part of business groups. This can create incentive problems that result in lending on preferential terms. More generally, banks in many countries lend to firms controlled by the bank's owners. This type of lending is known as "insider lending" or "related lending." In chapter 9, "Related Lending," Rafael La Porta, Florencio Lopez-de-Silanes, and Guillermo Zamarripa examine the benefits of related lending, using data on bank-borrower relationships in Mexico. The authors show that related lending in Mexico is prevalent and takes place on better terms than arm's-length lending. This could still be consistent with an efficient allocation of resources, but the authors show that related loans are significantly more likely to default and that when they default, they have lower recovery rates than unrelated loans. Their evidence for Mexico supports the view that related lending is often a manifestation of looting, particularly in weak institutional environments. The costs of this are often incurred by the government and taxpayers, as happened in Mexico when many of the private banks experienced financial distress and had to be rescued by the government, which provided fiscal resources for their recapitalization.

However, close ties between banks and industrial groups need not be inefficient; they can create valuable relationships, particularly in environments where hard information on borrowers is sparse. As such, relationships can substitute for a weaker institutional environment. In chapter 10, "The Value of Durable Bank Relationships: Evidence from Korean Banking Shocks," Kee-Hong Bae, Jun-Koo Kang, and Chan-Woo Lim examine the value of durable bank relationships in the Republic of Korea, using a sample of exogenous events that negatively affected Korean banks during the financial crisis of 1997–98. The authors show that adverse shocks to banks have a negative effect not only on the value of the banks themselves but also on the value of their client firms. They also show that this adverse effect on firm value is a decreasing function of the financial health of both the banks and their client firms. These results indicate that bank relationships were valuable to this group of firms; however, whether the relationship supported an efficient allocation of resources is not clear.

Given the importance of banks in developing countries' financial intermediation, it is essential that banks be properly supervised and monitored, a task most often assigned to the bank supervisory agency. When bank supervisors fail to discipline banks, however, it is up to the depositors to monitor banks and punish banks for bad behavior by withdrawing deposits. In chapter 11, "Do Depositors Punish Banks for Bad Behavior? Market Discipline, Deposit Insurance, and Banking Crises," Maria Soledad Martinez Peria and Sergio Schmukler study whether this form of market discipline is effective and whether it is affected by the presence of deposit insurance. They focus on the experiences of Argentina, Chile, and Mexico during the 1980s and 1990s. They find that depositors discipline banks by withdrawing deposits and by requiring higher interest rates, and their responsiveness to bank risk taking increases in the aftermath of crises. Deposit insurance does not appear to diminish the extent of market discipline. This suggests that in a weak institutional environment, where bank supervision fails to mitigate excessive risks taking by banks, depositors and other bank claimholders can play an important role in the monitoring of financial institutions.

Volume II. Part I. Capital Markets

Volume II opens with a selection of articles on capital markets. Equity and bond finance raised in capital markets (as an alternative to bank finance) has become increasingly important for corporations around the world. The increase in the use of markets for raising capital are in part resulting from rising equity prices that have triggered new issuance. Lower interest rates have also caused many firms to opt for corporate bonds. Also important, especially in developing countries, as institutional fundamentals are improving substantially, there has been an improved willingness on the part of international investors to invest and provide funds. As emerging stock markets have been liberalized, global investors have been increasingly seeking to diversify assets in these markets. The effects of these measures have been researched in a number of papers.

Stock market liberalization (that is, the decision by a country's government to allow foreigners to purchase shares in that country's stock market) has been found to have real effects on the economic performance of a country. In chapter 1, "Stock Market Liberalization, Economic Reform, and Emerging Market Equity Prices," Peter Blair Henry shows that a country's aggregate equity price index experiences substantial abnormal returns during the period leading up to the implementation of its initial stock market liberalization. This result is consistent with the prediction of standard international asset-pricing models that stock market liberalization reduces a country's cost of equity capital by allowing for risk sharing between domestic and foreign agents. This reduced cost of capital in turn can be expected to lead to greater investment and growth.

Stock market liberalization has indeed been found to have positive ramifications for overall investment and economic growth. In chapter 2, "Does Financial Liberalization Spur Growth?" Geert Bekaert, Campbell Harvey, and Christian Lundblad show that equity market liberalizations, on average, lead to a 1 percent increase in annual real economic growth. This effect appears to have been most pronounced in countries with a strong institutional environment, suggesting that liberalization must be accompanied by a strengthening of the institutional environment to reap all of the benefits.

Other evidence confirms the need for additional policy measures besides liberalization. Not all stock markets work as efficiently as they should. In particular, insider trading is a common feature of many stock markets. Although most stock markets have established laws to prevent insider trading, enforcement is poor in many countries, and investors get worse prices and rates of return. In chapter 3, "The World Price of Insider Trading," Utpal Bhattacharya and Hazem Daouk analyze the quality of enforcement of insider trading laws. They show that while insider trading laws exist in the majority of countries with stock markets, enforcement—as evidenced by actual prosecutions of people engaging in insider trading—has taken place in only about one-third of these countries. Their empirical analysis shows that the cost of equity in a country does not change after the introduction of insider trading laws, but only decreases significantly after the first prosecution, suggesting that enforcement of the law is critical, rather than just the adoption of the insider trading law.

The question remains, however, whether stock markets should be regulated by relying mostly on the government using public enforcement by securities commissions and the like or whether the emphasis should be on self-regulation, relying on private enforcement by giving individuals the legal tools to litigate in case of abuses. In chapter 4, "What Works in Securities Laws?" Rafael La Porta, Florencio Lopez-De-Silanes, and Andrei Shleifer tackle this complex matter by examining the effect of different designs of securities laws on stock market development in 49 countries. The authors find little evidence that public enforcement benefits stock markets, but strong evidence that laws mandating disclosure and facilitating private enforcement through liability rules benefit stock markets' development—with regard to the size of the market, the number of firms listed, and the new issuance. Their results echo those analyzing the banking system, where it has been found that supervision by government authorities often does not deliver the results desired, but that private sector oversight can be effective, especially in weak institutional environments.

A well-functioning stock market should allow firms not only to raise financing but also to produce more informative stock prices. Where stock prices are more informative, this induces better governance and more efficient capital investment decisions. However, in many developing countries, the cost of collecting information on firms is high, resulting in less trading by investors with private information, leading to less informative stock prices. In chapter 5, "Value-Enhancing Capital Budgeting and Firm-Specific Stock Return Variation," Art Durnev, Randall Morck, and Bernard Yeung introduce a method to gauge the informativeness of a company's stock price. They base their measure of informativeness on the magnitude of firm-specific return variation. The idea is that a more informative stock displays a higher stock variation because stock variation occurs because of trading by investors with private information. The authors document this measure of stock price informativeness for a large number of countries. They then go on to show that the economic efficiency of corporate investment, as measured by Tobin's Q (the ratio of the market value of a firm's assets to the replacement value of its assets—a measure of firm efficiency and growth prospects), is positively related to the magnitude of firm-specific variation in stock returns, suggesting that more informative stock prices facilitate more efficient corporate investment.

Volume II. Part II. Capital Structure and Financial Constraints

Because of large institutional differences and differences in the relative importance of the banking system and the equity and bond markets, it will come as no surprise that capital structures of firms vary widely across countries. In chapter 6, "Capital Structures in Developing Countries," Laurence Booth, Varouj Aivazian, Asli Demirguc-Kunt, and Vojislav Maksimovic document capital structure choices of firms in 10 developing countries and then analyze the determinants of these structures. They find that although some of the factors that are important in explaining capital structure in developed countries (such as profitability and asset tangibility of the firm) carry over to developing countries, there are persistent differences across countries, indicating that specific country factors are at work. The authors explore obvious candidates such as the institutional framework governing bankruptcy, accounting standards, and the availability of alternative forms of financing, but their smaller set of countries does not allow them to explain in a definite way which of these may be more important.

More generally, it is difficult to disentangle the impact of different institutional features on capital structure choices in a cross-country setting because there are so many country-specific factors to control for. In chapter 7, "A Multinational Perspective on Capital Structure Choice and Internal Capital Markets," Mihir Desai, Fritz Foley, and James Hines therefore take advantage of a unique dataset on the capital structure of foreign affiliates of U.S. multinationals to further our understanding of the institutional determinants of capital structure. The authors find that capital structure choice is significantly affected by three institutional factors: tax environment, capital market development, and creditor rights. They show that financial leverage of subsidiaries is positively affected by local tax rates. They also find that multinational affiliates are financed with less external debt in countries with underdeveloped capital markets or weak creditor rights, likely reflecting the disadvantages of higher local borrowing costs. Instrumental variable analysis—to control for other factors driving these results—indicates that greater borrowing from parent companies substitutes for three-quarters of reduced external borrowing induced by weak local capital market conditions. Multinational firms therefore appear to employ internal capital markets opportunistically to overcome imperfections in external capital markets. As such, globalization and internationalization of financial services can offer some benefits for countries with weak institutional environments.

Besides a limited way to control for cross-country differences, another complication of studying the determinants of capital structure is that not all firms demand external finance. Many successful firms finance their investments internally and do not need to access outside finance. For these firms, financial sector development thus matters less. The important question is whether those firms that are financially constrained are better able to obtain external finance in more developed financial systems, with positive ramifications for firm growth. Here the difficulty arises in how to measure which firms are financially constrained. In chapter 8, "Financial Development and Financing Constraints: International Evidence from the Structural Investment Model," Inessa Love addresses this question by using an investment Euler equation to infer the degree of financing constraints of individual firms. She provides evidence that financial development affects growth by reducing the financing constraints of firms and in that way improving the efficient allocation of investment. The magnitude of the changes, which run through changes in the cost of capital, is large: in a country with a low level of financial development, the cost of capital is twice as large as in a country with an average level of financial development.

In chapter 9, "Financial and Legal Constraints to Growth: Does Firm Size Matter?" Thorsten Beck, Asli Demirguc-Kunt, and Vojislav Maksimovic expand on the analysis of what financial sector development means for the growth prospects of individual firms. They use firm-level survey data covering 54 countries to construct a self-reported measure of financing constraints to address the question of how much faster firms might grow if they had more access to financing. The authors find that financial and institutional development weakens the constraining effects of financing constraints on firm growth in an economically and statistically significant way and that it is the smallest firms that benefit most from greater financial sector development.

Volume II. Part III. Political Economy of Finance

Politics plays an important role in finance. Financial development and financial reform are often driven by political economy considerations, and where finance is a scarce commodity, political connections are often especially valuable for firms in need of external finance. Whether these connections are good, in the sense that they support an efficient allocation of resources, is one question that has been more closely analyzed recently. Also, a number of papers have also researched from various angles how political economy factors affect the institutions necessary for financial sector development.

In chapter 10, "The Great Reversals: The Politics of Financial Development in the 20th Century," Raghuram Rajan and Luigi Zingales show that financial development does not change monotonically over time. By most measures, countries were more financially developed in 1913 than in 1980 and only recently have many countries surpassed their 1913 levels. To explain these changes, they propose an interest group theory of financial development wherein incumbents oppose financial development because it fosters greater competition through lowering entry barriers for newcomers. The theory predicts that incumbents' opposition will be weaker when an economy allows both cross-border trade and capital flows because then their hold on the allocation of rents is less. Consistent with this theory, they find that trade and capital flows can explain some of the cross-country and time-series variations in financial development. This in turn suggests that liberalization of trade and capital flows can be an important means of fostering greater financial sector development because they weaken the political economy factors holding back an economy.

The last two chapters in Volume II provide further empirical evidence of the value of political connections in developing countries, but now using firm-level data for particular countries. In chapter 11, "Estimating the Value of Political Connections," Raymond Fisman shows that the market value of politically connected firms in Indonesia under President Suharto declined more when adverse rumors circulated about the health of the president. Because the same firms did not perform better than other firms, this suggests that these connected firms obtained favors, yet allocated resources less efficiently. In chapter 12, "Cronyism and Capital Controls: Evidence from Malaysia," Simon Johnson and Todd Mitton provide empirical evidence for Malaysia that the imposition of capital controls during the Asian financial crises benefited primarily firms with strong connections to Prime Minister Mahathir, again without an improved performance when compared with other firms. These chapters indicate that the operation of corporations in developing countries, including their financing and financial structure, importantly depends on their relationships with politicians. As such, financial sector reform cannot avoid considering how to address political economy issues.

THE JOURNAL OF FINANCE • VOL. LV, NO. 2 • APRIL 2000

Stock Market Liberalization, Economic Reform, and Emerging Market Equity Prices

PETER BLAIR HENRY*

ABSTRACT

A stock market liberalization is a decision by a country's government to allow foreigners to purchase shares in that country's stock market. On average, a country's aggregate equity price index experiences abnormal returns of 3.3 percent per month in real dollar terms during an eight-month window leading up to the implementation of its initial stock market liberalization. This result is consistent with the prediction of standard international asset pricing models that stock market liberalization may reduce the liberalizing country's cost of equity capital by allowing for risk sharing between domestic and foreign agents.

A stock market liberalization is a decision by a country's government to allow foreigners to purchase shares in that country's stock market. Standard international asset pricing models (IAPMs) predict that stock market liberalization may reduce the liberalizing country's cost of equity capital by allowing for risk sharing between domestic and foreign agents (Stapleton and Subrahmanyan (1977), Errunza and Losq (1985), Eun and Janakiramanan (1986), Alexander, Eun, and Janakiramanan (1987), and Stulz (1999a, 1999b)).

This prediction has two important empirical implications for those emerging countries that liberalized their stock markets in the late 1980s and early 1990s. First, if stock market liberalization reduces the aggregate cost of equity capital then, holding expected future cash flows constant, we should observe an increase in a country's equity price index when the market learns that a stock market liberalization is going to occur. The second implication is

* Assistant Professor of Economics, Graduate School of Business, Stanford University, Stanford, CA 94305-5015. This paper is a revised version of Chapter 1 of my Ph.D. thesis at the Massachusetts Institute of Technology. I thank Christian Henry and Lisa Nelson for their support and encouragement. I am grateful to Steve Buser, Paul Romer, Andrei Shleifer, Jeremy Stein, René Stulz (the editor), and two anonymous referees for helpful comments on earlier drafts. I also thank Olivier Blanchard, Rudi Dornbusch, Stanley Fischer, Jeffrey Kling, Don Lessard, Tim Opler, Jim Poterba, Peter Reiss, Ken Singleton, Robert Solow, Ingrid Werner, and seminar participants at Harvard, MIT, Northwestern, Ohio State, Stanford, UNC-Chapel Hill, and the University of Virginia. I am grateful to Nora Richardson and Joanne Campbell for outstanding research assistance and to Charlotte Pace for superb editorial assistance. The International Finance Corporation and the Research Foundation of Chartered Financial Analysts generously allowed me to use the Emerging Markets Database. Ross Levine generously shared his extensive list of capital control liberalization dates. Finally, I would like to thank the National Science Foundation, The Ford Foundation, and the Stanford Institute for Economic Policy Research (SIEPR) for financial support. All remaining errors are my own.

that we should observe an increase in physical investment following stock market liberalizations, because a fall in a country's cost of equity capital will transform some investment projects that had a negative net present value (NPV) before liberalization into positive NPV endeavors after liberalization. This second effect of stock market liberalization should generate higher growth rates of output and have a broader impact on economic welfare than the financial windfall to domestic shareholders (see Henry (1999a)). This paper examines whether the data are consistent with the first of these two implications. Specifically, an event study approach is used to assess whether stock market liberalization is associated with a revaluation of equity prices and a fall in the cost of equity capital.

In the sample of 12 emerging countries examined in this paper, stock markets experience average abnormal returns of 4.7 percent per month in real dollar terms during an eight-month window leading up to the implementation of a country's initial stock market liberalization. After controlling for comovements with world stock markets, economic policy reforms, and macroeconomic fundamentals, the average abnormal return, 3.3 percent per month over the same horizon, is smaller but still economically and statistically significant. Estimates using five-month, two-month, and implementation-month-only windows are all associated with statistically significant stock price revaluation. The largest monthly estimate, 6.5 percent, is associated with the implementation-month-only estimate.

These facts are consistent with a fundamental prediction of the standard IAPM. If an emerging country's stock market is completely segmented from the rest of the world, then the equity premium embedded in its aggregate valuation will be proportional to the variance of the country's aggregate cash flows. Once liberalization takes place and the emerging country's stock market becomes fully integrated, its equity premium will be proportional to the covariance of the country's aggregate cash flows with those of a world portfolio. If, in spite of foreign ownership restrictions, the emerging market is not completely segmented (Bekaert and Harvey (1995)) then the emerging market's equilibrium valuation will incorporate an equity premium that lies somewhere between the autarky and fully integrated premium.[1]

The general consensus (see Stulz (1999a, 1999b), Tesar and Werner (1998), Bekaert and Harvey (2000), and Errunza and Miller (1998)) is that the local price of risk (the variance) exceeds the global price of risk (the covariance). Therefore, we expect the equity premium to fall when a completely or mildly segmented emerging country liberalizes its stock market.[2] Holding expected

---

[1] See also Errunza, Losq, and Padmanabhan (1992), who demonstrate that emerging markets are neither fully integrated nor completely segmented. Even if the emerging country prohibits developed-country investors from investing in its domestic equity market, developed-country investors may be able to construct portfolios of developed-country securities that mimic the returns on the emerging country's stock market.

[2] Markets that are mildly segmented ex ante should experience a smaller decline than fully segmented markets. See Errunza and Losq (1989).

future cash flows constant, this fall in the equity premium will cause a permanent fall in the aggregate cost of equity capital and an attendant re-valuation of the aggregate equity price index.[3]

One of the key issues in constructing estimates of the cumulative abnormal returns associated with a country's initial stock market liberalization lies in establishing the date of the initial liberalization and picking an appropriate time interval around this date. After providing a detailed description of the dating procedure and the reasons for using an eight-month event window, the empirical analysis in this paper begins by focusing on the behavior of stock prices during the eight-month window. After controlling for comovements with world stock returns, macroeconomic reforms, and macroeconomic fundamentals, the average monthly revaluation effect associated with the eight-month stock market liberalization window is 3.3 percent, which implies a total revaluation of 26 percent.

Although these results suggest a revaluation of equity prices in anticipation of the initial stock market liberalization, using a relatively long window is problematic because policymakers may behave like managers who issue equity following a run-up in stock prices (Ritter (1991) and Loughran and Ritter (1995)). Using an eight-month event window may overstate the liberalization effect if policymakers try to liberalize during a period of unusually high returns. To address this problem, the paper also presents estimates based on shorter event windows. Estimates using five-month, two-month, and one-month (implementation-month-only) windows are all associated with a statistically significant stock price revaluation. The largest effect, 6.5 percent, is associated with the implementation-month-only estimate, which suggests that the revaluation associated with a country's initial stock market liberalization is not an artifact of using long windows. Further checks of robustness of the results are performed by estimating the revaluation effect using implementation-month-only windows and alternative liberalization dates that have been proposed by other authors. These results are quantitatively and qualitatively similar to the benchmark results. Finally, the paper also demonstrates that stock market liberalizations that follow the initial liberalization are associated with much smaller and statistically insignificant revaluations.

This paper presents the first careful empirical estimates of the impact of stock market liberalization on emerging market equity prices. A number of papers examine the effect of stock market liberalization on market integra-

---

[3] This is the case of an unanticipated liberalization. If the liberalization is announced before it actually occurs, then there will be a jump in price upon announcement followed by mild price appreciation until the liberalization is implemented. The reason for price appreciation between announcement and implementation is as follows: Let $P^* > P$ be the integrated capital market equilibrium price. Upon announcement of a future liberalization at time T, the current price will jump only part of the way to P^* because no risk sharing takes place until T^*. However, since the price at T^* must be P^* and there can be no anticipated price jumps, the price must gradually appreciate between T and T^*. Also, if there is uncertainty as to whether the announced stock market liberalization is going to occur, there may be significant price appreciation, as news confirming the liberalization becomes public knowledge.

tion (Errunza et al. (1992), Buckberg (1995), Bekaert (1995), and Bekaert and Harvey (1995)); however, none of these papers estimate the valuation impact of stock market liberalization. Kim and Singal's (2000) evidence that emerging market stock returns are abnormally high in the months leading up to liberalization provides crucial initial evidence on the valuation question, but they acknowledge that there were confounding events throughout the sample period for which they do not control. In a related paper, Bekaert and Harvey (2000) show that liberalization tends to decrease aggregate dividend yields and argue that the price change reflects a change in the cost of capital rather than a change in earnings or profits of firms.[4] They control for the potentially confounding effect of economic reforms by using proxy variables such as credit ratings.

An important contribution of this paper relative to Bekaert and Harvey (2000) is that rather than using ready-made proxy variables to control for economic reforms, I construct a novel data set of economic policy reforms (Henry (1999b)) for each of the 12 countries in my sample. Using this time series of economic policy changes to control explicitly for economic reforms provides transparent evidence on the impact of stock market liberalization.

Specifically, in addition to disentangling the effect of stock market liberalization from the effects of macroeconomic stabilization, trade liberalization, privatization, and the easing of exchange controls, the paper also provides a first set of estimates of the impact of these macroeconomic reforms on the stock market. For example, in the sample of countries considered here, stock markets experience average abnormal returns of 2.1 percent per month in real dollar terms during the eight months leading up to trade liberalization. The trade reform window frequently overlaps with the window for stock market liberalization. Therefore, estimating the effect of stock market liberalization without controlling for trade reforms may result in upward biased estimates. Moreover, the stock price responses to trade and other macroeconomic reforms are of independent interest.

The remainder of this paper proceeds as follows. Section I presents the data and descriptive findings. Section II describes the methodology that is used to identify a country's initial stock market liberalization and measure its valuation impact. Section III presents the empirical results. Section IV discusses some potential interpretation problems. Section V summarizes the main results and conclusions.

I. Data and Descriptive Findings

A. Stock Market Data

The sample examined in this paper includes 12 emerging markets: Argentina, Brazil, Chile, Colombia, Mexico, and Venezuela in Latin America, and India, Malaysia, Korea, the Philippines, Taiwan, and Thailand in Asia. These

---

[4] Errunza and Miller (1998) and Foerster and Karolyi (1999) provide firm level evidence on the related topic of ADR issuance.

countries were chosen because of the general interest in the two regions. Indonesia was excluded from the Asian list because Indonesian stock market data are available only after the date on which its stock market was liberalized. All emerging stock market data are taken from the International Finance Corporation's (IFC) Emerging Markets Data Base (EMDB). Returns for individual countries come from the *IFC Total Return Index* (U.S. dollar denominated). The Morgan Stanley Capital Index for Europe, Asia, and the Far East is also from the EMDB. Data on the S&P 500 come from the IMF's *International Financial Statistics* (IFS). Each country's U.S. dollar total return index is deflated by the U.S. consumer price index, which comes from the IFS. All of the data are monthly. All returns are logarithmic.

B. Stock Market Liberalization Dates

B.1. Implementation Dates

Testing the hypothesis that a country's first stock market liberalization causes equity price revaluation requires a systematic procedure for identifying the date of each country's first stock market liberalization. Official policy decree dates are used when they are available; otherwise, two alternatives are pursued. First, many countries initially permitted foreign ownership through country funds. Since government permission is presumably a necessary condition for establishment of these funds, the date when the first country fund is established is a proxy for the official implementation date. The second way of indirectly capturing official implementation dates is to monitor the IFC's Investability Index. The investability index is the ratio of the market capitalization of stocks that foreigners can legally hold to total market capitalization. A large jump in the investability index is evidence of an official liberalization. In what follows, the date of a country's first stock market liberalization is defined as the first month with a verifiable occurrence of any of the following: liberalization by policy decree, establishment of the first country fund, or an increase in the investability index of at least 10 percent.

Table I lists the date on which each of the 12 countries first liberalized its stock market, as well as the means by which it liberalized. In particular, where the initial liberalization is through a country fund, the specific name of the country fund is given. Table II provides a comparison of the liberalization dates in Table I with other liberalization dates in the literature. Specifically, column (2) of Table II lists the liberalization dates identified using the procedure outlined in the preceding paragraph. Columns (3) through (5) list the official liberalization dates of Bekaert and Harvey (2000), Kim and Singal (2000), and Buckberg (1995) respectively. Column (6) lists the earliest date of the preceding four columns. Three of the 12 dates in column (2) are preceded by dates in column (6). An investigation of the three dates preceding those given in column (2) yielded no confirmation of the September 1987 opening for Thailand or the December 1988 opening for Venezuela. The February 1991 date for Colombia actually refers to *La Apertura*, which was a trade liberalization not a stock market liberalization. Hence, the liberaliza-

Table I

First Stock Market Liberalization

The stock market liberalization dates are based on information obtained from the following sources: Levine and Zervos (1994); The *Wilson Directory of Emerging Market Funds*; IFC Investable Indices; Park and Van Agtmael (1993); Price (1994); *The Economist Intelligence Unit*, various issues; *The Economist Guide to World Stock Markets* (1988); and the IMF's *Exchange Arrangements and Restrictions*, various issues.

Country	Date of First Stock Market Liberalization	Details about the Liberalization
Argentina	November 1989	Policy Decree: The liberalization began with the New Foreign Investment Regime in November 1989. Legal limits on the type and nature of foreign investments are reduced (Park and Van Agtmael (1993), p. 326).
Brazil	March 1988	Country Fund Introduction: "The Brazil Fund Incorporated" (*The Wilson Directory of Emerging Market Funds*, p. 17).
Chile	May 1987	Country Fund Introduction: "The Toronto Trust Mutual Fund" (*The Wilson Directory of Emerging Market Funds*, p. 17).
Colombia	December 1991	Policy Decree: Resolution 52 allowed foreign investors to purchase up to 100 percent of locally listed companies (Price (1994)).
India	June 1986	Country Fund Introduction: "The India Fund" (*The Wilson Directory of Emerging Market Funds*, p. 12).
Korea	June 1987	Country Fund Introduction: "The Korea Europe Fund Limited" (*The Wilson Directory of Emerging Market Funds*, p. 13).
Malaysia	May 1987	Country Fund Introduction: "The Wardley GS Malaysia Fund" (*The Wilson Directory of Emerging Market Funds*, p. 14).
Mexico	May 1989	Policy Decree: Restrictions on foreign portfolio inflows were substantially liberalized (Levine and Zervos (1994)).
The Philippines	May 1986	Country Fund Introduction: "The Thornton Philippines Redevelopment Fund Limited" (*The Wilson Directory of Emerging Market Funds*, p. 15).
Taiwan	May 1986	Country Fund Introduction: "The Taipei Fund" (*The Wilson Directory of Emerging Market Funds*, p. 15).
Thailand	January 1988	Country Fund Introduction: "The Siam Fund Limited" (*The Wilson Directory of Emerging Market Funds*, p. 16).
Venezuela	January 1990	Policy Decree: Decree 727 completely opened the market to foreign investors except for bank stocks ((Levine and Zervos (1994)).

Table II
Comparison of Official Liberalization Dates across Authors

The dates in column (2) are constructed using the dating procedure described in the paper. The dates in columns (3) through (5) are taken from Bekaert and Harvey (2000), Kim and Singal (2000), and Buckberg (1995), respectively. Column 6 shows the earliest date given for a country in the preceding four columns.

(1) Country	(2) Dating Procedure	(3) Bekaert & Harvey	(4) Kim & Singal	(5) Buckberg	(6) Earliest
Argentina	11-89	11-89	11-89	10-91	11-89
Brazil	3-88	5-91	5-91	5-91	3-88
Chile	5-87	1-92	9-87	10-89	5-87
Colombia	12-91	2-91	2-91	10-91	2-91
India	6-86	11-92	11-92	NA	6-86
Korea	6-87	1-92	1-92	NA	6-87
Malaysia	5-87	12-88	12-88	NA	5-87
Mexico	5-89	5-89	11-89	5-89	5-89
The Philippines	5-86	6-91	7-86	10-89	5-86
Taiwan	5-86	1-91	1-91	NA	5-86
Thailand	1-88	9-87	8-88	NA	9-87
Venezuela	1-90	1-90	1-90	12-88	12-88

tion dates in column (2) also represent the earliest verifiable stock market liberalization dates listed in Table I. This is important because the goal here is to identify the first stock market liberalization in any particular country. The empirical analysis in Section III begins with the dates in column (2) but, for comparison, results based on the other dates are also presented.

B.2. Announcement Dates

A search for announcement dates corresponding to the implementation dates listed in Table I was conducted using the database Lexis/Nexis Research Software version 4.06. Consultations with library science staff suggested that Lexis/Nexis offers two distinct advantages relative to Bloomberg and the Dow Jones News Retrieval. First, Bloomberg has relatively little coverage prior to 1991. Second, Dow Jones News Retrieval covers a subset of the news sources spanned by Lexis/Nexis. Lexis/Nexis covers more than 2,300 full-text information sources from U.S. and overseas newspapers, magazines, journals, newsletters, wire services, and broadcast transcripts. It also covers abstract material from more than 1,000 information sources.

The search algorithm used was as follows. If the initial stock market liberalization came via a country fund, the search was conducted using the name of the country fund. If the initial stock market liberalization was not a country fund, then the following search phrases were used: *stock market liberalization, stock market opening, capital market liberalization, capital market opening, restrictions on foreign capital, foreign investment,* and *foreign portfolio investment.*

Table III presents the complete results of the search. The first column of the table lists the country and the implementation date of its first stock market liberalization. Column 2 lists all announcement dates that were uncovered by the search. For seven of 12 countries the earliest news of stock market liberalization comes on or after the actual implementation date. Of the five countries for which the announcement date precedes the actual liberalization date, three have announcements occurring only one month in advance. Given the legal, political, and logistical complexities of enacting such a policy, it is hard to believe that the market first learns of the undertaking only a month before it happens. By way of comparison, the average time between announcement and listing for American Depositary Receipts (ADRs) is three months, and ADRs are issued in markets that have already been liberalized. For the remaining two countries, Colombia and Taiwan, only Taiwan's announcement date seems reasonable. The headline for Colombia actually corresponds not to the stock market, but to its major trade liberalization, *La Apertura*. The central point of Table III is that announcement dates uncovered using a source such as Lexis/Nexis are likely to be poor proxies for the date at which information about the liberalization first reached market participants. In the absence of credible announcement dates, the only reliable way of capturing all of the price changes associated with the liberalization is to estimate abnormal returns over a generous window of time preceding the liberalization. A detailed discussion of the construction of such a window is postponed until Section II.

C. Descriptive Findings

Figure 1 motivates the analysis by plotting the average cumulative abnormal return (triangles) across all 12 countries in event time. T^* is the month in which the stock market liberalization was implemented (see the dates in Table I). Figure 1 suggests a revaluation of aggregate equity prices in anticipation of stock market liberalization; the cumulative abnormal return from $T^* - 12$ to T^* is on the order of 40 percent.[5]

As a way of checking the consistency of the cumulative abnormal return plot with other work, Figure 1 also plots the cumulative abnormal change in the log of the dividend yield (squares). As one would expect, the respective plots are near mirror images: Realized returns increase as the dividend yield decreases. The cumulative decline in dividend yields from $T^* - 12$ to T^* is on the order of 30 percent. Since the average level of the dividend yield in these countries prior to liberalization is about four percent, the 30 percent decline reported in Figure 1 suggests an average fall in the dividend yield of about 100 basis points.[6] This estimate of 100 basis points is slightly larger

---

[5] Kim and Singal (2000) also find that emerging countries experience positive abnormal returns in the months leading up to stock market liberalization. Errunza and Miller (1998) find similar results using firm level data.

[6] Ln(0.04) − Ln(0.03) is approximately equal to 0.3. Therefore, a 30 percent fall in the dividend yield from a level of four percent implies a fall of approximately 100 basis points.

Stock Market Liberalization   537

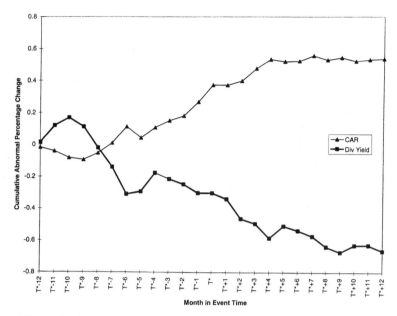

Figure 1. The behavior of stock returns and dividend yields around the first stock market liberalization. The variable on the y-axis is the continuously compounded abnormal percentage change. T^* is the month in which the stock market liberalization was implemented. The upward trending series (triangles) is a plot of the cumulative residuals from a panel regression of the real dollar return from all 12 countries on a constant and 11 country-specific dummies. The downward trending series (squares) is a plot of the cumulative residuals from a panel regression of the change in the natural log of the dividend yield on a constant and 11 country-specific dummies.

than the range of declines (5 to 90 basis points) reported by Bekaert and Harvey (2000), but once controls are introduced in Section III, this number falls well within the range of Bekaert and Harvey's estimates.

Though Figure 1 suggests a causal channel from stock market liberalization to stock prices and the cost of equity capital, the graph needs to be interpreted with caution because it does not control for any other reforms. In particular, note that there is a stock price revaluation of about 20 percent from T^* to $T^* + 4$. The dividend yield also continues to fall after implementation of the liberalization. Since there is no theoretical reason to expect a stock-market-liberalization-induced revaluation after implementation, Figure 1 suggests that favorable, unanticipated macroeconomic events tend to occur following stock market liberalizations. Macroeconomic reforms are the focus of the next subsection.

D. Economic Reforms

Conducting an event study is the most direct and transparent way of assessing the impact of stock market liberalization on emerging market equity prices. However, unlike the typical event study in finance where the econo-

Table III

Announcement Dates for First Stock Market Liberalizations

The announcements were procured via Lexis-Nexis Software version 4.06 using the search procedure described in the paper.

(1) Country and Implementation Date	(2) Announcement Date(s)	(3) Source	(4) Headline
Argentina (November 1989)	December 11, 1989	*The Financial Times*	Argentina fund aims at privatised companies.
Brazil (March 1988)	March 23, 1988	*The Toronto Financial Post*	Some like it hot: Shares in the fund will be offered to the public shortly by first Boston Corporation and Merrill Lynch Capital Markets
	March 31, 1988 April 4, 1988	PR Newswire Institutional Investor, Inc.	Brazil Fund Common Stock Offered Brazil Fund is Hot
Chile (May 1987)	February 7, 1996	*The Reuter European Business Report*	Micropal names best 1995 emerging market funds. The Toronto Trust Chile Fund, launched in 1987, is Micropal's best performing emerging market fund over the past seven years
Colombia (December 1991)	February, 1991	National Trade Data Bank Market reports	Colombia-Economic Policy and Trade Practices. The administration of President Gaviria has embarked on "la apertura" (the opening), a bold plan to lower tariffs and other barriers to foreign trade
India (June 1986)	May 12, 1986	*The Financial Times*	Maverick Brings in the Savings. The government approved the Unit trust of India's (UTI) collaboration with Merrill Lynch to launch the India Fund
	June 17, 1986	*The Financial Times*	More Details Given for India Fund. The Indian government last week approved the proposal which for the first time will allow foreigners to invest in the Indian stock markets

Stock Market Liberalization　539

Korea (June 1987)	March 21, 1987	*The Economist*	South Korean Securities; Authorised Entry Only
Malaysia (May 1987)	April 8, 1987	*Jiji Press Limited*	Arab-Malaysian Merchant Bank—IFC Move to Tap U.S. Market.
	May 11, 1987	*U.P.I.*	Malaysian Fund Offering Increased
Mexico (May 1989)	May 15, 1989	*Reuters*	Mexico Announces New Foreign Investment Rules
	July 8, 1989	*The New York Times*	Mexico Eases Foreign Curb. The government has opened Mexico's stock exchange to foreign investment
Philippines (May 1986)	September 22, 1986	*Business Week*	For Aquino, U.S. Business Will Be a Tough Sell. *Text:* Hong Kong-based Thornton Management (Asia) Ltd. recently launched the Philippines Redevelopment Fund which invests in Philippine stocks
Taiwan (May 1986)	July 3, 1985	*Central News Agency*	Local Securities Investment Company Formed in Taipei *Details:* A 25 million dollar investment fund to be called the Taipei Fund will be raised soon
	June 28, 1986	*The Economist*	Asian Funds *Details:* The Taipei Fund was formed on May 22nd
Thailand (January 1988)	April 27, 1988	*The Financial Times*	Another Thai Fund to Join the Market *Details:* the fund was established in January
Venezuela (January 1990)	December, 1989	*South Magazine*	Scramble at the Fringe; Third World Stock Markets *Details:* Liberalisation is proceeding in Argentina and Venezuela

metrician can be reasonably certain that the event in question is isolated from other influential events, the shift from closed to open capital markets usually coincides with four equally important changes in economic policy: macroeconomic stabilization, trade liberalization, privatization, and the easing of exchange controls.

Table IV, which lists all confounding macroeconomic events occurring within a 15-month window around the initial stock market liberalization, forcefully illustrates this point. Argentina provides a good illustration of why attention to concurrent economic reforms is a critical part of this event study. At least part of the dramatic increase in Argentine stock prices during 1989 was probably due to the implementation of a sweeping stabilization plan. There are many other conspicuous examples: IMF negotiations, a free trade agreement, and the overthrow of Marcos in the Philippines (1986); privatization in Malaysia (1987); a Brady debt reduction deal in Venezuela (1990); privatization and tariff reductions in Colombia (1992).[7]

The theory used to explain the stock price effects of a capital market liberalization assumes that everything else is held constant when this change is made. To construct an estimate that we can use to test the theory, it is necessary to hold constant the other reform measures and isolate a pure capital market effect. Additionally, the stock market's response to the other reforms is interesting in its own right. Using the full list of events allows for measurement of the price response to each of the four major reforms.

In addition to the problem of confounding macroeconomic reforms, four other methodological issues are involved in measuring the impact of stock market liberalization on equity prices: construction of the event windows in the absence of announcement dates, multiple stock market liberalizations, and accounting for macroeconomic fundamentals and policy endogeneity. The next section discusses these issues in detail.

II. Methodological Issues

A. *Construction of Event Windows*

In the absence of reliable announcement dates, the average time between announcement and listing for American Depositary Receipts (three months)[8] provides an announcement proxy. Suppose the government announces in month $T^* - 3$ that it will open the stock market to foreign investors in month T^*. Since there can be no anticipated price jumps, the price must jump on the announcement and then gradually appreciate in such a way that there is no jump in price when the liberalization occurs at T^*. Measuring the impact of stock market liberalization in this textbook world would be straightforward: Regress real returns on a constant, a set of control variables, and two dummies.

---

[7] For a complete chronological listing of events in each country see Henry (1999b). The complete list of events is also available at http://www.afajof.org.

[8] I thank an anonymous referee for bringing this fact to my attention.

The first dummy would pick up the level effect of the initial jump at $T^* - 3$, and the second dummy would measure the slope effect due to gradual price appreciation in months $T^* - 2$, $T^* - 1$, and T^*.[9]

Errunza and Miller (1998) argue that, unlike the canonical example where all market participants learn about the future opening at the same time, in practice there is likely to be widespread information leakage prior to any official announcement in emerging markets.[10] Given that learning about a future liberalization is a gradual process in which market participants receive the news at different times, and given the theoretical expectation of no revaluation implementation, an event window of $T^* - 7$ to T^* is used to test for a revaluation effect. Again, T^* refers to the implementation dates in Table I.

The magnitude and statistical significance of abnormal returns during the liberalization window are evaluated by estimating the following panel regression:

$$R_{it} = \alpha_i + \gamma \cdot Liberalize_{it} + \epsilon_{it}. \tag{1}$$

The α_i are country-specific dummies. $Liberalize_{it}$ is a dummy variable that takes on the value one in each of the eight months from $T^* - 7$ to T^* associated with country i's first stock market liberalization.[11] Hence, the parameter γ measures the average monthly abnormal return across all 12 countries during the eight-month stock market liberalization window.

B. Multiple Stock Market Liberalizations

Table AI shows that most countries' initial stock market liberalization did not constitute a complete opening to foreign investors. Rather, stock market liberalization is a gradual process generally involving several liberalizations subsequent to the first. Inasmuch as it is part of a broader set of economic reforms geared toward increased openness, news of the first stock market liberalization is also implicit news about the entire future schedule of stock market liberalizations. Consequently, future stock market liberalizations are

---

[9] Footnote 3 explains why there will be an initial jump followed by price appreciation.

[10] They give an example of the leakage problem in the context of Indian ADRs.

[11] If all market participants learned about the liberalization at the same time and there was no uncertainty about when the liberalization was going to occur, then the *Liberalize* variable would only need to be on during the month in which the announcement occurred. In reality, however, learning about an impending liberalization is a gradual process. The technique of allowing the dummy variable to be on during the entire announcement window is well established (see, e.g., MacKinlay (1997)). This dummy variable method is a variant of standard event study methodology. Standard event studies are unable to take into account exogenous shifts in the equation parameters that may occur during the event window. The dummy variable method avoids specification errors while yielding the same information on returns that would be obtained from the cumulative abnormal residual in event studies (see Ozler (1989) and Binder (1998)).

542   The Journal of Finance

Table IV

First Stock Market Liberalizations and Contemporaneous Economic Reforms

T^* is the date of the country's stock market liberalization in event time. For example, in Argentina any event listed in the $T^* - 6$ box occurred on or between June and August of 1989. All events are taken from *The Economist Intelligence Unit: Quarterly Economic Reports*. A full chronology of events is presented in Henry (1999b).

Country, Date of Liberalization	Type of Liberalization	T^*-12	T^*-9	T^*-6	T^*-3	T^*	T^*+3
Argentina November 1989	Limits on foreign capital reduced	Airline privatization; dual exchange rate system fails	Structural adjustment funds frozen; economic team resigns	Privatization stabilization plan	IMF agreement	Exchange rate devalued by 35 percent	IMF agreement frozen
Brazil March 1988	Country Fund	Finance minister resigns	Second Cruzado Plan	New proposals submitted to creditors	None	Capital goods duties reduced	Tariffs reduced
Chile May 1987	Country Fund	None	Attempt on Pinochet's life	None	Largest banks privatized; new debt repayment terms	None	Two floods and an earthquake
Colombia December 1991	Investability Index jumps 46 percent	Restrictions on profit remittance eased	Tariffs reduced; external debt refinanced	Tariffs cut; credit controls relaxed	Exchange controls eased	Privatization of telecom industry begins	None
India June 1986	Country Fund	None	None	None	None	None	Attempt on Prime Minister's life

Stock Market Liberalization   543

Country							
Korea June 1987	Country Fund	None	None	False rumors of Kim II Sung's death	Tariffs reduced on consumer durables	Protracted student protests	Tariff cuts announced
Malaysia February 1987	Country Fund	None	National Economic Plan (NEP) frozen	NEP to be extended past 1990	Privatization of telecom industry	Rubber price stabilization pact reached	None
Mexico May 1989	Investability index jumps 410 percent	Salinas elected; U.S. govt. gives $3.5B to boost reforms	Pacto extended	Privatization of two state mines	Brady Plan approved by U.S. Congress; IMF agreement	None	Brady agreement with creditors
The Philippines May 1986	Country Fund	Debt rescheduling signed	IMF targets missed	$2.9 billion of public debt rescheduled	Marcos overthrown	Import restrictions lifted	Talks open with IMF
Taiwan May 1986	Country Fund	None	None	Investment in foreign securities allowed	None	Import bans lifted	Exchange controls eased
Thailand January 1988	Country Fund	General Yongchaiyut calls for reforms	None	ASEAN free trade agreement extended	None	None	None
Venezuela January 1990	Full market access except bank stocks	Trade liberalization; adjustment loan approved	None	None	Easier profit remittance for foreign firms	$680 million structural adjustment loan	Brady deal; Agricultural tariffs reduced

probably anticipated at the time of the first stock market liberalization. Because subsequent liberalizations are probably anticipated, there are two relevant states of the world to consider:

State 1: When the first stock market liberalization occurs, future liberalizations are anticipated, and it is known that they will take place with a probability of 1.

State 2: When the first stock market liberalization occurs, future liberalizations are anticipated, but there is some positive probability that each of the subsequent liberalizations will not occur.

If State 1 is the true state of the world, then the only revaluation occurs when the first stock market liberalization is announced. Although there will be a gradual appreciation of prices until the entire liberalization process is completed, this slope effect[12] will be hard to detect given the noise in the data. If State 2 is the true state of the world, then in addition to the first price jump there may also be revaluations as each scheduled liberalization date approaches and market participants receive news confirming that it will take place according to schedule.

These two distinct states of the world raise the important question of how to measure the effects of the initial stock market liberalization versus those of subsequent liberalizations. Testing for revaluation effects by using a dummy variable that takes on the value one during the event window of each and every stock market liberalization is likely to understate the true effects of stock market liberalization if S1 is the true state of the world. On the other hand, it is also important to know whether subsequent stock market liberalizations induce revaluation effects. This discussion argues for creating two dummy variables. The first, called *Liberalize*, takes on the value one during the event window of the first stock market liberalization. The second, called *Liberalize2*, takes on the value one during all liberalization windows subsequent to the first.

C. Macroeconomic Fundamentals and Policy Endogeneity

As the ultimate goal is to estimate the size of the aggregate equity price response to stock market liberalization holding expected future cash flows constant, equation (1) will need augmentation. In Sections III.C and III.D I control for expected future cash flows by adding a set of economic reform dummies and macroeconomic fundamentals as right-hand-side variables. More generally, a fundamental concern with estimating the stock price response to liberalization is that policymakers have an incentive to liberalize the stock market when it is doing well. A policymaker who liberalizes the stock market when prices are depressed risks being accused of selling off the country at fire-sale prices. Summers (1994) makes a similar point in the context of

---

[12] Footnote 3 explains why there may be a slope effect.

privatization. To the extent that stock market performance depends on economic conditions, the decision to liberalize depends on the economy's current and expected future performance. Although controlling for macroeconomic fundamentals partially controls for this concern, the standard event study approach may yield upward-biased estimates if policymakers time liberalizations to coincide with news about positive future macroeconomic shocks. On the other hand, some liberalizations have been undertaken during crises. Nevertheless, the potential endogeneity of the liberalization decision requires cautious interpretation of the estimated revaluation effect. This issue is raised again in Section III.E.

III. Results

Sections A through D estimate the average cumulative impact of a country's first stock market liberalization on aggregate market returns over the eight-month liberalization window described in Section II. Section A begins with a benchmark specification, equation (1), that is comparable to Kim and Singal's (2000) earlier work. Sections B through D pose three alternative specifications that take seriously the notion that comovements with foreign stock markets, contemporaneous economic reforms, or a favorable shock to macroeconomic fundamentals might be responsible for the sharp increase in valuations. Section E discusses some of the interpretation difficulties involved in using a relatively long event window, and also presents results based on shorter windows. All of the estimates in Sections F and G use implementation-month-only windows. Section F also tests for a revaluation effect using alternative event dates. Specifically, the implementation dates of all the authors in Table II are used along with exactly the same battery of controls as in Sections A through E. Section G estimates the average effect of the second and all subsequent stock market liberalizations.

A. Benchmark Estimates

The results from estimating equation (1) are given in column (1a) of Table V. The coefficient of 0.047 on *Liberalize* is highly significant. On average, a country's first stock market liberalization is preceded by a total revaluation of 38 percent in U.S. dollar terms. The total revaluation number is calculated by multiplying the average monthly abnormal return during the window by the length of the window (4.7 percent per month × eight months = 37.6 percent). Panel B of Table V provides estimates of the impact of liberalization on dividend yields. The specification is identical to equation (1) except that the left-hand-side variable is the change in the log of the dividend yield. The dividend yield results are not as strong as those for returns. Specifically, the coefficient of -0.024 on *Liberalize* in the dividend yield specification implies an average fall in dividend yields of about 50 basis points. Again, this is consistent with Bekaert and Harvey (2000) who also

A Reader in International Corporate Finance

The Journal of Finance

Table V

Stock Market Reactions to First Stock Market Liberalization

The regressions are performed using monthly stock market data from December 1976 to December 1994 for Argentina, Brazil, Chile, India, Korea, Mexico, and Thailand. For the other countries the data are monthly from December 1984 to December 1994. The dividend yield data are also monthly and cover the period from December 1984 to December 1994. *Liberalize* is a dummy variable for the event window of the first stock market liberalization. The event window begins seven months prior to the implementation month and ends in the implementation month. For example, for a stock market liberalization that was implemented in November 1989, the event window begins in April 1989 and ends in November 1989. R^{LDC}, R^{US}, and R^{EAFE} are the dividend-inclusive monthly return on the IFC global index, the S&P 500, and the Morgan Stanley Capital Index for Europe, Asia, and the Far East, respectively. *Stabilize, Trade, Privatize,* and *Exchange* are dummy variables for the event windows of macroeconomic stabilization, trade opening, privatization, and exchange controls, respectively. Each of the event windows for these economic reform variables begins seven months prior to the implementation of the reform and ends in the implementation month. A constant plus 11 country dummies were also estimated but not reported. Heteroskedasticity-consistent (White) standard errors are in parentheses.

	Panel A: Stock Returns				Panel B: $\Delta\ln(D/P)$			
	(1a)	(2a)	(3a)	(4a)	(1b)	(2b)	(3b)	(4b)
Liberalize	0.047***	0.041***	0.039***	0.033***	−0.024*	−0.019	−0.015	−0.010
	(0.010)	(0.0124)	(0.012)	(0.011)	(0.015)	(0.015)	(0.015)	(0.017)
R^{LDC}		0.522***	0.517***	0.525***		−0.350***	−0.341***	−0.339***
		(0.148)	(0.015)	(0.142)		(0.114)	(0.110)	(0.115)
R^{US}		0.250***	0.278***	0.278***		−0.355*	−0.365*	−0.446**
		(0.102)	(0.109)	(0.109)		(0.200)	(0.205)	(0.200)
R^{EAFE}		−0.008	−0.006	−0.018		−0.043**	−0.045**	−0.027
		(0.044)	(0.044)	(0.042)		(0.020)	(0.022)	(0.024)
Stabilize			0.003	0.003			−0.003	0.003
			(0.010)	(0.010)			(0.010)	(0.010)
Trade			0.025***	0.021***			−0.039***	−0.037**
			(0.005)	(0.048)			(0.015)	(0.016)
Privatize			0.016**	0.010			−0.029	−0.030
			(0.007)	(0.008)			(0.019)	(0.021)
Exchange			−0.005	−0.002			0.010	0.007
			(0.015)	(0.015)			(0.049)	(0.045)
$\bar{R}^2$	0.007	0.076	0.083	0.147	0.000	0.018	0.023	0.027
No. of obs.	2292	2292	2292	2292	1569	1569	1569	1569

*, **, and *** indicate significant difference at the 10, 5, and 1 percent levels, respectively.

find a small fall in dividend yields around liberalization. Errunza and Miller (1998) also report dividend yield results that are not as significant as those for stock returns. Nevertheless, the negative coefficient on *Liberalize* in column (1b) of the dividend yield regressions is qualitatively consistent with a one-time equity price revaluation resulting from a fall in the cost of equity capital.

B. Controlling for World Stock Returns

A glaring omission associated with specification (1) is the effect of comovements with foreign stock markets. The following specification measures the abnormal return associated with a country's first stock market liberalization after controlling for the effects of foreign stock market fluctuations:

$$R_{it} = \alpha_i + \beta_1 R_t^{LDC} + \beta_2 R_t^{US} + \beta_3 R_t^{EAFE} + \gamma \cdot Liberalize_{it} + \epsilon_{it}, \qquad (2)$$

where R_t^{LDC} = the continuously compounded real dollar return on an index of emerging market funds at time t; R_t^{US} = the continuously compounded real return on the S&P 500 index at time t; and R_t^{EAFE} = the continuously compounded real dollar return on Morgan Stanley's Europe, Asia, and Far East (EAFE) stock market index at time t. If the run-up in emerging market equity prices is the result of booming foreign stock markets, then the coefficient on the *Liberalize* dummy in equation (2) should be significantly reduced relative to specification (1).

Column (2a) of Table V shows the results. As evidenced by the sharp increase in adjusted R^2 as compared with that in column (1a), the inclusion of world stock returns dramatically improves the regression fit. Not surprisingly, the largest beta is associated with other emerging market returns; own-country returns are most sensitive to movements in other emerging markets.[13] On average, when the aggregate emerging market index rises by one percentage point, an individual country's index will rise by 0.5 percentage points. The U.S. beta is smaller than the emerging market beta, but is also significant. The EAFE beta is not significant. Although comovements with foreign stock markets are an important explanatory factor for emerging market returns, their inclusion has little effect on the *Liberalize* coefficient. The monthly point estimate is now 0.041. The coefficient on *Liberalize* in the dividend yield specifications is still negative, but is no longer significant.

C. Controlling for Concurrent Economic Reforms

Four variables are constructed to control for the effect of the following economic reforms: macroeconomic stabilization, trade liberalization, privatization, and the easing of exchange controls. These variables are denoted *Stabilize*, *Trade*, *Privatize*, and *Exchange* respectively. The underlying data used to construct these variables are the policy events in Tables IV and V, and the full event list. For example, Table IV indicates that in May of 1986 the Philippines lifted import restrictions. Thus, May of 1986 is T^* for this particular trade liberalization, and the variable *Trade* takes on the value

---

[13] It is possible that the strong correlation results from the fact that each country in the sample is also a part of the emerging market index. Excluding the LDC returns from the right-hand side does not alter the sign or magnitude of the other betas.

one in each of the eight months from October 1985 through May 1986. The exact same methodology is followed for every occurrence of each type of reform in all 12 countries. The following panel model is then estimated:

$$R_{it} = \alpha_i + \beta_1 R_t^{LDC} + \beta_2 R_t^{US} + \beta_3 R_t^{EAFE} + \gamma_1 Liberalize_{it} + \gamma_2 Stabilize_{it}$$

$$+ \gamma_3 Trade_{it} + \gamma_4 Privatize_{it} + \gamma_5 Exchange_{it} + \epsilon_{it}. \tag{3}$$

Column (3a) of Table V shows the results. After controlling for world stock returns and macroeconomic reforms, the *Liberalize* coefficient is now 0.039. Although they barely affect the *Liberalize* coefficient, the macroeconomic reforms are themselves associated with equity price revaluation. For instance, the coefficient on *Trade* is 0.025 and the *Privatize* coefficient is 0.016. This implies that trade liberalization and privatization are associated with cumulative revaluations of 20 percent and 13 percent respectively. The *Stabilize* coefficient also has the expected sign, but does not have a statistically significant effect on stock returns.[14] The coefficient on *Exchange* is negative, but also insignificant.

It is interesting to ask whether the estimated stock market revaluation effects of liberalization are statistically distinguishable from those of the economic reforms. The null hypothesis that the *Liberalize* coefficient is equal to the *Trade* and *Privatize* coefficients is rejected at the 10 percent level.

Given their magnitude and significance, the *Trade* and *Privatize* coefficients merit some further discussion. The *Trade* result is consistent with recent studies, such as that of Sachs and Warner (1995), which find trade liberalization to be the single economic reform most closely tied to future growth. Trade liberalization may reduce the cost of imported intermediate inputs, thereby increasing expected future profitability.[15] This interpretation, that trade liberalization signals higher future profitability, is also consistent with the negative and significant coefficient on *Trade* in the dividend yield specification in column (3b). The sign of the *Privatize* coefficient is consistent with a story that says placing state enterprises in private hands raises their efficiency and expected future profitability.[16] Indeed, this story is corroborated by Boubakri and Cosset (1998) who find evidence that privatization leads to improved firm performance.

---

[14] Every IMF agreement is counted as a stabilization plan, but in reality some agreements are not so much "news" in the sense of being a new stabilization plan as they are a continuation of an already existing plan. This may bias against finding a significant effect of stabilization, but is favorable to omitting some agreements and running the risk of attributing to liberalization that which is due to stabilization.

[15] For a formal model along these lines see Basu and Morey (1998).

[16] The efficiency argument is one of two competing effects of privatization on equity prices. The other effect is that the news that privatization is coming may increase the supply of shares in the country, driving down equity prices in some models. That privatization positively impacts the stock market would seem to suggest that the efficiency effect dominates.

D. Controlling for Macroeconomic Fundamentals

After controlling for comovements with foreign markets and concurrent economic reforms, the first stock market liberalization still has a point estimate of 0.039. However, macroeconomic factors have not been accounted for. This is a potentially serious problem because of the possibility that exogenous macroeconomic shocks unrelated to reform might cause a run-up in equity prices. Therefore, not accounting for country fundamentals might lead to an overstatement of the effects of stock market liberalization. This critique is addressed by adding distributed lags and leads of the growth rates of country macroeconomic fundamentals[17] to the right-hand side of regression (3) as in Fama (1981). Let F_{it} be a vector of country fundamentals. The following regression is estimated:

$$R_{it} = \alpha_i + \beta_1 R_t^{LDC} + \beta_2 R_t^{US} + \beta_3 R_t^{EAFE} + \gamma_1 Liberalize_{it} + \gamma_2 Stabilize_{it}$$
$$+ \gamma_3 Trade_{it} + \gamma_4 Privatize_{it} + \gamma_5 Exchange_{it} + \delta(L)\Delta(\ln F_{it}) + \epsilon_{it}. \tag{4}$$

The results are listed in column (4a) of Table V. (To conserve space, the estimates of the fundamentals are not included since they are not of direct interest.)

This time the story is substantially altered. After controlling for the fundamentals, the *Liberalize* coefficient falls to 0.033. At first glance this may not seem like much of a discrepancy from the 0.047 in specification (1). However, cumulated over the entire eight-month liberalization window, the new estimate implies a total revaluation of 26 percent, or two-thirds of the total revaluation implied by the original point estimate. Furthermore, the *Privatize* coefficient is no longer significant. One possible explanation for the attenuation of the *Privatize* coefficient is that governments decide to privatize when macroeconomic conditions are strong. In the absence of fundamentals on the right-hand side, the *Privatize* dummy simply picks up this correlation. Finally, the hypothesis that the *Liberalize* and *Trade* coefficients are the same can no longer be rejected. After accounting for the effects of macroeconomic activity on the stock market, trade opening has as large a revaluation effect as stock market liberalization. That the effects of stock market liberalization are substantially diminished by adding macroeconomic fundamentals to the right-hand side supports the argument in Section II that policymakers time market openings to coincide with good economic conditions.

E. Shorter Window Lengths

In the absence of verifiable announcement dates, the four preceding subsections (A–D) use an event window of eight months to capture potential announcement effects and to allow for the possibility of information leakage.

---

[17] The fundamentals are domestic industrial production, the U.S. Treasury bill rate, domestic inflation, the real exchange rate, and a political stability index. After trying a number of specifications I ended up including one-month lagged, current, and one-month leads of the fundamentals.

The use of this relatively long event window raises the following problem in interpreting the results. Policymakers may time stock market liberalization in the same way that managers time equity issuance to follow a period of significant run-up in their firm's equity price (Ritter (1991), Loughran and Ritter (1995)). If this is the case then the results in Table V may be an artifact of the relatively long event window. This section reestimates the response of equity prices to liberalization using shorter event windows. Specifically, equation (4) is reestimated using windows of three different lengths for the *Liberalize* variable: five months ($T^* - 4$ to T^*), two months ($T^* - 1$ to T^*), and one month (T^* only). The reform variables remain exactly as described in Section III.C.

The results, which are presented in Table VI, indicate that the equity price revaluation associated with stock market liberalization is relatively robust to the choice of window length. Although the statistical significance is not as strong as for the eight-month window, the *Liberalize* coefficient of 0.030 for the five-month window ($T^* - 4$ to T^*) is almost identical to the eight-month coefficient of 0.033. Interestingly, the point estimate for the two-month window ($T^* - 1$ to T^*), 0.050, is larger than that for both the five-month and eight-month windows. The implementation-month-only (T^*) point estimate, 0.065, is the largest of all. The fact that the strongest results are those for the window that is least susceptible to the market-timing critique is indeed suggestive of a revaluation effect of stock market liberalization. Given that the interpretation difficulties are least severe with the implementation-month-only estimation windows, all of the results in Sections III.F and III.G will rely on estimates using T^* only windows.

F. Other Initial Stock Market Liberalization Dates

Sections III.A through III.E present results based on the stock market liberalization dates in Table I. Now I estimate the impact of stock market liberalization using the other liberalization dates. The Appendix provides, in Table AII, a chronological listing of all the unique liberalization dates in Table II, columns (2) through (5). A variable called *LiberalizeAll*, which takes a value of one on each of the implementation dates listed in column (1) of Table AII, is created. The specifications given in equations (1) through (4) are reestimated, replacing *Liberalize* with *LiberalizeAll*. The *LiberalizeAll* coefficient can be interpreted as the average implementation-month-only revaluation across all the unique liberalization dates in Table II.

Table AIII, columns (1a) through (4a), presents the results. The *Liberalize* coefficient is highly significant in all stock return regressions. After controlling for all relevant factors, the coefficient of 0.052 on *LiberalizeAll* is slightly smaller than the coefficient of 0.065 on the *Liberalize* variable in Table VI.[18] The fall in dividend yields is only statistically significant in the first regression (1b), but the results in specifications (2b) through (4b) are qualitatively

---

[18] That the point estimate for *LiberalizeAll* is somewhat smaller than that for *Liberalize* is consistent with the fact that a number of the stock market liberalization dates used in constructing *LiberalizeAll* occur later than those used to construct *Liberalize*.

Table VI

Stock Market Reactions to First Stock Market Liberalization, Alternative Event Window Lengths

The regressions are performed using monthly stock market data from December 1976 to December 1994 for Argentina, Brazil, Chile, India, Korea, Mexico, and Thailand. For the other countries the data are monthly from December 1984 to December 1994. The dividend yield data are also monthly and cover the period from December 1984 to December 1994. *Liberalize* is a dummy variable for the event window of the first stock market liberalization. For $T^* - 4$ to T^*, the event window begins four months prior to the implementation month and ends in the implementation month. For example, for a stock market liberalization that was implemented in November 1989, the event window begins in July 1989 and ends in November 1989. For $T^* - 1$ to T^*, the event window begins in the month before the implementation month. For T^*, the event window is the implementation month only. R^{LDC}, R^{US}, and R^{EAFE} are the dividend-inclusive monthly return on the IFC Global Index, the S&P 500, and the Morgan Stanley Capital Index for Europe, Asia, and the Far East, respectively. *Stabilize*, *Trade*, *Privatize*, and *Exchange* are dummy variables for the event window of macroeconomic stabilization, trade opening, privatization, and exchange controls, respectively. Each of the event windows for these economic reform variables begins seven months prior to the implementation of the reform and ends in the implementation month. A constant plus 11 country dummies were also estimated but not reported. Heteroskedasticity-consistent (White) standard errors are in parentheses.

	Panel A: Stock Returns			Panel B: $\Delta\ln(D/P)$		
	$T^* - 4$ to T^*	$T^* - 1$ to T^*	T^*	$T^* - 4$ to T^*	$T^* - 1$ to T^*	T^*
Liberalize	0.030*	0.050*	0.065*	0.017	−0.008	−0.003
	(0.018)	(0.028)	(0.039)	(0.032)	(0.051)	(0.076)
R^{LDC}	0.520***	0.522***	0.522***	−0.340***	−0.340***	−0.339***
	(0.058)	(0.058)	(0.059)	(0.118)	(0.111)	(0.116)
R^{US}	0.283***	0.280***	0.281***	−0.451**	−0.367*	−0.448**
	(0.091)	(0.091)	(0.094)	(0.200)	(0.204)	(0.197)
R^{EAFE}	−0.016	−0.0150	−0.014	−0.028	−0.0276	−0.0281
	(0.036)	(0.036)	(0.033)	(0.024)	(0.021)	(0.024)
Stabilize	0.003	0.003	0.003	0.002	0.003	0.003
	(0.010)	(0.010)	(0.010)	(0.008)	(0.008)	(0.008)
Trade	0.021**	0.020**	0.020**	−0.037**	−0.037**	−0.037**
	(0.009)	(0.009)	(0.009)	(0.016)	(0.017)	(0.017)
Privatize	0.010	0.011	0.011	−0.030	−0.030	−0.030
	(0.009)	(0.009)	(0.009)	(0.021)	(0.021)	(0.0210)
Exchange	−0.002	−0.002	−0.003	0.008	0.008	0.008
	(0.014)	(0.014)	(0.014)	(0.045)	(0.045)	(0.045)
$\bar{R}^2$	0.146	0.146	0.146	0.027	0.027	0.027
No. of obs.	2292	2292	2292	1569	1569	1569

*, **, and *** indicate significant difference at the 10, 5, and 1 percent levels, respectively.

consistent with the stock return results. As in Tables V and VI, the *Trade* co-efficient is highly significant in all dividend yield regressions, indicating that a move toward freer trade is seen as improving future growth prospects. Column (2) of Table AII lists all of the unique dates in columns (3) through (5) of Table II. Column (5a) of Table AIII presents stock return estimates using these dates. The coefficient on *LiberalizeAll* in this case is 0.051.

G. Stock Market Liberalizations Subsequent to the First

Sections III.A through III.F analyze whether revaluations occur in anticipation of the first stock market liberalization. In order to test whether revaluations occur in anticipation of subsequent stock market liberalizations, a second set of regressions is run which no longer looks at countries' first stock market liberalization in isolation. A new variable called *Liberalize2* is created which takes on the value one during the implementation month of all the stock market liberalizations listed in Table AI. Again, as in Section III.F, since the dummy variable is on during the implementation month only, the total revaluation effect is the same as the point estimate. The analysis begins by estimating

$$R_{it} + \alpha_i + \gamma_1 Liberalize_{it} + \gamma_2 Liberalize2 + \epsilon_{it}, \tag{5}$$

and proceeds to augment specification (5) with the identical set of right-hand side variables used as controls in Sections III.B through III.D.

The results are reported in Table AIV in the Appendix. Regression (1a) indicates that the coefficient on *Liberalize2* is 0.030, but it is statistically insignificant. The *Liberalize* coefficient is now 0.101, and the hypothesis that the estimated *Liberalize* and *Liberalize2* coefficients are statistically the same is rejected at the 5 percent level. On average, subsequent stock market liberalizations have less of a valuation effect than the first. Regression (2a) illustrates that including world stock returns on the right-hand side does not change either set of coefficients very much.

Regression (3a) of Table AIV demonstrates that after including contemporaneous reforms the *Liberalize* coefficient is not affected much. *Liberalize2* continues to be statistically insignificant, and the *Trade* and *Privatize* coefficients are similar in magnitude to the estimates in Table V. Regression (4a), which includes the macroeconomic fundamentals, shows that the *Liberalize* coefficient has fallen from 0.101 in regression (1a) to 0.066. The true implementation-month-only revaluation effect of the first stock market liberalization is about two-thirds of what one is led to believe in the absence of controls. This corroborates the story that emerged from Table V where the true cumulative eight-month revaluation effect also was about two-thirds as large as in the absence of controls. The *Liberalize2* coefficient has fallen from 0.030 in regression (1a) to 0.022 and is still statistically insignificant.

The statistically insignificant *Liberalize2* coefficient lends itself to two possible interpretations. First, it could be that the revaluation effects of subsequent stock market liberalizations are not detectable at the time they occur because they are anticipated at the time of the first stock market liberalization (Urias (1994) makes a similar argument in the context of ADRs). Second, it is possible that once the initial liberalization occurs, new country funds (the majority of subsequent liberalizations) provide minimal diversification benefits because they are spanned by existing funds (Diwan, Errunza, and Senbet (1993)). In other words, it is possible that the first liberalization effectively integrates the market.

IV. Alternative Explanations

The central message from Sections III.A to III.F is that a substantial appreciation of aggregate share prices occurs both in the months leading up to the implementation of a country's initial stock market liberalization as well as in the implementation month itself. On average, in the eight-month window preceding its initial stock market liberalization, a country's aggregate share price index experiences a 38 percent increase in real dollar terms. After controlling for relevant factors, the revaluation is about 26 percent. About 6.6 percent of this revaluation takes place in the actual implementation month. The macroeconomic reforms are themselves a significant source of share price revaluation. In particular, the stock market experiences a total revaluation of 2.1 percent per month in each of the eight months leading up to a trade liberalization. These results certainly suggest a revaluation of aggregate share prices in anticipation of future stock market liberalization and trade liberalization. Nevertheless, it is not clear that we can infer causation.

Suppose a trade reform occurs before a stock market liberalization. We might end up attributing any associated stock market revaluation to the trade reform and not to the stock market liberalization. However, the revaluation might really be due to the stock market liberalization, but the market knows that stock market liberalizations usually follow trade reforms. In fact, the sequencing literature (Dornbusch (1983), Edwards (1984), and McKinnon (1991)) advocates trade liberalization first, followed by capital account liberalization. Given the influence of this literature on the policy reform debate in developing countries during the 1980s, it is more than plausible that trade liberalizations were seen as a harbinger of future stock market liberalizations. Analogously, the possibility remains that when a stock market liberalization is implemented, equity prices jump because stock market liberalization is interpreted as a signal of future macroeconomic reforms.

V. Conclusions

The standard IAPM makes a salient prediction about an emerging country that does not allow foreigners to purchase shares in its stock market: The country's aggregate cost of equity capital will fall when it opens its stock market to foreign investors. Equivalently stated, holding expected future cash flows constant, we should see an increase in an emerging country's equity price index when the market learns of an impending future stock market liberalization. This paper examines whether the data are consistent with this theoretical prediction.

The paper attempts to hold expected future cash flows constant by augmenting the standard event study analysis with a set of right-hand-side variables that control for major economic policy changes such as macroeconomic stabilization programs, trade liberalizations, privatizations, and the easing of exchange controls. The analysis also controls for comovements with foreign stock markets and macroeconomic fundamentals. Finally, the paper confronts the potential endogeneity problem that arises out of policymakers' incentive to liberalize the stock market in response to a prolonged run-up in equity prices.

Bearing in mind all of the caveats about inferring causality, it is instructive to do some simple calculations. Suppose that the preliberalization discount rate on equity is 20 percent and that the entire revaluation effect is 26 percent—the size of the response to the first stock market liberalization. Since we are holding expected future cash flows constant and using logarithmic returns, this revaluation means that the cost of equity capital also falls by 26 percent. This implies a fall in the level of the discount rate to about 15 percent. If one uses the more conservative, implementation-month-only revaluation effect of 6.5 percent, the implied level of the postliberalization discount rate is on the order of 19 percent. Stulz (1999a, 1999b) argues that the magnitudes of the fall in the level of the discount rate implied by such estimates are small relative to what we would expect in a world where (1) there was no home bias and (2) liberalizations were implemented in a fully credible, once-and-for-all fashion.

An important question for future research lies in assessing whether what seems like a relatively small revaluation effect has any economic significance. At the macroeconomic level, Henry (1999a) finds that stock market liberalizations are consistently followed by a surge in the growth rate of private physical investment. Although this suggests significant economic effects of stock market liberalization, further research is needed. In particular, future research should work to uncover the sector-specific, valuation, cost of capital, and investment effects of stock market liberalization.

The fact that aggregate valuation seems to increase in anticipation of future trade liberalizations also points to a potentially fruitful line of research. Trade liberalization has heterogeneous effects on exporters and importers; an analysis of firm level data would deepen our understanding of the sector-specific valuation impacts of trade liberalization. More generally, if the goal is to understand emerging financial markets, then the fact that emerging stock markets respond to macroeconomic reforms suggests that there is positive value added to careful documentation and explicit statistical use of macroeconomic policy changes.

Appendix

Details of the stock market liberalization dates studied in addition to those in Table I are provided in the following four tables. Table AI shows that most countries' initial stock market liberalizations did not constitute a complete opening to foreign investors, Table AII provides a listing of all the unique liberalization dates in Table II, and Tables AIII and AIV provide details of regressions of stock market reactions to alternative initial liberalization dates and subsequent liberalization dates, respectively.

Table A1

Subsequent Stock Market Liberalizations and Contemporaneous Economic Reforms

T^* is the date of the country's stock market liberalization in event time. All events are taken from *The Economist Intelligence Unit: Quarterly Economic Reports*. A full chronology of events is presented in Henry (1999b).

Country, Opening Date	Type of Opening	$T^* - 12$	$T^* - 9$	$T^* - 6$	$T^* - 3$	T^*	$T^* + 3$
Argentina							
January 91	Investable Index jumps 19 percent	None	Airline and ship privatizations begin	Structural adjustment funds unfrozen	IMF agreement; privatizations	Domingo Cavallo appointed finance minister	Tariff reductions
January 92	Country Fund	None	Privatizations	IMF stand by loan	None	IMF approves economic plan	IMF agreement; Brady deal
Brazil							
October 88	Country Fund	None	None	None	IMF approves economic program; import ban lifted	Creditors ratify new loan agreement	Third Cruzado Plan
April 90	Investability Index jumps 33 percent	IMF talks open; stock market scandal	Tariffs reduced	Privatization process frozen	None	Collor takes office, sweeping deregulations	Tariffs reduced; curb on profit remittance removed
January 91	Investability Index jumps 34 percent	None	None	IMF talks open	Deregulation measures announced; debt restructuring rejected	Second Collor Plan	None
July 91	Investability Index jumps 185 percent;	None	None	None	Agreement on payment of arrears	IMF negotiations begin; privatizations	None
May 92	Country Fund	None	None	IMF approves a new stand by loan	Negotiations begin on Brady deal	Brady debt deal signed; official charges of corruption against Collor	None

continued

Table AI—*Continued*

Country, Opening Date	Type of Opening	$T^* - 12$	$T^* - 9$	$T^* - 6$	$T^* - 3$	T^*	$T^* + 3$
Chile							
June 88	Country Fund	None	None	Telefonos de Chile privatized	Privatization of state electricity company begins	Poll shows Pinochet to win plebiscite	None
January 89	Investability Index jumps 15 percent	None	None	None	Pinochet defeated in plebiscite	None	None
February 90	Country Fund	None	IMF mission visits	IMF loan; Central Bank independent	Patricio Alwyn takes over as President	Foreign exchange controls eased	Alwyn announces commitment to reforms
January 91	Investability Index jumps 42 percent	None	None	Debt rescheduling	None	None	Capital outflow restrictions eased
January 92	Investability Index jumps 46 percent	None	None	Free trade agreement with Mexcio	None	Peso revalued by 5 percent	Foreign exchange controls eased
India							
May 87	Country Fund	None	None	Stock market scandal	None	None	None
August 88	Country Fund	None	Talks on trade liberalization begin	Import liberalization package	Government declares support for privatization	None	None
December 88	Country Fund	None	None	None	None	None	None
October 89	Country Fund	None	None	None	None	Gandhi congress ousted	None
June 90	Country Fund	None	None	None	None	None	None
May 92	Country Fund	Rao elected PM; rupee devalued	None	None	Exchange controls eased; import duties decreased	Illegal stock trading exposed	Import liberalization

India (*continued*)							
May 94	Country Fund	Government faces no confidence vote	None	None	None	Foreigners can enter telecom industry	None
September 94	Country Fund	None	None	None	None	None	None
Korea							
December 88	Government announces plan to open stock market	Roh Tae Woo elected president	Tariffs reduced on consumer durables	None	Minimum wage increased by 23 percent	Interest rates deregulated	Investment in foreign real estate allowed
July 90	Country Fund	None	None	None	North Korea proposes disarmament	Diplomatic relations with USSR	None
March 91	Country Fund	None	None	None	None	None	None
January 92	Foreigners allowed to hold up to 10 percent of market	None	None	Foreign firms allowed to hold retail outlets	Limit on foreign banks issue of cds eased	Bank bailout of $680 million	North Korea agrees to military inspection
October 92	Investability Index jumps 23 percent	None	None	None	Pension funds urged to buy more equity	Kim Young Sam elected president	None
July 93	Country Fund	None	None	Governor of Bank of Korea is sacked	Financial reform plan published	Foreigners can buy convertible bonds	Real name financial system decree
December 93	Country Fund	None	None	None	Lending rates liberalized	GATT, tariff reduction agreements	Foreign banks admitted
December 94	Foreign equity ceiling raised to 12 percent	None	Manufacturing firms can issue unlimited corporate bonds	Kim Il Sung dies	None	None	None
Malaysia							
December 87	Country Fund	None	None	Possible cut in corporate tax rate announced	90 arrests under Internal Security Act	None	$1 billion rescue plan for depositors
April 89	Country Fund	Most favored nation trade pact with China	None	ASEAN-Japan Development Fund loans	None	None	Hiatus on restructuring foreign equity
April 90	Country Fund	None	Banks allowed to purchase stock	152 firms delist from Singapore Stock Exchange	None	Plan for electricity privatization	None

Table AI—*Continued*

Country, Opening Date	Type of Opening	$T^* - 12$	$T^* - 9$	$T^* - 6$	$T^* - 3$	T^*	$T^* + 3$
Malaysia *(continued)*							
January 91	Investability Index jumps 29 percent	None	None	None	Prime Minister Mathir's party retains power in general elections	None	None
Mexico							
October 90	Country Fund	Brady term sheet submitted	None	Privatization of banks approved None	Salinas requests NAFTA talks; Telmex to be privatizatized	None	None
January 92	Investability Index jumps 51 percent	None	NAFTA talks begin; $2.2B of Telmex privatized	Election: strong PRI showing boosts reforms	Bancomer privatized	None	Environmental concerns about NAFTA
The Philippines							
May 87	Country Fund	None	Import controls lifted	Paris Club debt rescheduling of $870 million	$10.5 billion structural adjustment loan; debt rescheduling	Agrarian land reform plan is approved	Coup attempt; bombings of businesses in Makati
November 89	Country Fund	IMF approves stabilization plan	None	Debt rescheduling $2.2 billion	Brady deal reached in principle	Coup attempt	None
October 93	Country Fund	None	Airline privatization announced	IMF negotiations begin	Privatization of copper and shipyards	Privatization of steel company approved	IMF agreement reached
Taiwan							
December 86	Country Fund	None	None	None	Import tariffs reduced	None	Restrictions imposed on capital inflows
May 89	Country Fund	None	Capital gains tax imposed	Privatization of China Steel announced	More flexible exchange rate regime	Central bank governor resigns; trade restrictions lifted	Exchange controls lifted; privatizations

Taiwan (*continued*)							
January 91	Foreigners allowed to hold up to 10 percent of market	Bank privatizations announced	Han Pei-Tsun elected prime minister	Pension funds allowed to invest in stock market	None	None	Privatizations
August 93	Investability Index jumps 115 percent	None	Privatizations	Lien Chan becomes prime minister	None	None	None
March 94	Investability Index jumps 33 percent	None	None	None	Tariffs cut by an average of 100 percent	288 million shares of China Steel sold	Banking opened to foreign banks
Thailand							
December 88	Country Fund	None	None	Chartchai Choonhavan takes office	None	Ceiling on foreign borrowing raised	U.S. imposes restrictions on imports from Thailand
December 89	Country Fund	None	None	Accusations of corruption	None	Strikes protesting privatization	Ceiling on loan rates raised
June 90	Country Fund	None	None	None	None	None	Twenty ministers sacked in corruption scandal
January 91	Investability Index jumps 35 percent	None	None	None	None	Coup overthrows government	Exchange controls eased
Venezuela							
January 94	Investability Index jumps 33 percent	Perez accused of misusing public funds	Free trade agreement with Chile; rampant coup rumors	Perez suspended from presidency	Privatization process frozen	Price controls imposed; Banco Latino collapses	None

The Journal of Finance

Table AII

Unique Stock Market Liberalization Dates

This table lists the unique liberalization dates from Table II. Column (1) lists all of the unique liberalization dates in Table II. Column (2) lists the unique liberalization dates from columns (3) through (5) of Table II.

Country	(1) All Unique Stock Market Liberalization Dates from Table II	(2) Unique Stock Market Liberalization Dates from Table II, Columns (3)–(5) only
Argentina	November 1989 October 1991	October 1991
Brazil	March 1988 May 1991	May 1991
Chile	May 1987 September 1987 October 1989 January 1992	September 1987 October 1989 January 1992
Colombia	February 1991 October 1991 December 1991	February 1991 October 1991
India	June 1986 November 1992	November 1992
Korea	June 1987 January 1992	January 1992
Malaysia	May 1987 December 1988	December 1988
Mexico	May 1989 November 1989	November 1989
The Philippines	May 1986 July 1986 June 1991 October 1989	July 1986 June 1991 October 1989
Taiwan	May 1986 January 1991	January 1991
Thailand	January 1988 September 1987	September 1987
Venezuela	January 1990 December 1988	December 1988

Table AIII
Stock Market Reactions to First Stock Market Liberalization, Alternative Event Dates

The regressions are performed using monthly stock market data from December 1976 to December 1994 for Argentina, Brazil, Chile, India, Korea, Mexico, and Thailand. For the other countries the data are monthly from December 1984 to December 1994. The dividend yield data are also monthly and cover the period from December 1984 to December 1994. *Liberalize* is a dummy that takes on the value one during the implementation month of the first stock market liberalization. R^{LDC}, R^{US}, and R^{EAFE} are the dividend-inclusive monthly return on the IFC Global Index, the S&P 500, and the Morgan Stanley Capital Index for Europe, Asia, and the Far East, respectively. *Stabilize, Trade, Privatize,* and *Exchange* are dummy variables for the event windows of macroeconomic stabilization, trade opening, privatization, and exchange controls respectively. Each of the event windows for these variables begins seven months prior to the implementation of the reform and ends in the implementation month. A constant plus 11 country dummies were also estimated but not reported. Heteroskedasticity-consistent (White) standard errors are in parentheses.

	Panel A: Stock Returns					Panel B: Δln(D/P)				
	(1a)	(2a)	(3a)	(4a)	(5a)	(1b)	(2b)	(3b)	(4b)	(5b)
Liberalize	0.072*** (0.024)	0.057** (0.025)	0.056** (0.024)	0.052** (0.024)	0.051* (0.027)	-0.051* (0.029)	-0.041 (0.030)	-0.041 (0.030)	-0.034 (0.035)	-0.040 (0.041)
R^{LDC}		0.512*** (0.063)	0.507*** (0.062)	0.516*** (0.059)	0.519*** (0.143)		-0.343*** (0.103)	-0.334*** (0.103)	-0.334*** (0.104)	-0.335*** (0.116)
R^{US}		0.266*** (0.100)	0.272*** (0.100)	0.293*** (0.094)	0.293*** (0.108)		-0.363*** (0.140)	-0.372*** (0.140)	-0.452*** (0.156)	-0.453*** (0.205)
R^{EAFE}		-0.004 (0.036)	-0.002 (0.036)	-0.014 (0.033)	-0.015 (0.042)		-0.045 (0.054)	-0.047 (0.055)	-0.029 (0.056)	-0.029 (0.024)
Stabilize			0.004 (0.013)	0.003 (0.011)	0.003 (0.005)			-0.003 (0.024)	0.003 (0.023)	0.003 (0.008)
Trade			0.025*** (0.008)	0.021*** (0.008)	0.021*** (0.005)			-0.039** (0.016)	-0.037** (0.017)	-0.037** (0.016)
Privatize			0.017* (0.010)	0.011 (0.008)	0.011 (0.001)			-0.030* (0.018)	-0.030 (0.017)	-0.030 (0.022)
Exchange			-0.007 (0.015)	-0.003 (0.014)	-0.003 (0.016)			0.008 (0.037)	0.008 (0.037)	0.008 (0.046)
$\bar{R}^2$	0.001	0.066	0.070	0.147	0.145	0.000	0.010	0.010	0.030	0.030
No. of obs.	2292	2292	2292	2292	2292	1569	1569	1569	1569	1569

*, **, and *** indicate significance at the 10, 5, and 1 percent levels, respectively.

Table AIV

Stock Market Reaction to First and All Subsequent Stock Market Liberalizations

The regressions are performed using monthly data from December 1984 to December 1994. *Liberalize* is a dummy variable that takes on the value one during the month that the first stock market liberalization is implemented. *Liberalize2* is a dummy variable that takes on the value 1 during the implementation month of all stock market liberalizations subsequent to the first. R^{LDC}, R^{US}, and R^{EAFE} are the monthly return on the IFC Global Index, the S&P 500, and the Morgan Stanley Capital Index for Europe, Asia, and the Far East, respectively. *Stabilize*, *Trade*, *Privatize*, and *Exchange* are dummy variables for the event windows of macroeconomic stabilization, trade opening, privatization, and exchange controls respectively. Each of the event windows for these variables begins seven months prior to the implementation of the reform and ends in the implementation month. A constant plus 11 country dummies were also estimated but not reported. Heteroskedasticity-consistent (White) standard errors are in parentheses.

	Panel A: Stock Returns				Panel B: Δln(D/P)			
	(1a)	(2a)	(3a)	(4a)	(1b)	(2b)	(3b)	(4b)
Liberalize	0.101*** (0.038)	0.082** (0.041)	0.078 (0.039)	0.066 (0.036)	-0.060 (0.049)	-0.043 (0.050)	-0.037 (0.049)	-0.003 (0.081)
Liberalize2	0.030 (0.022)	0.030 (0.022)	0.028 (0.021)	0.022 (0.018)	-0.056 (0.059)	-0.057 (0.060)	-0.055 (0.060)	-0.074 (0.062)
R^{LDC}		0.520*** (0.150)	0.514*** (0.147)	0.524*** (0.143)		-0.353*** (0.120)	-0.343*** (0.116)	-0.325*** (0.115)
R^{US}		0.251*** (0.102)	0.258*** (0.101)	0.280*** (0.110)		-0.349* (0.195)	-0.359* (0.200)	-0.385** (0.191)
R^{EAFE}		-0.002 (0.044)	-0.001 (0.044)	-0.013 (0.042)		-0.049 (0.021)	-0.051 (0.022)	-0.041 (0.025)
Stabilize			0.005 (0.011)	0.003 (0.010)			-0.003 (0.011)	-0.001 (0.005)
Trade			0.025*** (0.005)	0.021*** (0.005)			-0.040*** (0.015)	-0.039** (0.017)
Privatize			0.016** (0.006)	0.010* (0.007)			-0.027 (0.019)	-0.026 (0.021)
Exchange			-0.007 (0.015)	-0.003 (0.016)			0.008 (0.050)	0.009 (0.046)
$\bar{R}^2$	0.000	0.070	0.070	0.147	0.000	0.010	0.011	0.031
No. of obs.	2292	2292	2292	2292	1569	1569	1569	1569

*, **, and *** indicate significance at the 10, 5, and 1 percent levels, respectively.

Stock Market Liberalization   563

REFERENCES

Alexander, Gordon, Cheol Eun, and Sundaram Janakiramanan, 1987, Asset pricing and dual listing on foreign capital markets: A note, *Journal of Finance* 42, 151–158.

Basu, Parantap, and Matthew Morey, 1998, Trade liberalization and the behavior of emerging stock market prices, Working paper, Fordham Institute for Research in Economics.

Bekaert, Geert, 1995, Market integration and investment barriers in emerging equity markets, *World Bank Economic Review* 9, 75–107.

Bekaert, Geert, and Campbell R. Harvey, 1995, Time-varying world market integration, *Journal of Finance* 50, 403–444.

Bekaert, Geert, and Campbell R. Harvey, 2000, Foreign speculators and emerging equity markets, *Journal of Finance* 55, 565–613.

Binder, John, 1998, The event study methodology since 1969, *Review of Quantitative Finance and Accounting*, forthcoming.

Boubakri, Narjess, and Jean-Claude Cosset, 1998, The financial and operating performance of newly privatized firms: Evidence from developing countries, *Journal of Finance* 53, 1081–1111.

Buckberg, Elaine, 1995, Emerging stock markets and international asset pricing, *World Bank Economic Review* 9, 51–74.

Diwan, Ishac, Vihang Errunza, and Lemma Senbet, 1993, Empirical perspectives on national index funds, Working paper, World Bank, Washington, D.C.

Dornbusch, Rudiger, 1983, Panel discussion on the southern cone, *International Monetary Fund Staff Papers* 30, 164–184.

Edwards, Sebastian, 1984. The order of liberalization of the external sector in developing countries, *Princeton Essays in International Finance*, 156.

Errunza, Vihang, and Etienne Losq, 1985, International asset pricing under mild segmentation: Theory and test, *Journal of Finance* 40, 105–124.

Errunza, Vihang, and Etienne Losq, 1989, Capital flow controls, international asset pricing, and investors welfare: A multi-country framework, *Journal of Finance* 44, 1025–1037.

Errunza, Vihang, Etienne Losq, and Prasad Padmanabhan, 1992, Tests of integration, mild segmentation, and segmentation hypotheses, *Journal of Banking and Finance* 16, 949–972.

Errunza, Vihang, and Darius P. Miller, 1998, Market segmentation and the cost of capital in international equity markets, Working paper, McGill University and Texas A&M University.

Eun, Cheol, and Sundaram Janakiramanan, 1986, A model of international asset pricing with a constraint on foreign equity ownership, *Journal of Finance* 41, 897–914.

Fama, Eugene F., 1981, Stock returns, real activity, inflation, and money, *American Economic Review* 71, 545–565.

Foerster, Stephen R., and G. Andrew Karolyi, 1999, The effects of market segmentation and investor recognition on asset prices: Evidence from foreign stocks listing in the United States, *Journal of Finance* 54, 981–1013.

Henry, Peter Blair, 1999a, Do stock market liberalizations cause investment booms? *Journal of Financial Economics*, forthcoming.

Henry, Peter Blair, 1999b, Appendix of major policy changes in selected developing countries, mimeo, Stanford University Graduate School of Business.

Kim, E. Han, and Vijay Singal, 2000, Stock market openings: Experience of emerging economies, *Journal of Business* 73, 25–66.

Levine, Ross, and Sara Zervos, 1994, Capital control liberalization and stock market development: Data annex of country policy changes, World Bank, Washington, D.C.

Loughran, Timothy, and Jay Ritter, 1995, The new issues puzzle, *Journal of Finance* 50, 23–51.

McKinlay, A. Craig, 1997, Event studies in economics and finance, *Journal of Economic Literature* 35, 13–39.

McKinnon, Ronald I., 1991, *The Order of Economic Liberalization* (Johns Hopkins University Press, Baltimore).

Ozler, Sule, 1989, On the relationship between reschedulings and bank value, *American Economic Review* 12, 1117–1131.

Park, Keith, and Antoine W. Van Agtmael, 1993, *The World's Emerging Stock Markets: Structure, Development, Regulations and Opportunities* (Probus Publishing Company, Chicago).

Price, Margaret M., 1994, *Emerging Stock Markets* (McGraw Hill, Inc., New York).

Ritter, Jay, 1991, The long-run performance of initial public offerings, *Journal of Finance* 46, 3–27.

Sachs, Jeffrey, and Andrew Warner, 1995, Economic reform and the process of global integration, *Brookings Papers on Economic Activity* 1, 1–113.

Stapleton, Richard, and Marti Subrahmanyam, 1977, Market imperfections, capital market equilibrium, and corporate finance, *Journal of Finance* 32, 307–319.

Stulz, René M., 1999a, International portfolio flows and security markets, Working paper, Dice Center for Financial Economics, The Ohio State University.

Stulz, René M., 1999b, Globalization and the cost of equity capital, Working paper, The New York Stock Exchange.

Summers, Lawrence H., 1994, A changing course toward privatization; in Ahmed Galal and Mary Shirley, eds.: *Does Privatization Deliver?* (The World Bank, Washington, D.C.).

Tesar, Linda L., and Ingrid M. Werner, 1998, The internationalization of securities markets since the 1987 crash; in Robert E. Litan and Anthony M. Santomero, eds.: *Brookings-Wharton Papers on Financial Services* (Brookings Institution Press, Washington).

Urias, Michael, 1994, The impact of security cross-listing on the cost of capital in emerging markets, Unpublished dissertation, Stanford University.

ELSEVIER

Available online at www.sciencedirect.com

SCIENCE @ DIRECT®

Journal of Financial Economics 77 (2005) 3–55

JOURNAL OF Financial ECONOMICS

www.elsevier.com/locate/econbase

Does financial liberalization spur growth? [☆]

Geert Bekaert[a,b], Campbell R. Harvey[b,c,*], Christian Lundblad[d]

[a]*Columbia University, New York, NY 10027, USA*
[b]*National Bureau of Economic Research, Cambridge, MA 02138, USA*
[c]*Fuqua School of Business, Duke University, Durham, NC 27708-0120, USA*
[d]*Indiana University, Bloomington, IN 47405, USA*

Received 3 February 2003; received in revised form 27 October 2003; accepted 24 May 2004
Available online 20 January 2005

Abstract

We show that equity market liberalizations, on average, lead to a 1% increase in annual real economic growth. The effect is robust to alternative definitions of liberalization and does not reflect variation in the world business cycle. The effect also remains intact when an exogenous measure of growth opportunities is included in the regression. We find that capital account liberalization also plays a role in future economic growth, but, importantly, it does not subsume the contribution of equity market liberalizations. Other simultaneous reforms only

[☆]We appreciate the helpful comments of Wayne Ferson, Peter Henry, Ross Levine, Graciela Kaminsky, Han Kim, Luc Laeven, Michael Pagano, Vicente Pons, Tano Santos, Sergio Schmukler, Bill Schwert (Editor), Andrei Shleifer, René Stulz, Jeffrey Wurgler, seminar participants at the University of Chicago, Georgetown University, Ohio State University, University of Michigan, Boston College, Washington University in St. Louis, Missouri, the World Bank, Princeton University, University of California at Los Angeles, Fordham University, Instituto Superior de Ciencias do Trabalho e da Empresa in Lisbon, Portugal, University of Porto, Cass Business School – London, the International Monetary Fund, the London School of Economics, and the participants at the American Finance Association meetings in Atlanta, Georgia, the Conference on Financial Systems and Crises at the Yale School of Management, the Western Finance Association meetings in Tuscon, Arizona, the Conferencia Regional para América Latina y el Caribe meetings in Monterrey, Mexico, the European Finance Association Meetings in Barcelona, Spain, and the Atlanta Federal Reserve Bank/Inter-American Development Bank Conference, and especially those of an anonymous referee.

*Corresponding author. Fuqua School of Business, Duke University, Durham, NC 27708-0120, USA. Tel.: +1 919 660 7768; fax: +1 919 660 8030.

E-mail address: cam.harvey@duke.edu (C.R. Harvey).

partially account for the equity market liberalization effect. Finally, the largest growth response occurs in countries with high-quality institutions.

JEL classification: E32; F30; F36; F43; G15; G18; G28

Keywords: Equity market liberalization; Financial development; Capital account openness; Quality of institutions; GDP growth

1. Introduction

The last 25 years have witnessed the financial liberalization of equity markets across the world. Equity market liberalizations give foreign investors the opportunity to invest in domestic equity securities and domestic investors the right to transact in foreign equity securities. We find that equity market liberalizations increase subsequent average annual real economic growth by about 1%, even after controlling for other variables that are commonly used in the economic growth literature.

From a neoclassical perspective, our results are to be expected. Improved risk sharing post-liberalization should decrease the cost of equity capital (see, for example, Bekaert and Harvey, 2000) and increase investment. When markets are imperfect, equity market liberalization could have strong effects as well. Financing constraints (see, e.g., Hubbard, 1997, and Gilchrist and Himmelberg, 1999), make external finance more costly than internal finance and cause investment to be sensitive to cash flows. Equity market liberalization directly reduces financing constraints in the sense that more foreign capital becomes available, and foreign investors could insist on better corporate governance, which indirectly reduces the cost of internal and external finance. Hence, the cost of capital could go down because of improved risk sharing or because of the reduction in financing constraints or both. Moreover, better corporate governance and investor protection should promote financial development (La Porta et al., 1997) and hence growth (King and Levine, 1993, for example).

From at least two alternative perspectives, our results may be more surprising. First, alternative theories do not imply positive growth effects after financial liberalization, for example, because of reduced precautionary savings (Devereux and Smith, 1994) or because informational asymmetries prevent foreign capital to be profitably invested (Stiglitz, 2000). Second, a rapidly growing literature on the growth effects of capital account liberalization finds mixed results (see Eichengreen, 2002, for a survey).

We conduct a number of empirical exercises that instill confidence in our results.

- Our results survive an extensive number of econometric robustness experiments, including controlling for world business cycle variation.

G. Bekaert et al. / Journal of Financial Economics 77 (2005) 3–55   5

- Our results are robust to alternative measurements of the liberalization variable. The use of a homogeneous measure of international openness, focusing on equity markets, could explain why our results are so different from the capital account openness literature. We confirm that the standard International Monetary Fund (IMF) measure of whether the capital account is free of restrictions (see Rodrik, 1998, and Kraay, 1998) does not give rise to a robust growth effect. When capital account restrictions are more finely measured, as in Quinn (1997) and Edwards (2001), there is a significant growth effect. However, the growth effect from equity market liberalization remains important even after controlling for a more finely measured capital account liberalization indicator.
- We take seriously the possibility that liberalization could be a strategic decision correlated with growth opportunities. However, when we control for growth opportunities, the liberalization effect remains intact.
- Our growth effect is large which likely cannot be fully ascribed to equity market liberalization. Most importantly, equity market liberalization could coincide with other reforms that improve the growth prospects of the country. We closely investigate several possibilities such as macro reforms, financial reforms, legal reforms (including reforms regarding insider trading), and the coincidence of equity market liberalizations with post-banking crisis reforms.
- It is unlikely that the liberalization effect is the same in all liberalizing countries. We relate the heterogeneity of the growth effect to the comprehensiveness of reforms, the legal environment, the quality of institutions, the investment conditions, and the degree of financial development.

The paper is organized as follows. Section 2 describes our data, the summary statistics and the econometric framework. Section 3 examines the role of equity market liberalization as a determinant of economic growth. Section 4 explores whether the equity market liberalization effect can be accounted for by macroeconomic and other regulatory reforms. Section 5 sheds light on why the growth response to financial liberalization differs across countries. Some concluding remarks are offered in Section 6.

2. Data and preliminary analysis

This section introduces the key data that we use throughout the paper. Section 2.1 introduces our measures of equity market liberalization. Section 2.2 provides an unconditional analysis, i.e., not controlling for other factors, of how equity market liberalization impacts the key variables in our research.

2.1. Equity market liberalizations

Our tests involve regressions of real per capita gross domestic product (GDP) growth on an equity market liberalization indicator using panel data. Table 1 contains the descriptions and sources of all the variables used in the paper.

Table 1
Description of the variables
All data are employed at the annual frequency.

Variable	Description
	Dating equity market liberalization
Official equity market liberalization indicator (Official Liberalization)	Corresponding to a date of formal regulatory change after which foreign investors officially have the opportunity to invest in domestic equity securities. Official Liberalization dates, presented in Table 2, are based on Bekaert and Harvey (2002) *A Chronology of Important Financial, Economic and Political Events in Emerging Markets*, http://www.duke.edu/~charvey/chronology.htm. This chronology is based on over 50 different source materials. A condensed version of the chronology, along with the selection of dates for a number of countries appears in Bekaert and Harvey (2000). We have extended their official liberalization dates to include Japan, New Zealand, and Spain. For the liberalizing countries, the associated Official Liberalization indicator takes a value of one when the equity market is officially liberalized and thereafter, and zero otherwise. For the remaining countries, fully segmented countries are assumed to have an indicator value of zero, and fully liberalized countries are assumed to have an indicator value of one. These dates appear in Appendix A.
First sign equity market liberalization indicator (First Sign)	"First Sign" equity market liberalization dates denote the year associated with the earliest of three dates: Official Liberalization, first American Depositary Receipt (ADR) announcement and first country fund launch. The First Sign indicator takes a value of one on and after the First Sign year, and zero otherwise. As with the Official Liberalization indicator, fully segmented countries are assumed to have an indicator value of zero, and fully liberalized countries are assumed to have an indicator value of one. These dates are reported in Appendix A.
Intensity equity market liberalization indicator (Liberalization Intensity)	Following Bekaert (1995) and Edison and Warnock (2003), the Liberalization Intensity measure is based on the ratio of the market capitalization of the constituent firms comprising the IFC Investable index to those that comprise the IFC Global index for each country. The IFC Global index, subject to some exclusion restrictions, is designed to represent the overall market portfolio for each country, whereas the IFC Investable index is designed to represent a portfolio of domestic equities that are available to foreign investors. A ratio of one means that all of the stocks are available to foreign investors. We denote this measure: *Liberalization Intensity*. We also explore a related measure, *Alternative Intensity*, by calculating the ratio of the number of firms in the investable and global indices for each country. In both cases, fully segmented countries have an intensity measure of zero, and fully liberalized countries have an intensity measure of one.
	Other important dates
IMF capital account openness indicator	We measure capital account openness by employing the IMF's *Annual Report on Exchange Arrangements and Exchange Restrictions* (AREAER). This publication reports six categories of information. The

G. Bekaert et al. / Journal of Financial Economics 77 (2005) 3–55   7

Table 1 (*continued*)

Variable	Description
	capital account openness indicator takes on value of zero if the country has at least one restriction in the "restrictions on payments for the capital account transaction" category. These dates are reported in Appendix A.
Quinn Capital account openness indicator	Quinn's (1997) capital account openness measure is also created from the text of the annual volume published by the International Monetary Fund (IMF), *Exchange Arrangements and Exchange Restrictions.* Rather than the indicator constructed by the IMF that takes a 1 if any restriction is in place, Quinn's openness measure is scored 0–4, in half integer units, with 4 representing a fully open economy. The measure hence facilitates a more nuanced view of capital account openness, and is available for 76 countries in our study. We transform each measure into a 0 to 1 scale.
Banking sector crisis indicator	Caprio and Klingebiel (2001) document systemic and borderline banking sector crises. We construct banking crisis indicators that take a value of one when (a) a country is undergoing a systemic banking sector crisis or (b) when a country is undergoing either a systemic or borderline banking sector crisis. We also construct post-banking crisis indicators that take a value of one in the last year and each subsequent year following (a) a systemic banking sector crisis or (b) either a systemic or borderline banking sector crisis.
Insider trading law indicator	Bhattacharya and Daouk (2002) document the enactment of insider trading laws and the first prosecution of these laws. We construct two indicator variables. The first takes the value of one following the introduction of an insider trading law. The second takes the value of one after the law's first prosecution.

Macroeconomic and demographic measures

Variable	Description
Gross domestic product (GDP) growth	Growth of real per capita gross domestic product. Available for all countries from 1980 through 1997. Source: *World Bank Development Indicators* CD-ROM.
Initial GDP	Logarithm of real per capita gross domestic product in 1980. Available for all countries. Source: *World Bank Development Indicators* CD-ROM.
Government consumption/GDP	Government consumption divided by gross domestic product. General government final consumption expenditure includes all government current expenditures for purchases of goods and services (including compensation of employees). It also includes most expenditures on national defense and security, but excludes government military expenditures that are part of government capital formation. Available for all countries from 1980 through 1997. Source: *World Bank Development Indicators* CD-ROM.
Secondary school enrollment	Secondary school enrollment ratio is the ratio of total enrollment, regardless of age, to the population of the age group that officially corresponds to the secondary level of education. Accordingly, the reported value can exceed (or average) more than 100%. Available for all

Table 1 (*continued*)

Variable	Description
	countries from 1980 through 1997. Source: *World Bank Development Indicators* CD-ROM.
Populationgrowth	Growth rate of total population which counts all residents regardless of legal status or citizenship. Available for all countries from 1980 through 1997. Source: *World Bank Development Indicators* CD-ROM.
Log life expectancy	Life expectancy at birth indicates the number of years a newborn infant would live if prevailing patterns of mortality at the time of its birth were to stay the same throughout its life. Available for all countries from 1980 through 1997. Source: *World Bank Development Indicators* CD-ROM.
OECD GDP growth	Growth of real per capita gross domestic product for high-income OECD members. High-income economies are those in which 1998 GNP per capita was $9,361 or more. Source: *World Bank Development Indicators* CD-ROM.
World real interest rate	Constructed from each country's real interest rates. The GDP weighted real interest rate for the G-7 countries, where the real rate for each country is the lending interest rate adjusted for inflation as measured by the GDP deflator. Source: *World Bank Development Indicators* CD-ROM.
	Macroeconomic reforms
Trade/GDP	The trade dependency ratio is the sum of exports and imports of goods and services measured as a share of gross domestic product. Available for all countries from 1980 through 1997. Source: *World Bank Development Indicators* CD-ROM.
Inflation	Inflation as measured by the log annual growth rate of the gross domestic product implicit deflator. We use the CPI if the GDP-deflator is not available. Available for all countries from 1980 through 1997. Source: *World Bank Development Indicators* CD-ROM.
Black market premium	The black market premium is defined as (parallel FXrate/officialFXrate − 1) ∗ 100, where parallel FXrate is the black market rate. The variable measures the premium market participants must pay, relative to the official exchange rate, to exchange the domestic currency for dollars in the black market. Available for all countries from 1980 through 1997. Source: Easterly (2001).
Fiscal deficit	The overall budget deficit is total expenditure and lending minus repayments less current and capital revenue and official grants received; shown as a percentage of GDP. Data are available for central governments only. Available for 28 countries from 1980 through 1997. Source: *World Bank Development Indicators* CD-ROM.
Growth Opportunities	An implied measure of country-specific growth opportunities that reflects the growth prospects for each industry (at the global level) weighted by

G. Bekaert et al. / Journal of Financial Economics 77 (2005) 3–55 9

Table 1 (*continued*)

Variable	Description
	the industrial composition for each country. We construct an annual measure of the 3-digit SIC industry composition for each country by their output shares according to UNIDO Industrial Statistics Database. For each SIC code, we also measure price-earnings (PE) ratios for that industry at the global level, from which we construct an implied measure of growth opportunities for each country by weighting each global industry PE ratio by its relative share for that country. We subtract from this measure the overall world market PE ratio to remove the world discount rate effect (and we remove a 5-year moving average), and call the difference "growth opportunities" (GO). Available for 92 countries from 1980 through 1997. Source: Bekaert et al. (2004b).

Financial development

Variable	Description
Private credit/GDP	Private credit divided by gross domestic product. Credit to private sector refers to financial resources provided to the private sector, such as through loans, purchases of non-equity securities, and trade credits and other accounts receivable that establish a claim for repayment. Available for all countries from 1980 through 1997. Source: *World Bank Development Indicators* CD-ROM.
Equity market turnover	The ratio of equity market value traded to the market capitalization. The data are available for 50 countries from 1980 through 1997. Source: Standard and Poor's/International Finance Corporation's *Emerging Stock Markets Factbook*.

Legal environment

Variable	Description
Legal origin	Identifies the legal origin of the company law or commercial code of each country (English, French, Socialist, German, Scandinavian). We construct three indicators that take the value of one when the legal origin is Anglo-Saxon (English Law), French (French Law), or other (Law Other), and zero otherwise; legal origin is available for all countries. This variable is purely cross-sectional, and available for all countries. Source: La Porta et al. (1999) .
Judicial Efficiency	Assessment of the "efficiency and integrity of the legal environment as it affects business, particularly foreign firms" produced by the country risk rating agency Business International Corp. It may be taken to "represent investors' assessments of conditions in the country in question." Average between 1980 and 1983. Scale from 0 to 10, with lower scores, lower efficiency levels. This variable is purely cross-sectional, and available for 47 countries. Source: La Porta et al. (1998).
Speed of Judicial Process	The total estimated speed in calendar days of the procedure (to evict a tenant for nonpayment of rent or to collect a bounced check) under the factual and procedural assumptions provided. It equals the sum of (i) duration until completion of service of process, (ii) duration of trial, and (iii) duration of enforcement. This variable is purely cross-sectional, and available for 69 countries. Source: Djankov et al. (2003).

10   *G. Bekaert et al. / Journal of Financial Economics 77 (2005) 3–55*

Table 1 (*continued*)

Variable	Description
	Quality of Institutions
Quality of Institutions	The sum of the International Country Risk Guide (ICRG) Political Risk (ICRGP) subcomponents: Corruption, Law and Order, and Bureaucratic Quality.
Corruption	ICRGP quality of institutions sub-component. This is a measure of corruption within the political system. Such corruption: distorts the economic and financial environment, reduces the efficiency of government and business by enabling people to assume positions of power through patronage rather than ability, and introduces an inherent instability into the political process. The most common form of corruption met directly by business is financial corruption in the form of demands for special payments and bribes connected with import and export licenses, exchange controls, tax assessments, police protection, or loans. Although the PRS measure takes such corruption into account, it is more concerned with actual or potential corruption in the form of excessive patronage, nepotism, job reservations, "favor-for-favors," secret party funding, andsuspiciously close ties between politics and business. In PRS's view these sorts of corruption create risk to foreign business, potentially leading to popular discontent, unrealistic and inefficient controls on the state economy, and encourage the development of the black market.
Law and Order	ICRGP quality of institutions sub-component. PRS assesses Law and Order separately, with each sub-component comprising zero to three points. The Law sub-component is an assessment of the strength and impartiality of the legal system, while the Order sub-component is an assessment of popular observance of the law. Thus, a country can enjoy a high rating (3.0) in terms of its judicial system, but a low rating (1.0) if the law is ignored for a political aim.
Bureaucratic Quality	ICRGP quality of institutions sub-component. The institutional strength and quality of the bureaucracy can act as a shock absorber that tends to minimize revisions of policy when governments change. Therefore, high points are given to countries where the bureaucracy has the strength and expertise to govern without drastic changes in policy or interruptions in government services. In these low-risk countries, the bureaucracy tends to be somewhat autonomous from political pressure and to have an established mechanism for recruitment and training. Countries that lack the cushioning effect of a strong bureaucracy receive low points because a change in government tends to be traumatic in terms of policy formulation and day-to-day administrative functions.
	Investment environment
Economic risk rating	ICRG Economic Risk indicator (which ranges between 0 and 50). The risk rating is a combination of 5 subcomponents: GDP levels and growth, respectively, inflation, balanced budgets, and the current account. The minimum number of points for each component is zero, while the

Table 1 (*continued*)

Variable	Description
	maximum number of points depends on the fixed weight that component is given in the overall economics risk assessment.
Anti-director rights	An index aggregating different shareholder rights. The index is formed by adding 1 when: (1) the country allows shareholders to mail their proxy vote to the firm; (2) shareholders are not required to deposit their shares prior to the General Shareholders' Meeting; (3) cumulative voting or proportional representation of minorities in the board of directors is allowed; (4) an oppressed minorities mechanism is in place; (5) the minimum percentage of share capital that entitles a shareholder to call for an Extraordinary Shareholders' Meeting is less than or equal to 10 percent (the sample median); or (6) shareholders have preemptive rights that can only be waved by a shareholders' vote. The index ranges from 0 to 6. This variable is purely cross-sectional, and available for 47 countries. Source: La Porta et al. (1998).
Investment Profile	ICRG Political Risk (ICRGP) sub-component (12% weight in overall ICRGP index). This is a measure of the government's attitude to inward investment. The investment profile is determined by PRS's assessment of three sub-components: (i) risk of expropriation or contract viability; (ii) payment delays; and (iii) repatriation of profits. Each sub-component is scored on a scale from zero [very high risk] to four [very low risk].
Creditor rights	An index aggregating different creditor rights. The index is formed by adding 1 when (1) the country imposes restrictions, such as creditors'consent or minimum dividends to file for reorganizations; (2) secured creditors are able to gain possession of their security once the reorganization petition has been approved (no automatic stay); (3) secured creditors are ranked first in the distribution of the proceeds that results from the disposition of the assets of a bankrupt firm; and (4) the debtor does not retain the administration of its property pending the resolution of the reorganization. The index ranges from 0 to 4. This variable is purely cross-sectional, and available for 45 countries. Source: La Porta et al. (1998).
Accounting Standards	Index created by examining and rating companies' 1990 annual reports on their inclusion or omission of 90 items. These items fall into seven categories (general information, income statements, balance sheets, funds flow statements, accounting standards, stock data, and special items). A minimum of three companies in each country were studied. The companies represent a cross section of various industry groups; industrial companies represented 70 percent, and financial companies represented the remaining 30 percent. This variable is purely cross-sectional, and available for 39 countries. Source: La Porta et al. (1998).

Perhaps the most important variable in our paper is the indicator variable, Official Liberalization. This variable is based on the Bekaert and Harvey (2002) detailed chronology of important financial, economic, and political events in many

12 *G. Bekaert et al. / Journal of Financial Economics 77 (2005) 3–55*

developing countries. The variable takes the value of one when foreign portfolio investors can own the equity of a particular market and zero otherwise. We augment this analysis with liberalization dates for five developed countries: Iceland, Japan, Malta, New Zealand, and Spain (see Appendix A).

We investigate the robustness of the liberalization effect to an alternative measure of financial liberalization: First Sign. This measure is based on the earliest of three possibilities: a launching of a country fund, an American Depositary Receipt (ADR) announcement, and an Official Liberalization. It might be possible for a foreign investor to access the market through a country fund well before foreigners are allowed to directly transact in the local equity market. For example, consider the case of Thailand. Bekaert and Harvey (2002) date the Official Liberalization in September 1987. This was the first month of operation of the Thai Alien Board, which allowed foreigners to directly transact in Thai securities. However, foreigners could indirectly access the Thai market earlier. In July 1985, the Bangkok Fund Ltd. was launched on the London Stock Exchange, and in December 1986, Morgan Stanley launched the Thailand Fund. Thailand announced its first ADR in January 1991. So, for our analysis, the Official Liberalization is dated in 1987, and the First Sign date is 1985.

We also consider an alternative continuous measure of liberalization. Bekaert (1995) and Edison and Warnock (2003) propose a measure of equity market openness based on the ratio of the capitalization of the International Finance Corporation (IFC) investable to the global stocks in each country. The IFC's global stock index seeks to represent the local stock market, and the investable index corrects market capitalization for foreign ownership restrictions. A ratio of one means that all of the stocks are available to foreign investors. In Table 3, we call this measure Liberalization Intensity.[1] Table 1 has more details on the construction of this variable.

Finally, we contrast equity market liberalization with capital account liberalization and two measures of capital account openness; one based on IMF information and the other proposed by Quinn (1997) and Quinn and Toyoda (2003). The various liberalization measures are presented in Appendix A. All other data are discussed when they are introduced in the analysis.

Our regression analysis uses four different country samples, which are determined by data availability. Economic growth rates, the basic control variables, and the Official Liberalization indicator are available for all samples. Our largest samples cover 95 and 75 countries, respectively, and employ primarily macroeconomic and demographic data. Our smallest samples, cover 50 and 28 countries, respectively, and employ, in addition to the macroeconomic and demographic information, data describing the state of banking and equity market development in each country. We report results based on the largest overall sample (95 countries, Sample I) and the largest sample that includes financial information (50 countries, Sample II). We sometimes refer to the results for the two alternative samples which are available on request.

---

[1] We also explore a related measure by calculating the ratio of the number of firms in the investable and global indices for each country (Alternative Intensity). Given the high volatility of emerging market equity returns, this measure could be less noisy. These results are similar and are available on request.

G. Bekaert et al. / Journal of Financial Economics 77 (2005) 3–55 13

2.2. Unconditional effects of liberalization

Tables 2 and 3 present a summary analysis of some of the main variables in our study. We analyze the data from two perspectives. First, in Table 2, we consider means of the variables five years before and after equity market liberalizations. However, for real GDP growth, we also examine three- and seven-year intervals. We

Table 2

Summary statistics. We explore the three, five, and seven-year averages of the growth rate of real per capita gross domestic product (GDP) and the five-year averages of the other variables employed in the paper (and summarized in Table 1) before and after the equity market liberalization (including the liberalization year in the after period). For some countries, we do not have a full three, five, or seven years available given the timing of the liberalization, so we simply take the available years in the average. For all variables, unless otherwise stated, the summary statistics reflect data for 95 countries from 1980 to 1997. Official Liberalization means that the equity market is liberalized. Fully liberalized denotes countries that are fully liberalized throughout our sample. Never liberalized denotes countries that never undergo financial liberalization. ICRG is the International Country Risk Guide. Statistical significance is denoted by * for 10%, ** for 5%, and *** for 1%. NA denotes variables for which the test is not available.

Variable	Pre-liberalization	Post-liberalization	Never liberalized	Fully liberalized
Real GDP growth (three-year)	0.0160	0.0265**	−0.0016	0.0201***
Real GDP growth (five-year)	0.0159	0.0276***		
Real GDP growth (seven-year)	0.0153	0.0264***		
Government/GDP	0.1379	0.1328	0.1581	0.1885***
Enrollment	0.5573	0.6115**	0.3439	0.9974***
Population growth	0.0203	0.0169**	0.0255	0.0060***
Life expectancy	65.7	67.7**	56.9	75.7***
Growth opportunity	−0.0301	0.0076***	−0.0012	−0.0016
Trade/GDP	0.6229	0.6383	0.6970	0.8429***
Log(1 + inflation) (Latin)	0.1890	0.1411	0.0596	NA
Log(1 + inflation) (not Latin)	0.0993	0.0857	0.0934	0.0411***
Log(1 + black market premium)	0.1499	0.0724***	0.2211	0.0007***
Fiscal Deficit (28 countries)	0.0606	0.0333***	NA	0.0307
Private credit/GDP	0.3831	0.4263	0.2286	0.8095***
Turnover (50 countries)	0.1814	0.2664	NA	0.4938
Banking crisis (systematic)	0.3243	0.2941	0.3300	0.1131***
Banking crisis (systematic and borderline)	0.5243	0.5784	0.4190	0.3891
Law and order (75 countries)	0.4875	0.6065***	0.4472	0.9510***
Insider trading law	0.4205	0.7241***	0.0836	0.6540***
Insider trading prosecution	0.0667	0.1149*	NA	0.4325
Judicial efficiency (47 countries)			NA	0.9456
Speed of process (checks + eviction) (69 countries)			363.4	408.3
Quality of institutions (75 countries)	0.5273	0.6033***	0.4158	0.9333***
ICRG economic index (75 countries)	0.5895	0.6765***	0.5909	0.7845
Investment profile (75 countries)	0.4660	0.5312***	0.4680	0.6494***
Anti-director rights (47 countries)			NA	0.4902
Creditor rights (45 countries)			NA	0.4853
Accounting standards (39 countries)			NA	0.6950

14   *G. Bekaert et al. / Journal of Financial Economics 77 (2005) 3–55*

Table 3
Preliminary analysis of the impact of liberalization. For all estimates, the dependent variable is the one-year average growth rate of real per capita gross domestic product (GDP). Regressions include time effects, fixed effects, or both, as indicated (not reported in the interest of space); no other controls are included. In Panel A, we focus on equity market liberalization across the 40 countries that liberalize in our sample. The Official Liberalization variable takes a value of one when the equity market is liberalized, and zero otherwise. We consider an additional regression that includes China (41 countries). The First Sign liberalization indicator takes the value of one after the first of the following events: the Official Liberalization date, the introduction of American Depository Receipts, or the introduction of a country fund. The Liberalization Intensity measure is the ratio of the market capitalizations for the International Finance Corporation's investables to global indices.

In Panel B, we consider more general measures of capital account openness. The International Monetary Fund capital account openness indicator takes on value of zero if the country has at least one reported capital account restriction. The Quinn capital account liberalization indicator takes a value between one and zero depending upon the intensity of the reported capital account liberalization or openness; these regressions include 76 countries. For both measures, we perform regressions for the same 40 liberalizing countries for comparison, as well as for the full set of countries for which the measures are available.

	Estimate	Standard Error	Adjusted R^2
Panel A: Equity market liberalization			
Official Liberalization indicator (40 countries)			
Fixed effects	0.0124	0.0032	0.208
Time effects	0.0202	0.0048	0.052
Fixed and time effects	0.0105	0.0053	0.229
Official Liberalization indicator plus China (41)			
Fixed effects	0.0128	0.0031	0.251
Time effects	0.0210	0.0049	0.048
Fixed and time effects	0.0117	0.0053	0.270
First Sign indicator (40)			
Fixed effects	0.0129	0.0033	0.208
Time effects	0.0185	0.0041	0.055
Fixed and time effects	0.0080	0.0050	0.228
Liberalization Intensity (40)			
Fixed effects	0.0205	0.0051	0.209
Time effects	0.0137	0.0064	0.033
Fixed and time effects	0.0151	0.0064	0.231
Panel B: Capital account liberalization			
IMF capital account openness indicator (40)			
Fixed effects	0.0036	0.0065	0.190
Time effects	0.0057	0.0043	0.029
Fixed and time effects	0.0017	0.0065	0.224
IMF capital account openness indicator (95)			
Fixed effects	0.0041	0.0051	0.110
Time effects	0.0071	0.0029	0.024
Fixed and time effects	−0.0017	0.0053	0.133
Quinn capital account openness indicator (37)			
Fixed effects	0.0154	0.0192	0.169
Time effects	0.0218	0.0086	0.030
Fixed and time effects	−0.0016	0.0203	0.196

G. Bekaert et al. / Journal of Financial Economics 77 (2005) 3–55   15

Table 3 (*continued*)

	Estimate	Standard Error	Adjusted R^2
Quinn capital account openness indicator (76)			
Fixed effects	0.0122	0.0123	0.143
Time effects	0.0193	0.0047	0.033
Fixed and time effects	0.0019	0.0129	0.167

look at the difference in means between countries that are fully liberalized and countries that were never liberalized (segmented countries). Second, in Table 3, we conduct regression analysis.

Using a sample of liberalizing countries, Table 2 shows that the real annual GDP growth rate is more than 1% higher in the post-liberalization period for all intervals. A much sharper difference in growth exists between fully liberalized countries and those that did not experience a liberalization, of approximately 2.2%.

The next group of variables serves as control variables in the growth regressions. In the neoclassical growth model, they can be viewed as determinants of steady-state GDP. The control variables experience changes after liberalization that would typically indicate a higher steady state GDP. The most striking and statistically significant differences occur for the fully liberalized and segmented countries. The never-liberalized countries have: lower secondary school enrollment, lower life expectancy, and higher population growth.

Table 3 presents a complementary analysis to Table 2. Here we estimate an ordinary least squares (OLS) regression of one-year GDP growth rates on the different measures of liberalization. We estimate these regressions with fixed effects, time effects, and both fixed and time effects and, therefore, focus only on liberalizing countries. Essentially, the regression identifies average GDP growth post- versus pre-liberalization controlling for country-specific time-invariant growth circumstances and global business cycle effects. Panel A focuses on our measures of equity market liberalization, and Panel B considers various measures of capital account liberalization. We discuss Panel B in Section 3.3.

The first and third parts of Panel A consider the impact of the Official Liberalization indicator and the First Sign indicator. Even with both fixed and time effects, the impact of the equity market liberalization variables is positive and around 1%. The second subpanel adds China to the analysis with a liberalization date of 1991. Unfortunately, we do not have enough data coverage to add China to the analysis in the other tables. The addition of this country in the analysis here increases both the size and the significance of the liberalization coefficient. In the fourth part of this table, we consider a measure of liberalization intensity. This variable provides the strongest and most significant impact, about 1.5% per year, but this number must be interpreted as the effect of a full, comprehensive liberalization.

G. Bekaert et al. / *Journal of Financial Economics* 77 (2005) 3–55

The differences in means reported in Table 2 and the fixed effects regressions in Table 3 suggest liberalization is associated with increased growth.

3. Liberalization and economic growth

This section contains the main results. We start by outlining the econometric framework we employ in Section 3.1, and report the main results in Section 3.2. Section 3.3 contrasts capital account with equity market liberalization, and Section 3.4 considers several robustness exercises. Section 3.5 explicitly discusses the possibility of endogeneity bias.

3.1. Econometric framework

Define the logarithmic growth in real GDP per capita for country i between t and $t + k$ as:

$$y_{i,t+k,k} = \frac{1}{k} \sum_{j=1}^{k} y_{i,t+j} \quad i = 1, \ldots, N, \tag{1}$$

where

$$y_{i,t} = \ln\left(\frac{\text{GDP}_{i,t}}{\text{POP}_{i,t}} \Big/ \frac{\text{GDP}_{i,t-1}}{\text{POP}_{i,t-1}}\right)$$

and N is the number of countries in our sample. Denote the initial level of log GDP per capita as Q_{it} and the country's long-run (steady state) per capita GDP as Q_i^*. Taking a first-order approximation to the neoclassical growth model (see, e.g., Mankiw, 1995), we can derive $y_{i,t+k,k} = -\lambda[Q_{it} - Q_i^*]$, where λ is a positive conditional convergence parameter. The literature often implicitly models Q_i^* as a linear function of a number of structural variables such as the initial level of human capital. Hence a prototypical growth regression can be specified as

$$y_{i,t+k,k} = -\lambda Q_{i,t} + \gamma' \mathbf{X}_{it} + \varepsilon_{i,t+k,k}, \tag{2}$$

where $\mathbf{X}_{it}$ are the variables controlling for different levels of long-run per capita GDP across countries. Our main addition to the literature is to examine the effect of adding an equity market liberalization variable, $\text{Lib}_{i,t}$, to the growth regression

$$y_{i,t+k,t} = \beta Q_{i,1980} + \gamma' \mathbf{X}_{i,t} + \alpha \text{Lib}_{i,t} + \varepsilon_{i,t+k,k}, \tag{3}$$

where $Q_{i,1980}$ represents the logarithm of per capita real GDP in 1980 and serves as an initial GDP proxy. Because it is critical to capture the temporal dimension of the liberalization process, we combine time-series with cross-sectional information.

We estimate Eq. (3) with two approaches. First, we consider an OLS regression on non-overlapping five-year intervals. We consider both a homoskedastic, diagonal

G. Bekaert et al. / Journal of Financial Economics 77 (2005) 3–55   17

and a seemingly unrelated regression (SUR) error structure for these regressions. While this approach does not capture all of the information in the data, it has the advantage of being transparent and providing a baseline estimate for our more general procedure. Second, we identify the parameters using a generalized method of moments (GMM) estimator described and analyzed in Bekaert et al. (2001). The estimator maximizes the time-series content in our regression by making use of overlapping data. We adjust the standard errors for the resulting moving average component in the residuals using a cross-sectional extension to Hansen and Hodrick (1980). Our regressors are all predetermined. While the GMM estimator looks like an instrumental variable estimator, it reduces to pooled OLS under simplifying assumptions on the weighting matrix.

Our GMM framework raises four issues: the construction of the weighting matrix, the choice of k, the specification of the control variables, and the construction of the liberalization indicator.

First, growth regressions have been criticized for being contaminated by multicollinearity (see Mankiw, 1995). In a pure cross-sectional regression, the regressors could be highly correlated (highly developed countries score well on all proxies for long-run growth), the data could be measured with error, and every country's observation is implicitly viewed as an independent draw. Therefore, standard errors likely underestimate the true sampling error. In our panel approach, we can accommodate heteroskedasticity both across countries and across time and correlation between country residuals by choosing the appropriate weighting matrix. In the tables, we report results using the method that accommodates overlapping observations and groupwise heteroskedasticity but does not allow for temporal heteroskedasticity or SUR effects. We report robustness checks later. Also, the growth effect survives the inclusion of fixed effects (see Table 3).

Second, because our sample is relatively short, starting only in 1980, and because many liberalizations only occurred in the 1990s, we use $k = 5$, instead of $k = 10$, which is typical in the literature. However, Islam (1995) and Caselli et al. (1996) find similar results using $k = 5$ versus $k = 10$, and we check the robustness to the alternative k's and the introduction of variables controlling for the world business cycle.

Third, Levine and Renelt (1992) find that most of the independent variables in standard growth regressions are, in a particular sense, fragile. We are primarily interested in the robustness of any effect the liberalization dummy could have on growth. We minimize the data mining biases for the other regressors by closely mimicking the regression in Barro (1997b). In addition, given the documented fragility of some of these variables, our initial analysis adds the control variables one by one to the growth regression.

Fourth, perhaps the main methodological issue regarding our sample is the construction of the equity market liberalization indicator variable. Although timing capital market reforms is prone to errors, the use of annual data reduces the impact of small timing errors. Nevertheless, we conduct several robustness experiments with respect to the definition of the liberalization variable.

18 *G. Bekaert et al. / Journal of Financial Economics 77 (2005) 3–55*

3.2. The liberalization effect in a standard growth regression

Panel A of Table 4 describes the results of the standard growth regression for our largest sample (95 countries). Panels B and C are discussed in Section 3.3. The regression uses nonoverlapping five-year growth rates.[2] The coefficients are OLS estimates, and we report OLS standard errors with the exception of the very last line, which reports restricted SUR standard errors. We restrict the off-diagonal elements of the weighting matrix to be identical. It is not feasible to do a full SUR estimation because the number of countries is much larger than the number of time-series observations. The SUR estimates are close to the OLS estimates.

The explanatory variables in Table 4 include a constant, initial GDP (1980), government consumption to GDP, secondary school enrollment, population growth, and life expectancy. In contrast to Table 3, this regression contains control variables and, as a result, we do not include the fixed or time effects. We add the variables one by one and eventually all together. When initial GDP is the only regressor, it enters with a positive coefficient. When paired with the other control variables, which can now proxy for the steady state level of GDP, it enters with a negative sign, as expected given the standard results on conditional convergence.

The results for the full regression [see Eq. (2)] are broadly consistent with the previous literature (see Barro, 1997a, b and Barro and Sala-i-Martin, 1995). Initial GDP enters with a significant negative coefficient suggesting that low initial GDP levels imply higher growth rates, conditional on the other variables. Life expectancy has a significant positive coefficient suggesting that long life expectancy is associated with higher economic growth. Population growth has a significantly negative coefficient in the regression with the SUR standard errors but is insignificant in the regression with the OLS standard errors. However, secondary school enrollment has the wrong sign and the government size variable is insignificant. The SUR standard errors are generally smaller than the OLS standard errors, because of the heteroskedasticity adjustment.

Most important, the liberalization coefficient is positive and at least 1.85 standard errors above zero in all the regressions. For example, in the full regression, the liberalization coefficient is 0.0120 and approximately three standard errors from zero with the OLS standard errors and close to five standard errors from zero using the SUR standard errors. This suggests that, on average, a liberalization is associated with a 1.20% increase in the real per capita growth rate in GDP. The effect ranges from 0.74% to 1.82% across all specifications.

Table 5 presents results from our GMM estimation with overlapping observations. In addition, this table assesses sensitivity of our results to the specification of the equity market liberalization variable. We also consider both the largest sample (95 countries) and a smaller sample (76 countries) that closely resembles the sample in Quinn (1997) and Quinn and Toyoda (2003).

---

[2] We have three different sample choices for the nonoverlapping regression, 1981–1995, 1982–1996, and 1983–1997. We report the averages of the coefficients and standard errors from three separate nonoverlapping estimations.

G. Bekaert et al. / Journal of Financial Economics 77 (2005) 3–55   19

Table 4

The impact of liberalization in pooled ordinary least squares (OLS) growth regressions. For all estimates, the dependent variable is the five-year nonoverlapping average growth rate of real per capita gross domestic product (GDP). Log(GDP) is the log real per capita GDP level in 1980. Govt/GDP is the ratio of government consumption to GDP; enrollment is the secondary school enrollment ratio; population growth is the growth rate of total population; Log(life) is the log life expectancy of the total population. In Panel A, the Official Liberalization variable takes a value of one when the equity market is liberalized, and zero otherwise; these regressions cover 95 countries.

In Panel B, the International Monetary Fund (IMF) capital account openness indicator takes on value of zero if the country has at least one reported capital account restriction; these regressions cover 95 countries. In Panel C, the Quinn capital account liberalization indicator takes a value between one and zero depending upon the intensity of the reported capital account liberalization or openness; these regressions include 76 countries. We first consider each control variable separately, then all together. For each case, we report the simple average of three coefficients (with standard errors and adjusted R^2's) associated with separate pooled OLS regressions (over 1981–1995, 1982–1996, and 1983–1997) for which the dependent variable is three nonoverlapping five-year GDP average growth rates. That is, each pooled OLS regression has three time-series observations with no overlap; we conduct each regression separately and then average the resulting coefficients. For the last entry of each panel, we also include restricted seemingly unrelated regression (SUR) standard errors (all off-diagonal elements are assumed to be equal) as a robustness check.

Constant	Initial log(GDP)	Gov/GDP	Secondary school enrollment	Population growth	Log(life)	Official Liberalization indicator	IMF capital account openness	Quinn capital account openness	Adjusted R^2
Panel A: Official Liberalization (95 countries)									
0.0048 (0.0021)						0.0181 (0.0029)			0.082
0.0020 (0.0104)	0.0004 (0.0015)					0.0173 (0.0048)			0.079
0.0072 (0.0052)		−0.0152 (0.0332)				0.0182 (0.0030)			0.081
−0.0011 (0.0035)			0.0145 (0.0073)			0.0119 (0.0048)			0.094
0.0135 (0.0041)				−0.3568 (0.1479)		0.0127 (0.0038)			0.106

Table 4
(continued)

	Constant	Initial log(GDP)	Gov/GDP	Secondary school enrollment	Population growth	Log(life)	Official Liberalization indicator	IMF capital account openness	Quinn capital account openness	Adjusted R^2
	−0.1939					0.0488	0.0074			0.149
	(0.0415)					(0.0103)	(0.0039)			
	−0.3093	−0.0084	−0.0007	−0.0029	−0.2616	0.0935	0.0120			0.217
OLS standard errors	(0.0606)	(0.0024)	(0.0318)	(0.0138)	(0.1947)	(0.0159)	(0.0044)			
Restricted SUR standard errors	(0.0337)	(0.0012)	(0.0159)	(0.0061)	(0.1129)	(0.0089)	(0.0025)			
Panel B: IMF capital account liberalization (95 countries)										
	−0.3081	−0.0079	−0.0060	0.0023	−0.3540	0.0929		0.0033		0.197
	(0.0585)	(0.0021)	(0.0252)	(0.0109)	(0.1447)	(0.0159)		(0.0042)		
	−0.3085	−0.0085	−0.0004	−0.0028	−0.2667	0.0935	0.0117	0.0010		0.214
OLS standard errors	(0.0606)	(0.0025)	(0.0321)	(0.0138)	(0.2020)	(0.0159)	(0.0043)	(0.0044)		
Restricted SUR standard errors	(0.0339)	(0.0012)	(0.0163)	(0.0062)	(0.1165)	(0.0090)	(0.0026)	(0.0020)		
Panel C: Quinn sample (76 countries)										
	−0.2875	−0.0121	−0.0267	0.0107	−0.4709	0.0929			0.0247	0.266
	(0.0645)	(0.0023)	(0.0332)	(0.0122)	(0.2366)	(0.0171)			(0.0078)	
	−0.2805	−0.0121	−0.0248	0.0065	−0.3759	0.0913	0.0102		0.0185	0.279
OLS standard errors	(0.0643)	(0.0023)	(0.0332)	(0.0127)	(0.2311)	(0.0171)	(0.0047)		(0.0081)	
Restricted SUR standard errors	(0.0395)	(0.0013)	(0.0192)	(0.0066)	(0.1467)	(0.0102)	(0.0028)		(0.0048)	

Table 5

Equity market and capital account liberalization. The dependent variable is the overlapping five-year average growth rate of real per capita gross domestic product (GDP). In addition to the control variables, we report the coefficient on the official Liberalization Indicator that takes a value of one when the equity market is liberalized, and zero otherwise. The First Sign liberalization indicator takes the value of one after the first of the following events: the Official Liberalization date, the introduction of an American Depository Receipt, or the introduction of a country fund. The Liberalization Intensity is the ratio of the market capitalizations for the International Finance Corporation's investables and global indices. The International Monetary Fund (IMF) capital account liberalization indicator takes on a value of zero if the country has at least one reported capital account restriction; these regressions cover 95 countries. In Panel B, the Quinn capital account liberalization indicator takes a value between one and zero depending upon the intensity of the reported capital account liberalization or openness; these regressions cover 76 countries. All standard errors (in parentheses) provide a correction for cross-sectional heteroskedasticity and account for the overlapping nature of the data.

	(1)	(2)	(3)	(4)
Panel A: Full sample (95 countries)				
Constant	−0.3277	−0.3240	−0.3370	−0.3267
	(0.0286)	(0.0278)	(0.0288)	(0.0287)
Initial log(GDP)	−0.0082	−0.0082	−0.0086	−0.0083
	(0.0010)	(0.0010)	(0.0011)	(0.0011)
Gov/GDP	−0.0144	−0.0102	−0.0135	−0.0142
	(0.0131)	(0.0122)	(0.0131)	(0.0133)
Secondary school enrollment	0.0004	−0.0019	−0.0003	0.0006
	(0.0048)	(0.0048)	(0.0049)	(0.0049)
Population growth	−0.1911	−0.1874	−0.1923	−0.1935
	(0.0774)	(0.0753)	(0.0776)	(0.0783)
Log(life)	0.0975	0.0966	0.1007	0.0974
	(0.0076)	(0.0074)	(0.0078)	(0.0077)
Official Liberalization indicator	0.0097			0.0094
	(0.0020)			(0.0021)
First Sign liberalization indicator		0.0122		
		(0.0020)		
Liberalization Intensity			0.0107	
			(0.0023)	
IMF capital account openness indicator				0.0010
				(0.0017)
Adjusted R^2	0.207	0.215	0.206	0.207

	(1)	(2)	(3)	(4)	(5)
Panel B: Quinn sample (76 countries)					
Constant	−0.2962	−0.2908	−0.3072	−0.2947	−0.2997
	(0.0350)	(0.0341)	(0.0344)	(0.0349)	(0.0334)
Initial log(GDP)	−0.0101	−0.0101	−0.0110	−0.0104	−0.0117
	(0.0011)	(0.0011)	(0.0011)	(0.0012)	(0.0011)

22 *G. Bekaert et al. / Journal of Financial Economics 77 (2005) 3–55*

Table 5 (*continued*)

	(1)	(2)	(3)	(4)	(5)
Gov/GDP	−0.0352 (0.0162)	−0.0305 (0.0155)	−0.0320 (0.0160)	−0.0334 (0.0165)	−0.0377 (0.0161)
Secondary school enrollment	0.0026 (0.0050)	−0.0007 (0.0049)	0.0008 (0.0050)	0.0024 (0.0052)	0.0037 (0.0054)
Population growth	−0.4241 (0.1056)	−0.4241 (0.1036)	−0.4313 (0.1053)	−0.4424 (0.1088)	−0.4530 (0.1107)
Log(life)	0.0947 (0.0089)	0.0933 (0.0087)	0.0991 (0.0088)	0.0948 (0.0089)	0.0966 (0.0085)
Official Liberalization indicator	0.0120 (0.0022)			0.0115 (0.0022)	0.0077 (0.0023)
First Sign liberalization indicator		0.0149 (0.0021)			
Liberalization Intensity			0.0147 (0.0025)		
IMF capital account openness indicator				0.0020 (0.0017)	
Quinn capital account openness indicator					0.0179 (0.0040)
Adjusted R^2	0.270	0.286	0.271	0.270	0.284

The first two sets of estimates in Panels A and B in Table 5 show the results for the Official Liberalization and the First Sign indicator variables, respectively. The OLS results in Table 3 were suggestive that these two specifications of the liberalization variable would produce similar results. This is confirmed in Table 5. In the sample of 95 countries, the coefficient on the First Sign indicator is 1.22% compared with 0.97% for the Official Liberalization indicator. In the smaller sample (76 countries), the First Sign coefficient is 1.49% compared with 1.20% for the Official Liberalization coefficient. The third set of estimates shows the results for the Liberalization Intensity variable. The magnitude and significance of this variable is similar to the other two liberalization proxies. Indeed, in all six regressions, the liberalization coefficients are always significant with T-ratios exceeding 4.5. With the exception of the insignificant secondary school enrollment coefficient, the signs and magnitudes of the coefficients on the control variables are stable across these three definitions of equity market liberalization.

3.3. Capital account versus equity market liberalization

The effect of capital account openness on economic growth is the topic of considerable debate. Grilli and Milesi-Ferretti (1995), Kraay (1998), Rodrik (1998), and Edison et al. (2002a) claim that no correlation exists between capital account liberalization and growth prospects. In contrast, Quinn (1997), Klein and Olivei (1999), and Quinn and Toyoda (2003) find a positive relation between capital account liberalization and growth. Many papers, such as Edison et al. (2002b), Chandra (2003), and Arteta et al. (2003) find that the effect is mixed or fragile. Edwards (2001) finds a positive effect that is driven by the higher income countries in his sample. Klein (2003) finds an inverted U-shaped effect: Capital account liberalization has no impact on the poorest and the richest countries but a substantial impact on the middle-income countries.

We consider two measures of capital account openness in Tables 3–5: one from IMF's *Annual Report on Exchange Arrangements and Exchange Restrictions* (AREAER) (see also Grilli and Milesi-Ferretti, 1995) and one following Quinn (1997) and Quinn and Toyoda (2003). The IMF publication reports several categories of information, mostly on current account restrictions. The capital account openness dummy variable takes on a value of zero if the country has at least one restriction in the "restrictions on payments for the capital account transactions" category.[3]

The Quinn (1997) and Quinn and Toyoda (2003) capital account openness measure is also created from the annual volume published by the IMF's AREAER. In contrast to the IMF indicator that takes a value of zero if any restriction is in place, Quinn's openness measure is scored from 0 to 4, in half integer units, with 4 representing a fully open economy. The measure facilitates a more nuanced view of capital account openness and is available for 76 countries in our study. We transformed each measure into a 0 to 1 scale. [See Eichengreen (2002) for a review of this and other measures.] Some summary statistics for both the IMF and Quinn variables are presented in Appendix A.

We begin with the fixed and time effects regressions in Table 3. In Panel B of Table 3, we find the coefficient on IMF capital account liberalization measure to be insignificantly different from zero in the 40-country sample. The coefficient on the Quinn measure is large in both the fixed and time effects regressions (when estimated separately). However, in the regression that combines the fixed and time effects, the impact is diminished.

The last two parts of Table 3 consider larger samples. With our full set of 95 countries, capital account openness according to the IMF measure has no significant effect on growth. When measured using the Quinn measure (76 countries), the magnitude of the coefficients is large when fixed and time effects are considered separately, but small and insignificant when the effects are combined.[4] The evidence suggests that measuring capital account openness at a finer level as Quinn (1997) does leads to stronger growth effects than using the standard measure but the growth effect does not survive the inclusion of fixed and time effects. Clearly, the effects of equity market liberalization are less fragile.

---

[3]The IMF changed the reporting procedures in 1996 and included subcategories for capital account restrictions (see the discussion in Miniane, 2004), but we follow the bulk of the literature in using the 0/1 variable.

[4]We also estimated a regression with the IMF capital account liberalization measure in the identical 76-country sample as the Quinn measure. The results for this sample are similar to the 95 country results.

24   *G. Bekaert et al. / Journal of Financial Economics 77 (2005) 3–55*

Panels B and C of Table 4 present multivariate counterparts to the last part of Table 3. In this nonoverlapping five-year growth regression, we consider the capital account liberalization measures and the equity market liberalization both separately and together. Panel B considers the IMF measure for 95 countries. In each specification, the coefficient on this measure is indistinguishable from zero. Panel C considers the Quinn measure for 76 countries. The results suggest that the Quinn measure is correlated with growth. In the specification that includes all the control variables and both equity market and capital account liberalization, the coefficient on the Quinn variable is large and is more than two standard errors from zero. Importantly, while the coefficient on the Quinn variable is significant, this variable does not diminish the impact of the equity market liberalization. The coefficient on the equity market liberalization indicator is 1.02% and is more than 3.5 standard errors from zero even when competing directly against the capital account openness indicator.[5]

Finally, Table 5 provides the GMM estimation with overlapping observations. Consistent with the previous analysis, Panel A of Table 5 shows that the IMF measure of capital account liberalization does not significantly impact economic growth. However, the results in Panel B which focus on a sample of 76 countries, show that the Quinn variable is more successful. In the joint estimation, the coefficient on the Quinn variable is more than four standard errors above zero. The equity market liberalization variable, while diminished in magnitude, remains more than three standard errors from zero.

We draw three conclusions from our analysis of capital account openness. First, in our sample of 95 countries, the IMF capital account openness measure does not appear to be correlated with growth. However, consistent with Edwards (2001), the capital account measure does best in our smallest sample, which is more heavily weighted toward high-income countries (the 28-country sample results are available on request). Overall, our evidence supports the conclusion in Arteta et al. (2003) that the relation between the IMF measure and growth is fragile. Second, the Quinn measure, which scores the intensity of controls, is correlated with growth. Third, and most important for our research, the growth effect of the equity market liberalization indicator is robust to including measures of capital account openness. Further, all three sets of results appear to be consistent across varying degrees of econometric complexity with the proviso that the Quinn capital account openness measure is no longer significantly associated with growth when fixed and time effects are introduced.

3.4. Other robustness checks

We establish that equity market liberalization generates a significant growth effect, which is robust to alternative dating of the liberalization and distinct from the effects

---

[5]The performance of the Quinn capital account openness indicator has one unusual aspect. The significance of this measure is dependent on including initial GDP in the regression. In contrast, the significance of the equity market liberalization variable is robust to inclusion or exclusion of initial GDP. These results are available on request.

of capital account liberalization. Here, we conduct seven additional robustness checks. First, we compare Latin American liberalizations to non-Latin American liberalizations. The results in Panel A of Table 6 suggest that the Latin American region is not driving the growth effect. Second, we control for variation in the world business cycle and interest rates. Panel B of Table 6 shows that, Organization for Economic Cooperation and Development (OECD) economic growth exerts a strong positive influence in our growth regression, but the liberalization effect is not diminished by the inclusion of the business cycle variables. In each of our samples, the growth effect from liberalization increases once we add these variables. Third, consistent with our analysis in Table 3, we include time effects variables in the main regression in Table 5, and no discernable impact is evident on the liberalization coefficients. Fourth, we estimate the regressions with three alternative growth horizons: three, seven, and ten years. While the liberalization effect is present at all horizons, this analysis suggests that most of the impact occurs in the first five years after liberalization which is consistent with the convergence literature. (The seven-year horizon regressions suggest that 88% of the growth impact of a liberalization takes place in the first five years.) Fifth, we test the sensitivity of our results to setting initial GDP at 1980 levels. As alternatives, we reset GDP to 1990 levels and also consider using the initial GDP at the time when a country liberalizes. Again, the inference did not change. Sixth, we alter our assumptions about the weighting matrix. In particular, we consider an estimation with restricted SUR effects and an estimation that imposed homoskedasticity with no SUR effects. The liberalization result is resilient to such changes.[6]

Finally, we conduct a Monte Carlo analysis of the liberalization effect. For each replication, we draw 95 uniform random numbers and randomly assign one of the existing liberalization dummies to each country. We re-run the growth regression with the same control variables but with purely random liberalization events. We repeat this experiment one thousand times. The 97.5th percentile of the distribution shows a coefficient of 0.0057 and a T-statistic of 3.25 as reported in Appendix B. This is well below our estimated coefficient of 0.0097 and T-statistic of 4.8 reported in Table 5. Hence, the empirical P-value is less than 0.001. The Monte Carlo evidence shows that the impact of the liberalization indicator is not a statistical artifact and not simply associated with the clustering of liberalizations in the late 1980s and early 1990s. It also shows that a standard T-test could slightly over-reject at asymptotic critical values, which we should take into account in our inference.

3.5. Endogeneity

As with the effect of financial development on growth, endogeneity issues loom large. Is the liberalization decision an exogenous political decision, or do countries liberalize when they expect improved growth opportunities? These concerns are highly relevant for countries that join a free market area, such as Spain and Portugal in the European Union, in which membership simultaneously requires relaxing

---

[6]A full record of the results of the robustness checks is available on request.

Table 6

Analysis of the liberalization effect. Samples I and II refer to samples of 95 and 50 countries, respectively. The dependent variable is the overlapping five-year average growth rate of real per capita gross domestic product (GDP). In addition to the control variables, we report the coefficient on the Official Liberalization indicator that takes a value of one when the equity market is liberalized, and zero otherwise. In Panel A, Latin refers to an indicator that takes the value of one if the country is in Latin America. In Panel B, the world real interest rate is the contemporaneous GDP-weighted real interest rate for the G-7 countries. OECD GDP growth is the five-year average real GDP growth of Organization for Economic Cooperation and Development countries. In Panel C, we augment the control group to include a measure of implied growth opportunities detailed in Table 1. All standard errors (in parentheses) provide a correction for cross-sectional heteroskedasticity and account for the overlapping nature of the data.

	Panel A: regional influences		Panel B: world growth and real interest rates		Panel C: growth opportunities	
	Sample I	Sample II	Sample I	Sample II	Sample I	Sample II
Constant	−0.3293 (0.0291)	−0.2793 (0.0472)	−0.3323 (0.0279)	−0.2954 (0.0495)	−0.3252 (0.0288)	−0.2679 (0.0460)
Initial log(GDP)	−0.0082 (0.0010)	−0.0106 (0.0012)	−0.0085 (0.0010)	−0.0114 (0.0012)	−0.0084 (0.0010)	−0.0107 (0.0012)
Gov/GDP	−0.0150 (0.0132)	−0.0705 (0.0166)	−0.0154 (0.0126)	−0.0700 (0.0157)	−0.0115 (0.0128)	−0.0661 (0.0160)
Secondary school enrollment	0.0000 (0.0049)	0.0028 (0.0055)	−0.0001 (0.0045)	0.0060 (0.0050)	0.0010 (0.0048)	0.0047 (0.0053)
Population growth	−0.1905 (0.0777)	−0.4390 (0.1228)	−0.1885 (0.0729)	−0.3965 (0.1056)	−0.2053 (0.0768)	−0.4697 (0.1170)
Log(life)	0.0980 (0.0777)	0.0937 (0.0126)	0.0098 (0.0073)	0.0974 (0.0129)	0.0974 (0.0077)	0.0909 (0.0124)
Official Liberalization indicator			0.0108 (0.0019)	0.0112 (0.0021)	0.0092 (0.0020)	0.0087 (0.0021)

G. Bekaert et al. / Journal of Financial Economics 77 (2005) 3–55

27

Official Liberalization indicator (Latin)	0.0065 (0.0041)	0.0052 (0.0051)				
Official Liberalization indicator (not Latin)	0.0100 (0.0022)	0.0098 (0.0022)				
OECD GDP growth (contemporaneous)			0.5049 (0.0846)	0.6552 (0.0942)		
World real interest rate (contemporaneous)			−0.2240 (0.0670)	−0.1734 (0.0735)		
Growth opportunities					0.0106 (0.0038)	0.0122 (0.0039)
Adjusted R^2	0.207	0.225	0.216	0.221	0.211	0.209

28   *G. Bekaert et al. / Journal of Financial Economics 77 (2005) 3–55*

capital controls and favorable growth conditions. However, such liberalizations are rare in our sample.

Addressing endogeneity concerns in this context is difficult because finding a suitable instrument for liberalization is nearly impossible. Instead, we try to directly control for growth opportunities. However, this is a formidable task. Any local variable that is correlated with growth opportunities could indicate an increase in growth opportunities because of the planned equity market liberalization. Hence, including the growth opportunity variable into the regression is not informative. Following Bekaert et al. (2004b), our approach is to look for exogenous growth opportunities.

More specifically, we view each country as composed of a set of industries with time-varying growth opportunities and assume that these growth prospects are reflected in the price to earnings (PE) ratios of global industry portfolios. We then create an implied measure of country-specific growth opportunities that reflects the growth prospects for each industry (at the global level) weighted by the industrial composition for each country. We construct an annual measure of the three-digit Standard Industrial Classification (SIC) industry composition for each country by its output shares according to the United National Industrial Development Organization (UNIDO) Industrial Statistics Database. For each SIC code, we also measure price-earnings ratios for that industry at the global level, from which we construct an implied measure of growth opportunities for each country by weighting each global industry PE ratio by its relative share for that country. We divide this measure by the overall world market PE ratio to remove the world discount rate effect, and we also measure this variable relative to its past five-year moving average. We call the difference "growth opportunities" (GO).

$$
\mathrm{GO}_{i,t} = \ell n\left[\frac{\mathrm{IPE}_t \times w'_{i,t}}{\mathrm{WDPE}_t}\right] - \frac{1}{60}\sum_{s=t-60}^{t-1} \ell n\left[\frac{\mathrm{IPE}_s \times w'_{i,s}}{\mathrm{WDPE}_s}\right], \tag{4}
$$

where IPE_t is a vector of global industry price-earning ratios,[7] $w_{i,t}$ is a vector of country-specific industry weights, and WDPE_t is the price-earning ratio of the world market.

When we introduce this variable into a growth regression, Panel C of Table 6 shows that it predicts growth but does not drive out the liberalization effect. The fact that the GO measure is significant in the regressions indicates that it is a good measure of growth opportunities. Comparing the growth effect of liberalization in this regression (0.92%) with the original effect in Table 5 (0.97%), both the coefficient and its statistical significance are essentially unchanged. Whereas this analysis perhaps does not completely resolve the endogeneity problem, it does give us more confidence that our results are not being driven by an endogeneity issue.

---

[7]All price-earnings ratios are taken from Datastream. We use the December value for our annual measures. The Datastream world market is the value-weighted sum of the global industry portfolios.

G. Bekaert et al. / Journal of Financial Economics 77 (2005) 3–55 29

4. Accounting for the liberalization effect

Our growth effect is surprisingly large. One potential interpretation is that reforms are multifaceted. Countries could liberalize equity markets at the same time as they remove restrictions on foreign exchange, deregulate the banking system, and undertake steps to develop the equity market. In this section, we introduce proxies for other contemporaneous reforms into the main regressions.

We investigate three types of reforms: macro-reforms, financial reforms, and legal reforms. We do not have sufficient information to determine the exact time lines of reforms for all our countries in most instances. Consequently, we follow an indirect approach by inserting as control variables into our growth regression continuous variables that measure the direct effect of the reforms. An example would be the level of inflation for macro-reforms. The third bloc of variables examined in Table 2 is made up of the variables used in this section. Table 2 shows that, in most instances, these variables change in the required direction after an equity liberalization and that liberalized economies score better on measures of macroeconomic stability, financial development and rule of law. This is an indication of the potential simultaneity of reforms directly affecting these variables, on the one hand, and equity market liberalization, on the other hand, or perhaps equity market liberalization contributes to a better macroeconomic environment, promotes financial development, or instigates legal reforms that improve the legal environment. In fact, Rajan and Zingales (2003) point out that financial development may be blocked by groups (incumbents) interested in maintaining their monopoly position (in goods and capital markets). They argue that this is less likely to be the case if the country has open trade and free capital flows and hence financial openness may instigate other reforms.

If there are simultaneous reforms, the introduction of these continuous variables into our regression is likely to drive out the liberalization effect, which is a coarse measurement of the extent and quality of the reforms. We do have detailed time-line information on one type of reform: the introduction of insider trading rules and their enforcement. We examine whether these reforms impact growth. Finally, we conjecture that a big reform package is likely after a major financial crisis, such as a banking crisis, and use information on the timing of banking crises to create another control for reform simultaneity effects.

4.1. Macroeconomic reforms

Mathieson and Rojaz-Suarez (1993) and Henry (2000) discuss how policy reforms, including equity market liberalization, in developing countries typically involve domestic macro-reforms. We consider three variables that proxy for macroeconomic reforms: trade openness, the level of inflation, and the black market foreign exchange premium.

Our measure of trade openness is the ratio of exports plus imports to GDP. The effect of trade integration and trade liberalization on growth is the subject of a large literature. Dollar (1992), Lee (1993), Edwards (1998), Sachs and Warner (1995), and

30 *G. Bekaert et al. / Journal of Financial Economics 77 (2005) 3–55*

Wacziarg (2001) establish that lower barriers to trade induce higher growth. Rodriguez and Rodrik (2001) criticize these studies on many grounds. However, Rodriguez and Rodrik primarily question whether trade policy instead of trade volume has affected growth. In our study, we are interested in the effect of financial market liberalization not in testing the impact of trade policy. The results in Table 7, Panel A, show that, in both samples (95 and 50 countries, respectively), the coefficient on trade openness is highly significant and positive, suggesting countries that are open have higher growth than countries that are relatively closed.

Barro (1997a, b) finds a significant negative relation between inflation and economic growth and concludes that the result primarily stems from a strong negative relation between very high inflation rates (over 15%) and economic growth. We use the natural logarithm of one plus the inflation rate to diminish the impact of some outlier observations. Given that the extreme skewness in inflation primarily results from inflation in Latin American countries, we also introduce a dummy for Latin America.

The results in Table 7 for the inflation variable are mixed. We find that three of the four coefficients on inflation are not significantly different from zero. Inflation is never significant for the Latin American countries. In one of the non-Latin American samples, the sign is positive and significant for Sample I. We also estimate a regression without the Latin American indicator. The coefficient on the single inflation variable is not significantly different from zero. We also consider a regression with dummies for Brazil and Argentina only, the largest outliers in inflation data. Here, we find negative but insignificant coefficients, whereas the effect for Argentina and Brazil is negative and significant.[8]

We also examine the effect of introducing black market foreign exchange premiums. The black market premium is taken from Easterly (2001). This variable measures the premium market participants must pay, relative to the official exchange rate, to exchange the domestic currency for dollars in the parallel market. The black market premium is often used as an indicator of macroeconomic imbalances and would consequently be sensitive to macro-reforms. It is also a direct indicator of the existence of foreign exchange restrictions, and it should therefore not be surprising that it is closely correlated with market integration and equity market liberalization (see, for instance, Bekaert, 1995). Hence the black market premium could also be an inverse indicator of the quality and comprehensiveness of the equity market liberalization. Table 2 shows that the black market premium substantially decreases from a pre-liberalization level of 0.150 to a post-liberalization premium of 0.072. As with the inflation indicator, we use the natural logarithm of one plus the black market premium to dampen the influence of outliers. The results in Table 7 show that the premium has a strong negative relation to economic growth in our samples.

The regression reported in Panel A of Table 7 shows that the liberalization coefficient decreases by about 25 basis points but remains significantly different from zero. For example, in Sample I, the coefficient is reduced from 0.97% (Table 5) to 0.74% but remains significantly different from zero. Hence, our results indicate that

---

[8]These results are available on request.

Table 7

The influence of the reform environment on liberalization. Samples I and II refer to samples of 95 and 50 countries, respectively. We report analysis from a regression that has the overlapping five-year average growth rate of real per capita gross domestic product (GDP) as the dependent variable. In addition to the control variables, we report the coefficients for the Official Liberalization indicator, which takes a value of one when the equity market is liberalized, and zero otherwise. In Panel A, we augment the control group to include the openness of the trade sector measured by the sum of exports plus imports divided by GDP, the log of one plus the level of inflation and the log of one plus the level of the black market premium for foreign exchange. In Panel B, we consider financial development variables: the ratio of private credit to GDP, which is a banking development indicator, and the value of trading scaled by market capitalization. In Panel C, we consider law and order (higher values denoting improvements, rescaled to fall between zero and one) taken from the International Country Risk Guide (ICRG), and in Panel D, insider trading law and insider trading prosecution, which are indicators representing either the introduction of laws prohibiting insider trading or actual prosecutions, respectively. For law and order, the * by Sample I denotes that this variable is available for only 75 countries. In Panel E, we include two indicators of banking crises: systemic and systemic and borderline. In the first case, we introduce a dummy variable that is set to one during a banking crisis contemporaneously with the left-hand side variable. In the second case, we add a variable that takes on a value of one after a banking crisis. All standard errors (in parentheses) provide a correction for cross-sectional heteroskedasticity and account for the overlapping nature of the data.

	Panel A: macroeconomic reforms		Panel B: financial development		Panel C: law and order		Panel D: insider trading			
	Sample I	Sample II	Sample I	Sample II	Sample I*	Sample II	Sample I	Sample II	Sample I	Sample II
Constant	−0.3262 (0.0279)	−0.1957 (0.0504)	−0.3155 (0.0282)	−0.2273 (0.0426)	−0.3177 (0.0343)	−0.2714 (0.0413)	−0.3189 (0.0288)	−0.2524 (0.0453)	−0.3265 (0.0281)	−0.2594 (0.0461)
Initial log(GDP)	−0.0084 (0.0010)	−0.0104 (0.0013)	−0.0093 (0.0011)	−0.0120 (0.0011)	−0.0070 (0.0013)	−0.0124 (0.0013)	−0.0080 (0.0010)	−0.0104 (0.0013)	−0.0084 (0.0010)	−0.0112 (0.0012)
Gov/GDP	−0.0289 (0.0124)	−0.0801 (0.0176)	−0.0166 (0.0131)	−0.0559 (0.0157)	−0.0374 (0.0151)	−0.0679 (0.0161)	−0.0143 (0.0129)	−0.0636 (0.0165)	−0.0144 (0.0129)	−0.0656 (0.0163)
Secondary school enrollment	−0.0006 (0.0051)	0.0050 (0.0058)	−0.0005 (0.0049)	0.0007 (0.0051)	0.0019 (0.0051)	0.0055 (0.0056)	−0.0003 (0.0049)	0.0026 (0.0056)	0.0008 (0.0047)	0.0051 (0.0050)
Population growth	−0.1979 (0.0722)	−0.6259 (0.1194)	−0.1994 (0.0765)	−0.6066 (0.1246)	−0.2009 (0.0820)	−0.4611 (0.1193)	−0.1952 (0.0770)	−0.5118 (0.1250)	−0.1936 (0.0757)	−0.5149 (0.1217)

Table 7 (continued)

	Panel A: macroeconomic reforms		Panel B: financial development		Panel C: law and order		Panel D: insider trading			
	Sample I	Sample II	Sample I	Sample II	Sample I*	Sample II	Sample I	Sample II	Sample I	Sample II
Log(life)	0.0970 (0.0075)	0.0730 (0.0131)	0.0957 (0.0076)	0.0828 (0.0113)	0.0937 (0.0090)	0.0933 (0.0111)	0.0950 (0.0077)	0.0867 (0.0121)	0.0976 (0.0075)	0.0899 (0.0123)
Official Liberalization indicator	0.0074 (0.0019)	0.0066 (0.0021)	0.0077 (0.0020)	0.0069 (0.0019)	0.0090 (0.0022)	0.0070 (0.0020)	0.0087 (0.0020)	0.0080 (0.0021)	0.0088 (0.0020)	0.0077 (0.0021)
Trade	0.0106 (0.0014)	0.0100 (0.0017)								
Log(1 + inflation) (Latin)	-0.0006 (0.0023)	0.0008 (0.0027)								
Log(1 + inflation) (not Latin)	0.0092 (0.0042)	0.0127 (0.0078)								
Log(1 + black market premium)	-0.0092 (0.0018)	-0.0067 (0.0032)								
Private credit			0.0125 (0.0031)	0.0084 (0.0032)						
Turnover				0.0152 (0.0026)						
ICRG law and order					-0.0001 (0.0007)	0.0020 (0.0008)				
Insider trading law							0.0003 (0.0014)	-0.0003 (0.0015)		
Insidertrading prosecution									0.0032 (0.0024)	0.0033 (0.0024)
Adjusted R^2	0.265	0.276	0.207	0.262	0.209	0.228	0.209	0.231	0.209	0.235

G. Bekaert et al. / Journal of Financial Economics 77 (2005) 3–55   33

Panel E: banking crises

	Sample I	Sample II	Sample I	Sample II	Sample I	Sample II	Sample I	Sample II
Constant	−0.3047 (0.0281)	−0.2602 (0.0444)	−0.3057 (0.0285)	−0.2852 (0.0495)	−0.3170 (0.0291)	−0.2621 (0.0470)	−0.3168 (0.0286)	−0.2471 (0.0455)
Initial log(GDP)	−0.0080 (0.0010)	−0.0105 (0.0010)	−0.0080 (0.0010)	−0.0107 (0.0011)	−0.0078 (0.0010)	−0.0104 (0.0012)	−0.0080 (0.0010)	−0.0107 (0.0012)
Gov/GDP	−0.0211 (0.0129)	−0.0745 (0.0150)	−0.0178 (0.0133)	−0.0652 (0.0161)	−0.0128 (0.0124)	−0.0648 (0.0160)	−0.0127 (0.0125)	−0.0611 (0.0156)
Secondary school enrollment	0.0010 (0.0049)	0.0022 (0.0054)	0.0012 (0.0049)	0.0011 (0.0057)	0.0007 (0.0047)	0.0041 (0.0053)	0.0010 (0.0046)	0.0040 (0.0050)
Population growth	−0.1896 (0.0774)	−0.4666 (0.1161)	−0.1854 (0.0754)	−0.4516 (0.1157)	−0.1855 (0.0747)	−0.4804 (0.1201)	−0.1926 (0.0743)	−0.5805 (0.1149)
Log(life)	0.0925 (0.0075)	0.0901 (0.0118)	0.0929 (0.0077)	0.0971 (0.0132)	0.0939 (0.0078)	0.0891 (0.0126)	0.0943 (0.0077)	0.0861 (0.0122)
Official Liberalization indicator	0.0094 (0.0021)	0.0084 (0.0020)	0.0101 (0.0019)	0.0081 (0.0021)	0.0097 (0.0020)	0.0087 (0.0021)	0.0091 (0.0020)	0.0076 (0.0021)
During systemic crisis	−0.0072 (0.0014)	−0.0085 (0.0015)						
During systemic and borderline crisis			−0.0081 (0.0011)	−0.0126 (0.0013)				
Post systemic crisis					0.0058 (0.0019)	0.0022 (0.0027)		
Post systemic and borderline crisis							0.0056 (0.0014)	0.0062 (0.0017)
Adjusted R^2	0.218	0.246	0.225	0.295	0.211	0.223	0.212	0.233

part of the equity market liberalization effect is accounted for by these four different proxies for macro-reforms.[9]

4.2. Financial reforms

Regulatory changes furthering financial development could occur simultaneously with the equity market liberalization. A significant literature studies the relation between financial development and growth with contributions as early as McKinnon (1973) and Patrick (1966). Rousseau and Sylla (1999, 2003) show that early U.S. growth in the 1815–1840 period and early growth in other countries was finance led. We examine two financial development indicators: the size of the banking sector and stock exchange trading activity.

King and Levine (1993) study the impact of banking sector development on growth prospects.[10] Kaminsky and Schmukler (2002) study the timing and impact of equity market, capital account, and banking reforms. Panel B of Table 7 examines the role of the banking sector by adding private credit to GDP to the growth regression. Private credit to GDP enters significantly in both samples.

Atje and Jovanovic (1989), Demirgüç-Kunt and Levine (1996), Demirgüç-Kunt and Maksimovic (1996), and Levine and Zervos (1996, 1998a) examine the effect of stock market development on economic growth. In Panel B, we also add, as an independent variable, equity turnover (a measure of trading activity).[11] This financial variable is available only for the 50-country sample. The results in Panel B of Table 7 show that the coefficient on the turnover variable is positive and significant. This implies a positive relation between stock market development and economic growth, consistent with previous studies.

In both samples, the liberalization effect is somewhat diminished. However, the liberalization coefficient continues to be significantly different from zero. Clearly, equity market liberalization is more than just another aspect of more general financial development, not deserving of special attention.

4.3. Legal environment

In a series of influential papers, La Porta et al. (1997, 1998, 1999, 2000) and Djankov et al. (2003) stress the cross-country differences in the legal environment

---

[9]We also considered a fourth policy variable, the size of the country's fiscal deficit. Unfortunately, these data were available only for the smallest of our samples. Edwards (1987) argues that financial openness can be beneficial only when countries first have government finances under control. The coefficient on the deficit variable is significant and negatively influences growth prospects. The coefficient on the equity market liberalization remains significantly different from zero.

[10]Jayaratne and Strahan (1996) find that banking deregulation led to higher regional economic growth within the United States whereas Beck et al. (2000) and Levine et al. (2000) measure the growth effect of the exogenous component of banking development.

[11]We do not consider market capitalization to GDP because this variable is hard to interpret. Having a measure of overall equity values in the numerator, it could simply be a forward-looking indicator of future growth or it could be related to the cost of capital. In addition, Rousseau and Wachtel (2000) find market capitalization to GDP to have a weaker impact than value traded in their cross-country analysis of growth.

G. Bekaert et al. / Journal of Financial Economics 77 (2005) 3–55   35

(either laws or their enforcement) in general and the legal environment regarding investor protection in particular. Reforms improving investor protection could promote financial development (see La Porta et al. (1997) for a direct test) and hence growth. The recent literature on financing constraints suggests a concrete channel through which this could occur. If capital markets are imperfect, external capital is likely to be more costly than internal capital and a shortage of internal capital would reduce investment below first-best levels. Recent empirical work shows that financial development (see Rajan and Zingales, 1998; Love, 2003) and the liberalization of the banking sector (Laeven, 2003) could help relax these financing constraints and increase investment. Financial liberalization would make available more foreign capital, but this does not necessarily resolve the market imperfections that lead to a wedge between the internal and external finance cost of capital. Reforms improving corporate governance and reducing the ability of insiders to extract resources from the firm could directly affect the external cost of capital. More generally, a better legal environment could increase steady state GDP. While the presence of foreign investors could promote financial reforms that help reduce financing constraints and the external finance cost of capital premium, reforms improving the legal environment and investor protection perhaps are the real source of the improved growth prospects.

To examine this issue, we follow La Porta et al. (1997) and use a variable that measures the rule of law in general, which is the rule of law subcomponent of the International Country Risk Guide (ICRG) political risk rating. Table 2 indicates that this variable significantly increases post-liberalization. When we add this measure to the growth regression (see Panel C of Table 7), the growth effect of equity market liberalization slightly increases for Sample I, but decreases 18 basis points in Sample II. In Sample II, law and order generates small but significant growth effects.

Second, we use the insider trading law dummies created by Bhattacharya and Daouk (2002). They argue that the enforcement of insider trading laws makes developing markets more attractive to international investors. They present evidence that associates insider trading laws with a lower cost of capital in a sample of 95 countries. Bhattacharya and Daouk distinguish between the enactment of insider trading laws and the enforcement of these laws.

Insider trading laws, and especially their enforcement, could be closely related to the corporate governance problems that lead to the external finance premium. Enforcement of insider trading laws could be a good instrument for reduced external financing constraints. It is possible that the enactment of such rules are particularly valued and perhaps demanded by foreigners before they risk investing in emerging markets. The enforcement of insider trading laws could proxy for a more general state of law enforcement that could be correlated with policy reforms introducing equity market liberalization.

Panel D of Table 7 examines the relation between the enactment and enforcement of insider trading laws and economic growth. The existence of these laws has no significant relation to economic growth, as evidenced in the first set of results. While the coefficients on insider trading prosecutions are also not significantly different from zero, the coefficients are positive in both samples. Importantly, the equity market liberalization remains significantly different from zero in the presence of the insider trading variable and drops by at most 11 basis points.[12]

4.4. Banking crises

A major crisis of an economic nature could induce a plethora of reforms, one of which being an equity market liberalization.[13] If this is the case, a crisis indicator could be a useful control for the policy simultaneity problem. Caprio and Klingebiel (2001) provide the necessary information to create such an indicator. They survey and date banking crises for about 90 countries, differentiating between systemic and nonsystemic banking crises. A banking crisis can bias our regressions in two distinct ways.

First, if policy reforms are clustered right after a crisis, the presence of a crisis negatively affects growth just before the reforms take place – biasing the growth effect upward. We use a contemporaneous banking crisis dummy to control for this effect. Panel E of Table 7 shows that, in both samples and across the two definitions, growth is significantly lower during crisis times. However, the introduction of the crisis dummy does not affect the magnitude of the equity market liberalization effect.

Second, we control for policy simultaneity by adding a dummy variable for the post-crisis period. The variable takes the value of one in the last year of the crisis and each year afterward. In most samples, there is significantly higher economic growth in the post crisis period (either systemic or systemic/borderline). This is particularly true for the broader definition of crisis. The equity market liberalization effect, however, is largely unaffected by the inclusion of the post-banking crisis variable.

Intuition would suggest that some of the increment to economic growth resulting from an equity market liberalization could be attributed to simultaneous policy reforms. While the incremental growth resulting from a liberalization is smaller in the presence of proxies for reforms, they do not subsume the equity market liberalization effect.

5. Why do countries respond differently to liberalizations?

Equity market liberalization, or the more general reforms it could proxy for, likely does not have the same impact in every country. The growth effect should depend on two factors: how much additional investment the reforms generate (e.g., because the cost of capital goes down) and the efficiency of new investments. Countries with a relatively high physical and human capital stock, relatively efficient financial markets, good legal institutions, and so on, might see highly efficient investment and

---

[12]Bhattacharya and Daouk (2002) examine the differential impact of insider trading laws and financial liberalizations on the cost of capital. While they find that both factors are important, the liberalization effect is more prominent.

[13]For example, Drazen and Easterly (2001) find that reforms are more likely to occur when inflation and black market premiums are at extreme values. Kaminsky and Reinhart (1999) examine the interrelation between banking and currency crises and financial liberalizations.

G. Bekaert et al. / Journal of Financial Economics 77 (2005) 3–55 37

a large growth response. From a broad historical perspective, Acemoglu et al. (2003) argue that the quality of political institutions played an important role in how European countries took advantage of Atlantic trade and were propelled to higher growth. But one could also make the case that countries with relatively bad institutions, an inefficient legal system, and serious corporate governance problems could experience the largest drop in the cost of capital and generate larger investment increases. Overall, the signs of interaction effects between liberalization and domestic factors are ex ante unclear.

First, we provide an exploratory analysis of what differentiates the liberalization effects across countries. Next, we follow La Porta et al. (1997, 1998, 1999, 2000) and consider institutional factors that measure the quality of the legal environment both overall and specifically for equity investors.

5.1. Financial development

We explore the differences across countries in the equity market liberalization effect by breaking up the indicator variable into three pieces:

$$
\begin{aligned}
y_{i,t+k,t} = {} & \beta Q_{i,1980} + \gamma' X_{i,t} + \alpha \text{LibFull}_{i,t} + \alpha_L \text{LibLow}_{i,t} \\
& + \alpha_H \text{LibHigh}_{i,t} + \delta \text{Char}_{i,t} + \varepsilon_{i,t+k,k},
\end{aligned}
\tag{5}
$$

where $\text{LibFull}_{i,t}$ represents an indicator for countries that are fully liberalized throughout our sample; $\text{LibLow}_{i,t}$ denotes the countries that liberalize but have a characteristic, such as financial development, that falls below the median of the liberalizing countries; and $\text{LibHigh}_{i,t}$ is the analogous definition for countries with a higher than median value of the characteristic. The regression also includes the own-effect of the characteristic, which is denoted by $\text{Char}_{i,t}$. We report the coefficients on the high and low characteristic indicators as well as a Wald test of whether the coefficients are significantly different. We also report the coefficient on the own effect.[14]

Table 2 suggests that financial development indicators substantially improve post equity market liberalizations. Table 8 shows that countries with a higher than median private credit to GDP ratio experience significantly higher growth after liberalization (1.05% for higher than average private credit to GDP and 0.48% for low level of private credit to GDP). The results suggest that a strong banking system provides the foundation whereby a country can have a larger increment to growth following an equity market liberalization. Table 8 shows similar results for our proxy for the development of equity markets: turnover. If a country has less than average turnover, then the effect of an equity market liberalization is a modest 0.17%. Countries with more than median turnover experience an average 0.94% boost in growth.

---

[14]We also estimate, but do not report, a more complex specification whereby the characteristics are interacted with the liberalization variables. Given that the results are similar, we elect to report the more intuitive analysis.

Table 8

Why does the growth effect from liberalizations differ across countries? For each interaction variable, we separately conduct regressions that have the five-year average growth rate of real per capita gross domestic product (GDP) as the dependent variable. We include in the regressions the same control variables as presented in Table 4. We also separate the liberalization effect for fully liberalized and liberalizing countries. For liberalizing countries, we estimate interaction effects with the financial development, legal, and investment condition variables. We report the associated impact on GDP growth for a liberalizing country for a low level (below the median of the associated interaction variable for liberalizing countries) and for a liberalizing country at a high level (above the median of the associated interaction variable for liberalizing countries).

We provide the significance of a Wald test, for which the null hypothesis is that the high-low effects are equivalent. We also report the statistical significance of the interaction coefficient; statistical significance is denoted by a * for 10%, ** for 5%, and *** for 1%. Significance levels are based on standard errors that correct for cross-sectional heteroskedasticity and account for the overlapping nature of the data.

The financial development variables are the ratio of private credit to GDP and equity market turnover. The legal environment variables are legal origin (English, French, or other), judicial efficiency, and the combined speed of the process to resolve a bounced check or tenant eviction (longer duration implies a lower speed). The International Country Risk Guide (ICRG) political risk quality of institutions subcomponent is the sum of the following ICRG subcomponents: corruption, law and order, and bureaucratic quality, detailed in Table 1. For all interaction indices, larger values denote improvements. ICRGE is the ICRG economic risk indicator. The investment conditions variables are a measure of economic risk, the investment profile, anti-director (minority shareholders) rights, creditor rights, and accounting standards. The number of countries for which the interaction variable is available is also provided. Finally, some of the variables are available as time series, while others are only available in the cross section; we denote this in the time-series available column.

Impact on growth resulting from liberalization	Fully liberalized	From low level of variable	From high level of variable	Direct effect of interaction variable	Number of countries	Time-series available
Financial development						
Private credit	0.0084**	0.0048	0.0105***	0.0116**	95	Yes
Turnover	0.0134***	0.0017	0.0094***	0.0152***	50	Yes
Legal environment						
French versus English law	0.0072**	0.0068	0.0124**		95	No
Other versus English law	0.0072**	0.0097	0.0124		95	No
Judicial efficiency	0.0105**	0.0069	0.0099	0.0057	47	No
Speed of process (combined)	0.0065	0.0029	0.0084	−0.0002	69	No
Quality of institutions						
ICRGP quality of institutions	0.0098**	0.0045	0.0129**	−0.0003	75	Yes
Investment conditions or protection						
ICRGE	0.0049	0.0071	0.0075	0.0696***	75	Yes
Investment profile	0.0060	0.0019	0.0085***	0.0210***	75	Yes
Anti-director rights	0.0117**	0.0018	0.0089**	0.0084***	47	No
Creditor rights	0.0102**	0.0035	0.0089	0.0190***	45	No
Accounting standards	0.0094**	0.0004	0.0110***	0.0058	39	No

G. Bekaert et al. / Journal of Financial Economics 77 (2005) 3–55 39

The financial development results provide the following two insights. First, equity market liberalization adds something over and above the impact of a change in a variable that proxies for financial development (Table 7). Second, the level of financial development matters. Liberalizations have a greater effect on economic growth if the country starts with above average financial development (Table 8).

5.2. Legal, investment and institutional environment

We look at a number of variables that proxy for the legal environment. We start with the classification of legal systems based on their origins, in La Porta et al. (1997): English, French, and other. They argue that the type of legal regime is a good proxy for the degree of investor protection. We use a measure of judicial efficiency from La Porta et al. (1998), which is based on Business International Corporation's assessment of the "efficiency and integrity of the legal environment as it affects business, particular foreign firms." We also consider the Djankov et al. (2003) measure of the duration of the legal process, both for collection of bad checks and tenant eviction. They argue that this measure is a good instrument for judicial formalism, which is inversely related to court quality. One disadvantage of these variables is that they are purely cross-sectional. Liberalization and the presence of foreign investors might affect the legal system. Alternatively, foreign investors could be reluctant to invest in countries with poorly developed legal systems. We find some evidence in favor of the latter interpretation in that all the interaction effects are positive.

For example, according to the results in Table 8 the growth impact of a liberalization is significantly greater for countries with English versus French legal origins (1.24% versus 0.68%). Although English legal origins are associated with higher growth than other legal origins, the difference is not statistically significant. A higher growth effect is associated with countries with a speedier judicial processes (0.84% for speedy and 0.29% for slow judicial processes), but the difference is not significant (the P-value is 0.14).

The legal environment is only one aspect of the quality of institutions. Acemoglu et al. (2002) argue that an institutional environment encouraging investment is more important than geographic factors in explaining economic development. To investigate the role of institutions, we construct a quality of institutions measure using three sub-components of the ICRG political risk rating (see Table 1). Our results support Acemoglu, Johnson, and Robinson's thesis. The growth prospects from a liberalization are almost three times higher for countries with a higher than median level of the quality of institutions index (1.29% versus 0.45%).

Finally, we examine the state of the investment environment. First, using the ICRG economic risk rating (which includes current level of GDP per capita, inflation, and current account and budget balances), we find that the current state of the economy has an insignificant impact on the heterogeneity of the growth effect. Second, we investigate the investment profile subcategory in the ICRG political risk ratings (which includes contract viability, profit repatriation, and payment delays). We find a highly significant difference when sorting by this characteristic. Countries with better than average investment profiles experience a 0.85% increment in growth whereas a lower than average profile shows only a 0.19% increase.

We also use, following La Porta et al. (1997), direct proxies for investor protection: anti-director rights, creditor rights and accounting standards. Countries with better shareholder rights or creditor rights or accounting standards experience higher economic growth. However, the effect for creditor rights is not significant at conventional levels. Some of these effects are striking. For example, the growth increment for countries with higher than average-rated accounting standards is 1.1%; it is only 0.04% for countries with below average accounting standards.

Table 8 also includes information on the own effect of each characteristic. Both of the financial development indicators have a positive effect in the regression, which is not surprising given the results in Table 7. The own effect for the speed of the judicial process is not significant at conventional significance levels. The current state of the economy has a strongly significant own effect along with the investment profile. Finally, all three of the investor protection variables have positive own effects. However, the accounting standards effect is not significantly different from zero.

Our analysis of heterogeneity of the growth effect has a simple message. First, not all countries experience the same increment to growth after equity market liberalizations. Second, the countries that benefit the most in terms of growth are those with higher than average financial development, English instead of French or other legal origins, good institutions, a favorable investment profile for foreign direct and portfolio investors, and higher than average investor protection.

6. Conclusions

Although substantial research has been conducted on the relation between financial development and economic growth, both the finance and development literature lacks a comprehensive analysis of the effects of the equity market liberalization process on economic growth.

Our research demonstrates that equity market liberalization (allowing foreign investors to transact in local securities and vice versa) did increase economic growth. We augment the standard set of variables used in economic growth research with an indicator variable for equity market liberalization. We find that equity market liberalization leads to an approximate 1% increase in annual real per capita GDP growth and find this increase to be statistically significant. This result is robust to a wide variety of experiments, including an alternative set of liberalization dates, different groupings of countries, regional indicator variables, business cycle effects, different weighting matrices for the calculation of standard errors, and four different time-horizons for measuring economic growth.

The approximately 1% increment in real growth following an equity market liberalization is surprisingly large. It is reasonable to expect that equity market

G. Bekaert et al. / Journal of Financial Economics 77 (2005) 3–55 41

liberalizations are intertwined with both macroeconomic reforms and financial development. Our evidence to some degree supports this point of view. Importantly, after controlling for either macro-reforms, financial development, banking crises, legal reforms, or the ability of a country to enforce its laws, we still find a statistically significant impact on economic growth from equity market liberalizations.

Most of our specifications, by construction, force a common coefficient relating liberalizations to growth in every country. It makes sense that there are country-specific deviations from the average. It is of great interest to investigate what might make a country have a greater (or lesser) response to a financial liberalization. In his book on trade openness, Rodrik (1999) argues that openness perhaps is not suitable for all countries. Likewise financial liberalization perhaps does not bring the anticipated benefits depending on the strength of the domestic institutions and other factors. Whereas, in recent work, Edwards (2001) and Quinn and Toyoda (2003) suggest that the benefits of capital account liberalization are restricted to more developed countries, we do not find the growth effect to depend positively on development levels. We do find that countries that are further along in terms of financial development experience a larger than average boost from equity market liberalization. In addition, countries with better legal systems, good institutions, favorable conditions for foreign investment, and investor protection generate larger growth effects.

Although our regressions are predictive, they reveal association not causality. While our analysis describes a number of plausible channels through which the liberalization effect could have occurred, the answer to the question "Does" (not "Did") financial liberalization affect economic growth? remains difficult to answer definitively. Our broad cross-country growth results appear consistent with scattered micro-evidence and event studies. Levine and Zervos (1998b) find that stock markets become more liquid following stock market liberalizations in a study of 16 countries. Karolyi (1998) surveys a rich ADR literature, which shows that ADRs, which can be viewed as investment liberalizations, lead to reduced costs of capital. Chari and Henry (2004) show that individual firms experience reductions in the costs of capital post-equity market liberalization. Lins et al. (2005) show that firms from emerging markets listing in the United States are able to relax financing constraints. Galindo et al. (2001) show that financial liberalization improves the efficiency of capital allocation for firms in 12 developing countries. Gupta and Yuan (2003) show that industries depending more on external finance experience significantly higher growth following liberalization and grow faster through the creation of new plants (instead of investing in existing ones).

Finally, we measure an average growth effect. There are potential costs. For example, the distribution of the welfare gain is an important social issue. Das and Mohapatra (2003) show that the income share of the highest quintile rises at the cost of the middle income quintiles post liberalization. Many argue that the cost of financial liberalization is increased economic growth volatility. However, the empirical evidence in Bekaert et al. (2004a) casts doubt on this view.

Appendix A

Dating financial liberalization. The Official Liberalization dates, date of the first American Depository Receipt (ADR) issuance, and first country fund are based on Bekaert and Harvey (2000), augmented to include ten additional emerging markets, plus Iceland, Japan, Malta, New Zealand, and Spain. The ADR announcement dates are from Miller (1999). For South Africa, the first ADR introduction date is associated with the post-apartheid period. We ignore many ADRs from the early 1980s. All other countries are considered fully liberalized (industrialized) with a * or fully segmented (less developed) with no entry from 1980 to 1997. Liberalization Intensity is the ratio of International Finance Corporation (IFC) investable to global market capitalization. The numbers presented here are time-series averages for each country. International Monetary Fund (IMF) and Quinn capital account openness measures are discussed in Table 1. The numbers presented here for the Quinn data are time-series averages for each country.

Country	Official Liberalization	First ADR	First country fund	Liberalization Intensity (average)	IMF capital account openness	Quinn capital account openness (average)	Reason for Official Liberalization dating
Algeria				0.000		0.132	
Argentina	1989	1991	1991	0.508	1993–	0.361	Free repatriation of capital and remittance of dividends and capital gains (November).
Australia	*			1.000	*	0.694	
Austria	*			1.000	1993–	0.813	
Bangladesh	1991			0.000			Purchases of Bangladesh shares and securities by nonresidents, including nonresident Bangladeshis, in stock exchange in Bangladesh were allowed, subject to meeting procedural requirements (June).
Belgium	*			1.000	*	0.847	
Barbados				0.000		0.306	
Benin				0.000			
Botswana	1990			0.000		0.632	
Brazil	1991	1992	1992	0.315		0.382	Foreign investment law changed. Resolution 1832 Annex IV stipulates that foreign institutions can now own up to 49 of voting stock and 100% of nonvoting stock. Economy ministers approved rules allowing direct foreign investments; 15% tax on distributed earnings and dividends but no tax on capital gains. Foreign investment capital must remain in country for six years as opposed to 12 years under previous law. Bank debt restructuring agreement (May).
Burkina Faso				0.000			
Cameroon				0.000			
Canada	*			1.000	*	0.910	

G. Bekaert et al. / Journal of Financial Economics 77 (2005) 3–55   43

Country	Official Lib.	First ADR	First Country Fund		Dates		Events
Central African Republic				0.000			
Chad	1992			0.000		0.382	Liberalization of foreign investment, reducing the minimum holding period and tax on investment income (January).
Chile	1992	1990	1989	0.195		0.403	Foreigners have the same rights as domestic investors (January).
Colombia	1991	1992	1992	0.306		0.403	
Congo, Republic of				0.000		0.250	
Costa Rica				0.000	1980–1981, 1995–	0.514	
Cote d'Ivoire	1995	1995		0.000		0.278	National Assembly approved a new Ivoirian Investment Code. For all practical purposes, there are no significant limits on foreign investment (or difference in the treatment of foreign and national investors) either in terms of levels of foreign ownership or sector of investment.
Denmark	*			1.000		0.889	
Dominican Republic				0.000	1988–	0.410	
Ecuador 0.604	1994	1994		0.000	1980–1985,1988–1992, 1995–		IFC frontier market as of 1995.
Egypt	1996	1996	1992	0.000		0.403	Capital Market Law 95 grants foreign investors full access to capital markets. No restrictions are placed on foreign investment in the stock exchange.
El Salvador				0.000	1996–	0.292	
Fiji	*			0.000		0.229	
Finland	*			1.000	1991–	0.715	
France	*			1.000	1990–	0.785	
Gabon				0.000		0.500	
Gambia				0.000	1991–	0.653	
Germany	*			1.000	*	0.993	
Ghana	1993	1995		0.000		0.361	Nonresidents were allowed to deal in securities listed on the Ghana Stock Exchange, subject to a 10% limit for an individual and 14% limit for total holdings by nonresidents in any one listed securities (June).

Appendix A (continued)

Country	Official Liberalization	First ADR	First country fund	Liberalization Intensity (average)	IMF capital account openness	Quinn capital account openness (average)	Reason for Official Liberalization dating
Greece	1987	1988	1988	0.502	1996–	0.674	Liberalization of currency controls allowed foreigners to participate in the equity market and to repatriate their capital gains.
Guatemala				0.000	1989–	0.833	
Guyana				0.000			
Haiti				0.000		0.278	
Honduras				0.000	1993–1995	0.563	
Iceland	1991			0.389		0.285	First shares trade on the Iceland Stock Exchange.
India	1992	1992	1986	0.079		0.278	Government announces that foreign portfolio investors will be able to invest directly in listed Indian securities (September).
Indonesia	1989	1991	1989	0.228	1980–1995	0.632	Minister of finance allows foreigners to purchase up to 49% of all companies listing shares on the domestic exchange excluding financial firms (September).
Iran				0.000		0.375	
Ireland	*			1.000	1992–	0.813	
Israel	1993	1987	1992	0.000	1996–	0.438	Nonresidents allowed to deposit into nonresident accounts all incomes receive from Israeli securities and real estate even if these were purchased from sources other than nonresident accounts (November).
Italy	*			1.000	1990–	0.868	
Jamaica	1991	1993		0.000	1996–	0.396	All inward and outward capital transfers were permitted, except that financial institutions must match their Jamaica dollar liabilities to their clients with Jamaica dollar assets (September).
Japan	1983	*		0.944	*	0.667	Finance Ministry announces easing restrictions on investments by stocks by foreigners (September).
Jordan	1995	1997		0.051		0.382	Foreign investment bylaws passed allowing foreign investors to purchase shares without government approval (December).

G. Bekaert et al. / Journal of Financial Economics 77 (2005) 3–55   45

Country							
Kenya	1995			0.000	1996–	0.278	Restrictions on investment by foreigners in shares and government securities were removed. The Capital Market Authority Act was amended to allow foreign equity participation of up to 40% of listed companies, while individuals are allowed to own up to 5% of listed companies (January).
Korea, Republic of	1992	1990	1984	0.067		0.479	Partial opening of the stock market to foreigners. Foreigners can now own up to 10% of domestically listed firms. Five hundred sixty-five foreign investors registered with the Securities Supervisory Board (January).
Kuwait				0.000			
Lesotho				0.000			
Madagascar				0.000			
Malawi				0.000			
Malaysia	1988	1992	1987	0.432	1980–1995	0.597	Budget calls for liberalization of foreign ownership policies to attract more foreign investors (October).
Mali				0.000			
Malta	1992	1998		0.333			Malta Stock Exchange was established by an act of Parliament in 1990.
Mauritius	1994			0.000	1996–	0.535	The stock market was opened to foreign investors following the lifting of exchange control. Foreign investors do not need approval to trade shares, unless investment is for the purpose of legal or management control of a Mauritian company or for the holding of more than 15% in a sugar company. Foreign investors benefit from numerous incentives such as revenue on sale of shares can be freely repatriated and dividends and capital gains are tax-free.
Mexico	1989	1989	1981	0.462	1980–1981	0.479	Restrictions on foreign capital participation in new direct foreign investments were liberalized substantially.
Morocco	1988	1996		0.000	1996–	0.132	The repatriation of capital and income from the investments into Morocco was granted (June).
Nepal	*			0.000	*	0.375	
Netherlands				1.000		0.958	
New Zealand	1983	1983		0.611	1983–	0.826	Major reforms initiated in 1986.
Nicaragua				0.000	1996–		
Niger	1987			0.000	1995–	0.382	

Appendix A (continued)

Country	Official Liberalization	First ADR	First country fund	Liberalization Intensity (average)	IMF capital account openness	Quinn capital account openness (average)	Reason for Official Liberalization dating
Nigeria	1995	1998		0.000		0.389	Nigerian market was open to foreign portfolio investment.
Norway	1999			1.000	1995–	0.778	
Oman				0.000	*		A stand-alone global index for Oman was added to the Standard & Poor's Emerging Market Indices, which has a base date of December 31, 1998. S & P tracks both global and investable indices for Oman.
Pakistan	1991	1994	1991	0.206		0.319	No restriction on foreigners or nonresident Pakistanis purchasing shares of a listed company or subscribing to public offerings of shares subject to some approvals (November).
Paraguay				0.000	1982–1983, 1996–	0.438	
Peru	1992	1994		0.300	1980–1983, 1993–	0.271	A Decree on the Private Sector Investment Guarantee Regime was enacted, under which the rights and guarantees that are accorded to domestic investors would be extended to foreign investors (December).
Philippines	1991	1991	1987	0.292		0.278	Foreign Investment Act is signed into law. The Act removes, over a period of three years, all restrictions on foreign investments (June).
Portugal	1986	1990	1987	0.519	1993–	0.646	All restrictions on foreign investment removed except for arms sector investments (July).
Rwanda				0.000		0.271	
Saudi Arabia	1999		1997	0.000	*	0.750	The Ministry of Finance announced the groundbreaking decision to allow non-Saudi investors to own shares in the local market through mutual funds (October).
Senegal				0.000		0.507	
Sierra Leone				0.000		0.264	
Singapore	*			1.000	*	0.972	

G. Bekaert et al. / Journal of Financial Economics 77 (2005) 3–55   47

Country							Details
South Africa	1996	1994	1994		0.354	0.333	Restrictions on foreign membership in the Johannesburgh Stock Exchange lifted.
Spain	1985		1988	1994–	0.681	0.722	Joins the European Economic Community, which attracts an influx of foreign capital.
Sri Lanka	1991		1994		0.146	0.333	Companies incorporated abroad were permitted to invest in securities traded at the Colombo Stock Exchange, subject to the same terms and conditions as those applicable to such investments by approved national funds, approved regional funds, and nonresident individuals (May).
Swaziland	*					0.000	
Sweden	*			1993–	0.806	1.000	
Switzerland				*	1.000	1.000	
Syria		1985			0.521	0.000	
Thailand	1987		1991		0.375	0.180	Inauguration of the Alien Board on Thailand's Stock Exchange. The Alien Board allows foreigners to trade stocks of those companies that have reached their foreign investment limits (September).
Togo				1994–		0.000	
Trinidad and Tobago	1997				0.285	0.000	Under the Companies Ordinance and the Foreign Investment Act, a foreign investor could purchase shares in a local corporation. However, foreign investors currently must obtain a license before they can legally acquire more than 30% of a publicly held company (April).
Tunisia	1995		1998		0.382	0.000	Inward portfolio investment was partially liberalized (June).
Turkey	1989	1989	1990		0.333	0.675	Foreign investors were permitted to trade in listed securities with no restrictions at all and pay no withholding or capital gains tax provided they are registered with the Capital Markets Board and the Treasury (August).
United Kingdom	*				1.000	1.000	
United States	*				1.000	1.000	
Uruguay				1980–1992, 1996–	0.896	0.000	
Venezuela	1990		1991		0.639	0.297	Decree 727 opened foreign direct investment for all stocks except bank stocks (January).
Zambia				1996–		0.000	
Zimbabwe	1993			1996–		0.058	Zimbabwe Stock Exchange was open to foreign portfolio investment subject to certain conditions (June).

Appendix B

Monte Carlo analysis of the liberalization effect. This table presents evidence from a Monte Carlo procedure (with one thousand replications) that mimics the generalized method of moments (GMM) estimation presented in Table 2, for our largest sample of 95 countries. The dependent variable is the five-year average growth rate of real per capita gross domestic product. The independent variables are the ones used in Table 2, but the liberalization variable is randomized using the procedure documented in the text. The weighting matrix we employ in our GMM estimation provides a correction for cross-sectional heteroskedasticity. We present the 2.5, 5.0, 50, 95, and 97.5 percentile for the estimated coefficients and t-statistics on the liberalization coefficient.

| | Randomized liberalization indicator | |
	Coefficient	t-statistic
Mean	0.0000	0.03
Median	0.0002	0.16
2.50%	−0.0059	−3.23
5.00%	−0.0052	−2.95
95.00%	0.0048	2.94
97.50%	0.0057	3.25

Appendix C

Summary Statistics. All variables and data sources are in Table 1. Under the category legal origin, F denotes French, AS denotes Anglo-Saxon, and O denotes other.

Country	Real GDP growth	Initial GDP per capita	Gov/GDP	Secondary school enrollment	Population growth	Life expectancy	Growth opportunities	Trade/GDP	Inflation	Black market premium	Government deficit	Private credit/GDP	Equity turnover	ICRG law & order	Insider law	Insider prosecution	Legal origin	Judicial efficiency	Speed or process (checks + eviction)	Economic risk	Investment profile	Anti-director rights	Creditor rights	Accounting standards
Algeria	-0.87%	$1,433	15.9%	53.9%	2.7%	64.7	0.00%	48.4%	17.1%	133.2%	36.6%	29.07	37.0		1991	1995	F	60	740	55.3	54.6	66.7	25	45
Argentina	0.44	8,132	6.58	67.82	1.41	71.1	0.06	15.60	5.29	21.93	22.03	28.88	59.3		1991	1996	F	60	363	44.4	42.6	66.7	25	45
Australia	1.65	14,074	17.72	92.88	1.36	76.4	-0.72	35.71	3.26	0.00	71.49	46.50	100.0		1991	1996	AS	100	981	75.0	56.0	66.7	25	75
Austria	1.87	18,852	19.33	100.11	0.37	74.9	-0.72	75.86	0.00	0.00	87.24		100.0		1993	1996	O	95		80.6	70.4	33.3	75	54
Bangladesh	2.35	210	3.33	18.51	2.11	52.8	-0.50	21.14	7.06	70.70	14.46	13.10	25.9		1995	1998	AS		660	59.2	39.4			
Belgium	1.65	19,093	15.80	112.80	0.20	75.2	-0.72	130.52	3.80	0.00	42.31		99.1		1990	1994	F	95	240	76.6	66.7	0.0	50	61
Barbados	0.46	4,992	18.52	87.10	0.40	74.2	-1.06	110.02	4.81	8.14	43.31	4.48					AS		203					
Benin	0.75	355	11.79	16.11	3.02	50.9	-0.28	62.66	5.60	2.11	20.51						F		140					
Botswana	4.93	1,049	24.16	38.62	3.12	57.0	-0.44	99.36	11.68	14.68	11.65						AS							
Brazil	0.75	3,371	14.04	39.16	1.77	64.6	-0.28	17.66	635.50	29.48	48.29	50.73	61.1		1976	1978	F	58	300	46.7	44.9	50.0	25	54
Burkina Faso	0.98	193	14.05	5.88	2.40	45.0	0.28	40.51	5.01	2.18	13.58						F							
Cameroon	-1.08	569	10.41	24.75	2.80	53.0	-0.28	47.00	6.22	2.18	21.31		47.2				F			61.1	47.7			
Canada	1.15	14,485	22.28	99.43	1.23	76.7	-0.39	57.74	3.92	0.00	76.23	33.92	100.0		1966	1976	AS	93	464	78.3	66.2	83.3	25	74
Central African Republic	-1.58	476	14.82	12.64	2.30	47.0	-2.28	47.95	7.69	2.07	7.86						F							
Chad	0.81	236	10.81	7.38	2.74	45.0	-0.83	45.27	5.51	2.18	9.90						F							
Chile	3.99	2,112	11.44	66.85	1.59	72.5	1.11	55.60	16.68	13.44	58.66	7.16	70.4		1981	1996	F	73	440	61.6	50.5	83.3	50	52
Colombia	1.59	1,396	11.55	49.62	2.02	68.2	-0.39	31.08	24.03	8.76	29.50	9.32	25.0		1990	1990	F	73	1027	59.5	51.9	50.0	0	50
Congo, Republic of	1.03	676	17.42	64.26	2.85	49.7	-0.33	111.33	6.43	1.32	15.96						F							
Costa Rica	0.28	2,248	16.10	43.78	2.48	74.7	0.11	77.46	23.45	37.43	18.53		15.7		1990		F		510	55.3	31.9			
Cote d'Ivoire	-2.37	985	15.58	20.89	3.27	49.6	-0.39	70.04	6.02	2.18	33.07	2.39	66.7				F		280	57.7	48.6			
Denmark	1.84	23,610	26.29	109.74	0.18	74.7	-0.33	68.12	4.52	0.00	42.13	24.00	58.3		1991	1996	O	100	308	77.7	63.0	33.3	75	62
Dominican Republic	1.61	1,149	6.55	44.54	2.09	67.7	0.39	70.06	19.33	24.85	28.27		100.0				F		425	61.4	40.3			
Ecuador	0.25	1,269	11.18	54.76	2.41	66.7	-0.22	52.60	35.34	22.93	24.96		54.6		1993		F	63	441	50.7	40.7	33.3	75	
Egypt	2.68	475	13.72	66.50	2.30	60.5	-0.50	55.82	12.61	7.55	32.56	8.78	66.7		1992		F	65	434	61.9	46.8	33.3	100	24
El Salvador	-0.44	1,772	12.17	27.81	1.51	62.6	-0.56	52.09	13.43	46.10	29.14		49.1				F		210	58.7	37.5			
Fiji	0.06	2,117	17.66	57.05	1.51	70.3	0.50	105.12	5.71	2.56	30.37		28.7				AS							
Finland	1.94	17,482	20.92	110.33	0.42	74.8	-0.11	58.22	5.17	0.00	68.91	20.99	100.0		1989	1993	O	100	360	72.7	68.1	50.0	25	77
France	1.40	18,868	18.97	96.45	0.50	76.1	-0.28	44.52	4.87	0.00	92.67	36.42	88.0		1967	1975	F	80	407	77.0	63.0	50.0	0	69
Gabon	-0.61	5,622	16.40	42.23	3.02	50.7	-0.28	93.76	7.36	2.18	15.10		40.7				F			74.5	48.6			
Gambia	-0.25	327	19.74	17.95	3.56	46.2	1.17	115.35	10.85	8.70	15.34						AS							
Germany	1.60	28,566	19.64	100.31	0.28	74.5	-0.61	54.08	2.93	0.00	93.07	88.21	90.7		1994	1995	O	90	485	82.8	67.6	16.7	75	62
Ghana	-0.14	480	10.15	38.58	2.99	56.0	1.83	37.97	39.05	70.54	3.96				1993		O		340					
Greece	1.18	7,684	13.95	91.12	0.54	76.2	-0.67	41.99	15.89	6.70	38.76	14.87	65.7		1988	1996	F	70	562	62.5	43.1	33.3	25	55

Guatemala	-0.30%	$1,381	6.8%	21.8%	2.5%	60.2	0.06%	38.5%	14.4%	17.0%		16.8%		25.9	1996		F		500	60.7	42.6			
Guyana	0.07	800	20.22	75.79	0.66	62.2		155.21	32.84	104.17		30.30					AS							
Haiti	-2.51	521	8.82	19.14	1.96	52.4		39.09	14.68	54.60		13.49					F							
Honduras	-0.35	626	13.38	33.57	3.06	64.7	0.11	67.52	12.54	21.68		30.40		33.3	1988		F		300	55.2	45.8			
Iceland	1.53	17,574	18.92	95.89	1.02	77.7	0.72	69.34	23.10	2.43		42.18		100.0	1989		O		315	65.4	52.3			
India	3.61	192	10.86	40.99	2.00	58.2	-0.33	19.11	8.76	10.52	6.42	28.07	41.83	43.5	1992	1996	AS	80	318	60.9	52.3	83.3	100	57
Indonesia	4.89	371	9.37	43.00	1.79	59.6	0.11	49.90	10.07	6.13		33.21	26.39	46.3	1991	1996	F	25	450	66.4	56.0	33.3	100	
Iran	-0.43	1,986	14.33	53.98	2.65	64.3	-0.56	30.93	23.41	189.55		30.93		45.4			F			56.8	42.1			
Ireland	4.25	8,245	16.47	102.06	0.46	74.3	0.17	115.84	5.50	0.00	6.01	51.77	51.86	78.7	1990		AS	88	251	76.8	62.5	66.7	25	
Israel	2.08	10,482	32.70	82.81	2.40	75.4	-0.50	87.18	77.25	5.82		64.61	60.22	50.9	1981	1989	AS	100	725	64.4	48.1	50.0	100	64
Italy	1.73	12,305	16.71	80.47	0.12	76.1	-0.56	43.66	8.90	0.00	10.49	52.66	31.94	86.1	1991	1996	F	68	1275	72.9	60.2	16.7	50	62
Jamaica	0.01	1,849	15.87	63.70	1.08	72.5	0.78	111.29	23.84	20.26		32.00	8.44	38.9	1993		AS		307	56.1	45.8			
Japan	2.52	22,962	9.53	96.54	0.47	78.3	-0.33	21.34	1.63	0.50	3.19	178.26	45.77	88.9	1988	1990	O	100	423	85.7	72.2	66.7	50	65
Jordan	0.04	1,002	25.92	52.26	4.16	67.1	-0.83	124.47	5.10	3.77		67.57	14.84	48.1			F	87	284	70.1	49.5	16.7		
Kenya	0.05	310	17.32	23.12	3.25	56.2	0.44	58.89	11.64	18.46		31.42	2.49	58.3	1989		AS	58	510	55.3	50.0	50.0	100	
Korea, Republic of	6.22	2,578	10.54	90.64	1.13	69.3	-0.56	67.58	7.46	1.59	0.70	62.56	105.25	56.5			O	60	378	75.3	64.4	33.3	75	62
Kuwait	0.60	25,246	29.91	74.49	1.85	73.9	-0.83	100.75	2.00	0.47		65.42		59.3			F		450	82.1	58.8			
Lesotho	2.50	261	21.73	24.68	2.38	56.1	0.61	149.49	11.92	6.54		17.64					AS							
Madagascar	-2.18	369	8.79	22.56	2.73	53.5	-0.78	39.88	19.20	17.65		16.63					F							
Malawi	-0.21	151	17.10	8.29	3.00	44.6	-0.11	57.51	21.69	35.03		13.40		40.7			AS		143	53.1	49.5			
Malaysia	4.15	1,777	14.53	55.11	2.65	69.6	0.72	140.04	3.24	1.04		91.46	33.13	74.1	1973	1996	AS	90	360	78.8	57.4	66.7	100	76
Mali	-0.34	214	11.81	7.82	2.60	46.0		52.18	6.75	3.12		15.12					F							
Malta	4.06	2,564	18.56	82.04	0.22	75.0	-1.28	176.38	3.43	3.03		69.44			1990		F		1275					
Mauritius	3.52	1,539	12.36	53.38	1.04	68.5	0.83	119.04	9.37	5.22		33.04			1988		F							
Mexico	0.45	2,766	9.54	55.62	1.99	69.3	-0.33	36.56	46.92	8.95	4.54	20.21	52.06	54.6	1975		F	60	463	56.1	56.0	16.7	0	60
Morocco	1.33	876	16.68	34.90	2.03	62.0	-1.17	55.01	5.95	4.41		31.20	8.26	51.9	1993		F		937	63.1	47.7			
Nepal	1.81	151	8.78	30.22	2.54	52.0	1.67	39.26	10.28	23.44		13.59					AS							
Netherlands	1.62	18,729	15.44	116.95	0.59	76.7	-0.11	103.27	2.20	0.00	3.90	89.93	40.75	100.0	1991		F	100	91	84.1	66.7	33.3	50	64
New Zealand	1.06	14,487	16.27	91.85	1.06	74.8	0.33	58.85	7.13	0.00		50.51	17.49	100.0	1988		AS	100	140	72.0	65.3	66.7	75	70
Nicaragua	-0.40	1,040	24.85	41.17	2.79	62.7	0.22	66.23	1615.88	145.55		35.69		36.1			F			28.4	33.8			
Niger	-2.92	315	13.19	5.95	3.31	44.3	-2.78	44.61	5.03	2.24		12.78					F							
Nigeria	-0.95	329	13.55	30.19	2.98	48.5	-0.61	58.79	26.38	80.40		12.34	0.93	28.7	1979		AS	73	607	54.5	44.4	50.0	100	59
Norway	2.64	18,362	20.14	103.64	0.43	76.7	0.33	73.61	4.97	0.00	0.15	69.00	36.37	100.0	1985	1990	O	100	452	85.2	65.7	66.7	50	74
Oman	2.73	2,945	30.21	39.09	4.28	66.6	-0.33	88.54	1.81	1.65		22.61		63.0	1989	1999	F			73.2	58.8			

G. Bekaert et al. / Journal of Financial Economics 77 (2005) 3–55 51

Country																								
Pakistan	2.86%	$271	12.7%	20.3%	2.6%	58.0	-0.17%	35.0%	8.9%	11.0%		27.6%	21.7%	36.1	1995	1994	AS	50	730	63.4	45.4	83.3	100	
Paraguay	0.54	1,254	7.56	32.86	2.90	67.8	0.00	48.31	20.63	30.41		19.09		44.4	1999		F	68	424	59.1	62.0	50.0	0	38
Peru	-0.21	2,822	9.01	64.50	2.04	64.2	0.17	29.93	603.64	28.96		14.28	24.47	26.9	1991		F	48	687	50.4	43.5	50.0	0	65
Philippines	-0.05	947	9.53	70.94	2.45	64.1	0.28	62.22	12.47	6.23		34.60		32.4	1982		F	55	328	59.4	38.4	50.0	0	36
Portugal	2.70	6,542	11.83	69.63	0.16	73.4	-0.67	68.49	13.49	5.10		63.99	18.25	86.1	1986		F		750	74.3	50.0	50.0	25	
Rwanda	-2.10	246	31.02	7.59	2.54	42.4	0.17	31.77	10.43	38.67		7.18					O							
Saudi Arabia	-3.01	9,180	15.48	43.28	4.54	66.3	-0.83	83.78	0.65	1.10		61.59		70.4	1990		AS			74.9	59.3			
Senegal	-0.23	584	11.58	14.60	2.72	48.3	-0.22	66.11	6.28	2.18		29.64		36.1			F		490	61.3	53.2			
Sierra Leone	-3.95	317	10.32	17.49	2.24	35.4	0.78	35.88	50.35	59.54		3.75		49.1			AS			48.0	30.1			
Singapore	5.63	9,045	18.19	65.29	1.86	73.7	0.44	370.31	3.40	1.22	-7.29	98.93	33.84	87.0	1973	1978	AS	100	106	82.2	66.7	66.7	100	78
South Africa	-0.57	3,967	15.36	71.13	2.28	60.5	-0.56	50.83	12.94	1.96	4.80	91.67	6.53	42.6	1989		AS	60	293	69.1	55.6	83.3	75	70
Spain	2.09	10,089	9.52	103.16	0.32	76.5	-0.39	40.97	7.80	2.73	4.79	75.57	38.36	76.9	1994	1998	F	63	330	73.3	66.7	66.7	50	64
Sri Lanka	3.21	365	20.53	67.72	1.38	70.5	-0.17	71.42	11.92	12.74		21.32	5.69	24.1			AS	70	1170	59.3	48.6	50.0	75	
Swaziland	2.11	970	27.53	44.16	3.11	55.2	0.78	160.41	11.40	11.35		21.31					AS		80					
Sweden	1.10	20,712	13.71	101.64	0.36	77.2	0.06	64.72	6.05	0.00	5.75	95.85	33.16	100.0	1971	1990	O	100	350	76.8	62.5	50.0	50	83
Switzerland	0.84	38,763	17.28	97.86	0.61	77.2	-0.22	69.96	3.01	0.00	0.63	150.62	50.59	100.0	1988	1995	O	100	490	86.2	75.5	33.3	25	68
Syria	0.99	784	11.10	51.00	3.17	65.0	-1.83	53.59	13.26	122.72		8.29		47.2			F			54.2	42.1			
Thailand	5.47	845	15.20	35.02	1.57	67.0	-1.00	67.11	5.10	0.23	0.60	82.00	55.42	64.8	1984	1993	AS	33	840	74.4	56.5	33.3	75	64
Togo	-0.93	411		24.80	2.98	50.2	-1.56	85.85	6.85	2.18		23.39					F							
Trinidad and Tobago	-0.08	3,154	16.12	77.87	1.14			78.68				45.32												
Tunisia	1.89	1,309	16.39	43.41	2.19	70.2	-0.11	84.17	6.13	27.25		60.19	9.01	66.7	1981	1996	AS		386	65.8	53.2			
Turkey	2.32	1,798	10.25	45.71	2.12	65.4	-0.94	34.07	7.17	6.44		18.47	6.34	47.2	1994	1981	F	40	40	64.8	48.1	33.3	50	51
United Kingdom	1.76	13,028	21.33	97.75	0.27	64.7	-0.28	53.23	61.16	5.51	3.02	84.54	46.01	54.6	1981	1981	F	100	405	56.4	50.9	83.3	100	78
United States	1.57	19,688	17.18	96.04	0.96	75.2	-0.56	20.76	5.86	0.00	3.44	94.96	33.64	85.2	1980	1961	AS	100	216	71.8	63.4	83.3	25	71
Uruguay	1.16	4,066	13.61	75.55	0.67	75.0	-0.33	42.67	4.54	9.15		39.63	57.92	100.0	1934	1996	F	100	103	76.8	71.8	83.3	50	31
Venezuela	-1.08	4,225	9.58	30.82	2.46	70.3	-0.06	49.13	56.00	34.42		35.78	12.91	50.0	1996		F	65	690	62.3	53.7	16.7	50	
Zambia	-1.73	682	20.40	22.08	2.95	49.5	-0.39	72.61	34.13	58.16		14.59		39.8	1998		AS	65	720	63.2	44.9			40
Zimbabwe	0.98	721	19.09	40.17	2.91	55.7	-0.22	53.42	16.47	39.88	6.83	24.40	7.92	38.9	1993		AS	75	394	51.7	43.1	50.0	100	

References

Acemoglu, D., Johnson, S., Robinson, J., 2002. Reversal of fortune: geography and institutions in the making of the modern world income distribution. Quarterly Journal of Economics 117, 1231–1294.

Acemoglu, D., Johnson, S., Robinson, J., 2003. The rise of Europe: Atlantic trade, institutional change, and economic growth. Unpublished working paper, Massachusetts Institute of Technology, Cambridge, MA.

Arteta, C.O., Eichengreen, B., Wyplosz, C., 2003. On the growth effects of capital account liberalization. In: Helpman, E., Sadka, E. (Eds.), Economic Policy in the International Economy: Essays in Honor of Assaf Razin. Cambridge University Press, Cambridge.

Atje, R., Jovanovic, B., 1989. Stock markets and development. European Economic Review 37, 632–640.

Barro, R.J., 1997a. Determinants of Economic Growth. MIT Press, Cambridge, MA.

Barro, R.J., 1997b. Determinants of economic growth: a cross-country empirical study. Discussion paper 579. Harvard Institute for International Development.

Barro, R., Sala-i-Martin, X., 1995. Economic Growth. McGraw-Hill, New York.

Beck, T., Levine, R., Loayza, N., 2000. Finance and sources of growth. Journal of Financial Economics 58, 261–300.

Bekaert, G., 1995. Market integration and investment barriers in emerging equity markets. World Bank Economic Review 9, 75–107.

Bekaert, G., Harvey, C.R., 2000. Foreign speculators and emerging equity markets. Journal of Finance 55, 565–614.

Bekaert, G., Harvey, C.R., 2002. Chronology of important financial, economic and political events in emerging markets. http://www.duke.edu/~charvey/chronology.htm.

Bekaert, G., Harvey, C.R., Lundblad, C., 2001. Emerging equity markets and economic development. Journal of Development Economics 66, 465–504.

Bekaert, G., Harvey, C.R., Lundblad, C., 2004a. Growth volatility and financial liberalization. Unpublished working paper, Duke University, Durham, North Carolina.

Bekaert, G., Harvey, C.R., Lundblad, C., Siegel, S., 2004b. Growth opportunities and market integration. Unpublished working paper, Columbia University, New York.

Bhattacharya, U., Daouk, H., 2002. The world price of insider trading. Journal of Finance 57, 75–108.

Caprio Jr., G., Klingebiel, D., 2001. Bank insolvencies: cross-country experience. Unpublished Working Paper 1620, World Bank, Washington, DC.

Caselli, F., Esquivel, G., Lefort, F., 1996. Reopening the convergence debate: a new look at cross-country growth empirics. Journal of Economic Growth 1, 363–389.

Chandra, A., 2003. The influence of capital controls on long-run growth: where and how much? Unpublished working paper, North Carolina State University, Raleigh, NC.

Chari, A., Henry, P.B., 2004. Risk sharing and asset prices: evidence from a natural experiment. Journal of Finance 59, 1295–1324.

Das, M., Mohapatra, S., 2003. Income inequality: the aftermath of stock market liberalization in emerging markets. Journal of Empirical Finance 10, 217–248.

Demirgüç-Kunt, A., Levine, R., 1996. Stock market development and financial intermediaries: stylized facts. World Bank Economic Review 10, 291–322.

Demirgüç-Kunt, A., Maksimovic, V., 1996. Stock market development and financing choices of firms. World Bank Economic Review 10, 341–370.

Devereux, M.B., Smith, G.W., 1994. International risk sharing and economic growth. International Economic Review 35, 535–551.

Djankov, S., La Porta, R., Lopez-de-Silanes, F., Shleifer, A., 2003. Courts. Quarterly Journal of Economics 118, 453–518.

Dollar, D., 1992. Outward-oriented developing countries really do grow more rapidly: evidence from 95 LDCs, 1976-85. Economic Development and Cultural Change 40, 523–544.

Drazen, A., Easterly, W., 2001. Do crises induce reform? Simple empirical tests of conventional wisdom. Economics and Politics 13, 129–158.

G. Bekaert et al. / Journal of Financial Economics 77 (2005) 3–55

53

Easterly, W., 2001. The lost decades: developing countries' stagnation in spite of policy reform 1980–1998. Journal of Economic Growth 6, 135–157.

Edison, H., Warnock, F., 2003. A simple measure of the intensity of capital controls. Journal of Empirical Finance 10, 81–104.

Edison, H., Levine, R., Ricci, L.A., Slok, T.M., 2002a. International financial integration and economic growth. Journal of International Money and Finance 21, 749–776.

Edison, H., Klein, M.W., Ricci, L.A., Slok, T.M., 2002b. Capital account liberalization and economic performance: survey and synthesis. Unpublished Working Paper 9100, National Bureau of Economic Research, Cambridge, MA.

Edwards, S., 1987. Sequencing of economic liberalization in developing countries. Finance and Development 24, 26–29.

Edwards, S., 1998. Openness, productivity, and growth: what do we really know? Economic Journal 108, 383–398.

Edwards, S., 2001. Capital mobility and economic performance: are emerging economies different. In: Siebert, H. (Ed.), The World's New Financial Landscape: Challenges for Economic Policy. Springer, Berlin, pp. 219–244.

Eichengreen, B., 2002. Capital account liberalization: what do the cross-country studies tell us? World Bank Economic Review 15, 341–366.

Galindo, A., Schiantarelli, F., Weiss, A., 2001. Does financial liberalization improve the allocation of investment. Unpublished working paper, Boston College, Boston, MA.

Gilchrist, S., Himmelberg, C., 1999. Investment, fundamentals and finance. In: Bernanke, B.S., Rotemberg, J. (Eds.), NBER Macroeconomics Annual 1998. National Bureau of Economic Research, Cambridge, MA, pp. 223–274.

Grilli, V., Milesi-Ferretti, G.M., 1995. Economic effects and structural determinants of capital controls. IMF Staff Papers 42, 517–551.

Gupta, N., Yuan, K., 2003. Financial dependence and growth: evidence from stock market liberalizations. Unpublished working paper, University of Michigan, Ann Arbor, MI.

Hansen, L.P., Hodrick, R., 1980. Forward exchange rates as optimal predictors of future spot rates: an econometric analysis. Journal of Political Economy 88, 829–853.

Henry, P.B., 2000. Stock market liberalization, economic reform, and emerging market equity prices. Journal of Finance 55, 529–564.

Hubbard, G., 1997. Capital market imperfections and investment. Journal of Economic Literature 36, 193–225.

Islam, N., 1995. Growth empirics: a panel data approach. Quarterly Journal of Economics 107, 1127–1170.

Jayaratne, J., Strahan, P.E., 1996. The finance-growth nexus: evidence from bank branch deregulation. Quarterly Journal of Economics 111, 639–670.

Kaminsky, G.L., Reinhart, C., 1999. The twin crises: the causes of banking and balance of payments problems. American Economic Review 89, 473–500.

Kaminsky, G.L., Schmukler, S.L., 2002. Short-run pain, long-run gain: the effects of financial liberalization. Unpublished working paper, George Washington University, Washington, DC.

Karolyi, A., 1998. Why do companies list their shares abroad? (A survey of the evidence and its managerial implications), Salomon Brothers Monograph Series 7. New York University, New York.

King, R.G., Levine, R., 1993. Finance, entrepreneurship, and growth. Journal of Monetary Economics 32, 513–542.

Klein, M.W., 2003. Capital account openness and the varieties of growth experience. Unpublished Working Paper 9500, National Bureau of Economic Research, Cambridge, MA.

Klein, M.W., Olivei, G., 1999. Capital account liberalization, financial depth and economic growth. Unpublished Working Paper 7384, National Bureau of Economic Research, Cambridge, MA.

Kraay, A., 1998. In search of the macroeconomic effects of capital account liberalizations. Unpublished working paper, World Bank, Washington, DC.

La Porta, R., Lopez-de-Silanes, F., Shleifer, A., Vishny, R.W., 1997. Legal determinants of external finance. Journal of Finance 52, 1131–1150.

La Porta, R., Lopez-de-Silanes, F., Shleifer, A., Vishny, R.W., 1998. Law and finance. Journal of Political Economy 106, 1113–1155.

La Porta, R., Lopez-de-Silanes, F., Shleifer, A., Vishny, R.W., 1999. The quality of government. Journal of Law, Economics, and Organization 15, 222–279.

La Porta, R., Lopez-de-Silanes, F., Shleifer, A., Vishny, R.W., 2000. Investor protection and corporate governance. Journal of Financial Economics 58, 3–28.

Laeven, L., 2003. Does financial liberalization reduce financing constraints. Financial Management 32, 1–12.

Lee, J.W., 1993. International trade, distortions, and long-run economic growth. IMF Staff Papers 40, 299–328.

Levine, R., Renelt, D., 1992. A sensitivity analysis of cross-country growth regressions. American Economic Review 82, 942–963.

Levine, R., Zervos, S., 1996. Stock market development and economic growth. World Bank Economic Review 10, 323–340.

Levine, R., Zervos, S., 1998a. Stock markets, banks, and economic growth. American Economic Review 88, 537–558.

Levine, R., Zervos, S., 1998b. Capital control liberalization and stock market development. World Development, 1169–1183.

Levine, R., Loayza, N., Beck, T., 2000. Financial intermediation and growth: causality and causes. Journal of Monetary Economics 46, 31–77.

Lins, K., Strickland, D., Zenner, M., 2005. Do non-U.S. firms issue equity on U.S. exchanges to relax capital constraints? Journal of Financial and Quantitative Analysis, forthcoming.

Love, I., 2003. Financial development and financing constraints: international evidence from the structural investment model. Review of Financial Studies 16, 765–791.

Mankiw, N.G., 1995. The growth of nations. Brookings Papers on Economic Activity 1, 275–310.

Mathieson, D., Rojaz-Suarez, L., 1993. Liberalization of the capital account: experiences and issues. Occasional paper 103. International Monetary Fund, Washington, DC.

McKinnon, R.I., 1973. Money and Capital in Economic Development. Brookings Institution, Washington, DC.

Miller, D., 1999. The market reaction to international cross listings: evidence from depositary receipts. Journal of Financial Economics 51, 103–123.

Miniane, J., 2004. A new set of measures on capital account restrictions. IMF Staff Papers 51, 276–308.

Patrick, H., 1966. Financial development and economic growth in underdeveloped countries. Economic Development Cultural Change 14, 174–189.

Quinn, D., 1997. The correlates of changes in international financial regulation. American Political Science Review 91, 531–551.

Quinn, D., Toyoda, A.M., 2003. Does capital account liberalization lead to economic growth? an empirical investigation. Unpublished working paper, Georgetown University, Washington, DC.

Rajan, R.G., Zingales, L., 1998. Financial dependence and growth. American Economic Review 88, 559–586.

Rajan, R.G., Zingales, L., 2003. The great reversals: the politics of financial development in the 20th century. Journal of Financial Economics 69, 5–50.

Rodriguez, F., Rodrik, D., 2001. Trade policy and economic growth: a skeptic's guide to the cross-national evidence. In: Bernanke, B.S., Rogoff, K.S. (Eds.), NBER Macroeconomics Annual 2000. MIT Press, Cambridge, MA.

Rodrik, D., 1998. Who needs capital account convertibility? Princeton Essays in International Finance 207, 1–10.

Rodrik, D., 1999. Determinants of Economic Growth. Overseas Development Council, Washington, DC.

Rousseau, P.L., Sylla, R., 1999. Emerging financial markets and early U.S. growth. Unpublished Working Paper 7448, National Bureau of Economic Research, Cambridge, MA.

Rousseau, P.L., Sylla, R., 2003. Financial systems economic growth and globalization. In: Bordo, M.D., Taylor, A.M., Williamson, J.G. (Eds.), Globalization in Historical Perspective. University of Chicago Press, Chicago, IL, pp. 373–413.

Rousseau, P.L., Wachtel, P., 2000. Equity markets and growth: cross-country evidence on timing and outcomes, 1980–1995. Journal of Banking and Finance 24, 1933–1958.

Sachs, J.D., Warner, A.M., 1995. Economic reform and the process of global integration. Brookings Papers on Economic Activity, 1–118.

Stiglitz, J.E., 2000. Capital market liberalization, economic growth, and instability. World Development 25, 1075–1086.

Wacziarg, R., 2001. Measuring the dynamic gains from trade. World Bank Economic Review 15, 393–429.

THE JOURNAL OF FINANCE • VOL. LVII, NO. 1 • FEB. 2002

The World Price of Insider Trading

UTPAL BHATTACHARYA and HAZEM DAOUK*

ABSTRACT

The existence and the enforcement of insider trading laws in stock markets is a phenomenon of the 1990s. A study of the 103 countries that have stock markets reveals that insider trading laws exist in 87 of them, but enforcement—as evidenced by prosecutions—has taken place in only 38 of them. Before 1990, the respective numbers were 34 and 9. We find that the cost of equity in a country, after controlling for a number of other variables, does not change after the introduction of insider trading laws, but decreases significantly after the first prosecution.

An Insider (Primary or Secondary Insider) may not, by utilizing knowledge of Insider Information, acquire or dispose of Insider Securities for his or her own account or for the account of another person, or for another person.
—Section 14 of the WpHG, Germany, 1994

LAWS PROHIBITING INSIDER TRADING came late to Germany. They had to come because the European Union required all its members to implement the European Community Insider Trading Directive (89/592/EEC of November 13, 1989). The lateness of Germany in establishing laws prohibiting insider trading, however, was not an exception. Posen (1991) notes that in the beginning of the 1990s, insider trading was not illegal in most European countries.

The purpose of this paper is twofold. First, we carry out a comprehensive survey on the existence and the enforcement of insider trading laws around the world. Stamp and Welsh (1996, page x), in a study of insider trading laws in a small subset of developed countries, did not like what they found. We quote them: "[I]n conclusion, it is clear that a number of jurisdictions are either not interested in, or are not prepared to devote the necessary re-

---

* Both authors are from the Kelley School of Business, Indiana University. This paper would not be possible without the information we received from the regulators and the representatives of the 103 stock markets that we contacted. We are deeply indebted to them. The first author is grateful to KAIST, South Korea, for allowing him the use of their Datastream data source when he was a visiting scholar there in the summer of 1999. Thanks are also due to seminar participants at Amsterdam, Arizona State, Bocconi, Cincinnati, Concordia, COPPEAD, Georgia State, Harvard Business School, HKUST, Indiana, McGill, Michigan State, NBER, Peking, Pittsburgh, NYSE, Queens, Shanghai Jiao Tong, Vanderbilt, University of Washington, Western Ontario, Yale, and York. Any remaining errors in this paper are our own.

sources to implementing their insider dealing legislation." We update their data set by obtaining information on insider trading laws in every country that has a stock market. To preclude any selection bias, we began the second part of the paper only after we had obtained information from *all* countries that have stock markets.

The second purpose of this paper is to ask whether the existence and enforcement of insider trading laws matter. To be precise, the research question is whether prohibitions against insider trading affect the cost of equity. This is an important question because, as a major purpose of stock markets is to make it easier for corporations to raise financing through equity, corporations would like to know if they have to pay an extra return in stock markets where insiders trade with impunity. If yes, it would be in the benefit of corporations to avoid paying this extra borrowing cost by having their equity traded in stock markets that limit insider trading, everything else constant. To put it in another way, if insider trading is found to increase the cost of equity, corporations would pay stock exchanges a premium to limit insider trading, everything else being constant.

Scores of law, economics, and finance papers have argued the pros and cons of insider trading regulations. Bainbridge (2000), besides providing a comprehensive list of papers that have discussed insider trading, succinctly summarizes the arguments for and against allowing insider trading. Considering the richness and the complexity of issues involved in the debate on insider trading—historical, cultural, economic, and legal—this paper, by choice, restricts its attention to one key economic aspect: the cost of equity.

Consider a stock market in which insiders trade with impunity. The liquidity providers in such a market would protect themselves by increasing their sell price and decreasing their buy price.[1] This increases the transaction cost, which in turn induces a stock trader to require an even higher return on equity.[2] A second, and a generally neglected, reason why the cost of equity would be higher in such a market is that controlling large shareholders could easily be tempted by management to make profits from stock tips rather than profits from hard-to-do monitoring.[3] Knowing this, shareholders would demand an even higher return on equity. It is important to note that the first reason predicts a higher cost of equity because of an implicit transaction tax inherent in high bid-ask spreads, whereas the second reason does not depend on such an illiquidity premium. Could the cost of equity be lower in a market where insiders trade freely? Manne (1966) first provided the argument why the cost of equity could be higher in markets that do not allow insider trading: No insider trading means less effi-

---

[1] See Glosten and Milgrom (1985) and Kyle (1985) for formal models.

[2] See Amihud and Mendelson (1986) for a formal model on why this should happen for riskless assets. Jacoby, Fowler, and Gottesman (2000) and Easley, Hvidkjaer, and O'Hara (2000) extend this to risky assets. Brennan and Subrahmanyam (1996) provide convincing empirical evidence.

[3] See Maug (1999) for a model formalizing this perspective. Beny (1999) provides some empirical evidence.

The World Price of Insider Trading   77

cient markets, and less efficient markets means that shareholders would demand an even higher return to compensate for the fact that they find it difficult to analyze firms.

The above paragraph lists the reasons how insider trading and the cost of equity can be linked through the suppliers of equity funds—the shareholders. Lombardo and Pagano (1999) argue that legal variables can also affect the demanders of equity funds—the firms—and, therefore, the relationship between these legal variables and the equilibrium cost of equity is difficult to interpret. For example, if a supply shock emanating from shareholders causes the cost of equity to fall, more firms will find that hitherto negative NPV projects become positive NPV projects, and more equity will be issued. This will decrease equity prices and raise the cost of equity (if you believe that the demand curve for equity is downward sloping) or it will increase equity prices and lower the cost of equity (if you do not believe that the demand curve for equity is downward sloping, but you believe that more equity means more diversification opportunities of firm-specific risk, and so a lower risk premium).

The debate about the effect of insider trading on the cost of equity will eventually have to be settled empirically. However, as Bainbridge (2000) notes, serious empirical research on insider trading is hindered by the subject's illegality. The only source of data concerning legal trades are the trading reports filed by corporate insiders, and it is unlikely that managers will willingly report their violations. Even if they do, it is improbable that managers are the only insiders. The only source of data concerning illegal trades is confidential, and if any researcher (e.g., Meulbroek (1992)) obtains them, the study will suffer from a selection bias. It should also be mentioned here that because of availability of data, and because of a long evolution of common law on insider trading, nearly all empirical research on insider trading has been concentrated in the Unites States.[4]

Our comprehensive survey finds that 103 countries had stock markets at the end of 1998. Insider trading laws existed in 87 countries, but enforcement, as evidenced by prosecutions, had taken place in only 38 of them. Before 1990, the respective numbers were 34 and 9. This leads us to conclude that the existence and the enforcement of insider trading laws in stock markets is a phenomenon of the 1990s.

Do prohibitions against insider trading affect the cost of equity in a country? In this paper, we measure the effect of insider trading laws on the cost of equity using four different approaches. Each of these approaches has its advantages and disadvantages, and these we discuss in other sections of this paper.

The first approach is simply descriptive statistics. We look at mean returns, turnover, and volatility five years before the introduction of insider trading laws and five years afterwards. We repeat this exercise around the

---

[4] The first prosecution for insider trading occurred in the United States under state law as early as 1903 (Oliver v. Oliver, 45 S.E. 232 Georgia, 1903).

date of the first prosecution. We find that mean returns decrease after the introduction of insider trading laws, but this decrease is less than the decrease that is observed after the first prosecution. Turnover increases after insider trading enforcement, but does not change much after the introduction of insider trading laws. There is a small increase in volatility.

The second approach uses an international asset pricing factor model. It is a simplified version of Bekaert and Harvey (1995). Their empirical specification allows for partial integration of a country to the world equity markets. After controlling for a world factor, a local factor, a foreign exchange factor, a liquidity factor, and other variables like an indicator for liberalization and an indicator for shareholder rights, we find that enforcement has a negative effect on the cost of equity that is significant both statistically and economically. On the other hand, insider trading laws have an insignificant effect.

The third approach is a simplified version of Bekaert and Harvey (2000), who use changes in dividend yields to measure changes in the cost of equity. After controlling for an indicator for liberalization, we find that insider trading laws have an insignificant effect on the cost of equity. On the other hand, enforcement has a negative and significant effect.

The fourth approach follows Erb, Harvey, and Viskanta (1996). They find that surveys of country risk forecasts are good predictors of the cross section of expected equity returns. After controlling for other variables, like an indicator for liberalization, we find that insider trading laws have an insignificant effect on country credit ratings. On the other hand, enforcement has a positive and significant effect on country credit ratings.

To summarize, whichever approach we use, we find that insider trading enforcement is associated with a significant decrease in the cost of equity.[5] The numerical estimate of this decrease in the cost of equity ranges from a low of 0.3 percent (the credit rating approach) to a high of 7 percent (the international asset pricing model approach). More importantly, we find that the mere existence of insider trading regulations does not affect the cost of equity.

The paper is structured as follows. In Section I, we describe our data. Section II gives descriptive statistics of our findings from our comprehensive survey of stock markets around the world. Section III, which is the main section of this paper, tests the null hypothesis that the existence and enforcement of insider trading laws does not affect the cost of raising equity in a country. The four different approaches we use in our testing are four subsections in Section III. We conclude in Section IV. It is in this section that we lay out the limitations of our research, and argue that although we would like to stress our finding of a reduction in the cost of equity that is associated with the enforcement of insider trading laws, our point estimates should not be overemphasized.

---

[5] There is also a fifth approach: estimating liquidity and cost of capital at the level of the firm. This approach has been used by Errunza and Miller (2000) and Jain (2001). Unfortunately, we did not have access to this data.

The World Price of Insider Trading 79

I. Data

We are interested in finding out whether the existence and enforcement of insider trading laws affect the cost of equity in a country. To this end, we collect primary and secondary data from different sources. The data could broadly be classified into three categories: data on the existence and the enforcement of insider trading in various stock markets of the world, stock market returns, and other variables that may affect the cost of equity in a country.

A. Data on the Existence and the Enforcement of Insider Trading Laws

The first thing we did was to count the number of countries that had stock markets. Assuming that every stock market had its own web site in this information age, we counted the number of web sites.[6] According to this criterion, there were 103 countries that had stock markets at the end of 1998, of which 22 are classified as developed markets, and 81 are classified as emerging markets. This list included all the 88 countries covered in the *International Encyclopedia of the Stock Market* (1988), and it included all the 94 countries included in the *Handbook of World Stock, Derivative and Commodity Exchanges* (1998). The 81 emerging markets we identify include all the 28 emerging markets that Morgan Stanley Capital International (MSCI) follows, as well as the 33 that the International Financial Corporation (IFC) of the World Bank tracks.[7] The first column in Table I gives a list of all the countries. We then sent e-mails, letters, and faxes to all the 103 stock markets, as well as to their national regulators.[8] The reason we contacted two sources is because we wanted to cross-check the information that was provided. We asked in our letter if the stock market had insider trading laws and, if yes, from when. If they had insider trading laws, we asked if there had been a prosecution under these laws— successful or unsuccessful—and, if yes, when was the first prosecution. The reason we asked the second question is because Bhattacharya et al. (2000) show in the case of one emerging market that the existence of insider trading laws without their enforcement—as proxied by a prosecution— does not deter insiders. Wherever possible, and this was only possible for a small subset of developed countries, the answers were cross-checked against the findings of Posen (1991) and Stamp and Welsh (1996).

---

[6] The Yahoo web site (http://dir.yahoo.com/Business_and_Economy/Finance_and_Investment/ Exchanges/Stock_Exchanges) gives a comprehensive list of stock markets of the world. So does the web site of the International Federation of Stock Exchanges (http://www.fibv.com). The third source is a list compiled by Ken Loder of Seattle University (http://www2.jun.alaska.edu/ ~jfdja/common/markq.html).

[7] Portugal is a developed country in the MSCI database, whereas it is an emerging market in the IFC database.

[8] The e-mail and postal addresses of the stock markets, as well as their facsimile numbers, were obtained from their respective web sites. The e-mail and postal addresses of the national regulators, as well as their facsimile numbers, were obtained from the membership list of the International Organization of Securities Commissions (IOSCO) (http://www.iosco.org/iosco.html). Some countries did not have national regulators.

Table I

Stock Markets Around the World

Stock markets of 103 countries had web sites. We assumed this to be the universe of all countries that had stock markets. The list is given in Column 1. The numbers in Columns 2 and 3 are from *The Handbook of Stock, Derivative and Commodity Exchanges* (1998). If not available, the source was the web site of the stock exchange. The numbers in Column 4 are from FIBV, International Federation of Stock Exchanges (http://www.fibv.com). Whenever they were not available, the source was *The Handbook of Stock, Derivative and Commodity Exchanges* (1998). All local currency units were converted to USD by using the appropriate exchange rate on 12/31/97. This exchange rate came from the Currency Converter available in http://www.oanda.com/converter/classic. The numbers in Column 5 are from *The Handbook of Stock, Derivative and Commodity Exchanges* (1998). They have been reconciled with the figures obtained from FIBV. All local currency units were converted to USD by using the appropriate exchange rate on 12/31/97. This exchange rate came from the Currency Converter available in http://www.oanda.com/converter/classic. Turnover in Column 6 is defined as Dollar Volume divided by Market Capitalization. The numbers in Columns 7 and 8 came from the answers given to two questions we sent to all the national regulators and officials of stock markets of the world in March 1999. The two questions were: (1) When (mm/yy), if at all, were insider trading laws established in your exchange? (2) If answer to (1) above is YES, when (mm/yy), if at all, was the first prosecution under these laws? Wherever possible, the answers were cross-checked with the following books in our law library: Posen (1991) and Stamp and Welsh (1996). The index measuring shareholder rights in Column 9 is obtained by adding one when: (a) there is one share-one vote rule; (b) the country allows shareholders to mail their proxy vote to the firm; (c) shareholders are not required to deposit their shares prior to the General Shareholders' Meeting; (d) cumulative voting or proportional representation of minorities in the board of directors is allowed; (e) an oppressed minorities mechanism is in place; and (f) the minimum percentage of share capital that entitles a shareholder to call for an Extraordinary Shareholders' Meeting is less than or equal to 10 percent (the sample median). The index ranges from 0 to 6. This data is obtained from Table 2 in La Porta et al. (1998). The official liberalization dates in Column 10 come from Table I in Bekaert and Harvey (2000). We assume that all the developed countries were liberalized before our sample period, except for Japan (December 1980), New Zealand (July 1984), and Spain (January 1978). The liberalization dates of these three countries were identified by a Lexis/Nexis search as in Henry (2000).

The World Price of Insider Trading 81

(1) Country	(2) Establishment of Main Exchange	(3) Company Listings in Main Exchange (end-1997)	(4) Market Capitalization of Main Exchange (USD billion in end-1997)	(5) Dollar Volume in Main Exchange (USD billion in 1997)	(6) Turnover in Main Exchange	(7) IT Laws Existence	(8) IT Laws Existence	(9) Index of Shareholder Rights	(10) Official Liberalization Date
Developed countries									
Australia	1859	1216	295	150	0.51	1991	1996	4	Before 12/69
Austria	1771	109	37.3	12.412	0.33	1993	No	2	Before 12/69
Belgium	1801	141	138.9	28.9	0.21	1990	1994	0	Before 12/69
Canada	1878	1420	568	304	0.54	1966	1976	4	Before 12/69
Denmark	1919	237	93.76	37.4	0.40	1991	1996	3	Before 12/69
Finland	1912	127	73.3	34.55	0.47	1989	1993	2	Before 12/69
France	1826	717	676.3	394.9	0.58	1967	1975	2	Before 12/69
Germany	1585	1461	825.2	1966.4	2.38	1994	1995	1	Before 12/69
Hong Kong	1891	658	413.3	489	1.18	1991	1994	5	Before 12/69
Ireland	1793	69	52.97	32.36	0.61	1990	No	3	Before 12/69
Italy	1808	209	344.67	193.89	0.56	1991	1996	0	Before 12/69
Japan	1878	1805	2160.58	834.45	0.39	1988	1990	4	Dec 80
Luxembourg	1929	62	33.89	0.56	0.02	1991	No		Before 12/69
Netherlands	1600's	434	468.896	256.581	0.55	1989	1994	2	Before 12/69
New Zealand	1870	146	29.889	9.29	0.31	1988	No	4	Jul 84
Norway	1819	196	66.5	46.27	0.70	1985	1990	3	Before 12/69
Singapore	1930	294	106.317	74.137	0.70	1973	1978	4	Before 12/69
Spain	1831	133	290.383	424.086	1.46	1994	1998	2	Jan 78
Sweden	1863	261	264.711	164.623	0.62	1971	1990	2	Before 12/69
Switzerland	1938	216	575.339	468.462	0.81	1988	1995	1	Before 12/69
United Kingdom	1773	2157	1996.225	833.194	0.42	1980	1981	4	Before 12/69
United States	1792	2691	8879.631	5777.6	0.65	1934	1961	5	Before 12/69

continued

Table I—*Continued*

(1) Country	(2) Establishment of Main Exchange	(3) Company Listings in Main Exchange (end-1997)	(4) Market Capitalization of Main Exchange (USD billion in end-1997)	(5) Dollar Volume in Main Exchange (USD billion in 1997)	(6) Turnover in Main Exchange	(7) IT Laws Existence	(8) IT Laws Existence	(9) Index of Shareholder Rights	(10) Official Liberalization Date
Emerging markets									
Argentina	1854	107	59.2	37.8	0.64	1991	1995	4	Nov 89
Armenia	1993	59	0.0131	0.0028	0.21	1993	No		
Bahrain	1987	42	20.783	1.272	0.06	1990	No		
Bangladesh	1954	219	1.5	3.8	2.53	1995	1998		
Barbados	1987	18	1.14	0.0233	0.02	1987	No		
Bermuda	1971	33	47	0.0964	0.00	No	No		
Bolivia	1979	11	0.337	0.004	0.01	No	No		
Botswana	1989	12	0.613	0.0565	0.09	No	No		
Brazil	1890	536	255.4	191.1	0.75	1976	1978	4	May 91
Bulgaria	1991	285	0.388 (1998)	0.1268 (1998)	0.33	No	No		
Chile	1893	92	72	7.328	0.10	1981	1996	4	Jan 92
China	1990	383	111.4	166.7	1.50	1993	No		
Colombia	1928	318	16.2	1.67	0.10	1990	No	1	Feb 91
Costa Rica	1976	114	0.8199	0.018	0.02	1990	No		
Croatia	1918	82	4.265	0.2427	0.06	1995	No		
Cyprus	1996	49	2.7	0.35	0.13	1999	No		
Czech Republic	1871	300	14.36	21.54	1.50	1992	1993		
Ecuador	1969	128	2.02	62.6	30.99	1993	No	2	
Egypt	1890	650	20.9	7.12	0.34	1992	No	2	
El Salvador	1992	29	0.501	5.545	11.07	No	No		
Estonia	1996	22	1.09	1.52	1.39	1996	No		
Ghana	1989	21	1.135	0.1256	0.11	1993	No		
Greece	1876	207	33.8	20	0.59	1988	1996	2	Dec 87
Guatemala	1986	5	0.002	NA	NA	1996	No		
Honduras	1992	120	0.4477	0.348	0.78	1988	No		
Hungary	1864	49	15	33	2.20	1994	1995		
Iceland	1985	49	73.3	93.24	1.27	1989	No		
India	1875	5843	127.72	49.9	0.39	1992	1998	2	Nov 92

continued

Indonesia	1912	282	29.05	21.87	0.75	1991	1996	2	Sep 89
Iran	1966	263	11.468	0.915	0.08	No	No	3	
Israel	1953	659	44.37	13.58	0.31	1981	1989		Dec 95
Jamaica	1961	49	2.29	0.132	0.06	1993	No	1	
Jordan	1978	139	5.45	0.5	0.09	No	No	3	
Kazakhstan	1997	13	1.335	0.002	0.00	1996	No		
Kenya	1954	50	1.9	0.1	0.05	1989	No		
Kuwait	1984	65	25.88	NA	NA	No	No		
Latvia	1993	50	0.338	0.083	0.25	No	No		
Lebanon	1920	113	2.904	0.639	0.22	1995	No		
Lithuania	1926	607	2.5	0.36	0.14	1996	No		
Macedonia	1996	2	0.0086	0.0252	2.93	1997	No		
Malawi	1996	3	NA	NA	NA	No	No		
Malaysia	1973	708	93.18	101.3	1.09	1973	1996	3	Dec 88
Malta	1992	8	5	0.0205	0.00	1990	No	0	
Mauritius	1988	45	0.224	0.018	0.08	1988	No		
Mexico	1894	155	156.2	52.8	0.34	1975	No		
Moldova	1994	NA	NA	NA	NA	1995	No		
Mongolia	1991	433	0.054	0.015	0.28	1994	No		
Morocco	1929	49	12.23	3.33	0.27	1993	No		
Namibia	1992	33	31.85	0.185	0.01	No	No		
Nigeria	1960	182	3.67	0.147	0.04	1979	1999	3	May 89
Oman	1988	119	8.738	4.196	0.48	1989	No	5	
Pakistan	1947	781	13.1	11.469	0.88	1995	No		
Palestine	1995	19	0.503	0.0252	0.05	No	No		
Panama	1990	21	2.246	0.055	0.02	1996	No		
Paraguay	1977	64	0.383	0.091	0.24	1999	No		
Peru	1951	293	17.38	4.295	0.25	1991	1994	3	Aug 95
Philippines	1927	221	31.211	20.35	0.65	1982	No	4	
Poland	1817	137	12.134	7.455	0.61	1991	1993	2	Feb 91
Portugal	1825	159	39.3	20.14	0.51	1986	No		
Romania	1882	84	0.633	0.26	0.41	1995	No		
Russia	1994	149	71.592	16.634	0.23	1996	No		
Saudi Arabia	1984	70	59.37	16.55	0.28	1990	No		
Slovakia	1991	14	5.29	2.37	0.45	1992	No		
Slovenia	1924	86	1.99	0.32	0.16	1994	1998		June 91
South Africa	1887	615	211.599	38.71	0.18	1989	No	4	
South Korea	1956	776	41.88	95.73	2.29	1976	1988	3	July 86
Sri Lanka	1896	239	2.09	0.297	0.14	1987	1996	2	Jan 92

Table I—Continued

(1) Country	(2) Establishment of Main Exchange	(3) Company Listings in Main Exchange (end-1997)	(4) Market Capitalization of Main Exchange (USD billion in end-1997)	(5) Dollar Volume in Main Exchange (USD billion in 1997)	(6) Turnover in Main Exchange	(7) IT Laws Existence	(8) IT Laws Existence	(9) Index of Shareholder Rights	(10) Official Liberalization Date
Emerging markets (continued)									
Swaziland	1990	4	0.13	0.357	2.75	No	No		
Taiwan	1961	404	296.808	1290.92	4.35	1988	1989	3	Jan 91
Tanzania	1998	2	0.236	0.0003	0.00127	1994	No		
Thailand	1974	431	22.792	24.421	1.07	1984	1993	3	Sep 87
Trinidad and Tobago	1981	26	1.74	0.135	0.08	1981	No		
Tunisia	1969	304	2.3	0.2	0.09	1994	No		
Turkey	1866	258	61.095	58.104	0.95	1981	1996	2	Aug 89
Ukraine	1992	6	0.212	NA	NA	No	No		
Uruguay	1867	18	0.211	0.004	0.02	1996	No	2	
Uzbekistan	1994	63	0.041	0.028	0.68	No	No		
Venezuela	1840	159	14.6	3.923	0.27	1998	No	1	Jan 90
Yugoslavia	1894	21	0.048	NA	NA	1997	No		
Zambia	1994	10	0.502	0.008	0.02	1993	No		
Zimbabwe	1896	67	2.32	0.35	0.15	No	No	3	Jun 93
Descriptive statistics									
Median for entire sample	1953	128	14.8	4.92	0.34	1991	1994		
Median for developed countries	1859	249	292.6915	179.2565	0.55	1989	1993.5		
Median for emerging markets	1973	85	3.9675	0.777	0.25	1992	1995.5		
Range for entire sample	1585 to 1998	2 to 5843	0.002 to 8879.631	0.0003 to 5777.6	0.00127 to 30.99	1934 to 1999	1961 to 1999		
Range for developed countries	1585 to 1938	62 to 2691	29.889 to 8879.631	0.56 to 5777.6	0.0165 to 2.3829	1934 to 1994	1961 to 1998		
Range for emerging markets	1817 to 1998	2 to 5843	0.002 to 296.808	0.0003 to 191.1	0.00127 to 30.99	1973 to 1999	1978 to 1999		
Entire sample (today)						87 (84.5%)	38 (36.9%)		
Developed countries (today)						22 (100%)	18 (81.8%)		
Emerging markets (today)						65 (80.2%)	20 (24.7%)		
Entire sample (pre-1990s)						34 (43%)	9 (11.4%)		
Developed countries (pre-1990s)						12 (54.5%)	5 (22.7%)		
Emerging markets (pre-1900s)						22 (38.6%)	4 (7%)		

The World Price of Insider Trading   85

As consistent enforcement is economically more meaningful than just the first enforcement, the reader may be wondering why we focused only on obtaining data about the first prosecution. This is because it is extremely difficult to obtain data on any prosecution. In an earlier paper, which focused on insider trading in just one country, we could not get this data from the country's regulators even after a year of repeated requests. In this paper, as we were acutely sensitive of the fact that responses were more likely from countries that had enforced insider trading laws which would lead to a severe selection bias in our results, we had to obtain information from every country that had a stock market. So we simply asked the regulators about the first prosecution cases. After one year, and sometimes as many as five reminders, we obtained this information from *all* the 103 countries that had stock markets.

It is important to note that the first enforcement of a law, however perfunctory it might be, is an event of paramount importance. The first prosecution signals to the world that we have gone from a regime where there had been no prosecutions to a regime where there has been at least one prosecution; this implies that the probability of future prosecutions has had a discrete jump up.[9]

B. Stock Market Returns

Data on monthly equity indices of 22 developed countries were obtained from Morgan Stanley Capital International (MSCI). Though MSCI has data on monthly equity indices of emerging markets as well, we chose to obtain these from the International Financial Corporation (IFC) of the World Bank, because the IFC covers more emerging markets—33—and their data begin earlier in most cases.[10] The first column in Table AI in the Appendix gives a list of the countries for which we have MSCI/IFC data. All our data extend to December 1998. The second column in Table AI gives us the sample period that was available for these 55 monthly stock market indices. These indices are value weighted, and are calculated with dividend reimbursement. As noted by Harvey (1991), the returns computed on the basis of these indices are highly correlated with popular country indices.

---

[9] We had historical data on all prosecutions for only three countries. This allowed us to use a panel time-series regression for these three countries to check the importance of the first prosecution. The regressions use adjusted dividend yields as proxies for the cost of capital, and these are the dependent variables. The regressions are conducted with country-fixed effects and corrections for cohort heteroskedasticity and cohort autocorrelation. First, the regression is run with respect to the first prosecution. The analysis is replicated for the second prosecution. The estimated impact of the first prosecution on the cost of equity for the three countries is a decrease of 2.9 percent (not statistically significant). The estimated impact using the second prosecution is also negative. However, the impact of the first prosecution is around 25 percent more than the impact of the second prosecution.

[10] In a previous version of this paper, we ran all our tests using the MSCI database for both developed as well as emerging markets. As the results are similar, we do not report it in this paper.

The MSCI value-weighted World Index was used as a proxy for the market portfolio.[11]

Descriptive statistics about the stock markets for 1997 were obtained from the *Handbook of World Stock, Derivative and Commodity Exchanges* (1998). We obtained the following information about 94 countries: the year of establishment, the number of firms listed at year-end 1997, the market capitalization in USD at year-end 1997, and the volume of trade in USD in 1997. Data on the missing 9 countries as well as cross-checks of the above data were obtained from the 103 stock market web sites.

C. Other Variables That May Affect the Cost of Equity in a Country

Liquidity, as demonstrated by Amihud and Mendelson (1986), and Brennan and Subrahmanyam (1996), may affect the cost of equity. The measure of liquidity that we adopted was turnover, and this is defined as the volume of trade in the stock market divided by the market capitalization of the stock market. We could obtain monthly data on the volume of trade and market capitalization for 35 of the 55 countries from the vendor Datastream. The third and fourth columns in Table AI give the sample period that was available for these 35 monthly market capitalization and volume time series.

Bekaert and Harvey (2000) use changes in dividend yield to measure changes in the cost of equity. We obtained monthly data on the dividend yield for 38 of the 55 countries from the vendor Datastream. The dividend yield was on the Datastream-constructed indices. The fifth column in Table AI gives us the sample period that was available for these 38 monthly dividend yield time series.

Bekaert and Harvey (1997) divide the sum of exports and imports with a country's gross domestic product to obtain a variable that proxies the level of integration of a country with the rest of the world. This is because the level of globalization does affect the cost of equity (see Stulz (1999a)). We use the same method. Monthly data on exports and imports for the 55 countries were obtained from the International Financial Statistics provided by the International Monetary Fund. For some countries, the frequency of GDP was quarterly and for some it was yearly. To obtain monthly GDP, we divided by 3 in the former case, and by 12 in the latter case. The sixth, seventh, and eighth columns in Table AI give us the sample period that was available for these 55 GDP, exports, and imports time series.

Monthly data on foreign exchange rates were obtained from the International Financial Statistics. The ninth column in Table AI gives us the sample period that was available for these 55 monthly foreign exchange rate time series.

---

[11] The MSCI World Index is actually an index of only developed countries. It begins in December 1969. In principle, we should have used the MSCI All-Country World Index, but since this only begins only in December 1987 and has a correlation of 0.996767 with the developed country index, it is better to use the developed country index in practice. The results in this paper are with respect to this developed country index. We ran all our tests using the AC World Index as well. As all the results are similar, we do not report them in this paper.

As there has been some recent literature documenting that better legal institutions are associated with more efficient equity markets (see, e.g., La Porta et al. (1997, 1998), Levine (1997), Demirguc-Kunt and Maksimovic (1998), and Lombardo and Pagano (1999)), we need to control for these other legal factors. We computed an index measuring shareholder rights by adding one when: (1) there is one share–one vote; (2) the country allows shareholders to mail their proxy vote to the firm; (3) shareholders are not required to deposit their shares prior to the General Shareholders' Meeting; (4) cumulative voting or proportional representation of minorities in the board of directors is allowed; (5) an oppressed minorities mechanism is in place; and (6) the minimum percentage of share capital that entitles a shareholder to call for an Extraordinary Shareholders' Meeting is less than or equal to 10 percent (the sample median). The index ranges from 0 to 6. This data are obtained from Table 2 in La Porta et al. (1998). The ninth column in Table I gives us this computed index value for the 49 countries they track.

Erb et al. (1996) found that country credit ratings are a very good proxy for the ex ante risk exposure, particularly of segmented emerging economies. Country credit ratings come from Institutional Investor's semiannual survey of bankers. The survey represents the responses of 75 to 100 bankers. Respondents rate the credit quality of each country on a scale of 0 to 100. They rate them once every six months. The data, with a few exceptions, begin in September 1979 and end in September 1999. The data exist not only for the 55 countries for which we have stock market data—the tenth column in Table AI gives us the sample period that was available for the 55 biannual country credit ratings time-series—but for 42 other countries as well. This data can be downloaded from Harvey's web site (http://www.duke.edu/~charvey).

Liberalization, as Stulz (1999b) points out, reduces cost of equity through two routes. It reduces required return because risk sharing improves, and it reduces required return because corporate governance improves. Bekaert and Harvey (2000) and Henry (2000) empirically confirm that liberalization reduces the cost of equity. We obtain official liberalization dates from Table I in Bekaert and Harvey (2000). These are given in the tenth column in Table I. We control for the confounding effects of liberalization in all our tests.

II. Stock Markets and Insider Trading Regulations Around the World

A. Stock Markets Around the World

Table I gives descriptive statistics of the main stock markets in the 103 countries that have stock markets.

The stock markets exhibit a bewildering diversity. The ages of the stock markets range from a few months (1998, Tanzania) to hundreds of years (1585, Germany), with the median year of establishment being 1953. As expected, stock markets in the developed countries (median year of establishment is 1859) are older than stock markets in the emerging markets (median year of establishment is 1973). The number of listed firms on the main exchange ranged from

2 (1997, Macedonia) to 5,843 (1997, India), with the median number of listed firms being 128. As expected, stock markets in the developed countries (median number of listed firms is 249) list more firms than stock markets in the emerging economies (median number of listed firms is 85). Market capitalization of the stock markets ranged from 0.002 billion USD (1997, Guatemala) to 8879.631 billion USD (1997, New York Stock Exchange), with the median being 14.8 billion USD. As expected, the size of the stock markets in the developed countries (median size is 292.692 billion USD) is bigger than the size of the stock markets in the emerging economies (median size is 3.968 billion USD). Dollar volume of trade ranged from 0.0003 billion USD (1998, Tanzania) to 5777.6 billion USD (1997, New York Stock Exchange), with the median dollar volume being 4.92 billion USD. As expected, there is more trade in the stock markets of the developed countries (median dollar volume is 179.3 billion USD) than in the stock markets of the emerging economies (median dollar volume is 0.777 billion USD). Turnover, which is defined as volume divided by market capitalization, ranged from 0.00127 (1998, Tanzania) to 30.99 (1997, Ecuador), with the median being 0.338. As expected, the liquidity of the stock markets in the developed countries (median turnover is 0.547) is bigger than the liquidity of the stock markets in the emerging economies (median turnover is 0.246).

B. The Existence and Enforcement of Insider Trading Laws around the World

The seventh and eighth columns in Table I give us information on the existence and enforcement of insider trading laws for every country that has a stock market. Insider trading laws were first established in the United States (1934). Until 1967, when France established these laws, the United States was the only country that had insider trading laws. The latest country to establish insider trading laws is Cyprus (1999). The median year of establishment of these laws is 1991. Developed countries (median year of establishment of insider trading laws is 1989) have had these laws on their books longer than emerging markets (median year of establishment of insider trading laws is 1992). Today, 100 percent of developed countries have insider trading laws on their books, but only 80 percent of emerging markets do. Before 1990, the respective numbers were 55 percent and 39 percent.

The enforcement of insider trading laws is difficult to measure. If we assume that a law is not enforced unless a charge is brought under it, a reasonable way to measure enforcement is to date the first prosecution, and assume that enforcement begins after that date. This is what we did. We found that the first case under federal insider trading laws took place in the United States (1961).[12] Until 1990, only nine countries had brought any charges

[12] In 1961, the Securities and Exchange Commission of the United States had an enforcement action against Cady, Roberts and Company. The case involved tipping: An insider (the tipper), who does not trade, discloses information to an outsider (the tippee), who trades. The classic insider trading case, which set precedents for the common law in the United States, was Texas Gulf Sulphur (1968). See Bainbridge (2000) for a lucid description on the evolution of common law on insider trading in the United States.

The World Price of Insider Trading   89

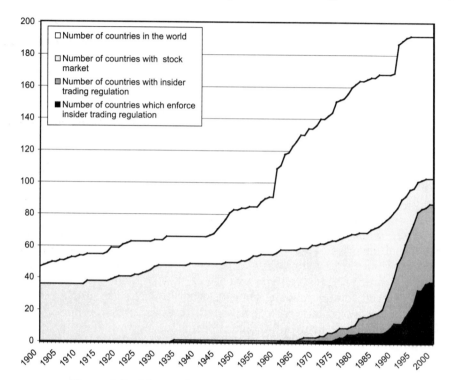

Figure 1. Insider trading regulations in the 20th century.

under these laws. The latest country to prosecute under insider trading laws is Oman (1999). The median year of the first prosecution is 1994. Though the median year for the first prosecution was the same for both developed countries and emerging economies, 82 percent of developed countries have prosecuted till today, but only 25 percent of emerging markets have prosecuted till today. Before 1990, the respective numbers were 23 percent and 7 percent.

Figure 1 graphically demonstrates the history of the existence and the enforcement of insider trading laws in the 20th century. It plots the time series of the number of countries in the world, the number of countries with stock markets, the number of countries that have insider trading laws, and the number of countries that enforce their insider trading laws.[13] It is apparent from this graph that in the first third of this century, these laws did not exist anywhere; in the second third of this century, these laws existed in only one country (the United States); and in the last third of this century,

---

[13] The data for the number of countries in the world were obtained from the CIA's *World Factbook* (1999). We obtained the date of incorporation of a stock market from *The Handbook of Stock, Derivative and Commodity Exchanges* (1998) and, if not available there, the source was the web site of the stock exchange. Note that the number of countries with stock markets includes also the countries whose stock markets were temporarily closed due to some crisis. See Table IV of Jorion and Goetzmann (1999) for a list of such countries.

existence and enforcement of insider trading laws accelerated. This acceleration was particularly pronounced in the 1990s.

Figure 1 also tells us that if we use the argument of revealed preferences of governments around the world, it seems that a consensus has been achieved among governments: insider trading laws are good for society. Since Bettis, Coles, and Lemmon (2000) find in their sample of U.S. firms that 92 percent of them have policies restricting insider trading, it could be argued that even firms agree that insider trading is undesirable. So the debate about the pros and cons of insider trading laws seems to have been settled. Every developed country today has these insider trading laws, and four out of five emerging market economies have it.

The enforcement of these laws, however, is a different issue. Only one in three countries has enforced these laws. Why? We quote Stamp and Welsh (1996, page ix) here: "In a number of common law jurisdictions . . . the burden of proof on the prosecution is onerous, making it difficult to secure a conviction. In other jurisdictions, . . . this problem is exacerbated by the legislatures' attempt to provide an exhaustive list . . . which can be exploited by the experienced insider dealer. On the other hand, in a number of other countries, . . . there is no real political will to enforce the legislation."

Do the existence and the enforcement of insider trading laws in stock markets affect the cost of equity? We attempt to answer this question in the next section.

III. Does Insider Trading Increase the Cost of Equity?

We use two variables related to insider trading regulation. The first one is related to the existence of laws prohibiting insider trading in the country of interest (*IT laws*). The second variable relates to legal prosecution for insider trading in the country of interest (*IT enforcement*). These insider trading variables are coded as follows. The indicator variable *IT laws* changes from zero to one in the year after the insider trading laws are instituted. The indicator variable *IT enforcement* changes from zero to one in the year after the first prosecution is recorded. We use one variable related to liberalization. This variable is coded as follows. The indicator variable *liberalization* changes from zero to one in the month after the official liberalization date that was obtained from Bekaert and Harvey (2000).

The effect of the insider trading variables on the cost of equity is measured using four different approaches.

A. Using Simple Descriptive Statistics

If equity markets are informationally efficient, and if insider trading laws affect the cost of equity, it follows that there will be an immediate impact on trading statistics on the day insider trading laws are changed. This is the approach that Henry (2000) used to study the effect of liberalization on the cost of equity, and this is the first approach we would like to use to study the effect of insider trading laws on the cost of equity.

The World Price of Insider Trading   91

An advantage of this event-study approach is that it directly tries to measure the discrete equity price change that is supposed to occur if there is a change in the cost of equity caused by a change in the insider trading laws. There are two disadvantages of the event-study approach. First, if there is an equity price change, it is difficult to conclude that this came about because there was a change in the cost of equity or because there was a change in expected dividend growth. This, as Henry (2000) admits, makes interpretation difficult in the case of liberalization. In the case of insider trading laws, however, it could be argued that growth opportunities of a firm are not likely to change much if there is a change in insider trading laws. The second disadvantage is more severe. It is difficult to date the change in the insider trading law precisely.[14] This makes it impossible for us to conduct a classical event study. Defining the year of introduction of insider trading laws as year t, we look at mean returns, turnover, and volatility five years before the introduction of insider trading laws (year $t - 5$ through year $t - 1$), and five years afterwards (year $t + 1$ through year $t + 5$, or less if data were not available). We repeat this exercise around the date of the first prosecution.

Figure 2a plots the mean returns, volatility, and turnover five years before and five years after the year in which insider trading laws were introduced; Figure 2b plots the mean returns, volatility, and turnover five years before and five years after the year in which the first prosecution under these laws occurred.

The figures tell us that mean returns decrease after the introduction of insider trading laws, but the percentage decrease is less than the decrease that is observed after the first prosecution. Volatility increases slightly in both cases, which tells us that the welfare effects of insider trading laws are not unambiguous. Turnover increases in the case of insider trading enforcement, but not in the case of insider trading laws.

Table II provides formal confirmation of our observations in Figures 2a and 2b. We use the natural logarithm of the ratio of volume to market capitalization as a measure of liquidity. Call this variable *liq*. Compute the monthly realized rate of equity return. Call this variable *rawret*.

Using *liq* as the dependent variable, we run a panel time-series regression with country-fixed effects. We correct for country-specific heteroskedasticity and country-specific autocorrelation. The regressions use data from our 35 countries for which we have data for the *liq* variable.

Panel A of Table II presents the results from this panel time-series regression. In regression (1a), when *IT laws* is the independent variable, the coefficient on *IT laws* is positive and statistically significant at the one percent level. In regression (2a), when *IT enforcement* is the independent variable, the coefficient on *IT enforcement* is positive and statistically significant at the one percent level. These conclusions do not change—see regressions (3a) and (4a)—if we add the *liberalization* indicator as a control variable. These results provide evidence in favor of a testable implication drawn from

---

[14] Nearly all the regulators gave us the year their insider trading law was passed and/or was enforced, and not the month. Also, as discussed before, it is not clear that the enforcement date of insider trading laws is the date of the first prosecution.

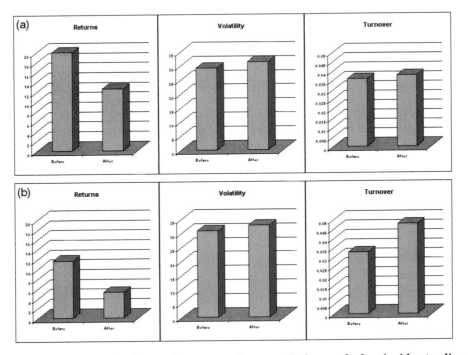

Figure 2. Returns, volatility, and turnover five years before and after insider trading laws (a) and insider trading enforcement (b).

the theoretical models of Kyle (1985), Glosten and Milgrom (1985), and Bhattacharya and Spiegel (1991): the curbing of insider trading improves liquidity in a market. Judging by the coefficients, the effect of enforcement of insider trading laws on liquidity seems to be stronger than the effect of their mere existence.

Panel B of Table II presents the results from a similar panel time-series regression when *rawret* is the dependent variable. In regression (1b), when *IT laws* is the independent variable, the coefficient on *IT laws* is negative and statistically significant at the 10 percent level. In regression (2b), when *IT enforcement* is the independent variable, the coefficient on *IT enforcement* is negative and statistically significant at the 1 percent level. When we add the *liberalization* indicator as a control variable—see regressions (3b) and (4b)—the coefficient on *IT laws* is no longer significant (*p*-value of 0.26), but the coefficient on *IT enforcement* remains significant at the 5 percent level. The magnitude of the coefficient on *IT enforcement* suggests a drop of 7 percent in the annual cost of equity.

A conclusion we can draw from Table II is that the enforcement of insider trading laws affects the cost of equity indirectly through its positive effect on liquidity (seen in Panel A, 4a), and directly (seen in Panel B, 4b). This provides evidence in support of hypotheses we laid out in the beginning of this paper: Lower insider trading reduces cost of equity indirectly by increasing

Table II
Effect of Insider Trading Laws on Liquidity and Raw Returns

The panel regressions with country-fixed effects are based on monthly data. The first dependent variable is *liq*, and it is the natural logarithm of the ratio of volume to market capitalization. The second dependent variable is *rawret*, defined as raw returns, and is computed as continuously compounded returns. The first two independent variables are the insider trading variables. They are coded as follows. The indicator variable *IT laws* changes from zero to one in the year after the insider trading laws are instituted. The indicator variable *IT enforcement* changes from zero to one in the year after the first prosecution was recorded. The third independent variable is the liberalization variable. It is coded as follows. The indicator variable *liberalization* changes from zero to one in the month after the official liberalization date that was obtained from Bekaert and Harvey (2000). It is assumed to be one for all developed countries, except for the three noted in Table I. The equity data for developed countries are from Morgan Stanley Capital International, and the equity data for emerging markets are from International Financial Corporation. The *p*-values are in parentheses. We correct for country-specific heteroskedasticity and country-specific autocorrelation.

Panel A: Liquidity; Dependent Variable: *Liq.*				
Independent Variables	(1a)	(2a)	(3a)	(4a)
IT laws	0.2568		0.2879	
	(0.0000)		(0.0000)	
IT enforcement		0.4276		0.4385
		(0.0000)		(0.0000)
Liberalization			−0.0104	0.0141
			(0.6785)	(0.5745)

Panel B: Raw Returns; Dependent Variable: *Rawret.*				
Independent Variables	(1b)	(2b)	(3b)	(4b)
IT laws	−0.0043		−0.0027	
	(0.0805)		(0.2611)	
IT enforcement		−0.0082		−0.0063
		(0.0074)		(0.0345)
Liberalization			−0.0041	−0.0039
			(0.2405)	(0.2421)

liquidity, that is, it reduces the illiquidity premium; and lower insider trading reduces cost of equity directly by improving corporate governance.

A disadvantage of using ex post average excess return to measure ex ante risk premium is that we can be led to dramatically wrong conclusions with our short sample periods. For example, we can easily conclude from rising (falling) stock prices, that risk premiums are rising (falling), whereas it may be that the only reason that stock prices are rising (falling) is because ex ante risk premiums are falling (rising).

B. Using an International Asset Pricing Model

The major determining feature of the cost of equity is risk. We, therefore, need to control for risk in order to measure the marginal impact of insider-trading laws. What do we use for a risk measure? Solnik (1974a, 1974b) made a strong case for using the world market portfolio as the risk factor in the international capital asset pricing model (ICAPM). Though Harvey and Zhou (1993) fail to reject the ICAPM, more general models that allow time variations (like Harvey (1991)) or multifactors and time variations (like Ferson and Harvey (1993)), reject some aspects of the ICAPM. The consensus seems to be that a country's beta with respect to the world market portfolio has some merit to explain expected returns for developed countries; the variance of return of the country's stock market does better in explaining expected returns for emerging markets (see Harvey (1995)).

We adopt a simplified version of Bekaert and Harvey (1995) as our international asset pricing model. Their empirical specification allows for partial integration of a country to the world equity markets. Their model is very appealing because it permits a country to evolve from a developing segmented market (where risk is measured by the country's variance) to a developed country which is integrated to world equity markets (where risk is measured by the sensitivity of a country's equity returns to movements in the world market portfolio). The special case of complete integration, where the world factor is the only factor, is nested in their model. This international asset pricing model is expressed as follows:

$$(r_{i,t} - r_{f,t}) = \alpha_0 + \phi_{i,t} \lambda_{\mathrm{cov}} h_{i,w,t} + (1 - \phi_{i,t}) \lambda_{\mathrm{var}} h_{i,t} + e_{i,t} \tag{1}$$

where

$r_{i,t}$ = the dollar monthly return of the stock market index of country i at time t,

$r_{f,t}$ = the monthly return of the one month U.S. T-bill at time t,

α_0 = a constant that would be estimated,

$\phi_{i,t}$ = a measure of the level of integration of country i at time t, $0 \leq \phi_{i,t} \leq 1$,

λ_{cov} = the price of the covariance risk that would be estimated,

$h_{i,w,t}$ = the conditional covariance of the monthly return of the stock market index of country i with the monthly return of the world index at time t,

λ_{var} = the price of own country variance risk that would be estimated (which we are restricting to be the same across all countries),

$h_{i,t}$ = the conditional variance of the monthly return of the stock market index of country i at time t, and

$e_{i,t}$ = the residual error term.

The independent variables in model (1)—conditional covariance $h_{i,w,t}$ and conditional variance $h_{i,t}$—are separately estimated pair-wise for each country i and world pair from the multivariate ARCH model specified below:

$$r_{i,t} = c_1 + \epsilon_{i,t},$$

$$r_{w,t} = c_2 + \epsilon_{w,t},$$

The World Price of Insider Trading 95

$$h_{i,t} = b_1 + a_1(\tfrac{1}{2}\epsilon_{i,t-1}^2 + \tfrac{1}{3}\epsilon_{i,t-2}^2 + \tfrac{1}{6}\epsilon_{w,t-3}^2),$$

$$h_{w,t} = b_2 + a_2(\tfrac{1}{2}\epsilon_{w,t-1}^2 + \tfrac{1}{3}\epsilon_{w,t-2}^2 + \tfrac{1}{6}\epsilon_{w,t-3}^2),$$

$$h_{i,w,t} = b_3 + a_3(\tfrac{1}{2}\epsilon_{i,t-1}\epsilon_{w,t-1} + \tfrac{1}{3}\epsilon_{i,t-2}\epsilon_{w,t-2} + \tfrac{1}{6}\epsilon_{i,t-3}\epsilon_{w,t-3}),$$

$$\epsilon_{i,t}, \epsilon_{w,t} \sim N\left(\begin{bmatrix} 0 \\ 0 \end{bmatrix}, \begin{bmatrix} h_{i,t} & h_{i,w,t} \\ h_{i,w,t} & h_{w,t} \end{bmatrix}\right)$$

(2)

where

$r_{w,t}$ = the dollar monthly return of the stock market index of the world at time t,

$\epsilon_{i,t-j}$ = the innovation in monthly return of the stock market index of country i at time $t - j$, $j \in \{0,1,2,3\}$,

$\epsilon_{w,t-j}$ = the innovation in monthly return of the stock market index of the world at time $t - j$, $j \in \{0,1,2,3\}$, and

$h_{w,t}$ = the conditional variance of the monthly return of the stock market index of the world at time t.

Model (2) was first introduced by Bollerslev, Engle, and Wooldrige (1988). As in Engle, Lilien, and Robins (1987), the weights of the lagged residual vectors are taken to be $\tfrac{1}{2}$, $\tfrac{1}{3}$, and $\tfrac{1}{6}$, respectively. The constants a_2, b_2, and c_2 are constrained to be identical for all country-world pairs. Maximum likelihood is used to estimate model (2).[15]

The other independent variable in model (1), $\phi_{i,t}$, measures the level of integration of country i at time t. We define it as follows:

$$\phi_{i,t} = \frac{\exp\left(\alpha_1\left(\dfrac{exports_{i,t} + imports_{i,t}}{gdp_{i,t}}\right)\right)}{1 + \exp\left(\alpha_1\left(\dfrac{exports_{i,t} + imports_{i,t}}{gdp_{i,t}}\right)\right)}.$$

(3)

The definition of $\phi_{i,t}$ implies that it is a function of the ratio of the sum of exports and imports to gross domestic product. It is designed to take values between zero and one. When its value is zero, the country is not integrated with world equity markets, and its equity is exposed only to local risk (own variance). When its value is one, the country is fully integrated with world equity markets, and its equity is exposed only to global risk (covariance with

---

[15] This type of ARCH estimation has some problems because of nonnormalities in the data. Bekaert and Harvey (1995) use a semiparametric ARCH model, which is basically a mixture of normal distributions.

world factor). Bekaert and Harvey (1997) find that increases in this ratio are empirically associated with increased importance of world factor relative to local risk factors.[16]

Model (1) is estimated using nonlinear least squares. The regressions use data from our 55 countries from December 1969 to December 1998 (some countries do not have data for the full time period). The results are given in Panel A of Table III.

Panel A of Table III tells us that covariance risk seems to have a positive price (λ_{cov} is positive) and is statistically significant at the five percent level. It also tells us that though own country variance risk has a positive price (λ_{var} is positive), the estimates are significant only at the six percent level.

If the insider trading variables have no incremental effect on the cost of equity, then those variables will be orthogonal to the residuals from the model in (1).[17] We therefore test the hypothesis that the insider trading variables do not affect the cost of equity by regressing the residuals from model (1) on the insider trading variables.[18] We use a panel time-series regression with country-fixed effects. We correct for country-specific heteroskedasticity and country-specific autocorrelation. The result from this test is given in Panel B1 of Table III.

Panel B1 in Table III tells us that the coefficient on *IT laws* is statistically insignificant. On the other hand, Panel B1 in Table III tells us that the *IT enforcement* dummy has a negative effect on the cost of equity. It is significant at the five percent level.

At this point, we investigate whether our finding—the enforcement of insider trading laws is associated with a decrease in the cost of equity—is robust to the inclusion of other factors. The other factors that we control for are liquidity, the liberalization indicator, a foreign exchange factor, and a variable measuring other shareholder rights.[19]

---

[16] The specification of the ratio ϕ in Bekaert and Harvey (1997) has not just trade/GDP but also market capitalization/GDP.

[17] Insider trading will affect the cost of equity through Φ if the foreign investor is marginal; insider trading will affect the cost of equity through λ_{var} if the domestic investor is marginal. In the former case, a correct specification of Φ should pick this up and we should not see any effect on residuals; in the latter case, as we have restricted λ_{var} to be the same for all countries, the effect will be seen on the residuals. As we do not know ex ante which investor, foreign or domestic, is marginal, and as it is likely that our specification of Φ is not complete, we measure the effect of insider trading by its effect on the residuals.

[18] We do not include the insider trading variables in the model in (1) directly for the following reason. The insider trading variables are dummy variables that take on the value of zero or one. Including a dummy variable in a nonlinear estimation is subject to computational problems as the convergence of the optimization becomes more difficult and the results more unstable. This is especially the case for our model, which is large and complex. In any case, it should be noted that the two approaches are similar and should yield the same outcome for the test. Moreover, Section III.E presents results from Fama–MacBeth linear regressions, where the insider trading dummies are directly included in the risk-adjustment model. Those results are very similar to the ones shown here.

[19] As purchasing power parity is not observed in the data, standard models like Ferson and Harvey (1993) and Dumas and Solnik (1995) have a foreign exchange factor (FX factor). So does our model. However, because of convergence problems, our estimation is a two-step procedure. Therefore, unlike the standard models, in the first step, we strip out the effects of the local

The World Price of Insider Trading   97

We regress the residuals from model (1) against the insider trading enforcement variable, liquidity, the liberalization indicator, and a foreign exchange factor. We do not include the variable measuring other shareholder rights because it does not change over time. Since we are using a panel regression with country-fixed effects, a variable that does not change over time will have a value of zero by definition. However, we will account for this variable in the next regression. Panel B2 of Table III tells us that the coefficient on the insider trading enforcement variable factor continues to remain negative and significant at the five percent level after we control for the above factors.

If we annualize the coefficient on the insider trading enforcement variable factor from panel B2 in Table III, which is -0.0056, we find that the enforcement of insider trading is associated with a 7 percent reduction in the cost of equity. This might appear to be unrealistically large. However, we need to keep in mind that the majority of the countries in our sample are emerging markets, and these have yearly returns ranging from -18 percent to 28 percent. With this respect, our estimate of the impact of enforcing insider trading laws on the cost of equity does not seem extreme.[20] Nevertheless, there may be a few reasons why our estimate of 7 percent may be too high. First, many emerging markets had their first enforcement in the 1990s, and they also had negative equity returns in the late 1990s. However, when we controlled for this by truncating our sample period at 1995, our estimate of 7 percent was reduced by only 50 basis points. Second, as governments probably enforce insider trading laws when the cost of equity becomes too high, there is an endogeneity problem. We do not correct for this.

As argued before, we were not able to include the *shareholders' rights* variable because of country-fixed effects. However, we still would like to control for this variable. Therefore, we run the previous regression and add the *shareholders' rights* variable without demeaning it. This is not strictly speaking the correct way to do panel regressions with fixed effects. However, we argue that this is an approximate way to control for *shareholders' rights*. Panel B3 of Table III tells us that the coefficient on the insider trading enforcement variable factor continues to remain negative and significant at the five percent level.

Interestingly, from both Panel B2 and Panel B3, the impact of liberalization on returns is observed to be economically more significant. This is consistent with the findings in Bekaert and Harvey (2000) and Henry (2000).

---

variance factor and the world factor, and in the second step, to isolate the effect of insider trading, we strip out the effects of other factors like the FX factor. The FX factor that we use is the conditional covariance of the return of the stock market index of the country with the return a U.S. investor would get if she held the foreign currency. This conditional covariance is obtained by using the multivariate ARCH model we previously discussed in equation (3)—just replace the world portfolio (w) by the foreign exchange portfolio (ifx).

[20] We attempted to measure the differential impact of insider trading laws on developed countries and emerging markets by using a dummy variable to denote an emerging market, and interacting this with the IT enforcement dummy. The coefficient of the IT enforcement dummy becomes statistically insignificant, whereas the coefficient of the interaction variable becomes statistically significant at the five percent level. We conclude that the reduction in the cost of capital that is associated with the enforcement of insider trading laws comes about mainly from emerging markets.

Table III

Effect of Insider Trading Laws on the Cost of Equity
(Using an International Asset Pricing Model)

Panel A: Adjusting for risk. The panel regressions are based on monthly data from 1969:12 through 1998:12. The international asset pricing model used is

$$(r_{i,t} - r_{f,t}) = \alpha_0 + \phi_{i,t}\lambda_{\mathrm{cov}}h_{i,w,t} + (1 - \phi_{i,t})\lambda_{\mathrm{var}}h_{i,t} + e_{i,t} \tag{A1}$$

where the measure of integration of country i at time t, $\Phi_{i,t}$, is defined as follows:

$$\phi_{i,t} = \frac{\exp\left(\alpha_1\left(\dfrac{exports_{i,t} + imports_{i,t}}{gdp_{i,t}}\right)\right)}{1 + \exp\left(\alpha_1\left(\dfrac{exports_{i,t} + imports_{i,t}}{gdp_{i,t}}\right)\right)} \tag{A2}$$

and λ_{cov} is the price of the covariance risk with the world, and λ_{var} is the price of own country variance risk. The independent variables are the conditional covariances and variances, $h_{i,w,t}$ and $h_{i,t}$, respectively, and these are obtained from the multivariate ARCH model below:

$$r_{i,t} = c_1 + \epsilon_{i,t},$$

$$r_{w,t} = c_2 + \epsilon_{w,t},$$

$$h_{i,t} = b_1 + a_1(\tfrac{1}{2}\epsilon_{i,t-1}^2 + \tfrac{1}{3}\epsilon_{i,t-2}^2 + \tfrac{1}{6}\epsilon_{i,t-3}^2),$$

$$h_{w,t} = b_2 + a_2(\tfrac{1}{2}\epsilon_{w,t-1}^2 + \tfrac{1}{3}\epsilon_{w,t-2}^2 + \tfrac{1}{6}\epsilon_{w,t-3}^2),$$

$$h_{i,w,t} = b_3 + a_3(\tfrac{1}{2}\epsilon_{i,t-1}\epsilon_{w,t-1} + \tfrac{1}{3}\epsilon_{i,t-2}\epsilon_{w,t-2} + \tfrac{1}{6}\epsilon_{i,t-3}\epsilon_{w,t-3}),$$

$$\epsilon_{i,t}, \epsilon_{w,t} \sim N\left(\begin{bmatrix} 0 \\ 0 \end{bmatrix}, \begin{bmatrix} h_{i,t} & h_{i,w,t} \\ h_{i,w,t} & h_{w,t} \end{bmatrix}\right) \tag{A3}$$

where $\epsilon_{i,t-j}$ is the innovation in monthly return of the stock market index of country i at time $t - j$, $j \in \{0,1,2,3\}$, and $\epsilon_{w,t-j}$ is the innovation in monthly return of the stock market index of the world at time $t - j$, $j \in \{0,1,2\}$.

Panel B: Effect on residuals. The panel regressions with country-fixed effects are based on monthly data from 1969:12 through 1998:12. The dependent variable is the residual, e_{it}, from the international asset pricing model estimated in Panel A. The independent variables are as follows. The indicator variable *IT laws* for existence changed from zero to one in the year after the insider trading laws were instituted. The indicator variable *IT enforcement* for enforcement changed from zero to one in the year after the first prosecution was recorded. The indicator variable *liberalization* changes from zero to one in the month after the official liberalization date that was obtained from Bekaert and Harvey (2000). It is assumed to be one for all developed countries, except for the three noted in Table I. The liquidity variable is the natural logarithm of the ratio of volume to market capitalization. The shareholders' rights variable is computed from Table 2 in La Porta et al. (1998). The last independent variable is the foreign exchange variable. It is defined as $h_{i,ifx,t}$, which is the conditional covariance of the return of the stock market index with the depreciation of the ith foreign currency with respect to the dollar at time t. We estimate this conditional covariance variable from the multivariate ARCH model below.

continued

The World Price of Insider Trading   99

Table III—*Continued*

$$r_{i,t} = f_1 + \epsilon_{i,t},$$

$$r_{ifx,t} = f_2 + \epsilon_{ifx,t},$$

$$h_{i,t} = e_1 + d_1(\tfrac{1}{2}\epsilon_{i,t-1}^2 + \tfrac{1}{3}\epsilon_{i,t-2}^2 + \tfrac{1}{6}\epsilon_{i,t-3}^2),$$

$$h_{ifx,t} = e_2 + d_2(\tfrac{1}{2}\epsilon_{ifx,t-1}^2 + \tfrac{1}{3}\epsilon_{ifx,t-2}^2 + \tfrac{1}{6}\epsilon_{ifx,t-3}^2),$$

$$h_{i,ifx,t} = e_3 + d_3(\tfrac{1}{2}\epsilon_{i,t-1}\epsilon_{ifx,t-1} + \tfrac{1}{3}\epsilon_{i,t-2}\epsilon_{ifx,t-2} + \tfrac{1}{6}\epsilon_{i,t-3}\epsilon_{ifx,t-3}),$$

$$\epsilon_{i,t}, \epsilon_{ifx,t} \sim N\left(\begin{bmatrix} 0 \\ 0 \end{bmatrix}, \begin{bmatrix} h_{i,t} & h_{i,ifx,t} \\ h_{i,ifx,t} & h_{ifx,t} \end{bmatrix} \right) \tag{A4}$$

where $\epsilon_{i,t-j}$ is the innovation in monthly return of the stock market index of country i at time $t - j$, $j \in \{0,1,2,3\}$, and $\epsilon_{ifx,t-j}$ is the innovation in monthly depreciation of the ith foreign currency with respect to the dollar at time $t - j$, $j \in \{0,1,2,3\}$. We correct for country-specific heteroskedasticity and country-specific autocorrelation.

Panel A: Adjusting for Risk		
Parameter	Coefficient	p-value
α_0	0.0011	0.5534
α_1	15.6094	0.0283
λ_{cov}	2.2157	0.0471
λ_{var}	2.3984	0.0615

Independent Variable	Coefficient	p-value
Panel B1: Effect on Residuals (Risk adjusted); Dependent Variable: Residual from Risk Adjustment Model		
IT laws	−0.0021	0.4038
IT enforcement	−0.0082	0.0135
Panel B2: Effect on Residuals (Risk, Foreign Exchange Factor, Liquidity Factor, and Liberalization Adjusted); Dependent Variable: Residual from Risk Adjustment Model		
Foreign exchange, $h_{i,ifx,t}$	7.2922	0.0003
Liquidity	0.0047	0.0001
Liberalization	−0.0063	0.0987
IT enforcement	−0.0056	0.0361
Panel B3: Effect on Residuals (Risk, Foreign Exchange Factor, Liquidity Factor, Shareholder Rights, and Liberalizations Adjusted); Dependent Variable: Residual from Risk Adjustment Model		
Foreign exchange, $h_{i,ifx,t}$	7.2639	0.0003
Liquidity	0.0048	0.0000
Shareholders' rights	0.0003	0.3124
Liberalization	−0.0077	0.0587
IT enforcement	−0.0064	0.0218

C. Using the Dividend Yield

An approximate method to compute the cost of equity by backing it out from the classical constant growth dividend discount model is given in all finance textbooks. It turns out to be the sum of the forecast of the dividend yield and the forecast of the growth rate of dividends. Appendix A in Bekaert and Harvey (2000) explores in great detail the relationship between dividend yields and the cost of equity for more general models. The advantages of using dividend yields to measure cost of equity are many. Dividend yields are observable, stationary, and do not move much. A sharp change in cost of equity should lead to a sharp change in dividend yields. The disadvantage of using dividend yields is that changes in dividend yields may come about because of repurchases of stock, and may come about because of changes in growth opportunities. The first factor is not much of a problem in emerging markets because repurchases are minor. The second factor, though a concern in the papers of Bekaert and Harvey (2000) and Henry (2000), who look at the effect of liberalization, may not be an issue in our paper. The reason is that changes in insider trading laws would only have, at most, a second-order effect on the growth opportunity of firms.

Define k as the cost of equity implied by the Gordon growth model. Assuming that the best forecast for future growth rates in dividends is the most current dividend growth rate, g, the cost of equity, k, is computed as the sum of the forecast of the dividend yield ($(1 + g)$ multiplied by current dividend yield) and the forecast of the growth rate of dividends, g. Using k as the dependent variable, we run a panel time-series regression with country-fixed effects. We correct for country-specific heteroskedasticity and country-specific autocorrelation. The regressions use data for the 38 countries for which we have dividend yield data from January 1973 to December 1998 (some countries do not have data for the full time period).

Table IV presents the results from this panel time-series regression. When *IT laws* is the independent variable, the coefficient on *IT laws* is negative and statistically insignificant. When *IT enforcement* is the independent variable, the coefficient on *IT enforcement* is negative and statistically significant at the five percent level. These conclusions do not change if we add the *liberalization* indicator as a control variable.

If we annualize the coefficient on the insider trading enforcement variable factor in Table IV, which is -0.0049, we find that the enforcement of insider trading is associated with a reduction in the cost of equity by about six percent per year. Note that we obtained a seven percent estimate when we used an explicit international asset pricing model in the previous section. As the previous methodology to estimate the cost of equity was different than the current methodology, we may conclude that our result is robust.

D. Using Country Credit Ratings

Erb et al. (1996) found that country credit ratings are a very good proxy for ex ante risk exposure, particularly of segmented emerging economies. Country credit ratings predict both expected returns and volatility. They argue that

Table IV

Effect of Insider Trading Laws on the Cost of Equity (Using Dividend Yields)

The panel regressions with country-fixed effects are based on monthly data from 1973:01 through 1998:12. The dependent variable is k, the cost of equity, defined as the sum of the dividend yield forecast and the growth rate of the dividend. The independent variables are the insider trading and liberalization variables. They are coded as follows. The indicator variable *IT laws* changes from zero to one in the year after the insider trading laws are instituted. The indicator variable *IT enforcement* changes from zero to one in the year after the first prosecution was recorded. The indicator variable *liberalization* changes from zero to one in the month after the official liberalization date that was obtained from Bekaert and Harvey (2000). It is assumed to be one for all developed countries, except for the three countries noted in Table I. The equity data for developed countries are from Morgan Stanley Capital International, and the equity data for emerging markets are from International Financial Corporation. The p-values are in parentheses. We correct for country-specific heteroskedasticity and country-specific autocorrelation.

Independent Variables	(1)	(2)	(3)	(4)
IT laws	−0.0023		−0.0017	
	(0.2995)		(0.4489)	
IT enforcement		−0.0052		−0.0049
		(0.0449)		(0.0401)
Liberalization			−0.0024	−0.0019
			(0.5626)	(0.6224)

it might be better to use this risk measure since it is not directly associated with the stock market. This approach has another advantage: As there are many more countries for which we have data on ratings than countries for which we have data on stock market returns, our sample size is roughly doubled from 55 to 97. The disadvantage of this approach is that it uses survey data as the independent variable, and survey data, where people do not put their money where their mouths are, may have their own biases.

We call the log of this country credit rating variable cr. Using cr as the dependent variable, we run a panel time-series regression with country-fixed effects. We correct for country-specific heteroskedasticity and country-specific autocorrelation. The regressions use data from our 97 countries from September 1979 to September 1998 (some countries do not have data for the full time period).

Table V presents the results from this panel time-series regression. When *IT laws* is the independent variable, the coefficient on *IT laws* is positive and statistically significant at the five percent level. When *IT enforcement* is the independent variable, the coefficient on *IT enforcement* is positive and statistically significant at the five percent level. When we add the *liberalization* indicator as a control variable, the coefficient on *IT laws* is no longer significant. On the other hand, the coefficient on *IT enforcement* continues to remain significant at the five percent level.

Table V also tells us that the enforcement of insider trading laws increases the log of a country's credit rating by 0.0257. As Exhibit 4 in Erb et al. (1996) tells us that an increase of one in the log of a country's credit rating decreases

Table V

Effect of Insider Trading Laws on Country Credit Rating

The panel regressions with country-fixed effects are based on biannual data from 1979:2 through 1998:2. The dependent variable is *cr*, which represents the natural log of a country credit rating. Country credit ratings come from Institutional Investor's semiannual survey of bankers. The survey represents the responses of 75 to 100 bankers. Respondents rate each country on a scale of 0 to 100. The independent variables are the insider trading and liberalization variables, which are coded as follows. The indicator variable *IT laws* for existence changed from zero to one in the year after the insider trading laws were instituted. The indicator variable *IT enforcement* for enforcement changed from zero to one in the year after the first prosecution was recorded. The indicator variable *liberalization* changes from zero to one in the month after the official liberalization date that was obtained from Bekaert and Harvey (2000). It is assumed to be one for all developed countries, except for the three countries noted in Table I. The *p*-values are in parentheses. We correct for country-specific heteroskedasticity and country-specific autocorrelation.

Independent Variables	(1)	(2)	(3)	(4)
IT laws	0.0788		−0.0018	
	(0.0000)		(0.8967)	
IT enforcement		0.1056		0.0257
		(0.0000)		(0.0329)
Liberalization			0.0466	0.0408
			(0.0449)	(0.0730)

the cost of equity by 10.47 percent, this implies that the enforcement of insider trading is associated with a reduction in the cost of equity by about 0.0257×10.4 percent, that is about 30 basis points per year. This may not seem large, but one must remember two points. First, country credit ratings, unlike country equity returns, do not move much. The standard deviation of country credit ratings for the typical country is only one and a half points. Second, the above computation assumes that insider trading enforcement affects the cost of equity only through credit ratings, which is a conservative assumption.

E. Robustness Checks

The tests we ran under our four different approaches to estimating the cost of equity were panel time-series regressions. As these tests assume that the returns or risk-adjusted returns or dividend yields or credit ratings across countries are independent draws, they may overstate the statistical significance of the estimated coefficient on the *IT enforcement* variable. The Fama–MacBeth (1973) procedure, on the other hand, does not require the assumption of independence. This procedure runs each regression cross-sectionally for each month, and then aggregates the individual coefficients across the months.[21] Significance of the aggregated coefficients is obtained by a simple

---

[21] The Fama–MacBeth regressions for our international asset pricing model are, however, slightly different from the Fama–MacBeth regressions for the other three approaches. This is because, unlike in the other three approaches, we have to use estimates as independent vari-

Table VI
Effect of Insider Trading Enforcement—A Summary

The column "Panel Regressions" reproduces the coefficient and p-value of the IT enforcement dummy from our previous tables. The column "Fama–MacBeth Regressions" gives the coefficient and p-value of the IT enforcement dummy from the corresponding Fama–MacBeth cross-sectional regressions. The Fama–MacBeth procedure runs each regression cross-sectionally for each month, and then aggregates the individual coefficients across the months. Significance of the aggregated coefficients is obtained by a simple t-test. The Fama–MacBeth regressions for our international asset pricing model are, however, slightly different. Here we use estimates—conditional covariances and conditional variances—and these are computed from (3). We use a linear model. We incorporate the *IT enforcement* dummy as well as all the other controls directly into the linear regression.

| | Coefficient of the IT Enforcement Dummy (p-value) | |
Dependent Variable	Panel Regressions	Fama–MacBeth Regressions
Liquidity (Table II, Panel A)	0.4385	0.5707
	(0.0000)	(0.0000)
Raw returns (Table II, Panel B)	−0.0063	−0.0030
	(0.0345)	(0.1797)
Risk-adjusted return (Table III, Panel B3)	−0.0056	−0.0053
	(0.0361)	(0.0287)
Adjusted dividend yield (Table IV)	−0.0049	−0.0012
	(0.0401)	(0.5076)
Credit rating (Table V)	0.0257	0.1686
	(0.0329)	(0.0000)

t-test. A particular disadvantage of the Fama–Macbeth procedure in our case is that as we have a number of missing emerging market variables, especially in the early years, we cannot do cross-sectional regressions for those years. This reduction in power is particularly acute when we use dividend yields.

The results are given in Table VI, which is a useful summary of the main results of the paper. The column "Panel regressions" reproduces the coefficient and p-value of the IT enforcement dummy from our previous tables. The column "Fama-MacBeth regressions" gives the coefficient and p-value of the IT enforcement dummy from the corresponding Fama–MacBeth cross-

ables. These estimates—the conditional covariances and conditional variances—are computed as before using (3). This is not a problem because, as these estimates are generated country by country, they do not suffer from the assumption of independence. In the Fama–MacBeth procedure, our nonlinear model (1) demands a reasonable convergence of the optimization problem for every time period separately. This is impossible here due to the relatively small number of country observations per period, and the effort and time required to ensure that the optimization has correctly converged to the right parameters. For these reasons, we use a linear model, more in the spirit of the model used in the original Fama and MacBeth (1973). The linear model will not explicitly allow for partial integration of a country to the world equity. Given that the model is now linear, we can incorporate the *IT enforcement* dummy as well as all the other controls directly into the regression, without resorting to a two-step procedure as before.

sectional regressions. Notice that, with the exception of the dividend yield regressions, the p-values are broadly similar. The reason for the lack of significance of the coefficient in the dividend yield Fama–MacBeth regression is because we have less time periods with nonmissing dividend yields data than we have for returns.

The second robustness check we carried out was to check for outliers in all our tests. Removing these did not affect our p-values significantly.

IV. Concluding Remarks

Though the debate about the pros and cons of allowing insider trading in stock markets has been quite contentious in the law, economics, and finance literature, it seems that from the point of view of actual practice, the debate seems to have been settled. In a comprehensive survey of insider trading regulations in every country that had a stock market at the end of 1998, this paper finds that all of the 22 developed countries and four out of five of the 81 emerging markets had insider trading laws in their books.

The enforcement of these laws, however, has been spotty. We find that there has been a prosecution in only one out of three countries. Developed countries have a better record of prosecution than emerging markets (82 percent of developed countries, and 25 percent of emerging markets have had prosecutions).

The paper then goes on to show that the easy part—the establishment of insider trading laws—is not associated with a reduction in the cost of equity. It is the difficult part—the enforcement of insider trading laws—that is associated with a reduction in the cost of equity in a country.

Two qualifications are in order. First, as governments probably enforce insider trading laws when the cost of equity becomes too high, there is an endogeneity problem. We do not correct for this. This implies that our estimates of the reduction in equity associated with an enforcement of insider trading laws may be too high. Second, though we find that there is a statistically and economically significant drop in the cost of equity after the first insider trading enforcement action, we are reluctant to attribute causality. The reason for our reluctance to attribute causality is our finding that the first insider trading enforcement action is also related to an increase in country credit ratings. As there is no reason to suspect that these two variables are directly linked, we believe that these two variables are correlated with an unobservable causal variable—the attractiveness of the stock market to outside investors. Though we controlled for liberalization and controlled for other shareholder rights that have been used in the literature, and still obtained significance for our insider trading enforcement variable, we would not like to overemphasize our point estimates.

Appendix

Table AI gives a description of the data used.

Table AI

Description of Data Used

Data on monthly stock market indices for the 22 developed countries were obtained from Morgan Stanley Capital Market International (MSCI). Data on monthly stock market indices for the 33 emerging markets were obtained from the International Financial Corporation (IFC). The sample periods are given in Column 2. Data on monthly market capitalization, dollar volume, and monthly dividend yields were obtained from Datastream. The sample periods are given in Columns 3, 4, and 5. Data on quarterly/annual GDP, monthly exports, monthly imports, and monthly foreign exchange rates were from the International Financial Statistics of the International Monetary Fund. The statistics for Taiwan come from Datastream. The sample periods are given in Columns 6, 7, 8, and 9. Data on 55 biannual country credit ratings is obtained from the web site of Harvey (http://www.duke.edu/~charvey). The sample periods are given in Column 10. Harvey has data on 42 more emerging markets, and we use these as well.

					Sample Period				
(1) Country	(2) Indices of Stock Markets (Monthly)	(3) Market Capitalization of Main Exchange (Monthly)	(4) Dollar Volume in Main Exchange (Monthly)	(5) Dividend Yield (Monthly)	(6) GDP of Country (Quarterly or Annual)	(7) Exports of Country (Monthly)	(8) Imports of Country (Monthly)	(9) Exchange Rate (Monthly)	(10) Country Credit Rating (Bi-annual)
Developed countries									
Australia	12/69–12/98	1/73–12/98	1/84–12/98	1/73–12/98	69Q4–98Q4	12/69–12/98	12/69–12/98	12/69–12/98	9/79–9/98
Austria	12/69–12/98	1/73–12/98	8/86–12/98	1/73–12/98	69Q4–98Q4	12/69–12/98	12/69–12/98	12/69–12/98	9/79–9/98
Belgium	12/69–12/98	1/73–12/98	1/86–12/98	1/73–12/98	69Y–98Y	1/93–12/98	1/93–12/98	12/69–12/98	9/79–9/98
Canada	12/69–12/98	1/73–12/98	1/73–12/98	1/73–12/98	69Q4–98Q4	12/69–12/98	12/69–12/98	12/69–12/98	9/79–9/98
Denmark	12/69–12/98	1/73–12/98	4/88–12/98	1/73–12/98	69Y–98Y	12/69–12/98	12/69–12/98	12/69–12/98	9/79–9/98
Finland	12/87–12/98	3/88–12/98	NA	3/88–12/98	69Y–98Y	12/69–12/98	12/69–12/98	12/69–12/98	9/79–9/98
France	12/69–12/98	1/73–12/98	6/88–12/98	1/73–12/98	69Q4–98Q4	12/69–12/98	12/69–12/98	12/69–12/98	9/79–9/98
Germany	12/69–12/98	1/73–12/98	6/88–12/98	1/73–12/98	69Q4–98Q4	12/69–12/98	12/69–12/98	12/69–12/98	9/79–9/98
Hong Kong	12/69–12/98	1/73–12/98	6/88–12/98	1/73–12/98	69Y–98Y	12/69–12/98	12/69–12/98	12/69–12/98	9/79–9/98
Ireland	12/87–12/98	1/73–12/98	NA	1/73–12/98	69Y–98Y	12/69–12/98	12/69–12/98	12/69–12/98	9/79–9/98
Italy	12/69–12/98	1/73–12/98	7/86–12/98	1/73–12/98	69Q4–98Q4	12/69–12/98	12/69–12/98	12/69–12/98	9/79–9/98
Japan	12/87–12/98	1/73–12/98	1/90–12/98	1/73–12/98	69Y–98Y	1/71–12/98	1/71–12/98	12/69–12/98	9/91–9/98
Luxembourg	12/69–12/98	1/73–12/98	NA	NA	69Y–98Y	12/69–12/98	12/69–12/98	12/69–12/98	9/79–9/98
Netherlands	12/69–12/98	1/73–12/98	2/86–12/98	1/73–12/98	69Y–98Y	12/69–12/98	12/69–12/98	12/69–12/98	9/79–9/98
New Zealand	12/87–12/98	1/88–12/98	1/90–12/98	1/88–12/98	69Q4–98Q4	12/69–12/98	12/69–12/98	12/69–12/98	9/79–9/98
Norway	12/69–12/98	1/80–12/98	1/80–12/98	1/80–12/98	69Y–98Y	12/69–12/98	12/69–12/98	12/69–12/98	9/79–9/98
Singapore	12/69–12/98	1/73–12/98	1/83–12/98	1/73–12/98	69Y–98Y	12/69–12/98	12/69–12/98	12/69–12/98	9/79–9/98
Spain	12/69–12/98	3/87–12/98	2/90–12/98	3/87–12/98	69Y–98Y	12/69–12/98	12/69–12/98	12/69–12/98	9/79–9/98
Sweden	12/69–12/98	1/82–12/98	1/82–12/98	1/82–12/98	69Y–98Y	12/69–12/98	12/69–12/98	12/69–12/98	9/79–9/98
Switzerland	12/69–12/98	1/73–12/98	1/89–12/98	1/73–12/98	69Y–98Y	12/69–12/98	12/69–12/98	12/69–12/98	9/79–9/98
United Kingdom	12/69–12/98	1/70–12/98	10/86–12/98	1/70–12/98	69Q4–98Q4	12/69–12/98	12/69–12/98	12/69–12/98	9/79–9/98
United States	12/69–12/98	1/73–12/98	1/73–12/98	1/73–12/98	69Q4–98Q4	12/69–12/98	12/69–12/98	12/69–12/98	9/79–9/98

continued

Table AI—*Continued*

Sample Period

(1) Country	(2) Indices of Stock Markets (Monthly)	(3) Market Capitalization of Main Exchange (Monthly)	(4) Dollar Volume in Main Exchange (Monthly)	(5) Dividend Yield (Monthly)	(6) GDP of Country (Quarterly or Annual)	(7) Exports of Country (Monthly)	(8) Imports of Country (Monthly)	(9) Exchange Rate (Monthly)	(10) Country Credit Rating (Bi-annual)
Emerging markets									
Argentina	12/75–12/98	1/88–12/98	8/93–12/98	8/93–12/98	69Y–98Y	12/69–12/98	12/69–12/98	12/69–12/98	9/79–9/98
Brazil	12/75–12/98	7/94–12/98	NA	7/94–12/98	69Y–98Y	12/69–12/98	12/69–12/98	12/69–12/98	9/79–9/98
Chile	12/75–12/98	7/89–12/98	7/89–12/98	7/89–12/98	69Y–98Y	12/69–12/98	12/69–12/98	12/69–12/98	9/79–9/98
China	12/92–12/98	8/91–12/98	8/91–12/98	3/94–12/98	79Y–98Y	1/77–12/98	1/77–12/98	12/69–12/98	9/79–9/98
Colombia	12/84–12/98	NA	NA	NA	69Y–98Y	12/69–12/98	12/69–12/98	12/69–12/98	9/79–9/98
Czech Republic	12/93–12/98	NA	NA	NA	93Y–98Y	1/93–12/98	1/93–12/98	1/93–12/98	3/93–9/98
Egypt	12/94–12/98	NA	NA	NA	69Y–98Y	12/69–12/98	8/90–12/98	12/69–12/98	9/79–9/98
Greece	12/75–12/98	1/88–12/98	1/88–12/98	1/90–12/98	69Y–98Y	12/69–12/98	12/69–12/98	12/69–12/98	9/79–9/98
Hungary	12/92–12/98	NA	NA	NA	70Y–98Y	1/76–12/98	1/76–12/98	12/69–12/98	9/79–9/98
India	12/75–12/98	1/90–12/98	1/95–12/98	1/90–12/98	69Y–98Y	12/69–12/98	12/69–12/98	12/69–12/98	9/79–9/98
Indonesia	12/89–12/98	4/90–12/98	4/90–12/95	4/90–12/98	69Y–98Y	12/69–12/98	12/69–12/98	12/69–12/98	9/79–9/98
Israel	12/96–12/98	NA	NA	NA	69Y–98Y	12/69–12/98	12/69–12/98	12/69–12/98	9/79–9/98
Jordan	12/78–12/98	NA	NA	NA	69Y–98Y	12/69–12/98	12/69–12/98	12/69–12/98	9/79–9/98
Malaysia	12/84–12/98	1/86–12/98	1/86–12/98	1/86–12/98	69Y–98Y	12/69–12/98	12/69–12/98	12/69–12/98	9/79–9/98
Mexico	12/75–12/98	1/88–12/98	1/88–12/98	5/89–12/98	69Y–98Y	12/69–12/98	12/69–12/98	12/69–12/98	9/79–9/98
Morocco	12/95–12/98	NA	NA	NA	69Y–98Y	12/69–12/98	12/69–12/98	12/69–12/98	9/79–9/98
Nigeria	12/84–12/98	NA	NA	NA	69Y–98Y	12/69–12/98	12/69–12/98	12/69–12/98	9/79–9/98
Pakistan	12/84–12/98	NA	NA	NA	69Y–98Y	12/69–12/98	12/69–12/98	12/69–12/98	9/79–9/98
Peru	12/92–12/98	NA	NA	NA	69Y–98Y	12/69–12/98	12/69–12/98	12/69–12/98	9/79–9/98
Philippines	12/84–12/98	9/87–12/98	1/90–12/98	11/88–12/98	69Y–98Y	12/69–12/98	12/69–12/98	12/69–12/98	9/79–9/98
Poland	12/92–12/98	3/94–12/98	3/94–12/98	3/94–12/98	79Y–98Y	12/69–12/98	1/86–12/98	12/69–12/98	9/79–9/98
Portugal	1/86–12/98	1/90–12/98	1/90–12/98	1/90–12/98	69Y–98Y	12/69–12/98	12/69–12/98	12/69–12/98	9/79–9/98
Russia	12/95–12/98	NA	NA	NA	90Y–98Y	1/92–12/98	1/92–12/98	6/92–12/98	9/92–9/98
Saudi Arabia	12/97–12/98	NA	NA	NA	69Y–98Y	12/69–12/98	12/69–12/98	12/69–12/98	9/79–9/98
Slovakia	12/95–12/98	NA	NA	NA	93Y–98Y	1/93–12/98	1/93–12/98	1/93–12/98	3/93–9/98
South Africa	12/92–12/98	1/73–12/98	1/90–12/98	1/73–12/98	69Q4–98Q4	12/69–12/98	12/69–12/98	12/69–12/98	9/79–9/98
South Korea	12/75–12/98	9/87–12/98	9/87–12/98	9/87–12/98	69Q4–98Q4	12/69–12/98	12/69–12/98	12/69–12/98	9/79–9/98
Sri Lanka	12/92–12/98	NA	NA	NA	69Y–98Y	12/69–12/98	12/69–12/98	12/69–12/98	9/82–9/98
Taiwan	12/84–12/98	9/87–12/98	4/91–12/98	5/88–12/98	69Q4–98Q4	1/88–12/98	1/88–12/98	12/93–12/98	9/79–9/98
Thailand	12/75–12/98	1/87–12/98	1/87–12/98	1/87–12/98	69Y–98Y	12/69–12/98	12/69–12/98	12/69–12/98	9/79–9/98
Turkey	12/86–12/98	1/88–12/98	1/88–12/98	6/89–12/98	87Q1–98Q4	12/69–12/98	12/69–12/98	12/69–12/98	9/79–9/98
Venezuela	12/84–12/98	NA	NA	NA	69Y–98Y	12/69–12/98	12/69–12/98	12/69–12/98	9/79–9/98
Zimbabwe	12/75–12/98	NA	NA	NA	69Y–98Y	1/78–12/98	1/78–12/98	12/69–12/98	9/79–9/98

The World Price of Insider Trading 107

REFERENCES

Amihud, Yakov, and Haim Mendelson, 1986, Asset pricing and the bid-ask spread, *Journal of Financial Economics* 15, 223–249.

Bainbridge, Stephen, 2000, Insider trading, in *Encyclopedia of Law and Economics III* (Edward Elgar Publishing, Cheltenham, U.K.), 772–812.

Bekaert, Geert, and Campbell Harvey, 1995, Time varying world market integration, *Journal of Finance* 50, 403–444.

Bekaert, Geert, and Campbell Harvey, 1997, Emerging equity market volatility, *Journal of Financial Economics* 43, 29–77.

Bekaert, Geert, and Campbell Harvey, 2000, Foreign speculators and emerging equity markets, *Journal of Finance* 55, 565–613.

Beny, Laura, 1999, A comparative empirical investigation of agency and market theories of insider trading, Working paper, Harvard Law School.

Bettis, J. Carr, Jeffrey Coles, and Michael Lemmon, 2000, Corporate policies restricting trading by insiders, *Journal of Financial Economics* 57, 191–200.

Bhattacharya, Utpal, Hazem Daouk, Brian Jorgenson, and Carl-Heinrich Kehr, 2000, When an event is not an event: The curious case of an emerging market, *Journal of Financial Economics* 55, 69–101.

Bhattacharya, Utpal, and Matthew Spiegel, 1991, Insiders, outsiders, and market breakdowns, *Review of Financial Studies* 4, 255–282.

Bollerslev, Tim, Robert Engle, and Jeffrey Wooldrige, 1988, A capital asset pricing model with time-varying covariances, *Journal of Political Economy* 96, 116–131.

Brennan, Michael, and Avanidhar Subrahmanyam, 1996, Market microstructure and asset pricing: On the compensation for illiquidity in stock returns, *Journal of Financial Economics* 41, 441–464.

Demirguc-Kunt, Asli, and Vojislav Maksimovic, 1998, Law, finance, and firm growth, *Journal of Finance* 53, 2107–2137.

Dumas, Bernard, and Bruno Solnik, 1995, The world price of foreign exchange risk, *Journal of Finance* 50, 445–479.

Easley, David, Soeren Hvidkjaer, and Maureen O'Hara, 2000, Is information risk a determinant of asset returns? Working paper, Cornell University.

Engle, Robert, David Lilien, and Russell Robins, 1987, Estimating time varying risk premia in the term structure: The ARCH-M model, *Econometrica* 55, 391–407.

Erb, Claude, Campbell Harvey, and Tadas Viskanta, 1996, Expected returns and volatility in 135 countries, *Journal of Portfolio Management*, Spring, 46–58.

Errunza, Vihang, and Darius Miller, 2000, Market segmentation and the cost of capital in international equity markets, *Journal of Financial and Quantitative Analysis* 35, 577–600.

Fama, Eugene, and James MacBeth, 1973, Risk, return, and equilibrium: Empirical tests, *Journal of Political Economy* 81, 607–636.

Ferson, Wayne, and Campbell Harvey, 1993, The risk and predictability of international equity returns, *Review of Financial Studies* 6, 527–566.

Glosten, Lawrence, and Paul Milgrom, 1985, Bid, ask and transaction prices in a specialist model with heterogeneously informed traders, *Journal of Financial Economics* 14, 71–100.

Handbook of World Stock, Derivative and Commodity Exchanges, 1998 (International Financial Publications, London).

Harvey, Campbell, 1991, The world price of covariance risk, *Journal of Finance* 46, 111–157.

Harvey, Campbell, 1995, Predictable risk and returns in emerging markets, *Review of Financial Studies* 8, 773–816.

Harvey, Campbell, and Guofu Zhou, 1993, International asset pricing with alternative distribution assumptions, *Journal of Empirical Finance* 1, 107–131.

Henry, Peter, 2000, Stock market liberalization, economic reform, and emerging market equity prices, *Journal of Finance* 55, 529–564.

International Encyclopedia of the Stock Market, 1998, vol. 1 and 2, (Fitzroy Dearborn Publishers, Chicago).

Jacoby, Gady, David Fowler, and Aron Gottesman, 2000, The capital asset pricing model and the liquidity effect: A theoretical approach, *Journal of Financial Markets* 3, 69–81.

Jain, Pankaj, 2001, Institutional design and liquidity on stock exchanges, Working paper, Indiana University.

Jorion, Philippe, and William Goetzmann, 1999, Global stock markets in the twentieth century, *Journal of Finance* 54, 953–980.

Kyle, Albert, 1985, Continuous auctions and insider trading, *Econometrica* 53, 1315–1335.

La Porta, Rafael, Florencio Lopez-de-Silanes, Andrei Shleifer, and Robert Vishny, 1997, Legal determinants of external finance, *Journal of Finance* 52, 1131–1150.

La Porta, Rafael, Florencio Lopez-de-Silanes, Andrei Shleifer, and Robert Vishny, 1998, Law and finance, *Journal of Political Economy* 106, 1113–1155.

Levine, Ross, 1997, Financial development and economic growth: Views and agenda, *Journal of Economic Literature* 35, 688–726.

Lombardo, Davide, and Marco Pagano, 1999, Legal determinants of the return on equity, Working paper, Stanford University.

Manne, Henry, 1966, *Insider Trading and the Stock Market* (Free Press, New York).

Maug, Ernst, 1999, Insider trading legislation and corporate governance, Working paper, Duke University.

Meulbroek, Lisa, 1992. An empirical analysis of illegal insider trading, *Journal of Finance* 47, 1661–1699.

Posen, Norman, 1991, *International Securities Regulation* (Little, Brown and Company, Boston).

Solnik, Bruno, 1974a, An equilibrium model of the international capital market, *Journal of Economic Theory* 8, 500–524.

Solnik, Bruno, 1974b, The international pricing of risk: An empirical investigation of the world capital market structure, *Journal of Finance* 29, 48–54.

Stamp, Mark, and Carson Welsh eds., 1996, *International Insider Dealing* (FT Law and Tax, Biddles Limited, Guildford, U.K.).

Stulz, René, 1999a, Globalization of equity markets and the cost of capital, Working paper, National Bureau of Economic Research.

Stulz, René, 1999b, Globalization, corporate finance, and the cost of capital, *Journal of Applied Corporate Finance*, Fall, 8–25.

World Factbook, 1999 (Central Intelligence Agency, Langley, VA).

THE JOURNAL OF FINANCE • VOL. LXI, NO. 1 • FEBRUARY 2006

What Works in Securities Laws?

RAFAEL LA PORTA, FLORENCIO LOPEZ-DE-SILANES,
and ANDREI SHLEIFER[*]

ABSTRACT

We examine the effect of securities laws on stock market development in 49 countries. We find little evidence that public enforcement benefits stock markets, but strong evidence that laws mandating disclosure and facilitating private enforcement through liability rules benefit stock markets.

IN THIS PAPER, WE EXAMINE SECURITIES LAWS OF 49 COUNTRIES, focusing specifically on how these laws regulate the issuance of new equity to the public. Security issuance is subject to the well-known "promoter's problem" (Mahoney (1995))—the risk that corporate issuers sell bad securities to the public—and as such is covered in all securities laws.[1] We analyze the specific provisions in securities laws governing initial public offerings in each country, examine the relationship between these provisions and various measures of stock market development, and interpret the evidence in light of the available theories of securities laws.

For securities markets, alternative theories of optimal legal arrangements can be distilled down to three broad hypotheses. Under the null hypothesis, associated with Coase (1960) and Stigler (1964), the optimal government policy is to leave securities markets unregulated. Issuers of securities have an incentive to disclose all available information to obtain higher prices simply because failure to disclose would cause investors to assume the worst (Grossman (1981), Grossman and Hart (1980), Milgrom and Roberts (1986)). Investors can

* La Porta is at Tuck School of Business, Dartmouth College; Lopez-de-Silones is at the University of Amsterdam; and Shleifer is at Harvard University. We are grateful to the Inter-American Development Bank, the Gildor Foundation, the BSI Gamma Foundation, the NSF, the International Institute for Corporate Governance at Yale University, and the Doing Business project of the World Bank for financial support; to Alfredo Larrea-Falcony and Qian Sun for significant contributions to this work; to Constanza Blanco, John C. Coates IV, Luis Leyva Martinez, Carlos Orta Tejeda, Tuffic Miguel Ortega, Jorge Gabriel Taboada Hoyos, Annette L. Nazareth, and Robert Strahota for assistance in developing the questionnaire; to Douglas Baird, Jack Coffee, Frank Easterbrook, Richard Epstein, Merritt Fox, Edward Glaeser, Simon Johnson, Lawrence Katz, Paul Mahoney, Mark Ramseyer, Kevin Murphy, Eric Posner, Richard Posner, Roberta Romano, Luigi Spaventa, the editor, and two referees of this journal for helpful comments; and to Jeffrey Friedman, Mario Gamboa-Cavazos, Amy Levin, Anete Pajuste, and Vasudev Vadlamudi for excellent research assistance. The data used in this paper can be downloaded from http://post.economics.harvard.edu/faculty/shleifer/papers/securities_data.xls.

[1] Teoh, Welch, and Wong (1998) and Dechow, Sloan, and Sweeney (1996) present evidence consistent with the view that U.S. firms manipulate accounting figures to raise capital on favorable terms. Leuz, Nanda, and Wysocki (2003) show that earnings manipulation is more extensive in countries with weak investor protection.

rely on these disclosures when there are reputational, legal, and contractual penalties for misreporting, verification of accuracy is costless, or reporting accuracy is backed by warranties. When verification is costly, issuers of "good" securities can resort to additional mechanisms to signal their quality (Ross (1979)). For example, auditors and underwriters can credibly certify the quality of the securities being offered to safeguard their reputation and avoid liability under contract or tort law (Benston (1985), Chemmanur and Fulghieri (1994), De Long (1991)). Similarly, private stock exchanges can mandate optimal disclosure and monitor compliance by listed firms to facilitate trading (Benston (1973), Fischel and Grossman (1984), Miller (1991)). These market and general legal mechanisms suffice for securities markets to prosper. Securities law is either irrelevant (to the extent that it codifies existing market arrangements or can be contracted around), or damaging, in so far as it raises contracting costs and invites political interference in markets (Coase (1975), Macey (1994), Romano (2001)).

The two alternative hypotheses hold that securities laws "matter." Both reputations and contract and tort law are insufficient to keep promoters from cheating investors because the payoff from cheating is too high and because private tort and contract litigation is too expensive and unpredictable to serve as a deterrent. To reduce the enforcement costs and opportunistic behavior, the government can introduce a securities law that specifies the contracting framework.[2] The two alternative hypotheses differ in what kind of government intervention would be optimal within such a framework.

Under the first alternative, the government can standardize the private contracting framework to improve market discipline and private litigation. Without such standardization, litigation is governed by contract and tort law, with grave uncertainty about outcomes because such matters as intent and negligence need to be sorted out in court (Easterbrook and Fischel (1984)). We examine two aspects of standardization. First, the law can mandate the disclosure of particular information, such as profitability and ownership structure, in the prospectus. If followed, such mandates make it easier for investors to value companies and therefore more willing to invest. If violated, these mandates create a prima facie liability of issuers or intermediaries. Second, the law can specify the liability standards facing issuers and intermediaries when investors seek to recover damages from companies that follow affirmative disclosure rules but fail to reveal potentially material information. The law can thereby reduce the uncertainties and the costs of private litigation, in turn benefiting markets.[3]

Under the final hypothesis, even given a securities law that describes both the disclosure obligations of various parties and the liability standards, private enforcement incentives are often insufficient to elicit honesty from issuers. A public enforcer such as a Securities and Exchange Commission is needed to

---

[2] See Landis (1938), Friend and Herman (1964), Coffee (1984, 1989, 2002), Simon (1989), Mahoney (1995), Fox (1999), Stulz (1999), Black (2001), Beny (2002), and Reese and Weisbach (2002).

[3] This view is developed in Black and Kraakman (1996), Hay, Shleifer, and Vishny (1996), Hay and Shleifer (1998), Glaeser and Shleifer (2001, 2002), and Bergman and Nicolaievsky (2002).

support trade. Such an enforcer might be able to intervene ex ante, by clarifying legal obligations or ex post, by imposing its own penalties or bringing lawsuits. Public enforcement might work because the enforcer is *independent and focused* and thus can regulate markets free from political interference, because the enforcer can *introduce regulations of market participants*, because it can *secure information* from issuers and market participants—through subpoena, discovery, or other means—more effectively than private plaintiffs, or because it can *impose sanctions*.[4] Under this hypothesis, the strength of public enforcement introduced by securities laws is most beneficial for market development.

To distinguish these hypotheses, we cooperate with attorneys from 49 countries to assemble a database of rules and regulations governing security issuance. We use the data to produce quantitative measures of securities laws and regulations, with a focus on mandatory disclosure, liability standards, and public enforcement. Finally, we examine the relationship between our measures of securities laws and a number of indicators of stock market development. In the analysis below, we first motivate our data collection effort using an example of an actual dispute. We then present the data on securities laws around the world, and finally investigate whether and how these laws matter for stock market development.

I. A Motivating Example

We focus on the agency problem between prospective investors in an initial public offering and the "promoter" who offers shares for sale. In modern days, this promoter is usually the owner or founder of a private company acting in concert with his distributors (or underwriters) and accountants. But at least some of the law developed historically as a way to control share sales by specialized promoters, who bought companies and then sold their equity to the public (Mahoney (1995)). The promoter's problem is fraught with potential conflicts of interest. The promoter wants to sell the shares at the highest possible price while concealing bad information about the company and diverting its cash flows and assets to himself. Both the adverse selection and the moral hazard problems are severe, and if not addressed can undermine and possibly stop fund-raising in the stock market.

Grossman and Hart (1980) show, however, that with perfect law enforcement (i.e., automatic sanctions for not telling the truth), promoters have an incentive to reveal everything they know, at least in a particular model. The reason is that without such revelation, potential investors assume the absolute worst. To the extent that the circumstances of the company are better or the conflicts of interest less severe, promoters have every reason to disclose such information, and they cannot say anything more optimistic than the truth because of the automatic sanctions. Grossman and Hart also note that without perfect enforcement, these favorable results for the market solution do not hold.

---

[4] These themes are developed in Landis (1938), Becker (1968), Polinsky and Shavell (2000), Glaeser, Johnson, and Shleifer (2001), Glaeser and Shleifer (2003), and Pistor and Xu (2002).

Contrast this theoretical paradigm with an actual example of a securities issue from the Netherlands (Velthuyse and Schlingmann (1995)). In 1987–1988, the Dutch bank ABN Amro underwrote some bonds of Coopag Finance BV, a Dutch financial company wholly owned by Co-op AG, a diversified German firm. The bonds were guaranteed by Co-op AG. The prospectus was drafted in accordance with the requirements of the Amsterdam Stock Exchange and included audited annual accounts provided by the issuer to ABN Amro. In conformity with the law on annual accounts, the (consolidated) financial statements included in the prospectus omitted 214 affiliated companies of Co-op AG with debts of DM 1.5 billion. Shortly after the issue, Dutch newspapers published negative information about Co-op AG and the bond prices of Coopag Finance BV plummeted. The creditors of Coopag Finance sued the underwriter, ABN Amro, for losses due to its failure to disclose material information about the finances of Co-op AG. ABN Amro claimed in response that "the damages, if any, did not result from the alleged misleading nature of the prospectuses. . . . ," but rather from unfavorable events that took place after the offering. In addition, the distributor argued that "an investigation by ABN Amro, however extensive, could not have led to the discovery of deceit, because even the accountants appeared not to have discovered in time that something was wrong . . . " (Velthuyse and Schlingmann (1995), p. 233). The successive Dutch courts, however, ruled the distributor liable and recognized explicitly that the distributor's duty in presenting the prospectus to investors went beyond merely relying on the information provided by the issuer. Rather, to avoid liability, the Supreme Court ruled that a distributor must conduct an independent investigation of the issuer and prove that it cannot be blamed for the damages caused by the misleading prospectus.

As this example illustrates, a country as developed as the Netherlands, as recently as 15 years ago, did not have clearly defined responsibilities and automatic penalties for issuers and underwriters as required by Grossman and Hart (1980). Some of the differences between the example and their model are worth emphasizing. First, reputational concerns did not suffice to induce either the issuer to disclose the omitted information or the underwriter to carry out an independent investigation of the issuer's financial condition. Second, the problem for private enforcement was not that of inaccurate disclosure—in fact, the issuer complied with the affirmative disclosure requirements—but rather, the omission of material information from the prospectus. This omission did not cause investors to assume the worst; after all, they bought the bonds. Third, this omission raised the question for the court of whether the distributor or the issuer was liable, with the distributor rather than the bankrupt issuer having the assets to compensate investors. Fourth, and perhaps most importantly, the court had to resolve the crucial question of the standard of liability for the distributor, namely, what were its affirmative obligations to investors. The court did not presume, as in the model, that failure to disclose automatically caused liability. Resolving this issue required extensive and expensive litigation, leading to a particular standard of care. These differences between the case and the model suggest that in reality, enforcement of good conduct is costly, and hence we should not necessarily expect efficient outcomes from unregulated markets.

This enforcement-based reasoning forms the analytical foundation of the case for securities laws. Market mechanisms and litigation supporting private contracting may be too expensive. Since investors, on average, are not tricked, they pay lower prices for the equity when they are unprotected, and the amount of equity issued is lower (Shleifer and Wolfenzon (2002), La Porta et al. (2002b)). Securities laws, in so far as they reduce the costs of contracting and resolving disputes, can encourage equity financing of firms and stock market development. The Dutch example also suggests that solving the promoter's problem is important not only for equity markets but for debt markets as well.

II. The Variables

Our data on the regulation of the promoter's problem are based on answers to a questionnaire by attorneys in the sample of 49 countries with the largest stock market capitalization in 1993 (La Porta et al. (1998)). We invited one attorney from each country to answer the questionnaire describing the securities laws (including actual laws, statues, regulations, binding judicial precedents, and any other rule with force of law) applicable to an offering of shares listed in the country's largest stock exchange in December 2000.[5] All 49 authors returned answered questionnaires, and subsequently confirmed the validity of their answers as we recorded them. All the variables derived from the questionnaires and other sources are defined in Table I.

A. Disclosure and Liability Standards

As James Landis, the principal author of U.S. securities laws, recognized, making private recovery of investors' losses easy is essential to harness the incentives of market participants to enforce securities laws (Landis (1938), Seligman (1995)). Efficiency considerations suggest that the lowest cost provider of information about a security should collect and present this information, and be held accountable if he omits or misleads. In the Grossman and Hart model (1980), for example, the lowest cost providers are not the investors, but the issuers, distributors, and accountants.[6] An efficient system would provide these agents incentives to collect and present information to investors,

---

[5] We first approached authors who had published country reports on securities laws in publications such as *International Securities Regulation* and *International Securities Laws*. When countries were not covered in such publications or authors declined our invitation, we searched the *Martindale Law Directory* to identify leading law firms practicing in the area of securities laws and invited them to answer the questionnaire. The respondents received a questionnaire designed by the authors with the help of practicing lawyers in Argentina, Japan, and the United States.

[6] Two other features of initial public offerings make "buyer-beware" rules unattractive. First, the scope for fraud is very large. Second, the damages resulting from investing in reliance of a defective prospectus are much easier to calculate than those that result from, for example, the use of a defective appliance.

6 *The Journal of Finance*

Table I

Description of the Variables

This table describes the variables in the paper. The *Supervisor* is the main government agency in charge of supervising stock exchanges. The *Issuer* is a domestic corporation that raises capital through an initial public offering of common shares. The newly issued shares will be listed on the country's largest stock exchange. The *Distributor* advises the *Issuer* on the preparation of the prospectus and assists in marketing the securities but does not authorize (or sign) the prospectus unless required by law. The *Accountant* audits the financial statements and documents that accompany the prospectus. Unless otherwise specified, the source for the variables is the questionnaire of law firms and the laws of each country. The edited answers to the question-naire are posted at http://post.economics.harvard.edu/faculty/shleifer/papers/securities_documentation.pdf.

Variable	Description
	I. Disclosure requirements
Prospectus	Equals one if the law prohibits selling securities that are going to be listed on the largest stock exchange of the country without delivering a prospectus to potential investors; and equals zero otherwise.
Compensation	An index of prospectus disclosure requirements regarding the compensation of the *Issuer*'s directors and key officers. Equals one if the law or the listing rules require that the compensation of *each* director and key officer be reported in the prospectus of a newly listed firm; equals one half if only the *aggregate* compensation of directors and key officers must be reported in the prospectus of a newly listed firm; and equals zero when there is no requirement to disclose the compensation of directors and key officers in the prospectus for a newly listed firm.
Shareholders	An index of disclosure requirements regarding the *Issuer*'s equity ownership structure. Equals one if the law or the listing rules require disclosing the name and ownership stake of each shareholder who, directly or indirectly, controls 10% or more of the *Issuer*'s voting securities; equals one half if reporting requirements for the *Issuer*'s 10% shareholders do not include indirect ownership or if only their aggregate ownership needs to be disclosed; and equals zero when the law does not require disclosing the name and ownership stake of the *Issuer*'s 10% shareholders. We combine large shareholder reporting requirements imposed on firms with those imposed on large shareholders themselves.
Inside ownership	An index of prospectus disclosure requirements regarding the equity ownership of the *Issuer*'s shares by its directors and key officers. Equals one if the law or the listing rules require that the ownership of the *Issuer*'s shares by *each* of its director and key officers be disclosed in the prospectus; equals one half if only the *aggregate* number of the *Issuer*'s shares owned by its directors and key officers must be disclosed in the prospectus; and equals zero when the ownership of the *Issuer*'s shares by its directors and key officers need not be disclosed in the prospectus.
Irregular contracts	An index of prospectus disclosure requirements regarding the *Issuer*'s contracts outside the ordinary course of business. Equals one if the law or the listing rules require that the terms of material contracts made by the *Issuer* outside the ordinary course of its business be disclosed in the prospectus; equals one half if the terms of only *some* material contracts made outside the ordinary course of business must be disclosed; and equals zero otherwise.
Transactions	An index of the prospectus disclosure requirements regarding transaction between the *Issuer* and its directors, officers, and/or large shareholders (i.e., "related parties"). Equals one if the law or the listing rules require that *all* transactions in which related parties have, or will have, an interest be disclosed in the prospectus; equals one half if *only some* transactions between the *Issuer* and related parties must be disclosed in the prospectus; and equals zero if transactions between the *Issuer* and related parties need not be disclosed in the prospectus.
Disclosure requirements index	The index of disclosure equals the arithmetic mean of (1) prospectus; (2) compensation; (3) shareholders; (4) inside ownership; (5) contracts irregular; and (6) transactions.

(continued)

What Works in Securities Laws?   7

Table I—*Continued*

Variable	Description
	II. Liability standard
Liability standard for the issuer and its directors	Index of the procedural difficulty in recovering losses from the *Issuer* and its directors in a civil liability case for losses due to misleading statements in the prospectus. We first code separately the liability standard applicable to the *Issuer* and its directors and then average the two of them. The liability standard applicable to the *Issuer*'s directors equals one when investors are only required to prove that the prospectus contains a misleading statement. Equals two thirds when investors must also prove that they relied on the prospectus and/or that their loss was caused by the misleading statement. Equals one third when investors must also prove that the director acted with negligence. Equals zero if restitution from directors is either unavailable or the liability standard is intent or gross negligence. The liability standard applicable to the *Issuer* is coded analogously.
Liability standard for distributors	Index of the procedural difficulty in recovering losses from the *Distributor* in a civil liability case for losses due to misleading statements in the prospectus. Equals one when investors are only required to prove that the prospectus contains a misleading statement. Equals two thirds when investors must also prove that they relied on the prospectus and/or that their loss was caused by the misleading statement. Equals one third when investors must also prove that the *Distributor* acted with negligence. Equals zero if restitution from the *Distributor* is either unavailable or the liability standard is intent or gross negligence.
Liability standard for accountants	Index of the procedural difficulty in recovering losses from the *Accountant* in a civil liability case for losses due to misleading statements in the audited financial information accompanying the prospectus. Equals one when investors are only required to prove that the audited financial information accompanying the prospectus contains a misleading statement. Equals two thirds when investors must also prove that they relied on the prospectus and/or that their loss was caused by the misleading accounting information. Equals one third when investors must also prove that the *Accountant* acted with negligence. Equals zero if restitution from the *Accountant* is either unavailable or the liability standard is intent or gross negligence.
Liability standard index	The index of liability standards equals the arithmetic mean of (1) liability standard for the issuer and its directors; (2) liability standard for distributors; and (3) liability standard for accountants.
	III.1 Characteristics of the Supervisor of securities markets
Appointment	Equals one if a majority of the members of the *Supervisor* are not unilaterally appointed by the Executive branch of government; and equals zero otherwise.
Tenure	Equals one if members of the *Supervisor* cannot be dismissed at the will of the appointing authority; and equals zero otherwise.
Focus	Equals one if separate government agencies or official authorities are in charge of supervising commercial banks and stock exchanges; and equals zero otherwise.
Supervisor characteristics index	The index of characteristics of the *Supervisor* equals the arithmetic mean of (1) appointment; (2) tenure; and (3) focus.
	III.2 Power of the Supervisor to issue rules
Rule-making power index	An index of the power of the *Supervisor* to issue regulations regarding primary offerings and listing rules on stock exchanges. Equals one if the *Supervisor* can generally issue regulations regarding primary offerings and/or listing rules on stock exchanges without prior approval of other governmental authorities. Equals one half if the *Supervisor* can generally issue regulations regarding primary offerings and/or listing rules on stock exchanges only with the prior approval of other governmental authorities. Equals zero otherwise.

(continued)

8   *The Journal of Finance*

Table I—*Continued*

Variable	Description
	III.3 Investigative powers of the Supervisor of securities markets
Document	An index of the power of the *Supervisor* to command documents when investigating a violation of securities laws. Equals one if the *Supervisor* can generally issue an administrative order commanding all persons to turn over documents; equals one half if the *Supervisor* can generally issue an administrative order commanding publicly traded corporations and/or their directors to turn over documents; and equals zero otherwise.
Witness	An index of the power of the *Supervisor* to subpoena the testimony of witnesses when investigating a violation of securities laws. Equals one if the *Supervisor* can generally subpoena all persons to give testimony; equals one half if the *Supervisor* can generally subpoena the directors of publicly traded corporations to give testimony; and equals zero otherwise.
Investigative powers index	The index of investigative powers equals the arithmetic mean of (1) document; and (2) witness.
	III.4 Sanctions
Orders issuer	An index aggregating stop and do orders that may be directed to the *Issuer* in case of a defective prospectus. The index is formed by averaging the subindexes of orders to stop and to do. The subindex of orders to stop equals one if the *Issuer* may be ordered to refrain from a broad range of actions; equals one half if the *Issuer* may only be ordered to desist from limited actions; and equals zero otherwise. The subindex of orders to do equals one if the *Issuer* may be ordered to perform a broad range of actions to rectify the violation; equals one half if the *Issuer* may only be ordered to perform limited actions; and equals zero otherwise. We disregard orders that may be issued by Courts at the request of a private party in a civil lawsuit.
Orders distributor	An index aggregating stop and do orders that may be directed to the *Distributor* in case of a defective prospectus. The index is formed by averaging the subindexes of orders to stop and to do. The subindex of orders to stop equals one if the *Distributor* may be ordered to refrain from a broad range of actions; equals one half if the *Distributor* may only be ordered to desist from limited actions; and equals zero otherwise. The subindex of orders to do equals one if the *Distributor* may be ordered to perform a broad range of actions to rectify the violation; equals one half if the *Distributor* may only be ordered to perform limited actions; and equals zero otherwise. We disregard orders that may be issued by Courts at the request of a private party in a civil lawsuit.
Orders accountant	An index aggregating stop and do orders that may be directed to the *Accountant* in case of a defective prospectus. The index is formed by averaging the subindexes of orders to stop and to do. The subindex of orders to stop equals one if the *Accountant* may be ordered to refrain from a broad range of actions; equals one half if the *Accountant* may only be ordered to desist from limited actions; and equals zero otherwise. The subindex of orders to do equals one if the *Accountant* may be ordered to perform a broad range of actions to rectify the violation; equals one half if the *Accountant* may only be ordered to perform limited actions; and equals zero otherwise. We disregard orders that may be issued by Courts at the request of a private party in a civil lawsuit.
Orders index	The index of orders equals the arithmetic mean of (1) orders issuer; (2) orders distributor; and (3) orders accountant.
Criminal director/officer	An index of criminal sanctions applicable to the *Issuer's* directors and key officers when the prospectus omits material information. We create separate subindexes for directors and key officers and average their scores. The subindex for directors equals zero when directors cannot be held criminally liable when the prospectus is misleading. Equals one half if directors can be held criminally liable when *aware* that the prospectus is misleading. Equals one if directors can *also* be held criminally liable when negligently *unaware* that the prospectus is misleading. The subindex for key officers is constructed analogously.

(continued)

What Works in Securities Laws? 9

Table I—*Continued*

Variable	Description
Criminal distributor	An index of criminal sanctions applicable to the *Distributor* (or its officers) when the prospectus omits material information. Equals zero if the *Distributor* cannot be held criminally liable when the prospectus is misleading. Equals one half if the *Distributor* can be held criminally liable when *aware* that the prospectus is misleading. Equals one if the *Distributor* can *also* be held criminally liable when *negligently* unaware that the prospectus is misleading.
Criminal accountant	An index of criminal sanctions applicable to the *Accountant* (or its officers) when the financial statements accompanying the prospectus omit material information. Equals zero if the *Accountant* cannot be held criminally liable when the financial statements accompanying the prospectus are misleading. Equals one half if the *Accountant* can be held criminally liable when *aware* that the financial statements accompanying the prospectus are misleading. Equals one if the *Accountant* can *also* be held criminally liable when *negligently* unaware that the financial statements accompanying the prospectus are misleading.
Criminal index	The index of criminal sanctions equals the arithmetic mean of (1) criminal director; (2) criminal distributor; and (3) criminal accountant.

III.5 Summary index of public enforcement

Public enforcement index	The index of public enforcement equals the arithmetic mean of (1) supervisor characteristics index; (2) rule-making power index; (3) investigative powers index; (4) orders index; and (5) criminal index.

IV. Outcome variables

External cap/GDP	The average ratio of stock market capitalization held by small shareholders to gross domestic product (GDP) for the period 1996 to 2000. The stock market capitalization held by small shareholders is computed as the product of the aggregate stock market capitalization and the average percentage of common shares not owned by the top three shareholders in the 10 largest nonfinancial, privately owned domestic firms in a given country. A firm is considered privately owned if the State is not a known shareholder in it. Source: La Porta et al. (1999b), Hartland-Peel (1996) for Kenya, *Bloomberg*, and various annual reports for Ecuador, Jordan, and Uruguay.
Domestic firms/pop	Logarithm of the average ratio of the number of domestic firms listed in a given country to its population (in millions) for the period 1996 to 2000. Source: International Finance Corporation (2001) and World Bank (2001).
IPOs	The average ratio of the equity issued by newly listed firms in a given country (in thousands) to its GDP (in millions) over the period 1996 to 2000. Source: *Securities Data Corporation,* World Bank (2001).
Block premia	"The block premia is computed taking the difference between the price per share paid for the control block and the exchange price 2 days after the announcement of the control transaction, dividing by the exchange price and multiplying by the ratio of the proportion of cash flow rights represented in the controlling block." We use the country's sample median. Source: Dyck and Zingales (2004, p. 547).
Access to equity	Index of the extent to which business executives in a country agree with the statement "Stock markets are open to new firms and medium-sized firms." Scale from 1 (strongly agree) though 7 (strongly disagree). Source: Schwab et al. (1999).
Ownership concentration	The average percentage of common shares owned by the top three shareholders in the 10 largest nonfinancial, privately owned domestic firms in a given country. A firm is considered privately owned if the State is not a known shareholder in it. Source: La Porta et al. (1998), Hartland-Peel (1996) for Kenya, *Bloomberg*, and various annual reports for Ecuador, Jordan, and Uruguay.
Liquidity	The average total value of stocks traded as a percentage of GDP for the period 1996 to 2000. Source: World Development Indicators at http://devdata.worldbank.org/dataonline/.

(continued)

Table I—*Continued*

Variable	Description
	V. Control variables and instruments
Anti-director rights	This index of anti-director rights is formed by adding one when: (1) the country allows shareholders to mail their proxy vote; (2) shareholders are not required to deposit their shares prior to the General Shareholders' Meeting; (3) cumulative voting or proportional representation of minorities on the board of directors is allowed; (4) an oppressed minorities mechanism is in place; (5) the minimum percentage of share capital that entitles a shareholder to call for an Extraordinary Shareholders' Meeting is less than or equal to 10% (the sample median); or (6) when shareholders have preemptive rights that can only be waived by a shareholders' meeting. The range for the index is from 0 to 5. Source: La Porta et al. (1998).
Efficiency of the judiciary	Assessment of the "efficiency and integrity of the legal environment as it affects business, particularly foreign firms" produced by the country risk rating agency International Country Risk (ICR). It may be "taken to represent investors' assessment of conditions in the country in question." Average between 1980 and 1983. Scale from 0 to 10, with lower scores representing lower efficiency levels. Source: *International Country Risk Guide* (Political Risk Services (1996)).
Log GDP per capita	Logarithmic of per capita GDP (in U.S. dollars) in 2000.
Legal origin	Identifies the legal origin of the company law or commercial code of each country. Source: La Porta et al. (1998).
Investor protection	Principal component of the indices of disclosure requirements, liability standards, and anti-director rights. Scale from 0 to 10.

and would hold them liable if they do not. In securities laws, this strategy generally takes the form of disclosure requirements and liability standards that make it cheaper for investors to recover damages when information is wrong or omitted—the two features we try to capture empirically.

We collect six proxies for the strength of specific disclosure requirements pertaining to the promoter's problem.[7] The first and most basic question is whether promoters can issue securities without delivering a prospectus describing the securities to potential investors in advance. Since every country requires a prospectus before securities are sold and listed, the operational word here is "delivering." In some countries, it is possible to sell securities after a prospectus is deposited at the company, or with the Supervisor, without delivering it to investors. Delivering a prospectus to potential investors is an affirmative step in making disclosures to them. In addition, we keep track of affirmative disclosure requirements in the following five areas: (1) insiders' compensation; (2) ownership by large shareholders; (3) inside ownership; (4) contracts outside

---

[7] A detailed study of the impact of substantive disclosure rules is beyond the scope of this paper. However, we examine the robustness of our findings to the inclusion of less selective measures of disclosure. Bushman, Piotroski, and Smith (2003) present data on firms' actual disclosures in the following four areas: (1) segments, R&D, capital expenditures, accounting policies, and subsidiaries; (2) major shareholders, management, board, director, and officer remuneration, and director and officer shareholding; (3) consolidation and discretionary reserves; and, (4) frequency of reporting, consolidation of interim reports, and number of disclosed items. None of these variables has additional explanatory power in our regressions.

the normal course of business; and (5) transactions with related parties. We calculate the index of "disclosure requirements" as the average of the preceding six proxies.

In addition to specific disclosure requirements, nearly every country has a residual disclosure requirement that the prospectus must include all material information necessary to assess the value of the securities being offered. When bad news hits after security issuance, the question becomes whether this information was known or knowable to the issuer, the distributor, and/or the accountant and omitted from the prospectus. As legal scholars including Black (2001) and Coffee (2002) emphasize, and as the Dutch example illustrates, the liability standard in the cases of such omission is central to private enforcement of securities laws.[8]

There are basically four liability standards. In the base case, the standard is the same as in torts, namely negligence: the plaintiff must show that the issuer, the distributor, or the accountant was negligent in omitting information from the prospectus. The tort standard also requires that investors prove that they relied on the prospectus to invest (reliance) or that their losses were caused by the misleading information in the prospectus (causality). Some countries rule out recovery in a prospectus liability case or make it harder than the tort standard by requiring the plaintiffs to show that the defendants either knew about the omission or acted with intent or gross negligence (e.g., while "drunk") in omitting the information from the prospectus. In contrast, the burden of proof is less demanding than tort in countries in which investors must prove reliance or causality or both, but not negligence. Finally, burden of proof is lowest where plaintiffs only need to show that the information in the prospectus was misleading (but not prove reliance or causality). The defendants are either strictly liable (i.e., they cannot avoid liability if the prospectus omitted information) or they must themselves show that they exercised due diligence in preparing the prospectus. This shift in the burden of proof from plaintiffs to defendants can, in principle, significantly reduce the cost to the former of establishing liability.

In our empirical analysis, we distinguish among these four liability standards in cases against issuers and directors, distributors, and accountants, and compute a "liability standard" index.

B. Public Enforcement

In the context of securities markets, a public enforcer can be a securities commission, a central bank, or some other supervisory body. For concreteness, we call the main government agency or official authority in charge of supervising

---

[8] We have been asked to examine whether the availability of class action suits and contingency fees is associated with the development of securities markets. A dummy equal to one if class actions are available in a prospectus liability case is an insignificant predictor of the development of securities markets. Similarly, a dummy equal to one if contingency fees are generally available is an insignificant predictor of the development of securities markets. Finally, the interaction of class actions and contingency fees is also insignificant.

securities markets the Supervisor. We focus on five broad aspects of public enforcement.

The first aspect covers the basic attributes of the Supervisor, which we capture with three variables. First, an effective Supervisor may need to be insulated from interference by the Executive, both to facilitate recruiting professional staff and to prevent political interference on behalf of influential issuers. To measure the Supervisor's independence, we keep track of whether its key members are appointed through a system of checks-and-balances or unilaterally by the Executive. Second, the independence of the Supervisor may be enhanced when its key members may be dismissed only after due process rather than at the will of the appointing authority. Third, an effective Supervisor may need to be focused on securities markets, rather than on both these markets and banking, so that his success is more closely tied to that of the securities market. Accordingly, we measure whether the Supervisor's mandate covers securities markets alone. We combine these three variables into a subindex of "Supervisor attributes."

The second issue is whether the power to regulate securities markets be delegated to the Supervisor, rather than remain with the legislature or the Ministry of Finance (Spiller and Ferejohn (1992)). We measure whether the Supervisor has the power to regulate primary offerings and/or listing rules on stock exchanges.

The third aspect covers the investigative powers of the Supervisor. Unless the issuer, the distributor, and the auditor are strictly liable for all false and misleading statements in the prospectus (which never happens), the question arises as to why the information revealed to investors was inaccurate. Did the issuer, distributor, or auditor have the information? If not, could they have had it? At what cost? Did the issuer hide the information from the distributor or the auditor? Answering these questions is costly, especially for private plaintiffs. A Supervisor can be empowered to command documents from issuers, distributors, or accountants, and to subpoena testimony of witnesses. Such powers can in principle enable the Supervisor to ascertain the reasons for inaccuracy which can then—as a public good—become the basis for sanctions, or for criminal or civil litigation. We summarize the powers of the Supervisor to subpoena documents and witnesses by forming a subindex of "Investigative powers."

The fourth aspect—perhaps most directly intended to substitute for the weakness of private enforcement—covers noncriminal sanctions for violations of securities laws. These sanctions may involve ordering the directors of a public firm to rectify noncompliance with disclosure requirements, to institute changes recommended by outside reviewers, and/or to compensate investors for their losses. Such sanctions could be imposed separately on issuers, distributors, and accountants, and we keep track of each category. We then average the scores for the sanctions against the various parties to create a subindex of "Orders."

Finally, the fifth aspect covers criminal sanctions for violations of securities laws. We keep track of whether criminal sanctions are applicable, to whom they apply, and what conduct invokes them. We average the scores for criminal sanctions against directors, distributors, and accountants to obtain a subindex of "criminal sanctions." These variables are of special interest since a popular sentiment sees criminal sanctions as essential to enforce good practices in security issuance. We average the preceding five subindexes to form the index of "Public enforcement."

C. Other Variables

We are interested in understanding the effects of the various provisions in securities laws on financial development. We use seven proxies for the development of securities markets in different countries. The first variable is the ratio of stock market capitalization to gross domestic product (GDP) scaled by the fraction of the stock market held by outside investors. (The results are qualitatively similar for the unadjusted ratio of market capitalization to GDP.) The second variable is the (logarithm of the) number of domestic publicly traded firms in each country relative to its population. The third variable is the value of initial public offerings in each country relative to its GDP. All three variables are 5-year averages of yearly data for the period 1996 to 2000. Theoretically, the first of these three measures is the most attractive, since in theory better investor protection is associated with both a higher number of listed firms and a higher valuation of capital (Shleifer and Wolfenzon (2002)). Except for some differences in scaling and timing, these three variables are used in La Porta et al. (1997) to study the consequences of investor protection through corporate law on stock market development.

The fourth variable is a qualitative assessment of the ability of new and medium-sized firms to raise equity in the stock market based on a survey of business executives by the *Global Competitiveness Report 1999* (Schwab et al. (1999)). The fifth variable is the (median) premium paid for control in corporate control transactions. In several theoretical models, this variable has been interpreted as a measure of the private benefits of control, which are higher in countries with weaker investor protection (Grossman and Hart (1988), Dyck and Zingales (2004), Nenova (2003)). The sixth variable is a proxy for ownership concentration among the largest firms in the country. Both theory (Shleifer and Wolfenzon (2002)) and prior empirical work (La Porta, Lopez-de-Silanes, and Shleifer (1999a)) suggest that ownership concentration is lower in countries with better investor protection. Finally, the seventh variable is a proxy for stock market liquidity, as measured by the ratio of traded volume to GDP. Levine and Zervos (1998) show that this variable predicts the growth in per capita income.

To isolate the effect of securities laws on financial markets, we control for several factors identified by previous research. The first of these is the level of economic development, which we measure as the (logarithm of) per capita GDP. Economic development is often associated with capital deepening. In addition, richer countries might have higher quality institutions in general, including better property rights and rule of law, which could be associated with better financial development regardless of the content of the laws (North (1981),

La Porta et al. (1999b)).[9] To further address this issue, we use the measure of the efficiency of the judiciary from the *International Country Risk Guide* (Political Risk Services (1996)) as an additional control.

La Porta et al. (1997, 1998) present evidence that measures of investor protection derived from corporate law are associated with stock market development. This evidence raises the question of which laws, if any, make a difference. Accordingly, in all our regressions, we include the anti-directors rights index of the protection afforded to shareholders through statutory corporate law as an additional control.

As in many other studies in this area, the causal effect of securities laws on financial development cannot be established with certainty. Following La Porta et al. (1997, 1998), we use the legal origin of commercial laws as an instrument. The commercial laws of most countries originate in one of four legal families: English (common) law, French civil law, German civil law, and Scandinavian law, which have spread throughout the world through conquest, colonization, and occasionally voluntary transplantation. England developed a common law tradition, characterized by independent judges and juries, relatively weaker reliance on statutes, and the preference for contracts and private litigation as a means of dealing with social harms. France, in contrast, developed a civil law tradition, characterized by state-employed judges, great reliance on legal and procedural codes, and a preference for state regulation over private litigation. This makes legal origin a suitable instrument for the stance of the law regarding alternative regulatory strategies.

Table II presents our data on securities laws. Countries are arranged by legal origin, and we report means by legal origin as well as tests of the differences in these means. There is large cross-country variation in our measures of securities laws. Common and civil law countries differ significantly in our measures of disclosure, liability standards, and public enforcement. Common law countries both have more extensive mandatory disclosure requirements, and make it easier for investors to recover damages. In the public enforcement area, these differences are smaller for Supervisor attributes and rule-making power, and greater for investigative powers, orders, and criminal sanctions. In the next section, we examine which aspects of the securities law, as well as corporate law, matter for financial development.

III. Securities Laws and Financial Development

Table III presents the results of regressions of our various measures of financial development on the anti-director rights index, efficiency of the judiciary, logarithm of GDP per capita, disclosure (Panel A), liability standards (Panel B),

---

[9] In practice, per capita GDP is very highly correlated with survey measures of the quality of institutions such as perceptions of property rights, rule of law, and the prevalence of corruption. In our sample, the pair-wise correlation of (log) per capita GDP with property rights, corruption, and rule of law is 0.754, 0.882, and 0.892, respectively. The results reported in the paper are robust to replacing log per capita GDP by any of these three measures.

Table II
Indices of Regulation of Securities Markets

This table classifies countries by legal origin and shows the securities law variables for each country covering the areas of (1) disclosure requirements; (2) liability standards; (3) supervisor characteristics; (4) rule-making power of the supervisor; (5) investigative powers of the supervisor; (6) orders to issuers, distributors, and accountants; (7) criminal sanctions applicable to directors, distributors, and accountants; and (8) public enforcement. All variables are described in Table I.

Country	Symbol	Disclosure Requirements	Liability Standard	Supervisor Characteristics	Rule-Making Power	Investigative Powers	Orders	Criminal Sanctions	Public Enforcement
English legal origin									
Australia	AUS	0.75	0.66	0.67	1.00	1.00	1.00	0.83	0.90
Canada	CAN	0.92	1.00	0.67	0.50	1.00	1.00	0.83	0.80
Hong Kong	HKG	0.92	0.66	0.33	1.00	1.00	1.00	1.00	0.87
India	IND	0.92	0.66	0.33	0.50	1.00	0.67	0.83	0.67
Ireland	IRL	0.67	0.44	0.00	1.00	0.00	0.00	0.83	0.37
Israel	ISR	0.67	0.66	0.67	0.00	1.00	1.00	0.50	0.63
Kenya	KEN	0.50	0.44	0.33	1.00	0.50	1.00	0.67	0.70
Malaysia	MYS	0.92	0.66	0.33	0.50	1.00	1.00	1.00	0.77
New Zealand	NZL	0.67	0.44	0.33	0.00	1.00	0.00	0.33	0.33
Nigeria	NGA	0.67	0.39	0.67	0.50	0.00	0.00	0.50	0.33
Pakistan	PAK	0.58	0.39	0.67	1.00	1.00	0.17	0.08	0.58
Singapore	SGP	1.00	0.66	0.33	1.00	1.00	1.00	1.00	0.87
South Africa	ZAF	0.83	0.66	0.33	0.00	0.50	0.00	0.42	0.25
Sri Lanka	LKA	0.75	0.39	0.33	1.00	0.50	0.00	0.33	0.43
Thailand	THA	0.92	0.22	0.67	1.00	1.00	0.33	0.58	0.72
USA	USA	1.00	1.00	1.00	1.00	1.00	1.00	0.50	0.90
United Kingdom	GBR	0.83	0.66	0.00	1.00	1.00	1.00	0.42	0.68
Zimbabwe	ZWE	0.50	0.44	1.00	0.00	0.00	0.08	1.00	0.42
Mean		**0.78**	**0.58**	**0.48**	**0.67**	**0.75**	**0.57**	**0.65**	**0.62**
French legal origin									
Argentina	ARG	0.50	0.22	0.67	1.00	1.00	0.08	0.17	0.58
Belgium	BEL	0.42	0.44	0.00	0.00	0.25	0.00	0.50	0.15
Brazil	BRA	0.25	0.33	0.33	1.00	0.50	0.75	0.33	0.58
Chile	CHL	0.58	0.33	0.33	1.00	0.75	0.42	0.50	0.60
Colombia	COL	0.42	0.11	0.33	1.00	0.75	0.33	0.50	0.58
Ecuador	ECU	0.00	0.11	1.00	1.00	0.25	0.08	0.42	0.55
Egypt	EGY	0.50	0.22	0.67	0.00	0.25	0.17	0.42	0.30
France	FRA	0.75	0.22	1.00	0.50	1.00	1.00	0.33	0.77
Greece	GRC	0.33	0.50	0.67	0.00	0.25	0.17	0.50	0.32
Indonesia	IDN	0.50	0.66	0.33	1.00	1.00	0.25	0.50	0.62

(*continued*)

Table II—*Continued*

Country	Symbol	Disclosure Requirements	Liability Standard	Supervisor Characteristics	Rule-Making Power	Investigative Powers	Orders	Criminal Sanctions	Public Enforcement
Italy	ITA	0.67	0.22	0.67	1.00	0.25	0.00	0.50	0.48
Jordan	JOR	0.67	0.22	0.33	1.00	1.00	0.67	0.00	0.60
Mexico	MEX	0.58	0.11	0.00	1.00	0.25	0.00	0.50	0.35
Netherlands	NLD	0.50	0.89	0.33	1.00	0.50	0.00	0.50	0.47
Peru	PER	0.33	0.66	0.67	1.00	0.75	1.00	0.50	0.78
Philippines	PHL	0.83	1.00	0.67	1.00	1.00	1.00	0.50	0.83
Portugal	PRT	0.42	0.66	0.67	1.00	1.00	0.25	0.00	0.58
Spain	ESP	0.50	0.66	0.67	0.00	0.50	0.00	0.50	0.33
Turkey	TUR	0.50	0.22	0.67	1.00	1.00	0.00	0.50	0.63
Uruguay	URY	0.00	0.11	0.67	1.00	0.25	0.50	0.42	0.57
Venezuela	VEN	0.17	0.22	0.33	1.00	1.00	0.08	0.33	0.55
Mean		**0.45**	**0.39**	**0.52**	**0.79**	**0.64**	**0.32**	**0.40**	**0.53**
German legal origin									
Austria	AUT	0.25	0.11	0.33	0.00	0.00	0.00	0.50	0.17
Germany	DEU	0.42	0.00	0.33	0.00	0.25	0.00	0.50	0.22
Japan	JPN	0.75	0.66	0.00	0.00	0.00	0.00	0.00	0.00
Korea	KOR	0.75	0.66	0.33	0.00	0.50	0.08	0.33	0.25
Switzerland	CHE	0.67	0.44	0.33	1.00	0.00	0.00	0.33	0.33
Taiwan	TWN	0.75	0.66	0.33	1.00	0.25	0.17	0.83	0.52
Mean		**0.60**	**0.42**	**0.28**	**0.33**	**0.17**	**0.04**	**0.42**	**0.25**
Scandinavian legal origin									
Denmark	DNK	0.58	0.55	0.00	1.00	0.50	0.33	0.00	0.37
Finland	FIN	0.50	0.66	0.67	0.00	0.25	0.17	0.50	0.32
Norway	NOR	0.58	0.39	0.00	0.00	0.25	0.33	1.00	0.32
Sweden	SWE	0.58	0.28	0.00	1.00	0.25	0.67	0.58	0.50
Mean		**0.56**	**0.47**	**0.17**	**0.50**	**0.31**	**0.38**	**0.52**	**0.38**
Mean of all countries		**0.60**	**0.47**	**0.45**	**0.66**	**0.60**	**0.38**	**0.50**	**0.52**
Tests of means (t-stats)									
English vs. Civil Law		−5.01[a]	−2.45[b]	−0.60	−0.04	−2.23[b]	−2.60[a]	−3.18[a]	−2.72[a]
English vs. French		−5.31[a]	−2.48[b]	0.48	0.90	−0.92	−1.87[c]	−3.46[a]	−1.43
English vs. German		−2.19[b]	−1.44	−1.67	−1.59	−3.45[a]	−2.70[a]	−1.77[c]	−3.85[a]
English vs. Scandinavian		−2.60[b]	−0.99	−1.94[c]	−0.67	−2.17[b]	−0.80	−0.76	−2.22[b]
French vs. German		1.49	0.28	−2.13[b]	−2.27[b]	−3.32[a]	−1.87[c]	0.18	−3.66[a]
French vs. Scandinavian		1.03	0.58	−2.34[b]	−1.21	−1.94[c]	0.29	1.05	−1.82[c]
German vs. Scandinavian		−0.32	0.28	−0.75	0.48	1.26	3.70[a]	0.49	1.35

[a] significant at 1%; [b] significant at 5%; and [c] significant at 10%.

Table III
Securities Laws and the Development of Stock Markets

Ordinary least squares regressions of the cross-section of countries. The dependent variables are (1) external market capitalization; (2) log of domestic firms per capita; (3) value of the IPO-to-GDP ratio; (4) block premium; (5) access to equity; (6) ownership concentration; and (7) the stock-market-volume-to-GDP ratio. All regressions include anti-director rights, efficiency of the judiciary, and log of GDP per capita. In addition, regressions include disclosure requirements (Panel A); liability standards (Panel B); and public enforcement (Panel C). All variables are described in Table I. Robust standard errors are shown in parentheses.

Panel A: Disclosure Requirements

	Market Capitalization	Number of Firms	IPOs	Block Premia	Access to Equity	Ownership Concentration	Liquidity
Disclosure requirements	0.5813[a]	1.1103[b]	4.6983[a]	-0.2682[b]	1.8032[a]	-0.1930[b]	97.2050[a]
	(0.1377)	(0.4127)	(1.4395)	(0.1145)	(0.4834)	(0.0871)	(34.0413)
Anti-director rights	0.0420	0.1195	0.1371	-0.0180	-0.0715	-0.0209[c]	1.7897
	(0.0308)	(0.0946)	(0.2772)	(0.0204)	(0.0856)	(0.0123)	(5.5914)
Ln GDP per capita	0.0957[a]	0.2789[b]	1.1393[a]	-0.0028	0.1543[c]	-0.0285[b]	20.2746[a]
	(0.0229)	(0.1075)	(0.2439)	(0.0195)	(0.0903)	(0.0139)	(6.4414)
Efficiency of the judiciary	0.0386[c]	0.2302[a]	-0.0843	-0.0070	0.1824[a]	-0.0070	-4.0440
	(0.0204)	(0.0664)	(0.2106)	(0.0114)	(0.0649)	(0.0093)	(5.3761)
Constant	-1.2056[a]	-2.6758[a]	-9.5765[a]	0.4067[b]	1.4312[c]	0.9540[a]	-160.1500[a]
	(0.2037)	(0.6693)	(1.8551)	(0.1492)	(0.7266)	(0.1036)	(37.7904)
Observations	49	49	49	37	44	49	49
Adjusted R^2	54%	69%	38%	32%	52%	36%	27%

(continued)

Table III—*Continued*

	Market Capitalization	Number of Firms	IPOs	Block Premia	Access to Equity	Ownership Concentration	Trading
Panel B: Liability Standards							
Liability standards	0.4481ᶜ	0.7522ᶜ	3.7150ᵃ	-0.1302ᶜ	1.4655ᵃ	-0.1104	90.3188ᵃ
	(0.1289)	(0.4245)	(1.3750)	(0.0673)	(0.4755)	(0.0699)	(31.4726)
Anti-director rights	0.0515	0.1474	0.2049	-0.0276ᵇ	-0.0545	-0.0277ᵇ	1.9140
	(0.0330)	(0.0883)	(0.3216)	(0.0133)	(0.0823)	(0.0125)	(5.3484)
Ln GDP per capita	0.0878ᵃ	0.2665ᵇ	1.0733ᵃ	-0.0121	0.1534	-0.0268ᶜ	18.5645ᵃ
	(0.0240)	(0.1089)	(0.2370)	(0.0219)	(0.1082)	(0.0150)	(6.0737)
Efficiency of the judiciary	0.0457ᵇ	0.2439ᵃ	-0.0275	-0.0040	0.1916ᵃ	-0.0095	-2.9061
	(0.0226)	(0.0768)	(0.2031)	(0.0126)	(0.0663)	(0.0106)	(5.0634)
Constant	-1.0818ᵃ	-2.4459ᵃ	-8.5704ᵃ	0.3950ᵇ	1.7065ᵇ	0.9152ᵃ	-138.5010ᵃ
	(0.2026)	(0.7360)	(1.7468)	(0.1647)	(0.8231)	(0.1000)	(35.2721)
Observations	49	49	49	37	44	49	49
Adjusted R^2	51%	67%	36%	22%	50%	31%	27%
Panel C: Public Enforcement							
Public enforcement	0.3446ᶜ	0.6422	3.7220ᵇ	-0.0087	0.0069	0.0560	39.5648
	(0.1990)	(0.4813)	(1.5531)	(0.0651)	(0.5736)	(0.0940)	(30.0063)
Anti-director rights	0.0711ᵇ	0.1761ᵇ	0.3098	-0.0414ᵃ	0.0895	-0.0420ᵃ	7.8568
	(0.0347)	(0.0861)	(0.2434)	(0.0148)	(0.1056)	(0.0121)	(4.7260)
Ln GDP per capita	0.1041ᵃ	0.2949ᵃ	1.2210ᵃ	-0.0133	0.1835	-0.0289ᶜ	21.4326ᵃ
	(0.0218)	(0.1052)	(0.2687)	(0.0216)	(0.1222)	(0.0153)	(7.0790)
Efficiency of the judiciary	0.0518ᵇ	0.2551ᵃ	0.0355	-0.0041	0.1916ᵇ	-0.0090	-2.0959
	(0.0236)	(0.0750)	(0.2168)	(0.0120)	(0.0740)	(0.0112)	(5.4241)
Constant	-1.2999ᵃ	-2.8470ᵃ	-10.8554ᵃ	0.3898ᵇ	1.7103ᶜ	0.8912ᵃ	-165.9368ᵃ
	(0.2169)	(0.7578)	(2.0799)	(0.1791)	(0.9944)	(0.1173)	(40.4056)
Observations	49	49	49	37	44	49	49
Adjusted R^2	48%	66%	34%	15%	38%	29%	18%

ᵃsignificant at 1%; ᵇsignificant at 5%; and ᶜsignificant at 10%.

and public enforcement (Panel C).[10] Both higher per capita GDP and efficiency of the judiciary tend to be associated with more developed stock markets, and these effects are quantitatively large. To interpret the results on Table III, note that when securities laws are excluded from the regression, stronger anti-director rights are associated with better stock market development for all dependent variables except the index of access to equity (results not reported). In contrast, anti-director rights are only significant in one of the regressions that controls for disclosure (ownership concentration) and two of the regressions that control for liability standards (ownership concentration and block premium). The results for anti-director rights are more consistent in the regressions that control for public enforcement. In those regressions, anti-director rights have predictive power for market capitalization, number of firms, block premium, and ownership concentration.

Perhaps most interestingly, both disclosure requirements and liability standards are positively correlated with larger stock markets. In Panel A, disclosure is associated with more developed stock markets for all seven dependent variables. The estimated coefficients predict that a two-standard deviation increase in disclosure (roughly the distance from the Netherlands to the United States) is associated with an increase of 0.27 in the external-market-to-GDP ratio, a 52% rise in listed firms per capita, a 2.22 increase in the IPO-to-GDP ratio, a 13 percentage point drop in the block premium, a 0.85 point improvement in the access-to-equity index, a 9 percentage point drop in ownership concentration, and a 45.9 point increase in the volume-to-GDP ratio.[11]

The results on liability standards are also consistently strong. The estimated coefficients predict that a two-standard deviation increase in this variable (roughly the distance from Denmark to the United States) is associated with an increase of 0.23 percentage points in the external-market-to-GDP ratio, a 28% rise in listed firms per capita, a 1.88 increase in the IPO-to-GDP ratio, a 6.6 percentage point drop in the block premium, a 0.75 point improvement in the access-to-equity index, a decrease of 6.6 percentage points in ownership concentration (but with a t-stat of only 1.58), and a 45.8 point increase in the volume-to-GDP ratio.

Figures 1 and 2 illustrate the impact on the external-market-capitalization-to-GDP ratio of disclosure and liability standards, respectively. In our sample, the external-market-capitalization-to-GDP ratio ranges from 0.002 in Uruguay

[10] We obtain similar results replacing each of our three indices of securities laws by the principal component of the variables included in the relevant index. The most important change is that the principal component of public enforcement only predicts IPOs.

[11] The effect of efficiency of the judiciary on financial markets is comparable to that of disclosure. The estimated coefficients predict that a two-standard deviation increase in the efficiency of the judiciary (roughly the distance from Korea or Mexico to the United States) is associated with an increase of 0.16 in the external-market-to-GDP ratio, a 94% rise in listed firms per capita, and a 0.75 point improvement in the access-to-equity index, a 12 percentage point drop in ownership concentration, and an 83 point increase in the volume-to-GDP ratio. The effect of efficiency of the judiciary on financial development is similar in the specifications that control for liability standards (Panel B) and public enforcement (Panel C).

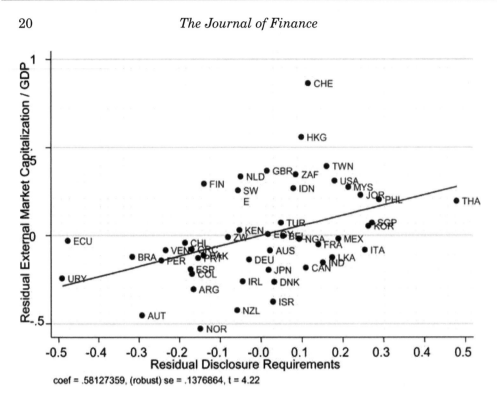

coef = .58127359, (robust) se = .1376864, t = 4.22

Figure 1. Partial regression plot of external-market-capitalization-to-GDP and disclosure requirements. The independent variables include anti-director rights, log of GDP per capita, and efficiency of the judiciary. Table II lists the country symbols.

to 1.44 in Switzerland. Thus, the roughly 0.25 point increase in the external-market-capitalization-to-GDP ratio associated with a two-standard deviation improvement in either disclosure or liability standards is economically large. Note also that the strength of disclosure and liability standards is not driven by outliers; we obtain qualitatively similar results using median regressions.

The results for public enforcement (Panel C) are less consistent. Public enforcement only matters for the external-market-capitalization-to-GDP ratio and IPOs, although it has a large economic effect on both variables (see Figure 3). A two-standard deviation increase in public enforcement (roughly, from the Netherlands to the United States) is associated with an increment of 0.15 points in the external-market-capitalization-to-GDP ratio and adds 1.6 firms in the IPO-to-GDP ratio. In contrast, anti-director rights, but not public enforcement, matter for the number of firms, block premium, and ownership concentration.

These results suggest a preliminary view of what works, and what does not, in securities laws. Public enforcement plays a modest role at best in the development of stock markets. In contrast, the development of stock markets is strongly associated with extensive disclosure requirements and a relatively low burden of proof on investors seeking to recover damages resulting from omissions of material information from the prospectus.

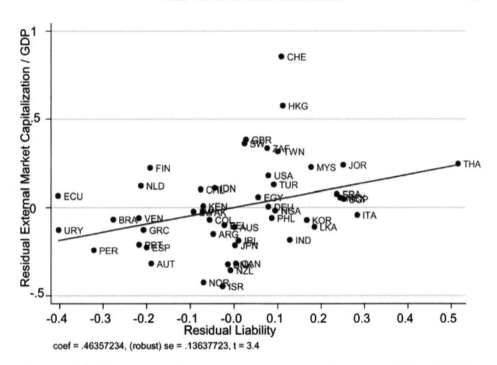

coef = .46357234, (robust) se = .13637723, t = 3.4

Figure 2. Partial regression plot of external-market-capitalization-to-GDP and liability standards. The independent variables include anti-director rights, log of GDP per capita, and efficiency of the judiciary. Table II lists the country symbols.

In the remainder of this section, we explore these preliminary findings from a range of perspectives. We first examine whether the weakness of public enforcement is due to our aggregation procedure. Table IV presents the results of regressing external market capitalization on the components of the public enforcement index. The power to make rules is the only element of public enforcement that is statistically significant. The results using other proxies for stock market development are similar (we do not report them to save space). First, neither the characteristics of the Supervisor (i.e., its independence and focus) nor its power to make rules matter for any of the other outcome variables. Second, the Supervisor's investigative power is only associated with more domestic firms. Third, the Supervisor's power to issue orders is only associated with more IPOs (and weakly—*t*-stat of 1.65—with more domestic firms). Fourth, criminal sanctions only matter for IPOs. Criminal deterrence may be ineffective because proving criminal intent of directors, distributors, or accountants in omitting information from the prospectus is difficult. In sum, no dimension of public enforcement consistently matters for the development of stock markets.

Table V presents the results of a horse race between disclosure requirements, liability rules, and public enforcement. Disclosure is significant in all regressions. In contrast, public enforcement is never significant. Liability standards

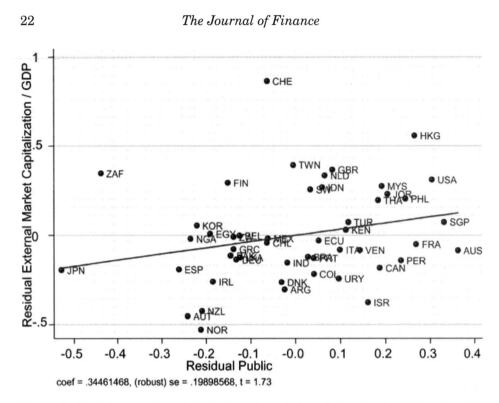

coef = .34461468, (robust) se = .19898568, t = 1.73

Figure 3. Partial regression plot of external-market-capitalization-to-GDP and public enforcement. The independent variables include anti-director rights, log of GDP per capita, and efficiency of the judiciary. Table II lists the country symbols.

are significant in the regressions for external capitalization, access to equity, and liquidity. However, multicollinearity between disclosure and liability standards may be of concern as the correlation between the two variables is 0.55 (the correlation between public enforcement and either disclosure or liability standards is only around 0.3). Finally, consistent with Table III, the anti-director rights index is never significant.

One of our key results is that disclosure and liability standards are stronger than the anti-director rights index. Why? One possibility is that we have found the "true" channel through which legal origin matters: it is correlated with the development of stock markets because it is a proxy for the effectiveness of private contracting as supported by securities laws. Note in this regard that legal origin typically loses its strong predictive power for the development of stock markets when we include anti-directors rights, disclosure, or liability standards in the regression. A second possibility is that investor protection through corporate law (which also works through private litigation) also matters, but we simply have cleaner measures of disclosure and liability standards. A third, more nuanced, possibility is that corporate and securities laws often rely on similar rules (e.g., regarding liability standards in civil cases), and it is the presence of these rules that is essential for the ability of private investors to seek remedy for expropriation by corporate insiders. For example, the U.S. system of mandatory disclosure evolved out of common law principles applicable

What Works in Securities Laws? 23

Table IV
External Market Capitalization and Public Enforcement

Ordinary least squares regressions of the cross-section of countries. The dependent variable is external market capitalization. We report five regressions successively controlling for the following securities laws variables: (1) supervisor attributes; (2) rule-making powers; (3) investigative powers; (4) orders; and (5) criminal sanctions. In addition to a securities laws variable, all regressions include anti-director rights, efficiency of the judiciary, and log of GDP per capita. Robust standard errors are shown in parentheses. All variables are described in Table I.

	Supervisor Characteristics	Rule-Making Powers	Investigative Powers	Orders	Criminal Sanctions
Securities regulation	−0.0111	0.1986[c]	0.1207	0.0525	0.1336
variable	(0.1312)	(0.1008)	(0.1112)	(0.1236)	(0.1643)
Anti-director	0.0944[a]	0.0889[a]	0.0803[b]	0.0878[a]	0.0877[a]
rights	(0.0325)	(0.0316)	(0.0312)	(0.0310)	(0.0303)
Efficiency of	0.0465[c]	0.0590[b]	0.0412[c]	0.0496[c]	0.0430[c]
the judiciary	(0.0247)	(0.0249)	(0.0243)	(0.0249)	(0.0252)
Ln GDP per	0.0990[a]	0.0992[a]	0.1041[a]	0.0987[a]	0.1018[a]
capita	(0.0245)	(0.0234)	(0.0219)	(0.0245)	(0.0265)
Constant	−1.1002[a]	−1.3177[a]	−1.1129[a]	−1.1377[a]	−1.1506[a]
	(0.2342)	(0.2350)	(0.2003)	(0.2021)	(0.2410)
Observations	49	49	49	49	49
Adjusted R^2	44%	50%	46%	45%	45%

[a]significant at 1%; [b]significant at 5%; and [c]significant at 10%.

to agents dealing adversely with their principals (Mahoney (1995)). In fact, the correlations of the anti-director index with disclosure requirements and liability standards are 0.52 and 0.50, respectively (see the Appendix). On this view as well, our results do not imply that corporate law is unimportant.

IV. Robustness

In this section, we address three issues of robustness using some additional data. First, is the weakness of our results on public enforcement due to inadequate measures of the Supervisor's strength? Second, what omitted variables may explain the strength of our results on disclosure and liability standards? Third, are securities laws endogenous?

Public enforcement may only be effective in countries with efficient government bureaucracies. To address this concern, we have rerun our regressions for the subsample of countries with per capita GDP above the median. We find that in these countries, public enforcement is correlated with more developed financial markets as proxied by the market-capitalization-to-GDP ratio, the number of listed firms, and the value of IPOs (and weakly—t-stat of 1.72—with stock market liquidity).[12] The effect of public enforcement in rich countries is

---

[12] Results are qualitatively similar if we break up the sample using survey measures of the quality of government (including either judicial efficiency or the Kaufmann, Kraay, and Mastruzzi (2003) proxy for bureaucratic quality). We also find that public enforcement is correlated with better access to equity markets in countries in which insider trading laws were enforced before 1995 (Bhattacharya and Daouk (2002)).

Table V

Disclosure, Liability Standards, and Public Enforcement

Ordinary least squares regressions of the cross-section of countries. The dependent variables are (1) external market capitalization; (2) log of domestic firms per capita; (3) value of the IPO-to-GDP ratio; (4) block premium; (5) access to equity; (6) ownership concentration; and (7) the stock-market-volume-to-GDP ratio. All regressions include disclosure requirements, liability standards, public enforcement, anti-director rights, efficiency of the judiciary, and log of GDP per capita. All variables are described in Table I. Robust standard errors are shown in parentheses.

	Market Capitalization	Number of Firms	IPOs	Block Premia	Access to Equity	Ownership Concentration	Liquidity
Disclosure requirements	0.4316[a]	0.8735[c]	3.2784[b]	-0.2667[b]	1.5815[a]	-0.1912[b]	68.5580[b]
	(0.1391)	(0.4919)	(1.6017)	(0.1296)	(0.4548)	(0.0887)	(30.0254)
Liability standards	0.2646[c]	0.3849	2.1213	-0.0790	1.1350[b]	-0.0656	64.9247[b]
	(0.1386)	(0.4961)	(1.6166)	(0.0713)	(0.4827)	(0.0647)	(30.4823)
Public enforcement	0.1900	0.3627	2.5228	0.0864	-0.7054	0.1130	9.9240
	(0.1812)	(0.4946)	(1.6761)	(0.0653)	(0.6908)	(0.0994)	(32.3549)
Anti-director rights	0.0176	0.0799	-0.1054	-0.0157	-0.1133	-0.0224	-2.4741
	(0.0333)	(0.0976)	(0.2861)	(0.0175)	(0.0847)	(0.0136)	(5.6187)
Ln GDP per capita	0.0925[a]	0.2757[b]	1.1296[a]	0.0025	0.1080	-0.0252[c]	18.9326[a]
	(0.0213)	(0.1071)	(0.2445)	(0.0205)	(0.0840)	(0.0132)	(5.9055)
Efficiency of the judiciary	0.0427[b]	0.2377[a]	-0.0341	-0.0070	0.1790[a]	-0.0053	-3.6729
	(0.0201)	(0.0684)	(0.2105)	(0.0114)	(0.0577)	(0.0099)	(5.3006)
Constant	-1.2694[a]	-2.8131[a]	-10.6035[a]	0.3437[b]	1.9522[a]	0.8872[a]	-156.8780[a]
	(0.2222)	(0.7724)	(2.2086)	(0.1611)	(0.6737)	(0.1219)	(39.7945)
Observations	49	49	49	37	44	49	49
Adjusted R^2	56%	68%	40%	31%	58%	37%	29%

[a]significant at 1%; [b]significant at 5%; and [c]significant at 10%.

narrowly confined to the rule-making power of the Supervisor. In contrast, public enforcement does not predict the development of securities markets in countries with below-median GDP per capita.

A related concern is that public enforcement may be ineffective if the Supervisor lacks adequate resources. To address this concern, we collect data on the number of employees that work for the Supervisor. We find that the (log of) the number of employees is insignificant in our regressions. To get at the interaction between public enforcement and the resources of the Supervisor, we break up the sample according to whether the number of employees working for the Supervisor is above or below the sample median and run separate regressions for both groups of countries. Public enforcement is statistically significant only for IPOs in countries with well-staffed regulators (and for domestic firms in countries with poorly staffed regulators). All the evidence suggests that relying on pubic enforcement is unlikely to be a useful strategy for jump-starting the development of securities markets in poor countries.

One set of omitted variable stories holds that investor protection picks up the effect of political ideology. Roe (2000) argues that the emphasis on investor protection for the development of financial markets is misplaced. In his view, social democracies have weak investor protection and arrest the development of financial markets. To examine this issue, we use the Botero et al. (2004) measure of political ideology as the fraction of years between 1928 and 1995 that the office of the chief executive is held by a member of a leftist party. This proxy for left power is uncorrelated with both disclosure and liability standards (correlations of −0.06 and −0.13, respectively). We find (results not reported) that the power of the left is associated with smaller external market capitalization when controlling for either disclosure or liability standards, and with a higher block premium when controlling for liability standards. However, including left power in the regressions does not diminish the strength of the results on either disclosure or liability standards.

It might also be argued that financial markets are small where the state is large. For example, few firms may be publicly traded in countries in which the state owns most of the capital. Omitted variable bias may account for the strength of our results if disclosure or liability standard is negatively correlated with the role of the state in the economy. To address this concern, we have included two measures of the role of the state in the economy in our regressions: (1) the fraction of the capital stock in the hands of state-owned companies from La Porta et al. (1999b); and (2) the fraction of the banking assets controlled by government-owned banks from La Porta et al. (2002a). Our results on securities laws remain qualitatively unchanged.

Another omitted variable story holds that countries with large capital markets may come to rely on disclosure and private litigation because their institutions are more democratically responsive to the interests of small investors. However, measures of democracy and political rights are uncorrelated with securities laws. Moreover, these measures are not significant predictors of financial development in our regressions. A related concern is that securities laws may proxy for social capital. The most commonly used measure of social

Table VI
Instrumental Variables Regressions

Panel A presents two-stage least squares regressions of the cross-section of countries. The dependent variables are (1) external market capitalization; (2) log of domestic firms per capita; (3) value of the IPO-to-GDP ratio; (4) block premia; (5) access to equity; (6) ownership concentration; and (7) the stock-market-volume-to-GDP ratio. Investor protection is the principal component of: (1) anti-director rights; (2) disclosure requirements; and (3) liability standards. In addition to investor protection, all regressions include efficiency of the judiciary and log of GDP per capita. Panel B presents results from the first-stage regression. The instrument is a dummy equal to one if the country's legal origin is common law. All variables are described in Table I. Robust standard errors are shown in parentheses.

	Market Capitalization	Number of Firms	IPOs	Block Premia	Access to Equity	Ownership Concentration	Liquidity
			Panel A: Second Stage Regression Results				
Investor protection	0.5800[b]	2.0147[a]	6.3885[a]	-0.2118[b]	1.3533[b]	-0.1651[c]	55.9974
	(0.2615)	(0.6917)	(2.3353)	(0.0942)	(0.6068)	(0.0973)	(40.5738)
Efficiency of the judiciary	0.0443[b]	0.2137[a]	-0.1488	-0.0076	0.1638[b]	-0.0115	-2.6144
	(0.0211)	(0.0773)	(0.1961)	(0.0115)	(0.0704)	(0.0096)	(4.5972)
Ln GDP per capita	0.0908[a]	0.2741[b]	1.1539[a]	-0.0067	0.1762	-0.0253[c]	19.8192[a]
	(0.0209)	(0.1089)	(0.2468)	(0.0191)	(0.1049)	(0.0146)	(6.3732)
Constant	-1.0052[a]	-2.4332[a]	-8.9957[a]	0.3303[b]	1.6148[c]	0.8601[a]	-130.0414[a]
	(0.1855)	(0.7313)	(1.6992)	(0.1436)	(0.8141)	(0.0935)	(32.1144)
Observations	49	49	49	37	44	49	49
R^2	59%	71%	43%	36%	54%	39%	31%
		Panel B: First Stage Regression Results for Investor Protection					
English legal origin	0.3448[a]						
	(0.0598)						
Efficiency of the judiciary	-0.0064						
	(0.0176)						
Ln GDP per capita	0.0521[b]						
	(0.0255)						
Constant	-0.0644						
	(0.1876)						
Observations	49						
R^2	0.45						

[a]significant at 1%; [b]significant at 5%; and [c]significant at 10%.

capital—a survey measure of trust among strangers—is available for 27 of our countries and is always insignificant.[13]

Finally, it is possible that governments adopt better securities laws in countries with buoyant financial markets (Cheffins (2001, 2003), Coffee (2001)). This argument is undermined by the systematic differences in investor protection across legal origins. Reverse causality is also undermined by the fact that the dimensions of the law that are expensive to implement—for example, having an independent and focused regulator—do not seem to matter. On the contrary, what matters is legal rules that are cheap rather than expensive to introduce. A second reverse causality argument holds that regulators swarm toward large securities markets because there are bigger rents to secure from regulating them. This argument is also undermined by the fact that it is precisely the regulations that render the regulators unimportant, namely, those that facilitate private contracting and that have the tightest association with stock market development.

We can partially address endogeneity problems using instrumental variables. In practice, legal origin is the only suitable instrument, but we have several legal variables that influence stock market development. To get around this problem, we replace disclosure, liability standards, and anti-director rights with the principal component of these three variables, which we call investor protection. This principal component accounts for roughly 70% of the variation in disclosure, liability standards, and anti-director rights. Table VI presents the two-stage least squares results using common law as an instrument. Investor protection is statistically significant for all seven proxies of stock market development (Panel A). Moreover, legal origin is a strong predictor of investor protection (Panel B).[14] These results should partially mitigate endogeneity concerns.

V. Conclusion

In the introduction, we describe three hypotheses concerning the effect of securities laws on stock market development. Our findings provide clear evidence bearing on these hypotheses.

First, the answer to the question of whether securities laws matter is a definite yes. Financial markets do not prosper when left to market forces alone. Second, our findings suggest that securities laws matter because they facilitate private contracting rather than provide for public regulatory enforcement. Specifically, we find that several aspects of public enforcement, such as having

---

[13] We also use the percentage of the population that belongs to a protestant denomination as a proxy for trust (the correlation between the two variables is 0.762). In the specifications that include our three indices of securities laws, the percentage of the population that is protestant predicts more access to equity and a lower control premium but disclosure and liability standards retain their predictive power.

[14] The F-statistic for the exclusion of English legal origin from the first-stage regression is 33.3, suggesting that there is no problem of weak instruments (Staiger and Stock (1997)). The Hausman test rejects the unbiasedness of the OLS estimated coefficients in the regressions for domestic firms, IPOs, and trading.

an independent and/or focused regulator or criminal sanctions, do not matter, and others matter in only some regressions. In contrast, both extensive disclosure requirements and standards of liability facilitating investor recovery of losses are associated with larger stock markets. Our results on the benefits of disclosure support similar findings of Barth, Caprio, and Levine (2003), who find that their proxy for private monitoring is positively correlated with the size of the banking sector.

These results point to the importance of regulating the agency conflict between controlling shareholders and outside investors to further the development of capital markets. They also point to the need for legal reform to support financial development, and cast doubt on the sufficiency of purely private solutions in bridging the gap between countries with strong and weak investor protection. Finally, our findings further clarify why legal origin predicts stock market development. The results support the view that the benefit of common law in this area comes from its emphasis on market discipline and private litigation. The benefits of common law appear to lie in its emphasis on private contracting and standardized disclosure and in its reliance on private dispute resolution using market-friendly standards of liability.

Appendix
Table of Correlations

This appendix shows the correlations among the variables used in the paper. All variables are described in Table I.

	Disclosure requirements	Liability standards	Supervisor characteristics	Rule-making power	Orders	Investigative Power	Criminal sanctions	Public enforcement	Anti-Directors rights	Efficiency of the judiciary	Ln GDP per capita	UK Legal Origin	French Legal Origin	German Legal Origin	Scandinavian Legal Origin	Market capitalization	Domestic firms	IPOs	Block premia	Access to equity	Ownership concentration
Liability standards	0.5496[a]																				
Supervisor characteristics	-0.1099	0.0481																			
Rule-making power	0.0196	-0.0427	-0.0149																		
Orders	0.3847[a]	0.4082[b]	0.1399	0.2837[b]																	
Investigative power	0.3759[a]	0.3100[b]	0.2142	0.3465[b]	0.5750[a]																
Criminal sanctions	0.3121[b]	0.2184	-0.0053	-0.0778	0.3208[b]	-0.0292															
Public enforcement	0.3305[b]	0.3091[b]	0.3821[a]	0.6179[a]	0.8067[a]	0.7575[a]	0.3193[b]														
Anti-directors rights	0.5236[b]	0.4999[b]	0.0559	0.0177	0.4129[a]	0.3554[b]	0.2811[c]	0.3691[a]													
Efficiency of the judiciary	0.2542[c]	0.2241	-0.3128[b]	-0.2600[c]	0.2215	-0.1588	0.2038	-0.1130	0.2113												
Ln GDP per capita	0.1378	0.1805	-0.2821[b]	-0.1798	0.0263	-0.1263	0.0489	-0.1709	0.0349	0.6618[a]											
English Legal Origin	0.5902[b]	0.3369[b]	0.0878	0.0058	0.3548[b]	0.3091[b]	0.4212[a]	0.3687[a]	0.5890[a]	0.1826	-0.1967										
French Legal Origin	-0.5509[a]	-0.2830[b]	0.2297	0.2384[c]	-0.1322	0.1054	-0.3393[b]	0.0639	-0.4463[a]	-0.4742[a]	-0.1815	-0.6599[a]									
German Legal Origin	0.0005	-0.0687	-0.2267	-0.2771[c]	-0.3175[b]	-0.4259[a]	-0.1237	-0.4719[a]	-0.1925	0.1611	0.3078[b]	-0.2846[b]	-0.3235[b]								
Scandinavian Legal Origin	-0.0440	0.0006	-0.2983[b]	-0.1094	-0.0057	-0.2247	0.0198	-0.1996	0.0001	0.3428[b]	0.3059[b]	-0.2272	-0.2582[c]	-0.1114							
Market capitalization	0.5412[a]	0.5046[a]	-0.1773	0.0885	0.3030[b]	0.0691	0.2447[c]	0.1869	0.3909[a]	0.5771[a]	0.5646[a]	0.2041	-0.4058[a]	0.1828	0.1552						
Domestic firms	0.4596[a]	0.4152[a]	-0.1876	-0.2464[c]	0.3378[b]	0.1476	0.2209	0.0805	0.3598[b]	0.7454[a]	0.6760[a]	0.2681[c]	-0.4770[a]	0.1084	0.2602[c]	0.6315[a]					
IPOs	0.4372[b]	0.4241[a]	-0.1209	0.0637	0.2813[c]	0.0037	0.4162[b]	0.2021	0.2459[c]	0.3960[a]	0.5426[a]	0.1795	-0.3407[b]	0.2181	0.0387	0.7144[a]	0.5664[a]				
Block premia	-0.5845[a]	-0.4523[b]	-0.1100	0.1326	-0.1658	-0.1439	-0.2334	-0.1309	-0.4662[b]	-0.3103[c]	-0.2586	-0.3209[c]	0.3936[b]	0.0592	-0.2258	-0.5334[a]	-0.5055[a]	-0.4641[a]			
Access to equity	0.5173[b]	0.4802[a]	-0.1462	-0.2757[c]	0.2103	-0.0425	0.2659[c]	-0.0443	0.2659[c]	0.6234[a]	0.5498[a]	0.3401[b]	-0.5624[a]	0.1121	0.2892[c]	0.6727[a]	0.6985[a]	0.5139[a]	-0.5942[a]		
Ownership concentration	-0.5005[a]	-0.4159[b]	0.1634	0.0535	-0.1080	-0.0335	-0.0147	0.0093	-0.4024[a]	-0.4301[a]	-0.4243[a]	-0.1572	0.5163[a]	-0.3526[b]	-0.2343	-0.5623[a]	-0.4267[a]	-0.4743[a]	0.4993[a]	-0.5390[a]	
Liquidity	0.4154[a]	0.4404[a]	-0.0647	0.0968	0.1028	-0.0287	0.2766[c]	0.1187	0.2165	0.2829[b]	0.4390[a]	0.0269	-0.3233[b]	0.4180[a]	0.0365	0.7571[a]	0.4329[a]	0.6967[a]	-0.3944[b]	0.4736[b]	-0.5297[a]

[a]significant at 1%; [b]significant at 5%; and [c]significant at 10%.

30   *The Journal of Finance*

REFERENCES

Barth, James, Gerard Caprio, and Ross Levine, 2003, Bank supervision and regulation: What works best? *Journal of Financial Intermediation* 13, 205–248.

Becker, Gary, 1968, Crime and punishment: An economic approach, *Journal of Political Economy* 76, 169–217.

Benston, George, 1973, Required disclosure and the stock market: An evaluation of the Securities Market Act of 1934, *American Economic Review* 63, 132–155.

Benston, George, 1985, The market for public accounting services: Demand, supply and regulation, *Journal of Accounting and Public Policy* 4, 33–79.

Beny, Laura, 2002, A comparative empirical investigation of agency and market theories of insider trading, Harvard University mimeo.

Bergman, Nittai, and Daniel Nicolaievsky, 2002, Investor protection and the Coasian view, Harvard University mimeo.

Bhattacharya, Utpal, and Hazem Daouk, 2002, The world price of insider trading, *Journal of Finance* 57, 75–108.

Black, Bernard, 2001, The legal and institutional preconditions for strong securities markets, *UCLA Law Review* 48, 781–858.

Black, Bernard, and Reinier Kraakman, 1996, A self-enforcing model of corporate law, *Harvard Law Review* 109, 1911–1981.

Botero, Juan, Simeon Djankov, Rafael La Porta, Florencio Lopez-de-Silanes, and Andrei Shleifer, 2004, The regulation of labor, *Quarterly Journal of Economics* 119, 1339–1382.

Bushman, Robert, Joseph Piotroski, and Abbie Smith, 2003, What determines corporate transparency? *Journal of Accounting Research* 42, 207–252.

Cheffins, Brian R., 2001, Law, economics and the UK's system of corporate governance: Lessons from history, *Journal of Corporate Law Studies* 1, 71–89.

Cheffins, Brian R., 2003, Law as bedrock: The foundations of an economy dominated by widely held public companies, *Oxford Journal of Legal Studies* 23, 1–23.

Chemmanur, Thomas, and Paolo Fulghieri, 1994, Investment bank reputation, information production, and financial intermediation, *Journal of Finance* 49, 57–79.

Coase, Ronald, 1960, The problem of social cost, *Journal of Law and Economics* 3, 1–44.

Coase, Ronald, 1975, Economists and public policy, in J. F. Weston, ed.: *Large Corporations in a Changing Society* (New York University Press, New York).

Coffee, John, 1984, Market failure and the economic case for a mandatory disclosure system, *Virginia Law Review* 70, 717–753.

Coffee, John, 1989, The mandatory/enabling balance in corporate law: An essay on the judicial role, *Columbia Law Review* 89, 1618–1691.

Coffee, John, 2001, The rise of dispersed ownership: The roles of law and the state in the separation of ownership control, *Yale Law Review* 111, 1–82.

Coffee, John, 2002, Understanding Enron: It's about the gatekeepers, stupid, *Business Lawyer* 57, 1403–1420.

Dechow, Patricia, Richard Sloan, and Amy Sweeney, 1996, Causes and consequences of earnings manipulations: An analysis of firms subject to enforcement actions by the SEC, *Contemporary Accounting Research* 13, 1–36.

De Long, Bradford, 1991, Did J.P. Morgan's men add value? An economist's perspective on financial capitalism, in Peter Temin, ed.: *Inside the Business Enterprise: Historical Perspectives on the Use of Information* (University of Chicago Press, Chicago, IL).

Dyck, Alexander, and Luigi Zingales, 2004, Private benefits of control: An international comparison, *Journal of Finance* 59, 537–600.

Easterbrook, Frank, and Daniel Fischel, 1984, Mandatory disclosure and the protection of investors, *Virginia Law Review* 70, 669–715.

Fischel, Daniel, and Sanford Grossman, 1984, Customer protection in futures and securities markets, *Journal of Futures Markets* 4, 273–295.

Fox, Merritt, 1999, Retaining mandatory disclosure: Why issuer choice is not investor empowerment, *Virginia Law Review* 85, 1335–1419.

Friend, Irwin, and Edward Herman, 1964, The S.E.C. through a glass darkly, *Journal of Business* 37, 382–405.

Glaeser, Edward, Simon Johnson, and Andrei Shleifer, 2001, Coase versus the Coasians, *Quarterly Journal of Economics* 116, 853–899.

Glaeser, Edward, and Andrei Shleifer, 2001, A reason for quantity regulation, *American Economic Review Papers and Proceedings* 91, 431–435.

Glaeser, Edward, and Andrei Shleifer, 2002, Legal origins, *Quarterly Journal of Economics* 117, 1193–1230.

Glaeser, Edward, and Andrei Shleifer, 2003, The rise of the regulatory state, *Journal of Economic Literature* 41, 401–425.

Grossman, Sanford, 1981, The informational role of warranties and private disclosure about product quality, *Journal of Law and Economics* 24, 461–483.

Grossman, Sanford, and Oliver Hart, 1980, Disclosure laws and takeover bids, *Journal of Finance* 35, 323–334.

Grossman, Sanford, and Oliver Hart, 1988, One share-one vote and the market for corporate control, *Journal of Financial Economics* 20, 175–202.

Hartland-Peel, Christopher, 1996, *African Equities: A Guide to Markets and Companies* (Euromoney Publications, London, U.K.).

Hay, Jonathan, and Andrei Shleifer, 1998, Private enforcement of public laws: A theory of legal reform, *American Economic Review Papers and Proceedings* 88, 398–403.

Hay, Jonathan, Andrei Shleifer, and Robert Vishny, 1996, Toward a theory of legal reform, *European Economic Review* 40, 559–567.

International Finance Corporation, 2001, Emerging Markets Database, located online at: http://www.ifc.org/EMDB/EMDBHOME.HTM.

Kaufmann, Daniel, Aart Kraay, and Massimo Mastruzzi, 2003, Governance matters III: Updated governance indicators for 1996–02, Working paper draft for comments, Washington, D.C.: World Bank.

Landis, James, 1938, *The Administrative Process* (Yale University Press, New Haven, CT).

La Porta, Rafael, Florencio Lopez-de-Silanes, and Andrei Shleifer, 1999a, Corporate ownership around the world, *Journal of Finance* 54, 471–517.

La Porta, Rafael, Florencio Lopez-de-Silanes, and Andrei Shleifer, 2002a, Government ownership of banks, *Journal of Finance* 57, 265–301.

La Porta, Rafael, Florencio Lopez-de-Silanes, Andrei Shleifer, and Robert Vishny, 1997, Legal determinants of external finance, *Journal of Finance* 52, 1131–1150.

La Porta, Rafael, Florencio Lopez-de-Silanes, Andrei Shleifer, and Robert Vishny, 1998, Law and finance, *Journal of Political Economy* 106, 1113–1155.

La Porta, Rafael, Florencio Lopez-de-Silanes, Andrei Shleifer, and Robert Vishny, 1999b, The quality of government, *Journal of Law, Economics, and Organization* 15, 222–279.

La Porta, Rafael, Florencio Lopez-de-Silanes, Andrei Shleifer, and Robert Vishny, 2002b, Investor protection and corporate valuation, *Journal of Finance* 57, 1147–1170.

Leuz, Christian, Dhananjay Nanda, and Peter Wysocki, 2003, Earnings management and investor protection: An international comparison, *Journal of Financial Economics* 69, 505–528.

Levine, Ross, and Sara Zervos, 1998, Stock markets, banks, and economic growth, *American Economic Review* 88, 537–558.

Macey, Jonathan, 1994, Administrative agency obsolescence and interest group formation: A case study of the SEC at sixty, *Cardozo Law Review* 15, 909–949.

Mahoney, Paul, 1995, Mandatory disclosure as a solution to agency problems, *University of Chicago Law Review* 62, 1047–1112.

Milgrom, Paul, and John Roberts, 1986, Relying on the information of interested parties, *Rand Journal of Economics* 17, 18–32.

Miller, Merton, 1991, *Financial Innovations and Market Volatility* (Blackwell, Cambridge, MA).

Nenova, Tatiana, 2003, The value of corporate voting rights and control: A cross-country analysis, *Journal of Financial Economics* 68, 325–351.

North, Douglass, 1981, *Structure and change in Economic History* (Norton, New York).

Pistor, Katharina, and Chenggang Xu, 2002, Law enforcement under incomplete law: Theory and evidence from financial market regulation, Columbia Law School, mimeo.

Polinsky, Mitchell, and Steven Shavell, 2000, The economic theory of public enforcement of law, *Journal of Economic Literature* 38, 45–76.

Political Risk Services, 1996, *International Country Risk Guide* (Political Risk Services, East Syracuse, NY).

Reese, William, and Michael Weisbach, 2002, Protection of minority shareholder interests, cross-listings in the United States, and subsequent equity offerings, *Journal of Financial Economics* 66, 65–104.

Roe, Mark, 2000, Political preconditions to separating ownership from corporate control, *Stanford Law Review* 53, 539–606.

Romano, Roberta, 2001, The need for competition in international securities regulation, *Theoretical Inquiries in Law* 2, 1–179.

Ross, Stephen, 1979, Disclosure regulation in financial markets: Implication of modern finance theory and signaling theory, in Franklin Edwards, ed.: *Issues in Financial Regulation* (McGraw-Hill, New York).

Schwab, Klaus, Michael Porter, Jeffrey Sachs, Andrew Warner, Macha Levinson, The World Economics Forun of Geneva, and The Harvard University Center for International Development, eds., 1999, *The Global Competitiveness Report 1999* (Oxford University Press, New York).

Seligman, Joel, 1995, *The Transformation of Wall Street: A History of the Securities and Exchange Commission and Modern Corporate Finance* (Northeastern University Press, Boston, MA).

Shleifer, Andrei, and Daniel Wolfenzon, 2002, Investor protection and equity markets, *Journal of Financial Economics* 66, 3–27.

Simon, Carol, 1989, The effect of the 1933 Securities Act on investor information and the performance of new issues, *American Economic Review* 79, 295–318.

Spiller, Pablo, and John Ferejohn, 1992, The economics and politics of administrative law and procedures: An introduction, *Journal of Law, Economics and Organization* 8, 1–7.

Staiger, Douglas, and James Stock, 1997, Instrumental variables regression with weak instruments, *Econometrica* 65, 557–586.

Stigler, George, 1964, Public regulation of the securities market, *Journal of Business* 37, 117–142.

Stulz, René, 1999, Globalization of equity markets and the cost of capital, *Journal of Applied Corporate Finance* 12, 8–25.

Teoh, Siew Hong, Ivo Welch, and T. J. Wong, 1998, Earnings management and the long-run market performance of initial public offerings, *The Journal of Finance* 53, 1935–1974.

Velthuyse, Heleen, and Francine Schlingmann, 1995, Prospectus liability in The Netherlands, *Journal of International Banking Law*, 229–236.

World Bank, 2001, *World Development Indicators 2001*, [CD-ROM] (World Bank, Washington, D.C.).

THE JOURNAL OF FINANCE • VOL. LIX, NO. 1 • FEBRUARY 2004

Value-Enhancing Capital Budgeting and Firm-specific Stock Return Variation

ART DURNEV, RANDALL MORCK, and BERNARD YEUNG*

ABSTRACT

We document a robust cross-sectional positive association across industries between a measure of the economic efficiency of corporate investment and the magnitude of firm-specific variation in stock returns. This finding is interesting for two reasons, neither of which is a priori obvious. First, it adds further support to the view that firm-specific return variation gauges the extent to which information about the firm is quickly and accurately reflected in share prices. Second, it can be interpreted as evidence that more informative stock prices facilitate more efficient corporate investment.

CORPORATE CAPITAL INVESTMENT should be more efficient where stock prices are more informative. Informed stock prices convey meaningful signals to management about the quality of their decisions. They also convey meaningful signals to the financial markets about the need to intervene when management decisions are poor. Corporate governance mechanisms, such as shareholder lawsuits, executive options, institutional investor pressure, and the market for corporate control, depend on stock prices. Where stock prices are more informative, these mechanisms induce better corporate governance—which includes more efficient capital investment decisions.

Our objective in this paper is to examine empirically whether capital investment decisions are indeed more efficient where stock prices are more informative. To do this, we require a measure of the efficiency of investment and a measure of the informativeness of stock prices.

*Durnev is from the Department of Finance, University of Miami, Morck is the Stephen A. Jarislowsky Distinguished Professor of Finance at the School of Business, University of Alberta, and Yeung is the Abraham Krasnoff Professor of International Business, Professor of Economics, and Professor of Management at the Stern School of Business, New York University. We are grateful for helpful comments by the editor, Richard Green, an anonymous referee, Yakov Amihud, Luis Cabral, Serdar Dinc, Bernard Dumas, William Goetzmann, David Hirshleifer, Bjørne Jørgensen, Andrew Karolyi, Han Kim, Claudio Loderer, J.P. Mei, Roberta Romano, Robert Shiller, Andrei Shleifer, Richard Sloan, Rene Stulz, Jeremy Stein, Richard Thaler, Larry White and Daniel Wolfenzon; and to participants at the NBER Corporate Finance Seminar, le Centre Interuniversitaire de Recherche en Analyse des Organisations (CIRANO) in Montreal, the Econometric Society meeting at the University of California in Los Angeles, the European Financial Management Association meeting in Lugano, Baruch-CUNY, Columbia Business School, Indiana University, the University of Alberta, the University of Michigan, the University of Minnesota, MIT Sloan School, New York University, the Ohio State University, the University of North Carolina, the University of Chicago, Wharton School at the University of Pennsylvania, and Yale University; and to students in Andrei Shleifer's Research Seminar on Behavioral Finance at Harvard.

To gauge the efficiency of corporate investment, we directly estimate Tobin's marginal q ratio, the change in firm value due to unexpected changes in investment scaled by the expected change in investment, for U.S. industries. The deviation in Tobin's marginal q from its optimal level is our measure of investment efficiency—the smaller the deviation the greater the investment efficiency.

To gauge the informativeness of stock prices, we follow Morck, Yeung, and Yu (2000) and consider the magnitude of firm-specific return variation. We justify this on two grounds: one conceptual and the other empirical. On the conceptual level, stock variation occurs because of trading by investors with private information. Grossman and Stiglitz (1980) predict that a lower cost of private information leads to a higher intensity of informed trading, and hence to what they call "more informative pricing." Extending their reasoning, we suggest that, in a given time interval and all else being equal, higher firm-specific variation stems from more intensive informed trading due to a lower cost of information, and hence indicates a more informative price. We focus on firm-specific variation because Roll (1988) shows this could be associated with trading based on private information. At the empirical level, a growing empirical literature links firm-specific variation to stock price informativeness, e.g., Morck, Yeung, and Yu (2000), Durnev et al. (2001), and Bushman, Piotroski, and Smith (2002). We recognize that these conceptual arguments and empirical studies, which we discuss in detail in the next section, constitute a subtle case for accepting firm-specific return variation as a proxy for stock price informativeness that calls for further theoretical development. However, we feel they nonetheless justify further investigation of this possibility.

We find the proximity of marginal q to its optimal level and the magnitude of firm-specific return variation to be highly positively correlated across industries. This finding is notable for two reasons. First, it underscores the conceptual arguments and empirical evidence cited above, that firm-specific stock return variation merits serious consideration as a measure of the informativeness of stock prices. Second, taking firm-specific variation as a measure of the informativeness of stock prices, it can be interpreted as evidence that informativeness of stock prices facilitates efficient investment. That is, the information efficiency of the stock market matters to the real economy.

While we cannot categorically reject alternative possible explanations of our finding, we believe them to be less plausible. One possibility is that firm-specific variation and the deviation of marginal q from its optimum might have common factors having nothing to do with the informativeness of stock prices. We include a long list of control variables, introduced in Section III, to capture such factors. Our empirical results in Section IV lead us to exclude the most obvious of these possibilities. Another more abstruse possibility is that high firm-specific variation is noise or, in the words of Roll (1986), "frenzy unrelated to concrete information." In Section IV, we explore this possibility and ultimately reject it. Intuitively, our measure of the efficiency of capital investment decisions is actually a measure of how closely investment spending matches a change in market value. If firm-specific variation reflects investor frenzy, our finding has the disturbing implication that capital spending is better aligned with market value change where market values are less meaningful. We are not aware of any theoretical basis for postulating that managers' capital budgeting decisions are most aligned with observed market value change when market value is noisier. We cannot preclude the possibility that further work might expose a missing factor in our statistical work, or might lead to a theory that explains why capital budgeting decisions are more aligned with observed market value changes when stock prices are noisier. However, we believe Ockham's razor disfavors these lines of attack.

This paper is organized as follows. Section I describes our firm-specific return variation variables, while Section II explains our marginal q measure. Section III describes our empirical estimation techniques and our main control variables. Section IV presents our empirical results and robustness checks. Section V considers the validity and implications of our interpretations of our results and Section VI concludes. The Appendix describes our data and marginal q estimation technique in detail.

I. Measuring Firm-specific Return Variation

A. Motivation

We support our use of firm-specific return variation to measure stock price informativeness with a conceptual argument and with a body of empirical evidence.

On the conceptual level, variation in a firm's stock return in any given time period is due to public news and to trading by investors with private information. Grossman and Stiglitz (1980, p. 405) argue that "because [acquiring private] information is costly, prices cannot perfectly reflect the information which is available, since if it did, those who spent resources to obtain it would receive no compensation." In their model, traders invest in a risk-free asset and a single risky asset, and decide whether or not to pay for private information about the fundamental value of the risky asset. Grossman and Stiglitz derive the result that informed trading becomes more prevalent as the cost of private information falls, which increases the informativeness of the price system (p. 399). We take this reasoning a step further, and suggest the following: In a market with many risky stocks, during any given time interval, information about the fundamental values of some firms might be cheap, while information about the fundamental values of others might be dear. Traders, ceteris paribus, obtain more private information about the former and less about the latter. Consequently, the stock prices of the former, moving in response to informed trading, are both more active and more informative than the stock prices of the latter.

Consider decomposing the variation of a firm's return into a systematic portion, explained by market and industry return, and a firm-specific residual variation. Roll (1988) shows that firm-specific variation, so defined, is largely unassociated with public announcements, and argues that firm-specific return variation is therefore chiefly due to trading by investors with private information. Accordingly, even if the argument of Grossman and Stiglitz (1980)

A Reader in International Corporate Finance

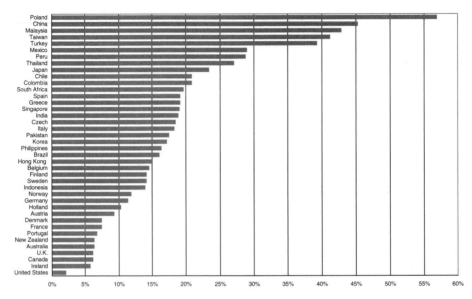

Source: Morck, Yeung, and Yu (2000).

Figure 1. Stock return synchronicity in various countries as measured by the average R^2 of regressions of firm returns on domestic and U.S. market returns.

were not applicable to "free" macroeconomic information such as trade or money supply statistics, it surely applies to much of the firm-specific information. Thus, if the cost of firm-specific information varies across firms, ceteris paribus, the intensity and completeness of trading on private firm-specific information should also vary. Extending the argument of Roll (1988), we hypothesize that greater firm-specific variation indicates more intensive informed trading and, consequently, more informative pricing.

Empirically, a range of evidence already points in this direction.

First, Figure 1 shows the average R^2 statistics of regressions of firm-level stock return on local and U.S. market return using 1995 data for a range of countries, as reported by Morck, Yeung, and Yu (2000). These R^2's are very low for countries with well-developed financial systems, such as the United States, Canada, and the United Kingdom, but are very high for emerging markets such as Poland and China. Morck, Yeung, and Yu (2000) show that these results are clearly not due to differences in country or market size, and that they are unlikely to be due to more synchronous fundamentals in emerging economies. They find that government disrespect of private property rights and lack of shareholder protection laws actually explain the low level of firm-specific stock return variation. They propose that in countries with less corruption and better shareholder protection, traders have more incentive to trade based on firm-specific information. This is consistent with the argument that low average market model R^2's reflect greater activity by the informed traders, as posited by Roll (1988).

Capital Budgeting and Firm-specific Stock Return Variation 69

Second, Wurgler (2000) shows capital flows to be more responsive to value addition in countries with less synchronous stock returns. This suggests that capital moves faster to its highest value uses where stocks move more asynchronously. That is, stock markets in which firm-specific variation is a larger fraction of total variation are functionally more efficient in the sense of Tobin (1982).

Third, Bushman, Piotroski, and Smith (2002) show that stock returns exhibit greater firm-specific return variation in countries with more developed financial analysis industries and with a freer press.

Fourth, Durnev et al. (2001) show that stock returns predict future earnings changes more accurately in industries with less synchronous returns, as measured by market-model R^2 statistics. Collins, Kothari, and Rayburn (1987), and others in the accounting literature, regard such predictive power as gauging the "information content" of stock prices. In this sense, stock prices have greater information content when firm-specific variation is a larger fraction of total variation.

We believe these conceptual arguments and empirical results justify the use of firm-specific return variation as an indicator of timely and accurate incorporation of firm-specific information into stock prices. However, we realize that this view is based on theoretical conjecture and indirect empirical evidence. Indeed, Roll (1988) allows that firm-specific return variation may be due to "investors' frenzy," unrelated to information. We therefore remain ecumenical at the outset, and ultimately let the data suggest an interpretation of firm-specific return variation.

B. *Measuring Firm-specific Return Variation*

This section describes the estimation of our firm-specific return variation measures. We use daily total returns for 1990 through 1992 for the 4,029 firms in the intersection of CRSP and COMPUSTAT. These span 196 three-digit SIC industries. The Appendix provides further details. Since we estimate our other important variable, the efficiency of corporate investment decisions, using a 1993-to-1997 panel of annual data for each industry, estimating industry-average firm-specific variations over this period lets us match predetermined firm-specific return variation of an industry with the same industry's investment efficiency measure, and thereby mitigate endogeneity problems.

We gauge firm-specific return variation by regressing firm j's return on industry i, $r_{i,j,t}$, on market and industry returns, $r_{m,t}$ and $r_{i,t}$, respectively:

$$r_{i,j,t} = \beta_{j,0} + \beta_{j,m} r_{m,t} + \beta_{j,i} r_{i,t} + \varepsilon_{i,j,t}, \tag{1}$$

where $\beta_{j,0}$ is the constant, $\beta_{j,m}$ and $\beta_{j,i}$ are regression coefficients and $\varepsilon_{i,j,t}$ is the noise term. The market index and industry indices are value-weighted averages excluding the firm in question. This exclusion prevents spurious correlations between firm and industry returns in industries that contain few firms. One minus the average R^2 of (1) for all firms in an industry measures the importance

A Reader in International Corporate Finance

of firm-specific return variation in that industry. We use industry aggregate rather than firm-level estimates to facilitate comparison with our marginal q estimates which we shall explain below.

Note that we follow Roll (1988) in distinguishing "firm-specific" variation from the sum of market-related and industry-related variation. For simplicity, we refer to the latter sum as "systematic" variation. We decompose return variation in this way because Roll (1988) specifically links arbitrage that capitalizes private information to firm-specific variation, so defined.

A standard variance decomposition lets us express an industry-average R^2 as

$$R_i^2 = \frac{\sigma_{m,i}^2}{\sigma_{\varepsilon,i}^2 + \sigma_{m,i}^2}, \tag{2}$$

where

$$\begin{aligned} \sigma_{\varepsilon,i}^2 &= \frac{\sum_{j \in i} SSR_{i,j}}{\sum_{j \in i} T_j} \\ \sigma_{m,i}^2 &= \frac{\sum_{j \in i} SSM_{i,j}}{\sum_{j \in i} T_j} \end{aligned} \tag{3}$$

for $SSR_{i,j}$ and $SSM_{i,j}$, the unexplained and explained variations of (1), respectively. The sums in (3) are scaled by $\sum_{j \in i} T_j$, the number of daily observations available in industry i.

Since $\sigma_{\varepsilon,i}^2$ and $\sigma_{m,i}^2$ have skewness of 2.27 and 3.51, respectively, and kurtoses of 9.76 and 19.93, respectively, we apply a logarithmic transformation. Both $\ln(\sigma_{\varepsilon,i}^2)$ and $\ln(\sigma_{m,i}^2)$ are more symmetric (skewness $= -0.37$, 0.07) and normal (kurtosis $= 3.66$, 3.52).

The distribution of $1 - R_i^2$ is also negatively skewed (skewness $= -1.00$) and mildly leptokurtic (kurtosis $= 4.79$). Moreover, it has the econometrically undesirable characteristic of being bounded within the unit interval. As recommended by Theil (1971, Chapter 12), we circumvent the bounded nature of R^2 with a logistic transformation of $1 - R_i^2 \in [0, 1]$ to $\Psi_i \in \Re$,

$$\Psi_i = \ln\left(\frac{1 - R_i^2}{R_i^2}\right). \tag{4}$$

We thus use the Greek letter Ψ to denote firm-specific stock return variation measured relative to variations due to industry- and market-wide variation. The transformed variable is again less skewed (skewness $= 0.03$) and less leptokurtic (kurtosis $= 3.80$). The hypothesis that Ψ_i is normally distributed cannot be rejected in a standard W-test ($p = 0.13$).

The transformed variable Ψ_i also possesses the useful characteristic that

$$\Psi_i = \ln\left(\frac{1 - R_i^2}{R_i^2}\right) = \ln\left(\frac{\sigma_{\varepsilon,i}^2}{\sigma_{m,i}^2}\right) = \ln\left(\sigma_{\varepsilon,i}^2\right) - \ln\left(\sigma_{m,i}^2\right). \tag{5}$$

Intuitively, a higher Ψ_i indicates the greater the power of firm-specific variation, $\sigma_{\varepsilon,i}^2$, *relative to* market- and industry-wide variation, $\sigma_{m,i}^2$, in explaining the stock price movements of firms in industry i.

We let $\ln(\sigma_{\varepsilon,i}^2)$ denote absolute firm-specific stock return variation, $\ln(\sigma_{m,i}^2)$ absolute systematic stock return variation, and Ψ_i relative firm-specific stock return variation.

Table I briefly describes these variables, and others used in this study. Panel A of Table II presents univariate statistics for $\ln(\sigma_{\varepsilon,i}^2)$, $\ln(\sigma_{m,i}^2)$, and Ψ_i. The substantial standard deviations and spreads of these three variables attest to their substantial variation across industries. Moreover, higher firm-specific and systematic return variations tend to occur together ($\rho = 0.773, p = 0.00$).[1]

II. Tobin's Marginal q Ratio

A. Motivation

We now turn to our measure for the proximity of capital budgeting to value maximization. Optimal capital budgeting requires undertaking all positive expected net present value (NPV) projects and avoiding all those with negative expected NPV. The NPV of a project is the present value of the net cash flows, cf_t. The project will produce at all future times t less its set-up cost, C_0. Thus, optimal capital budgeting requires undertaking projects if and only if

$$E[NPV] = E\left[\sum_{t=1}^{\infty} \frac{cf_t}{(1+r)^t} - C_0\right] > 0, \tag{6}$$

where E is the expectations operator. Under ordinary circumstances, managers are the decision makers, and the E operator should be based on the manager's information set.

To compare NPVs across firms, we scale by set-up cost, obtaining profitability indexes (*PI*). Optimality entails undertaking a project if and only if its expected *PI* surpasses 1,

$$E_{mgt}[PI] = \frac{1}{C_0} E_{mgt}\left[\sum_{t=1}^{\infty} \frac{cf_t}{(1+r)^t}\right] = 1 + \frac{E_{mgt}[NPV]}{C_0} > 1, \tag{7}$$

where we now explicitly use E_{mgt} to denote management's expectations.

The change in the market value of a firm associated with an unexpected unit increase in its stock of capital goods (replacement cost) is the firm's marginal

---

[1] In our sample, examples of high firm-specific stock return variation industries include: "Apparel, Piece Goods, and Notions," "Video Tape Rental," "Miscellaneous Industrial and Commercial," "Periodicals: Publishing, or Publishing and Printing," and "Miscellaneous Chemical Products." Examples of low firm-specific stock return variation industries include "Combination Electric and Gas, and Other Utility," "Automotive Rental and Leasing," "Paperboard Mills," "Mailing, Reproduction, Commercial Art," "Women's, Misses', Children's, and Infants."

Table I

Definitions of Main Variables

Variables		Definition
		Panel A. Firm-specific Stock Return Variation Variables
Absolute firm-specific stock return variation	$\ln(\sigma_\varepsilon^2)$	Logarithm of residual sum of squares (scaled by the number of firm-year observations) from regressions of firm return on market and three-digit industry value-weighted indices (constructed excluding own return) run on daily data by three-digit industry from 1990 through 1992.
Relative firm-specific stock return variation	Ψ	Logarithm of residual sum of squares minus logarithm of explained sum of squares (both scaled by the number of firm-year observations) from the regressions described above.
		Panel B. Quality of Capital Budgeting Variables
Marginal q	$\dot{q}$	A coefficient in the regression of the change in the market value of a firm (scaled by a lagged value of its stock of capital goods) on an unexpected unit increase in its stock of capital goods (scaled by a lagged value of its stock of capital goods) and controls by three-digit industry using annual data from 1993 through 1997. Tangible assets are defined in (A5) and are equal to the sum of real property, plant, and equipment estimated using recursive formula in (A7), and real inventory.
		Panel C. Control Variables
Absolute systematic stock return variation	$\ln(\sigma_m^2)$	Logarithm of explained sum of squares (scaled by the number of firm-year observations) from the regressions described above.
Absolute firm-specific fundamentals variation	$\ln(_{ROA}\sigma_\varepsilon^2)$	Logarithm of residual sum of squares (scaled by the number of firm-year observations) from regressions of firm ROA on market and three-digit industry value-weighted ROA indices (constructed excluding own return) run on annual data by three-digit industry from 1983 through 1992. ROA is equal to the sum of income, interest expenses, and depreciation over tangible assets. Tangible assets are defined as in (A5).

Absolute systematic fundamentals variation	$\ln(_{ROA}\sigma_m^2)$	Logarithm of explained sum of squares (scaled by the number of firm-year observations) from the regressions described above.
Relative firm-specific fundamentals variation	$_{ROA}\Psi$	Logarithm of residual sum of squares minus logarithm of explained sum of squares (both scaled by the number of firm-year observations) from the regressions described above.
Average q	$\bar{q}$	Average q is three-digit industry average from 1990 through 1992. The average q for a given industry in a specified period is the sum of the market values of all firms over the sum of all their replacement costs of tangible assets. The market value and the replacement costs of tangible assets are described in the Appendix.
Corporate diversification	segs	It is 1990-to-1992 average of total assets weighted-average number of three-digit industries a firm operates in.
Herfindahl index	H	It is 1990-to-1992 average of three-digit industry Herfindahl indices constructed using sales data.
Size	$\ln(K)$	Log of the average from 1990 to 1992 of real property, plant, and equipment, estimated using the recursive formula in (A7).
Liquidity	λ	The ratio of the difference between current assets and current liabilities to tangible assets from 1990 through 1992. Tangible assets are defined as in (A5).
Leverage	lev	It is 1990-to-1992 market value of net long-term debt over tangible assets. Tangible assets are defined as in (A5).
Advertising spending	adv	Total, from 1990 through 1992, of inflation adjusted advertising expenditures over tangible assets. Tangible assets are defined as in (A5).
R&D spending	r&d	Total, from 1990 through 1992, of inflation adjusted R&D expenditures over tangible assets. Tangible assets is defined as in (A5).

Table II
Univariate Statistics for Main Variables

This table reports the mean, median, standard deviation, min, and max of main variables. Refer to Table I for variable definitions. The sample is 196 three-digit industries for all variables. The return variation measures, σ_ε^2, σ_m^2, R^2, $\ln(\sigma_\varepsilon^2)$, $\ln(\sigma_m^2)$, and Ψ, are constructed using 1990-to-1992 data for a sample of 196 three-digit industries spanned by 4,029 firms. The quality of capital budgeting variables, $(\bar{q}-1)^2$ and $|\bar{q}-1|$, are constructed using 1993-to-1997 data for 196 three-digit industries spanned by 16,735 firm-year observations. The controls, $\bar{q}$, seg, H, $\ln(K)$, λ, lev, adv, and $r\&d$, are constructed using 1990-to-1992 data for 196 three-digit industries spanned by 4,029 firms. The fundamentals variation controls, $\ln(_{ROA}\sigma_\varepsilon^2)$, $\ln(_{ROA}\sigma_m^2)$, and $_{ROA}\Psi$ are constructed using 1983-to-1992 data for 196 three-digit industries spanned by 4,705 firms. To utilize as much information as possible to capture fundamental comovements, we include firms that might not last throughout the period, but had at least 6 years of continuous data. Finance industries (SIC code 6000–6999) are omitted.

Variables		Mean	Median	Standard Deviation	Minimum	Maximum
		Panel A. Stock Return Variation Variables				
Firm-specific stock return variation	σ_ε^2	0.029	0.024	0.025	0.001	0.154
Systematic stock return variation	σ_m^2	0.007	0.006	0.007	0.001	0.056
Systematic rel. to firm-specific stock return variation	R^2	0.219	0.206	0.087	0.040	0.560
Absolute firm-specific stock return variation	$\ln(\sigma_\varepsilon^2)$	−3.826	−3.731	0.807	−6.775	−1.873
Absolute systematic stock return variation	$\ln(\sigma_m^2)$	−5.169	−5.153	0.728	−7.265	−2.875
Relative firm-specific stock return variation	Ψ	1.343	1.347	0.523	−0.242	3.170
		Panel B. Quality of Capital Budgeting Variables				
Marginal q	$\dot{q}$	0.907	0.867	0.872	−3.333	3.886
Squared deviation of marginal q from 1	$(\dot{q}-1)^2$	0.765	0.379	2.107	0.000	18.775
Absolute deviation of marginal q from 1	$|\dot{q}-1|$	0.575	0.143	0.660	0.006	4.333
		Panel C. Control Variables				
Absolute firm-specific fundamentals variation	$\ln(_{ROA}\sigma_\varepsilon^2)$	−5.888	−5.757	0.866	−9.058	−4.348
Absolute systematic fundamentals variation	$\ln(_{ROA}\sigma_m^2)$	−5.943	−5.858	0.811	−8.817	−4.184
Relative firm-specific fundamentals variation	$_{ROA}\Psi$	0.055	0.115	0.550	−2.052	1.605
Average q	$\bar{q}$	1.775	1.363	1.518	0.215	12.251
Corporate diversification	$segs$	2.033	1.809	0.917	1.000	5.937
Herfindahl index	H	0.338	0.297	0.198	0.044	0.991
Size	$\ln(K)$	9.010	9.090	1.681	4.267	13.811
Liquidity	λ	0.274	0.236	0.231	−0.108	1.409
Leverage	lev	0.297	0.262	0.189	0.004	1.208
Advertising spending	adv	0.018	0.004	0.031	0.000	0.178
R&D spending	$r\&d$	0.030	0.011	0.045	0.000	0.237

Tobin's q ratio, and is denoted by

$$\dot{q} = \frac{\Delta V}{\Delta K} = \frac{1}{C_0} E\left[\sum_{t=1}^{\infty} \frac{cf_t}{(1+r)^t}\right] = 1 + \frac{E[NPV]}{C_0} = E[PI], \qquad (8)$$

where all capital spending during each year is aggregated into a project with set-up cost C_0, cf_t is the total cash flows this project yields at times t, and E here reflects investors' expectations.

Thus, marginal q is investors' estimate of the marginal project's profitability index. Ignoring taxes and other complications, value maximization implies $\dot{q} = 1$. In this idealized situation, $\dot{q} > 1$ implies underinvestment and $\dot{q} < 1$ implies overinvestment. We discuss the effects of taxes and other complexities on the threshold $\dot{q}$, here denoted h, after we have explained our estimation of $\dot{q}$.

B. Measuring Tobin's Marginal q Ratio

We now summarize our estimation procedure (a full description is provided in the Appendix). We operationalize (8) by writing the marginal q of firm j as the ratio

$$\dot{q}_{j,t} = \frac{V_{j,t} - E_{t-1}V_{j,t}}{A_{j,t} - E_{t-1}A_{j,t}} = \frac{V_{j,t} - V_{j,t-1}(1 + \hat{r}_{j,t} - \hat{d}_{j,t})}{A_{j,t} - A_{j,t-1}(1 + \hat{g}_{j,t} - \hat{\delta}_{j,t})}, \qquad (9)$$

where $V_{j,t}$ and $A_{j,t}$ are the market value (equity plus debt) and stock of capital goods, respectively, of firm j at time t, and E_t is the expectations operator using all information extant at time t.[2] The expected market value of the firm in t is its market value in $t - 1$ augmented by both the expected return from owning the firm, $\hat{r}_{j,t}$, and its disbursements to investors, $\hat{d}_{j,t}$, which includes cash dividends, share repurchases, and interest expenses.[3] The expected value of the firm's capital assets in period t is the value of its capital assets in period $t - 1$ augmented by both its expected rate of spending on capital goods, $\hat{g}_{j,t}$, and the expected depreciation rate on those capital goods, $\hat{\delta}_{j,t}$.

---

[2] An alternative approach would be to use equity value only as the numerator of marginal q. This would be consistent with the view that managers maximize shareholder value, rather than firm value, but ignores many legal requirements that managers consider as of creditors' interests as well if bankruptcy is a reasonable possibility. Focusing on equity value also highlights the issue of whether managers should maximize the value of existing shareholders' wealth or that of existing and new shareholders. We assume the latter and also add the value of creditors' claims in (9), so that our implicit maximand is V_t rather than shareholder value. However, we shall point out later that the alternative approach leads to qualitatively similar results.

[3] We can omit interest if debt is assumed to be perpetual so that periodic repayments do not affect the principal. Omitting interest expenses does not affect our results. Since we are calculating the return from owning the entire firm, not from owning a single share, stock repurchases must be included as part of cash payments to investors.

Cross-multiplying and simplifying (9) leads to

$$\frac{V^i_{j,t} - V^i_{j,t-1}}{A^i_{j,t-1}} = -\dot{q}_j(g_j - \delta_j) + \dot{q}_j \frac{A^i_{j,t} - A^i_{j,t-1}}{A^i_{j,t-1}} + r_j \frac{V^i_{j,t-1}}{A^i_{j,t-1}} + \xi_j \frac{D^i_{j,t}}{A^i_{j,t-1}} + u^i_{j,t},$$

(10)

where $D_{j,t} \equiv \dot{d}_{j,t} V_{j,t-1}$ and ξ allows for a tax wedge. (Theoretically, ξ should be equal to -1. However, the valuation of dividends, share repurchases, and bond interest payments may be different from market value changes because of the difference in the tax brackets of various recipients of disbursement.)

It follows that the coefficient β^i_0 of the regression across all firms j in industry i at times t

$$\frac{\Delta V^i_{j,t}}{A^i_{j,t-1}} = \alpha^i + \beta^i_0 \frac{\Delta A^i_{j,t}}{A^i_{j,t-1}} + \beta^i_1 \frac{V^i_{j,t-1}}{A^i_{j,t-1}} + \beta^i_2 \frac{D^i_{j,t}}{A^i_{j,t-1}} + u^i_{j,t},$$

(11)

is an estimate of an industry-average marginal q. We estimate (11) using the generalized least squares method to allow error correlation across time for each firm and across firms in each period.

To relate $\dot{q}$ to predetermined firm-specific variation (measured from 1990 to 1992), we estimate (11) using a 1993-to-1997 panel of annual data for each industry. We use industry, not firm-level, $\dot{q}$ estimates for two reasons. First, firm-level estimation of (11) requires many years of data, inducing a survival bias. Second, using long time windows means that shifting technological constraints, market conditions, and governance changes might make our estimates unreliable. Since nonsynchronous $\Delta V^i_{j,t}$ and $\Delta A^i_{j,t}$ can add noise, we define the change in firm value according to a firm's fiscal-year window.[4]

The average estimated α^i, β^i_1, and β^i_2 also broadly match their interpretations in (10). The mean and median $\alpha^i = -\dot{q}_j(g_{j,t} - \delta_{j,t})$ are -0.129 and -0.089, respectively, and α^i differs insignificantly from zero ($p < 10\%$) in 110 of 196 industries. Also, α^i is negatively and significantly correlated with estimated growth rates of capital assets. The mean β^i_1, 0.127, implies an average cost of capital of 12.7 percent, the median β^i_1 is 0.129. The second regression coefficient, β^i_1, is significantly positively correlated with estimated weighted average costs of capital. The mean and median β^i_2 are -0.680 and -0.668, respectively; β^i_2 differs significantly from negative one ($p < 10\%$) in 146 of 196 industries.

The sample mean $\dot{q}$ is 0.91, and the median is 0.87.[5] The correspondence of capital budgeting to value maximization depends on the distance of $\dot{q}$ from

---

[4] The firm value is defined as a fiscal year-end number of common shares outstanding (COMPUSTAT, data series #25) times a fiscal year-end common shares price (COMPUSTAT, data series #199).

[5] The five-lowest marginal q industries are: "Asphalt Paving, Roofing Materials," "Health Services," "Chemicals and Allied Products," "Fabricated Rubber Products," and "Accounting, Auditing and Bookkeeping Services." The five-highest marginal q industries are: "Power, Distribution, Special Transformers," "Pens, Pencils, Other Office Materials," "Motion Picture Theaters," "Mailing, Reproduction, Commercial Art," and "Air Transport, Nonscheduled."

its optimal value, h, which we initially set to 1. We measure the distance of $\dot{q}$ from h as either a squared deviation, $(\dot{q} - h)^2$, or an absolute deviation, $|\dot{q} - h|$. For simplicity, we say $(\dot{q} - h)^2$ and $|\dot{q} - h|$ gauge *capital budgeting quality*, though they are more properly regarded as measuring investors' aggregated opinions about capital budgeting quality; that is, their opinions about corporate investment efficiency. Panel B of Table II provides summary statistics of $\dot{q}$, $(\dot{q} - 1)^2$ and $|\dot{q} - 1|$ for our 196 industries.

C. Complications

Taxes and other complications can push h, the optimal value of the estimated $\dot{q}$, away from 1. (Let the optimal value of the estimated $\dot{q}$ be $\hat{\dot{q}}$.) In this section, we consider these complications, and discuss their importance in this analysis.

First, h may deviate from 1 because of taxes. Suppose a firm unexpectedly increases its stock of capital assets by plowing back $(A_{j,t} - E_{t-1}A_{j,t})$ of after-tax corporate earnings. The cost to investors of the firm not disbursing this is $(1 - T_D)(A_{j,t} - E_{t-1}A_{j,t})$, where T_D is the personal tax on disbursements. This gives investors an after-tax capital gain of $(1 - T_{CG})(V_{j,t} - E_{t-1}V_{j,t})$, where T_{CG} is the effective personal capital gains tax rate, adjusted for the timing of realizations. For this capital investment to add value, $(1 - T_{CG})(V_{j,t} - E_{t-1}V_{j,t})$ must exceed $(1 - T_D)(A_{j,t} - E_{t-1}A_{j,t})$. Repeating the algebra used to derive (10) now yields

$$\frac{V^i_{j,t} - V^i_{j,t-1}}{A^i_{j,t-1}} = \alpha_j + \dot{q}_j \frac{1 - T_D}{1 - T_{CG}} \frac{A^i_{j,t} - A^i_{j,t-1}}{A^i_{j,t-1}} + r_j \frac{V^i_{j,t-1}}{A^i_{j,t-1}} + \xi_j \frac{D^i_{j,t}}{A^i_{j,t-1}} + u^i_{j,t}. \quad (12)$$

This means that β^i_1 from (11) is actually an estimate of $\dot{q}_j(\frac{1-T_D}{1-T_{CG}})$. Reasonable figures for the 1990s are $T_D \cong 33$ percent and $T_{CG} \cong 14$ percent (half the statutory rate of 28 percent). Assuming the marginal investor is tax-exempt half of the time, these assumptions imply that $\dot{q} \cong 1.15\beta^i_1$, moving our mean $\dot{q}$ to $0.91 \times 1.15 = 1.05$, and the median to $0.87 \times 1.15 = 1.00$.

Needless to say, this comparison is further clouded by the corporate tax advantages from various sorts of capital spending, the endogeneity of capital structure and disbursement policies, the timing of capital gains realization, the substitution of repurchases for dividends, and the wide range of personal tax rates paid by different investors.

Second, capital spending is disclosed annually (unaudited quarterly data are less reliable), so the aggregation of projects in (9) is unavoidable. If, as conditions change differentially, firms continuously adjust their capital budgeting, $\dot{q}$ should be near one. However, if discrete changes induce large capital budgeting changes, (9) may capture effects on value of inframarginal, as well as marginal, capital spending. This should bias $\dot{q}$ and h upward.

Third, C_0 (in (8)) is *unexpected* capital spending, but this is unobserved. In our operationalization in (9), we depict C_0 as observed capital spending minus an implicit estimate of expected capital spending. This estimate may be high or low, and thus induces noise, but not bias, in $\dot{q}$ and hence h.

Fourth, changes in firm value, ΔV, may arise from changes in the values of past investments or future investment options. This adds noise, but not necessarily bias—unless, for example, such options rise in value throughout our estimation window, inducing an upward bias in $\hat{q}$ and h for growth industries.

A priori, predicting the net effect of these complications is virtually impossible. However, since each affects observed $\hat{q}$ and thus h similarly, the distances between $\hat{q}$ and h may still be meaningful, and these are the quantities of primary interest to us.

III. Empirical Framework

Our empirical objective is to examine the relationship between firm-specific return variation and the alignment of capital budgeting to market value maximization. As we stated in Section II.A, where we motivate the use of firm-specific return variation as a measure for stock price informativeness, this variable could conceivably reflect either more or less informed stock prices. In the former case, greater firm-specific variation should be associated with an estimated marginal q, β_0^i in (11), closer to its theoretical optimum; the opposite should hold in the latter case.

Our $\dot{q}$ estimates could be affected by a variety of industry factors. Therefore, we must introduce a set of control variables. In this section, we first report simple correlations and then describe the control variables we use in our regressions.

A. Simple Correlation Coefficients

Table III reports the simple correlation coefficients between our capital budgeting quality measures and our firm-specific stock return variation variables. Ignoring for the moment taxes and other complications, we interpret $(\dot{q} - 1)^2$ and $|\dot{q} - 1|$ as indicators of the deviation of capital budgeting from the optimum.[6] Marginal q tends to be nearer one in industries where returns exhibit both greater absolute firm-specific variation, $\ln(\sigma_{\varepsilon,i}^2)$, and greater relative firm-specific variation, Ψ_i. These relationships are statistically significant. Also, the distance of $\dot{q}$ from 1 is insignificantly related to systematic variation, $\ln(\sigma_{m,i}^2)$; $\dot{q}$ itself is uncorrelated with all three return variation measures, $\ln(\sigma_{\varepsilon,i}^2)$, $\ln(\sigma_{m,i}^2)$, and Ψ_i.[7]

Figure 2 illustrates these patterns by grouping industries by their average R^2's. Regardless of whether we use the mean absolute or squared distance of $\dot{q}$ from one, $\dot{q}$ is nearer to 1 in industries with lower R^2's. Figure 3 shows that this pattern reflects a greater dispersion of $\dot{q}$ *both above and below* 1 in industries with higher R^2's.

---

[6] Instead of 1, we can take the "optimal" $\hat{q}$ to be the mean (0.91) or the median (0.87) of our estimated marginal q. The results for the simple correlations and the graphs that we shall depict in Figures 2 and 3 do not change qualitatively.

[7] Marginal q is negatively correlated with $(\dot{q} - 1)^2$ and $|\dot{q} - 1|$ because more than 62 percent of our $\dot{q}$ estimates are less than 1.

Capital Budgeting and Firm-specific Stock Return Variation 79

Table III
Simple Correlation Coefficients of Capital Budgeting Quality and Firm-specific Stock Return Variation Variables with Each Other and with Control Variables

This table reports correlation coefficients based on a 196 three-digit industries sample. Numbers in parentheses are probability levels at which the null hypothesis of zero correlation is rejected. Coefficients significant at 10 percent or better (based on the two-tailed test) are in boldface. Refer to Table I for variable definitions. The return variation measures, σ_ε^2, σ_m^2, R^2, $\ln(\sigma_\varepsilon^2)$, $\ln(\sigma_m^2)$, and Ψ, are constructed using 1990-to-1992 data for 196 three-digit industries spanned by 4,029 firms. The quality of capital budgeting variables, $(\dot{q} - 1)^2$ and $|\dot{q} - 1|$, are constructed using 1993-to-1997 data for 196 three-digit industries spanned by 16,735 firm-year observations. The controls, $\bar{q}$, seg, H, $\ln(K)$, λ, lev, adv, and $r\&d$, are constructed using 1990-to-1992 data for 196 three-digit industries spanned by 4,029 firms. The fundamentals variation controls, $\ln({}_{ROA}\sigma_\varepsilon^2)$, $\ln({}_{ROA}\sigma_m^2)$, and ${}_{ROA}\Psi$, are constructed using 1983-to-1992 data for 196 three-digit industries spanned by 4,705 firms. To utilize as much information as possible to capture fundamental comovements, we include firms that might not last throughout the period, but had at least 6 years of continuous data. Finance industries (SIC code 6000–6999) are omitted.

		$\dot{q}$	$(\dot{q} - 1)^2$	$|\dot{q} - 1|$	$\ln(\sigma_\varepsilon^2)$	Ψ
Panel A: Quality of Capital Budgeting Variables						
Marginal q	$\dot{q}$	–	**−0.249**	**−0.131**	–	–
			(0.00)	(0.07)		
Absolute deviation of marginal q from 1	$|\dot{q} - 1|$	–	**0.915**	–	**−0.140**	−0.113
			(0.00)		(0.05)	(0.12)
Panel B: Firm-Specific Stock Return Variation						
Absolute firm-specific stock return variation	$\ln(\sigma_\varepsilon^2)$	0.040	**−0.166**	–	–	**0.468**
		(0.58)	(0.02)			(0.00)
Relative firm-specific stock return variation	Ψ	0.025	**−0.129**	–	–	–
		(0.72)	(0.07)			
Panel C: Control Variables						
Absolute systematic return variation	$\ln(\sigma_m^2)$	0.026	−0.091	−0.075	**0.773**	**−0.199**
		(0.71)	(0.20)	(0.30)	(0.00)	(0.01)
Absolute firm-specific ROA variation	$\ln({}_{ROA}\sigma_\varepsilon^2)$	0.035	−0.059	−0.040	**0.608**	**0.524**
		(0.62)	(0.42)	(0.58)	(0.00)	(0.00)
Absolute systematic ROA variation	$\ln({}_{ROA}\sigma_m^2)$	−0.045	−0.032	0.043	**0.624**	**0.243**
		(0.53)	(0.65)	(0.55)	(0.00)	(0.00)
Relative firm-specific ROA variation	${}_{ROA}\Psi$	0.122	−0.044	−0.127	0.037	−0.028
		(0.09)	(0.54)	(0.08)	(0.61)	(0.70)
Average q	$\bar{q}$	0.018	−0.079	−0.054	**0.308**	0.083
		(0.80)	(0.27)	(0.45)	(0.00)	(0.25)
Corporate diversification	$segs$	−0.090	−0.078	−0.095	**−0.163**	0.060
		(0.21)	(0.28)	(0.18)	(0.02)	(0.41)
Herfindahl index	H	−0.134	**0.278**	**0.337**	−0.043	0.034
		(0.06)	(0.00)	(0.00)	(0.55)	(0.63)
Industry size	$\ln(K)$	0.014	**−0.282**	**−0.379**	**−0.187**	−0.037
		(0.85)	(0.00)	(0.00)	(0.01)	(0.61)
Liquidity	λ	−0.077	0.041	0.075	**0.172**	−0.027
		(0.29)	(0.57)	(0.30)	(0.02)	(0.71)
Leverage	lev	0.048	−0.114	−0.068	0.133	0.083
		(0.50)	(0.11)	(0.34)	(0.06)	(0.25)
Advertising spending	adv	−0.082	0.022	−0.037	**0.170**	0.035
		(0.26)	(0.76)	(0.61)	(0.02)	(0.63)
R&D spending	$r\&d$	−0.044	−0.025	−0.018	0.012	−0.038
		(0.54)	(0.73)	(0.80)	(0.87)	(0.59)

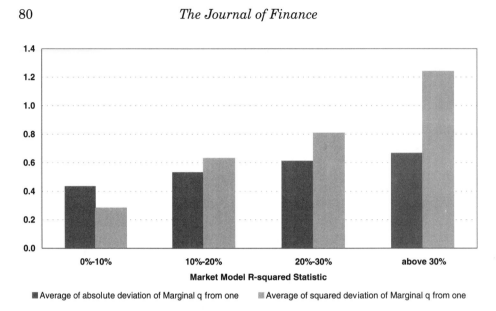

Figure 2. The deviation of marginal Tobin's q from 1 with industries grouped by industry-average firm-level market model R^2. A low R^2 indicates high firm-specific return variation relative to market and industry-related variation. The height of each bar is the group average deviation of marginal q below and above1.

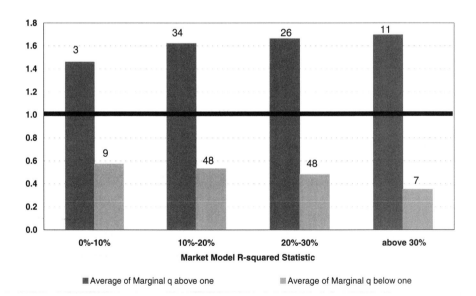

Figure 3. Mean marginal q for industries subsamples with marginal q above 1 and below 1, grouped by industry-average firm-level market model R^2. A low R^2 indicates high firm-specific return variation relative to market and industry-related variation. The height of each bar is the group mean marginal q. The number of observations in each group is listed at the top of each bar. The sample sizes for 0% to 10%, 10% to 20%, 20% to 30% and 30% to 40% are 3, 34, 26, and 11 industries with marginal q above 1 and 9, 48, 48, and 7 industries with marginal q below 1.

B. Multivariate Regression Specification

The simple correlations and graphical representations of our data suggest that greater firm-specific return variation is associated with higher-quality capital budgeting. To verify whether greater firm-specific return variation is associated, ceteris paribus, with capital budgeting quality, we control for other relevant factors.

Our regressions are thus of the form

$$
\begin{aligned}
&\text{either } (\dot{q}_i - h)^2 \text{ or } |\dot{q}_i - h| = b_\Psi \Psi + \mathbf{c}' \cdot \mathbf{Z_i} + u_i, \\
&\text{either } (\dot{q}_i - h)^2 \text{ or } |\dot{q}_i - h| = b_\varepsilon \ln\left(\sigma_{\varepsilon,i}^2\right) + b_m \ln\left(\sigma_{m,i}^2\right) + \mathbf{c}' \cdot \mathbf{Z_i} + u_i,
\end{aligned}
\tag{13}
$$

where $\mathbf{Z_i}$ is a list of control variables. To mitigate endogeneity problems, the controls—like return variation—are measures during the period 1990 through 1992. Absolute systematic variation, $\ln(\sigma_{m,i}^2)$, as explained below, is also considered a control.

We begin by setting h equal to 1. As discussed above, taxes, the discreteness of capital budgeting, the unobservability of expected capital spending, and changes in expected cash flows from prior or future investments can all push both estimated $\dot{q}$ and h up or down. We therefore reestimate (13) using nonlinear least squares to determine h and the regression coefficients simultaneously. Appendix A.4 and Amemiya (1985) provide details.

C. Control Variables

The controls are intended to capture several possibilities. First, exogenous factors might affect the quality of capital budgeting. For example, capital budgeting decisions might be better in concentrated industries with high barriers to entry because conditions in such industries are easier to predict. Not controlling for this obscures the true relationship between capital budgeting quality and firm-specific return variation by inducing heteroskedastic residuals. Although we use heteroskedasticity-consistent standard errors, including controls where possible is econometrically desirable.

Second, latent common factors related to both capital budgeting quality and firm-specific return variation might cause a spurious relationship between the two. Industry concentration again illustrates. Concentrated industries, in addition to having better-quality capital budgeting decisions, might also contain homogenous firms whose fundamentals (and therefore stock returns) exhibit relatively little firm-specific variation. A negative relationship between capital budgeting quality and firm-specific return variation might simply reflect the effects of industry concentration on both variables. Several such latent common factors could affect capital budgeting quality and fundamentals variation.

Note that we do not include corporate governance variables, such as board structure, ownership structure, and the like. Corporate governance variables are themselves rough proxies for the alignment of corporate decision-making with market value maximization, which we estimate directly (at least with regard to capital budgeting) with $\hat{q}$. Including corporate governance variables would amount to putting proxies for our dependent variable on the right-hand side of our regressions. We relegate the examination of the relationship between corporate governance variables, capital budgeting quality and firm-specific variation to future research.

The next two subsections describe our controls and our reasons for including each.

C.1. Specialized Control Variables

First, as argued above, industry concentration might matter. We therefore include a 1990-to-1992 average real-sales-weighted Herfindahl Index, denoted H_i.

Second, we control for industry size. Firms in large, established industries might have more internal cash, greater access to capital, and fewer value-creating investment opportunities. They might therefore be more prone to the overinvestment problems of Jensen (1986) than firms in smaller industries. Also, larger industries may be more mature, contain more homogenous firms, and so exhibit less firm-specific fundamentals variation. Firms in smaller industries might be subject to greater information asymmetry problems, and thus be more likely to ration capital and underinvest. We therefore include the logarithm of 1990-to-1992 industry property, plant, and equipment (PP&E), denoted $\ln(K_i)$, as our *Industry Size* control. The estimation of K_i is explained in detail in the Appendix equations (A6) and (A7).

Third, a large literature links corporate diversification with both corporate governance problems and access to capital.[8] Also, corporate diversification might also reduce firm-specific fundamentals variation. Our *corporate diversification* measure for industry i, denoted $segs_i$, is the 1990-to-1992 assets-weighted average diversification level of firms whose primary business is industry i. Firm diversification is the 1990-to-1992 average number of different three-digit segments reported in COMPUSTAT Industry Segment file.

Fourth, capital budgeting might be more error-prone in industries where intangible assets are important because the future cash flows they generate are harder to predict. Moreover, firms in these industries typically have fewer collateralizable assets, and thus may have more difficulty raising external funds. Also, Shiller (1989) implies that such firms might sometimes exhibit less firm-specific variation, as during R&D races, and then large firm-specific variation

---

[8] Lewellen (1971) proposes that diversification stabilizes earnings, and helps firms access debt financing on better terms, all else being equal. Matsusaka and Nanda (1994) and Stein (1997) argue that the head office of a diversified firm can act like a financial intermediary, investing surplus funds from one division with positive NPV projects in another, reducing the need for external funds. Amihud and Lev (1981), Morck, Shleifer, and Vishny (1990), May (1995), and Khorana and Zenner (1998) all propose that managerial utility maximization might explain value-destroying diversification, so more diversified firms might be firms with larger agency problems. Scharfstein and Stein (2000) argue that diversified firms shift income from cash-rich divisions to cash-poor ones out of a sense of "fairness." Rajan, Servaes, and Zingales (2000) propose that such transfers are due to self-interested divisional managers and weak head offices. Thus, different levels of corporate diversification could conceivably generate a spurious correlation between financing decisions and stock return variation in several ways.

Capital Budgeting and Firm-specific Stock Return Variation 83

when one wins. We therefore control for industry *research and development spending* (R&D) and *advertising spending*, denoted as *r&d* and *adv*, respectively. Both are measured per dollar of tangible assets in each industry, averaged across 1990 to 1992. Tangible assets are PP&E plus inventories, estimated as in Appendix equation (A5) and the description that follows. We take R&D to be negligible if not reported and all other financial data are reported.

Fifth, we control for average Tobin's q, the market value, $V_{j,t}$, over replacement cost, $A_{j,t}$,

$$\bar{q}_{j,t} \equiv \frac{V_{j,t}}{A_{j,t}}, \tag{14}$$

estimated using 1990-to-1992 data. Besides serving as a general proxy for the presence of intangibles, $\bar{q}$ also measures the importance of growth options. Changes in these option values during our estimation window could affect both $\dot{q}$ and σ_ε^2. Note that $\bar{q}$ is not the same as $\dot{q}$, marginal q. As a firm invests in ever more marginally value-increasing projects, its $\dot{q}$ falls to 1. Its average q, however, need not fall to 1, for $\bar{q}$ is investors' expected present value of cash flows from all its capital investments—including past inframarginal investments and future expected investments—scaled by the sum of the replacement costs of its existing assets.

To estimate each industry's $\bar{q}$, we sum the market values of all firms in that industry, and divide this by the sum of all their replacement costs. The market value and the replacement costs of tangible assets are as described in the Appendix. We then average this for each industry during the period 1990 through 1992. Although $\bar{q}$ is uncorrelated with $\dot{q}$ and negatively (insignificantly) correlated with $\dot{q}$'s deviation from 1, it is positively significantly related to both absolute and relative firm-specific return variation, measured by $\ln(\sigma_\varepsilon^2)$ and Ψ.

Sixth, liquidity could affect capital budgeting decisions. For example, cash-rich firms might overinvest, while cash-strapped firms might ration capital. We therefore include industry *liquidity*, 1990-to-1992 industry average net current assets over PP&E, denoted λ_i.

Seventh, the existing capital structure might affect capital budgeting. For example, Jensen (1986) argues that high leverage improves corporate governance—in part, by preventing overinvestment. Others, such as Myers (1977), argue that various bankruptcy cost constraints distort capital budgeting in highly levered firms. Since leverage might also affect fundamentals variation, we include *leverage*, lev_i, 1990-to-1992 industry average long-term debt over tangible assets (PP&E and real inventory). Details of the estimation of long-term debt and tangible assets are provided in Appendix A.2.

Eighth, capital budgeting quality may be affected by industry-specific factors, which the above controls do not fully capture. We therefore add one-digit industry fixed effects.

C.2. Firm-specific Fundamentals Variation Control Variables

Unfortunately, myriad industry characteristics might affect firm-specific fundamentals variation, and many cannot be measured readily. Therefore, we explicitly control for firm-specific fundamentals variation with two proxies—a precisely estimated, but indirect measure, and a direct measure that can be estimated only imprecisely.

Firm-specific changes in fundamental value may be larger and more frequent in industries where changes in market and industry-related fundamentals are larger and more frequent. If so, observed systematic variation might be a useful proxy for (unobserved) firm-specific fundamentals variation. We therefore tentatively interpret absolute systematic return variation, $\ln(\sigma_m^2)$, as a proxy for firm-specific fundamentals variation, and revisit this issue later.

If this interpretation of $\ln(\sigma_m^2)$ is valid, using relative, rather than absolute, firm-specific return variation is an alternative way of controlling for firm-specific fundamentals variation. Since relative firm-specific return variation, ψ, is the difference between $\ln(\sigma_\varepsilon^2)$ and $\ln(\sigma_m^2)$, using ψ as the independent variable is equivalent to using $\ln(\sigma_\varepsilon^2)$ as the independent variable and constraining the coefficient of $\ln(\sigma_m^2)$ to be the inverse of the coefficient of $\ln(\sigma_\varepsilon^2)$. We therefore include $\ln(\sigma_m^2)$ as a control variable in regressions of absolute firm-specific return variation, but not in regressions of relative firm-specific return variation.

We can also estimate fundamentals variation directly. Following Morck, Yeung, and Yu (2000), we construct variables analogous to our stock return variation measures $\ln(\sigma_\varepsilon^2)$, $\ln(\sigma_m^2)$, and Ψ, but using the annual return on assets (ROA) instead of stock returns. We define ROA as net income plus depreciation plus interest, all divided by tangible assets. The denominator is described in Appendix equation (A5).

To estimate firm-specific fundamentals variation for each industry, we run regressions of the form of (1), but using ROA rather than stock returns. That is, we run

$$ROA_{i,j,t} = \beta_{j,0} + \beta_{j,m}ROA_{m,t} + \beta_{j,i}ROA_{i,t} + \varepsilon_{i,j,t} \tag{15}$$

for each firm j in each industry i, with t an annual time index. The dependent variable, $ROA_{i,j,t}$ is firm j's ROA, $ROA_{m,t}$ is a value-weighted market average ROA, and $ROA_{i,t}$ is a value-weighted industry average ROA. Again, we exclude the firm in question from these averages. We run these regressions on our 1983-to-1992 sample of nonfinancial firms, described in the Appendix. We drop firms for which fewer than 6 years of data are available.

We follow the same step-by-step procedure outlined above with regards to (1) through (5). This variance decomposition lets us express an industry-average $_{ROA}R^2$ as

$$_{ROA}R_i^2 = \frac{_{ROA}\sigma_{m,i}^2}{_{ROA}\sigma_{\varepsilon,i}^2 + _{ROA}\sigma_{m,i}^2}, \tag{16}$$

where

$$
\begin{aligned}
_{ROA}\sigma_{\varepsilon,j}^2 &= \frac{\sum_{j \in i} SSR_{i,j}}{\sum_{j \in i} T_j} \\
_{ROA}\sigma_{m,j}^2 &= \frac{\sum_{j \in i} SSM_{i,j}}{\sum_{j \in i} T_j},
\end{aligned}
\tag{17}
$$

with $SSR_{i,j}$ and $SSM_{i,j}$ now the unexplained and explained variations, respectively, of regression (15) for firm j in industry i. The sum of $SSR_{i,j}$ and of $SSM_{i,j}$ for industry i is scaled by the number of annual return observations $\sum_{j \in i} T_j$.

We again apply logarithmic transformations to obtain our absolute firm-specific fundamentals variation measure, $\ln({}_{ROA}\sigma^2_{\varepsilon,i})$, our absolute systematic fundamentals variation measure, $\ln({}_{ROA}\sigma^2_{m,i})$, and our relative firm-specific fundamentals variation measure

$$
{}_{ROA}\Psi_i = \ln\left(\frac{1 - {}_{ROA}R_i^2}{{}_{ROA}R_i^2}\right) = \ln\left({}_{ROA}\sigma^2_{\varepsilon,i}\right) - \ln\left({}_{ROA}\sigma^2_{m,i}\right). \tag{18}
$$

Note that we again follow Roll (1988) in distinguishing firm-specific variation from the sum of market-related and industry-related variation, and we refer to the latter sum as systematic variation.

Since we have at most 10 annual observations per firm, our variance decomposition may be imprecise. Using more years reduces the number of usable firms in each industry, and risks making the fundamentals variation measures reflect conditions that no longer prevail.

Univariate statistics for these control variables are presented in Panel C of Table II, and their correlations with the marginal q, and our capital budgeting quality measures, the deviations of $\dot{q}$ from 1, are presented in the bottom panel of Table III. Table IV presents the correlations of the control variables with each other. The absolute value deviation of $\dot{q}$ from 1 is negatively correlated with industry size and positively correlated with industry concentration. Both correlations are highly significant (the p-values are 0.00). With these two exceptions, our capital budgeting quality variables are uncorrelated with our control variables.

This suggests that the simple correlation coefficients described above may in fact be meaningful as tests of our hypotheses. However, even though they are individually insignificantly correlated with capital budgeting quality, our control variables may be jointly significant in multiple regressions, to which we now turn.

IV. Regression Results

A. Main Results

Table V presents regressions of the distance of marginal q from one on firm-specific stock price variation and the controls. The central result is that higher firm-specific stock return variation is statistically significantly associated with marginal q nearer one. This is true whether we measure distance from one as absolute deviation, $|\dot{q} - 1|$, or squared deviation, $(\dot{q} - 1)^2$. It is also true whether we measure firm-specific return variation as absolute variation, $\ln(\sigma^2_\varepsilon)$, or as relative variation, Ψ_i, and regardless of whether the controls are included or not. The regression using relative firm-specific variation is weaker though. The coefficient of interest in regression 4.8 of Table V attains a 9 percent probability level, while that in regression 4.4 of Table V only achieves 11 percent.

Table IV

Simple Correlation Coefficients of Main Control Variables with Firm-specific Stock Return Variation Variables and with Each Other

This table reports correlation coefficients based on a 196 three-digit industries sample. Numbers in parentheses are probability levels at which the null hypothesis of zero correlation is rejected. Coefficients significant at 10 percent or better (based on two-tailed test) are in boldface. Refer to Table I for variable definitions. The sample is 196 three-digit industries for all variables. The return variation measures, σ_ε^2, σ_m^2, R^2, $\ln(\sigma_\varepsilon^2)$, $\ln(\sigma_m^2)$, and Ψ, are constructed using 1990-to-1992 data for a sample of 196 three-digit industries spanned by 4,029 firms. The controls, $\bar{q}$, seg, H, $\ln(K)$, λ, lev, adv, and $r\&d$, are constructed using 1990-to-1992 data for 196 three-digit industries spanned by 4,029 firms. The fundamentals variation controls, $\ln({}_{ROA}\sigma_\varepsilon^2)$, $\ln({}_{ROA}\sigma_m^2)$, and ${}_{ROA}\Psi$, are constructed using 1983-to-1992 data for 196 three-digit industries spanned by 4,705 firms. To utilize as much information as possible to capture fundamental comovements, we include firms that might not last throughout the period, but had at least six years of continuous data. Finance industries (SIC code 6000–6999) are omitted.

	R&D Spending	$\ln({}_{ROA}\sigma_\varepsilon^2)$	$\ln({}_{ROA}\sigma_m^2)$	${}_{ROA}\Psi$	$\bar{q}$	$segs$	H	$\ln(K)$	λ	lev	adv	$r\&d$
$\ln(\sigma_m^2)$	Absolute systematic stock return variation	**0.524** (0.00)	**0.518** (0.00)	0.061 (0.39)	**0.282** (0.00)	**-0.224** (0.00)	-0.073 (0.31)	**-0.182** (0.01)	**0.211** (0.00)	0.087 (0.22)	**0.164** (0.02)	0.041 (0.57)
$\ln({}_{ROA}\sigma_\varepsilon^2)$	Absolute firm-specific fundamentals variation		**0.787** (0.00)	**0.415** (0.00)	**0.338** (0.00)	**-0.167** (0.02)	-0.073 (0.31)	**-0.189** (0.01)	**0.328** (0.00)	0.087 (0.22)	**0.259** (0.00)	0.114 (0.11)
$\ln({}_{ROA}\sigma_m^2)$	Absolute systematic fundamentals variation			**-0.236** (0.00)	**0.362** (0.00)	-0.114 (0.11)	-0.019 (0.79)	**-0.256** (0.00)	**0.290** (0.00)	**0.142** (0.05)	**0.189** (0.01)	0.054 (0.45)
${}_{ROA}\Psi$	rel. firm-specific fundamentals variation				-0.001 (0.99)	-0.094 (0.19)	-0.087 (0.22)	0.080 (0.26)	0.090 (0.21)	-0.072 (0.32)	**0.129** (0.07)	0.100 (0.16)
$\bar{q}$	Average q					-0.069 (0.34)	-0.109 (0.13)	-0.042 (0.56)	**0.260** (0.00)	**0.175** (0.01)	**0.359** (0.00)	**0.160** (0.02)
$segs$	Corporate diversification						**0.233** (0.00)	**0.244** (0.00)	**-0.182** (0.01)	0.064 (0.37)	0.080 (0.26)	-0.112 (0.12)
H	Herfindahl index							**-0.293** (0.00)	-0.048 (0.50)	-0.024 (0.74)	-0.026 (0.72)	0.048 (0.51)
$\ln(K)$	Size								**-0.460** (0.00)	-0.052 (0.47)	**0.217** (0.00)	-0.076 (0.29)
λ	Liquidity									**-0.141** (0.05)	0.109 (0.13)	**0.305** (0.00)
Lev	Leverage										**-0.176** (0.01)	-0.078 (0.28)
Adv	Advertising spending											0.022 (0.76)

Table V
Ordinary Least Squares Regressions of Capital Budgeting Quality Variables (Measured as Deviation of Marginal q from One) on Firm-specific Stock Return Variation and Control Variables

This table reports Ordinary Least Squares regression estimation results. The dependent variables are capital budgeting quality measures $(\dot{q} - 1)^2$ (specifications 5.1–5.4) and $|\dot{q} - 1|$ (specifications 5.5–5.8). Regressions 5.1 and 5.5 include absolute firm-specific stock return variation, $\ln(\sigma_\varepsilon^2)$, absolute systematic stock return variation, $\ln(\sigma_m^2)$, absolute firm-specific fundamentals variation, $\ln(_{ROA}\sigma_\varepsilon^2)$, and absolute systematic fundamentals variation, $\ln(_{ROA}\sigma_m^2)$, as independent variables. Regressions 5.2 and 5.6 also include corporate diversification (*segs*), Herfindahl index (*H*), size ($\ln(K)$), liquidity (λ), leverage (*lev*), advertising spending (*adv*), and R&D spending (*r&d*) as control variables. Regressions 5.3 and 5.7 also include average q ($\bar{q}$) as a control variable. Regressions 5.4 and 5.8 include relative firm-specific stock return variation, Ψ, relative firm-specific fundamentals variation, $_{ROA}\Psi$; average q ($\bar{q}$) corporate diversification (*segs*); Herfindahl index (*H*); size ($\ln(K)$); liquidity (λ); leverage (*lev*); advertising spending (*adv*); and R&D spending (*r&d*) as independent variables. All regressions also include one-digit SIC industry fixed effects (coefficients are not reported). Finance industries (SIC code 6000–6999) are omitted. Numbers in parentheses are probability levels, based on Newey-West (robust) standard errors, at which the null hypothesis of a zero coefficient can be rejected. Coefficients significant at 10 percent level, based on 2-tail tests, are in boldface. The return variation measures, $\sigma_\varepsilon^2, \sigma_m^2, R^2, \ln(\sigma_\varepsilon^2), \ln(\sigma_m^2)$, and Ψ, is constructed using 1990-to-1992 data for a sample of 196 three-digit industries spanned by 4,029 firms. The quality of capital budgeting variables, $(\dot{q} - 1)^2$ and $|\dot{q} - 1|$, is constructed using 1993-to-1997 data for 196 three-digit industries spanned by 16,735 firm-year observations. The controls, $\bar{q}$, *seg*, H, $\ln(K)$, λ, *lev*, *adv*, and *r&d*, are constructed using 1990-to-1992 data for 196 three-digit industries spanned by 4,029 firms. The fundamentals variation controls, $\ln(_{ROA}\sigma_\varepsilon^2)$, $\ln(_{ROA}\sigma_m^2)$, and $_{ROA}\Psi$, are constructed using 1983-to-1992 data for 196 three-digit industries spanned by 4,705 firms. To utilize as much information as possible to capture fundamental comovements, we include firms that might not last throughout the period, but had at least six years of continuous data. Refer to Table I for variable definitions.

Dependent Variables		Squared Deviation of Marginal q from 1, $(\dot{q} - 1)^2$				Absolute Value of Deviation of Marginal q from 1, $|\dot{q} - 1|$			
		5.1	5.2	5.3	5.4	5.5	5.6	5.7	5.8
Absolute firm-specific stock return variation	$\ln(\sigma_\varepsilon^2)$	**-0.701**	**-0.760**	**-0.730**	—	**-0.231**	**-0.245**	**-0.239**	—
		(0.08)	(0.04)	(0.05)		(0.06)	(0.02)	(0.03)	
Absolute systematic stock return variation	$\ln(\sigma_m^2)$	0.310	0.306	0.295	—	0.083	0.080	0.077	—
		(0.39)	(0.39)	(0.40)		(0.44)	(0.44)	(0.45)	
Relative firm-specific stock return variation	Ψ	—	—	—	-0.531	—	—	—	**-0.158**
					(0.11)				(0.09)
Absolute firm-specific fundamentals variation	$\ln(_{ROA}\sigma_\varepsilon^2)$	0.001	0.073	0.070	—	-0.084	-0.059	-0.059	—
		(0.99)	(0.87)	(0.87)		(0.51)	(0.63)	(0.62)	
Absolute systematic fundamentals variation	$\ln(_{ROA}\sigma_m^2)$	0.212	0.087	0.140	—	**0.198**	0.145	0.156	—
		(0.52)	(0.80)	(0.67)		(0.07)	(0.15)	(0.12)	

Table V—*Continued*

Dependent Variables		Squared Deviation of Marginal q from 1, $(\hat{q}-1)^2$				Absolute Value of Deviation of Marginal q from 1, $|\hat{q}-1|$			
		5.1	5.2	5.3	5.4	5.5	5.6	5.7	5.8
Relative firm-specific fundamentals variation	ROA^{Ψ}	—	—	—	−0.030	—	—	—	−0.105
					(0.94)				(0.33)
Average q	$\bar{q}$	—	—	−0.193	−0.204	—	—	−0.041	−0.042
				(0.14)	(0.13)			(0.29)	(0.27)
Corporate diversification	$segs$	—	−0.173	−0.169	−0.134	—	**−0.076**	**−0.076**	−0.065
			(0.21)	(0.22)	(0.29)		(0.10)	(0.10)	(0.14)
Herfindahl index	H	—	**2.073**	**1.975**	**2.016**	—	**0.839**	**0.818**	**0.831**
			(0.03)	(0.03)	(0.02)		(0.01)	(0.00)	(0.00)
Size	$\ln(K)$	—	**−0.381**	**−0.374**	**−0.361**	—	**−0.131**	**−0.129**	**−0.125**
			(0.04)	(0.04)	(0.05)		(0.00)	(0.00)	(0.01)
Liquidity	λ	—	−0.859	−0.599	−0.472	—	−0.175	−0.120	−0.061
			(0.24)	(0.37)	(0.45)		(0.45)	(0.58)	(0.77)
Leverage	lev	—	**−1.306**	**−1.026**	**−1.120**	—	−0.319	−0.260	−0.285
			(0.02)	(0.07)	(0.05)		(0.12)	(0.21)	(0.17)
Advertising spending	adv	—	9.115	13.516	12.612	—	1.751	2.676	2.400
			(0.26)	(0.18)	(0.20)		(0.42)	(0.33)	(0.37)
R&D spending	$r\&d$	—	−1.916	−0.916	−0.840	—	−0.574	−0.364	−0.338
			(0.43)	(0.73)	(0.75)		(0.46)	(0.67)	(0.69)
F-statistics		**3.54**	**1.87**	**1.83**	**1.91**	**8.57**	**3.35**	**3.22**	**3.21**
		(0.00)	(0.02)	(0.02)	(0.02)	(0.00)	(0.00)	(0.00)	(0.00)
Regression R^2		0.124	0.278	0.288	0.277	0.121	0.326	0.330	0.314

Table V ignores taxes and other complications that can bias $\hat{q}$ and thus push h, the optimal $\dot{q}$, away from 1. When we consider the ways in which taxes and other factors can raise or lower both $\hat{q}$ and thus h, we note that these factors most likely affect our $\dot{q}$ estimates uniformly, or at least randomly. Consequently, our estimated distances between $\hat{q}$ and the similarly distorted optimum, h, may also be distorted uniformly, or at least randomly, and thus can still be used as an inverse indicator of capital budgeting quality.

Table VI therefore allows the $\dot{q}$ threshold value, h, to be estimated endogenously following the nonlinear procedure reported in Appendix A.4. Depending on the specification, h ranges from 0.715 to 0.908, and the Wald tests show it to differ significantly from one in all regressions save regression 5.8 of Table VI. The regression coefficients are similar to those reported in Table V, but have somewhat higher statistical significance.

Overall, these findings are consistent with the conjecture that greater firm-specific stock return variation is associated with higher quality capital budgeting.

B. Robustness

A battery of robustness checks generates qualitatively similar results to those presented above; that is, an identical pattern of signs and statistical significance arises across all of the checks. Space constraints limit us to a brief synopsis.

Although we use Newey–West heteroskedasticity-consistent standard errors, outliers could still affect our findings. Hadi's (1992, 1994) method (cut-off = 0.05) does not reveal outlier problems. Dropping observations for which Cook's D is greater than 1 or even 0.5 does not change our findings, nor does dropping the top and bottom 5 percent of observations of all our main variables.

We can estimate marginal q in a variety of ways. First, we modify (9), (10), and (11) to include *R&D* and *advertise* as capital expenditure in the estimation of $\dot{q}$.[9] Second, (A7) estimates fixed assets recursively assuming 10 percent economic depreciation. An alternative approach uses accounting depreciation, as in (A13). Third, we estimate $\dot{q}$ as the marginal change in shareholder value instead of firm (equity plus debt) value. Finally, we estimate industry $\dot{q}$ including fixed firm effects, so that each firm has its own expected asset growth rate net of depreciation, α^i in (11). Qualitatively similar results to those in the tables arise in each case.

We estimate σ_ε^2 in (1), (2), and (3) using daily data. Some listed firms may be thinly traded. Nontrading generates zero returns, and a string of zero returns can artificially raise our estimated σ_ε^2. To mitigate this problem, we also use weekly, bi-weekly, and monthly data. All three procedures generate qualitatively similar results to those reported in Tables V and VI.

---

[9] For consistency, this alternative requires that we also capitalize R&D and advertising spending into the replacement cost of total assets. We assume a 25 percent annual depreciation rate on both types of intangible investments to do this.

Table VI
Non-Linear Least Squares Regressions of the Capital Budgeting Quality Measures (Measured as Deviation from Threshold Value) on Firm-specific Stock Return Variation and Control Variables

This table reports nonlinear least squares regression estimation results. The dependent variables are capital budgeting quality measures $(\hat{q} - h)^2$ (specifications 6.1 – 6.4) and $|\hat{q} - h|$ (specifications 6.5–6.8) where the threshold level h is estimated endogenously. Regressions 6.1 and 6.5 include absolute firm-specific stock return variation, $\ln(\sigma_\varepsilon^2)$, absolute systematic stock return variation, $\ln(\sigma_m^2)$, absolute firm-specific fundamentals variation, $\ln(_{ROA}\sigma_\varepsilon^2)$, and absolute systematic fundamentals variation, $\ln(_{ROA}\sigma_m^2)$, as independent variables. Regressions 6.2 and 6.6 also include corporate diversification ($segs$), Herfindahl index (H), size ($\ln(K)$), liquidity (λ), leverage (lev), advertising spending (adv), and R&D spending ($r\&d$) as control variables. Regressions 6.3 and 6.7 also include average q ($\bar{q}$) as a control variable. Regressions 6.4 and 6.8 include relative firm-specific stock return variation, Ψ, relative firm-specific fundamentals variation, $_{ROA}\Psi$, average q, corporate diversification ($segs$), Herfindahl index (H), size ($\ln(K)$), liquidity (λ), leverage (lev), advertising spending (adv), and R&D spending ($r\&d$) as independent variables. All regressions also include one-digit SIC industry fixed effects (coefficients are not reported). The sample is 196 three-digit industries. Finance industries (SIC code 6000–6999) are omitted. Numbers in parentheses are probability levels at which the null hypothesis of zero coefficient can be rejected. Coefficients significant at 10 percent level (based on 2-tail test) are in boldface. For each specification, Wald test statistics of the hypothesis that the threshold level h is equal to one is reported. The return variation measures, σ_ε^2, σ_m^2, R^2, $\ln(\sigma_\varepsilon^2)$, $\ln(\sigma_m^2)$, and Ψ, are constructed using 1990-to-1992 data for 196 three-digit industries spanned by 4,029 firms. The quality of capital budgeting variables, $(\hat{q} - 1)^2$ and $|\hat{q} - 1|$, are constructed using 1993-to-1997 data for 196 three-digit industries spanned by 16,735 firm-year observations. The controls, $\bar{q}$, $segs$, H, $\ln(K)$, λ, lev, adv, and $r\&d$, are constructed using 1990-to-1992 data for 196 three-digit industries spanned by 4,029 firms. The fundamentals variation controls, $\ln(_{ROA}\sigma_\varepsilon^2)$, $\ln(_{ROA}\sigma_m^2)$, and $_{ROA}\Psi$, are constructed using 1983-to-1992 data for 196 three-digit industries spanned by 4,705 firms. To utilize as much information as possible to capture fundamental comovements, we include firms that might not last through out the period, but had at least six years of continuous data. Refer to Table I for variable definitions.

Dependent Variables		Squared Deviation of Marginal q from an Endogenously Estimated Threshold Value h, $(\hat{q} - h)^2$				Absolute Value of Deviation of Marginal q from an Endogenously Estimated threshold Value h, $|\hat{q} - h|$			
		6.1	6.2	6.3	6.4	6.5	6.6	6.7	6.8
Threshold value of marginal q	h	**0.755**	**0.773**	**0.780**	**0.777**	**0.715**	**0.820**	**0.868**	**0.908**
		(0.00)	(0.00)	(0.00)	(0.00)	(0.00)	(0.00)	(0.00)	(0.00)
F-statistics of Wald test to reject h equal to 1		**8.15**	**7.93**	**7.42**	**7.60**	**11.37**	**5.03**	**2.83**	1.35
		(0.00)	(0.01)	(0.01)	(0.01)	(0.00)	(0.03)	(0.09)	(0.25)
Absolute firm-specific stock return variation	$\ln(\sigma_\varepsilon^2)$	**−0.655**	**−0.717**	**−0.692**		**−0.754**	**−0.575**	**−0.538**	
		(0.04)	(0.02)	(0.02)		(0.00)	(0.00)	(0.00)	
Absolute systematic stock return variation	$\ln(\sigma_m^2)$	0.302	0.282	0.273		**0.693**	0.085	0.085	
		(0.35)	(0.36)	(0.37)		(0.00)	(0.59)	(0.61)	

Capital Budgeting and Firm-specific Stock Return Variation   91

	(1)	(2)	(3)	(4)	(5)	(6)	(7)	(8)
Relative firm-specific stock return variation — Ψ				−0.507 (0.05)				−0.410 (0.01)
Absolute firm-specific fundamentals variation — $\ln(_{ROA}\sigma_\varepsilon^2)$	0.079 (0.78)	0.146 (0.60)	0.141 (0.61)		0.803 (0.00)	0.280 (0.03)	0.485 (0.00)	
Absolute systematic fundamentals variation — $\ln(_{ROA}\sigma_m^2)$	0.105 (0.73)	−0.009 (0.97)	0.041 (0.89)		−0.740 (0.00)	−0.108 (0.47)	−0.275 (0.06)	
Relative firm-specific fundamentals variation — $_{ROA}\Psi$				0.054 (0.83)				0.311 (0.01)
Average q — $\bar{q}$			−0.170 (0.18)	−0.182 (0.14)			−0.245 (0.00)	−0.259 (0.00)
Corporate diversification — segs		−0.204 (0.23)	−0.200 (0.24)	−0.164 (0.32)		−0.178 (0.06)	−0.122 (0.19)	−0.129 (0.20)
Herfindahl index — H		1.813 (0.03)	1.735 (0.03)	1.773 (0.03)		1.041 (0.00)	0.771 (0.04)	1.023 (0.01)
Size — $\ln(K)$		−0.396 (0.00)	−0.389 (0.00)	−0.375 (0.00)		−0.315 (0.00)	−0.303 (0.00)	−0.274 (0.00)
Liquidity — λ		−0.962 (0.22)	−0.730 (0.36)	−0.624 (0.43)		−1.452 (0.00)	−0.910 (0.03)	−0.444 (0.28)
Leverage — lev		−1.235 (0.12)	−0.990 (0.22)	−1.092 (0.17)		−0.778 (0.08)	−0.866 (0.04)	−0.959 (0.02)
Advertising spending — adv		8.606 (0.11)	12.494 (0.04)	11.548 (0.06)		11.027 (0.00)	14.524 (0.00)	12.331 (0.00)
R&D spending — r&d		−2.257 (0.49)	−1.366 (0.68)	−1.297 (0.70)		−2.391 (0.24)	−1.745 (0.37)	−0.501 (0.82)
F-statistics	7.24 (0.00)	7.37 (0.00)	7.14 (0.00)	7.73 (0.00)	19.28 (0.00)	19.59 (0.00)	20.3 (0.00)	20.45 (0.00)
Regression R^2	0.341	0.457	0.463	0.455	0.597	0.702	0.720	0.699

We consider alternative constructs for our basic control. First, using Herfindahl indexes based on assets or employees, rather than sales, generates similar results. So does controlling for industry size using the logarithms of 1990-to-1992 average book assets or employees, or using fixed capital estimated recursively from reported depreciation, rather than a 10 percent depreciation rate. Controlling for liquidity using cash flow over assets and past external financing (described in Appendix A.3), rather than net current assets over tangible assets as in (A9), also yields comparable results. So does including all three liquidity measures. Finally, we can substitute variants of our basic fundamentals co-movement variables. For example, we use (A7) to adjust the denominator of *ROA* for inflation, construct *ROA* entirely from book values, or adjust PP&E with reported depreciation, as in (A13). All these procedures generate qualitatively similar results to those shown, as do a host of other variants.[10]

Another concern is that we miss important industry characteristics. First, rapidly growing industries, such as high-tech, might exhibit a variety of attributes that bias our $\dot{q}$ estimates. Although lagged average q and spending on intangibles already control for such industries, we can also include current average q and past stock returns. We also repeat our regressions using only industries that report zero R&D. Second, because an industry's exposure to foreign trade might affect the quality of capital budgeting, we include industry exports minus imports over sales and industry capital–labor ratios.[11] Third, firm size might be as important as industry size. Hence, we add *average* firm size in each industry: the logarithms of 1990-to-1992 average book assets, real sales, employees, or PP&E—estimated using either (A7) or (A13). Fourth, regulated utilities (SIC 4900 through 4999) may be subject to different constraints

---

[10] Dropping observations where $|ROA_{i,j,t} - ROA_{i,j,t-1}| > 25$ percent to avoid spurs in accounting *ROA* caused by transitory extraordinary events and tax saving practices. Doing so eliminates 869 firm-year observations from our sample. Leaving these observations in does not qualitatively affect our results. Another straightforward variant is to substitute comovement in return on equity (*ROE*), net income plus depreciation all over net worth, for *ROA* in (18). Constructing this alternative fundamentals comovement control variable necessitates dropping four observations where net worth is negative. Using comovement in *ROE* to control for fundamentals comovement yields results similar to those shown in the tables. Also, both *ROA* and *ROE* comovement can be estimated relative to an equal, rather than market value, weighting of the indices. Weightings based on sales, book assets, or book equity also yield qualitatively similar results to those shown in the tables. An issue with all the above direct measures of fundamentals variation is that while they are based on a long window, they are unreliable estimates because of changes in firm conditions and the like. Since our purpose is to estimate how similar fundamentals are among firms, we can use a panel variance of $ROA_{i,j,t}$ using all firms j in each industry i in 1990 to 1992 as an alternative control variable. This also produces qualitatively similar results. Using a time-series average of cross-sectional variances also yields qualitatively similar results.

[11] Industries more exposed to intensified international competition may make better capital budgeting decisions. In addition, international competition may have heterogeneous impacts on firm returns. Industry imports and exports are from the NBER-CES Manufacturing Industry Database. These data are available only for manufacturing (SIC codes from 2000 to 3999) industries, so our regressions are restricted to these industries. Capital–labor ratios are deviations from the economy-wide weighted average.

than unregulated firms despite liberalization in the 1980s. We therefore drop these industries. All these variations generate results qualitatively similar to those shown.

We can also ignore statistical propriety and change our empirical specification.

First, instead of using 1990-to-1992 return variation and 1993-to-1997 marginal q's, we can use contemporaneous data from either period. This yields results qualitatively similar to those shown.

Second, we split our sample by $\dot{q}$. In high-$\dot{q}$ subsamples ($\dot{q} > 1.0$, 0.9, 0.8, or 0.7), regressions analogous to those in Table V, but explaining $\dot{q}$, have significant negative coefficients on both $\ln(\sigma_\varepsilon^2)$ and Ψ. For low-$\dot{q}$ subsamples ($\dot{q} < 1.0$, 0.9, 0.8, or 0.7), these coefficients are positive and significant. The finding that $\dot{q}$ rises with firm-specific return variation in low-$\dot{q}$ subsamples, but falls with firm-specific variation in the high-$\dot{q}$ subsamples, makes it improbable that our results are artifacts of either liquidity constraints or inframarginal projects.

In conclusion, our results survive a battery of robustness checks. While we acknowledge that further analysis may overturn these results, we believe we have presented persuasive evidence that greater firm-specific stock return variation is associated with marginal q ratios better aligned to value maximization.

C. Economic Significance

Our results are highly economically significant. In regression 4.7, a one standard deviation increase in absolute firm-specific stock return variation, $\ln(\sigma_\varepsilon^2)$, reduces $|\dot{q} - 1|$ by 0.239×0.807 or 0.193, roughly 34 percent of the absolute distance of marginal q from one across industries. A one standard deviation increase in relative firm-specific stock return variation, Ψ, reduces the absolute distances of marginal q from one by 14 percent. The improvements, when measured by the squared distances of marginal q from one, are 28 percent and 13 percent, respectively.

V. Discussion

Our results show capital budgeting to be more aligned with market value maximization in industries where firm-specific return variation is higher. Our preferred interpretation of these findings extends the French and Roll (1986) and Roll (1988) contention that firm-specific variation reflects the intensity of informed trading with the additional contention that more intense informed trading is, the closer share prices are to fundamentals. We feel this is the simplest interpretation of our findings, and therefore the preferred interpretation by Ockham's razor.

In this section, we weigh alternative interpretations and possible underlying economic implications of, and explanations for, our preferred interpretation.

A. The Information Content of Stock Prices

Roll (1988) finds that firm-specific return variation is largely unrelated to public announcements, and contends that it reflects the capitalization of private information into share prices *via* informed trading. However, he concedes (p. 56) that it might also reflect "occasional frenzy unrelated to concrete information." We argued above that other research makes the latter interpretation unlikely. We now consider the plausibility of this interpretation in the context of our results.

First, greater error in stock prices should cause our $\dot{q}$ estimates to deviate more from their "true" value as assessed by investors. This, ceteris paribus, would raise the likelihood of finding a positive correlation (not the observed negative one) between firm-specific return variation and the distance of $\dot{q}$ from h.

Second, more error-laden share prices should cause corporate governance mechanisms to misfire, and perhaps to be disarmed. Yet capital investment is more, not less, aligned with market value maximization in higher firm-specific return variation industries. This is consistent with high firm-specific variation indicating large pricing errors only if managers' decisions are more aligned with shareholder value maximization where share prices are less informed. This seems improbable.

Third, more erroneous stock prices should magnify information asymmetry problems, strengthening liquidity constraints. Yet we find less evidence of capital rationing in high-$\dot{q}$ industries with larger firm-specific return variation.

Of course, we can never exclude alternative explanations absolutely. For example, $\dot{q}$ might be higher where capital spending is less predicable. If higher $\ln(\sigma_\varepsilon^2)$ and Ψ are associated with less predictable capital budgeting in low-$\dot{q}$ industries (where capital budgeting is already highly predictable), but with greater predictability in high-$\dot{q}$ industries (where capital budgeting is already less predictable), our findings could ensue. Alternatively, capital spending might become lumpier as $\ln(\sigma_\varepsilon^2)$ and Ψ rise for low-$\dot{q}$ industries, but less lumpy as $\ln(\sigma_\varepsilon^2)$ and Ψ rise for high-$\dot{q}$ industries. Or, some interaction of such effects might be devised. While such stories are didactically possible, they are—in our view—improbable.

If the preferred interpretation of our findings is valid, some inferences follow.

First, our preferred interpretation is also consistent with the use of return asynchronicity to measure the intensity of informed trading, as implied by French and Roll (1986) and Roll (1988), and as used by Bushman, Piotroski, and Smith (2002), Morck, Yeung, and Yu (2000), and others.

Second, our preferred interpretation is consistent with the use of return asynchronicity as a measure of the functional-form efficiency of the stock market, in the sense of Tobin (1982) and as proposed by Wurgler (2000). Our results suggest that capital allocation is more aligned with shareholder value maximization where share prices are more asynchronous. If shareholder value maximization, in turn, corresponds to economic efficiency, a positive correlation between Ψ and higher return asynchronicity follows.

Third, many industries have estimated $\dot{q}$ well above our estimated h, and so appear to underinvest. Many others have $\dot{q} < h$, and so appear to overinvest. Underinvestment could be due to liquidity constraints arising from information asymmetries, or to managerial risk aversion. Overinvestment could be due to a

Capital Budgeting and Firm-specific Stock Return Variation   95

variety of agency problems, such as Jensen's (1986) free cash flow hypothesis or Roll's (1988) hubris hypothesis, and become more important when share prices are less informed. These deviations of $\hat{q}$ estimates from h suggest that these stories are economically important, and that some are more important than others in specific industries.

This discussion begs the question of how stock prices should track fundamentals more closely in industries whose stocks move less synchronously (i.e., have higher Ψ). Morck, Yeung, and Yu (2000), Wurgler (2000), and Bushman, Piotroski, and Smith (2002) stress differences in institutional environments across countries. All U.S. firms are presumably subject to the same institutional environment, so cross-industry differences within the United States must be due to other factors.

B. Incomplete Arbitrage?

In this section, we speculate about how stock prices might come to track fundamentals more closely in industries with more asynchronous stock returns. We do this very tentatively, as we are uncertain of the validity of these ideas, and we welcome other explanations of our findings.

Grossman and Stiglitz (1980) argue that arbitrage is limited by the cost of obtaining and analyzing the information needed to estimate fundamental values. In addition, they make the point that greater risk aversion of the informed traders will also limit arbitrage and thus price informativeness (p. 399). Shleifer and Vishny (1997) and Shleifer (2000, Chapter 4) expand on these ideas. Arbitrageurs' risk aversion matters because arbitrageurs must hold large undiversified portfolios and bear *holding period risk*—the risk that new information will send the price in the wrong direction before the stock price has time to move to the arbitrageur's previously correct estimate of its fundamental value. Information gathering, processing costs, and holding period risk matter because arbitrageurs do not gather and process information if their expected return from doing so does not justify the cost and risk.

These considerations raise the possibility that arbitrage might be more severely limited in some industries than in others. We now consider some specific ways in which this might happen.

B.1. The Absence of Firm-specific Arbitrage

First, such differences might arise if the basic business activities of firms in some industries are intrinsically harder for arbitrageurs to predict. If so, arbitrage limits might more severely curtail firm-specific arbitrage plays in those industries. Since French and Roll (1986) and Roll (1988) find that firm-specific stock price fluctuations mainly reflect private information being incorporated into prices by informed trading, an absence of arbitrage on firm-specific information might be associated with depressed firm-specific return variation—at least over short intervals.

Over long intervals, the cost of firm-specific information about different firms might rise and fall exogenously. In this case, informed arbitrage on each stock would happen when firm-specific information about that stock is cheap. If we observe stocks for longer time intervals, differences in the extent of informed trading should wash out. Even if information about some firms is always more costly than information about other firms, a longer interval might mitigate differences in the extent of informed trading. This is because a steadily increasing divergence of the firm-specific component of a stock return from its fundamental value should eventually induce arbitrage, and a consequent discrete jump as the price finally moves to its fundamental value. That is, uncapitalized firm-specific information is "built up and discharged." This *capacitance theory of information* capitalization implies that differences in firm-specific return variation should fade if we measure them over sufficiently long intervals. We use a 3-year window to estimate $\ln(\sigma_\varepsilon^2)$ and Ψ. As we extend our estimation window, the differences across industries decrease and the statistical significance of these variables in the regressions falls, though their signs do not change. A 10-year window is sufficient to render all the coefficients statistically insignificant.

Unfortunately, this might also merely reflect a greater use of stale data, and so cannot be taken as clear confirmation of this explanation. We are pursuing this in a subsequent paper.

However, a lack of firm-specific arbitrage might not lead to a steadily increasing divergence of the share price from its fundamental value if the firm-specific component of fundamental value is mean reverting. This might occur if firm-specific differences in returns are due to firm-specific corporate governance problems, which are corrected over the longer term, or to exceptional firm-specific corporate governance, which does not last. If old firm-specific information grows stale, or depreciates, in this way, an absence of informed trading might not cause an uncapitalized information build-up. This *depreciation theory of information* means the gap between true value and market value need not grow with elapsed time and need not eventually trigger arbitrage. Some firm-specific events might pass into irrelevance without ever being capitalized into share prices.

If this hypothesis underlies our results, we might expect the firm-specific component of earnings to exhibit more mean reversion than industry or market-wide earnings averages. We are pursuing this possibility in a subsequent paper.

B.2. Agency Problems and Firm-specific Arbitrage

A second, closely related possibility is that management might more readily appropriate cash flows in some industries than in others. If management appropriates abnormally high cash flows due to abnormally high market-wide or industry-wide earnings, this is obvious to shareholders unless all the managers of other firms do likewise. However, if management appropriates abnormally high firm-specific cash flows, shareholders may never know. Arbitrageurs, however, might come to rationally expect such appropriations, and thus view predicting firm-specific fundamentals changes as of little value. If so, firm-specific return variation would be depressed.

If insiders' misappropriation raises operating costs, we should see a corresponding effect on firm-specific fundamentals variation, $_{ROA}\sigma_\varepsilon^2$. However, if insiders' pilfering unlinks earnings from dividends, earnings variation might be unaffected. This effect, however, might be distinguishable as a negative skewness in the firm-specific components of individual stock returns, for insiders would tend to appropriate positive firm-specific return, but not negative ones. We are pursuing this possibility elsewhere.

B.3. Noise Traders and Firm-specific Arbitrage

A third possibility is that noise traders concentrate their trading in certain "fad" industries. Black (1986) shows that noise traders are required for the stock market to function. De Long et al. (1990) show that noise trader induced stock price movements need not immediately be dampened by arbitrageurs, and they argue that this is especially likely when noise traders' mispricing errors are systematic. They consequently propose that noise trading induces market-wide return variation unrelated to fundamentals—which we would observe as an elevated $\ln(\sigma_m^2)$ and a depressed Ψ. This noise trader induced systematic variation increases the holding period risk that arbitrageurs must bear, and this deters arbitrage, lowering our measured $\ln(\sigma_\varepsilon^2)$ and Ψ.

However, this interpretation would seem inconsistent both with the typical insignificance of systematic variation, $\ln(\sigma_m^2)$, in our results, and with firm-specific variation relative to systematic variation, Ψ_i, not working as well as absolute firm-specific variation, $\ln(\sigma_\varepsilon^2)$, in some of the our regressions. Nonetheless, our incomplete understanding of the real importance and nature of noise trading prevents a categorical rejection of this hypothesis at present.

B.4. Qualification

The idea that different stock prices might track their fundamental values with different degrees of precision underlies our interpretation of the empirical findings. If valid, this notion itself is potentially quite important. We recognize that extensive further empirical investigation is needed to fully ascertain its validity, and to deduce the nature of the information economics that must underlie it. Moreover, we recognize that our interpretation of the findings may be erroneous. Consequently, we welcome other explanations of our empirical finding that industries in which stock returns are less synchronous have marginal q ratios closer to its optimal value.

VI. Conclusions

Our main conclusion is capital budgeting seems more closely aligned with market value maximization in industries whose stocks exhibit greater firm-specific return variation. That is, we find fewer marginal q ratios far above or far below a theoretical optimum in industries exhibiting higher firm-specific stock return variation. This finding is highly statistically and economically significant. It is also robust and survives controlling for firm-specific fundamentals variation and other factors that might affect stock return synchronicity.

This is of interest for several reasons.

First, Roll (1988) attributes the low R^2 statistics common in asset pricing models to high firm-specific return variation, and this firm-specific variation is not associated with public information releases. He concludes (p. 56) that it rather reflects "either private information or else occasional frenzy unrelated to concrete information." Our preferred interpretation of the findings is inconsistent with firm-specific return variation reflecting investor frenzy. Indeed, our findings imply that firm-specific return variation is due to informed trading, and that share prices are actually closer to fundamental values where firm-specific return variation is higher! One possibility is that activity by informed traders reduces noise trader induced errors in share prices, as in De Long et al. (1990).

Second, the extent to which corporate capital budgeting decisions maximize market value is a crucial issue in finance. Managers may make capital budgeting decisions that do not maximize market value because of corporate governance problems associated with managerial self-interest, ignorance, or incompetence. Suboptimal capital budgeting decisions can also result from costly external financing (due to information asymmetry between managers and investors) or other sorts of liquidity constraints. If our interpretation of the results is correct, firms follow capital budgeting policies more aligned with market value maximization where stock prices are more informed.

Third, our interpretation of the results raises the possibility that stock prices track fundamental values with differing degrees of accuracy in different industries. That is, rather than being "efficient" or "inefficient," the stock market exhibits a range of efficiency levels in different industries. How could this be? We speculate that such differences might arise because arbitrage is complete to different degrees across industries. But this begs the question of what determines the completeness of arbitrage. We speculate about possible roles for differences in transparency, arbitrage costs, arbitrage risks, monitoring costs, agency problems, and noise trading activity. Our findings suggest that a better understanding of what determines the limits to arbitrage is of fundamental importance.

Fourth, if we follow Tobin (1982) and define the stock market as *functional-form efficient* if stock price movements bring about economically efficient capital budgeting, our results suggest stock prices are more functionally efficient where firm-specific return variation is larger. This *functional form of the efficient markets hypothesis* is important because the quality of corporate capital allocation decisions has major ramifications for the real economy.

Finally, although we believe this interpretation of our finding is sound, we recognize that this work is preliminary and we welcome other explanations of

Capital Budgeting and Firm-specific Stock Return Variation 99

our finding that greater firm-specific return variation coincides with marginal Tobin's q ratios closer to optimal values.

Appendix

A.1. Construction of the Data Sets

Our sample begins with all companies listed in the WRDS CRSP/ COMPUSTAT Merged Database from 1990 to 1992. We discard duplicate entries for preferred stock, class B stock, and the like by deleting entries whose CRSP CUSIP identifiers append a number other than 10 or 11. Since accounting data for financial and banking firms (SIC codes from 6000 through 6999) are not comparable, we exclude them.

Since the analysis below requires more than one firm in each industry in constructing the firm-specific stock return variables, we drop industries that contain fewer than three firms. We also drop firm-year observations with fewer than 30 days of daily stock return data. When firms are delisted and COMPUSTAT indicates that a bankruptcy occurred, we assume a final daily return of −100 percent. When firms are delisted and COMPUSTAT indicates that a corporate control event occurred the final return is taken as given.

After these procedures, our final "1990 to 1992 sample" contains 4,066 firms spanning 205 three-digit SIC industries. We use this sample to construct our firm-specific stock return variation variables and most of our control variables.

Constructing some control variables requires a longer panel, starting prior to 1993. For these, we expand the 1990-to-1992 sample backward to 1983 by retaining sample firms that remain listed in COMPUSTAT in the period demarcated by those years. This "1983-to-1992 sample" contains 4,747 firms spanning 204 industries.

We use data from a "1993-to-1997 sample" to construct our capital budgeting quality variables. This sample consists of all firms listed in COMPUSTAT during those years in the industries spanned by our 1990-to-1992 sample. Our final 1993-to-1997 sample contains 16,782 firm-year observations spanning 199 three-digit industries. (The length of this window is arbitrary; our results hold if we use a shorter data window, e.g., 1993 to 1995.)

When COMPUSTAT reports a value as "insignificant," we set it to zero. When companies change their fiscal years, COMPUSTAT records one fiscal year with fewer than 12 months and another with more than 12 months. Under some circumstances, this causes COMPUSTAT to report a missing year observation. If a firm's fiscal year ends before June 15, COMPUSTAT reports it as data for the previous year on the grounds that more than half of the fiscal year occurred in the previous calendar year. This convention causes missing values if no fiscal year has the majority of its months in the calendar year of the change. We drop such firms.

In all three samples, we define *industries* as sets of firms that share the same primary three-digit SIC code in the COMPUSTAT Business Segment file. Firms need not have data for all time periods to be included in any of the samples. Hence, ours samples are all unbalanced panels.

A.2. Marginal Tobin's q Estimation Procedure

We define marginal q as the unexpected change in firm value during period t divided by the unexpected increase in capital goods during period t. We write this as

$$q_j = \frac{V_{j,t} - E_{t-1}V_{j,t}}{A_{j,t} - E_{t-1}A_{j,t}} = \frac{V_{j,t} - V_{j,t-1}(1 + \hat{r}_{j,t} - \hat{d}_{j,t})}{A_{j,t} - A_{j,t-1}(1 + \hat{g}_{j,t} - \hat{\delta}_{j,t})}, \tag{A1}$$

where $\hat{r}_{j,t}$ is the expected return from owning the firm, $\hat{d}_{j,t}$ is the firm's expected disbursement rate (including cash dividends, share repurchases, and interest expensive), $\hat{g}_{j,t}$ is the expected rate of spending on capital goods, and $\hat{\delta}_{j,t}$ is the expected depreciation rate on those capital goods.

Rewriting (A1), normalizing by $A_{j,t-1}$, we obtain

$$V_{j,t} - V_{j,t-1} = \dot{q}_j[A_{j,t} - A_{j,t-1}(1 + g_{j,t} - \delta_{j,t})] + V_{j,t-1}(\hat{r}_{j,t} - \hat{d}_{j,t}), \tag{A2}$$

or

$$\frac{V_{j,t} - V_{j,t-1}}{A_{j,t-1}} = -\dot{q}_j(g_j - \delta_j) + \dot{q}_j\frac{A_{j,t} - A_{j,t-1}}{A_{j,t-1}} - \xi_j\frac{div_{j,t-1}}{A_{j,t-1}} + r_j\frac{V_{j,t-1}}{A_{j,t-1}}, \tag{A3}$$

where $div_{j,t-1}$ is dollar disbursements.

Note that the intercept in (A3) is an estimate of $-\dot{q}_j(g_j - \delta_j)$, where the subscript j indicates a time average. The coefficients of lagged disbursements and lagged *average* q can be loosely interpreted as a tax correction factor and an estimate of the firm's weighted-average cost of capital.

We estimate $V_{j,t}$ and $A_{j,t}$ as

$$V_{j,t} = P_t(CS_{j,t} + PS_{j,t} + LTD_{j,t} + SD_{j,t} - STA_{j,t}), \tag{A4}$$

where

$$A_{j,t} \equiv K_{j,t} + INV_{j,t}. \tag{A5}$$

$CS_{j,t} =$ the end of fiscal year-t market value of the outstanding common shares of firm j,

$PS_{j,t} =$ the estimated market value of preferred shares (the preferred dividends paid over the Moody's *baa* preferred dividend yield),

$LTD_{j,t} =$ estimated market value of long-term debt,

$SD_{j,t} =$ book value of short-term debt,

$STA_{j,t} =$ book value of short-term assets,

$P_t =$ inflation adjustment using the GDP deflator,

$K_{j,t} =$ estimated market value of firm j's PP&E, and

$INV =$ estimated market value of inventories.

Capital Budgeting and Firm-specific Stock Return Variation   101

Before continuing, we provide details on the estimation of the market values of long-term debt, PP&E, and inventories.

We estimate the market value of long-term debt recursively. We construct a 15-year age profile of each firm's debt each year based on changes in book values. We estimate the market value of each vintage of each firm's debt in each year assuming all bonds to be 15-year coupon bonds issued at par. We use Moody's *Baa* bond rates to proxy for all bond yields.

We use a recursive algorithm to estimate the value of PP&E, $K_{j,t}$. This is necessary because historical cost accounting makes simple deflators questionable in adjusting for inflation. We begin by converting all figures to 1983 dollars. We assume that physical assets depreciate by 10 percent per year. Let $K_{j,t-10}$ be the book value of net PP&E (in 1983 dollars) for firm j in year t. (If a company's history is shorter than 10 years, we start the rolling equation with the first year available.) Accordingly, PP&E in year $t - 9$ is then

$$K_{j,t-9} = (1 - \delta)K_{j,t-10} + \frac{\Delta X_{j,t-9}}{1 + \pi_{t-9}}. \tag{A6}$$

More generally, we apply the recursive equation

$$K_{j,t+1} = (1 - \delta)K_{j,t} + \frac{\Delta X_{j,t+1}}{\prod_{\tau=0}^{t+1}(1 + \pi_\tau)}. \tag{A7}$$

Thus, PP&E in year $t + 1$ is PP&E from year t minus 10 percent depreciation plus current capital spending, denoted by $\Delta X_{j,t+1}$, deflated to 1983 dollars using π_t, the fractional change in the seasonally adjusted producer price index for finished goods published by the U.S. Department of Labor, Bureau of Labor Statistics.[12]

A similar recursive process is sometimes necessary to estimate the market value of inventories. The market value is taken as equal to the book value for firms using FIFO accounting. For firms using LIFO accounting, a recursive process analogous to that described in (A7) is used to estimate the age structure of inventories. Inventories of each age cohort are then adjusted for inflation using the GDP deflator.

We partition the 1993-to-1997 sample into three-digit industry subsamples of firms. For each subsample, we regress

$$\frac{\Delta V_{j,t}^i}{A_{j,t-1}^i} = \alpha^i + \beta_0^i \frac{\Delta A_{j,t}^i}{A_{j,t-1}^i} + \beta_1^i \frac{V_{j,t-1}^i}{A_{j,t-1}^i} + \beta_2^i \frac{D_{j,t-1}^i}{A_{j,t-1}^i} + u_{j,t}^i \tag{A8}$$

to obtain a marginal q estimate, $\dot{q}_i \cong \beta_0^i$, for that industry; $D_{j,t-1}^i$ is defined as dividends for common shares plus repurchases of common shares plus interest expenses.

---

[12] This index is available at http://www.stls.frb.org/fred/data/ppi/ppifgs.

Error terms are assumed to satisfy the following conditions: $u_{j,t}^i$ has zero mean, $\text{cov}(u_{j,t}^i, u_{j,s}^i) \neq 0 \, \forall \, t$ and s; and, $\text{cov}(u_{j,t}^i, u_{k,t}^i) \neq 0 \, \forall j$ and k. Equation (A8) (the same as Equation (11)) is estimated using the GLS method. All variables are scaled by $A_{j,t-1}^i$ to mitigate heteroskedasticity problems.

To mitigate the effect of outliers we drop companies with tangible assets less than $1 million and with absolute growth rates in tangible assets and value (scaled by tangible assets) greater than 300 percent. Dropping companies with absolute values of growth rates greater than 200 percent, 100 percent, or not dropping them at all does not change our results. We require at least 10 firm-year observations to estimate (A8). Finally, we omit two industries from our analysis for which the marginal q takes extremely high values of 4.79 and 6.88. Keeping them in our sample does not change the results.

The intersection of the "1983 to 1992," "1990 to 1992," and "1993 to 1997" samples results in the final sample of 196 three-digit industries we use in our analysis.

A.3. Additional Variables

Our basic liquidity measure is net current assets as a fraction of total assets

$$\hat{\lambda}_i = \frac{\sum_{j \in i, t \in [1990, 1992]} current\ assets_{j,t} - current\ liabilities_{j,t}}{\sum_{j \in i, t \in [1990, 1992]} tangible\ assets_{j,t}} \tag{A9}$$

for each industry i for the years from 1990 through 1992, where firm j is in industry i. The denominator is real PP&E, estimated using the recursive procedure in (A7), plus real inventories.

We define *cash flow over total assets* as

$$c_i = \frac{\sum_{j \in i, t \in [1990, 1992]} income_{i,j,t} + depreciation_{i,j,t}}{\sum_{j \in i, t \in [1990, 1992]} tangible\ assets_{i,j,t}}, \tag{A10}$$

where j is an index over firms that are members of industry i. The numerator is constructed by summing inflation-adjusted 1990, 1991, and 1992 data for all firms in each industry. The denominator is industry real PP&E, estimated using the recursive procedure in (A7), plus real inventory.

We define *past long-term debt* as

$$ltd_i = \max\left[0, \min\left[\frac{\sum_{j \in i, t \in [1990, 1992]} \Delta LD_{j,i}}{\sum_{j \in i, t \in [1990, 1992]} \Delta X_{j,t}}, 1\right]\right] \tag{A11}$$

where $\Delta LD_{j,t}$ is the book value of net long-term debt issued by firm j in industry i during year $t \in (1990, 1992)$, as reported in COMPUSTAT. The total value of capital spending by firm j in industry i in year $t \in [1990, 1992]$ is $\Delta X_{j,t}$. This variable is bounded within the unit interval.

Capital Budgeting and Firm-specific Stock Return Variation 103

We analogously define *past outside financing* as

$$d\,\&\,e_i = \max\left[0, \min\left[\frac{\sum_{j\in i, t\in[1990,1992]}(\Delta LD_{j,t}+\Delta SD_{j,t} + \Delta E_{j,t})}{\sum_{j\in i, t\in[1990,1992]}\Delta X_{j,t}}, 1\right]\right] \quad (A12)$$

where $\Delta LD_{j,t}$ and $X_{j,t}$ are defined as in (A11), $\Delta SD_{j,t}$ is net new short-term debt and accounts payable from the balance sheets of all firms j in industry i, and $\Delta E_{j,t}$ is net new equity issues by all firms j in industry i, both again from 1990 to 1992. This past outside financing variable is again bounded within the unit interval. In constructing lev_i and $d\&e_i$, we assume new debt or equity to be nil if these variables are not reported in COMPUSTAT but all major financial variables are reported.

As an *alternative estimate of the total value of property, plant and equipment*, we use reported accounting depreciation each year, $DEP_{j,t}$, rather than the assumed 10 percent economic depreciation rate used in (A7). The resulting recursive formula,

$$K_{j,t+1} = K_{j,t} - DEP_{j,t+1} + \frac{\Delta X_{j,t+1}}{\prod_{\tau=0}^{t+1}(1+\pi_\tau)}, \quad (A13)$$

generates an alternative panel of firm-level fixed assets. Using this measure throughout rather than that from (A7) does not qualitatively change our findings.

A.4. Nonlinear Estimation in Table VI

Consider a specification with dependent variable the squared deviation of marginal q from h,

$$(\dot{q}_i - h)^2 = b_\varepsilon \ln\left(\sigma_{\varepsilon,i}^2\right) + b_m \ln\left(\sigma_{m,i}^2\right) + \mathbf{c}' \cdot \mathbf{Z_i} + u_i. \quad (A14)$$

This is equivalent to

$$\dot{q}_i^2 = -h^2 + 2h\dot{q}_i + b_\varepsilon \ln\left(\sigma_{\varepsilon,i}^2\right) + b_m \ln\left(\sigma_{m,i}^2\right) + \mathbf{c}' \cdot \mathbf{Z_i} + u_i. \quad (A15)$$

Our aim is to estimate the vector of parameters $\mathbf{b} = \{h, b_\varepsilon, b_m, \mathbf{c}'\}$ using nonlinear least squares (NLS). In NLS, the following criterion function is minimized with respect to $\mathbf{b}$:

$$Q_i(\mathbf{b}) = \frac{1}{I}[\mathbf{y} - \mathbf{f}(\mathbf{x_1}, \mathbf{x_2}, \ldots, \mathbf{x}_I; \mathbf{b})]'[\mathbf{y} - \mathbf{f}(\mathbf{x_1}, \mathbf{x_2}, \ldots, \mathbf{x}_I; \mathbf{b})]$$

$$= \frac{1}{I}\sum_{i=1}^{I}[y_i - f(\mathbf{x}_i; \mathbf{b})]^2, \quad (A16)$$

where $y_i = \dot{q}_i^2$ and $f(x_i, \mathbf{b}) = -h^2 + 2h\dot{q}_i + b_\varepsilon \ln(\sigma_{\varepsilon,i}^2) + b_\varepsilon \ln(\sigma_{m,i}^2) + \mathbf{c}'\mathbf{Z}_i$. The NLS estimates are computed numerically using the Gauss–Newton algorithm.

Similarly, when the dependent variable is the absolute deviation of the marginal q from one,

$$|\dot{q}_i - h| = b_\varepsilon \ln\left(\sigma_{\varepsilon,i}^2\right) + b_m \ln\left(\sigma_{m,i}^2\right) + \mathbf{c}' \cdot \mathbf{Z_i} + u_i$$

is equivalent to

$$\dot{q}_i^2 = -h^2 + 2h\dot{q}_i + \left(b_\varepsilon \ln\left(\sigma_{\varepsilon,i}^2\right) + b_m \ln\left(\sigma_{m,i}^2\right) + \mathbf{c}' \cdot \mathbf{Z_i} + u_i\right)^2$$

because $(|x|)^2 = x^2$. In this case we estimate $y_i = f(\mathbf{x}_i; \mathbf{b}) + \varepsilon_i$ where $y_i = \dot{q}_i^2$ and

$$f(x_i, \mathbf{b}) = -h^2 + 2h\dot{q}_i + \left(b_\varepsilon \ln\left(\sigma_{\varepsilon,i}^2\right) + b_\varepsilon \ln\left(\sigma_{m,i}^2\right) + \mathbf{c}'\mathbf{Z}_i\right)^2.$$

Other specifications in Table VI and in the robustness checks section are estimated analogously.

REFERENCES

Amemiya, T., 1985, *Advanced Econometrics* (Harvard University Press, Cambridge, MA).

Amihud, Yakov, and Baruch Lev, 1981, Risk reductions as a managerial motive for conglomerate mergers, *Bell Journal of Economics* 12, 605–617.

Black, Fisher, 1986, Noise, *Journal of Finance* 41, 529–543.

Bushman, R., J. Piotroski, and A. Smith, 2002, What determines corporate transparency? Working paper, University of North Carolina.

Collins, Daniel W., S. P. Kothari, and Judy Rayburn, 1987, Firm size and the information content of prices with respect to earnings, *Journal of Accounting and Economics* 9, 111–138.

De Long, J. Bradford, Andrei Shleifer, Lawrence Summers, and Robert J. H. Waldmann 1990, Noise trader risk in financial markets, *Journal of Political Economy* 98, 703–738.

Durnev, Artyom, Randall Morck, Bernard Yeung, and Paul Zarowin, 2001, Does greater firm-specific return variation mean more or less informed stock pricing? Working paper, New York University.

French, Kenneth R., and Richard Roll, 1986, Stock return variances: The arrival of information and the reaction of traders, *Journal of Financial Economics* 17, 5–26.

Grossman, Sanford, and Joseph Stiglitz, 1980, On the impossibility of informationally efficient markets, *American Economic Review* 70, 393–408.

Hadi, A. S., 1992, Identifying multiple outliers in multivariate data, *Journal of the Royal Statistical Society Series B* 54, 761–771.

Hadi, A. S., 1994, A modification of a method for the detection of outliers in multivariate samples, *Journal of the Royal Statistical Society Series B* 56, 393–396.

Jensen, M., 1986, Agency costs of free cash flows, corporate finance and takeovers, *American Economic Review* 76, 323–329.

Khorana, Ajay, and Marc Zenner, 1998, Executive compensation of large acquirers in the 1980s, *Journal of Corporate Finance* 4, 209–240.

Lewellen, Wilbur G., 1971, A pure financial rationale for the conglomerate merger, *Journal of Finance* 26, 521–545.

Matsusaka, John G., and Vikram Nanda, 1994, Internal capital markets and corporate refocusing, *Journal of Financial Intermediation* 11, 176–211.

Capital Budgeting and Firm-specific Stock Return Variation 105

May Don O., 1995, Do managerial motives influence firm risk reduction strategies? *Journal of Finance* 50, 1291–1308.

Morck, Randall, Andrei Shleifer, and Robert W. Vishny, 1990, Do managerial objectives drive bad acquisitions? *Journal of Finance* 45, 31–48.

Morck, Randall, Bernard Yeung, and Wayne Yu, 2000, The information content of stock markets: Why do emerging markets have synchronous stock price movements?, *Journal of Financial Economics* 58, 215–238.

Myers, Stewart C., 1977, Determinants of corporate borrowing, *Journal of Financial Economics* 5, 147–175.

Rajan, Raghuram, Henri Servaes, and Luigi Zingales, 2000, The cost of diversity: The diversification discount and inefficient investment, *Journal of Finance* 55, 35–80.

Roll, Richard, 1986, The hubris hypothesis of corporate takeovers, *Journal of Business* 59, 197–216.

Roll, Richard, 1988, R^2, *Journal of Finance* 43, 541–566.

Scharfstein, David S., and Jeremy C. Stein, 2000, The dark side of internal capital markets: Divisional rent-seeking and inefficient investment, *Journal of Finance* 55, 2537–2564.

Shiller, Robert, 1989, Comovements in stock prices and comovements in dividends, *Journal of Finance* 44, 719–30.

Shleifer, Andrei, 2000, *Inefficient Markets: An Introduction to Behavioral Finance—Clarendon Lectures in Economics* (Oxford University Press, London, U.K.).

Shleifer, Andrei, and Robert W. Vishny, 1997, The limits of arbitrage, *Journal of Finance* 52, 35–55.

Stein, Jeremy C., 1997, Internal capital markets and the competition for corporate resources, *Journal of Finance* 52, 111–133.

Theil, Henri, 1971, *Principles of Econometrics* (Wiley, New York).

Tobin, James, 1982, On the efficiency of the financial system, *Lloyd's Banking Review* 153, 1–15.

Wurgler, Jeffrey, 2000, Financial markets and the allocation of capital, *Journal of Financial Economics* 58, 187–214.

THE JOURNAL OF FINANCE • VOL. LVI, NO. 1 • FEBRUARY 2001

Capital Structures in Developing Countries

LAURENCE BOOTH, VAROUJ AIVAZIAN, ASLI DEMIRGUC-KUNT,
and VOJISLAV MAKSIMOVIC*

ABSTRACT

This study uses a new data set to assess whether capital structure theory is portable across countries with different institutional structures. We analyze capital structure choices of firms in 10 developing countries, and provide evidence that these decisions are affected by the same variables as in developed countries. However, there are persistent differences across countries, indicating that specific country factors are at work. Our findings suggest that although some of the insights from modern finance theory are portable across countries, much remains to be done to understand the impact of different institutional features on capital structure choices.

OUR KNOWLEDGE OF CAPITAL STRUCTURES has mostly been derived from data from developed economies that have many institutional similarities. The purpose of this paper is to analyze the capital structure choices made by companies from developing countries that have different institutional structures.

The prevailing view, for example Mayer (1990), seems to be that financial decisions in developing countries are somehow different. Mayer is the most recent researcher to use aggregate flow of funds data to differentiate between financial systems based on the "Anglo-Saxon" capital markets model and those based on a "Continental-German-Japanese" banking model. However, because Mayer's data comes from aggregate flow of funds data and not from individual firms, there is a problem with this approach. The differences between private, public, and foreign ownership structures have a profound influence on such data, but the differences may tell us little about how profit-oriented firms make their individual financial decisions.

This paper uses a new firm-level database to examine the financial structures of firms in a sample of 10 developing countries. Thus, this study helps determine whether the stylized facts we have learned from studies of developed countries apply only to these markets, or whether they have more general applicability. Our focus is on answering three questions:

* Booth holds the Newcourt Chair in Structured Finance in the Rotman School of Management at the University of Toronto. Aivazian is Professor in the Department of Economics and Rotman School of Management at the University of Toronto. Demirguc-Kunt is a Principal Economist with the World Bank, and Maksimovic is Professor in the School of Business at the University of Maryland. This paper is the product of two independent papers submitted to the journal at approximately the same time, one by Booth and Aivazian and the other by Demirguc Kunt and Maksimovic. Our thanks to former journal editor René Stulz and an anonymous referee for comments that substantially improved on both the original papers. We would like to thank the International Finance Corporation for providing the data necessary for this study.

1. Do corporate financial leverage decisions differ significantly between developing and developed countries?
2. Are the factors that affect cross-sectional variability in individual countries' capital structures similar between developed and developing countries?
3. Are the predictions of conventional capital structure models improved by knowing the nationality of the company?

This last question is particularly important, because different institutional factors, such as tax rates and business risk, can result in different financing patterns, which then show up in firm data as well as the aggregate flow of funds data. Therefore, it is interesting to consider the added value of company analysis versus a simple country classification.

Very few studies have used cross-country comparisons to test theories of corporate financial leverage. Rajan and Zingales (1995) is a notable exception, where they use four key independent variables to analyze the determinants of capital structures across the G-7[1] countries: the tangibility of assets, market-to-book ratio, logarithm of sales as a size proxy, and a measure of profitability.

Our data are for 10 developing countries: India, Pakistan, Thailand, Malaysia, Turkey, Zimbabwe, Mexico, Brazil, Jordan, and Korea. These 10 countries include five former British colonies, two Latin American countries with a common inflationary experience, and three "others." Hence, as well as reflecting the Anglo-Saxon capital markets and the Continental-German-Japanese banking systems, there is a diversity of cultural and economic factors that should severely test whether extant capital structure models are portable.

The paper is organized as follows: Section I discusses the data set and the principal characteristics of the financing patterns in the 10 developing countries. Section II discusses the determinants of capital structure. Section III discusses the estimation of the capital structure model on a country-by-country basis. Section IV analyzes the data as a single data set to compare country factors with "economic factors." Section V concludes and offers suggestions for further research.

I. Data Sources and Macro Financial Information

Our primary source is data collected by the International Finance Corporation (IFC). The IFC data comprise abbreviated balance sheets and income statements for the largest companies in each country from 1980 to 1990, although all time periods are not available for every country. The criteria used by the IFC for choosing the countries were that quality data were available for a reasonably large sample of firms in the period from 1980 to 1991, and that developing countries from every continent were represented.

---

[1] The countries are the United States, Germany, Canada, Italy, France, Japan, and the United Kingdom.

Capital Structures in Developing Countries 89

The IFC collected annual financial statements and in some cases stock price data for a maximum of the 100 largest publicly traded firms in each country for which ongoing data were available throughout the sample period. The IFC chose large publicly traded firms in an effort to obtain high quality financial statements. For some of the smaller countries, fewer than 100 firms are traded or meet the data availability criteria, which resulted in smaller samples. For several countries, high-quality data for the early years of the sample were not available. For these countries, the sample starts after 1980.[2] The IFC database contains stock price data for 8 of the 10 countries. Unfortunately, stock price data are not available for any of the companies from Brazil or Mexico and are only available for some companies and/or years for several other countries.

Another drawback is that there are no data from the sources and uses-of-funds statement, and for most countries there is little useful data going from sales to earnings before tax. The IFC collected the data for reasons other than those of this research. Thus, as a practical matter it is impossible to go back and get data on alternative company variables that other studies have found useful. For example, there is no data on advertising and research and development (R&D) expenses that are known to give rise to intangible assets that are difficult to borrow against. Similarly, the data on corporate income taxes are rudimentary. Therefore, it is impossible to create sophisticated tax variables to handle the effect of loss carry-forwards or other tax incentives. As a result, the analysis cannot be as sophisticated as that contained in the best studies on U.S. data, such as, for example, Bradley, Jarrell, and Kim (1984), Titman and Wessels (1988), and Kale, Noe, and Ramirez (1992).

Despite these weaknesses, the IFC data set is still the most detailed data set available on capital structures in developing countries, and is much more comprehensive, in terms of company coverage, than competing commercial data sets. Moreover, it allows for the calculation of many variables that are known to be relevant from studies of firms in developed countries.

We calculate a firm's total book-debt ratio as its total liabilities divided by total liabilities and net worth. Although this ratio has some problems, it is the only ratio that can be calculated for all 10 countries, since there are no data available on Thailand's current liabilities. For the remaining nine countries, we can calculate long-term liabilities, divided by long-term liabilities plus net worth. For seven countries, we can calculate a market long-term debt ratio by substituting the average equity market value for net worth. These two ratios should help us analyze the empirical validity of capital structure models. Unlike the evidence for the G-7 countries used by Rajan and Zingales (1995), variables such as unfunded pension liabilities and deferred taxes are not a significant part of the liability structure of the companies in our sample.

---

[2] The data are described in detail, together with primary sources, in Singh et al. (1992). Capital structures are analyzed in Glen and Pinto (1994) and Booth (1995).

Table I
Debt Ratios

We define the total-debt ratio as total liabilities divided by total liabilities plus net worth. We define the long-term book-debt ratio as total liabilities minus current liabilities divided by total liabilities minus current liabilities plus net worth. The long-term market-debt ratio substitutes equity market value for net worth in the long-term book-debt ratio definition. The first row is for the complete time period available for each country, the second row is for the common period 1985 to 1987. The data for developing countries were collected by the International Finance Corporation (IFC) and consist primarily of abbreviated balance sheets and income statements for the largest companies in each country. Data for the United States, Japan, Germany, France, Italy, the United Kingdom, and Canada are from Rajan and Zingales (1995, Table IIIa) (note their estimate of the long-term debt ratio includes all nonequity liabilities). For Pakistan, Turkey, and Zimbabwe, we estimate debt ratios over the larger sample that includes firms without market-to-book or tangibility ratios.

	No. of Firms	Time Period	Total Debt Ratio (%)	Long-term Book-debt Ratio (%)	Long-term Market-debt Ratio (%)
Brazil	49	1985–1991	30.3	9.7	N/A
		1985–1987	30.7	8.4	N/A
Mexico	99	1984–1990	34.7	13.8	N/A
		1985–1987	35.4	15.6	N/A
India	99	1980–1990	67.1	34.0	34.7
		1985–1987	66.1	35.7	36.7
South Korea	93	1980–1990	73.4	49.4	64.3
		1985–1987	72.8	50.3	59.3
Jordan	38	1983–1990	47.0	11.5	18.6
		1985–1987	44.7	10.9	20.1
Malaysia	96	1983–1990	41.8	13.1	7.1
		1985–1987	40.9	13.1	7.7
Pakistan	96	1980–1987	65.6	26.0	18.9
		1985–1987	65.2	32.5	17.6
Thailand	64	1983–1990	49.4	N/A	N/A
		1985–1987	50.9	N/A	N/A
Turkey	45	1983–1990	59.1	24.2	10.8
		1985–1987	61.8	24.5	10.8
Zimbabwe	48	1980–1988	41.5	13.0	26.3
		1985–1987	40.3	11.4	26.0
United States	2,580	1991	58	37	28
Japan	514	1991	69	53	29
Germany	191	1991	73	38	23
France	225	1991	71	48	41
Italy	118	1991	70	47	46
United Kingdom	608	1991	54	28	19
Canada	318	1991	56	39	35

N/A: Not Available.

Table I provides summary data on the distribution of the three capital structure ratios across the 10 developing countries. For comparison, the table also includes the G-7 economies reported in Rajan and Zingales (1995). For the developing countries, we estimate the averages from the data for the entire period for all the available companies in each country.[3]

Based on total liabilities, the book-debt ratio varies from a low of 30.3 percent in Brazil to a high of 73.4 percent in South Korea. The countries seem to fall into a low-debt group, consisting of Brazil, Mexico, Malaysia, and Zimbabwe; a high-debt group, consisting of South Korea, India, and Pakistan; and a middle group consisting of Jordan, Turkey, and Thailand. We find a similar ranking in the long-term debt ratios when we use both book and market data. The only qualification is that companies in Zimbabwe (and to a lesser extent, Jordan) fall into a high-debt group based on market-debt ratios. Overall, except for South Korea (by far the most developed country in our sample), almost all the developing countries have a debt level, regardless of whether it is book or market, that is below the median of the G-7 countries.

We note that the difference between the total book-debt and long-term debt ratios is much more pronounced in developing countries than it is in the developed countries. Consistent with the findings of Demirguc-Kunt and Maksimovic (1999), a major difference between developing and developed countries is that developing countries have substantially lower amounts of long-term debt. To the extent that the theories of capital structure explain capital structures of firms in developed countries (e.g., we assume well-developed legal systems), this difference, in long versus short-term debt, might limit their explanatory power in developing countries.

We also note that the estimates in Table I come from different time periods. For example, the data from Pakistan is for the period 1980 to 1987, but that for Brazil covers 1985 to 1991. This introduces a potential business-cycle bias into the debt estimates, because book-debt ratios tend to increase during recessions and fall during expansionary periods. For this reason, beneath the estimates for the full time period we include the estimates for the single common period, 1985 to 1987. Although this three-year period is not likely to be a full business cycle, each country's debt-ratio estimate is substantially the same as for the full period. This finding indicates that the problem of differing time periods across countries is not likely to bias the estimates.

When we examine Tables I and II, we see that our sample contains a large proportion of the listed companies in all the countries except for Brazil and India. Table II also shows the percentage of equity market capitalization for all the companies included in the IFC Emerging Stock Markets Database. We note that in 1986, the sample of companies in the IFC Emerging Stock Markets Database formed a significant proportion of the total equity capitalization in all the economies in our sample, ranging from a low of 28.9 percent for Brazil to a high of 63.8 percent for Malaysia. The capitalization ratios for our sample should be at least as high, because our data contain

---

[3] The analysis makes extensive use of ratios, which sometimes results in extreme outliers. To alleviate the problem of spurious results based on these outliers, we discard all values that are at least three standard deviations from the average value for that country.

Table II
Macro Financial Data

The data are from the *Emerging Stock Market Fact Book* (International Finance Corporation, 1995), *Trends in Developing Economies: Extracts, Emerging Capital Markets*, Volume 2, (World Bank, 1993), *International Financial Statistics* (International Monetary Fund, 1999), and *World Development Report* (The World Bank, 1992). Turnover ratio is the value of stocks actually traded expressed as a percentage of the average total value of listed stocks. The Number and Value of Stocks pertain to stocks in the IFC Emerging Markets Database: a: 1986 to 1990; b: 1983 to 1985; c: 1987 to 1990; d: 1982 to 1985. Liquid liabilities/GDP data were provided by Ross Levine and come from King and Levine (1993). Accounting standards and investor protection are rated according to the following key: G = Good, of internationally acceptable quality; A = Adequate; P = Poor; requires reform; S = Functioning securities commission/government agency regulating market activity. The tax data are from the Price-Waterhouse and Ernst and Young, "Doing Business In . . . ," series, except for the United States, which is from Rajan and Zingales (1995, Table IV). The Miller tax term is, $1 - (1 - T_c)(1 - T_e)/(1 - T_i)$, where the equity tax rate is either that on capital gains or dividends.

		Brazil	Mexico	India	South Korea	Jordan	Malaysia	Pakistan	Thailand	Turkey	Zimbabwe	United States
No. of listed companies	1982	1,100	206	3,358	334	86	194	326	81	NA	62	6834
	1990	1,193	199	6,200	669	105	282	487	214	110	57	6342
Stock-market value	1982	10,261	1,719	7,058	4,408	2,845	13,903	877	1,260	NA	355	1,520,167
(millions of $)	1990	16,354	32,725	38,567	110,594	2,001	48,611	2,985	23,896	19,065	2,395	3,072,303
Turnover ratio (%)	1981–1985	44	50	64	68	10	16	NA	23	NA	6[b]	38
(Yearly average)	1986–1990	39	75	63	100	17	18[c]		82		4	68
Number of stocks	1986	29	26	47	23	10	40	9	10	18	11	
in IFC sample	1990	56	54	60	63	25	62	52	34	14	16	
Share of market value	1986	28.9	56.3	45.9	39.3	44.3	63.8	38.0	62.8	39.9	43.8	
of IFC sample (%)	1990	40.1	62.5	40.7	57.4	74.3	46.9	31.9	44.0	23.2	56.5	
GNP per capita ($U.S.)	1990	2,680	2,490	350	5,400	1,240	2,320	380	1,420	1,630	640	22,380
Real GDP growth rate (%)	1980–1985	0.9	1.2	5.2	8.5	NA	5.4	6.4	5.6	4.7	3.4	2.1
	1985–1989	1.9	1.6	6.2	9.6	-1.6	6.9	5.8	10.1	5.3	3.8	3.1
Stock-market value/GDP	1981–1985	9.7	2.1	4.2	6.7	66.3	59.7	3.8	3.9	NA	5.2[d]	52.8
(%) (Yearly Average)	1981–1989	10.0	4.6	5.8	21.3	57.0	68.0	4.8	9.9	NA	9.3[e]	56.2
Inflation rate (%)	1980	84.2	26.4	11.4	28.7	11.1	6.7	11.9	19.7	110.2	5.4	13.5
	1990	2,937.8	26.7	9.0	8.6	16.2	2.6	9.1	5.9	60.3	17.4	5.4
Liquid liabilities/GDP	1980–1989	0.10	0.25	0.40	0.37	1.14	0.94	0.4	0.54	0.24	0.39	0.64
Accounting standards		A	G	A	G	A	G	A	A	A	A	
Investor protection		AS	GS	AS	GS	AS	GS	AS	AS	AS	AS	
Corporate tax rate (T_c)		0.300	0.370	0.450	0.365	0.380	0.350	0.460	0.300	0.250	0.500	0.458
Highest personal tax rate (T_i)		0.250	0.400	0.400	0.500	0.450	0.400	0.350	0.370	0.550	0.600	0.358
Miller tax adv. of interest to dividends		0.142	0.482	0.000	0.635	0.380	-0.083	0.460	0.300	-0.360	0.000	0.450
Miller tax adv. of interest to cap. gains		0.300	0.203	0.340	0.794	0.380	-0.083	0.610	-0.110	-0.360	0.125	0.450

NA: Not Available.

more companies for each country than does the IFC Emerging Stock Markets Database, and our data pertain to the largest companies in each country. Hence, in terms of both the number of companies and equity market capitalization, our sample contains a significant proportion of the listed companies in these countries. Moreover, this coverage is much broader than that of other databases, which include some firms from developing countries, such as Worldscope.

It is not always clear whether the differences in book-debt ratios across countries reflect the differences in optimal capital structure policies, or differences in accounting practices. All countries in our sample, except for Korea and Thailand, follow accounting practices consistent with North American Generally Accepted Accounting Principles (GAAP). These principles flow from the capital markets perspective of Anglo-Saxon countries, which emphasize the information needed by external creditors. In contrast, Korea and Thailand use accounting systems similar to those of Germany and Japan, which reflect a banking orientation. One major difference between the two systems is that North American GAAP relies on fair-market valuation; the German and Japanese systems rely on strict historic cost accounting.

Because of these accounting differences, it is not always easy to compare financial statements across countries. For example, companies in Germany, Japan, South Korea, and Thailand might seem to be more leveraged than those in the United States, Canada, Brazil, and Mexico. This is because the first group uses strict historic cost accounting, which values many assets below their current market value. In contrast, and particularly for countries such as Brazil and Mexico, which have high inflation rates, adjustments to market values are especially important. These accounting differences could have an impact, especially on the book-debt ratios, although their impact on the market-value debt ratios is moot.

Table II provides information obtained from the IFC Emerging Stock Markets Fact Book on the quality of accounting standards for our sample of countries. Out of three possible quality rankings on accounting standards, most of the countries in our sample received a ranking of "adequate." Mexico, South Korea, and Malaysia received a ranking of "good." The table also indicates that all countries in our sample have either a functioning securities commission or an equivalent government agency.

Table II also provides some basic institutional information on macroeconomic variables. Several of the countries, such as Jordan, Brazil, and Mexico, have experienced relatively weak real economic growth. Others, such as Thailand and South Korea, show very high real-growth rates over the sample period. Although all of the countries have had relatively high inflation rates, Brazil and Mexico have been classic hyperinflationary environments. There are also unique combinations, such as low-inflation, low-growth countries like Jordan, low-inflation, high-growth countries like Malaysia, high-inflation, low-growth countries like Brazil and Mexico, and high-inflation, high-growth countries like South Korea, and there are middle-ground countries. Such a heterogeneity of economic environments poses a severe test for any model, even though macroeconomic variables supposedly play no role in most capital structure models. Certainly these factors do not affect the personal versus corporate leverage decision that is at the heart of the Modigliani and Miller (1958) capital structure framework.

Table II indicates that there are greater differences in financial-market institutions among the countries in our sample than there are in those of the G-7 countries studied by Rajan and Zingales (1995). For example, the ratio of stock market capitalization to GDP is a good approximation for the importance of the equity market. This ratio varies from a low of 2.1 percent in Mexico to a high of 78.5 percent in Malaysia. In most countries, the ratio of stock market capitalization to GDP increases over time, but for some countries the trend is imperceptible. We note that the two highest GDP growth countries, South Korea and Thailand, have the most dramatic jump in stock market capitalization from 6.7 percent and 3.9 percent of GDP to 39.6 percent and 17.4 percent of GDP, respectively. Over a similar period the market capitalization in the lowest-growth country, Jordan, declined from 66.3 percent to 44.5 percent of GDP.

Although the actual amount of equity capitalization is important, so too is the volume of transactions. If a large amount of equity is not traded, it can be just as inhibiting to corporate financing as a small amount that is traded. The trading statistics indicate that several of the countries have active markets with turnover ratios equal to that of the United States (about 55 percent). For several countries, the turnover ratios are significantly lower. If we put the turnover ratios together with the market capitalization data, we see that the equity markets appear to be viable in South Korea and Thailand; that Jordan and Malaysia have relatively large amounts of equities available that are not traded very often; that Brazil, India, and Mexico trade a relatively small number of equities quite actively; and that Pakistan, Zimbabwe, and Turkey have relatively limited equity markets combined with lower levels of trading. It is important to note that the equity market data on the last three countries is sporadic, consisting of data limited for the number of years or companies.

Studies of corporate financing in advanced industrial economies, such as those by Mayer (1990) and Rajan and Zingales (1995), examine the differences in the development of banks versus financial markets as possible determinants of capital structure. However, as the Rajan and Zingales study shows, the relative importance of banking is less indicative of differences in corporate leverage than it is of differences in the relative amounts of private financing (bank loans) and arms-length financing through open-market securities.[4]

---

[4] Demirguc-Kunt and Maksimovic (1996) find a negative relation between the level of stock market development and the ratios of both long- and short-term debt to total equity of firms, and a positive relation between bank development and leverage. Furthermore, in developing countries, large firms become more leveraged as stock markets develop, but smaller firms do not appear to be significantly affected by market development.

Capital Structures in Developing Countries 95

The financial systems in our sample exhibit a variety of models. At one extreme, commercial banks in Malaysia and Pakistan are universal banks that are involved in merchant banking as well as commercial lending. At the other extreme, in countries such as India and Zimbabwe, banking and commerce are separated. Separate institutions provide different services.

Table II gives a summary measure of financial intermediary development and liquid liabilities as a percentage of GDP. The principal features of the financial systems and the extent of government intervention in credit allocation in each country are described in the Appendix. Table II indicates a relatively high development of the financial intermediary sector in Jordan, Malaysia, and Thailand. South Korea, Zimbabwe, Pakistan, and India have an average level of development. Turkey, Mexico, and Brazil show a relatively low level of development, but even in these countries, the banking systems are complex. For example, in Turkey in 1980, there were over 40 institutions, including publicly owned banks, private commercial banks, development banks, and foreign banks. However, in most of the countries, the banking system is concentrated. The top three or four banks frequently hold a substantial share of financial assets. (The ratio ranges from 100 percent in the case of Zimbabwe to 20 percent for South Korea in 1990.)

In developing countries, the distinction between bank and market-based financing is further complicated by extensive government ownership and regulation of the financial system. Controls on the prices in security markets, along with government-directed credit programs to preferred sectors, could have a significant impact on corporate financing patterns.[5] We detail each country's directed credit policy in the Appendix. However, to illustrate the types of distortions that occur, we note that in India, government-imposed ceilings on interest rates could have led to a greater reliance on debt financing. However, there were also controls on the issue price of equity which might have forced many companies to issue convertible debt to recoup part of their loss due to equity underpricing.[6] Similar credit policy measures are at work in most of the 10 developing countries.

La Porta et al. (1998) develop indexes for a large sample of countries to study the quality of legal protection for shareholders and creditors. They find that investor rights tend to be stronger in Anglo-Saxon common-law countries as compared to French civil-law countries, whereas German civil-law countries fall somewhere in the middle. La Porta et al. also find that

---

[5] Financial liberalization policies in the 1990s eased controls in some of these countries. Note also that most corporate debt in India is convertible into common shares. Controls on the issue price of equity in India was phased out in 1992.

[6] Glen and Pinto (1994, page 49) note "Most (Indian) corporate debt is really quasi-equity, being convertible into shares. This is explicable by the earlier controls on the issue price of shares. Partially convertible debentures were configured in such a way that the pure debt portion would carry a very low interest rate, say 12% when the market rate was 19%. The investor, who cared only for the equity portion (because of the huge initial gain owing to equity price controls) would sell the nonconvertible portion to a financial institution at a discount."

better investor protection in common-law countries is not offset, but rather reinforced, by stronger law enforcement. They also find that companies in countries with weak investor rights tend to have higher ownership concentration.

According to La Porta et al. (1998), overall creditor rights for our sample of countries are stronger in India, Malaysia, Pakistan, Thailand, Zimbabwe, and South Korea, and weaker for Brazil, Jordan, Mexico, and Turkey. Shareholder rights are also strongest in our sample of common-law countries and weakest for our civil-law countries. The only exception is Brazil, which has shareholder rights similar to those of common-law countries.

When we review some of the salient institutional factors, it is clear that there can be no simple "matching" of countries into neat, self-contained boxes. Our sample of developing countries encompasses too wide a range of institutional characteristics. Therefore, it is not surprising that Tables I and II show no strong relation between measures of bank and stock market development, broad macroeconomic factors, and aggregate capital structures for developing countries. For example, Malaysia, South Korea, and Thailand all have high measures of bank and stock market development, but different overall leverage ratios.

Table II also presents data on the tax advantages of debt financing for each country. For all 10 countries, interest on corporate debt is tax deductible, which induces a corporate tax advantage for debt financing. This corporate tax shield ranges from a high of 0.55 in Pakistan to a low of 0.3 in Thailand.

In contrast to the corporate tax shield, the Miller (1977) gains-to-leverage formula,

$$1 - \frac{(1 - T_c)(1 - T_e)}{(1 - T_i)} \tag{1}$$

takes into account not just the corporate tax rate, T_c, but also the personal tax rate on interest income, T_i, and equity income (T_e). By assuming the highest personal tax rate for equity income from listed securities, we can estimate the Miller tax shield for each of the countries in our sample with equity income coming from either dividends or capital gains.

Table II indicates that debt has a "Miller" tax advantage over equity in most of these developing countries. The possible exceptions are Malaysia and Turkey, and perhaps India and Zimbabwe, depending on source income. However, it is important to note that the ranking based on corporate tax-shield values differs from that on Miller tax shields. For example, Zimbabwe and India have high tax-shield values based purely on corporate income taxes, but low Miller tax advantages to debt financing when income is paid out in dividends. On the other hand, South Korea moves from a medium ranking on corporate tax-shield value to a very high Miller value. Some countries like Pakistan and Turkey remain high on both measures. Notice that there

Capital Structures in Developing Countries   97

Table III
Macroeconomic Influences on Capital Structure Choice

The table shows the results of regressions of various debt measures against a set of independent macroeconomic variables. We define the total-debt ratio as total liabilities divided by total liabilities plus net worth. We define the long-term book-debt ratio as total liabilities minus current liabilities, divided by total liabilities minus current liabilities plus net worth. The long-term market debt ratio substitutes equity market value for net worth in the long-term book-debt ratio definition. Macroeconomic variables are as defined in Table II and the Miller tax variable as in the text. The data for developing countries were collected by the International Finance Corporation (IFC) and consist primarily of abbreviated balance sheets and income statements for the largest companies in each country. Data for the United States, Japan, Germany, France, Italy, the United Kingdom, and Canada are from Rajan and Zingales (1995). t-statistics are in parentheses.

	Total-debt Ratio (%)	Long-term Book-debt Ratio (%)	Long-term Market-debt Ratio (%)
Intercept	46.05	20.32	31.5
	(3.49)	(1.35)	(1.86)
Stock market value/GDP	−0.16	−0.02	−0.03
	(−1.22)	(0.10)	(−0.19)
Liquid liabilities/GDP	0.14	0.17	−0.17
	(0.86)	(0.09)	(−0.98)
Real GDP growth rate	1.18	1.2	−0.11
	(0.96)	(−0.75)	(−0.07)
Inflation rate	−0.1	−0.1	0.01
	(−1.15)	(−1.18)	(0.02)
Miller tax term	0.21	0.26	0.3
	(1.92)	(2.00)	(1.09)
Number of observations	17	16	14
Adjusted R^2	27.5%	22.4%	25.8%

is a positive association between tax-shield ranking and the debt ratios for South Korea and Pakistan (in the high-debt country group) and for Malaysia (a low-debt country).[7]

Another interesting point is that, unlike the United States, although all these countries allow loss carryforwards, none allows loss carrybacks. As a result, a succession of profitable years with significant tax payments could be negated by a succession of bad years. The absence of loss carrybacks reduces the tax advantage of debt financing for a high-risk firm. It should also be remembered that the tax code has many attributes aside from the statutory tax rates and may not be well enforced.

Table III offers some preliminary conclusions on the relation between aggregate capital structure and institutional characteristics. These conclusions are generated by pooling the data from the developing and developed

---

[7] It is possible that the marginal taxpayer lives in another country. In this case, foreign, rather than domestic, tax rates would apply to the tax calculations. However, cross-border financing for these countries was not significant prior to 1990.

countries and creating an enhanced sample of 17 countries. Table III shows the results of the cross-sectional regressions in which the dependent variables are the three debt measures defined in Table I, and the independent variables are the main macroeconomic factors listed in Table II, plus the Miller (1977) tax-shield value.

The obvious caveat to the results in Table III is that with only 17 countries, the standard errors of the coefficients are too large for the coefficients to be judged significant at normal levels. This is particularly true when the sample size shrinks to 14, when we use the market long-term debt ratio. However, some interesting generalizations emerge; for example, all three debt ratios vary negatively with the equity market capitalization, whereas, except for the long-term market-debt ratio, the debt ratios vary positively with the proportion of liquid liabilities to GDP.

As equity markets become more developed, they become a viable option for corporate financing and firms make less use of debt financing. Similarly, more highly developed debt markets are associated with higher private sector debt ratios. The fact that we do not see this relation for the long-term market-debt ratio could be because we cannot calculate this ratio for companies from Brazil, Mexico, and Thailand, and as a result, companies from these low-debt countries are not included in the estimates.

Higher real economic growth tends to cause the two book-debt ratios to increase, and higher inflation causes them to decrease. This implies that companies can borrow against real, but not inflationary growth prospects. Despite inflation pushing up the monetary value of the firm's assets, the higher interest rate and monetary risk caused by inflation causes book-debt ratios to fall. These results do not hold when we use market values to calculate the debt ratio. However, the coefficients are not significant. The results could be due to sample selection problems, particularly because neither of the two hyperinflationary countries, Brazil and Mexico, have stock market data.

Finally, the Miller (1977) tax term is significant in two of the three regression equations. This indicates that more debt is used in those countries that assign a higher tax advantage to debt financing. This is interesting, because most studies use data from a single country, in which all companies face similar marginal tax rates. As a result, there is usually little heterogeneity in marginal tax rates.[8]

The institutional data and regression analysis offer tantalizing glimpses of what country factors really mean. Is Brazil special because it is Brazil, or because it is a hyperinflationary country with low real growth and poorly developed financial markets? We cannot answer this question definitively. However, there is enough circumstantial evidence to indicate that this is an important topic for future research.

---

[8] See Graham (1996).

Capital Structures in Developing Countries   99

II. Capital Structure Determinants
and Aggregate Values

We choose variables to explain capital structure differences by considering the three principal theoretical models of capital structure: the Static Trade-off Model (STO), the Pecking-Order Hypothesis (POH), and the Agency Theoretic Framework (ATF). In each model, the choice between debt and equity depends on both firm-specific and institutional factors. In the STO model, capital structure moves towards a target that reflects tax rates, asset type, business risk, profitability, and the bankruptcy code. In the ATF, potential conflicts of interest between inside and outside investors determines an optimal capital structure that trades off agency costs against other financing costs. The nature of the firm's assets and growth opportunities are important factors in the importance of these agency costs. In the POH, financial market imperfections are central. Transaction costs and asymmetric information link the firm's ability to undertake new investments to its internally generated funds. If the firm must rely on external funds, as in the Myers and Majluf (1984) model, then it prefers debt to equity due to the lesser impact of information asymmetries.

Empirically, distinguishing between these hypotheses has proven difficult. In cross-sectional tests, variables that describe the POH can be classified as STO or ATF variables and vice versa. Moreover, in time-series tests, Shyam-Sunder and Myers (1999) show that many of the current empirical tests lack sufficient statistical power to distinguish between the models. As a result, recent empirical research has focused on explaining capital structure choice by using cross-sectional tests and a variety of variables that can be justified using any or all of the three models. We consider in turn the impact of taxes, agency conflicts, financial distress, and the impact of informational asymmetries.

A. The Impact of Taxes

For individual firms, defining tax variables is difficult, because the marginal value of the tax shield should be either zero or positive for all firms. To serve as a proxy for these interactions, we calculate an average tax rate from data on both earnings before and earnings after tax. We do this for all countries except Malaysia, for which we use earnings before tax and taxes paid, as this is the only available data.

The advantage of the average tax rate is that it includes the impact of tax loss carryforwards and the use of corporations as a conduit for income flows. These average tax rates vary from a low of 13.9 percent in Brazil to a high of 40 percent in Zimbabwe, and are closely correlated with the statutory tax rates. The only notable exception is Pakistan, where the statutory tax rate of 46 percent works out to an average tax rate for our sample of firms of only 13.2 percent. This is a reminder that although the tax rate is important, so too is the base to which it is applied.

B. Agency Costs and Financial Distress

Conflicts between principals (shareholders) and their agents (managers) can also affect capital structure choice. For example, the decision to use large amounts of outside financing, such as common equity, can generate agency costs of managerial discretion. As Jung, Kim, and Stulz (1996) show, when management pursues growth objectives, external common equity is valuable for firms with strong investment opportunities, because management and shareholder interests coincide. In contrast, for firms without strong investment opportunities, debt serves to limit the agency costs of managerial discretion as explained by Jensen (1986) and Stulz (1990), and recently shown by Berger, Ofek, and Yermack (1997).

Although the use of debt controls the agency costs of managerial discretion, it also generates its own agency costs. A highly debt-financed firm might forgo good investment opportunities due to the debt overhang problem analyzed by Jensen and Meckling (1976) and Myers (1977). The problem is that with risky debt, the debt holders can share in any profitable future investment returns, thereby extracting some of the net present value. This transfer of wealth can cause the shareholders to turn down good investment opportunities. The value of the forgone opportunities plus the costs of enforcing contractual provisions constitute the agency cost of debt. As Aivazian and Callen (1980) point out, if recontracting costs are low, the underinvestment incentives are reduced. Moreover, to the extent that these recontracting costs differ across countries due to differences in legal systems, we would expect agency costs to differ. As a result, the solution to the capital structure problem may differ across countries, even though the theoretical model may be equally valid.

Improvements in a firm's growth opportunities lead to an increase in the agency costs of debt and a reduction in the agency costs of managerial discretion. Smith and Watts (1992) provide empirical evidence, using U.S. data, that support a negative relation between leverage and growth opportunities. Titman and Wessels (1988) also estimate a negative empirical relation between leverage and R&D expenses, in which R&D is frequently treated as a proxy for growth opportunities. Where the potential for corporate opportunism is high, for example, for small firms with largely intangible assets, debt levels will be low and will consist mainly of short-term debt.

The costs of financial distress in the STO model are closely related to the same factors that are important from the ATF. For example, the costs of financial distress can be thought of as the product of the probability of entering a distressed situation and the costs of resolving such a situation should it occur. A high proportion of hard tangible assets then increases debt capacity, not only because of the reduction in distress costs, but also because it can reduce the proportion of growth opportunities, and as a result the agency costs of managerial discretion.

We estimate the probability of financial distress as the variability of the return on assets over the available time period. This is our business risk proxy. We calculate the return on assets as the earnings before interest and

Capital Structures in Developing Countries   101

tax divided by total assets. Increased variability in the return on assets implies an increase in the short-term operational component of business risk. The drawback is that this variable cannot capture longer-term risks, such as competitive entry.

Table IV shows the averages for the business-risk proxy. The averages vary from a low of 3.04 percent for South Korea to a high of 9 percent for Brazil. Note from Table II that the lowest business-risk countries, South Korea and Malaysia, also have the highest real-growth rates, but the highest business-risk countries, Brazil and Jordan, have the lowest real-growth rates. A drawback to the business-risk proxy is that it is estimated as a single value for all years. By identifying each firm, it thus acts like a dummy variable in the time series estimates.

The tangibility of the firm's assets and its market-to-book ratio are proxies for agency costs and the costs of financial distress. The more tangible the firm's assets, the greater its ability to issue secured debt and the less information revealed about future profits. Myers (1977) notes that high market-to-book ratios indicate the presence of Miller and Modigliani (1961) growth opportunities, which can be thought of as real options. Given the agency costs attached to these options, it is relatively more difficult to borrow against them than against tangible fixed assets. Scott (1977) provides a similar rationale for the importance of collateral to secure a loan.

We define the tangibility of assets as total assets minus current assets, divided by total assets. Rajan and Zingales (1995) use a similar definition. However, given our three measures of debt financing, the influence of tangibility will differ between the long-term and total-debt ratios as firms match the maturity of their debt to the tangibility of their assets. We define the market-to-book ratio as the equity market value divided by net worth.

Table IV shows that the tangibility of assets is similar across countries at about 40 percent, with Brazil an outlier at 67.5 percent. In contrast, the market-to-book ratio varies from a discount in Pakistan, South Korea, and Zimbabwe to a premium in Malaysia and Thailand. South Korea, like Japan, uses strict historic cost accounting so that hidden assets, such as land, can exist on the balance sheet. South Korea also allows reserves to smooth out earnings, which could explain its low business-risk value. The market-to-book ratio in South Korea also shows a significant upward trend over time. These factors imply that the market-to-book ratio is only imperfectly correlated with Tobin's Q ratio, and that the degree of correlation will differ across countries according to the accounting principles adopted.

C. Financing Hierarchies and the Pecking-Order Hypothesis

Myers and Majluf (1984) point out that high-quality firms can reduce the costs of informational asymmetries by resorting to external financing only if financing cannot be generated internally. If external financing is necessary, the same argument implies that firms should issue debt before considering external equity. Informational asymmetries thus provide a justification for a

Table IV

Independent Variables: Averages and Standard Deviations

The data were collected by the International Finance Corporation (IFC) and consist primarily of abbreviated balance sheets and income statements for the largest companies in each country from 1980 to 1990, although all time periods are not available for each country. We estimate the average tax rate from before- and after-tax income. We measure asset tangibility by total assets less current assets divided by total assets. We define return on assets as earnings before tax divided by total assets, and measure business risk as the standard deviation of the return on assets. Size is the natural logarithm of sales both in local currency units and converted to U.S. dollars at year-end exchange rates divided by 100. The market-to-book-ratio is the market value of equity divided by the book value of equity. For each variable, the first row is the average and the second is the standard deviation.

	Brazil	Mexico	India	South Korea	Jordan	Malaysia	Pakistan	Thailand	Turkey	Zimbabwe
Tax rate	13.9	26.3	21.8	29.9	16.3	32.2	12.4	28.8	29.7	28.9
	16.7	57.1	20.9	19.7	17.9	44.4	20.1	8.7	18.5	21.2
Business risk	9.0	5.6	4.5	3.1	7.5	4.5	6.2	3.4	5.5	5.7
	4.7	2.9	2.6	1.8	4.2	3.3	3.8	2.7	2.6	5.7
Asset tangibility	67.5	32.8	41	48.9	47.3	57.6	38.2	36	41.1	44.4
	18.5	30.1	17.5	15.2	21.5	21.8	19.8	17.2	19.2	12.7
Size (local currency)	0.112	0.114	0.142	0.117	0.076	0.115	0.06	0.136	0.103	0.103
	0.043	0.017	0.009	0.008	0.015	0.013	0.010	0.011	0.017	0.010
Size (U.S. dollars)	0.131	0.112	0.184	0.189	0.098	0.174	0.171	0.167	0.172	0.167
	0.010	0.014	0.010	0.009	0.003	0.016	0.011	0.013	0.017	0.016
Return on assets	6.7	8.1	7.1	3.7	6.8	6.9	9.4	13	9.9	11.6
	11.5	8.1	6.7	3.8	10.6	7.3	9.7	7.1	8.8	8.8
Market-to-book ratio	N/A	N/A	1.4	0.7	1.4	2.3	0.9	3.2	1.9	0.6
			1.1	0.7	0.7	1.8	0.7	2.1	1.3	0.6

N/A: Not Available.

financing-hierarchies approach. Donaldson (1963) reaches a similar conclusion using a managerial theory of the firm and the agency costs of managerial discretion. In both cases, capital structure choice depends on the firm's investment opportunities and its profitability. Highly profitable firms might be able to finance their growth by using retained earnings and by maintaining a constant debt ratio. In contrast, less profitable firms will be forced to resort to debt financing.

In general, highly profitable slow-growing firms should generate the most cash, but less profitable fast-growing firms will need significant external financing. Higgins (1977) discusses these links between sales growth, profitability, and external financing needs. We note that there may be a further link with the agency cost arguments if the existence of strong investment opportunities is correlated with current levels of profitability.

We define the return on assets (ROA) as the earnings before tax divided by total assets. We use the ROA as our profitability measure, because it is the only variable that can be calculated across all 10 countries. Average profitability ranges from a low of 3.7 percent in South Korea to a high of 13 percent in Thailand. The South Korean figure looks low, but like the market-to-book ratio, it changes over time. Note that the same strict historic cost accounting and conservatism that produce hidden assets also tend to result in an understatement of profits.

D. Empirical Model

The basic empirical model is a cross-sectional regression of the three different measures of the firm's debt ratio against the firm's tax rate, the standard deviation of its return on assets, the tangibility of its assets, the natural logarithm of its sales, its return on assets, and its market-to-book ratio. This estimating equation extends the model used by Rajan and Zingales (1995) for the G-7 countries to include an average tax rate and business-risk variables.

Following Rajan and Zingales (1995) we include size as an independent variable, because it is associated with survival and the agency costs of both debt and equity. We define size in the conventional way as the natural logarithm of sales rescaled by multiplying by 100. Table IV presents means and standard deviations for all the independent variables.

III. What the Data Tell Us

Given the sometimes limited number of companies for some countries and time periods, we first use panel data techniques for the sample of firms within each country. Accordingly, the empirical model is expressed as

$$\frac{D_{i,t}}{V_{i,t}} = (\alpha_i + \alpha_t) + \sum_{j=1}^{n} \beta_j X_{i,j,t} \, \varepsilon_{i,t}, \qquad (2)$$

where $X_{i,j,t}$ is the *j*th explanatory variable for the *i*th firm at time *t*, $\varepsilon_{i,t}$ is the random error term for firm *i* at time *t*, $D_{i,t}/V_{i,t}$ is one of the three debt ratios for the *i*th firm at time *t* and α is the intercept. Note that the coefficients on the independent variables for each country are assumed to be the same, but the regression intercept $(\alpha_i + \alpha_t)$ can vary across companies and over time.

The simplest model is to pool the data in which case there is one fixed intercept. However, it is unlikely that the capital structure models are fully specified. For example, there are no available proxies for factors such as the magnitude of distress costs or industry effects that we know are important. As well, the data set is unbalanced, as the number of observations for each company is different. As a result, a simple pooling might not result in either efficient or unbiased parameter estimates.

The fixed-effects model allows us to use all the data, while the intercept is allowed to vary across firms and/or time. In this way the effects of omitted explanatory variables can be captured in the changing company intercept. Also, by including a fixed-time effect, the model automatically assesses the impact of the inflationary environment in Mexico and Brazil. In both cases, the marginal significance of the explanatory variables can still be tested. However, as Hsiao (1986) points out, in the presence of measurement error the fixed-effects model can produce more biased estimators than simple pooling. For this reason, we report both the pooled ordinary least squares as well as the fixed-effects estimates.[9]

Tables V through VII give the results based on the fullest possible data set with each explanatory variable included. However, because the tangibility or market-to-book data is missing for Zimbabwe, Pakistan, and Turkey, the number of observations is dramatically reduced. To increase sample size for these three countries, we present the estimates (as row B) without the constraining variable.

We draw three general conclusions from Tables V through VII. First, the adjusted R^2s look reasonable, varying significantly across countries (partly due to the differing degrees of freedom). Second, the adjusted R^2 for the fixed-effects model is uniformly higher than for the simple pooling model, indicating the existence of omitted variables. Finally, the results indicate that there is a story to tell about the determinants of capital structure for each country, as there are many significant *t* statistics. However, the story seems to vary across countries.

For the total book-debt ratio in Table V, the adjusted R^2 for the simple pooling model varies from 19 percent to 60 percent. This is in line with results obtained elsewhere, where the quality of the data is better. Only for Zimbabwe do the results look weak. Individually, each set of estimates would not look out of place in a separate country analysis.

---

[9] A third model, the random effects model, assumes that the company specific intercept is a random variable and uses a generalized least squares estimation procedure. For our sample, the Hausman (1978) specification test indicated that in almost all cases the assumptions of the model are violated.

Capital Structures in Developing Countries   105

However, the impact of the independent variables is not completely uniform across countries. For example, the sign on the average tax rate is generally negative, but turns positive for three countries when the fixed effects are introduced. Similarly, the sign on asset tangibility varies between the different estimation techniques, indicating that it is highly correlated with the fixed effects; only for Brazil, India, Pakistan, and Turkey is it consistently negative. This would suggest that knowing the industrial composition of these companies would be very useful. The coefficient on business risk is negative for six countries and positive for four. The size variable is generally positive and highly significant for many of the countries, particularly when the fixed effects are added. The sign on the market-to-book ratio is generally positive, except for South Korea and Pakistan. For South Korea, it becomes positive when fixed effects are allowed.

The most successful of the independent variables is profitability, as it is consistently negative and highly significant. The only exception is for the reduced Zimbabwe sample. We note also that, except for Thailand, the average tax rate is determined from pre- and after-tax income. Despite the existence of tax loss carryforwards, when firms are profitable they pay taxes, but from the data it is apparent that when they lose money they do not get a refund. As a result, the tax rate seems to be a proxy for profitability, rather than for tax-shield effects. This could explain why the tax variable, like the profitability variable, varies inversely with the amount of debt financing.

Overall, the strongest result is that profitable firms use less total debt. The strength of this finding is striking; it holds for all but the restricted Zimbabwe sample. Also, the size of the coefficient is generally around -0.6 for the fixed-effects model, indicating that a 10 percent difference in profitability is associated with a 6 percent reduction in the debt ratio. Cross-sectional differences across countries could then largely result from estimation error.

The importance of profitability is related to the significant agency and informational asymmetry problems in these countries, and to the relatively undeveloped nature of their long-term bond markets. It is also possible that profitability is correlated with growth opportunities, so that the negative correlation between profitability and leverage is a proxy for the difficulty in borrowing against intangible growth opportunities.[10] For the static trade-off model, which holds growth opportunities fixed, we would expect leverage to increase with profitability.

The results in Table VI for the long-term book-debt ratio are similar to those for the total-debt ratio, although in some cases a little weaker. The major exception is for the tangibility ratio, where the results are largely reversed. For the total-debt ratio, tangibility tends to be associated with decreases in the debt ratio, but with the long-term debt ratio, it is associated with increases in the debt ratio. This implies that a firm with more tangible

---

[10] Our thanks to Professor René Stulz, for pointing this out. See Jung et al. (1996) and Shyam-Sunder and Myers (1999).

Table V
Total Book-debt Ratio

The table shows regressions of total book-debt ratio on firm-specific variables. The first row is for the simple pooling, the second for the fixed-effects model. The R^2 for the pooling and fixed-effects models are adjusted for degrees of freedom. We could not calculate intercepts for the fixed-effects model, because it was estimated indirectly rather than directly, using dummy variables (see Judge et al. (1985)). The business-risk variable acts as a firm dummy and cannot be used in the fixed-effects model. The data were collected by the International Finance Corporation (IFC) and consist primarily of abbreviated balance sheets and income statements for the largest companies in each country from 1980 to 1990, although all time periods are not available for each country. We define the total-debt ratio as total liabilities divided by total liabilities plus net worth. We estimate the average tax rate from before- and after-tax income and measure asset tangibility by total assets less current assets divided by total assets. We define return on assets as earnings before tax divided by total assets. We measure business risk as the standard deviation of the return on assets. Size is the natural logarithm of local currency sales divided by 100. The market-to-book ratio is the market value of equity divided by the book value of equity. The B Set of estimates for Pakistan, Turkey, and Zimbabwe are without the market-to-book and tangibility ratios, respectively, which severely limit sample size. t-statistics are in parentheses.

	Intercept	Average Tax Rate	Asset Tangibility	Business Risk	Size	Return on Assets	Market-to-book Ratio	Observations	R^2
Brazil	0.638	−0.026	−0.45	−0.139	0.132	−0.223		335	31%
	(17.11)	(−0.56)	(−11.82)	(−0.98)	(0.8)	(−5.92)			
		−0.017	−0.392		0.014	−0.22		335	72%
		(−0.43)	(−6.60)		(0.02)	(−3.81)			
Mexico	0.353	−0.036	0.066	1.245	−0.328	−0.616		642	19%
	(8.23)	(−3.67)	(3.43)	(6.07)	(−0.97)	(−8.46)			
		−0.2	−0.244		6.529	−0.627		642	59%
		(−2.51)	(−3.47)		(5.56)	(−8.33)			
India	1.019	−0.095	−0.195	0.043	−1.319	−0.961	0.004	880	31%
	(17.24)	(−4.26)	(−7.93)	(0.30)	(−3.22)	(−14.63)	(1.21)		
		−0.021	−0.261		1.186	−0.664	0.015	880	75%
		(−1.44)	(−7.71)		(1.34)	(−12.70)	(5.06)		
South Korea	0.806	−0.01	−0.128	−1.61	0.938	−1.5	−0.019	965	36%
	(17.94)	(−0.41)	(−6.43)	(−9.17)	(2.45)	(−17.32)	(−4.07)		
		0.029	0.013		1.801	−0.934	0.014	965	74%
		(2.28)	(0.49)		(2.8)	(−13.07)	(2.18)		
Jordan	−0.189	−0.084	−0.126	0.888	7.860	−0.703	0.012	319	60%
	(−4.10)	(−2.06)	(−3.56)	(5.67)	(17.77)	(−9.44)	(6.08)		
		0.046	0.065		19.89	−0.31	0.016	319	88%
		(1.53)	(1.62)		(.24)	(−5.74)	(2.02)		

Capital Structures in Developing Countries 107

Malaysia	0.071 (1.17)	-0.011 (-0.87)	-0.312 (-11.16)	0.361 (1.93)	4.836 (10.54)	-1.30 (-15.36)	0.02 (5.96)	693	46%
		-0.019 (-2.31)	0.062 (1.3)		6.64 (8.33)	-0.52 (-6.74)	0.014 (4.98)	693	80%
A: Pakistan	0.686 (6.8)	-0.182 (-2.90)	-0.092 (-1.62)	-0.15 (-0.47)	2.21 (1.6)	-1.14 (-9.24)	-0.016 (-0.95)	204	45%
		-0.113 (-2.00)	-0.135 (-0.89)		3.376 (1.34)	-0.392 (-2.89)	-0.01 (-0.48)	204	80%
B: Pakistan	0.806 (20.04)	-0.128 (-4.81)	-0.18 (-6.89)	-0.172 (-1.31)	0.809 (1.46)	-1.079 (-19.50)		896	37%
		-0.068 (-.291)	-0.182 (-4.58)		3.192 (2.95)	-0.555 (-11.48)		896	76%
Thailand	0.217 (1.49)	0.251 (2.06)	0.076 (1.25)	-0.794 (-1.95)	2.497 (2.56)	-1.42 (-9.56)	0.015 (3.12)	191	39%
		0.216 (1.73)	0.326 (3.09)		3.855 (0.79)	-0.539 (-2.58)	0.019 (3.61)	191	71%
A: Turkey	0.64 (4.43)	-0.249 (-2.91)	-0.235 (-3.13)	-0.863 (-1.69)	2.110 (1.65)	-0.727 (-4.32)	0.025 (2.29)	58	53%
		-0.127 (-1.14)	0.011 (0.19)		3.243 (0.37)	-0.689 (-2.04)	0.005 (0.16)	58	73%
B: Turkey	0.922 (16.04)	-0.048 (-1.20)	-0.274 (-7.11)	-0.662 (-2.47)	-0.608 (-1.37)	-1.069 (-13.33)		374	42%
		0.048 (1.34)	-0.046 (-0.89)		4.367 (2.94)	-0.854 (-10.07)		374	70%
A: Zimbabwe	1.318 (3.34)	0.109 (0.85)	-0.259 (-1.63)	-2.32 (-2.56)	-7.061 (-2.18)	0.441 (1.57)	-0.051 (-1.74)	54	29%
		0.143 (2.21)	0.02 (0.27)		2.733 (0.76)	0.249 (1.16)	-0.027 (-1.08)	54	89%
B: Zimbabwe	0.268 (3.95)	-0.06 (-1.78)	-0.094 (-0.79)		1.690 (3.63)	-0.301 (-2.94)	0.054 (4.09)	407	7%
		0.0 (-0.04)			1.60 (3.67)	-0.407 (-5.67)	0.045 (3.72)	407	75%

Table VI
Long-term Book-debt Ratio

Regressions of long-term book-debt ratio on firm specific variables. First row is for the simple pooling, the second for the fixed-effects model. The R^2 for the pooling and fixed-effects models are adjusted for degrees of freedom. Intercepts could not be calculated for the fixed-effects model, because it was estimated indirectly rather than directly, using dummy variables (see Judge et al. (1985)). The business-risk variable acts as a firm dummy and cannot be used in the fixed-effects model. The data were collected by the International Finance Corporation (IFC) and consist primarily of abbreviated balance sheets and income statements for the largest companies in each country from 1980 to 1990, although all time periods are not available for each country. The long-term book-debt ratio is defined as total liabilities minus current liabilities divided by total liabilities minus current liabilities plus net worth. The average tax rate is estimated from before- and after-tax income; asset tangibility is measured by total assets less current assets divided by total assets; return on assets is defined as earnings before tax divided by total assets; business risk is measured as the standard deviation of the return on assets; size is the natural logarithm of local currency sales divided by 100; market-to-book ratio is the market value of equity divided by the book value of equity. The B set of estimates for Pakistan, Turkey, and Zimbabwe are without the market-to-book and tangibility ratios, respectively, which severely limit sample size. t-statistics are in parentheses.

	Intercept	Average Tax Rate	Asset Tangibility	Business Risk	Size	Return on Assets	Market-to-book Ratio	Observations	R^2
Brazil	0.161	−0.051	−0.084	−0.212	0.248	−0.135	N/A	330	8%
	(5.81)	(−1.49)	(−2.96)	(−2.01)	(2.01)	(−2.52)			
		−0.021	−0.045		−0.155	−0.109	N/A	330	57%
		(−0.69)	(−0.94)		(−0.23)	(−2.34)			
Mexico	0.138	−0.022	0.042	0.45	0.055	−0.469	N/A	633	9%
	(3.19)	(−2.17)	(2.15)	(2.13)	(0.16)	(−6.36)			
		−0.009	−0.092		5.289	−0.562	N/A	633	63%
		(−1.23)	(−1.45)		(4.98)	(−8.29)			
India	0.211	−0.216	0.428	0.741	0.073	−0.915	0.009	877	43%
	(2.45)	(−6.64)	(11.96)	(3.49)	(0.12)	(−9.51)	(2.98)		
		−0.111	0.116		0.697	−0.662	0.012	877	74%
		(−4.07)	(2.11)		(0.48)	(−7.76)	(2.54)		
Korea	0.545	−0.025	0.208	−1.69	−0.284	−1.66	0.001	970	31%
	(9.03)	(−1.11)	(7.77)	(−7.23)	(−0.55)	(−14.20)	(10.11)		
		0.038	0.316		−4.55	−1.108	0.034	970	61%
		(1.86)	(7.50)		(−4.56)	(−9.99)	(3.41)		
Jordan	−0.447	0.038	0.317	0.522	4.816	−0.031	−0.002	316	44%
	(−9.75)	(0.93)	(9.03)	(3.37)	(11.00)	(−0.42)	(−0.20)		
		0.063	0.189		8.328	−0.147	0.003	316	68%
		(1.51)	(3.36)		(7.18)	(−1.93)	(0.26)		

								N	
Malaysia	−0.23 (−3.97)	−0.011 (−0.81)	0.038 (1.4)	0.348 (1.94)	3.014 (7.15)	−0.737 (−9.05)	0.007 (2.11)	693	16%
		−0.011 (−1.50)	0.34 (7.24)		5.069 (6.48)	−0.283 (−3.67)	0.002 (0.64)	693	72%
A: Pakistan	0.883 (1.81)	−0.261 (−0.85)	0.088 (0.32)	−0.835 (−0.55)	−0.37 (−0.06)	−0.791 (−1.34)	−0.424 (−5.16)	206	20%
		−0.112 (−0.97)	0.164 (0.57)		6.766 (1.19)	−0.309 (−1.12)	−0.149 (−3.49)	206	95%
B: Pakistan	0.169 (0.77)	−0.073 (−0.51)	0.532 (3.74)	−0.005 (−0.01)	0.687 (0.23)	−1.471 (−5.02)		910	5%
		0.095 (0.45)	0.364 (1.02)		7.63 (0.78)	−1.256 (−2.91)		910	2%
A: Turkey	−0.219 (−0.92)	−0.093 (−0.66)	0.306 (2.48)	−0.937 (−1.12)	4.02 (1.92)	−0.504 (−1.82)	0.024 (1.35)	58	28%
		−0.465 (−2.61)	0.701 (1.35)		−4.32 (−0.32)	0.009 (0.19)	0.038 (0.77)	58	57%
B: Turkey	0.215 (3.06)	0.052 (1.01)	0.136 (2.78)	−0.016 (−0.05)	0.332 (0.59)	−0.783 (−7.92)		372	16%
		−0.017 (−0.36)	0.257 (3.60)		0.616 (0.3)	−0.641 (−5.62)		372	51%
A: Zimbabwe	1.18 (2.82)	0.205 (1.49)	0.14 (0.80)	−3.03 (−3.13)	−10.23 (−2.96)	0.477 (1.55)	−0.093 (−2.94)	53	26%
		0.071 (1.01)	0.389 (4.80)		8.404 (2.07)	0.199 (0.09)	−0.20 (−0.45)	53	89%
B: Zimbabwe	0.101 (1.56)	−0.162 (−5.06)		0.14 (1.24)	0.928 (1.52)	−0.27 (−2.77)	0.007 (0.58)	406	14%
		−0.068 (−2.69)			1.582 (0.93)	−0.31 (−4.16)	−0.002 (−0.13)	406	72%

N/A: Not Available.

Table VII
Long-term Market-debt Ratio

The table presents regressions of long-term market-debt ratio on firm-specific variables. The first row is for the simple pooling, the second is for the fixed-effects model. The R^2 for the pooling and fixed-effects models are adjusted for degrees of freedom. Intercepts could not be calculated for the fixed-effects model, because it was estimated indirectly rather than directly using dummy variables (see Judge et al. (1985)). The business-risk variable acts as a firm dummy and cannot be used in the fixed-effects model. The data were collected by the International Finance Corporation (IFC) and consist primarily of abbreviated balance sheets and income statements for the largest companies in each country from 1980 to 1990, although all time periods are not available for each country. The average tax rate is estimated from before- and after-tax income; asset tangibility is measured by total assets less current assets divided by total assets; return on assets is defined as earnings before tax divided by total assets; business risk is measured as the standard deviation of the return on assets; size is the natural logarithm of local currency sales divided by 100; market-to-book ratio is the market value of equity divided by the book value of equity. The fixed effects regression could not be estimated for Turkey due to insufficient degrees of freedom. The fixed effects estimates (B) for Zimbabwe are without the market-to-book and tangibility ratios, which severely limit sample size. t-statistics in parentheses.

	Intercept	Average Tax Rate	Asset Tangibility	Business Risk	Size	Return on Assets	Market-to-book Ratio	Observations	R^2
India	0.586	−0.207	0.492	0.097	−1.724	−0.693	−0.076	877	57%
	(6.56)	(−6.10)	(13.2)	(0.44)	(−2.77)	(−6.93)	(−14.20)		
		−0.088	0.234		−0.256	−0.438	−0.066	877	79%
		(−3.02)	(3.96)		(−0.23)	(−4.78)	(−12.81)		
Korea	1.15	−0.067	0.057	−1.410	−1.848	−1.197	−0.284	970	71%
	(18.66)	(−2.92)	(2.10)	(−5.86)	(−3.52)	(−10.10)	(−42.95)		
		0.049	0.312		1.584	−0.80	−0.202	970	84%
		(2.44)	(7.44)		(1.59)	(−7.23)	(−20.42)		
Jordan	−0.746	0.018	0.555	0.647	9.151	0.049	−0.074	316	40%
	(−7.63)	(0.21)	(7.42)	(1.96)	(9.8)	(0.31)	(−3.46)		
		0.089	0.325		13.47	−0.037	−0.087	316	68%
		(0.93)	(2.5)		(5.03)	(−0.21)	(−3.28)		

Capital Structures in Developing Countries   111

Malaysia	−0.113	−0.002	0.047	0.43	1.642	−0.42	−0.008	670	22%
	(−3.59)	(−0.25)	(3.19)	(4.38)	(6.75)	(−9.19)	(−4.70)		
		−0.005	0.155		2.93	−0.24	−0.011	670	66%
		(−0.92)	(5.14)		(5.76)	(−4.89)	(−6.26)		
Pakistan	0.098	−0.091	0.562	−1.22	1.06	−0.337	−0.039	172	47%
	(0.96)	(−1.57)	(9.2)	(−4.05)	(0.75)	(−2.95)	(−2.29)		
		−0.131	0.376		3.18	−0.055	−0.017	172	69%
		(−1.88)	(2.18)		(0.95)	(−0.34)	(−0.43)		
Turkey	−0.116	0.076	0.11	−0.232	2.73	−0.227	−0.032	45	19%
	(−0.76)	(0.91)	(1.41)	(−0.48)	(2.03)	(−1.47)	(−2.86)		
A: Zimbabwe	1.930	0.292	0.012	−3.780	−16.02	−0.634	−0.17	54	36%
	(3.11)	(1.45)	(0.05)	(−2.66)	(−3.16)	(−1.44)	(−3.64)		
		0.057	0.381		13.17	−0.239	0.002	54	81%
		(0.40)	(2.34)		(1.66)	(−0.51)	(0.04)		
B: Zimbabwe	0.472	−0.374		0.497	0.217	−800	−0.10	408	36%
	(4.17)	(−6.63)		(2.52)	(0.2)	(−4.68)	(−4.54)		
		−0.153			−0.066	−0.741	−0.045	408	73%
		(−3.00)			(−0.19)	(−4.88)	(−1.81)		

assets will use more long-term debt, but that overall its debt ratio goes down. This is consistent with a traditional matching argument that long-term assets should be financed with long-term liabilities and with the observation that less can be borrowed against long-term assets than from short-term assets. This result is consistent with the static trade-off model, in terms of distress costs. It also supports the pecking-order hypothesis and agency theoretic frameworks from the point of view of agency and informational asymmetry costs.

The overall importance and signs on the coefficients for size, tangibility, and profitability are similar to those in Rajan and Zingales (1995) in their sample of G-7 countries, except that the evidence in favor of a negative relation between profitability and leverage is much stronger. The business-risk proxy continues to have the same mixed effect.

Table VII presents the estimates for the long-term debt ratio using the market value of equity. These estimates should be treated more cautiously, because market data are not available for three of the 10 countries, and are limited for Turkey and Pakistan. However, the models continue to show consistency in supporting the determinants of leverage. For example, the ambiguity in the effects of the tangibility and size variables is largely removed, as now both have mostly significant positive signs. The notable exceptions are the size variable for India and possibly South Korea. Similarly, high levels of profitability continue to be uniformly associated with low levels of debt.

The only significant difference between the results in Tables VI and VII is in the influence of the market-to-book ratio, which changes from mixed, but largely positive, to uniformly negative and highly significant. Rajan and Zingales (1995) find a similar phenomenon for their G-7 countries, except with slightly stronger evidence of a negative influence for the long-term book-debt ratio. This result could be due to spurious correlation introduced by having market values in the numerator of the market-to-book ratio and the denominator of the market long-term debt ratio. Short-run market movements, absent immediate reaction by corporations, will automatically induce a negative correlation between the two. Given the frictions in the capital markets in these developing countries, this is likely to be a severe problem

One implication of these results is that the marginal borrowing power on a dollar of market value is less than that on book value. This implication supports the secured debt hypothesis of Scott (1977) and the growth option argument of Myers (1977).

Despite the standard caveats, there is a message in the data, which is as strong as the message from equivalent work for developed countries: Capital structure models do have predictive power. This means that in cross-sectional tests, the "normal" independent variables are significant and have similar explanatory power. This in part answers the second question posed in the introduction: The factors that influence capital structures choice are similar between developed and developing countries. However, the signs on some of the coefficients, particularly business risk and the market-to-book ratio, are sometimes the opposite of what we would expect. One explanation

Capital Structures in Developing Countries   113

could be the greater dependence of firms in developing countries on short-term debt and trade credit, which have different determinants than long-term debt.

IV. A Common World Model of Capital Structure

The individual country models in Tables V through VII generally support conventional capital structure models. However, apart from the profitability measure, the regression coefficients differ across the countries, both in size and sign. There are several possible reasons, some statistical and some financial.

First, there are different numbers of observations for different countries. For example, when we estimate the models over subsets of the data (for example, for Pakistan, Zimbabwe, and Turkey), the coefficients invariably change. This could be due to sampling problems, or it could indicate the effect of missing variables. Second, there could be different institutional factors that cause the coefficients to vary across countries. Even within a country, we would not expect the signs to be the same across different industries; for example, we normally insert a dummy variable for regulated industries to correct for the fact that we do not expect the coefficient on the business-risk variable to be the same across regulated and unregulated industries. For the same reason, it may be unreasonable to assume that business risk has the same impact across different legal systems.

Despite these concerns, it is interesting to consider the predictive ability of one pooled model across all countries. This model could then be compared to a simple null hypothesis that everything is institutional and that we can explain capital structure differences by knowing the nationality of a company. In this respect, the comparison is biased against the pooled capital structure model, because the coefficients should vary (in unknown ways) across countries.

Table VIII gives the results of three regression models using country dummies as the sole independent variables. We exclude the dummy for Turkey, which is a middle-level debt country, so the coefficients should be interpreted as the significance of debt ratio differences relative to Turkey. For the total debt ratio, all the coefficients are significant. The exceptions are for Pakistan and Thailand, which Table I shows as having the closest debt ratios to Turkey. Five countries have significantly lower total-debt ratios and two have significantly higher total-debt ratios. For the long-term book-debt ratio, the results are identical, except that the overall explanatory power of the country dummies is lowered. For the market-debt ratio, the explanatory power is the same as for the long-term book-debt ratio, but the higher debt ratio for both Zimbabwe and Jordan is evident.

The Table VIII estimates can be taken as the null hypothesis. For the total debt ratio we can explain 43.3 percent of the variability in debt ratios by knowing the nationality of the company. For the long-term book and market ratios, the explanatory power is 12 percent. There are three possible explanations for these results. First, the different debt ratios reflect differences in industrial structure and other company-specific factors, such as business

Table VIII

Country Factors in Capital Structures

The table presents regression of debt ratios using country dummies as sole explanatory variables. The excluded dummy is for Turkey. The total book-debt ratio is defined as total liabilities divided by total liabilities plus net worth. The long-term book-debt ratio is defined as total liabilities minus current liabilities, divided by total liabilities minus current liabilities plus net worth. The long-term market-debt ratio substitutes equity market value for net worth in the long-term book-debt ratio definition. The data were collected by the International Finance Corporation (IFC) and pertain to the the largest companies in each country from 1980 to 1990, although all time periods are not available for each country. First values are coefficients on country dummy variables and the numbers in parentheses are t-statistics.

	Total-debt Ratio	Long-term Book-debt Ratio	Long-term Market-debt Ratio
Intercept	0.593	0.241	0.108
	(70.87)	(12.78)	(3.31)
Brazil	−0.288	−0.145	N/A
	(−23.63)	(−5.26)	
Mexico	−0.247	−0.103	N/A
	(−23.44)	(−4.33)	
India	0.079	0.095	0.226
	(8.08)	(0.43)	(6.76)
Korea	0.14	0.254	0.014
	(14.31)	(11.5)	(4.32)
Jordan	−0.131	−0.114	−0.86
	(−11.2)	(−4.29)	(−2.45)
Malaysia	−0.169	−0.106	−0.38
	(−16.40)	(−4.53)	(−1.12)
Pakistan	0.065	0.023	0.078
	(6.53)	(1.05)	(2.11)
Thailand	(0.009)	N/A	N/A
	(0.81)		
Turkey	No dummy variable: base case		
Zimbabwe	−0.174	−0.111	0.157
	(−15.13)	(−4.26)	(4.54)
Observations	6403	5902	3702
Adjusted R^2	43.2%	11.6%	11.8%

N/A: Not Available.

risk. If this is true, once firm-specific factors are included, the influence of the country dummies should decline. Second, there are systematic differences in the effect of factors such as taxation, legal structures, and bankruptcy laws that affect the debt ratios. In this case, the coefficients on the independent variables should differ, and there should be country effects attributable to missing variables. However, the independent variables should still have marginal significance. Finally, the differences could be spurious either because of inadequate data or because Miller's (1977) neutral mutations theory applies. As a result, no additional explanatory variables should cause the dummies to change.

Capital Structures in Developing Countries 115

Table IX shows the results from pooling across all countries with both country dummies and independent variables. These results omit time and company fixed effects. One problem is that data on long-term debt are not available for Thailand, and market data are not available for Brazil and Mexico. This means that there are implicit country effects at work. To compensate for this, we estimate the models for the two book-debt ratios both with and without the market-to-book ratio. Thus we increase sample size and achieve greater comparability. Another problem is converting local currency sales to U.S. dollar sales, when exchange controls and fixed exchange rates periodically lead to dramatic currency revaluations and changes in the relative sizes of different companies.

For the total book-debt ratio, the adjusted R^2s are 40 percent and 56 percent, respectively, for the models with and without the country dummies. When we run the models on the same sample without the market-to-book ratio, the adjusted R^2s are 43 percent and 58 percent, respectively, indicating that the marginal predictive value of the market-to-book ratio is very low. The regression coefficients are also almost identical.

We also note that the firm-specific coefficients are almost identical in most cases. By firm specific, we mean the variables that are most apt to be determined by the unique characteristics of the firm. These are the firm's average tax rate, asset tangibility, firm size, and firm profitability. In contrast, the market-to-book ratio picks up the capital market's valuation of the company, which will in turn be affected by common conditions in the capital market. Consequently, the market-to-book ratio is most closely associated with external country factors. This could explain why its sign reverses as country dummies are added.

To a great extent capital structure theory has much to say that is portable across countries: total-debt ratios decrease with the tangibility of assets, profitability, and the average tax rate and increase with size. Put another way, small, profitable firms in a tax-paying position with large proportions of tangible assets tend to have less debt. Other factors, such as the market-to-book ratio and business risk, are important in isolation, but tend to be subsumed within country dummies. These results continue to hold when we drop the market-to-book ratio. This increases the sample size by including firms from Mexico and Brazil, as well as companies in some of the other countries.

For the long-term debt ratio, the message is much the same: long-term debt ratios decrease with higher tax rates, size, and profitability. However, similar to the individual country results, more tangible assets leads to higher long-term debt ratios. Because they lose or change their significance in the expanded model, the influence of the market-to-book ratio and the business-risk variables tends to be subsumed within the country dummies. These results are largely the same whether or not the sample includes all firms with market-to-book ratio data.

Finally, the long-term market-debt ratio is negatively correlated with average tax rates, profitability, and the market-to-book ratio, and positively correlated with the tangibility of assets. Again the influence of the business-

Table IX
Country Factors and Capital Structure

The table presents regressions of debt ratios using firm-specific explanatory variables, with and without country dummies. The total debt ratio is defined as total liabilities divided by total liabilities plus net worth. The long-term book-debt ratio is defined as total liabilities minus current liabilities divided by total liabilities plus net worth. The long-term market-debt ratio is defined as total liabilities divided by total liabilities plus equity market value. The average tax rate is estimated from before- and after-tax income; asset tangibility is measured by total assets less current assets divided by total assets; return on assets is defined as earnings before tax divided by total assets; business risk is measured as the standard deviation of the return on assets; market-to-book ratio is the market value of equity divided by the book value of equity; size is the natural logarithm of U.S. dollar sales divided by 100. Generally when the coefficient of size was significant, there were five decimal places before the first nonzero number. The first row indicates the model without country dummies, the second with country dummies, and the third without the market-to-book ratio or country dummies. t-statistics are in parentheses.

	Intercept	Tax Rate	Tangibility	Business Risk	Size	Return on Assets	Market-to-book Ratio	Observations	R^2
Total book-debt ratio	0.465	−0.056	−0.343	−0.013	2.363	−1.150	−0.014	3,386	40%
	(20.72)	(−5.48)	(−24.52)	(−0.136)	(22.41)	(−29.74)	(−7.42)		
(With country dummies)	0.463	−0.027	−0.216	−0.028	1.931	−1.070	0.015	3,386	57%
	(10.42)	(−3.03)	(−16.92)	(−0.34)	(8.53)	(−30.78)	(7.61)		
Without the market-to-book ratio	0.177	−0.067	−0.248	0.158	3.536	−0.994		5,573	43%
	(11.85)	(−9.12)	(−24.58)	(2.32)	(47.26)	(−35.82)			
(With country dummies)	0.458	−0.036	−0.167	0.138	1.704	−0.910		5,573	58%
	(14.48)	(−5.55)	(−17.67)	(2.22)	(9.94)	(−36.52)			
Long-term book-debt ratio	−0.106	−0.092	0.075	−0.093	3.049	−1.063	−1.02	3,196	22%
	(−2.68)	(−5.08)	(2.96)	(−0.55)	(16.44)	(−14.51)	(−14.59)		
(With country dummies)	0.037	−0.068	0.225	−0.001	1.258	−0.902	0.002	3,196	32%
	(0.43)	(−3.93)	(8.95)	(−0.00)	(2.83)	(−13.15)	(0.48)		
Without the market-to-book ratio	−0.129	−0.054	0.085	−0.242	2.813	−1.023		5,357	11%
	(−3.74)	(−3.24)	(3.42)	(−1.53)	(16.35)	(−15.77)			
(With country dummies)	−0.038	−0.048	0.187	0.197	1.68	−0.856		5,357	16%
	(−0.454)	(−2.88)	(7.44)	(1.21)	(3.71)	(−13.13)			
Long-term market-debt ratio	0.138	−0.072	0.075	−0.615	2.498	−0.978	−0.109	3,133	38%
	(3.63)	(−3.96)	(3.11)	(−3.75)	(14.08)	(−14.41)	(−29.40)		
(With country dummies)	0.456	−0.084	0.205	−0.084	−1.05	−0.597	−0.060	3,133	56%
	(5.93)	(−5.29)	(9.34)	(−0.60)	(−2.71)	(−9.98)	(−16.95)		

risk variable is subsumed within the country dummy, as is the size variable, which changes sign. Unlike the results for the book-debt ratios, the market-to-book ratio continues to be negatively related to the market-debt ratio, even when country dummies are introduced.

We note that the results for the long-term book and market-debt ratios are substantially the same. The only difference is that the explanatory power of the market-debt ratio model is much greater with or without country dummies. This result is consistent with other results from developed countries and could be due to either measurement error or slow capital structure adjustments to market prices.

We draw two major conclusions from the results in Table IX. First, there is support for the importance of variables such as profitability, the tangibility of assets, size, etc., across all the countries in this data set. This is encouraging news. It seems that the stylized facts we know to be true from research on developed-country data sets are also true for our more primitive data set for these 10 developing countries. This belies the notion that finance is not portable from developed to developing countries. In fact, the results in Table IX, even without the country dummies, would not look out of place in the Rajan and Zingales (1995) study of developed-country capital structures.

Second, and discouraging but not surprising, is that country factors clearly matter as much as the financial variables analyzed in this paper. The adjusted R^2 indicates that the dummy variables alone explain 43 percent, 12 percent, and 12 percent of the variation in the total-debt, long-term book-debt, and long-term market-debt ratios, respectively. In contrast, the financial variables alone explain 40 to 43 percent, 11 to 22 percent, and 38 percent of the variation, respectively, depending on whether we use the restricted or full-sample results. To predict the total-debt and sometimes the long-term book-debt ratios, it seems that knowing the values of these financial variables is less informative than knowing the firm's country. For the market-debt ratio, the opposite is true: knowing the financial variables, and in particular the market-to-book ratio, is more informative than the country of origin.

V. Conclusions

This paper partly answers the questions posed in the introduction. It offers some hope, but also some skepticism. We find that the variables that are relevant for explaining capital structures in the United States and European countries are also relevant in developing countries, despite the profound differences in institutional factors across these developing countries. Knowing these factors helps predict the financial structure of a firm better than knowing only its nationality.

A consistent result in both the country and pooled data results is that the more profitable the firm, the lower the debt ratio, regardless of how the debt ratio is defined. This finding is consistent with the Pecking-Order Hypothesis. It also supports the existence of significant information asymmetries. This result suggests that external financing is costly and therefore avoided by firms.

However, a more direct explanation is that profitable firms have less demand for external financing, as discussed by Donaldson (1963) and Higgins (1977). This explanation would support the argument that there are agency costs of managerial discretion. Also, this result does not sit well with the static trade-off model, under which we would expect that highly profitable firms would use more debt to lower their tax bill. We could argue that such firms also have large growth options and high market-to-book ratios, so that the agency costs of debt would imply low debt ratios. However, this possibility relies on an argument that high market-to-book ratios are associated with high levels of current profitability, which is not necessarily true. The importance of profitability also explains why the average-tax-rate variable tends to have a negative effect on debt ratios, because rather than being a proxy for debt tax-shield values, it seems to be an alternative measure of profitability.

There is also support for the role of asset tangibility in financing decisions. Clearly, asset tangibility affects total and long-term debt decisions differently. We would expect this from the long-standing argument concerning matching and from the emphasis in bank financing on collateral for shorter-term loans. Generally, the more tangible the asset mix, the higher the long-term debt ratio, but the smaller the total-debt ratio. This indicates that as the tangibility of a firm's assets increases, by say, one percent, although the long-term debt ratio increases, the total-debt ratio falls; that is, the substitution of long-term for short-term debt is less than one.

In the individual country data, we also find support for the impact of intangibles and growth options as discussed by Myers (1977) and Scott (1977). Although in the aggregate data it seems that companies reduce their debt financing, as measured by the book-debt ratios, when the market-to-book ratio increases, these effects seem to be proxies for general country factors. These effects do not remain when we include country dummies. Finally, the estimated empirical average tax rate does not seem to affect financing decisions, except as a proxy for corporate profitability.

Thus, the answer to the first two questions posed in the introduction is:

> In general, debt ratios in developing countries seem to be affected in the same way and by the same types of variables that are significant in developed countries. However, there are systematic differences in the way these ratios are affected by country factors, such as GDP growth rates, inflation rates, and the development of capital markets.

Why our skepticism? Because, although some of the independent variables have the expected sign, their overall impact is low and the signs sometimes vary across countries. This latter observation could be due to the differing sample sizes, but it could also imply significant institutional differences that affect the importance of the independent variables. To some extent, we expect this, because the institutional framework governing bankruptcy, the

Capital Structures in Developing Countries 119

preparation of financial statements, and the availability of different forms of financing is at least as important as the direct variables they measure. Therefore, there is a somewhat negative answer to the third question:

Knowing the country of origin is usually at least as important as knowing the size of the independent variables for both the total and long-term book-debt ratios. Only for the market-debt ratio is this not true.

Consequently, there is much that needs to be done, both in terms of empirical research as the quality of international databases increases, and in developing theoretical models that provide a more direct link between profitability and capital structure choice.

Appendix: Description of the Financial System and Government Intervention in Credit Allocation

The following information is summarized in Table AI.

Brazil

Financial Structure

The Brazilian financial system comprises the central bank, 28 state banks, and 74 private banks, of which 18 are foreign. There are also investment banks, consumer finance companies, housing finance institutions, and credit cooperatives. There are 15 development banks with assets as large as commercial banks.

Ownership

Both public and private banks. In 1987, public banks held 75 percent of commercial bank assets.

Concentration

Total assets of four largest banks as a percentage of banking assets were around 40 percent in 1980 and fell to 33 percent in 1987. Banks are generally very profitable. From 1980 to 1984 ROE was 66 percent. From 1985 to 1987 it was around 60 percent.

Banking Model

Until 1988, different institutions performed different functions (i.e., commercial banks, insurance, brokerage, leasing, etc.) but they were all interconnected through stock holdings. Several types of institutions were centered around commercial banks, creating financial conglomerates. This was true for both private and public banks. In 1988, banks became universal banks.

Table A1
Financial Institutions and Directed Credit Policies

Interest margin is average lending rate minus deposit rate. Foreign commercial banks is percent of total commercial bank assets. Public financial institutions is the sum of public banks and public specialized institutions as a percent of total financial assets minus central bank assets.

	Banking Model	Commercial Bank Ownership	Bank Concentration (% of Bank Assets)	Interest Margin (%)	Foreign Commercial Banks (%)	Directed Credit Policies	
						Public Financial Institutions in Total (%)	Commercial Bank Resources that are Directed (%)
Brazil 1980	Banking and commerce separate in 1980s. However, bank holding companies blurred the separation.	56% private	Top 4 banks: 40	1.6	n.a.	70	70 Mostly to agriculture and poor regions.
1990	In 1988 banks became universal.	56% private	Top 4 banks: 33	3.1	5	70	(Subsidy/gdp peaked in 1987 to 7–8% and later declined to 3–4%.)
Mexico 1980	Banking and commerce separate till later in 1980s.	100% public	Top 3 banks: 70	7.5	0 (only Citibank before NAFTA)	70	60–90 till 1989. Abolished in 1989.
1990	Universal	100% private after 1992.	Top 3 banks: 70	14	n.a.	23	Most of directed credit went to public enterprises and housing. Also very small amount to exporters.
India 1980	Universal	Public	Top 4 banks: 45	3	4	92	80
1990	Universal	8% private	Top 4 banks: 45	3	5	92	Credit is directed mostly to agriculture and small enterprises.
South Korea 1980	During 1980s banks could hold stock but could not underwrite.	Mostly public. Privatized by end of 1983.	Top 5 banks: 30	7	12	84	50 (has declined from 55 in the 1980s)
1990	In 1990s they are becoming universal.	100% private	Top 5 banks: 20	4.6	11	63	(Subsidy/GDP was 1% for 1980–1990.)

Country / Year	Bank regulation	Ownership	Concentration		Foreign banks		Directed credit
Jordan 1980	Banks can hold stock but cannot underwrite or trade.	Mostly private	n.a.	4	n.a.	20	8 — Credit is directed through government specialized banks to agriculture, housing, and only small start-up manufacturing businesses.
1990			Top 3 banks: 65% of deposits	3.25	5 foreign banks	23	
Malaysia 1980	Universal	Mostly private	Top 5 banks: 53	1.5	38	28	59 — Credit is directed to indigenous groups, low-cost housing and small enterprises.
1990	Universal	Mostly private	Top 5 banks: 53	1.26	24	27	
Pakistan 1980	Universal	90% public	n.a.	4.4	14	87	80 — Credit is directed mostly to agriculture, housing and small industrial firms.
1990	Universal	27% private after 1991	Top 5 banks: 86	2.4	11	76	
Thailand 1980 1990	Banks can hold stock but can underwrite through their affiliates only. However, affiliates are generally fully controlled although legally there is a 10% limit.	80% private	Top 3 banks: 59	4	6	25	25–30 — Credit is directed mostly to agriculture, small scale industry and exporters.
1990			Top 3 banks: 55	5.5	5	22	
Turkey 1980	Universal. Banks started getting involved in securities markets in the second half of 1980s.	53% private	Top 4 banks: 64% of deposits	17	3	55	In the 1980s, decreased from 50% to around 18% in 1990s.
1990	Universal	53% private	Top 4 banks: 64% of deposits	20	4	48	Directed credit mostly went to state enterprises, farmers, artisans and small firms, backward regions and small industrial firms.
Zimbabwe 1980	Banking and commerce separate	Mostly private. Dominated by foreign (U.K.) banks.	Top 4 banks: 100	14	Mostly foreign	6	Substantial directed credit, mostly to public sector.
1990			Top 4 banks: 100	3	5	5	Private firms do not receive much directed credit.

n.a.: Not Available.

Directed Credit Policies

In 1988, Brazil's reserve requirements ranged from 8 to 43 percent of demand deposits, based on the bank's size (lower for small banks) and location (lower in poor regions). Government credit programs accounted for more than 70 percent of credit outstanding to the public and private sectors. Commercial banks were required to lend 20 to 60 percent (depending on bank size) of their sight deposits for agriculture. Eighteen percent went to state enterprises. Analysts estimated that the implicit subsidy on a sample of largest directed credit programs was about seven to eight percent of GDP in 1987, but later declined to three to four percent. These directed credits are now being phased out.

Mexico

Financial Structure

In 1989, the financial system comprised the central bank, 18 state-owned commercial banks, 2 private banks, 8 state-owned development banks, and 25 privately owned brokerage firms. Between 1982 and 1989, the government consolidated the banks, reducing their numbers from 60 to 20.

Ownership

Mexican banks were nationalized in 1982 following the devaluation of the peso. The government sold the brokerage operations of the universal banks and their nonbank equity holdings. For the period 1982 to 1991, the banks remained publicly owned. Foreign banks were not allowed during this period. Banks were reprivatized in 1991 and 1992. They now operate as universal banks and maintain close ties to large industrial groups.

Concentration

The 3 largest banks account for over 62 percent of banking assets. In 1987, this figure was 80 percent. By 1990, it had dropped to 70 percent. From 1985 to 1989, banks were very profitable with real ROE of over 50 percent in some cases.

Banking Model

Between 1982 and 1991, commercial banks faced many restrictions on their operations. However, private brokers were left relatively free and encouraged to expand into banking activities. Restrictions were slowly eased and banks were privatized in 1991 and 1992. They now operate as universal banks.

Capital Structures in Developing Countries 123

Directed Credit Policies

Before 1989, there was a 10 percent reserve requirement on deposits and government required that 31 percent of deposits be held in government bonds. In addition, 16.2 percent of deposits were allocated for "development activities," 10 percent lent to development banks, 10 percent lent for housing, and 1.2 percent for exporters. In 1989, reserve requirements and directed credit programs were replaced by a 30 percent liquidity requirement held in the form of interest-bearing government paper or central bank deposits.

India

Financial Structure

Commercial banking is dominated by 20 public banks (nationalized in 1969 and 1980) and 196 regional rural banks. Public banks account for over 90 percent of commercial bank assets and deposits. Private commercial banks consist of 29 Indian scheduled banks, 21 foreign banks, and 3 small nonscheduled banks. There are also postal savings banks, three term-lending institutions, two insurance corporations, and an Exim bank, all of which are public.

Ownership

Mostly public. Very recently, there have been some efforts to privatize.

Concentration

Twenty national banks account for 92 percent of banking assets and the four-bank concentration ratio is 45 percent. Market shares remained virtually unchanged for a long time. Public sector banks do not compete among themselves. They are among the least profitable in the world.

Banking Model

Banks operate as universal banks with widespread branches. They can accept all types of deposits and offer many kinds of loans. Banks have established subsidiaries for leasing, underwriting, mutual funds, merchant banking, and other corporate services.

Directed Credit Policies

Forced investments in public debt are the largest portion of the government's credit allocation. Around 50 percent of bank deposits are invested in government paper to satisfy reserve and liquidity requirements at lower-than-market rates. The remaining resources of commercial banks (after cash and liquidity requirements) must be invested in priority sectors, such as agriculture and small enterprises, at subsidized rates of interest. Only about 20 percent of bank resources can be allocated freely.

124   *The Journal of Finance*

South Korea

Financial Structure

The financial system comprises the Bank of South Korea (central bank), 5 nationwide city banks, 10 regional banks, 6 specialized banks, 31 branches of foreign banks, and 3 development banks. There are also savings institutions, insurance companies, and investment companies.

Ownership

Bank privatization started in the early 1980s. By 1983, all city banks were privatized. Although banks are mostly private, the Bank of South Korea continues to have significant control over their operations.

Concentration

In 1980, the top 5 banks held 30 percent of financial assets. By 1990, this had dropped to around 20 percent. Compared to G-7 countries, South Korean banks are among the most profitable.

Banking Model

In the 1990s, South Korean banks started to own investment and finance companies as subsidiaries. In the 1980s, they were allowed to hold stock up to 25 percent of their liabilities (up to 10 percent of stock in any nonbank), but they could not underwrite stocks.

Directed Credit Policies

Banks traditionally lent large sums to the big business groups (chaebols). In 1988, 23.7 percent of bank loans went to the 30 largest chaebols. In 1987, the South Korean government introduced restrictions in the form of "moral suasion" to reduce corporate leverage and forced the chaebols to raise capital in the stock market. This was done to increase credit access by small and medium enterprises. By 1990, the 30 largest chaebols were getting only 19.8 percent of total bank loans.

The Korean banking system has always been the most important channel for implementing the directed credit policies of the government. Thus, the banks entered the 1980s with a substantial proportion of nonperforming loans. Most of the directed credit went to developing heavy and chemical industries. These loans, although still quite substantial, have been declining. The ratio of policy loans (directed credit) to total loans of banks, which was 60 percent at the end of the 1970s, declined to 50 percent by the mid-1980s and to 40 percent at the end of 1991. However, the yearly subsidy provided by directed credit as a ratio of GDP has been approximately one percent for the period from 1980 to 1990. There is an eight to 11 percent reserve requirement on bank deposits.

Capital Structures in Developing Countries 125

Jordan

Financial Structure

The Jordanian financial system consists of the Central Bank of Jordan, 19 commercial banks, 5 foreign banks, investment banks, and 4 specialized banks.

Ownership

Mostly private. The 4 public specialized institutions had around 15 percent of total financial assets.

Malaysia

Financial Structure

The Malaysian financial system comprises the central bank, 38 commercial banks (22 domestic, 16 foreign), finance companies, merchant banks, discount houses, development institutions, and various other nonbank institutions. The banking system is well developed and diverse.

Ownership

Mostly private.

Concentration

In 1959, the five largest commercial banks in the country were all foreign. By 1988, four of the five largest banks were domestic. In 1959, the 5 top banks held 72 percent of bank assets. By 1988, this had fallen to 53 percent.

Banking Model

Initially, banking activities were confined to financing of external trade. In the 1970s, and especially in the 1980s, diversified bank holding companies developed with subsidiaries engaged in merchant banking, hire-purchase finance, housing, factoring, leasing, and other specialized activities. Since 1986, banks have also been engaged in stockbroking.

Directed Credit Policies

Banks are required to keep around 25 percent of their resources as reserve and liquidity funds. Approximately half of this amount is invested in government securities. In addition, there is directed credit to indigenous groups, small-scale enterprises, and low-cost housing projects, which add up to around 47 percent of bank loans.

Pakistan

Financial Structure

In the 1980s, the Pakistani financial system consisted of the central bank, five state banks, and nine foreign banks. In 1991, two of the state banks were privatized and new private banks were established.

Ownership

Until 1991, all commercial banks were public (except for the nine foreign banks). With the privatization in 1991, 73 percent of assets still remain public. Fourteen percent are newly privatized and 13 percent are foreign.

Concentration

Banking has always been heavily concentrated. In 1991, the top 3 state banks held 72 percent of assets.

Banking Model

Banks are universal banks. Almost all financial institutions in Pakistan are involved in the securities business. All public and private banks are active in the underwriting business.

Directed Credit Policies

The public sector has a very large borrowing requirement, which leaves little credit for the private sector. Allocation of this credit to the private sector is heavily influenced by the directed credit policies. State banks have little autonomy, as the Pakistan Banking Council approves most important decisions and there is considerable political interference in all lending and collection efforts. In addition to directed credit through commercial banks, several development banks are operating to provide long-term credit to specific clients at subsidized rates. These serve the industry, housing, and agriculture sectors.

Thailand

Financial Structure

The Thai financial system comprises the central bank, 15 domestic banks, and 14 foreign commercial banks, specialized financial institutions, and nonbanks. Nonbanks have been gaining importance in recent years.

Ownership

Commercial banks are mostly private, with one government-owned bank, which holds eight percent of commercial bank assets. In 1900, banking in Thailand was controlled by foreign institutions. Domestic banks were later established by the government, the army, and rich families. Original ownership groups continue to maintain tight control over banks.

Capital Structures in Developing Countries 127

Concentration

Market concentration has been decreasing. In 1980, the top 3 banks held 59 percent of assets. In 1988, this became 55 percent.

Banking Model

Banks and corporations form financial groups through cross-ownership of stock. Banks cannot engage directly in investment banking, but do so through their affiliates.

Directed Credit Policies

As part of their reserve requirements, banks must hold 2 percent of their deposits in the form of deposits with Bank of Thailand, and 2.5 to 5 percent of their deposits as government securities. To satisfy the liquidity requirement, 16 percent of deposits must be invested in eligible securities.

The Thai government adopted directed credit policies out of concern that the agricultural sector might be discriminated against by the financial system. Commercial banks are required to lend 20 percent of their previous year's deposits to the agricultural sector. In addition, bank lending for exports, small-scale industry, and agricultural production are at subsidized rates. Also according to the "local lending requirement," each bank branch established outside Bangkok since 1975 must lend at least three-fifths of its deposit resources locally. Since 1988, there has been a sharp decline in directed credit.

Turkey

Financial Structure

In 1980, Turkey's financial system comprised the Central Bank, 12 publicly owned commercial banks, 24 private commercial banks, 4 foreign banks, and 2 development banks. Public banks accounted for 50.3 percent of the assets, private banks for 46.7 percent, and foreign banks accounted for only 3 percent. In 1990, the basic structure of the system was not much different. Foreign banks increased in number to 26, but their share of the assets only increased to 3.8 percent.

Ownership

Divided almost equally between public and private.

Concentration

In 1980, the top 4 banks accounted for more than 64 percent of deposits, and the top 4 private banks held 78 percent of private bank deposits. In 1990, the top 4 banks continued to hold more than half of all deposits, and the top 4 private banks held over 65 percent of private deposits. Profits in the banking sector increased substantially, particularly after the mid-1980s, and by the end of 1990 had reached levels more than three times the OECD average.

Banking Model

Banks and corporations form banking groups with interlocking ownership and management. With the development of stock markets in the late 1980s, banks became more involved in the securities markets and began operating as universal banks.

Directed Credit Policies

Directed credit and discounts made available by the Central Bank were reduced from 49 percent of total credit in 1980 to 18 percent in 1987. In the early 1980s, borrowers were public administration, state enterprises, farmers, exporters, artisans and small firms, backward regions, industrial investors, and so on. By the late 1980s, preferential credit was provided only for agriculture, industrial artisans, exports, and housing. There is currently a reserve requirement equal to 25 percent of deposits.

Zimbabwe

Financial Structure

The Zimbabwe financial system comprises the Central Bank, four commercial banks, four merchant banks, five finance houses, three discount houses, three building societies, a post office savings bank, a number of insurance companies and pension funds, and several development banks. Its financial system is diverse compared to other sub-Saharan countries with relatively significant nonbank financial sectors.

Ownership

Banks are private and predominantly foreign.

Concentration

The commercial banking sector is dominated by branches or subsidiaries of British banks. There are only four banks. Banks are quite profitable.

Banking Model

British model. Banking and commerce are separate. Separate institutions provide different services.

Capital Structures in Developing Countries   129

Directed Credit Policies

Most of the private savings are lent to the public sector in the form of short-term loans, and medium-to-long-term public bonds. This lending is facilitated by a range of required asset requirements that effectively channel the resources into these public liabilities. Private corporations do not receive much directed credit.

REFERENCES

Aivazian, Varouj, and Jeffrey Callen, 1980, Corporate leverage and growth: The game theoretic issues, *Journal of Financial Economics* 9, 379–399.

Berger, Philip, Eli Ofek, and David Yermack, 1997, Managerial entrenchment and capital structure decisions, *Journal of Finance* 50, 1411–1430.

Booth, Laurence, 1995, Capital structures in developing countries, Working paper, University of Toronto.

Bradley, Michael, Gregg Jarrell, and E. Han Kim, 1984, On the existence of an optimal capital structure: Theory and evidence, *Journal of Finance* 39, 857–878.

Demirguc-Kunt, Asli, and Vojislav Maksimovic, 1996, Stock market development and financing choices of firms, *World Bank Economic Review* 10, 341–369.

Demirguc-Kunt, Asli, and Vojislav Maksimovic, 1999, Institutions, financial markets and firm debt maturity, *Journal of Financial Economics* 54, 295–336.

Donaldson, Gordon, 1963, Financial goals: Management vs stockholders, *Harvard Business Review* 41, 116–129.

Glen, Jack, and Brian Pinto, 1994, Debt and equity? How firms in developing countries choose, Discussion paper #22, International Finance Corporation.

Graham, John, 1996, Proxies for the corporate marginal tax rate, *Journal of Financial Economics* 42, 187–221.

Hausman, Jerry, 1978, Specification tests in econometrics, *Econometrica* 46, 1251–1272.

Higgins, Robert, 1977, How much growth can a firm afford, *Financial Management*, 7–16.

Hsiao, Cheng, 1986, *Analysis of Panel Data* (Cambridge University Press, Cambridge, England).

International Finance Corporation, 1995, *Emerging Stock Markets Fact Book*, Washington, DC.

International Monetary Fund, 1999, *International Financial Statistics*.

Jensen, Michael, and William Meckling, 1976, Theory of the firm: Managerial behavior, agency costs and ownership structure, *Journal of Financial Economics* 3, 305–360.

Jensen, Michael, 1986, The agency costs of free cash flow, corporate finance and takeovers, *American Economic Review* 76, 323–329.

Judge, George, W. E Griffiths, R. Carter Hill, Helmut Lutkepohl, and Tsoung-Chao Lee, 1985, *Theory and Practice of Econometrics* (John Wiley, New York).

Jung, Kooyul, Yong-Cheol Kim, and René Stulz, 1996, Timing, investment opportunities, managerial discretion, and the security issue decision, *Journal of Financial Economics* 42, 159–185.

Kale, Jayant, Thomas Noe, and Gabriel Ramirez, 1992, The effect of business risk on corporate capital structure: Theory and evidence, *Journal of Finance* 46, 1693–1715.

King, Robert, and Ross Levine, 1993, Finance and growth: Shumpeter might be right, *Quarterly Journal of Economics* 108, 717–737.

La Porta, Rafael, Florencio Lopez-de-Silanes, Andrei Shleifer, and Robert W. Vishny, 1998, Law and finance, *Journal of Political Economy* 106, 1113–1155.

Mayer, Colin, 1990, Financial systems, corporate finance and economic development, in R. Glenn Hubbard, ed.: *Asymmetric Information, Corporate Finance and Investment* (University of Chicago Press, Chicago, IL).

Miller, Merton, and Franco Modigliani, 1961, Dividend policy, growth and the valuation of shares, *Journal of Business* 34, 411–433.

Miller, Merton, 1977, Debt and taxes, *Journal of Finance* 32, 261–275.

Modigliani, Franco, and Merton Miller, 1958, The cost of capital, corporation finance and the theory of investment, *American Economic Review,* 48, 261–297.

Myers, Stewart, and Nicholas Majluf, 1984, Corporate financing and investment decisions when firms have information that investors do not have, *Journal of Financial Economics* 13, 187–221.

Myers, Stewart, 1977, The determinants of corporate borrowing, *Journal of Financial Economics* 5, 147–175.

Rajan, Raghuram, and Luigi Zingales, 1995, What do we know about capital structure? Some evidence from international data, *Journal of Finance* 50, 1421–1460.

Scott, James, 1977, Bankruptcy, secured debt and optimal capital structure, *Journal of Finance* 32, 1–19.

Shyam-Sunder, Lakshmi, and Stewart Myers, 1999, Testing static tradeoff against pecking order models of capital structure, *Journal of Financial Economics* 51, 219–244.

Singh, Ajit, Javed Hamid, Bahram Salimi, and Y. Nakano, 1992, Corporate financial structures in developing countries, Technical paper #1, International Finance Corporation, Washington, DC.

Smith, Clifford, and Ross Watts, 1992, The investment opportunity set and corporate financing, dividend and compensation policies, *Journal of Financial Economics* 32, 263–292.

Stulz, René, 1990, Managerial discretion and optimal financing policies, *Journal of Financial Economics* 26, 3–27.

Titman, Sheridan, and Robert Wessels, 1988, The determinants of capital structure choice, *Journal of Finance* 43, 1–19.

World Bank, 1993, *Trends in Developing Economies: Extracts, Emerging Capital Markets,* Volume 2, Washington, DC.

World Bank, 1992, *World Development Report,* Washington, DC.

[2004]

*Selected Countries
United States*

F23
G32
H25

243-79

Chapter Seven

243

THE JOURNAL OF FINANCE • VOL. LIX, NO. 6 • DECEMBER 2004

A Multinational Perspective on Capital Structure Choice and Internal Capital Markets

MIHIR A. DESAI, C. FRITZ FOLEY, and JAMES R. HINES JR.*

ABSTRACT

This paper analyzes the capital structures of foreign affiliates and internal capital markets of multinational corporations. Ten percent higher local tax rates are associated with 2.8% higher debt/asset ratios, with internal borrowing being particularly sensitive to taxes. Multinational affiliates are financed with less external debt in countries with underdeveloped capital markets or weak creditor rights, reflecting significantly higher local borrowing costs. Instrumental variable analysis indicates that greater borrowing from parent companies substitutes for three-quarters of reduced external borrowing induced by capital market conditions. Multinational firms appear to employ internal capital markets opportunistically to overcome imperfections in external capital markets.

TO WHAT EXTENT DOES CORPORATE BORROWING increase due to the tax deductibility of interest expenses and decline in response to costs imposed by capital market underdevelopment or unfavorable legal systems? Do firms use internal capital markets to substitute for external finance when the latter is costly, and if so, how extensive is such substitution? Empirical attempts to answer these fundamental questions face significant challenges. Limited variation in tax incentives within countries makes it difficult to identify the effects of taxes, and detailed information on the workings of internal capital markets is scarce. Recent efforts using cross-country samples exploit the rich variation that international comparisons offer, but frequently face problems associated with nonstandardized measurement across countries and limited statistical power due to small sample sizes.

Cross-country studies of capital structure commonly ignore the distinctive and illuminating features of multinational firms. These firms face differing tax incentives and legal regimes around the world, making it possible to identify the impact of these factors on financing choices. Analysis of the behavior of

*Desai is from Harvard University and NBER, Foley is from Harvard University, and Hines is from the University of Michigan and NBER. The statistical analysis of firm-level data on U.S. multinational companies was conducted at the International Investment Division, Bureau of Economic Analysis, U.S. Department of Commerce under arrangements that maintain legal confidentiality requirements. The views expressed are those of the authors and do not reflect official positions of the U.S. Department of Commerce. We thank various seminar participants, the referees, Richard Green, René Stulz, and William Zeile for helpful comments, as well as the Lois and Bruce Zenkel Research Fund at the University of Michigan and the Division of Research at Harvard Business School for financial support.

multinational firms promises clean estimates of the sensitivity of capital structure choice to tax incentives, an understanding of the mechanisms by which weak capital markets affect financing choices, and insight into the ways in which internal capital markets can facilitate tax minimization and provide an alternate financing source when external financing is most costly.

This paper analyzes the determinants of the capital structures of foreign affiliates of U.S. multinational firms, thereby obtaining evidence of the workings of their internal capital markets. The use of confidential affiliate-level data makes it possible to distinguish the behavior of foreign affiliates of the *same* parent companies operating in markets with differing tax rates and capital market regimes and to differentiate the determinants of external borrowing and borrowing from parent companies. As a result, it is possible to obtain estimates of the impact of taxation and local capital market conditions, while implicitly controlling for considerations that are common to all affiliates of the same company. The sample includes information on the activities of roughly 3,700 U.S. multinational firms operating in more than 150 countries through approximately 30,000 affiliates in 1982, 1989, and 1994. Since all reporting follows generally accepted U.S. accounting principles, and all financial information is filed through U.S. entities familiar with such practices, it is not necessary to make problematic assumptions normally required in order to analyze financial information collected in different countries. Furthermore, since the data distinguish borrowing from external sources and borrowing from parent companies, it is possible to study aspects of capital markets that are internal to firms.

The analysis first examines the effect on total affiliate leverage of tax incentives and legal and capital market conditions. Then the analysis evaluates the determinants of borrowing from external sources and borrowing from parent companies, using legal and capital market conditions as instruments to measure the extent to which firms substitute loans from parent companies for loans from external sources. Next comes consideration of the effect of legal and capital market conditions on borrowing rates, including differences between interest rates on external debt and interest rates on loans from parent companies. The analysis concludes by measuring the extent to which induced variation in borrowing costs changes debt sourcing decisions of multinational affiliates.

Three main empirical findings emerge. First, there is strong evidence that affiliates of multinational firms alter the overall level and composition of debt in response to tax incentives. The estimates imply that 10% higher tax rates are associated with 2.8% greater affiliate debt as a fraction of assets, internal finance being particularly sensitive to tax differences. While the estimated elasticity of external borrowing with respect to the tax rate is 0.19, the estimated tax elasticity of borrowing from parent companies is 0.35.

Second, the level and composition of leverage are influenced by capital market conditions. In countries with weak creditor rights and shallow capital markets, affiliates borrow less externally and more from parent companies. This suggests that internal borrowing may substitute for costly external borrowing. Instrumental variables regressions in which creditor rights and capital market conditions serve as instruments for the quantity of external debt permit identification of the degree to which affiliates substitute internal borrowing from parent companies for external debt. The results indicate that affiliates increase internal borrowing to offset approximately three-quarters of the reduction in external borrowing due to adverse legal and capital market conditions. All of these results control for other determinants of leverage and the composition of debt, including political risk and inflation, that also appear to influence affiliate leverage and its composition. Increased political risk is associated with greater overall leverage in the form of expanded external borrowing, while inflation does not appear to affect overall leverage, though higher inflation is associated with greater external borrowing and reduced internal borrowing.

Third, the evidence indicates that external borrowing is more costly in environments in which creditor rights are weak and capital markets are shallow and that affiliates substitute parent for external borrowing in response to these costs. Interest rates on external debt differ for affiliates of the same American parent company located in different host countries in a manner that corresponds to measures of capital market depth and creditor rights; moreover, the wedge between the cost of borrowing from external lenders and the cost of borrowing from parent companies is larger where credit markets are poorly developed. Instrumental variables regressions in which creditor rights and capital market conditions serve as instruments for interest rates allow identification of the degree to which affiliates alter the mix of borrowing from external sources and parent companies in response to differences in borrowing costs. One percent higher interest rates on external debt due to legal and capital market conditions are associated with external borrowing that falls by 1.3% of assets and borrowing from parent companies that rises by 0.8% of assets.

Section I of the paper reviews the studies of the effect of tax incentives on capital structure, the impact of local capital market conditions on financing decisions, and the workings of internal capital markets. Section II describes the affiliate-level data and summarizes the leverage and interest rate measures used in the analysis. Section III analyzes the determinants of affiliate capital structure and the use of loans from parent companies to substitute for external sources of funds. Section IV concludes.

I. Motivation and Hypotheses

The financing of foreign affiliates is likely to be influenced by the effect of local tax rates and capital market conditions on the after-tax cost of funds and by the ability of affiliates to obtain resources from parent companies. As a result, affiliate financing illuminates the importance of taxes in influencing capital structure, the impact of institutions on financing choices, and the workings of internal capital markets.

A. *Taxes and Capital Structure*

Since interest payments to lenders usually are fully deductible from taxable income, while dividend payments to shareholders are not, tax systems typically encourage the use of debt rather than equity finance.[1] This incentive grows as the corporate tax rate rises, so high corporate tax rates are often expected to be associated with greater corporate indebtedness. As Auerbach (2002) and Graham (2003) note, however, estimating the sensitivity of capital structure to tax incentives has proven remarkably difficult, due in part to measurement problems. Consequently, it is not surprising that several studies find no effect or unexpected relationships between tax incentives and the use of debt.[2] One problem in identifying tax effects stems from the lack of variation in corporate tax rates. By focusing on whether a firm is near tax exhaustion, Mackie-Mason (1990) avoids this constraint and identifies evidence of tax effects, in which the deductibility of interest expenses appears to encourage firms to use greater leverage than they otherwise would. Graham (1996), Graham, Lemmon, and Schallheim (1998), and Graham (1999) employ a sophisticated measure of the marginal tax rate in the United States based on simulations and prevailing tax rules to investigate further the use of debt and the relevance of personal taxation. The use of cross-country evidence has the potential to contribute further evidence by analyzing the outcomes when firms simultaneously select capital structures in several tax environments. This approach is able to overcome some of the difficulties that arise in identifying the marginal investor in general equilibrium and in accounting for the numerous factors that might give rise to deviations from a Miller (1977) equilibrium.

Hodder and Senbet (1990) extend the logic of a Miller equilibrium to an international setting to suggest that, in an integrated world capital market, all firms will locate debt in the most tax-advantaged jurisdictions.[3] As it is reasonable to posit that multinational firms operate in integrated capital markets, a

---

[1] There are subtle differences between the tax incentives of domestic and multinational firms. American multinational firms owe taxes to the United States on their foreign incomes, but they defer U.S. taxes until profits are repatriated and are entitled to claim credits for foreign income taxes paid. The upshot of this system is that American firms typically can arrange their finances to benefit from the deductibility of interest expenses in high-tax countries; for analyses, see Hines and Rice (1994) and Hines (1999).

[2] These results have also generated considerable skepticism on the importance of taxes to capital structure as evidenced in Myers et al. (1998). Such skepticism does not conform to the survey results reported in Graham and Harvey (2001), in which 45% of respondents indicate that tax implications are important or very important determinants of leverage, led only by the implications of borrowing for financial flexibility, credit rating, and the volatility of earnings. Tax considerations were reported to be particularly salient for larger, public firms and for decisions concerning the financing of subsidiaries. Valuation effects of debt usage, as analyzed by Fama and French (1998) and Graham (2000), offer additional evidence of the impact of taxation but are less applicable to multinational affiliates, since they are usually not separately traded.

[3] While Hodder and Senbet (1990) predict extreme outcomes, there are other factors (some of which are considered below) that might constrain firms from corner solutions. Some countries impose "thin capitalization" rules that limit the tax deductibility of interest paid by firms deemed to have excessive debt. These rules are typically vaguely worded and seldom, though arbitrarily, imposed, making their effects difficult to analyze quantitatively; any impact they have is likely to reduce the estimated significance of factors influencing total indebtedness. Also, "thin capitalization" rules generally do not affect the choice between different kinds of debt. Other theoretical examinations of the effect of tax incentives on the use of debt within multinational firms include Hines (1994), Chowdry and Nanda (1994), and Chowdry and Coval (1998).

Multinational Capital Structure and Internal Capital Markets 2455

multinational firm faces a single cost of capital, and therefore the relative tax advantage of debt in any market is simply a function of local tax rates. As a result, the sensitivity of foreign affiliate capital structure to foreign tax rates offers a powerful and clean test of the response of leverage to differential tax advantages to debt.[4]

B. Institutions, Markets, and External Borrowing Conditions

A large body of work indicates that there are important differences in the ability of firms to raise capital in different countries. La Porta et al. (1998) trace these effects to differences in legal regimes, and create an index of creditor rights in bankruptcy for a large sample of countries. In La Porta et al. (1997), these authors show that legal regimes have large effects on the size and breadth of capital markets: countries with weak creditor rights have significantly smaller local debt markets. There is evidence of other important determinants of financial development (Rajan and Zingales (2003)), but there is little disagreement that financial development varies widely.

Weak local financial markets appear to be associated with lower rates of growth. Evidence of this effect is provided at the country level by King and Levine (1993), at the industry level by Rajan and Zingales (1998), and at the firm level by Demirguc-Kunt and Maksimovic (1998). However, existing work does not detail the extent to which weak capital market conditions affect the cost of external borrowing, capital structure choice, and the use of internal capital markets as substitutes for external capital markets. In their cross-country analysis of the determinants of capital structure choice, Rajan and Zingales (1995) focus on G-7 countries, finding limited evidence of systematic differences across these similar countries. Booth et al. (2001) analyze firms in 10 developing countries, finding that these firms use less long-term debt than do comparable firms in developed countries and that unspecified country factors are significant determinants of capital structure. These studies leave open questions of how capital market conditions might directly alter the cost of external debt and how these conditions might push firms to attempt to substitute for locally provided external capital.[5]

---

[4] Other studies examine specific aspects of the effect of taxation on the financing of multinational firms. See Froot and Hines (1995) and Newberry (1998) on the effects of limits to the deductibility of interest expenses due to the U.S. allocation rules, Desai and Hines (1999) on changes in joint venture capital structure in response to foreign tax credit limitations, Altshuler and Grubert (2003) on interaffiliate transactions motivated by tax rules, and Newberry and Dhaliwal (2001) on the decision to issue bonds through the parent or a foreign subsidiary as a function of foreign tax credit rules.

[5] Studies such as Eichengreen and Mody (2000a,b) examine the determinants of corporate borrowing spreads across countries and the impact of differing legal regimes on sovereign borrowing costs. The alternative of analyzing interest rates paid by multinational firms implicitly controls for a host of unobservable factors by comparing interest rates faced by the same company in different institutional environments. The absence of detailed data on affiliate borrowing makes it infeasible, however, to incorporate term structure considerations emphasized in papers such as Duffee (2002).

In order for multinational affiliate capital structure decisions to illuminate the mechanisms by which local contracting conditions impact borrowing costs, multinational bankruptcies must follow local bankruptcy rules rather than the bankruptcy rules of the home country. This is generally the case. There is a remarkable void in the laws governing multinational bankruptcies, but respect for the laws of the country in which a firm is operating implies that local bankruptcy rules apply to the resolution of insolvency proceedings involving a multinational affiliate.[6]

Because local bankruptcy rules prevail, a multinational firm effectively is faced with the opportunity of borrowing across a variety of creditor rights' regimes. Real interest rates should be higher (all other things equal) in countries in which lenders have fewer rights in the event of default. Shleifer and Wolfenzon (2002) analyze the impact of creditor rights on economic outcomes, and Noe (2000) provides an equilibrium model of capital structure choice for multinational affiliates facing different legal regimes. The ability to renegotiate strategically with creditors in times of fiscal distress is attractive to the distressed firm but reduces its incentive to avoid bankruptcy, creating an agency problem that is reflected in higher borrowing rates.

Since shareholders bear agency costs, they have incentives to minimize renegotiation opportunities and can do so by concentrating their borrowing in jurisdictions providing strong creditor rights. Moreover, internal capital markets can be used to fund subsidiaries in jurisdictions providing weak creditor rights, drawing on capital from operations located in countries offering strong creditor rights. In addition to these predictions on the level and composition of affiliate debt, the interest rates paid by multinational firms should reflect the fact that lenders in countries with weak legal protections receive less in adverse states of the world than do lenders in countries offering strong legal protections. Furthermore, since there is adverse selection in the lending market, and moral hazard once borrowers receive loans, local banks and other lenders need to expend resources to investigate potential borrowers, monitor their behavior once loans are granted, and deploy legal resources to enforce contracts. These are real resource costs that should be reflected in still higher interest rates paid by borrowers and received by lenders in countries with weak creditor rights.

C. Internal Capital Markets

The sensitivity of investment to internal cash flows noted since Meyer and Kuh (1957) has drawn attention to the role of internal capital markets and how they are used by firms in response to any differences between internal

---

[6] Desai et al. (2003) offer a detailed discussion of the workings of multinational bankruptcies and the reasons why local laws should dictate the bankruptcy terms of multinational affiliates. Additionally, Bebchuk and Guzman (1999) provide a useful analysis of the tension between local and universal principles for multinational bankruptcies with particular reference to the United States, and Tagashira (1994), Gitlin and Flaschen (1987), and Powers (1993) discuss various efforts at international bankruptcy cooperation and their shortcomings.

Multinational Capital Structure and Internal Capital Markets 2457

and external costs of funds. Many efforts to examine the role of internal capital markets have been limited by relatively small samples, as in Blanchard, Lopez-de-Silanes, and Shleifer (1994) and Lamont (1997), or, as noted by Kaplan and Zingales (1997), by questionable a priori assumptions about what characterizes firms that face sizable wedges between internal and external costs of funds. This paper considers a large sample of firms, looking across environments in which differences between internal and external costs of funds differ systematically for reasons related to the development of capital markets, analyzing the allocation of funds within firms in response to these costs.[7]

Tests of the extent of substitution of internal capital for external capital across different borrowing environments reveal the degree to which multinational firms can use internal markets to overcome shortcomings associated with external credit market conditions. These tests produce powerful evidence of whether weak local capital market conditions constrain local borrowers. If affiliates substitute parent-provided debt for external debt where creditor rights are weak and where locally provided debt is scarce or expensive, then the use of external debt must be a relatively unattractive option in those locations. If local firms rely primarily on local sources of debt, then access to large internal capital markets may give multinational affiliates cost advantages over local firms. Multinational firms are also able to respond to tax incentives by adjusting loans between parent companies and subsidiaries, thereby creating tax planning opportunities not available to local firms. The sensitivity of parent loans to tax rate differences indicates the extent to which firms manage their internal finances to exploit these opportunities.

II. Multinational Affiliate Data

The empirical work analyzes data collected by the Bureau of Economic Analysis (BEA) for its Benchmark Survey of U.S. Direct Investment Abroad in 1982, 1989, and 1994, which includes information on the financial and operating characteristics of U.S. firms operating abroad. As a result of confidentiality assurances and penalties for noncompliance, BEA believes that coverage is close to complete and levels of accuracy are high. The surveys ask reporters for details on each affiliates' income statement, balance sheet, employment, and a variety of transactions between U.S. parents and their foreign affiliates. The foreign affiliate survey forms that U.S. multinational enterprises are required to complete vary depending on the year, the size of the affiliate, and the U.S. parent's percentage of ownership of the affiliate. In each of the benchmark years considered (1982, 1989, and 1994), all affiliates with sales, assets, or net income in excess of $3 million in absolute value, and their parents, were required to file extensive reports. Reporters must abide by generally accepted U.S.

---

[7] Stein (1997), Shin and Stulz (1998), and Scharfstein and Stein (2000), among others, discuss how internal capital markets can either ameliorate or exacerbate other frictions. Hubbard and Palia (1999) emphasize empirically how conglomerates may use internal capital markets opportunistically in response to costly external financing.

accounting principles and follow FASB 52 when dealing with foreign currency translations.[8]

The top panel of Table I displays the descriptive statistics for the sample of affiliates in each of the three benchmark years. In 1994, 17,898 affiliates of 2,373 parent firms filed forms, and these affiliates had mean and median assets of $74 million and $13 million, respectively. The main measure of affiliate leverage used in the analysis that follows is the ratio of current liabilities and long-term debt to affiliate assets. This measure has a mean and median of approximately 0.55 over the sample period. The main reason for focusing the analysis on this measure of leverage is that the data allow this measure to be disaggregated into the amount owed to an affiliate's corporate parent and the amount owed to other lenders. Nonetheless, the analysis in Table II considers a more narrow definition of leverage that removes trade credit, and the ratio of this restricted definition of debt to assets has a mean value of 0.35 over the period.

As the data in Table I indicate, the vast majority of debt comes from nonparent sources. Borrowing from the parent/assets is the ratio of the difference between the level of current liabilities and long-term debt an affiliate borrows from, and lends to, its U.S. parent to total affiliate assets. This variable has a mean of approximately 0.08 over the sample period, and a median that is just larger than zero. External borrowing/assets, the ratio of the level of current liabilities and long-term debt an affiliate borrows from nonparent sources to total affiliate assets, has a mean of 0.44 and a median of 0.41 for the benchmark years. On average, less than 20% of current liabilities and long-term debt comes from parent sources.[9]

The BEA data also contain information on the interest expense associated with affiliate debt, and it is possible to use this information to calculate an affiliate's average interest rate in a year. Because the data do not contain detailed information on interest rates charged on individual loans or on which types of debt are interest-bearing, the analysis uses two estimates of interest rates. The first measure is the interest rate on external borrowing, which is calculated

---

[8] Majority-owned affiliates were required to report a broader set of accounting items than were minority-owned affiliates. Larger affiliates were required to file longer forms than were smaller affiliates in 1989 and 1994. Additional information on the BEA data can be found in Mataloni (1995) and Desai et al. (2003).

[9] Three data shortcomings potentially limit identification of external and parent borrowing. First, there is no information on the extent to which parent companies guarantee affiliate loans. Second, back-to-back loans, in which a parent lends to a multinational bank which in turn lends to an affiliate through a branch located abroad, are recorded as external debt despite significant parent involvement. Third, loans made by an affiliate to another affiliate of the same parent are classified as external borrowing. Since these shortcomings blur the distinction between external and parent borrowing, they may reduce the measured differences between these two forms of debt. As a result, tests that distinguish the responsiveness of external and parent debt to taxes and borrowing conditions that use these data, if anything, underestimate true differences, and tests of the substitution of parent provided debt for external debt, if anything, underestimate the extent of substitution.

Multinational Capital Structure and Internal Capital Markets   2459

Table I
Descriptive Statistics for Affiliates of U.S. Multinationals in 1982, 1989, and 1994

The top panel provides descriptive statistics for dependent variables for all affiliates of U.S. multinationals by year and for the entire sample. Affiliate leverage is the ratio of affiliate current liabilities and long-term debt to total affiliate assets. Affiliate nontrade account leverage is the ratio of affiliate current liabilities and long-term debt, less trade accounts and trade notes payable, to total affiliate assets. External borrowing/assets is the ratio of current liabilities and long-term debt an affiliate borrows from nonparent sources to total affiliate assets. Borrowing from the parent/assets is the ratio of net current liabilities and long-term debt an affiliate borrows from its U.S. parent to total affiliate assets. The interest rate on external borrowing is the ratio of the affiliate interest payments to nonparents to current liabilities and long-term debt borrowed from nonparent sources. The interest rate on nontrade account borrowing is the ratio of total affiliate interest payments to current liabilities and long-term debt, excluding trade accounts and trade notes payable. The bottom panel reports descriptive statistics for control variables for all affiliates across all years. Country Tax Rate is the median tax rate in an affiliate's host country measured on an annual basis in the manner described in the text. Private credit is the ratio of private credit lent by deposit money banks to GDP, as provided in Beck et al. (1999). Creditor rights is an index of the strength of creditor rights developed in LaPorta et al. (1998); higher levels of the measure, which ranges from 0 to 4, indicate stronger legal protections. Net PPE/assets is the ratio of affiliate net property, plant, and equipment to total affiliate assets. EBITDA/assets is the ratio of affiliate earnings before interest, taxes, depreciation and amortization to total affiliate assets. Log of sales is the natural log of affiliate sales. Political risk is the annual average of the monthly index of political risk presented in the International Country Risk Guide, rescaled to lie between 0 and 1 with higher numbers indicating higher risks. Rate of inflation is the contemporaneous percentage change in the GDP deflator of an affiliate's host country. Growth options is the compound annual growth rate of total affiliate sales in an affiliate's country and industry until the following benchmark year. Share of debt from nonparent sources is the share of affiliate current liabilities and long-term debt owed to lenders other than the affiliate's parent.

| | Benchmark Years | | | |
	1982	1989	1994	All Years
Number of affiliates	14,918	15,243	17,898	32,342
Number of parents	1,902	1,989	2,373	3,680
Assets				
Mean	39,213	57,209	73,762	57,861
Median	8,401	10,987	12,704	10,597
Standard deviation	181,507	290,062	356,849	291,098
Affiliate leverage				
Mean	0.5707	0.5434	0.5446	0.5518
Median	0.5574	0.5256	0.5277	0.5364
Standard deviation	0.2893	0.3000	0.3131	0.3023
Affiliate nontrade account leverage				
Mean	0.3435	0.3540	0.3627	0.3499
Median	0.2779	0.2989	0.3149	0.2885
Standard deviation	0.2856	0.2779	0.2749	0.2816
External borrowing/assets				
Mean	0.4626	0.4433	0.4306	0.4439
Median	0.4329	0.4098	0.3840	0.4074
Standard deviation	0.2798	0.2916	0.3008	0.2921

(continued)

Table I—*Continued*

	Benchmark Years			All Years
	1982	1989	1994	
Borrowing from the parent/assets				
Mean	0.0845	0.0705	0.0846	0.0801
Median	0.0077	0.0032	0.0022	0.0041
Standard deviation	0.2464	0.2357	0.2616	0.2490
Interest rate on external borrowing				
Mean	0.0595	0.0435	0.0298	0.0493
Median	0.0231	0.0138	0.0099	0.0163
Standard deviation	0.1010	0.0883	0.0642	0.0922
Interest rate on nontrade account borrowing				
Mean	0.0919	0.0659	0.0485	0.0765
Median	0.0397	0.0269	0.0180	0.0299
Standard deviation	0.1463	0.1196	0.0974	0.1322
Descriptive Statistics for All Affiliate Years	Mean	Median	SD	
Country tax rate	0.3431	0.3404	0.1228	
Private credit	0.7927	0.7945	0.4478	
Creditor rights	1.9953	2.0000	1.3211	
Net PPE/assets	0.2360	0.1623	0.2357	
EBITDA/assets	0.1479	0.1378	0.2138	
Log of sales	9.5549	9.5540	2.0431	
Political risk	0.2359	0.2050	0.1215	
Rate of inflation	0.5572	0.0571	3.1066	
Growth options	0.0726	0.0613	0.1788	
Share of debt from nonparent sources	0.8148	0.9706	0.2795	

by dividing affiliate interest payments to nonparents by current liabilities and long-term debt borrowed from nonparent sources. This variable has a mean of approximately 0.05 and a median of approximately 0.02 over the sample period. One of the reasons that these average interest rates appear low is that the broad measure of debt used in this calculation includes trade credit, which is often noninterest bearing.[10]

In order to ensure that the interest rate regressions do not produce spurious results driven by differences in the use of trade credit, the dependent variable in several of the regressions is the interest rate on nontrade account borrowing, which is the ratio of total interest paid to a measure of current liabilities

---

[10] Interest rates are based on current interest payments, and therefore exclude payments to creditors in the event of default. Capital market equilibrium implies that interest rates measured in this way should be higher in jurisdictions in which creditor rights are weaker, and expected default payments are lower. Interest payments are recorded in U.S. dollars. The currency denomination of debt may be important to financial decision making within a multinational firm, but it is impossible to tell from the BEA data in which currency debt is formally denominated. See Kedia and Mazumdar (2003) and Allayannis, Brown, and Klapper (2003) for analyses of the determinants of the currency denomination of debt.

and long-term debt that excludes trade accounts and trade notes payable. This alternative interest rate variable has a mean of 0.08 and a median of 0.03. This variable includes interest payments to parents and external sources in the numerator and total debt in the denominator.

The bottom panel of Table I provides summary statistics for independent variables used in the regression analysis. Included among these variables are measures of affiliate characteristics that other studies (Titman and Wessels (1988), Rajan and Zingales (1995)) have shown to be correlated with leverage. These are all drawn from BEA data and include a measure of the tangibility of affiliate assets (the ratio of affiliate net property, plant, and equipment to assets), the cash flow generating capacity of underlying assets (the ratio of affiliate EBITDA to assets), affiliate size (the natural logarithm of affiliate sales), and the scope of growth options (as proxied by future sales growth within a country/industry grouping).[11] In addition, the relevant country-level measures of tax incentives, capital market depth, legal protections, and macroeconomic and political stability are summarized. Tax rates are calculated from BEA data by taking the ratio of foreign income taxes paid to foreign pretax income for each affiliate and using the medians of these rates as country-level observations for each country and year.[12] Mean and median country tax rates are equal to approximately 34% over the sample period. Private credit is the ratio of private credit lent by deposit money banks to GDP, as provided in Beck, Demirguc-Kunt, and Levine (1999). Creditor rights is an index of the strength of creditor rights developed in La Porta et al. (1998) that ranges from 0 to 4, with higher levels indicating stronger legal protections. Political risk is the annual average of monthly assessments from the International Country Risk Guide, rescaled to lie between 0 and 1, with higher values indicating greater risk. Since data for 1982 are unavailable, 1984 values are used in their place. The rate of inflation is the contemporaneous percentage change in a host country's GDP deflator.

III. Results

The first set of regressions reported in this section considers the determinants of total affiliate leverage, emphasizing the effects of local tax rates and

---

[11] The growth options variable is the compound annual rate of sales growth for all affiliates in a country/industry cell between the current and following BEA benchmark survey. For example, an observation for an affiliate in Germany in drug manufacturing in 1982 would have a corresponding growth options value equal to the annual percentage rate of sales growth for German drug manufacturing affiliates between 1982 and 1989. While this is not an ideal measure of growth options, standard alternatives, such as market-to-book ratios, are not feasible in the multinational setting.

[12] Affiliates with negative net income are excluded for the purposes of calculating country tax rates. For a more comprehensive description of the calculation of affiliate tax rates, see Desai et al. (2001). In particular, these income tax rates do not include withholding taxes on cross-border interest payments to related parties, since such taxes are endogenous to interest payments and in any case immediately creditable against home-country tax liabilities. Desai and Hines (1999) report that adjusting country tax rates for withholding taxes does not affect the estimated impact of taxation on affiliate borrowing, due to the combination of creditability and low withholding tax rates on related-party interest payments.

credit market conditions. This framework is then employed to examine whether these determinants have differential effects on internal and external borrowing and to test if affiliates substitute borrowing from parent companies for external borrowing in response to poorly functioning capital markets. Finally, the analysis considers how legal protections and capital depth affect the cost of external borrowing and tests if the composition of affiliate borrowing reflects the variation in these costs.

A. Determinants of Affiliate Leverage

Affiliates in countries with high local corporate tax rates face the strongest incentives to finance their investments with debt rather than equity. Figure 1 depicts the relationship between country tax rates and U.S. affiliate leverage in 1994. Leverage is the ratio of aggregate current liabilities and long-term debt to aggregate assets in each host country as measured in the 1994 BEA benchmark survey and reported by the U.S. Department of Commerce (1998). Figure 1 indicates that affiliates in high-tax countries generally make greater use of debt to finance their assets than do affiliates in low-tax countries. Affiliates in tax havens such as Bermuda and Barbados have aggregate leverage ratios of 0.30 or less, while affiliates in high-tax countries such as Japan and Italy have aggregate leverage ratios that exceed 0.53. Although the scatter plot in

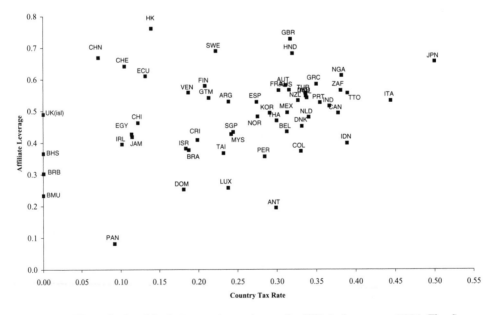

Figure 1. The relationship between tax rates and affiliate leverage, 1994. The figure provides a scatter plot of the relationship between affiliate leverage, on the y-axis, and local tax rates, on the x-axis, for 1994. Affiliate leverage is the ratio of current liabilities and long-term debt to total assets, as measured in the aggregate in the 1994 Benchmark Survey, and the tax rate is measured as the median tax rate, as defined in the text, for affiliates in a given country.

Multinational Capital Structure and Internal Capital Markets 2463

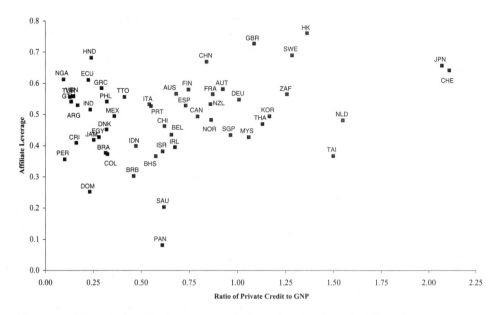

Figure 2. The relationship between capital market depth and affiliate leverage, 1994.
The figure provides a scatter plot of the relationship between affiliate leverage, on the y-axis, and the ratio of private credit to GNP, on the x-axis, for 1994. Affiliate leverage is the ratio of current liabilities and long-term debt to total assets, as measured in the aggregate in the 1994 Benchmark Survey, and the ratio of private credit to GNP is the ratio of private credit lent by deposit money banks to GNP, as provided in Beck et al. (1999).

Figure 1 does not control for characteristics of affiliates or nontax features of host countries, it does provide suggestive evidence that multinational parents capitalize their affiliates differentially in response to the incentives associated with the relative tax advantage of debt.

Figure 2 provides a similar descriptive scatter plot but emphasizes the relationship between capital market depth, measured as the ratio of private credit lent by deposit money banks in the host country to GDP, and aggregate leverage ratios of U.S. affiliates in 1994. The upward-sloping pattern in Figure 2 suggests that there is a positive correlation between levels of affiliate leverage and the local availability of credit. U.S. affiliates exhibit high leverage ratios in countries such as Japan and Switzerland, which have very deep credit markets, and considerably lower leverage ratios in countries such as Peru, the Dominican Republic, and Panama, where domestic private credit is scarce. There are exceptions to this pattern: affiliates have high leverage ratios in Honduras, Ecuador, Nigeria, Venezuela, and some other countries in which they seem to overcome shortcomings in local credit markets. In order to isolate more carefully the relationship between affiliate leverage, corporate tax incentives, and the strength of local credit markets, while also controlling for conflating factors, it is helpful to run regressions, the results of which are presented in Table II.

Table II

The Impact of Taxes and Capital Market Conditions on Multinational Affiliate Leverage

The dependent variable in columns 1 to 5 is the ratio of affiliate current liabilities and long-term debt to total affiliate assets; in columns 6 to 10, the dependent variable is the ratio of affiliate current liabilities and long-term debt, less trade accounts and trade notes payable, to total affiliate assets. All regressions are estimated by ordinary least squares and include parent, industry, and year fixed effects. Country tax rate is the median tax rate in an affiliate's host country. Private credit is the ratio of private credit lent by deposit money banks to GDP, as provided in Beck et al. (1999). Creditor rights is an index of the strength of creditor rights developed in LaPorta et al. (1998); higher levels of the measure, which ranges from 0 to 4, indicate stronger legal protections. Net PPE/assets is the ratio of affiliate net property, plant, and equipment to total affiliate assets. EBITDA/assets is the ratio of affiliate earnings before interest, taxes, depreciation and amortization to total affiliate assets. Log of sales is the natural log of affiliate sales. Political risk is the annual average of the monthly index of political risk presented in the International Country Risk Guide, rescaled to lie between 0 and 1 with higher numbers indicating higher risks. Rate of inflation is the contemporaneous percentage change in the GDP deflator of an affiliate's host country. Growth options is the compound annual growth rate of total affiliate sales in an affiliate's country and industry until the following benchmark year. Standard errors that correct for clustering of errors across observations in country/industry cells are presented in parentheses.

Dependent Variables	Affiliate Leverage					Affiliate Nontrade Account Leverage				
	(1)	(2)	(3)	(4)	(5)	(6)	(7)	(8)	(9)	(10)
Constant	0.6827	0.6878	0.5782	0.2906	0.4745	−0.2114	0.1470	0.7448	0.5849	0.6976
	(0.0665)	(0.0799)	(0.0496)	(0.1043)	(0.1558)	(0.0855)	(0.1659)	(0.0986)	(0.0598)	(0.0681)
Country tax rate	0.2646	0.2608	0.3206	0.2446	0.2698	0.1281	0.1257	0.1714	0.1297	0.1640
	(0.0205)	(0.0235)	(0.0226)	(0.0328)	(0.0314)	(0.0225)	(0.0257)	(0.0249)	(0.0274)	(0.0270)
Private credit		−0.0051		−0.0050			−0.0086		−0.0011	
		(0.0052)		(0.0076)			(0.0059)		(0.0072)	

Multinational Capital Structure and Internal Capital Markets   2465

	(1)	(2)	(3)	(4)	(5)	(6)	(7)	(8)	(9)	(10)
Creditor rights	0.0033		0.0044			0.0047		0.0082		
	(0.0019)		(0.0018)			(0.0024)		(0.0020)		
Net PPE/assets	0.0679	0.0717				-0.0242	-0.0207			
	(0.0163)	(0.0156)				(0.0176)	(0.0169)			
EBITDA/assets	-0.2764	-0.2755				-0.4377	-0.4304			
	(0.0150)	(0.0148)				(0.0175)	(0.0171)			
Log of sales	-0.0037	-0.0047				0.0028	0.0017			
	(0.0021)	(0.0021)				(0.0023)	(0.0023)			
Political risk	0.0703	0.0797				0.1441	0.1171			
	(0.0239)	(0.0254)				(0.0277)	(0.0277)			
Rate of inflation	0.0000	-0.0006				-0.0013	-0.0018			
	(0.0008)	(0.0008)				(0.0008)	(0.0008)			
Growth options	-0.0027	0.0077				0.0061	0.0202			
	(0.0166)	(0.0162)				(0.0174)	(0.0173)			
Parent, industry, and year fixed effects?	Y	Y	Y	Y	Y	Y	Y	Y	Y	Y
No. of obs.	18,132	18,775	23,795	25,179	26,580	17,527	18,109	39,995	42,639	44,460
R^2	0.2933	0.2859	0.2375	0.2253	0.2240	0.3516	0.3411	0.2460	0.2329	0.2286

The dependent variable in the specifications reported in columns 1 to 5 of Table II is the same measure of leverage employed in Figures 1 and 2 but is constructed at the affiliate level, so it equals the ratio of affiliate current liabilities and long-term debt to total assets. The data consist of affiliate-year observations for affiliates of U.S. firms in 1982, 1989, and 1994. Given that many potential determinants of affiliate leverage, particularly those that vary between companies and over time, might conflate this analysis, Table II reports the estimated coefficients from regressions that include a full set of year dummy variables, parent company dummy variables, and affiliate industry dummy variables. As a result, firm-specific considerations and industry-specific considerations implicitly do not affect the estimates reported in Table II (or those reported in subsequent tables); Desai et al. (2003) report the estimates of the same regression specifications without fixed effects, the results of which are broadly consistent with those reported in Tables II to VI. All regressions treat each affiliate-year observation in the panel as a separate observation; the standard errors in all of the tables correct for clustering of errors across observations in country/industry cells.

The regression reported in column 1 of Table II suggests that affiliate leverage responds strongly to local tax incentives. The 0.2646 estimated coefficient on the country tax rate implies that 10% higher tax rates are associated with affiliate leverage that is 2.6% greater as a fraction of assets. The specifications presented in columns 2 to 5 of Table II also consider the effect of capital market development and investor protections on levels of affiliate leverage. The specification reported in column 2 indicates that the level of private credit has a negative, but insignificant, effect on aggregate leverage. In contrast, the regression reported in column 3 indicates that stronger legal protections for creditors are associated with significantly greater use of debt. In the regression reported in column 3, a one-point increase in the (five-point) creditor rights index is associated with 0.82% greater affiliate leverage as a fraction of assets.

These regressions may in part reflect the impact of heterogeneous affiliate and country characteristics that are unrelated to tax rates and creditor rights, but happen to be correlated with them. It is possible to control for relevant observable aspects of heterogeneity, such as the tangibility of affiliate assets, the cash flow generating capacity of underlying assets, affiliate size, the scope of growth options, the political risk associated with operating in the affiliate's host country, and the annual inflation rate in the affiliate's host country. The regressions reported in columns 4 and 5 of Table II add these variables to the specifications reported in columns 2 and 3. The sample size in these specifications is significantly smaller because information required to construct the additional controls is collected only for a smaller set of affiliates.[13]

---

[13] The reduced sample includes all majority-owned affiliates that report in 1982, and all majority-owned affiliates that are large enough to file the long form in 1989 and 1994. As a result of reporting requirements, smaller samples are also used for many specifications in Tables III to VI.

Multinational Capital Structure and Internal Capital Markets 2467

These other affiliate and country characteristics appear also to influence leverage ratios. Affiliates with greater shares of assets in tangible property use less debt, but this effect is not statistically significant. Affiliates characterized by greater cash flow generating capacity have significantly lower levels of affiliate leverage, while inflation has only a modest effect on affiliate leverage. Multinationals use greater debt in politically risky countries, which is consistent with other evidence such as Novaes's (1998) study of foreign affiliates in Brazil. Finally, an affiliate's growth potential has limited influence on capital structure, suggesting, as one might expect, that the debt-overhang problem is ameliorated for subsidiaries of multinational parents. The inclusion of these additional affiliate and country variables has little effect on the estimated impact of taxation and creditor rights on affiliate leverage.[14]

The measure of affiliate leverage employed in columns 1 to 5 includes a component associated with trade credit. Given the distinct features of trade credit, it is useful to conduct similar analysis with trade credit stripped out of the numerator of the affiliate leverage measure, making it comparable to the nontrade account measures of leverage common in the literature. Unfortunately, this restriction comes at some cost, as this nontrade account measure of leverage can be calculated only for a subset of affiliates and cannot be broken into debt from external sources and debt from parents. Nonetheless, it is useful to repeat the analysis reported in columns 1–5, using this measure of debt as the dependent variable. The estimated sensitivity of borrowing to taxes, capital market depth, and creditor rights in the regressions reported in columns 6 to 10 of Table II are all consistent with those obtained using the more inclusive measure of debt as the dependent variable. Indeed, the only notable and significant distinction between the previous results and the results for the nontrade account measure of leverage is the impact of the tangibility of assets, as this variable now has a positive and significant coefficient. The negative estimated coefficients on the measure of asset tangibility in the regressions reported in columns 4 and 5 most likely reflect that affiliates within some industries that provide considerable trade credit also have low levels of tangible assets (e.g., manufacturing affiliates engaging in some wholesale trade), so the right panel of Table II provides clearer evidence of the link between asset tangibility and leverage, by emphasizing nontrade account borrowing. The similarity of the results with and without trade account credit as a component of leverage suggests that the subsequent analysis of borrowing from parents and external sources, for which data limitations make it impossible to strip out trade credit, is unlikely to harbor important biases.

---

[14] As an alternative to pooling observations across years and using year fixed effects, it is possible to conduct the same analysis for each year separately. Doing so significantly reduces the degrees of freedom in these regressions because each includes a full set of parent and industry fixed effects and because sample sizes are limited by reporting restrictions on the EBITDA variable. The regressions were rerun on annual cross-sections, using return on equity in place of EBITDA in order to obtain larger samples, and the results are broadly consistent with those reported in Tables II to VI.

B. The Composition of Affiliate Leverage and Substitutions in Quantities

The finding that aggregate affiliate leverage responds to tax incentives and capital market conditions may mask divergent responses of external borrowing and borrowing from parent companies. The evidence presented in Figures 3 and 4 suggests that legal and capital market conditions influence these two types of borrowing very differently. Figure 3 displays the relationship between the depth of local credit markets and aggregate borrowing from nonparent sources. The scatter plot implies a positive relationship between capital market depth and external borrowing. Comparing Figures 2 and 3 suggests that borrowing from nonparent sources is more sensitive to local capital market conditions than is total leverage. Affiliates located in many of the countries with weak credit markets, such as Honduras, Ecuador, Guatemala, Argentina, and Venezuela, rely heavily on their parents for debt.

Figure 4 offers additional evidence of the effect of the borrowing environment on the composition of debt by graphing the relationship between creditor rights and different types of debt. There is a subtle rise in the ratio of total current liabilities and long-term debt to assets as the creditor rights' index increases from 0 to 4. However, this aggregate measure obscures divergent effects of creditor rights on borrowing from parents and borrowing from nonparent sources. The

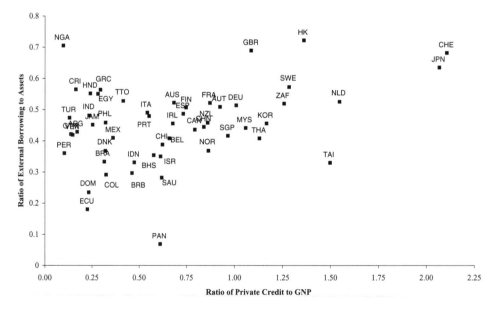

Figure 3. The relationship between capital market depth and external borrowing, 1994. The figure provides a scatter plot of the relationship between the ratio of external borrowing to assets, on the y-axis, and the ratio of private credit to GNP, on the x-axis, for 1994. The ratio of external borrowing to assets is the ratio of borrowings from unrelated parties to total assets, as measured in the aggregate in the 1994 Benchmark Survey, and the ratio of private credit to GNP is the ratio of private credit lent by deposit money banks to GNP, as provided in Beck et al. (1999).

Multinational Capital Structure and Internal Capital Markets   2469

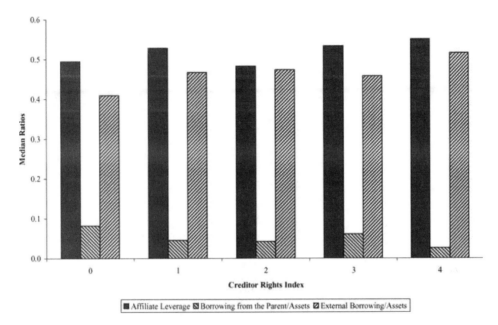

Figure 4. The relationship between creditor rights and affiliate leverage, 1994. The figure provides the median affiliate leverage ratio, median ratio of borrowing from the parent to assets, and median ratio of external borrowing to assets in 1994 by rating for creditor rights. Affiliate Leverage is the ratio of current liabilities and long-term debt to total affiliate assets, as measured in the aggregate in the 1994 Benchmark Survey. Borrowing from the Parent/Assets is the ratio of net current liabilities and long-term debt affiliates borrowed from U.S. parents to total assets, as measured in the aggregate in the 1994 Benchmark Survey. External Borrowing/Assets is the ratio of current liabilities and long-term debt borrowed from nonparent sources to total assets, as measured in the aggregate in the 1994 Benchmark Survey.

ratio of net parent borrowing to assets decreases as creditor rights improve, while the ratio of aggregate external borrowing to aggregate assets increases as creditor rights improve.

In order to analyze these differences, the two panels of Table III present regressions that evaluate the impact of tax incentives and measures of capital market depth on external borrowing and borrowing from parent companies. In the regressions reported in columns 1 to 5 of Table III, the dependent variable is the ratio of current liabilities and long-term debt owed to nonparents to total affiliate assets. In the regressions reported in columns 6 to 10 of Table III, the dependent variable is the ratio of the difference between the current liabilities and long-term debt an affiliate owes to and borrows from its parent to total affiliate assets. All specifications employ parent, industry, and year fixed effects so that firm-specific and industry-specific considerations implicitly do not affect the estimates.

The regressions reported in columns 1 and 6 indicate that borrowing from external sources and borrowing from parents are both sensitive to tax incentives; the regressions reported in columns 2 to 5 and 7 to 10 indicate that adding

Table III
The Impact of Taxes and Capital Market Conditions on the Composition of Leverage

The dependent variable in columns 1 to 5 is the ratio of current liabilities and long-term debt an affiliate borrows from nonparent sources to total affiliate assets; in columns 6 to 10, the dependent variable is the ratio of net current liabilities and long-term debt an affiliate borrows from its U.S. parent to total affiliate assets. All regressions are estimated by ordinary least squares and include parent, industry, and year fixed effects. Country tax rate is the median tax rate in an affiliate's host country. Private credit is the ratio of private credit lent by deposit money banks to GDP, as provided in Beck et al. (1999). Creditor rights is an index of the strength of creditor rights developed in LaPorta et al. (1998); higher levels of the measure, which ranges from 0 to 4, indicate stronger legal protections. Net PPE/assets is the ratio of affiliate net property, plant and equipment to total affiliate assets. EBITDA/assets is the ratio of affiliate earnings before interest, taxes, depreciation, and amortization to total affiliate assets. Log of sales is the natural log of affiliate sales. Political risk is the annual average of the monthly index of political risk presented in the International Country Risk Guide, rescaled to lie between 0 and 1 with higher numbers indicating higher risks. Rate of inflation is the contemporaneous percentage change in the GDP deflator of an affiliate's host country. Growth options is the compound annual growth rate of total affiliate sales in an affiliate's country and industry until the following benchmark year. Standard errors that correct for clustering of errors across observations in country/industry cells are presented in parentheses.

Dependent Variables	External Borrowing/Assets					Borrowing from the Parent/Assets				
	(1)	(2)	(3)	(4)	(5)	(6)	(7)	(8)	(9)	(10)
Constant	0.2535	0.2706	0.5963	0.4088	0.6867	−0.1683	−0.0649	0.1000	0.2552	0.1736
	(0.0292)	(0.0298)	(0.0633)	(0.1449)	(0.0976)	(0.1691)	(0.0387)	(0.0806)	(0.0452)	(0.0599)
Country tax rate	0.2831	0.2472	0.3218	0.2100	0.2461	0.0515	0.0689	0.0501	0.0841	0.0822
	(0.0197)	(0.0226)	(0.0229)	(0.0327)	(0.0323)	(0.0156)	(0.0162)	(0.0190)	(0.0249)	(0.0272)
Private credit		0.0218		0.0131			−0.0314		−0.0192	
		(0.0053)		(0.0079)			(0.0038)		(0.0063)	

Multinational Capital Structure and Internal Capital Markets   2471

	(1)	(2)	(3)	(4)	(5)	(6)	(7)	(8)	(9)	(10)
Creditor rights			0.0107			0.0057		−0.0042		
			(0.0024)			(0.0029)		(0.0013)		
Net PPE/assets					−0.0251	−0.0236			0.1047	0.0959
					(0.0168)	(0.0176)			(0.0152)	(0.0155)
EBITDA/assets					−0.2535	−0.2592			−0.2132	−0.2068
					(0.0168)	(0.0171)			(0.0136)	(0.0136)
Log of sales					0.0063	0.0066			−0.0027	−0.0032
					(0.0021)	(0.0022)			(0.0020)	(0.0018)
Political risk					0.0678	0.0704			0.0566	0.0750
					(0.0293)	(0.0286)			(0.0208)	(0.0231)
Rate of inflation					−0.0026	−0.0024			0.0012	0.0014
					(0.0007)	(0.0007)			(0.0007)	(0.0007)
Growth options					0.0432	0.0278			−0.0397	−0.0420
					(0.0172)	(0.0178)			(0.0142)	(0.0148)
Parent, industry, and year fixed effects?	Y	Y	Y	Y	Y	Y	Y	Y	Y	Y
No. of obs.	45,152	43,290	40,568	46,713	18,242	17,649	44,595	41,702	18,883	18,238
R^2	0.2293	0.2339	0.2453	0.2235	0.3013	0.3077	0.2352	0.2504	0.2868	0.2921

variables that capture capital market conditions and other affiliate controls does not change this result. Given the distinct shares of external and internal borrowing, it is useful to translate these coefficient estimates into corresponding elasticities in order to make them comparable. The 0.2461 estimated tax rate coefficient in the regression reported in column 5 of Table III, together with a sample mean external borrowing-to-assets ratio of 0.4439, and a sample mean tax rate of 0.3431, implies a tax elasticity of external borrowing equal to 0.19. While the estimated 0.0822 tax rate coefficient in the parent borrowing regression reported in column 10 of Table III is significantly smaller, the implied elasticity of parent borrowing is 0.35, reflecting the much smaller (0.0801) ratio of parent borrowing to total assets. The greater tax rate sensitivity of parent borrowing than external borrowing is consistent with the hypothesis that multinational firms fine-tune their internal financial transactions to avoid taxes.

While external and parent borrowing respond to tax incentives with different magnitudes but in similar ways, they respond to capital market depth and creditor rights in distinct ways. For example, the 0.0057 estimated coefficient reported in column 5 of Table III indicates that a one unit increase in the creditor rights' index raises borrowing from external sources by 0.57% of assets. In contrast, the −0.0035 estimated coefficient reported in column 10 of Table V implies that a one unit increase in the creditor rights' index is associated with borrowing from parents that falls by 0.35% of assets. A similar pattern appears in the regressions using capital market depth as the explanatory variable. These regressions imply that the aggregate borrowing behavior considered in the regressions reported in Table II masks distinct and contrary effects of capital market conditions on the components of borrowing. Estimated coefficients on other control variables are comparable between the regressions explaining external and parent borrowing with a few exceptions. Net PPE/Assets has a positive and significant coefficient in the specifications explaining parent borrowing but is insignificant in explaining external borrowing. One possible interpretation of this difference is that it reflects the purchase and financing of capital goods from multinational parents. Finally, external borrowing increases with affiliate size, while internal borrowing does not, suggesting that large affiliates are better able to access capital markets.

The fact that multinational affiliates use less external debt and more related party debt as capital markets weaken suggests that these forms of finance are substitutes. The extent to which firms substitute parent debt for external debt can be measured directly, and that is the purpose of the regressions reported in Table IV, in which borrowing from parent companies is the dependent variable and external borrowing is an independent variable. In this setting, a coefficient of −1.0 on external borrowing would correspond to perfect substitutability between parent and external debt. The regressions reported in columns 1 and 2 of Table IV imply a smaller, though statistically significant, degree of substitutability: borrowing from parent companies offsets between 12 and 16% of changes in external borrowing.

Multinational Capital Structure and Internal Capital Markets   2473

Table IV
The Substitutability of Parent and External Debt

The dependent variable is the ratio of net current liabilities and long-term debt an affiliate borrows from its U.S. parent to total affiliate assets. The specifications in columns 1 and 2 are estimated by ordinary least squares, and all specifications include parent, industry, and year fixed effects. External borrowing/assets is the ratio of current liabilities and long-term debt an affiliate borrows from nonparent sources to total affiliate assets. The specifications in columns 3 and 4 instrument for external borrowing/assets using private credit. Private credit is the ratio of private credit lent by deposit money banks to GDP, as provided in Beck et al. (1999). The specifications in columns 5 and 6 instrument for external borrowing/assets using creditor rights. Creditor rights is an index of the strength of creditor rights developed in LaPorta et al. (1998); higher levels of the measure, which ranges from 0 to 4, indicate stronger legal protections. The specificiations in columns 7 and 8 instrument for external borrowing/assets using both private credit and creditor rights. Country tax rate is the median tax rate in an affiliate's host country. Net PPE/assets is the ratio of affiliate net property, plant, and equipment to total affiliate assets. EBITDA/assets is the ratio of affiliate earnings before interest, taxes, depreciation, and amortization to total affiliate assets. Log of sales is the natural log of affiliate sales. Political risk is the annual average of the monthly index of political risk presented in the International Country Risk Guide, rescaled to lie between 0 and 1 with higher numbers indicating higher risks. Rate of inflation is the contemporaneous percentage change in the GDP deflator of an affiliate's host country. Growth options is the compound annual growth rate of total affiliate sales in an affiliate's country and industry until the following benchmark year. Standard errors are presented in parentheses, and in columns 1 and 2 these errors correct for clustering of errors across observations in country/industry cells.

Dependent Variable	Borrowing from the Parent/Assets							
	(1)	(2)	(3)	(4)	(5)	(6)	(7)	(8)
Constant	0.0824	0.3204	0.2478	1.3236	0.0588	0.0349	0.1110	-0.0160
	(0.0178)	(0.1845)	(0.2276)	(0.6527)	(0.1683)	(0.4131)	(0.1771)	(0.4295)
External borrowing/assets	-0.1177	-0.1619	-0.9693	-1.5245	-0.4758	-0.6309	-0.6111	-0.7557
	(0.0063)	(0.0099)	(0.1224)	(0.6913)	(0.0944)	(0.2356)	(0.0690)	(0.1612)
Country tax rate		0.1085		0.4007		0.2263		0.2388
		(0.0245)		(0.1479)		(0.0588)		(0.0390)

(continued)

Table IV—*Continued*

Dependent Variable	Borrowing from the Parent/Assets							
	(1)	(2)	(3)	(4)	(5)	(6)	(7)	(8)
Net PPE/assets		0.1111		0.0636		0.0779		0.0719
		(0.0162)		(0.0262)		(0.0128)		(0.0131)
EBITDA/assets		−0.2645		−0.6240		−0.3893		−0.4222
		(0.0140)		(0.1837)		(0.0641)		(0.0448)
Log of sales		−0.0012		0.0064		0.0008		0.0015
		(0.0022)		(0.0050)		(0.0021)		(0.0018)
Political risk		0.0782		0.1574		0.1169		0.1348
		(0.0207)		(0.0445)		(0.0241)		(0.0242)
Rate of inflation		0.0013		−0.0028		0.0000		−0.0005
		(0.0007)		(0.0022)		(0.0009)		(0.0008)
Growth options		−0.0296		0.0282		−0.0260		−0.0163
		(0.0151)		(0.0373)		(0.0151)		(0.0156)
Parent, industry, and year fixed effects?	Y	Y	Y	Y	Y	Y	Y	Y
IV w/private credit?	N	N	Y	Y	N	N	Y	Y
IV w/creditor rights?	N	N	N	N	Y	Y	Y	Y
No. of obs.	44,855	18,705	42,996	18,200	40,293	17,612	39,651	17,237
R^2	0.2490	0.3180						

Multinational Capital Structure and Internal Capital Markets 2475

Since borrowing from external sources and borrowing from parent companies are jointly determined, it is essential to instrument for the level of external borrowing in order to obtain unbiased measures of their degree of substitutability. Failure to do so, as in the regressions reported in columns 1 and 2 of Table IV, is likely to produce estimates that understate the true extent of substitution, given the many omitted variables that can be expected to affect external and parent company loans in the same direction. Fortunately, measures of capital market depth and creditor rights are suitable as instruments for external borrowing, since they affect the cost of external borrowing but are unlikely to affect the cost of borrowing from parent companies. Parent companies need not rely on local legal regimes in order to obtain appropriate compensation from their own affiliates, and they face internal costs of funds that are not functions of capital market conditions in individual foreign countries.[15] The instrumental variables regressions reported in columns 3 to 8 of Table IV impose that the estimated coefficients reflect the degree to which parent borrowing responds to changes in external borrowing induced by capital market depth or legal protections for creditors.[16]

The −0.9693 coefficient reported in column 3 of Table IV implies that parent debt substitutes almost perfectly for external debt. This estimated degree of substitution comes from using private credit as an instrument for the availability of external borrowing, and is larger (though still statistically indistinguishable from unity) once affiliate and country controls are included, as in the regression reported in column 4. Use of the creditor rights' variable as an alternative instrument produces estimated coefficients of −0.48 and −0.63 in the regressions reported in columns 5 and 6, corresponding to partial substitutability, in which parent lending makes up for roughly half of any external debt reduction due to weak legal protections. The regressions reported in columns 7 and 8 of Table IV use both instruments. The −0.7557 estimated coefficient on external borrowing/assets in column 8 implies that 75% of changes in external borrowing due to capital market conditions is compensated by parent lending. All of the specifications imply significant substitutability of parent borrowing for external borrowing in response to local capital market conditions. By

---

[15] One potential concern is that capital market conditions may influence borrowing from the parent through other channels. For example, it is possible that parents, like local credit providers, are reluctant to lend to firms in environments where it is difficult for lenders to recover their loans. This effect would increase the correlation of borrowing from parents and measures of credit market conditions. In this case, the estimated coefficient on external borrowing/assets would be biased upward, thereby reducing the estimated degree of substitutability. In order for bias to induce evidence of substitutability, it would have to be the case that parents would want to lend to affiliates in countries with poor capital markets for reasons other than the difficulties associated with obtaining external debt. This seems unlikely. As a result, potential shortcomings of the instruments should, if anything, reduce the estimated degree of substitutability between borrowing sources.

[16] *F*-tests of the significance of the first-stage specifications, which are similar to those shown in the left panel of Table III, are all significant at the 1% level. The right panel of Table III effectively provides a reduced-form version of the instrumental variable analysis that is provided in Table IV. This reduced form has the virtue of making more transparent the differences between the determinants of external and parent borrowing.

implication, local firms not affiliated with multinational parent companies, and without access to alternate sources of capital, face more difficulty obtaining credit.

Given that the measures of internal and external borrowing used in the regressions reported in Table IV are normalized by assets, and debt levels are highly correlated with total assets, it is conceivable that the measured substitutability of parent for external debt might simply be a function of the way in which the variables are constructed. For example, if all assets were financed with debt (which is not the case), then the sum of the parent debt ratio and the external debt ratio would equal 1, and the estimated coefficient in an OLS regression of parent debt on external debt would be -1. This issue does not arise in the instrumental variables estimates, which exploit only the part of the variation in external debt that is attributable to capital market considerations, but it is nevertheless useful to consider alternative specifications for which the concern would not arise even in an OLS setting. The Appendix Table I of Desai et al. (2003) presents regressions using specifications similar to those presented in Table IV, with the main difference that the parent and external debt measures are normalized by affiliate owners' equity instead of affiliate assets. The results are consistent with those reported in Table IV, suggesting that the measured substitutability of parent for external debt in the regressions reported in Table IV is not the product of the way in which the variables are constructed.

C. The Determinants of Interest Rates and Substitution in Response to Prices

To the extent that legal protections for creditors and capital market conditions influence the use of external debt and parent debt, they must do so by affecting the relative cost of external finance. This implication can be tested directly by measuring the impact of legal protections and capital market conditions on pretax interest rates faced by affiliates of the same parent and by examining whether affiliates substitute internal for external debt in response to these cost differences.

Table V presents estimated coefficients from regressions with interest rates as dependent variables. The dependent variable in columns 1 to 4 is the interest rate on external borrowing. Again, all specifications include parent, industry, and year fixed effects, and the reported standard errors control for clustering at the country/industry level. Since not all affiliates report every item to BEA, the sample used in these specifications is limited by data availability.

The estimated -0.0385 coefficient reported in column 1 indicates that 10% greater host country use of private credit as a fraction of GDP is associated with 0.4% lower interest rates. The results presented in column 2 suggest that stronger legal protections for creditors reduce interest rates, a one-point improvement in legal protections being associated with 0.9% lower interest rates. Columns 3 and 4 include controls for local tax rates and country-level variation in political risk and inflation. Greater private credit availability and stronger creditor rights continue to be associated with lower interest rates, though the magnitudes of the estimated effects are somewhat smaller in these regressions

Table V
Determinants of Local Interest Rates

The dependent variable in columns 1 to 4 is the ratio of the value of affiliate interest payments to nonparents to current liabilities and long-term debt borrowed from nonparent sources; in columns 5 to 8, the dependent variable is the ratio of total affiliate interest payments to current liabilities and long-term debt, excluding trade accounts and trade notes payable. All regressions are estimated by ordinary least squares and include parent, industry, and year fixed effects. Country tax rate is the median tax rate in an affiliate's host country. Private credit is the ratio of private credit lent by deposit money banks to GDP, as provided in Beck et al. (1999). Creditor rights is an index of the strength of creditor rights developed in LaPorta et al. (1998); higher levels of the measure, which ranges from 0 to 4, indicate stronger legal protections. Political risk is the annual average of the monthly index of political risk presented in the International Country Risk Guide, rescaled to lie between 0 and 1 with higher numbers indicating higher risks. Rate of inflation is the contemporaneous percentage change in the GDP deflator of an affiliate's host country. Standard errors that correct for clustering of errors across observations in country/industry cells are presented in parentheses.

Dependent Variables	Interest Rate on External Borrowing				Interest Rate on Nontrade Account Borrowing (from all sources)			
	(1)	(2)	(3)	(4)	(5)	(6)	(7)	(8)
Constant	−0.0387	0.0254	−0.0689	0.0538	−0.0690	0.0617	0.0051	−0.0202
	(0.0337)	(0.0223)	(0.0362)	(0.0253)	(0.0383)	(0.0212)	(0.0331)	(0.0215)
Country tax rate			−0.0277	−0.0275	−0.0149	−0.0092	−0.0177	−0.0093
			(0.0117)	(0.0127)	(0.0139)	(0.0148)	(0.0139)	(0.0147)
Private credit	−0.0385		−0.0119		−0.0099		0.0074	
	(0.0034)		(0.0023)		(0.0034)		(0.0085)	

(continued)

Table V—*Continued*

Dependent Variables	Interest Rate on External Borrowing				Interest Rate on Nontrade Account Borrowing (from all sources)			
	(1)	(2)	(3)	(4)	(5)	(6)	(7)	(8)
Creditor rights		−0.0093 (0.0008)		−0.0071 (0.0007)		−0.0079 (0.0009)		−0.0033 (0.0027)
Share of debt from external sources							0.0267 (0.0089)	0.0220 (0.0079)
Share of debt from external sources * private credit							−0.0213 (0.0091)	
Share of debt from external sources * creditor rights								−0.0056 (0.0030)
Political risk			0.1112 (0.0113)	0.1662 (0.0136)	0.1243 (0.0145)	0.1911 (0.0174)	0.1354 (0.0145)	0.2023 (0.0171)
Rate of inflation			0.0066 (0.0007)	0.0064 (0.0007)	0.0064 (0.0008)	0.0061 (0.0008)	0.0064 (0.0008)	0.0060 (0.0008)
Parent, industry, and year fixed effects?	Y	Y	Y	Y	Y	Y	Y	Y
No. of obs.	20,587	19,687	18,988	18,226	19,023	18,171	18,519	17,747
R^2	0.1791	0.1758	0.2338	0.2569	0.2505	0.2692	0.2524	0.2713

Multinational Capital Structure and Internal Capital Markets 2479

than in the corresponding regressions reported in columns 1 and 2. Higher levels of political risk and inflation also significantly increase local borrowing rates.

The regressions presented in columns 1 to 4 of Table V indicate that interest rates are higher in countries with underdeveloped capital markets and poor creditor legal rights. It is noteworthy that, since parent company fixed effects are included as independent variables, these interest rate effects appear between affiliates of the same companies. This evidence is, however, subject to two limitations. The first is that the denominator of the interest rate variable is total liabilities, including trade credits on which explicit interest is seldom paid. As a result, measured interest rates are somewhat low and may vary between countries due to trade financing practices. The second limitation is that borrowing from external sources and borrowing from parent companies are treated symmetrically, which while statistically appropriate nonetheless obscures what might be an important distinction. Since creditor rights are considerably less important for intrafirm contracting than they are for contracts between unrelated parties, it follows that the interest rate effects of creditor rights (or capital market development) should be much smaller in the case of borrowing from parent companies.

Columns 5 to 8 of Table V report estimated coefficients from regressions designed to address these issues. The dependent variable is again the interest rate, in this case constructed as the ratio of total affiliate interest payments to other current liabilities and long-term debt, excluding trade accounts. The estimated capital market effects obtained using this dependent variable, reported in columns 5 and 6 of Table V, have the same signs and almost exactly the same magnitudes as those obtained using the first interest rate variable and reported in columns 3 and 4 of Table V.

Data limitations make it impossible to measure average interest rates paid to external sources when the denominator of the calculated interest rate excludes trade account debt. It is nonetheless possible to evaluate circuitously the difference between interest rates on parent loans and external loans, and the effect of capital market conditions on this difference, using a measure of interest rates that does not include trade account debt. Columns 7 and 8 of Table V present estimated coefficients from regressions in which the dependent variable is the same as that in the regressions reported in columns 5 and 6, but adds two independent variables: the share of debt from external sources[17] and the interaction between this share and measures of capital market development or creditor rights. If the wedge between the costs of borrowing from external sources and borrowing from parents increases as capital market measures deteriorate, two patterns should emerge. First, the coefficient on the share of debt from external sources should be positive, indicating that when measures of creditor legal protections or credit market development are at extreme low values, affiliates pay higher interest rates on loans from external sources relative to borrowing from

---

[17] The share of debt from nonparent sources equals one minus the ratio of current liabilities and long-term debt owed to the parent to total current liabilities and long-term debt.

parents. Second, the coefficient on the interaction between the share of debt from external sources and measures of credit market development should be negative, signifying that the wedge between external and internal borrowing costs declines as credit markets improve.

The results indicate that greater borrowing from external sources is associated with higher interest rates where capital markets are poorly developed or creditor rights are weak. For example, the 0.0220 coefficient on the share of debt from nonparent sources reported in column 8 indicates that external debt carries 2.20% higher interest rates than does borrowing from parents in countries with creditor rights' indices of zero. The −0.0056 coefficient on the interaction of creditor rights and nonparent debt share in the same column implies that the higher interest rates associated with external relative to parent borrowing decline as creditor rights strengthen, disappearing at highest level of the creditor rights' index. The estimated effects of capital market development and creditor rights not interacted with the share of external debt do not differ significantly from zero in the equations reported in columns 7 and 8, suggesting that borrowing from parent companies is no more expensive due to these capital market considerations.

It is possible to apply these results to measure the extent to which changes in the composition of borrowing can be traced to differences in interest rates induced by credit market conditions. The regressions presented in Table VI identify the degree to which borrowing from external sources and borrowing from parent companies reflect interest rate differences. The left panel (columns 1 to 4) of Table VI presents regressions in which the dependent variable is external borrowing/assets, while the right panel (columns 5 to 8) presents regressions in which the dependent variable is borrowing from the parent/assets. The independent variable of most interest in these regressions is the interest rate on external borrowing. Columns 2 to 4 and 6 to 8 report estimated coefficients from instrumental variable regressions in which measures of creditor rights and capital market development are used as instruments for interest rates.[18] The advantage of specifying these equations as instrumental variable regressions is that doing so makes it possible to trace the effect of capital market conditions on the cost of external borrowing and its subsequent impact on leverage obtained from external sources and parent companies. In order for measures of creditor rights and credit market conditions to be valid instruments in the specifications in Table VI, they must affect external and parent lending only through their impact on costs of external borrowing.[19]

---

[18] F-tests of the significance of the first-stage specifications, which are similar to those shown in the left-hand panel of Table V, are all significant at the 1% level.

[19] This condition for the validity of the instruments corresponds to the intuition that costs of external borrowing fully reflect the variation in capital market conditions. If instead, credit markets are rationed, then credit market conditions could have a direct effect on external borrowing that is not fully mediated by interest rates. In this case, the estimated coefficients on the interest rate on external borrowing in specifications using external borrowing as a dependent variable would be biased downward and would overstate the extent to which affiliates avoid external borrowing in response to interest costs. However, as discussed in footnote 15, it is very unlikely that adverse

Multinational Capital Structure and Internal Capital Markets 2481

Table VI
The Responsiveness of External and Parent Debt to External Interest Rates

The dependent variable in columns 1 to 4 is the ratio of current liabilities and long-term debt an affiliate borrows from nonparent sources to total affiliate assets; in columns 5 to 8, the dependent variable is the ratio of net current liabilities and long-term debt an affiliate borrows from its U.S. parent to total affiliate assets. The specifications in columns 1 and 5 are estimated by ordinary least squares, and all the specifications include parent, industry, and year fixed effects. The interest rate on external borrowing is the ratio of the value of affiliate interest payments to nonparents to current liabilities and long-term debt borrowed from nonparent sources. The specifications in columns 2 and 6 instrument for the interest rate on external borrowing using private credit. Private credit is the ratio of private credit lent by deposit money banks to GDP, as provided in Beck et al. (1999). The specifications in columns 3 and 7 instrument for the interest rate on external borrowing using creditor rights. Creditor rights is an index of the strength of creditor rights developed in LaPorta et al. (1998); higher levels of the measure, which ranges from 0 to 4, indicate stronger legal protections. The specification in columns 4 and 8 instrument for interest rate on external borrowing using both private credit and creditor rights. Country tax rate is the median tax rate in an affiliate's host country. Net PPE/assets is the ratio of affiliate net property, plant, and equipment to total affiliate assets. EBITDA/assets is the ratio of affiliate earnings before interest, taxes, depreciation, and amortization to total affiliate assets. Log of sales is the natural log of affiliate sales. Political risk is the annual average of the monthly index of political risk presented in the International Country Risk Guide, rescaled to lie between 0 and 1 with higher numbers indicating higher risks. Rate of inflation is the contemporaneous percentage change in the GDP deflator of an affiliate's host country. Growth options is the compound annual growth rate of total affiliate sales in an affiliate's country and industry until the following benchmark year. Standard errors are presented in parentheses, and in columns 1 and 5 these errors correct for clustering of errors across observations in country/industry cells.

Dependent Variables	External Borrowing/Assets				Borrowing from the Parent/Assets			
	(1)	(2)	(3)	(4)	(5)	(6)	(7)	(8)
Constant	−0.4545	−0.4801	−0.4878	−0.4919	0.2203	0.3871	0.2441	0.3605
	(0.1751)	(0.4724)	(0.4509)	(0.4758)	(0.1600)	(0.4107)	(0.2079)	(0.3493)
Interest rate on external borrowing	0.0107	−1.1999	−0.8523	−1.3209	0.2544	1.6832	0.4887	0.8337
	(0.0286)	(0.5368)	(0.2332)	(0.2480)	(0.0274)	(0.4712)	(0.1795)	(0.1830)
Country tax rate	0.2240	0.1775	0.2259	0.1590	0.0844	0.1306	0.0887	0.1178
	(0.0303)	(0.0266)	(0.0224)	(0.0259)	(0.0242)	(0.0228)	(0.0171)	(0.0190)

(continued)

Table VI—*Continued*

Dependent Variables	External Borrowing/Assets				Borrowing from the Parent/Assets			
	(1)	(2)	(3)	(4)	(5)	(6)	(7)	(8)
Net PPE/assets	-0.0266	0.0372	0.0224	0.0412	0.0881	0.0018	0.0581	0.0402
	(0.0168)	(0.0325)	(0.0184)	(0.0193)	(0.0153)	(0.0283)	(0.0140)	(0.0141)
EBITDA/assets	-0.2553	-0.2629	-0.2672	-0.2729	-0.2087	-0.2031	-0.2034	-0.2006
	(0.0164)	(0.0122)	(0.0117)	(0.0126)	(0.0126)	(0.0103)	(0.0088)	(0.0091)
Log of sales	0.0038	0.0055	0.0050	0.0058	-0.0034	-0.0062	-0.0040	-0.0048
	(0.0022)	(0.0019)	(0.0017)	(0.0018)	(0.0019)	(0.0016)	(0.0013)	(0.0013)
Political risk	0.0309	0.2283	0.2271	0.3482	0.0372	-0.1714	-0.0174	-0.0953
	(0.0274)	(0.0827)	(0.0482)	(0.0535)	(0.0204)	(0.0724)	(0.0370)	(0.0393)
Rate of inflation	-0.0026	0.0051	0.0030	0.0055	-0.0008	-0.0105	-0.0024	-0.0044
	(0.0007)	(0.0036)	(0.0017)	(0.0018)	(0.0006)	(0.0032)	(0.0013)	(0.0013)
Growth options	0.0388	0.0369	0.0143	0.0162	-0.0293	-0.0230	-0.0311	-0.0263
	(0.0170)	(0.0157)	(0.0162)	(0.0171)	(0.0144)	(0.0135)	(0.0123)	(0.0125)
Parent, industry, and year fixed effects?	Y	Y	Y	Y	Y	Y	Y	Y
IV w/private credit?	N	Y	N	Y	N	Y	N	Y
IV w/creditor rights?	N	N	Y	Y	N	N	Y	Y
No. of obs.	18,404	17,912	17,335	16,962	18,469	17,975	17,399	17,026
R^2	0.2977				0.2978			

Multinational Capital Structure and Internal Capital Markets 2483

The results indicate that borrowing is highly responsive to interest rate differences induced by credit market conditions. The OLS regressions reported in column 1 of Table VI show little impact of interest rates on external borrowing, but this is neither surprising nor particularly informative, given the potential endogeneity of interest rates to borrowing levels. The instrumental variables results reported in columns 2 and 6 indicate that multinational firms reduce external borrowing and increase parent borrowing in response to higher interest rates driven by reduced capital market depth. One percent higher interest rates due to capital market underdevelopment are associated with 1.2% reduced external borrowing and 1.7% greater parent borrowing, as a fraction of total assets. The use of creditor rights as an instrument in the regressions reported in columns 3 and 7 produces somewhat smaller, but otherwise similar results. In these regressions, 1% higher interest rates due to poor creditor rights are associated with 0.9% reduced external borrowing and 0.5% greater parent borrowing, as a fraction of total assets. Finally, the use of both instruments suggests that 1% higher interest rates due to legal and capital market conditions are associated with 1.3% reduced external borrowing and 0.8% greater parent borrowing, as a fraction of total assets. The smaller estimated magnitude of the interest rate effect on parent borrowing implies that substitution of parent for external debt, while considerable, is incomplete—which is consistent with the results reported in Tables III and IV.

Estimated coefficients on control variables included in the regressions reported in Table VI are consistent with the substitutability of parent and external debt. While other variables have coefficients of the same sign in the regressions for parent and external borrowing, multinational parents are particularly likely to lend to smaller affiliates (as measured by sales) that may have difficulty borrowing locally. Affiliates borrow more externally and less internally in high-inflation countries. Assuming that external debt is more likely denominated in local currencies, greater external borrowing and reduced parent borrowing in high-inflation countries is consistent with the common claim that affiliates hedge inflation risk through greater local borrowing.[20] Similarly, estimated coefficients on the political risk index in the instrumental variables regressions suggest that multinational firms hedge political risk through greater external borrowing and somewhat reduced borrowing from the parent.

---

credit market conditions would increase borrowing from parent companies except through their effects on external borrowing. As a result, estimates of the coefficient on the interest rate on external borrowing in specifications using internal borrowing as an independent variable are unlikely to reflect possible shortcomings of the instruments.

[20] The estimated effect of inflation on the composition of borrowing in Table VI differs from that in Table III. Given that the results in Table III do not explicitly control for interest rates and that interest rates are positively correlated with inflation rates, the instrumental variables setting provided in Table VI is more appropriate for inferring the effect of inflation on borrowing levels.

IV. Conclusions

Understanding the causes and consequences of differences between external and internal costs of finance—whether they arise from informational asymmetries, government policies, poor contracting environments, or agency problems—is an important agenda in finance. While theory illuminates many possible responses of capital structure to cost differences, the empirical literature has struggled with the limited institutional variation available to study these determinants of financing choices. Even identifying the responsiveness of firms to the tax advantage of debt has proven challenging, much of the best evidence coming from subtle differences introduced by firms transiting between taxable and tax-loss status. One of the advantages of examining these issues across countries is that doing so permits the use of rich variation in tax rates and government policies. The common difficulty that cross-country studies encounter in comparing the behavior of heterogeneous firms whose actions are measured using very different accounting conventions is greatly attenuated by analyzing variation in the financing choices of affiliates of the same U.S. multinational parent operating in countries with varied tax incentives and capital market conditions.

Certain patterns appear consistently in the results. Higher tax rates increase the use of debt from all sources, with borrowing from parent firms exhibiting greater responsiveness to tax rate differences than borrowing from external sources. Affiliates borrow less from external sources and more from their parents in countries with underdeveloped credit markets and weak creditor protections, greater parent lending replacing approximately three-quarters of the reduction in external borrowing. Interest rates on external borrowing are higher, and differences between interest rates on external and parent borrowing greater, in countries with underdeveloped credit markets and weak creditor protections. Differences in the use of external and parent debt can be traced to differences in interest rates on external debt induced by legal protections and credit market conditions.

These findings not only offer evidence of the tax and capital market determinants of capital structure but also illustrate factors influencing the choice between external and internal finance. While the centrality of internal finance to investment is widely appreciated, the allocation of funding within a firm is not well understood. This paper illustrates that firms use internal capital markets opportunistically when external finance is costly and when there are tax arbitrage opportunities.

The results also suggest that their internal capital markets give multinational firms significant advantages over local firms where credit markets are poorly developed. Local firms that borrow from external sources face high costs of debt in countries with shallow capital markets or weak creditor rights. Although weak credit markets also reduce external borrowing by multinational firms, affiliates are able to compensate by borrowing more from parent companies. The use of internal capital markets to attenuate the impact of adverse local economic conditions appears in other contexts, such as when host

Multinational Capital Structure and Internal Capital Markets 2485

countries impose capital controls (Desai et al. (2004)). The ability to substitute internal funds for external funds gives multinational firms opportunities not available to local competitors with more limited access to global capital markets.

REFERENCES

Allayannis, George, Gregory W. Brown, and Leora F. Klapper, 2003,Capital structure and financial risk: Evidence from foreign debt use in East Asia, *Journal of Finance* 58, 2667–2710.

Altshuler, Rosanne, and Harry Grubert, 2003, Repatriation taxes, repatriation strategies and multinational financial policy, *Journal of Public Economics* 87, 73–107.

Auerbach, Alan J., 2002, Taxation and corporate financial policy, in Alan J. Auerbach, and Martin Feldstein, eds.: *Handbook of Public Economics Volume III* (North-Holland, New York).

Bebchuck, Lucian Ayre, and Andrew T. Guzman, 1999, An economic analysis of transnational bankruptcies, *Journal of Law and Economics* 42, 775–806.

Beck, Thorsten, Asli Demirguc-Kunt, and Ross Levine, 1999, A new database on financial development and structure, mimeo.

Blanchard, Olivier Jean, Florencio Lopez-de-Silanes, and Andrei Shleifer, 1994, What do firms do with cash windfalls?, *Journal of Financial Economics* 36, 337–360.

Booth, Laurence, Varouj Aivazian, Asli Demirguc-Kunt, and Vojislav Maksimovic, 2001, Capital structures in developing countries, *Journal of Finance* 56, 87–130.

Chowdry, Bhagwan, and Joshua D. Coval, 1998, Internal financing of multinational subsidiaries: Debt vs. equity, *Journal of Corporate Finance* 4, 87–106.

Chowdry, Bhagwan, and Vikram Nanda, 1994, Internal financing of multinational subsidiaries: Parent debt vs. external debt, *Journal of Corporate Finance* 1, 259–281.

Demirguc-Kunt, Asli, and Vojislav Maksimovic, 1998, Law, finance, and firm growth, *Journal of Finance* 53, 2107–2137.

Desai, Mihir A., C. Fritz Foley, and James R. Hines Jr., 2001, Repatriation taxes and dividend distortions, *National Tax Journal* 54, 829–851.

Desai, Mihir A., C. Fritz Foley, and James R. Hines Jr., 2003, A multinational perspective on capital structure choice and internal capital markets, NBER Working Paper No. 9715.

Desai, Mihir A., C. Fritz Foley, and James R. Hines Jr., 2004, Capital controls, liberalization and foreign direct investment, NBER Working Paper No. 10337.

Desai, Mihir A., and James R. Hines Jr., 1999, 'Basket' cases: Tax incentives and international joint venture participation by American multinational firms, *Journal of Public Economics* 71, 379–402.

Duffee, Gregory R., 2002, Term premia and interest rate forecasts in affine models, *Journal of Finance* 57, 405–443.

Eichengreen, Barry, and Ashoka Mody, 2000a, What explains spreads on emerging market debt? in Sebastian Edwards, ed.: *Capital Flows and the Emerging Economies: Theory, Evidence, and Controversies* (The University of Chicago Press, Chicago).

Eichengreen, Barry, and Ashoka Mody, 2000b, Would collective action clauses raise borrowing costs? NBER Working Paper No. 7458.

Fama, Eugene F., and Kenneth R. French, 1998, Taxes, financing decisions and firm value, *Journal of Finance* 53, 819–843.

Froot, Kenneth A., and James R. Hines, Jr., 1995, Interest allocation rules, financing patterns, and the operations of U.S. multinationals, in Martin Feldstein, James R. Hines Jr., and R. Glenn Hubbard, eds.: *The Effect of Taxation on Multinational Corporations* (University of Chicago Press, Chicago).

Gitlin, Richard A., and Evan D. Flaschen, 1987, The international void in the law of multinational bankruptcies, *Business Law* 42, 307–323.

Graham, John R., 1996, Debt and the marginal tax rate, *Journal of Financial Economics* 41, 41–73.

Graham, John R., 1999, Do personal taxes affect corporate financing decisions?, *Journal of Public Economics* 73, 147–185.

Graham, John R., 2000, How big are the tax benefits of debt?, *Journal of Finance* 55, 1901–1941.

Graham, John R., 2003, Taxes and corporate finance: A review, *Review of Financial Studies* 16, 1074–1128.

Graham, John R., and Campbell R. Harvey, 2001, The theory and practice of corporate finance: Evidence from the field, *Journal of Financial Economics* 60, 187–243.

Graham, John R., Michael L. Lemmon, and James S. Schallheim, 1998, Debt, leases, taxes, and the endogeneity of corporate tax status, *Journal of Finance* 53, 131–162.

Hines, James R. Jr., 1994, Credit and deferral as international investment incentives, *Journal of Public Economics* 55, 323–347.

Hines, James R. Jr., 1999, Lessons from behavioral responses to international taxation, *National Tax Journal* 52, 305–322.

Hines, James R. Jr., and Eric M. Rice, 1994, Fiscal paradise: Foreign tax havens and American business, *Quarterly Journal of Economics* 109, 149–182.

Hodder, James E., and Lemma W. Senbet, 1990, International capital structure equilibrium, *Journal of Finance* 45, 1495–1517.

Hubbard, R. Glenn, and Darius Palia, 1999, A reexamination of the conglomerate merger wave in the 1960s: An internal capital markets view, *Journal of Finance* 54, 1131–1152.

Kaplan, Steven N., and Luigi Zingales, 1997, Do investment–cashflow sensitivities provide useful measures of financing constraints?, *Quarterly Journal of Economics* 112, 169–216

Kedia, Simi, and Abon Mozumdar, 2003, Foreign currency denominated debt: An empirical examination, *Journal of Business* 76, 521–546

King, Robert G., and Ross Levine, 1993, Finance and growth: Schumpeter might be right, *Quarterly Journal of Economics* 108, 713–737.

La Porta, Rafael, Florencio Lopez-de-Silanes, Andrei Shleifer, and Robert W. Vishny, 1997, Legal determinants of external finance, *Journal of Finance* 52, 1131–1155.

La Porta, Rafael, Florencio Lopez-de-Silanes, Andrei Shleifer, and Robert W. Vishny, 1998, Law and finance, *Journal of Political Economy* 106, 1113–1155.

Lamont, Owen, 1997, Cash flow and investment: Evidence from internal capital markets, *Journal of Finance* 52, 83–109.

Mackie-Mason, Jeffrey K., 1990, Do taxes affect corporate financing decisions?, *Journal of Finance* 45, 1471–1493.

Mataloni, Raymond J. Jr., 1995, A guide to BEA Statistics on U.S. Multinational Companies, *Survey of Current Business* 75, 38–53.

Meyer, John R., and Edwin Kuh, 1957, *The Investment Decision: An Empirical Study* (Harvard University Press, Cambridge, MA).

Miller, Merton H., 1977, Debt and taxes, *Journal of Finance* 32, 261–275.

Myers, Stewart, John McConnell, Alice Peterson, Dennis Soter, and Joel Stern, 1998, Vanderbilt University Roundtable on the capital structure puzzle, *Journal of Applied Corporate Finance* 11, 8–24.

Newberry, Kaye J., 1998, Foreign tax credit limitations and capital structure decisions, *Journal of Accounting Research* 36, 157–166.

Newberry, Kaye J., and Dan S. Dhaliwal, 2001, Cross-jurisdictional income shifting by U.S. multinationals: Evidence from international bond offerings, *Journal of Accounting Research* 39, 643–662.

Noe, Thomas H., 2000, Creditor rights and multinational capital structure, Working paper, Tulane University.

Novaes, Walter, 1998, Political risk and capital structure choice of foreign subsidiaries: An empirical analysis, Working paper, University of Washington.

Powers, Timothy E., 1993, The model international insolvency co-operation act: A 21st century proposal for international insolvency co-operation, in *Multinational Commercial Insolvency*, American Bar Association.

Rajan, Raghuram G., and Luigi Zingales, 1995, What do we know about capital structure? Some evidence from international data, *Journal of Finance* 50, 1421–1460.

Multinational Capital Structure and Internal Capital Markets 2487

Rajan, Raghuram G., and Luigi Zingales, 1998, Financial dependence and growth, *American Economic Review* 88, 559–586.

Rajan, Raghuram G., and Luigi Zingales, 2003, Great reversals: The politics of financial development in the 20th century, *Journal of Financial Economics* 69, 5–50.

Scharfstein, David S., and Jeremy C. Stein, 2000, The dark side of internal capital markets: Divisional rent-seeking and inefficient investment, *Journal of Finance* 55, 2537–2564.

Shin, Hyun-Han, and René M. Stulz, 1998, Are internal capital markets efficient?, *Quarterly Journal of Economics* 113, 531–552.

Shleifer, Andrei, and Daniel Wolfenzon, 2002, Investor protection and equity markets, *Journal of Financial Economics* 66, 3–27.

Stein, Jeremy C., 1997, Internal capital markets and the competition for corporate resources, *Journal of Finance* 52, 111–133.

Tagashira, Shoichi, 1994, International effects of foreign insolvency proceedings: An analysis of 'ancillary' proceedings in the United States and Japan, *Texas International Law Journal* 29, 1–38.

Titman, Sheridan, and Roberto Wessels, 1998, The determinants of capital structure choice, *Journal of Finance* 43, 1–19.

United States Department of Commerce, 1998, *U.S. Direct Investment Abroad: 1994 Benchmark Survey, Final Results* (U.S. Department of Commerce, Washington, DC).

Financial Development and Financing Constraints: International Evidence from the Structural Investment Model

Inessa Love
World Bank

This article provides evidence that financial development impacts growth by reducing financing constraints that would otherwise distort efficient allocation of investment. The financing constraints are inferred from the investment Euler equation by assuming that the firm's stochastic discount factor is a function of the firm's financial position (specifically, the stock of liquid assets). The magnitude of the changes in the cost of capital is twice as large in a country with a low level of financial development as in a country with an average level of financial development. The size effect, business cycles, and legal environment effects are also considered.

The relationship between the financial and real sides of the economy has long been a topic of intense interest and debate. The potential importance of the financial sector in promoting economic growth was recognized as early as Schumpeter (1912), though this perspective was disputed by numerous economists over the decades that followed [most notably by Lucas (1988)]. Proper empirical work in assessing the relationship between financial development and the real economy began only much later, with the work of King and Levine (1993) who reported cross-country evidence which suggested that financial development affects economic growth by fostering productivity improvements. Since then, a large and growing literature has flourished that examines the relationship between financial market development and various economic outcomes. Although the early studies were almost entirely based on cross-country analysis, more recent studies use time-series dimensions to address the causality between finance

The views presented here are the author's own and not necessarily those of the World Bank or its member countries. I am grateful to Geert Bekaert, Laarni Bulan, Charles Calomiris, Raymond Fisman, Ann Harrison, Campbell Harvey (the editor), Charles Himmelberg, Robert Hodrick, Glenn Hubbard, Andrei Kirilenko, Luc Laeven, Margaret McMillan, Xavier Salai-Martin and Toni Whited for helpful comments and discussions. I am especially grateful to Charles Himmelberg for his advice and guidance and to Raymond Fisman for support and encouragement. I thank Matz Dahlberg for providing his Gauss code for GMM bootstrapping and Kari Labrie for proofreading the manuscript. This research was supported by a fellowship from the Social Science Research Council Program in Applied Economics with funds provided by the John D. and Catherine T. MacArthur Foundation. Address correspondence to Inessa Love, Research Department, Finance Group, World Bank, 1818 H St, NW, Washington, DC 20433, or e-mail: ilove@worldbank.org.

The Review of Financial Studies Fall 2003 Vol. 16, No. 3, pp. 765–791, DOI: 10.1093/rfs/hhg013
© 2003 The Society for Financial Studies

The Review of Financial Studies / v 16 n 3 2003

and growth and to study the channels through which finance affects growth.[1]

The micro-level examination of the link between real and financial decisions of firms has seen considerable work since the pioneering contribution of Modigliani and Miller (1958), who showed that in a world of perfect capital markets, finance is irrelevant for real decisions. This view has been amended and disputed by richer theoretical models and empirical studies that have found a strong relationship between firms' financial health and investment [see Hubbard (1998) for a recent survey]. These financing constraints are generally attributed to capital market imperfections, stemming from such factors as asymmetric information and incentive problems, which result in differences between the costs of internal and external financing.

The results contained in this article lie at the intersection of these two broad literatures. Utilizing firm-level data while taking advantage of the cross-country variation in financial market development, I show that financing constraints decrease with financial development. I evaluate the magnitude of financing constraints by estimating investment Euler equations.[2] Financing constraints interfere with the efficient intertemporal allocation of investment by modifying the stochastic discount factor. In particular, financial frictions cause firms to substitute investment tomorrow for investment today, that is, the financially constrained firm will postpone investment until the next period. Although the "constrained" discount factor is not directly observable, it can be inferred from the Euler equation by assuming the firm's stochastic discount factor is a function of the firm's financial position (specifically, the stock of liquid assets). My estimates show that the financial factors have a larger impact on the intertemporal allocation of investment in countries with less developed financial markets.

These findings are robust to a wide variety of specifications and to the consideration of a range of alternative explanations. I also find that small

---

[1] Beck et al. (2000), Neusser and Kugler (1998) and Rousseau and Wachtel (1998) use time-series analysis to address the causality issues. Bekaert, Harvey, and Lundblad (2001a, 2001b) use both cross-country and time-series analysis to study the effect of financial liberalization on economic growth.

[2] The investment Euler equation is obtained by rearranging the first-order conditions for the dynamic value optimization problem. It gives the intertemporal decision rule that governs accumulation of the capital stock in adjacent time periods. The optimal level of investment is determined by equalizing the marginal cost of investment in one period and the cost of waiting to invest in the next period (see Section 1.1 for derivation and further discussion). The investment Euler equations have been estimated by numerous authors, with most studies concentrating on U.S. firms. See Whited (1992), Hubbard and Kashyap (1992), Hubbard, Kashyap, and Whited (1995), and Calomiris and Hubbard (1995) among others. The limited work utilizing international data includes Bond and Meghir (1994) for the United Kingdom; Jaramilo, Schiantarelli, and Weiss (1996) for Ecuador; Harris, Schiantarelli, and Siregar (1994) for Indonesia; Gelos and Werner (1999) for Mexico, and Bond et al. (1997) for Belgium, France, Germany, and the United Kingdom.

firms are disproportionately more disadvantaged in less financially developed countries than are large firms, that is, they have relatively larger impact of financial factors on their stochastic discount factors. Together, these results provide a micro-level foundation for one of the commonly cited explanations for the observed cross-country relationship between financial development and economic growth. Namely, I provide evidence that an improvement in the functioning of financial markets will reduce firms' financing constraints. This will allow for easier access to external funds for firms with good investment opportunities and this improvement in capital allocation will in turn enhance growth.

This article builds on several recent studies that address similar issues of the role of the financial system in stimulating economic growth using microdata. Demirguc-Kunt and Maksimovic (1998) find that the proportion of firms in countries that were growing faster than they could have using only internally generated funds is positively related to financial development and to legal system indicators. Rajan and Zingales (1998) use industry-level data to show that industries that require more external finance grow faster in more developed capital markets. Wurgler (2000) finds that financial development improves capital allocation by increasing the industry-level sensitivity of investment growth to value-added growth. However, to argue that financial development improves the allocation of capital within a country requires identifying firms that "should" be growing, given their investment opportunities. The authors of the previous articles do not attempt to control for the growth opportunities available for each firm or industry at each point in time in each country. This article improves on the previous work because the structural model in the form of investment Euler equations explicitly controls for future growth opportunities and provides a theoretical framework for the identification of the financing constraints.

This article is also related to several recent studies on financial liberalizations and their effect on financing constraints and the cost of external finance. Using Euler equation methodology, Laeven (2003) finds that progress in financial liberalization reduces firms financing constraints, especially for small firms. Galindo, Schiantarelli, and Weiss (2001) find that financial reform has led to an increase in the efficiency with which investment funds are allocated. Using different methodologies, Bekaert and Harvey (2000) and Henry (2000) find that the cost of equity capital decreases significantly after financial liberalizations. In addition, Bekaert, Harvey, and Lundblad (2001a) find that equity market liberalizations are associated with increases in real economic growth of approximately 1% per year. They also find that financial liberalization affects growth partially through its effect on financial development, thus reemphasizing the importance of financial development for growth, which is consistent with the results presented in this article.

The Review of Financial Studies / v 16 n 3 2003

The rest of the article is as follows. Section 1 presents the structural investment model based on a dynamic optimization problem and discusses financing constraints. Section 2 discusses the empirical model and estimation methodology. Section 3 describes the data. Section 4 provides the main results including the analysis of structural parameters. Section 5 presents several tests of alternative explanations, including the size effect, business cycles, and the legal system. Section 6 presents the auxiliary results using single-country regressions. Section 7 concludes.

1. The Model of Investment

Numerous studies have used the Q-theory of investment[3] to study financing constraints [see Hubbard (1998) for a recent survey]. Although the Q-theory and Euler equation models of investment come from the same optimization problem (the two models are just different ways to rearrange the first-order conditions), the assumptions required to *estimate* the Q-model are stronger than those required to estimate the Euler equation model. The main difficulty with implementing the Q-theory is finding a proxy for the unobservable marginal q. A commonly used proxy is the market value of assets relative to the book value. Among other assumptions, this proxy requires the market's valuation of capital to equal the manager's valuation. However, the divergence in these valuations is likely to be related to the degree of market imperfections, that is, the measurement error would be systematically related to the level of financial development. This assumption makes the Q-model unusable in the cross-country setting. In addition, several recent articles emphasize severe problems with the Q-methodology such as measurement error and identification problems [see Kaplan and Zingales (1997), Erikson and Whited (2000), Bond and Cummins (2001), Cooper and Ejarque (2001), and Gomes (2002)]. Therefore I choose to use the Euler equation methodology.

1.1 The Euler equation model
The dynamic model of the firm value optimization is reproduced in this section. This model is similar to models used in previous studies (listed in note 2), and follows closely the specification in Gilchrist and Himmelberg (1998). The model is simplified here because it ignores the possibility of debt financing. However, this simplification does not affect the resulting

---

[3] The "Q-theory," pioneered by Tobin (1969) and further developed by Hayashi (1982), refers to the first-order condition which states that the marginal adjustment cost of investment is equal to the shadow price of capital, denoted by Q. Both the Q-model and Euler equation model are two different ways to rearrange the first-order conditions for the same optimization problem (reproduced in Section 1.1).

Financial Development and Financing Constraints

first-order conditions for investment, which are the focus of this article.[4] In this model, shareholders (or managers) are maximizing the present value of the firm, which is equal to the expected discounted value of dividends subject to the capital accumulation and external financing constraints. The firm value is given by

$$V_t(K_t, \xi_t) = \max_{\{I_{t+s}\}_{s=0}^{\infty}} D_t + E_t \left[\sum_{s=1}^{\infty} \beta_{t+s-1} D_{t+s} \right] \qquad (1)$$

subject to

$$D_t = \Pi(K_t, \xi_t) - C(I_t, K_t) - I_t \qquad (2)$$

$$K_{t+1} = (1 - \delta)K_t + I_t \qquad (3)$$

$$D_t \geq 0 \qquad (4)$$

Here D_t is the dividend paid to shareholders and is given by the "sources equal uses" constraint of Equation (2); β_{t+s-1}, is a discount factor from the period $t + s$ to period t. In the capital accumulation constraint of Equation (3), K_t is the beginning of the period capital stock, I_t is the investment expenditure, and δ is the depreciation rate. The restricted profit function (i.e., it is already maximized with respect to variable costs) is denoted by $\Pi(K_t, \xi_t)$, where ξ_t is a productivity shock.[5] The adjustment cost of investment is given by the function $C(I_t, K_t)$, and is assumed to result in a loss of a portion of investment. The financial frictions are introduced via a nonnegativity constraint on dividends [Equation (4)], and the multiplier on this constraint is denoted λ_t. This multiplier equals the shadow cost associated with raising new equity, which implies that external (equity) financing is costly; this extra cost is due to information or contracting costs.[6]

---

[4] Formally including debt into the problem results in a separate Euler equation for debt, [see Gilchrist and Himmelberg (1998) for derivation]. However, the investment Euler equation is not directly related to the debt Euler equation and is not affected by adding debt into the model.

[5] The profit function depends on the beginning of period capital, and hence the implicit assumption is that investment becomes productive only in the next period (that is, a one-period time-to-build lag). I ignore the price of investment that is replaced by fixed and time effects in the estimation. I also ignore tax considerations due to data constraints.

[6] Several influential articles addressed the sources of information- or contracting-related frictions in detail (see, e.g., Jensen and Meckling (1976), Myers and Majluf (1984), Hart (1995), and others). Here these frictions are exogenous to the firm and are represented by the shadow value of external finance. Another way to introduce financial frictions is by exogenously limiting the amount of debt that the firm can raise at any point in time. This will create a shadow value of debt, which has the same effect in the Euler equation as the shadow value of equity.

The Review of Financial Studies / v 16 n 3 2003

The first-order conditions to the above maximization problem are rearranged to obtain the Euler equation (derivations are available on request from the author). It is given by

$$1 + \left(\frac{\partial C}{\partial I}\right)_t = \beta_t E_t \left[\Theta_t \left\{ \left(\frac{\partial \Pi}{\partial K}\right)_{t+1} + (1 - \delta)\left(1 + \left(\frac{\partial C}{\partial I}\right)_{t+1}\right) \right\} \right]. \quad (5)$$

Here $\partial C/\partial I$ is the marginal adjustment cost of investment, $\partial \Pi/\partial K$ is the marginal "profit" of capital, referred to as MPK (the contribution of an extra unit of capital to the firm's profits), and $\Theta_t = (1 + \lambda_{t+1}/1 + \lambda_t)$ is the relative shadow cost of external finance in periods t and $t + 1$, discussed in detail in the next section. The intuition behind this Euler equation is that the marginal cost of investing today on the left-hand side (given by the adjustment cost and the price of investment goods, normalized to one) is equal to the discounted marginal cost of postponing investment until tomorrow, on the right-hand side. The latter is equal to the sum of the foregone marginal benefit of an extra unit in capital, given by MPK, plus the adjustment cost and price of investment tomorrow (again normalized to one).

1.2 Financing constraints

The firm's intertemporal allocation of investment depends on its effective discount factor, which is given by the product of β_t, the internal discount factor, and Θ_t, the discount factor associated with the external finance premium. If a firm is constrained, which in the model is equivalent to the inability to pay negative dividends (i.e., issue new equity), the shadow value of these funds rises today relative to tomorrow (i.e., $\lambda_t > \lambda_{t+1}$). Since Θ_t depends negatively on this shadow value, the firm's effective discount factor drops and the firm postpones investment to the next period.

In perfect capital markets, $\lambda_t = \lambda_{t+1} = 0$ for all t and hence $\Theta_t = 1$, and the firm is never constrained. With capital market imperfections, Θ_t depends on a vector of state variables, and could be identified with some observable firm characteristics. Unfortunately the model does not provide a formula for this factor, and to identify it previous literature relied on ad hoc parameterization of this factor with observable indicators of a firm's financial health [see Whited (1992)].[7] Similarly, I parameterize Θ_t as a function of the stock of liquid assets, specifically stock of cash and marketable securities scaled by total assets (hereafter referred to as cash stock). One theoretical justification for this measure appears in the Myers and Majluf (1984) model, where the amount of cash holdings, which the authors call "financial slack," has a direct effect on investment in the

---

[7] Such ad hoc addition to the model is justified using two arguments. First, there are no rigorous testable theoretical models of the interaction of finance and investment. Second, the test of overidentifying restrictions described below is used to verify the validity of this assumption.

presence of asymmetric information. This slack allows firms to undertake positive net present value (NPV) projects, which they would pass if they do not have any internal funds.

I parameterize factor Θ_t as a linear function of the cash stock, Cash_{it-1},[8] given by $\Theta_{it} = a_{0i} + a\text{Cash}_{it-1}$, where a_{0i} is a firm-specific level of financing constraints, which enters in the firm fixed effect. It is important to note that this parameterization does not allow for an explicit error term. This is a strong assumption, but it can be tested with the overidentification test, which provides an important check on the validity of the model. If this test does not indicate the rejection, the omitted error term is not empirically important. I discuss this test in more detail in Section 2.1.

In this model the cash stock affects the rate of intertemporal substitution between investment today and investment tomorrow. If a firm is not constrained $\Theta_{it} = 1$, and the effective discount factor is given by β_t, the impact of cash stock on the intertemporal allocation decision will be zero. The more constrained the firm is, the larger will be the impact of the cash stock on its discount factor. Alternatively, an increase in cash stock will increase the effective discount factor, or equivalently, lower the implied cost of capital, making investment today more attractive than investment tomorrow.

The main hypothesis of this article is that financial development decreases financing constraints. This will be reflected in a decreased impact of internal funds on the stochastic discount factor, formally:

$$\Theta_{it} = a_{0i} + (a_1 + a_2 FD_c)\text{Cash}_{it-1}. \qquad (6)$$

Thus, the focus is on the interaction of *FD* (country-level measure of financial development) and *Cash*, that is, the coefficient a_2, and it is expected to be negative.[9]

1.3 MPK and adjustment costs

The marginal product of capital, MPK, can easily be derived from the profit maximization problem as a function of sales to capital ratio: $\text{MPK} = \theta(S/K)$, where $\theta = \alpha_k/\mu$, α_k is the capital share in the production function, and μ is a markup. The derivations and arguments in support of this measure over other alternative measures can be found in Gilchrist and

---

[8] I assume that the firm makes its decision for period t investment at the beginning of that year (or, equivalently, the end of previous year). Therefore the appropriate timing of the cash stock is $t-1$, because the investment decision depends on how much cash a firm has before starting the investment.

[9] An alternative way to test this hypothesis is to allow each country to have its own estimate of the cash stock, a_c, and then regress these coefficients on the *FD* index. I present these results in Section 6. Note that in this article FD_c is a country-level measure, and therefore the implicit assumption is that the level of financial development is relatively constant. This is a reasonable assumption in a sample with short time dimension, which is the case in this article. Because the *FD* index is not time-varying, its effect on the intercept is captured by the firm fixed effects.

The Review of Financial Studies / v 16 n 3 2003

Himmelberg (1998). In the definition used here, the parameter θ is likely to be firm specific, which is empirically captured by the firm fixed effects using the following approximation:

$$\text{MPK}_{it} = \theta_i \frac{S}{K_{it}} \approx const. + \theta_i + \bar{\theta} \frac{S}{K_{it}}, \tag{7}$$

where $\bar{\theta}$ can be thought of as the average of all θ_i. This representation focuses on the variation in the sales to capital level around the firm-specific mean, that is, the within-firm variation in the productivity of capital. The fixed effects alleviate concerns with the measurement error associated with the unobserved differences in the capital share and market power parameters.

I assume a linear marginal adjustment cost of investment, given by

$$\frac{\partial C}{\partial I_{it}} = \alpha \left(\frac{I}{K_{it}} - g \frac{I}{K_{it-1}} - \nu_i \right). \tag{8}$$

This adjustment cost function is slightly more general than the one used in the traditional models because it includes the lagged investment-to-capital ratio with an additional parameter g. It is added to capture strong persistence in investment-to-capital ratios present in the data. This extended functional form allows for the more common form with $g = 0$, which could be tested empirically. The intuition for this added term is that it may be easier for the firm to continue investment at some fraction g of the previous period ratio, since, for example, it has hired workers or made some other arrangements that would be costly to cancel. Parameter ν_i could be interpreted as a firm-specific level of investment at which adjustment costs are minimized.

2. Empirical Model and Estimation

The empirical model is obtained by substituting Equations (6)–(8) into Equation (5). However, this produces a highly nonlinear equation, which contains several firm-specific parameters: a_{0i}, θ_i, and ν_i, discussed above. To capture these parameters in a single firm fixed effect, I linearize the model. The linear model allows me to concentrate on the within-firm variation in the intertemporal allocation of investment. Similarly, linearization allows the discount factor β_t to be captured by country- and time-specific effects. Following Gilchrist and Himmelberg (1998), I linearize the product of β_t, Θ_t, and the marginal benefit of investment (the expression in curly brackets in Equation (5), here denoted as $\{.\}_t$] using a first-order Taylor approximation around the means. Since Θ_t could be above or below one, its mean should be a value around one. Denoting the unconditional mean of the expression in curly brackets as γ, and the average discount factor as $\bar{\beta}$ the approximation is given by

$$\beta_t \Theta_t \{.\}_t \approx const. + \bar{\beta}\gamma\Theta_t + \bar{\beta}\{.\}_t + \gamma\beta_t. \tag{9}$$

I assume that the conditional covariance between the financing constraints factor and the marginal benefit of investment, as well as the higher-order terms in the approximation, are captured, to a large extent, by the country-time and firm fixed effects. The overidentification tests, discussed in the next section, are used as an indication of the validity of this assumption.

After the required substitutions, linearization, and replacing the expectation with realized values plus an error term (i.e., rational expectations assumption), the empirical model is given by:

$$\frac{I}{K_{it}} = \beta_1 \frac{I}{K_{i,t+1}} + \beta_2 \frac{I}{K_{i,t-1}} + \beta_3 \frac{S}{K_{it}} + \beta_4 \text{Cash}_{it-1}$$
$$+ \beta_5 \text{Cash}_{i,t-1}\text{FD}_c + f_i + d_{c,t} + e_{it}, \tag{10}$$

where the coefficients are related to the structural parameters as

$$\beta_1 = \frac{\bar{\beta}(1-\delta)}{d}, \quad \beta_2 = \frac{g}{d}, \quad \beta_3 = \frac{\bar{\beta}\theta}{\alpha d}, \quad \beta_4 = \frac{\bar{\beta}\gamma}{\alpha d}a_1, \quad \beta_5 = \frac{\bar{\beta}\gamma}{\alpha d}a_2, \tag{11}$$
$$\text{and} \quad d = 1 + \bar{\beta}(1-\delta)g.$$

Here f_i denotes fixed effects and $d_{c,t}$ denotes country-time dummies that capture interest rates and aggregate macro shocks that are allowed to be different for each country.

With respect to the coefficients in Equation (10), the main hypothesis of this article is formally stated as

$$\beta_4 \geqslant 0 \quad \text{and} \quad \beta_5 < 0. \tag{12}$$

That is, financing constraints are nonzero (for at least some countries) and they decrease with financial development.[10]

2.1 Estimation issues
The first issue in estimating this model concerns the presence of fixed effects. Since the regressors are predetermined rather than strictly exogenous, mean-differencing would create biased estimates. To remove fixed effects I use forward mean differencing, discussed in Arellano and Bover (1995), which removes only the forward mean, that is, the mean of all the future observations available for each firm-year. The forward mean

---

[10] Note that β_4 and β_5 depend on previously defined structural parameters a_1 and a_2.

The Review of Financial Studies / v 16 n 3 2003

differencing preserves orthogonality between transformed errors and untransformed original variables, which are used as instruments.[11] The country-time dummies, $d_{c,t}$, are removed by country-time differencing prior to estimation (i.e., all instruments and all regressors are differenced by subtracting the mean for each country and each time period).

The rational expectation error, e_{it}, is orthogonal to any information available at the time when the investment decision is made, which I assume to be the beginning of the year. Therefore the orthogonality conditions for this model are given by $E[e_t|x_{t-s}] = 0$ for $s \geqslant 1$. I estimate the model by GMM with an optimal weighting matrix,[12] using as instruments $t-1$ and $t-2$ lags of all the variables in the regression, plus cash flow, cost of goods sold, industry dummies, and the interactions of cash, sales, and investment with FD (see Table 1 for variable definitions).

As discussed in the next section, the sample is very unbalanced and the less-developed countries are underrepresented. The countries with a small number of observations will have disproportionately little influence on the interaction term. To correct for this, I use either the rank-based approach or the weighted regressions approach. The rank-based regressions include only the largest firms within each country, ranked by the size of their fixed capital. Since there is no a priori criteria to select any specific number of firms, I experiment with different cutoff points and report results for 25, 50, and 150 firms. The weighted regression approach assigns a country-specific weight, which is equal to the inverse of the number of observations in each country. This effectively balances the number of observations across countries. This method is preferable, as it uses all available observations.

To test the overidentifying restrictions of the model I use the Sargan *J*-statistic, which equals to the value of the GMM objective function evaluated at the estimated parameter values. This statistic has an asymptotic chi-square distribution with degrees of freedom equal to the difference in the number of instruments and regressors. Two caveats apply to this test statistic. First, it is commonly established that its asymptotic distribution is a poor approximation to the finite sample distributions [see Hall and Horowitz (1996)]. Second, the asymptotic distribution of this

---

[11] Forward mean differencing, also referred to as "orthogonal deviations," was used to estimate investment models by Bond and Meghir (1994) and Gilchrist and Himmelberg (1998).

[12] The weighting matrix takes into account the panel structure of the data. It is given by $\mathbf{W} = (\sum_{i=1}^{N} \mathbf{Z}_i' \hat{\mathbf{u}}_i \hat{\mathbf{u}}_i' \mathbf{Z}_i)^{-1}$, where $\hat{\mathbf{u}}_i = (\hat{u}_{i1}, \ldots, \hat{u}_{iT_i})'$ is a vector of first-stage residuals and $\mathbf{Z}_i = (\mathbf{z}_{i1}', \ldots, \mathbf{z}_{iT_i}')'$ is a $T_i \times K$ matrix of instruments for firm i. It allows for conditional heteroscedasticity and SUR effects on the firm level (i.e., temporal heteroscedasticity within the firm), but does not allow any correlation across firms (which is captured by the country-time dummies). The weighting matrix employed here is akin to the weighting matrix II used in Bekaert, Harvey, and Lundblad (2001b). However, they have relatively small cross-sectional dimension and overlapping time periods and so they stack their observations by time, while here they are stacked by firm. This allows the most efficient use of my data, which have very large cross-sectional dimensions and small temporal dimensions.

Financial Development and Financing Constraints

Table 1
Variable definitions

Abbreviation	Description
Firm-level variables (from Worldscope)	
PPENT	Property plant and equipment, net of depreciation
CAPEX	Capital expenditure
DA	Depreciation and amortization expense
K	Beginning period capital = PPENT − CAPEX + DA
IK, I/K	Investment to capital ratio = CAPEX/K
SK, S/K	Sales to capital ratio = sales/K
Cash	Cash plus equivalents scaled by total assets (or scaled by K for robustness checks)
CF	Cash flow (net income + DA), scaled by K
COGS	Cost of goods sold, scaled by K
Size	Log of total assets in U.S. dollars
Rank	Ranking based on size of PPENT (first, ranked by year, then averaged over the years), largest firm in each country has rank equal to one.
Weight	Weight is a country-level variable equal to one over the number of valid observations per country.
Industry dummies	For manufacturing industries the dummies are on a two digit SIC level and for the rest of industries they are on a one digit level.
Country-level variables	
STKMKT	Stock market development is Index1 from Demurguc-Kunt and Levine (1996), equals to the sum of (standardized indices of) market capitalization to GDP, total value traded to GDP, and turnover (total value traded to market capitalization).
FININT	Financial intermediary development is Findex1 from Demurguc-Kunt and Levine (1996), equals to the sum of (standardized indices of) ratio of liquid liabilities to GDP, and ratio of domestic credit to private sector to GDP.
FD	Financial development = STKMKT + FININT.
Legal origin	Country's legal origin categorized into four groups: English, French, German or Scandinavian, from La Porta et al. (1998).
Efficiency, rule of law	Efficiency of legal system and rule of law are two measure of the quality of law enforcement, from La Porta et al. (1998).
Expropriation	Risk of expropriation is the risk of outright confiscation or forced confiscation by the government, from La Porta et al. (1998).
Corruption	The measure of corruption, from La Porta et al. (1998).
GNP PC	Log of GNP per capita in U.S. dollars in 1994, World Development Report 1996.
grGDP	Annual real growth rate of GDP, IFS.

statistic with the weighted regressions approach is unknown. To overcome these caveats I perform a bootstrap simulation to obtain the empirical distributions of the *J*-statistic.[13] I report the *p*-values, that is, the probability that the model is not rejected by the data (low *p*-values indicate rejection of the model).

3. Data

All firm-level data come from the Worldscope database, which contains data on large, publicly traded firms in which there is an investor interest.

---

[13] I follow the method of Hall and Horowitz (1996), who suggested recentering the bootstrap sample moments relative to the population moments. To capture the panel nature of the data, the sampling is done on the firm level. I report *p*-values given by the bootstrap distribution based on 200 repetitions. Increasing the number of repetitions for selected models produced qualitatively similar results. The Stata code for the GMM and bootstrap of the *J*-statistic are available from the author.

The Review of Financial Studies / v 16 n 3 2003

Table 2
Sample coverage across countries

Country	Country code	Number of observations	Percent of total observations	Number of firms
Argentina	AR	177	0.003	21
Austria	AT	424	0.008	45
Australia	AU	1359	0.026	135
Belgium	BE	474	0.009	50
Brazil	BR	593	0.012	68
Canada	CA	2950	0.057	283
Switzerland	CH	941	0.017	102
Chile	CL	390	0.007	46
Colombia	CO	108	0.003	10
Germany	DE	3688	0.067	379
Denmark	DK	927	0.018	97
Spain	ES	838	0.016	93
Finland	FI	656	0.013	65
France	FR	2794	0.055	296
United Kingdom	GB	8038	0.166	801
Indonesia	ID	464	0.009	59
Israel	IL	125	0.003	17
India	IN	1353	0.025	131
Italy	IT	1049	0.019	104
Japan	JP	3447	0.078	291
South Korea	KR	903	0.021	60
Mexico	MX	455	0.008	55
Malaysia	MY	1216	0.025	121
Netherlands	NL	1142	0.021	117
Norway	NO	607	0.011	59
New Zealand	NZ	280	0.005	28
Philippines	PH	222	0.005	20
Pakistan	PK	385	0.007	48
Portugal	PT	206	0.004	19
Sweden	SE	977	0.019	92
Singapore	SG	617	0.014	61
Thailand	TH	855	0.018	106
Turkey	TR	97	0.002	6
USA	US	8293	0.175	800
Venezuela	VE	74	0.001	8
South Africa	ZA	1008	0.019	101
Total		48,132		4794

Average number of firms per country	133
Average number of firms per country, excluding U.S. and U.K.	94
Median number of firms per country, excluding U.S. and U.K.	80

The firm data are available for 36 countries and cover about 5000 firms for the years 1988–1998 (however, the years before 1991 and the year 1998 have fewer observations). Details on the sample selection are given in Appendix A. The coverage within countries varies widely, from as little as 1% of all listed domestic firms included (for India) to as many as 82% (for Sweden), as calculated by La Porta et al. (1997) who use the same sample. Table 2 provides a list of countries in the sample, with the number of firms and observations per country, which varies widely across the countries. The United States and United Kingdom have about 800 firms each, while the average number of firms for the rest of the countries is 94.

The main firm-level variables are investment and sales, scaled by the beginning of period capital,[14] and stock of liquid assets (cash stock).

The main country-level indicator is an index of financial development, FD, which is an average of five standardized indices from Demirguc-Kunt and Levine (1996): market capitalization over gross domestic product (GDP), total value traded over GDP, total value traded over market capitalization, the ratio of liquid liabilities (M3) to GDP, and the credit going to the private sector over GDP. Thus the FD index combines five important characteristics of financial markets into a single measure, similar to the ones used in other studies. The value of this index corresponds to the beginning of my sample period and it is standardized to have mean zero and standard deviation of one.[15]

Other variables and their sources are defined in Table 1. Table 3 reports means and medians of the key variables, by country. Table 4 reports cross-country correlations of the country averages for these variables. Most of the country-level institutional characteristics are highly correlated with each other (panel B, Table 4).

4. Main Results

The main results are based on the model given in Equation (10) and are reported in Table 5. Models 1–3 use the rank-based approach with different cutoff points, and model 4 uses the weighted regression approach. All coefficients have their predicted signs and are significant at 1%. The coefficients in the weighted regression have the smallest standard errors because all the available observations are used, which results in efficiency gains. The main coefficients are cash and the interaction of cash with FD, and their signs are in line with the main hypothesis stated in Equation (12).

The interpretation of the magnitudes is best done in terms of the parameters of the underlying structural model, which are related to the reduced form coefficients by formulas given in Equation (11). There are five equations and eight parameters, therefore not all of the structural parameters can be identified. I choose to identify $(\bar{\beta}, g, \alpha, a_1, a_2)$ and assume the fixed values for the remaining parameters. I use the

---

[14] The model requires one to use the beginning of period capital stock as a scaling factor for calculating adjustment costs and MPK. One alternative is to use lagged capital stock (i.e., period $t-1$ used as the beginning of the period t capital stock). However, this would not be appropriate if there are mergers, acquisitions, divestitures, or other capital-changing events, which are hard to identify. I use the approximate value given by the ending period capital, minus investment and plus depreciation in that year, which is more robust to the capital-changing events, as discussed in Love (1999).

[15] Similar indicators were used in a recent article by Bekaert, Harvey, and Lundblad (2001a). They investigate the effect of financial liberalization and financial development on subsequent growth, measuring financial development at the begining of the five-year window. Similarly, in my article the financial development measure is taken at the begining of the period and the firm-level data actually used in regressions cover a five-year period (i.e., the effective sample after losing several years for instruments and transformations is 1991–1995).

The Review of Financial Studies / v 16 n 3 2003

Table 3
Descriptive statistics for key variables

Country	Cash Mean	Cash Median	I/K Mean	I/K Median	S/K Mean	S/K Median	FD	FININT	STKMKT
Argentina	0.08	0.04	0.19	0.13	1.6	1.2	−1.38	−0.79	−0.59
Austria	0.10	0.07	0.25	0.20	4.4	3.0	−0.27	−0.12	−0.15
Australia	0.08	0.05	0.26	0.18	3.3	2.3	0.42	0.23	0.19
Belgium	0.10	0.08	0.25	0.20	4.0	3.7	−0.82	−0.35	−0.47
Brazil	0.08	0.04	0.12	0.09	1.7	1.0	−1.04	−0.75	−0.29
Canada	0.07	0.02	0.23	0.18	3.1	1.5	0.03	−0.06	0.09
Switzerland	0.14	0.11	0.23	0.15	3.9	2.6	2.2	1.45	0.75
Chile	0.07	0.04	0.21	0.16	1.6	1.3	−0.75	−0.29	−0.46
Colombia	0.08	0.04	0.26	0.14	3.6	1.9	−1.6	−0.72	−0.88
Germany	0.08	0.05	0.31	0.25	5.5	4.8	1.68	0.3	1.38
Denmark	0.15	0.14	0.24	0.21	4.4	3.7	−0.49	−0.12	−0.37
Spain	0.06	0.04	0.14	0.09	2.8	1.8	−0.14	0.11	−0.25
Finland	0.09	0.08	0.38	0.21	5.0	3.2	−0.41	0.12	−0.53
France	0.12	0.09	0.27	0.21	6.5	6.0	0.1	0.31	−0.21
UK	0.09	0.06	0.22	0.17	4.6	4.0	1.68	0.45	1.23
Indonesia	0.14	0.10	0.37	0.23	3.9	2.6	−1.17	−0.46	−0.71
Israel	0.11	0.10	0.30	0.24	3.7	3.0	0.01	−0.07	0.08
India	0.04	0.03	0.27	0.19	3.5	2.6	−0.7	−0.44	−0.26
Italy	0.12	0.09	0.26	0.17	4.4	3.0	−0.64	−0.13	−0.51
Japan	*0.19*	*0.17*	0.22	0.19	4.1	3.3	*3.3*	1.31	2.02
South Korea	0.08	0.06	0.31	0.23	3.9	3.0	0.84	−0.21	1.05
Mexico	0.08	0.06	0.11	0.10	1.6	1.3	−0.85	−0.71	−0.14
Malaysia	0.08	0.05	0.23	0.16	2.7	1.8	1.19	0.29	0.9
Netherlands	0.10	0.05	0.24	0.20	5.1	3.8	0.66	0.34	0.32
Norway	0.14	0.12	0.33	0.22	3.6	2.1	−0.15	0.03	−0.18
New Zealand	0.04	0.02	0.17	0.13	3.3	2.8	−0.53	−0.2	−0.33
Philippines	0.12	0.07	0.37	0.22	2.6	1.4	−1.15	−0.61	−0.54
Pakistan	0.11	0.04	0.26	0.19	4.8	2.5	−1.28	−0.46	−0.82
Portugal	0.06	0.03	0.22	0.13	3.3	2.0	−0.67	−0.06	−0.61
Sweden	0.12	0.08	0.31	0.19	4.7	3.8	−0.31	−0.21	−0.1
Singapore	*0.19*	0.15	0.28	0.22	3.6	2.5	1.6	0.56	1.04
Thailand	0.06	0.03	0.40	0.23	4.5	2.5	0.36	−0.02	0.38
Turkey	0.13	0.07	*0.56*	*0.50*	*7.5*	5.8	−1.2	−0.59	−0.61
U.S.	0.09	0.04	0.24	0.19	4.8	3.8	1.35	0.14	1.21
Venezuela	0.09	0.06	0.21	0.13	1.5	1.1	−1.26	−0.52	−0.74
South Africa	0.09	0.06	0.22	0.19	4.7	3.8	0.25	−0.23	0.48
Mean	0.10	0.07	0.26	0.19	3.82	2.80	−0.03	−0.07	0.04
Median	0.09	0.06	0.25	0.19	3.87	2.62	−0.29	−0.12	−0.20
Std	0.04	0.04	0.08	0.07	1.33	1.22	1.14	0.50	0.73

Summary statistics by country for main variables. Variables definitions are given in Table 1. Outliers (far away maximum or minimum) are underlined.

minimum-distance estimator described in Appendix B, which also details the assumptions on fixed parameters. The parameters of the adjustment cost function imply a marginal adjustment cost in the range 0.25–0.9. These estimates are in line with previous evidence: for example, Whited (1998) cites articles that produced estimates in the range of 1% to 80% of the investment expenditure.

The magnitude of the financing constraints is given by the impact of the cash stock on the discount factor Θ, which was defined in Equation (6). The values for the structural parameters imply that for a firm in a country

Financial Development and Financing Constraints

Table 4
Panel A. Cross-country correlations of firm level variables

	Country means				Country medians			
	FD	Cash	IK	SK	FD	Cash	IK	SK
FD		0.15	0.02	0.34		0.21	0.21	0.44
		(0.35)	(0.87)	**(0.04)**		(0.22)	(0.22)	**(0.006)**
Cash	0.21		0.32	0.36	0.21		0.36	0.32
	(0.23)		**(0.04)**	**(0.02)**	(0.22)		**(0.02)**	**(0.04)**
IK	0.09	0.27		0.55	0.29	0.35		0.59
	(0.59)	*(0.099)*		**(0.0002)**	*(0.096)*	**(0.03)**		**(0.0001)**
SK	0.41	0.24	0.49		0.45	0.23	0.56	
	(0.015)	(0.14)	**(0.002)**		**(0.008)**	(0.15)	**(0.0003)**	

Panel B. Correlations of country-level institutional characteristics

	FD	FININT	STKMKT	Efficiency	Corruption	Expropr.	Accounting	GNPPC
FININT	0.90							
	(0)							
STKMKT	0.95	0.73						
	(0)	**(0)**						
Efficiency	0.52	0.52	0.45					
	(0.001)	**(0.001)**	**(0.005)**					
Corruption	0.51	0.55	0.40	0.83				
	(0.001)	**(0.001)**	**(0.01)**	**(0)**				
Expropriation	0.57	0.64	0.39	0.72	0.83			
	(0.001)	**(0)**	**(0.02)**	**(0)**	**(0)**			
Accounting	0.34	0.28	0.34	0.31	0.41	0.36		
	(0.05)	*(0.09)*	**(0.04)**	*(0.06)*	**(0.01)**	**(0.03)**		
GNP PC	0.56	0.61	0.46	0.74	0.87	0.84	0.46	
	(0)	**(0.0)**	**(0.004)**	**(0)**	**(0)**	**(0)**	**(0.005)**	
GDP US	0.54	0.41	0.49	0.20	0.26	0.46	0.15	0.42
	(0)	**(0.01)**	**(0.002)**	(0.22)	(0.11)	**(0.003)**	(0.39)	**(0.01)**

Correlations of country-level means and medians of the firm level variables and country's institutional characteristics. Variables definitions are in Table 1. Panel A: below the diagonal are Pearson correlation coefficients, with two outlier countries excluded: JP (Japan) and TR (Turkey). Above the diagonal are Spearman correlations (robust to outliers) with all observations included. Including outliers for Pearson correlations results in significant correlation for FD and Cash (due to JP which is an outlier on both of these) and nonsignificant correlation for SK and FD (due to TR, which has very high SK and low FD). Panel B: Pearson correlations with all countries. (Excluding Japan makes correlations of GDP PC with FD and FININT significant at 6% and 2%, respectively; also correlation between FININT and log GDP becomes insignificant.) *P*-values are in parenthesis; bold are significant at 5% or better, underlined are significant at 10%.

with an average FD, such as Spain, Norway, or Israel, a one standard deviation decrease in cash stock results in a change in the cost of capital of about 7%. The estimates also suggest that firms in countries with high FD (i.e., one standard deviation above the mean), such as the United States, the United Kingdom, and Japan, are not significantly financially constrained. This is not surprising given that the sample mainly consists of large publicly traded firms. On the other side, for firms in countries with low FD (i.e., one standard deviation below the mean), such as Mexico, Brazil, or Chile, a one standard deviation decrease in cash stock implies an increase in the cost of capital of about 14%. Although these estimates appear to be on the high side, the magnitude is definitely reasonable. What

The Review of Financial Studies / v 16 n 3 2003

Table 5
Main results on financial development and financing constraints

Model:	1 25 largest	2 50 largest	3 150 largest	4 All, weighted
I/K_{it+1}	0.733	0.643	0.638	0.353
	$(0.105)^{***}$	$(0.103)^{***}$	$(0.093)^{***}$	$(0.058)^{***}$
I/K_{it-1}	0.231	0.219	0.218	0.203
	$(0.025)^{***}$	$(0.017)^{***}$	$(0.013)^{***}$	$(0.008)^{***}$
S/K_{it}	0.021	0.017	0.013	0.033
	$(0.008)^{***}$	$(0.006)^{***}$	$(0.005)^{***}$	$(0.004)^{***}$
$Cash_{it-1}$	0.189	0.143	0.138	0.218
	$(0.063)^{***}$	$(0.047)^{***}$	$(0.039)^{***}$	$(0.034)^{***}$
$Cash_{it-1}{}^*FD_c$	−0.157	−0.113	−0.102	−0.183
	$(0.039)^{***}$	$(0.032)^{***}$	$(0.027)^{***}$	$(0.024)^{***}$
Constant	0.000	−0.002	−0.001	−0.002
	(0.001)	$(0.001)^{**}$	(0.001)	$(0.001)^{**}$
N observations	3533	6488	12474	21278
N firms	755	1436	2791	4794
p-value for J-statistic				
Chi-square	0.72	0.208	0.015	NA
Bootstrap	0.93	0.463	0.042	0.792

The dependent variable is IK_t, the model is given in Equation (10); variable definitions are in Table 1. The estimation is by GMM; country-time, and fixed effects are removed prior to estimation (see Section 2.1). Instruments are first and second lags of IK, SK, Cash, CFK, COGS, interactions of FD with IK, SK and Cash, and industry dummies. The firms are ranked based on the size of the capital stock. In the weighted regression, weights are equal to a value of one divided by the number of observations per country. P-values for J-statistic (test of overidentifying restrictions) are obtained using chi-square distribution or bootstrap simulation with 200 repetitions (the chi-square p-value is not available for weighted regressions). Heteroscedasticity adjusted standard errors in parentheses.
$^{***}, ^{**}$ and * represent significance at 1%, 5%, and 10%, respectively.

is important is that the constraints in a country with a low FD are almost twice as large as they are in a country with an average FD.[16] Although these calculations are rough approximations and should be used with caution, they suggest that financial development has a large and economically significant effect on financing constraints.

Another way to observe this relationship is by splitting the sample into financially developed and undeveloped subsamples (based on the median level of FD), given in Table 6. For the high-FD sample, the cash coefficient is small and insignificant, while it is large and significant for the low-FD sample.

The reported overidentification tests are used to verify the validity of the model. For rank-based regressions I report p-values (i.e., probability

---

[16] The effect on the cost of capital is calculated using structural parameters obtained from model 2 in Table 5. The numbers used in this calculation are $a_1 = 1.4$, $a_2 = -1.1$, FD = 0 for an average country and FD = −1 for a low-FD country, and a standard deviation of the change in the cash stock around its firm-level mean is 0.048 (calculated for the sample used in the regression). These numbers are substituted into Equation (6) to obtain the change in the discount factor which translates to the change in the cost of capital. The reported magnitudes depend on the assumptions of the fixed parameters described in Appendix B, which also contains a discussion of the sensitivity analysis. Relative to the rest of the investment literature, the range implied by the sensitivity tests seems reasonable. In addition, no matter what the assumptions on the fixed parameters, the magnitude of the constraints is about twice as large in a country with low financial development as it is in a country with average financial development.

Financial Development and Financing Constraints

Table 6
Sample splits

	High FD		Low FD	
	1	2	3	4
Model:	50 largest	150 largest	50 largest	150 largest
I/K_{it+1}	0.629	0.734	0.766	0.643
	$(0.064)^{***}$	$(0.094)^{***}$	$(0.105)^{***}$	$(0.126)^{***}$
I/K_{it-1}	0.257	0.231	0.184	0.181
	$(0.022)^{***}$	$(0.015)^{***}$	$(0.024)^{***}$	$(0.021)^{***}$
S/K_{it}	0.014	0.014	0.008	0.019
	$(0.007)^{***}$	$(0.005)^{***}$	(0.008)	$(0.009)^{**}$
$Cash_{it-1}$	0.041	0.035	0.210	0.258
	(0.044)	(0.036)	$(0.072)^{***}$	$(0.069)^{***}$
Constant	0.000	0.000	−0.001	−0.001
	(0.002)	(0.001)	(0.002)	(0.002)
N observations	4335	9377	2579	3596
N firms	861	1962	686	969
p-value for J-statistic				
Chi-square	0.907	0.348	0.518	0.495
Bootstrap	0.983	0.528	0.792	0.593

The dependent variable is IK_i; variable definitions are in Table 1. High FD and low FD are samples split on the median FD (reported in Table 3). The estimation is by GMM; country-time and fixed effects are removed prior to estimation (see Section 2.1). Instruments are first and second lags of IK, SK, Cash, CFK, COGS and industry dummies. The firms are ranked based on the size of the capital stock. *P*-values for *J*-statistic (test of overidentifying restrictions) are obtained using chi-square distribution or bootstrap simulation with 200 repetitions. Heteroscedasticity adjusted standard errors in parentheses.

***, ** and * represent significance at 1%, 5%, and 10%, respectively.

that the model is not rejected) using asymptotic and bootstrapped distributions, described in Section 2.1. It is interesting to note that the bootstrapped probabilities are always higher than the asymptotic ones, suggesting that the asymptotic tests tend to reject the model too often. However, both tests do not reject models 1 and 2 in Table 5 and all four models in Table 6, and both tests reject model 3 in Table 5.[17] For the weighted regression (model 4 in Table 5), only the bootstrapped test is available and it does not reject the model. These tests serve as evidence that the assumptions that I make in the model and estimation are not rejected by the data.

This section establishes the main claim of this article, that financial development decreases financing constraints, measured by the impact of internal funds on the effective discount factor, which in turn affects the rate of intertemporal substitution between investment in two subsequent periods.

---

[17] Increasing the cutoff point makes the sample more and more unbalanced, which is probably the reason for the rejection of the model (this is also true for models with different cutoff points that are not reported). However, in the sample splits in Table 6, even with 150 firms, neither sample is rejected (this is likely because the main imbalance is between developed and developing countries).

The Review of Financial Studies / v 16 n 3 2003

5. Tests of Alternative Explanations

5.1 Size and business cycles

Several robustness tests of the model are performed by adding other variables to the parameterization of the discount factor. The first variable is firm size. It is likely that small firms have larger information asymmetries which could lead to larger financing constraints, however, the empirical results on the effect of size on financing constraints have been mixed [see Schiantarelli (1996) for a survey of this evidence]. To test for the size effect, I add the interaction of size (measured by the log of total assets in U.S. dollars) with cash stock to the baseline model.[18] The results presented in model 1 of Table 7 show that larger firms are less constrained, as the impact of the cash stock on their discount factor is smaller. Next, I test the robustness of the FD result to inclusion of the size effect. If more financially developed countries have larger firms, as argued by Kumar, Rajan, and Zingales (1999), the estimated FD effect could be attributed to differences in firm size rather than financial development. Model 2 shows that this is not the case, as both interactions remain significant at 1%.

This methodology allows me to address another interesting empirical question: Is the size effect equal in all countries, or is it related to financial development? The intuition is that the largest firms in less financially developed countries could have easier access to external finance obtained through external capital markets or political connections, while smaller firms will be comparatively more disadvantaged. I test this by augmenting the model to add a triple interaction of cash, size, and FD. I find in model 3 that this interaction is negative and significant; that is, financial development affects the small firms significantly more than the large firms.[19] The size effect is about 35% larger for a country with low financial development relative to a country with average financial development.

Another potential concern is that my main results could reflect different stages in the countries' business cycles rather than the average level of financial development. External financing is easier to obtain during good times (when profits are high and balance sheets are healthy) and therefore financing constraints will vary over the business cycle.[20] To test this I include the interaction of the real GDP growth rate, $grGDP_{ct}$, with the

---

[18] Since my size measure is not time varying, it enters the Euler equation only as an interaction with the cash stock, as the level effect is captured by the firm fixed effects.

[19] Note that model 1 is rejected at the 5% level by the overidentification test, however, models 2 and 3 are not rejected. Model 1 could be rejected because it does not contain the interaction with financial development.

[20] This intuition has been formalized and tested on U.S. data by Gertler and Hubbard (1988), Bernanke and Gertler (1989) and Gertler and Gilchrist (1994), among others.

Financial Development and Financing Constraints

Table 7
Robustness: size effect and business cycles

Model:	Size Effect			Business Cycles	
	1	2	3	4	5
I/K_{it+1}	0.534	0.444	0.437	0.294	0.215
	$(0.061)^{***}$	$(0.057)^{**}$	$(0.058)^{**}$	$(0.071)^{**}$	$(0.063)^{***}$
I/K_{it-1}	0.197	0.200	0.199	0.189	0.194
	$(0.008)^{***}$	$(0.008)^{***}$	$(0.008)^{***}$	$(0.009)^{***}$	$(0.008)^{***}$
S/K_{it}	0.026	0.029	0.029	0.035	0.037
	$(0.004)^{***}$	$(0.004)^{***}$	$(0.004)^{***}$	$(0.004)^{***}$	$(0.004)^{***}$
$Cash_{it-1}$	0.443	0.493	0.617	0.226	0.254
	$(0.102)^{***}$	$(0.107)^{***}$	$(0.119)^{***}$	$(0.041)^{***}$	(0.042)
$Cash_{it-1}{}^*Size_i$	-0.057	-0.059	-0.083		
	$(0.017)^{***}$	$(0.018)^{***}$	$(0.021)^{***}$		
$Cash_{it-1}{}^*FD_c$		-0.172	-0.588		-0.164
		$(0.024)^{***}$	$(0.112)^{***}$		$(0.025)^{***}$
$Cash_{it-1}{}^*Size_i{}^*FD_c$			0.078		
			$(0.019)^{***}$		
$Cash_{it-1}{}^*grGDP_{ct}$				-1.420	-0.973
				$(0.622)^{**}$	$(0.632)^a$
Constant	-0.002	-0.002	-0.002	-0.002	-0.003
	$(0.001)^{***}$	$(0.001)^{***}$	$(0.001)^{***}$	$(0.001)^{***}$	$(0.001)^{***}$
N observations	21278	21278	21278	21009	21009
N firms	4794	4794	4794	4768	4768
Bootstraped *p*-value for *J*-statistic:	0.142	0.193	0.228	0.973	0.993

The dependent variable is IK_t. The size is equal to the (log of) total assets in U.S. dollars, grGDP is country-year real GDP growth rate. The estimation is by GMM; country-time and fixed effects are removed prior to estimation (see Section 2.1). Instruments are first and second lags of IK, SK, Cash, CF, COGS, size (GDP growth) and its interactions with Cash, IK and SK, interactions of FD with IK, SK, Cash, and size, and industry dummies. All the regressions are weighted regressions, weights are equal to a value of one divided by the number of observations per country. *P*-values for *J*-statistic (test of overidentifying restrictions) are obtained using bootstrap simulation with 200 repetitions. Heteroscedasticity adjusted standard errors in parentheses.
***, ** and * represent significance at 1%, 5%, and 10% level
^{a}in model (5) indicates, significance at 12% level.

firm-level measure of the cash stock. Model 4 in Table 7 shows that this interaction is negative, that is, economic boom periods (periods with high GDP growth) are associated with the lower level of financing constraints. The effect of financial development is not significantly affected by the addition of the GDP growth interaction: FD interaction remains significant at 1% in model 5.

5.2 Legal system indicators
Recent law and finance literature has focused on the differences in the rights of minority shareholders and the enforcement of laws across countries [most notably La Porta et al. (1997, 1998)]. They argue that "the [legal] protection investors receive determines their readiness to finance firms," and show that the legal environment has large effects on the level of financial development. Therefore better legal protection of investors will reduce the cost of external finance and should be reflected in the impact of internal funds on the firms' effective discount factor.

The Review of Financial Studies / v 16 n 3 2003

Previous research (La Porta et al. and others) identified several legal system indicators such as the efficiency of the legal system, the rule of law, the risk of expropriation, corruption, and legal origin (see Table 1 for variable definitions and original sources for these data). These indicators measure different aspects of the legal environment. For example, efficiency and the rule of law measure the quality of the law enforcement, that is, how well the laws on the books are enforced by the courts. Corruption measures the distortions introduced by the courts and government into the functioning of the financial and real sectors of the economy. The accounting standards measure the quality of information available to investors and should therefore reduce the external financing costs associated with information availability.

I use the baseline model in Equation (10) and replace FD with each of the legal indicators. As shown in Table 8, each indicator has a negative effect on the cash coefficient and countries of English legal origin appear to be less constrained, consistent with the previous evidence. When each indicator is included together with FD (all the even-numbered models in Table 8), FD interactions remain significant at 1% in all cases, as well as most legal indicators (only efficiency and English origin lose significance when included together with FD). Since FD and legal indicators are highly correlated, both variables drop in magnitude when included together. This could be taken as evidence that there are several aspects of the underlying contracting environment which are measured imperfectly with different indicators. However, financial development remains a robust indicator of the firm's financing constraints throughout the whole exercise.

6. Single-Country Regressions

An alternative way to address the relationship between financial development and financing constraints is to allow each country to have its own level of financing constraints, measured by the coefficient on cash stock. That is, the discount factor is now given by $\Theta_{it} = a_{0i} + a_c \text{Cash}_{it-1}$. I estimate Equation (10) without the interaction term for each country and obtain country-specific cash coefficients, $\hat{a}_c$. Then these coefficients are regressed on the country-level index of financial development:

$$\hat{a}_c = b_0 + b_1 \text{FD}_c + e_c. \tag{13}$$

The main hypothesis now is that $b_1 < 0$, that is, the first-stage cash coefficients are decreasing with financial development. These single-country regressions are not as efficient as cross-country regressions because they require estimating 180 coefficients [five per country for 36

Financial Development and Financing Constraints

Table 8
Legal system indicators and financing constraints

Model:	Indicator:	$Cash_{it-1}$	$Cash_{it-1}$ * Indicator$_c$	$Cash_{it-1}$ * FD$_c$	Bootstraped p-value for J-statistic:
1	Efficiency	0.685***	− 0.062***		0.792
		(0.101)	(0.012)		
2	Efficiency	0.392***	− 0.022	− 0.153***	0.853
		(0.122)	(0.016)	(0.030)	
3	Rule of law	0.712***	− 0.065***		0.738
		(0.100)	(0.012)		
4	Rule of law	0.564***	− 0.044***	− 0.139***	0.718
		(0.112)	(0.014)	(0.026)	
5	Corruption	0.716***	− 0.069***		0.818
		(0.098)	(0.012)		
6	Corruption	0.507***	− 0.039***	− 0.133***	0.802
		(0.117)	(0.015)	(0.029)	
7	Expropriation	1.510***	− 0.149***		0.643
		(0.175)	(0.019)		
8	Expropriation	1.210***	− 0.112***	− 0.111***	0.463
		(0.211)	(0.024)	(0.027)	
9	Accounting	1.140***	− 0.015***		0.302
		(0.158)	(0.002)		
10	Accounting	0.761***	− 0.009***	− 0.126***	0.387
		(0.193)	(0.003)	(0.027)	
11	English origin	0.263***	− 0.223***		0.313
		(0.039)	(0.061)		
12	English origin	0.245***	− 0.064	− 0.169***	0.568
		(0.039)	(0.066)	(0.025)	

The dependent variable is IK_t, the "baseline" model is given in Equation (10) with FD interactions replaced or supplemented with each of the indicator variable interactions (the rest of coefficients are not reported). Variable definitions are in Table 1. The estimation is by GMM, country-time and fixed effects are removed prior to estimation (see Section 2.1). Instruments are first and second lags of IK, SK, Cash, CFK, COGS, interactions of FD and appropriate indicator with IK, SK and Cash, and industry dummies. All the regressions are weighted regressions, weights are equal to a value of one divided by the number of observations per country. All regressions include 21,278 observations (4794 firms) except for models with accounting standards which include 21,032 observations (4687 firms). P-values for J-statistic (test of overidentifying restrictions) are obtained using bootstrap simulation with 200 repetitions. Heteroscedasticity adjusted standard errors in parentheses.
***, ** and * represent significance at 1%, 5%, and 10% respectively.

countries, the five coefficients are $\beta_1 - \beta_4$ in Equation (10) plus a constant] rather than estimating only 6. As a result, most of the individual cash coefficients are not significant at conventional levels (results of the first-stage estimation are available on request[21]). An advantage of this approach is in allowing all the coefficients to be country specific. Since the dependent variable is estimated in the first stage, the standard errors of the second-stage regression are not correct and the following results should be considered as "informal" and complementary to the formal inference performed in the previous sections.

---

[21] The cash stock coefficients range from zero (25th percentile) to 0.35 (75th percentile), with a mean of 0.17 and a median of 0.11. These statistics are in line with the cash coefficients estimated in the cross-country regressions, which varied from 0.13 to 0.21 (Table 5).

The Review of Financial Studies / v 16 n 3 2003

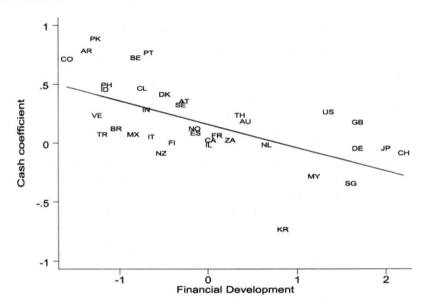

Figure 1
Cash coefficients and financial development
Regression line: -0.18, significant at 1% (the standard error is 0.05 and R^2 is 0.35). Without KR: -0.16, significant at 1% (the standard error is 0.04 and R^2 is 0.37).

In Figure 1 the cash coefficients estimated in the first stage are plotted against the FD index and a strong negative relationship is found. The OLS regression results in a coefficient of -0.18, significant at the 1% level with $R^2 = 0.35$. Keeping in mind the problem with standard errors in this regression, it is interesting to note that the magnitude of this coefficient (which is consistent) is much in line with the magnitude of the interaction term in cross-country regressions (see model 4 in Table 5). This makes the single-country regressions a useful robustness test, despite the problem of low efficiency of individual coefficients.

7. Conclusion

This article shows that financial development affects a firm's investment via their ability to obtain external finance. This effect is inferred from the investment Euler equation by assuming that the stochastic discount factor is a function of the firm's internal cash stock. I find that the impact of internal funds on the effective discount factor decreases with financial development. In other words, firms that face financing constraints behave as if they have low discount factors (i.e., high cost of capital) and tend to postpone investment to the next period. The magnitude of the changes in the cost of capital of financially constrained firms is twice as large in a country with a low level of financial development as it is in a country with an average level of financial development. The financial development effect remains significant after controlling for firm size and the country's business cycles, which also affect financing constraints. I also find that small firms are disproportionately more disadvantaged in less financially developed countries than are large firms. Finally, legal system indicators (the efficiency of the legal system, the risk of expropriation, corruption, or legal origin) are also associated with a reduction in financing constraints; however, the effect of financial development is robust to inclusion of any additional indicators.

This article makes contributions to two strands of literature. First, it contributes to the investment literature by estimating a structural investment model and confirming the presence of financing constraints for a broad range of countries. Second, and more importantly from a policy perspective, this article contributes to the economic development and growth literature by showing that financial development diminishes financing constraints by reducing information asymmetries and contracting imperfections. The decrease in financing constraints allows firms to invest according to their growth opportunities and therefore improves capital allocation.

Appendix 1: Sample Selection

All countries in the Worldscope database (May 1999 Global Researcher CD) excluding former socialist economies are included. This results in a sample of 36 countries. The sample does not include firms for which the primary industry is either financial (one-digit SIC code of 6) or service (one-digit SIC codes of 7 or above).

In addition, I delete the following (see Table 1 for variable definitions):

- All firms with three or fewer years of coverage.
- All firm-years with missing CAPEX, PPENT, sales, and cash.
  Observations with zero PPENT (200 observations).
- Observations with negative KBEG (277 observations), cash/total assets or COGS (27 observations).
- Observations with IK > 2.5 (1% of all observations).
- Observations with SK > 20 (5% of all observations).[22]
- Observations with Cogs/K > 20 (80 observations).
- Observations with cash/total assets > 0.6 (1% of all observations).
- 50% of all U.S. firms with at least four years of data available were selected by random sample.

In addition, to eliminate influential observations, I exclude 1% on each side of the distribution for each of the variables in the regression. The resulting dataset has about 5000 firms with about 48,000 observations; the number of observations by country is given in Table 2.

---

[22] This rule excludes firms for which capital is not a big factor in production. Half of these were in the United States and United Kingdom; Japan, France, and Denmark totaled 25%.

The Review of Financial Studies / v 16 n 3 2003

Appendix B: Identifying Structural Parameters Using Estimated Coefficients

The formulas that determine estimated coefficients as functions of the structural parameters are given in Equation (11). Denote $\boldsymbol{\beta} = (\beta_1, \beta_2, \beta_3, \beta_4, \beta_5)$, the vector of reduced-form coefficients estimated in the Euler equation. I choose to identify five parameters of interest, denoted $\boldsymbol{\sigma} = (\beta, g, \alpha, a_1, a_2)$ and assume the values for the remaining parameters. I assume a depreciation rate $\delta = 0.12$, which is the sample average of the depreciation expense to capital ratio. The coefficient θ, which translates the sales-to-capital ratio into MPK in Equation (7), is assumed to be equal to 0.2 (this corresponds to the values for the capital share $\alpha_k = 0.3$ and markup $\mu = 1.3$).[23] Finally, I assume the value for the linearization parameter $\gamma = 1.2$, which is equal to the average marginal benefit of investment.[24] The sensitivity analysis performed by varying the values of the fixed parameters results in the range of estimates that is reasonable in comparison to other articles in the literature.[25]

Denote the relationship between reduced-form coefficients and structural parameters as $\beta = f(\sigma)$. The minimum distance estimator is the argument of the following minimization problem:

$$\check{\sigma} = \arg\min_{\sigma}(\check{\beta} - f(\sigma))'\check{\Sigma}^{-1}(\check{\beta} - f(\sigma)),$$

where $\check{\beta}$ is the vector of estimates for the reduced-form coefficients and $\check{\Sigma}$ is its variance-covariance matrix. Let $F \equiv \mathrm{plim}\, \partial f(\sigma)/\partial \sigma'|_{\sigma = \check{\sigma}}$, which is a Jacobian matrix of derivatives of each of the functions with respect to each of the structural parameters. It can be shown that

$$\sqrt{N}(\check{\sigma} - \sigma_0) \to N(0, (F'\Sigma^{-1}F)^{-1})$$

where F and Σ can be consistently estimated by $\check{F}$ and $\check{\Sigma}$.

References

Arrelano, M., and O. Bover, 1995, "Another Look at the Instrumental Variable Estimation of Error Component Models," *Journal of Econometrics*, 68, 29–51.

Beck, T., R. Levine, and N. Loyaza, 2000, "Financial Intermediation and Growth: Causality and Causes," *Journal of Monetary Economics*, 46, 31–77.

Bekaert G., and C. Harvey, 2000, "Foreign Speculators and Emerging Equity Markets," *Journal of Finance*, 55, 565–613.

---

[23] The estimate of markup is taken from Hubbard, Kashyap, and Whited (1995), and it corresponds to a demand elasticity of -4.

[24] I assume that MPK is approximately equal to 0.2 [taken from Gilchrist and Himmelberg (1998)] and the marginal adjustment cost term is 0.2. Varying γ from 1.1 to 1.4 results in about 20% variation in parameter estimates. Since the value of γ depends on the values of other parameters, I experimented with an iterative procedure when γ was determined at every stage of minimization using the parameter values at that stage. This produced qualitatively similar results.

[25] The sensitivity analysis shows that the only parameter that results in significant variation in implied cost of capital is θ. For example, assuming $\theta = 0.1$ implies that the change in the cost of capital in a country with average financial development is about 5% and in a country with low financial development it is about 9%. Assuming $\theta = 0.3$ implies that the change in the cost of capital in a country with average financial development is about 17% and in a country with low financial development it is about 34%. Relative to the results reported in the text, this analysis implies ranges from 50% to 200%. These ranges seem reasonable relative to other articles in the investment literature, which is not known for producing precise estimates: for example Whited (1998) cites articles that estimate adjustment costs in the range from 0.01 to 0.8, that is, a difference of 8000%.

Financial Development and Financing Constraints

Bekaert G., C. Harvey, and C. Lundblad, 2001a, "Does Financial Liberalization Spur Growth," Working Paper W8245, NBER.

Bekaert G., C. Harvey, and C. Lundblad, 2001b, "Emerging Equity Markets and Economic Growth," *Journal of Development Economics*, 66, 465–504.

Bernanke, B., and M. Gertler, 1989, "Agency Costs, Net Worth, and Business Fluctuations," *American Economic Review*, 79, 14–31.

Bond, S., and J. G. Cummins, 2001, "Noisy Share Prices and the Q Model of Investment," working paper, Oxford University.

Bond, S., and C. Meghir, 1994, "Dynamic Investment Models and the Firm's Financial Policy," *Review of Economic Studies*, 61, 197–222.

Bond, S., J. Elston, J. Mairesse, and B. Mulkay, 1997, "Financial Factors and Investment in Belgium, France, Germany and the UK: A Comparison Using Company Panel Data," Working Paper 5900, NBER.

Calomiris, C., and G. Hubbard, 1995, "Internal Finance and Firm-Level Investment: Evidence from the Undistributed Profit Tax of 1936–1937," *Journal of Business*, 68, 443–482.

Cooper, R., and J. Ejarque, 2001, "Exhuming Q: Market Power versus Capital Market Imperfections," working paper, Boston University.

Demirguc-Kunt, A., and R. Levine, 1996, "Stock Market Development and Financial Intermediaries: Stylized Facts," *World Bank Economic Review*, 10, 291–321.

Demirguc-Kunt, A., and V. Maksimovic, 1998, "Law, Finance and Firm Growth," *Journal of Finance*, 53, 2107–2131.

Erickson, T., and T. Whited, 2000, "Measurement Error and the Relationship between Investment and q," *Journal of Political Economy*, 108, 1027–1057.

Galindo, A., F. Schiantarelli, and A. Weiss, 2001, "Does Financial Liberalization Improve the Allocation of Investment? Micro Evidence from Developing Countries," mimeo, Boston College.

Gelos, G., and A. Werner, 1999, "Financial Liberalization, Credit Constraints, and Collateral: Investment in the Mexican Manufacturing Sector," Working Paper WP/99/25, IMF.

Gertler, M., and S. Gilchrist, 1994, "Monetary Policy, Business Cycles, and the Behavior of Small Manufacturing Firms," *Quarterly Journal of Economics*, 109, 309–340.

Gertler, M., and G. Hubbard, 1988, "Financial Factors in Business Fluctuations," in *Financial Market Volatility: Causes, Consequences, and Policy Recommendations*, Federal Reserve Bank, Kansas City.

Gilchrist, S., and C. Himmelberg, 1998, "Investment, Fundamentals and Finance," *NBER Macroeconomics Annual*, MIT Press, Cambridge, Mass.

Gomes, J., 2002, "Financing Investment," forthcoming in *American Economic Review*.

Hall, P., and J. Horowitz, 1996, "Bootstrap Critical Values for Tests Based on Generalized Method-of-Moments Estimators," *Econometrica*, 64, 891–916.

Harris, J. R., F. Schiantarelli, and M. G. Siregar, 1994, "The Effect of Financial Liberalization on the Capital Structure and Investment Decisions of Indonesian Manufacturing Establishments," *World Bank Economic Review*, 8, 17–47.

Hart, O., 1995, *Firms, Contracts, and Financial Structure*, Oxford University Press, London.

Hayashi, F., 1982, "Tobin's Marginal q and Average q: A Neoclassical Interpretation," *Econometrica*, 50, 213–224.

Henry, P. B., 2000, "Stock Market Liberalization, Economic Reform and Emerging Market Equity Prices," *Journal of Finance*, 55, 529–564.

The Review of Financial Studies / v 16 n 3 2003

Hubbard, R. G., 1998, "Capital Market Imperfections and Investment," *Journal of Economic Literature*, 36, 193–225.

Hubbard, R. G., and A. Kashyap, 1992, "Internal Net Worth and the Investment Process: An Application to United States Agriculture," *Journal of Political Economy*, 100, 506–534.

Hubbard, R. G., A. Kashyap, and T. Whited, 1995, "Internal Finance and Firm Investment," *Journal of Money Credit and Banking*, 27, 683–701.

Jaramillo, F., F. Schianterelli, and A. Weiss, 1996, "Capital Market Imperfections Before and After Financial Liberalization: An Euler Equation Approach to Panel Data for Ecuadorian Firms," *Journal of Development Economics*, 51, 367–386.

Jensen, M., and W. Meckling, 1976, "Theory of the Firm: Managerial Behaviour, Agency Costs, and Ownership Structure," *Journal of Financial Economics*, 3, 305–360.

Kaplan, S., and L. Zingales, 1997, "Do Investment-Cash Flow Sensitivities Provide Useful Measures of Financing Constraints?" *Quarterly Journal of Economics*, 112, 169–215.

King, R. G., and R. Levine, 1993, "Finance and Growth: Schumpeter Might be Right," *Quarterly Journal of Economics*, 108, 717–737.

Kumar K. B., R. Rajan, and L. Zingales, 1999, "What Determines Firm Size," Working paper 7208, NBER.

Laeven, Luc, 2003, "Does Financial Liberalization Reduce Financing Constraints," forthcoming in *Financial Management*.

La Porta, R., F. Lopez-de-Silanes, A. Shleifer, and R. Vishny, 1997, "Legal Determinants of External Finance," *Journal of Finance*, 102, 1131–1150.

La Porta, R., F. Lopez-de-Silanes, A. Shleifer, and R. Vishny, 1998, "Law and Finance," *Journal of Political Economy*, 106, 1113–1155.

Love, I., 1999, "The Capital Accumulation Identity — How Well does it Hold in the Data: Evidence from Compustat and Worldscope Databases," working paper, Columbia University.

Lucas, R. E., 1988, "On the Mechanics of Economic Development," *Journal of Monetary Economics*, 22, 3–42.

Modigliani, F., and M. Miller, 1958, "The Cost of Capital, Corporate Finance, and the Theory of Investment," *American Economic Review*, 48, 261–297.

Myers, S., and N. Majluf, 1984, "Corporate Financing and Investment Decisions When Firms Have Information That Investors do not Have," *Journal of Financial Economics*, 13, 187–221.

Neusser, K., and M. Kugler, 1998, "Manufacturing Growth and Financial Development: Evidence from OECD countries," *Review of Economics and Statistics*, 80, 636–646.

Rajan, R., and L. Zingales, 1998, "Financial Dependence and Growth," *American Economic Review*, 88, 559–586.

Rousseau, P., and P. Wachtel, 1998, "Financial Intermediation and Economic Performance: Historical Evidence from Five Industrialized Countries," *Journal of Money Credit and Banking*, 30, 657–678.

Schiantarelli, F., 1996, "Financial Constraints and Investment: Methodological Issues and International Evidence," *Oxford Review of Economic Policy*, 12, 70–89.

Schumpeter, J. A., 1912, *The Theory of Economic Development*, trans. 1934, Harvard U.P., Cambridge, MASS.

Tobin, J., 1969, "A General Equilibrium Approach to Monetary Theory," *Journal of Money Credit and Banking*, 1, 265–293.

Financial Development and Financing Constraints

Whited, T., 1992, "Debt, Liquidity Constraints, and Corporate Investment: Evidence from Panel Data," *Journal of Finance*, 47, 1425–1460.

Whited, T., 1998, "Why do Investment Euler Equations Fail?" *Journal of Business and Economic Statistics*, 16, 479–488.

Wurgler, J., 2000, "Financial Markets and Allocation of Capital," *Journal of Financial Economics*, 58, 187–214.

THE JOURNAL OF FINANCE • VOL. LX, NO. 1 • FEBRUARY 2005

Financial and Legal Constraints to Growth: Does Firm Size Matter?

THORSTEN BECK, ASLI DEMIRGÜÇ-KUNT,
and VOJISLAV MAKSIMOVIC*

ABSTRACT

Using a unique firm-level survey database covering 54 countries, we investigate the effect of financial, legal, and corruption problems on firms' growth rates. Whether these factors constrain growth depends on firm size. It is consistently the smallest firms that are most constrained. Financial and institutional development weakens the constraining effects of financial, legal, and corruption obstacles and it is again the small firms that benefit the most. There is only a weak relation between firms' perception of the quality of the courts in their country and firm growth. We also provide evidence that the corruption of bank officials constrains firm growth.

CORPORATE FINANCE THEORY SUGGESTS that market imperfections, such as those caused by underdeveloped financial and legal systems, constrain firms' ability to fund investment projects. Using firm-level data, Demirgüç-Kunt and Maksimovic (1998) show that firms in countries with developed financial institutions and efficient legal systems obtain more external financing than firms in countries with less-developed institutions. Although these findings show a strong effect of financial institutions and the legal system on firm growth, their conclusions are based on a sample of the largest firms in each of the economies they study. Their study relies on inferring firms' demand for external financing from a financial model of the firm.

In this paper, we use a size-stratified survey of over 4,000 firms in 54 countries to assess (1) whether financial, legal, and corruption obstacles affect firms' growth; (2) whether this effect varies across firms of different sizes; (3) whether small, medium-sized, and large firms are constrained differently in countries with different levels of financial and institutional development; (4) the specific characteristics of the legal system that facilitate firm growth; and (5) the importance of corruption in financial intermediaries to firm growth.

*Beck and Demirgüç-Kunt are at the World Bank. Maksimovic is at the Robert H. Smith School of Business at the University of Maryland. This paper's findings, interpretations, and conclusions are entirely those of the authors and do not necessarily represent the views of the World Bank, its executive directors, or the countries they represent. We would like to thank Jerry Caprio, George Clarke, Simeon Djankov, Jack Glen, Richard Green, the editor, Luc Laeven, Florencio Lopez-de-Silanez, Inessa Love, Maria Soledad Martinez Peria, Raghuram Rajan, and seminar participants at the World Bank, American University, Case Western Reserve, Georgetown University, Oxford University, the University of Minnesota and Yale University, and an anonymous referee for helpful comments.

There is considerable evidence that firm size is related to a firm's productivity, survival, and profitability. As a result, understanding how financial, legal, and corruption obstacles affect firms of different sizes has policy implications. Significant resources are channeled into the promotion of small and medium-sized enterprises (SMEs). The World Bank alone has approved more than $10 billion in SME support programs in the past 5 years, $1.5 billion of it in the last year alone (World Bank Group Review of Small Business Activities (2002)).

A priori, it is not clear whether weak financial and legal institutions create greater obstacles to the growth of large or small firms. Large firms internalize many of the capital allocation functions carried out by financial markets and financial intermediaries. Thus, the development of financial markets and institutions should disproportionately benefit small firms. On the other hand, large firms are most likely to tax the resources of an underdeveloped financial or legal system, since they are more likely than small firms to depend on long-term financing and on larger loans. It is possible that financial development can disproportionately reduce the effect of institutional obstacles on the largest firms.

Our paper provides evidence relevant to reforming legal systems in developing countries. Although recent studies in international corporate finance predict a positive relation between the quality of the legal system and access to external financing, we actually know very little about how firms' perceptions conform to the conventional notions of what makes a legal system efficient (such as the impartiality of courts and whether court decisions are enforced). Moreover, we do not know whether these conventional notions help predict the effect of the legal system on firm growth. In this paper, we address both of these issues.

Our paper also provides evidence about the potential costs of monitoring by financial intermediaries. Several influential theoretical models and public policy prescriptions rely on monitoring by financial intermediaries to reduce misallocation of investment in economies with underdeveloped financial markets. Although the reduction of agency costs caused by firms' insiders is a major motivation for this monitoring, the models on which the policies are based typically do not consider the possibility of agency costs within banks. We examine evidence indicating that corrupt officials in financial intermediaries retard the efficient allocation of capital to smaller firms by relating firms' reports of bank corruption to the firms' growth rates.

Our paper builds on earlier studies, starting with La Porta et al. (1998), who argue that differences in legal and financial systems can explain much of the variation across countries in firms' financial policies and performance. Recent empirical evidence supports the view that the development of a country's financial system affects firm growth and financing. In addition to Demirgüç-Kunt and Maksimovic's (1998) firm-level results, Rajan and Zingales (1998a) show that industries that are dependent on external finance grow faster in countries with better developed financial systems.[1] Wurgler (2000) shows that

---

[1] In addition, Carlin and Mayer (2003) also argue that there exists a relation between a country's financial system and the characteristics of industries that prosper in the country. Demirgüç-Kunt

Financial and Legal Constraints to Growth   139

the rate at which resources are allocated to productive industries depends on the development of the financial system. Love (2003) shows that the sensitivity of investment to cash flow depends negatively on financial development. [2]

The richness of the survey's database allows us to go beyond earlier papers that infer the presence of institutional failures from past growth performance.[3] The firms that were surveyed reported whether specific features of the financial and legal systems in their countries and the corruption they faced were obstacles to their growth. Thus, we are able to analyze how firms in different financial and legal systems perceive obstacles to growth, and whether in fact there is a relation between these perceptions and firm growth. Our paper differs from earlier work in that we also examine the effect of corruption on firm growth.[4]

Second, the literature has less to say about how the state of a country's financial and legal institutions affects firms of different sizes.[5] We know that in developing economies, there are advantages in belonging to a business group (see Khanna and Palepu's (2000) study of India and Rajan and Zingales' (1998b) review of evidence on Asian capitalism). This finding contrasts with the prevailing view in the United States that the ability to escape market monitoring by recourse to internal capital markets makes large diversified firms inefficient (Scharfstein and Stein (2000), Rajan, Servaes, and Zingales (2000)).[6] However, studies of business groups in the emerging economies are limited to firms that choose to belong to such groups, and the extent to which these results generalize to other firms and to other institutional settings is unclear. Cross-country studies of financing choices have found different financing patterns for small and large firms, in the use of long-term financing and trade credit (Demirgüç-Kunt and Maksimovic (1999, 2001)). However, these studies rely on commercial databases of listed firms, so that even the "small" firms are relatively large.

The paper is organized as follows. Section I presents the data and summary statistics. Section II presents our main results. Section III presents conclusions and policy implications.

---

and Maksimovic (1999) show that the origin and efficiency of a legal system facilitates firms' access to external finance, particularly long-term finance. At the country level, King and Levine (1993), Levine and Zervos (1998), and Beck, Levine, and Loayza (2000) show that financial development promotes growth and that differences in legal origins explain differences in financial development.

[2] Rajan and Zingales (1998a) use the external financing by U.S. firms as a benchmark, under the assumption that firms in the same industries in other countries depend on similar amounts of external financing. Demirgüç-Kunt and Maksimovic (1998) rely on a financial planning model to identify firms that have access to long-term external financing.

[3] Exceptions are Schiffer and Weder (2001) who investigate different obstacles using WBES data and Clarke, Cull, and Peria (2003) who assess the impact of foreign bank entry on these obstacles.

[4] Empirical evidence based on cross-country comparisons does suggest that corruption has a major adverse effect on private investment and economic growth (Mauro (1996)). We look at whether corruption also has a significant impact in constraining firm growth.

[5] Except to study determinants of firm size by looking at the largest firms around the world (see Beck, Demirgüç-Kunt, and Maksimovic (2001b)).

[6] For evidence that large diversified firms in the U.S. economy do allocate resources efficiently, see Maksimovic and Phillips (2002).

I. Data and Summary Statistics

Our data set consists of firm survey responses from over 4,000 firms in 54 countries.[7] The main purpose of the survey is to identify obstacles to firm performance and growth around the world. Thus, the survey includes many questions on the nature of financing and legal obstacles to growth, as well as questions on corruption issues. General information on firms is more limited, but the survey includes data on numbers of employees, sales, industry, growth, and number of competitors. The survey also gives information on ownership, whether the firm is an exporter, and if it has been receiving subsidies from national or local authorities.

In addition to the detail on the obstacles, one of the greatest values of this survey is its wide coverage of SMEs. The survey covers three groups of firms. It defines small firms as those with 5–50 employees. Medium-sized firms are those that employ 51–500 employees, and large firms are those that employ more than 500 employees. Forty percent of our observations are from small firms, another 40% are from medium firms, and the remaining 20% are from large firms. Table AI in the Appendix reports the number of firms for each country in the sample. For each of the countries, we also use data on GDP per capita, GDP in U.S. dollars, growth rate of GDP, and inflation. We also use information on financial system development, legal development, and corruption. Country-level variables are 1995–1999 averages. To compile these averages, we follow Beck, Demirgüç-Kunt, and Levine (2000).

In Table I we summarize relevant facts about the level of economic development, firm growth, and firm-level obstacles in the sample countries. We provide details on our sources in Table AII in the Appendix. The countries in the sample show considerable variation in per-capita income. They range from Haiti, with an average GDP per capita of $369, to the United States and Germany, with per-capita incomes of around $30,000. We also provide the average annual growth rate of per-capita GDP as a control variable. If investment opportunities in an economy are correlated, there should be a relation between the growth rate of individual firms and the growth rate of the economy. The average inflation rate also provides an important control, since it is an indicator of whether local currency provides a stable measure of value in contracts between firms. The countries also vary significantly in their rates of inflation, from a low of 0% in Sweden and Argentina to 86% in Bulgaria.

In Table I, the column titled Firm Growth reports firm growth rates, which are sales growth rates for individual firms averaged over all sampled firms in each country. Firm growth rates also show a wide dispersion, from negative rates of −19% for Armenia and Azerbaijan to a positive 34% for Poland.

Table I also shows firm-level financing, legal, and corruption obstacles reported by firms averaged over all firms in each country. The World Business Environment Survey (WBES) asked enterprise managers to rate the extent to

---

[7] The WBES covers 80 economies. However, the sample is reduced because most firm-level or country-level variables are missing for 26 countries.

Table I
Economic Indicators and Obstacles to Firm Growth

GDP per capita is real GDP per capita in U.S. dollars. Inflation is the log difference of the consumer price index. Growth is the growth rate of GDP in current U.S. dollars. All country variables are 1995–1999 averages. Firm Growth is the percentage change in firm sales over the past 3 years (1996–1999). Financing, Legal, and Corruption are summary obstacles as indicated in the firm questionnaire. They take values between 1 and 4, with higher values indicating greater obstacles. We average firm variables over all firms in each country. Detailed variable definitions and sources are given in Table AII in the Appendix.

	GDP per Capita	Inflation	Growth	Firm Growth	Financing Obstacle	Legal Obstacle	Corruption Obstacle
Albania	806.78	0.15	0.03	0.25	3.04	2.76	3.40
Argentina	8000.15	0.00	0.02	0.10	3.03	2.27	2.59
Armenia	844.11	0.10	0.04	−0.19	2.48	1.51	1.99
Azerbaijan	407.75	0.03	0.05	−0.19	3.17	2.60	3.02
Belarus	2234.91	0.71	0.07	0.09	3.31	1.55	1.88
Belize	2737.70	0.01	0.00	0.13	3.14	1.54	2.00
Bolivia	938.55	0.06	0.01	0.07	3.00	2.81	3.53
Brazil	4491.67	0.07	0.00	0.04	2.67	2.58	2.49
Bulgaria	1414.61	0.86	−0.02	0.15	3.18	2.27	2.64
Canada	20548.97	0.01	0.02	0.17	2.11	1.46	1.40
Chile	5002.70	0.05	0.03	0.08	2.39	1.97	1.85
China	676.76	0.02	0.07	0.05	3.35	1.51	1.96
Colombia	2381.19	0.16	−0.01	0.04	2.71	2.41	2.87
Costa Rica	3692.47	0.12	0.04	0.25	2.63	2.24	2.59
Croatia	3845.27	0.05	0.05	0.09	3.32	2.69	2.56
Czech Republic	5158.04	0.07	0.00	0.10	3.17	2.18	2.07
Dominican Republic	1712.31	0.06	0.06	0.24	2.59	2.41	2.90
Ecuador	1538.48	0.30	−0.02	−0.03	3.34	3.09	3.52
El Salvador	1705.79	0.04	0.01	−0.01	2.98	2.37	2.80
Estonia	3663.49	0.10	0.05	0.61	2.44	1.70	1.92
France	27719.92	0.01	0.02	0.21	2.75	1.81	1.63
Germany	30794.03	0.01	0.01	0.10	2.60	2.14	1.86
Guatemala	1503.25	0.08	0.01	0.14	3.06	2.58	2.68
Haiti	368.73	0.14	0.00	−0.05	3.39	2.27	3.02
Honduras	707.52	0.16	0.00	0.13	2.93	2.40	2.93
Hungary	4705.65	0.15	0.04	0.29	2.61	1.30	1.94
Indonesia	1045.04	0.20	−0.02	−0.06	2.82	2.26	2.67
Italy	19645.96	0.02	0.01	0.16	1.98	2.27	1.90
Kazakhstan	1315.10	0.16	0.02	0.08	3.28	2.13	2.74
Kyrgizstan	800.34	0.22	0.04	−0.02	3.48	2.20	3.23
Lithuania	1907.93	0.09	0.03	0.08	3.00	2.24	2.44
Malaysia	4536.23	0.03	0.01	0.01	2.67	1.66	2.09
Mexico	3394.75	0.20	0.04	0.26	3.51	2.94	3.57
Moldova	667.74	0.18	−0.03	−0.14	3.39	2.47	2.90
Nicaragua	434.69	0.11	0.03	0.19	3.22	2.46	2.88
Pakistan	505.59	0.08	0.00	0.08	3.31	2.55	3.53
Panama	3123.95	0.01	0.02	0.07	2.13	2.36	2.74
Peru	2334.94	0.07	0.01	−0.01	3.10	2.55	2.85
Philippines	1125.81	0.08	0.01	0.07	2.69	2.24	3.13

(*continued*)

Table I—*Continued*

	GDP per Capita	Inflation	Growth	Firm Growth	Financing Obstacle	Legal Obstacle	Corruption Obstacle
Poland	3216.04	0.13	0.05	0.34	2.48	2.32	2.28
Portugal	11582.33	0.03	0.03	0.12	1.82	1.86	1.77
Romania	1372.02	0.53	−0.02	0.07	3.28	2.60	2.88
Russia	2223.57	0.35	0.00	0.28	3.21	2.18	2.62
Singapore	24948.09	0.01	0.02	0.11	1.96	1.33	1.29
Slovakia	3805.41	0.07	0.04	0.11	3.38	2.08	2.44
Slovenia	10232.73	0.08	0.04	0.29	2.30	2.29	1.64
Spain	15858.03	0.02	0.03	0.26	2.22	1.97	2.08
Sweden	28258.28	0.00	0.02	0.23	1.85	1.49	1.19
Trinidad & Tobago	4526.28	0.04	0.04	0.20	2.93	1.44	1.66
Turkey	2993.89	0.58	0.01	0.10	3.11	2.28	2.86
Ukraine	866.52	0.26	−0.03	0.03	3.46	2.18	2.54
United Kingdom	20186.56	0.03	0.02	0.31	2.21	1.51	1.24
United States	29250.32	0.02	0.03	0.14	2.39	1.79	1.86
Uruguay	6113.60	0.15	0.02	0.03	2.70	1.87	1.84
Venezuela	3482.51	0.40	−0.02	−0.02	2.57	2.65	2.98

which financing, legal, and corruption problems presented obstacles to the operation and growth of their businesses. A rating of 1 denotes no obstacle; 2, a minor obstacle; 3, a moderate obstacle; and 4, a major obstacle. These ratings provide a summary measure of the extent to which financing, legal systems, and corruption create obstacles to growth, and we refer to them below as "summary" obstacles.

Table I shows that in the large majority of countries, firms report that the financing obstacle is the most important summary obstacle to growth.[8] Also, in general, the reported obstacles tend to be lower in developed countries such as the United Kingdom and the United States compared to those in developing countries.

Table II contains the sample statistics of our variables. In addition to the financial, legal, and corruption summary obstacles described above, and in order to understand the nature of these obstacles to growth better, the survey asked firms more specific questions. We also investigate responses to these questions.

Table II reports unaudited self-reports by firms. In self-reporting it is possible that unsuccessful firms may blame institutional obstacles for their poor performance. This possibility must be balanced by the likelihood that alternative data sources used in cross-country firm-level research, such as accounting data, are also subject to distortion. With accounting data, the auditing process provides a measure of quality control. However, the quality of the audit may vary systematically across countries and firm size.[9] Moreover, the incentives

---

[8] This is consistent with other studies that use the WBES (see Schiffer and Weder (2001)).

[9] Financial data used in previous studies are also subject to potential biases because country institutional factors can affect the properties of accounting data (see Ball, Kothari, and Robin (2000) and Hung (2001)).

Table II
Summary Statistics and Correlations

Panel A presents summary statistics and Panel B presents correlations. N refers to firm-level observations for 54 countries. Firm Growth is given by the percentage change in firm sales. Government and Foreign are dummy variables that take the value of 1 if the firm has government or foreign ownership and 0 if not. Exporter is a dummy variable that indicates if the firm is an exporting firm. Subsidized is also a dummy variable that indicates if the firm receives subsidies from the national or local authorities. Manufacturing and Services are industry dummies. No. of Competitors is the logarithm of the number of competitors the firm has. Size is a variable that takes the value of 1 if firm is small, 2 if it is medium-sized, and 3 if it is large. Small firms employ 5–50 employees, medium-size firms employ 51–500 employees, and large firms employ more than 500 employees. Inflation is the log difference of the consumer price index. GDP per capita is real GDP per capita in U.S. dollars, GDP in millions of U.S. dollars. Growth is the growth rate of GDP. All country variables are 1995–1999 averages. The different financing, legal, and corruption issues are survey responses as specified in the firm questionnaire. Higher numbers indicate greater obstacles, with the exception of "Firms must make 'additional payments' to get things done" and "Firms know the amount of 'additional payments' in advance." Detailed variable definitions and sources are given in Table AII in the Appendix.

Panel A: Summary Statistics

	N	Mean	SD	Min	Max
Firm Growth	4,255	0.13	0.59	−1	2
Government	4,255	0.13	0.34	0	1
Foreign	4,255	0.17	0.37	0	1
Exporter	4,255	0.35	0.48	0	1
Subsidized	4,255	0.10	0.35	0	1
Manufacturing	4,255	0.37	0.48	0	1
Services	4,255	0.47	0.50	0	1
No. of competitors	4,255	0.80	0.33	0	1.39
Size	4,254	1.78	0.72	1	3
Inflation	54	17.41	19.30	0.11	86.05
GDP per capita	54	560	772	369	30,794
GDP (million $)	54	24.72	1.96	20.30	29.74
Growth	54	0.02	0.03	−0.03	0.07
Financing	4,213	2.87	1.13	1	4
Legal	3,976	2.17	1.05	1	4
Corruption	4,000	2.43	1.17	1	4

(continued)

Table II—*Continued*

Panel A: Summary Statistics

	N	Mean	SD	Min	Max
Collateral requirements	3,954	2.54	1.17	1	4
Bank paperwork/bureaucracy	4,078	2.54	1.10	1	4
High interest rates	4,112	3.24	1.03	1	4
Need special connections with banks	3,958	2.19	1.09	1	4
Banks lack money to lend	3,861	2.10	1.22	1	4
Access to foreign banks	3,489	1.99	1.17	1	4
Access to nonbank equity	3,470	2.06	1.16	1	4
Access to export finance	3,017	1.99	1.19	1	4
Access to financing for leasing equipment	3,532	2.02	1.14	1	4
Inadequate credit/financial information on customers	3,712	2.21	1.13	1	4
Access to long-term loans	3,937	2.63	1.27	1	4
Availability of information on laws and regulations	4,211	2.92	1.42	1	6
Interpretation of laws and regulations are consistent	4,225	3.42	1.37	1	6
Overall quality and efficiency of courts	3,521	3.73	1.31	1	6
Courts are fair and impartial	3,933	3.75	1.39	1	6
Courts are quick	3,991	4.77	1.22	1	6
Courts are affordable	3,910	3.92	1.45	1	6
Courts are consistent	3,918	4.04	1.36	1	6
Court decisions are enforced	3,905	3.67	1.48	1	6
Confidence in legal system to enforce contract & prop. rights	4,206	3.35	1.38	1	6
Confidence in legal system – 3 years ago	3,935	3.46	1.40	1	6
Corruption of bank officials	3,574	1.72	1.05	1	4
Firms have to make "additional payments" to get things done	3,924	4.36	1.62	1	6
Firms know the amount of "additional payments" in advance	2,310	3.38	1.59	1	6
If "additional payments" are made, services are delivered	2,269	3.01	1.53	1	6
It is possible to find honest agents to replace corrupt ones	3,602	3.58	1.75	1	6
Proportion of revenues paid as bribes	2,831	2.35	1.47	1	7
Prop. of contract value that must be paid for govt. contracts	1,733	2.51	1.73	1	6
Mgmt's time (%) spent with officials to understand laws & regs	3,990	2.24	1.39	1	6

Panel B: Correlation Matrix of Variables

	Firm Growth	Govt	Foreign	Exporter	Subsidized	Manuf.	Services	No. of Comp.	Size	Inflation	GDP/ Capita	GDP($)	Growth	Financing	Legal
Govt.	-0.0245*														
Foreign	0.0390***	-0.0258*													
Exporter	0.0844***	0.1001***	0.2368***												
Subsidized	-0.0049	0.1472***	0.0006	0.081***											
Manuf.	-0.0180	0.0855***	0.1165***	0.3448***	0.0219										
Services	0.0210	-0.0846***	-0.0312*	-0.2465***	-0.0759***	-0.7302***									
No. of Co.	0.0148	-0.0057	-0.1788***	-0.1211***	-0.0285*	-0.117***	0.0334**								
Size	0.0224	-0.0245*	0.0390***	0.0844***	0.0049	-0.0180	0.0210	0.0148							
Inflation	0.0010	0.1335***	-0.1231***	-0.1024***	0.0049	0.0280*	-0.1262***	0.2640***	0.0010						
GDP/Cap	0.0489***	-0.0808***	0.1262***	0.1223***	0.0675***	-0.0460***	0.0739***	-0.2228***	0.0489***	-0.3655***					
GDP($)	0.0551***	-0.0960***	0.0799***	0.0058	0.0625***	-0.0391***	0.0559***	-0.1178***	0.0551***	-0.0789***	0.5666***				
Growth	0.0751***	0.0673***	0.0237	0.1275***	0.0404***	0.0000	0.021	0.0281*	0.0751***	-0.3608***	0.1308***	-0.1007***			
Fin. Obst.	-0.0821***	0.0723***	-0.1732***	-0.052**	0.0231	0.0426***	-0.1317***	0.1039***	-0.0821***	0.1784***	-0.2518***	-0.1114***	-0.1226***		
Leg Obst.	-0.0676***	-0.0084	-0.0158	-0.0095	-0.0303**	0.0198	-0.0378**	0.0167	-0.0676***	0.0531***	-0.1737***	-0.0682***	-0.1411***	0.1901***	
Corruption	-0.0695***	-0.0713***	-0.0733***	-0.1025***	-0.0759***	-0.001	-0.0338**	0.0479***	-0.0695***	0.1314***	-0.3322***	-0.1635***	-0.1815***	0.2809***	0.5754***

*, **, *** indicate significance levels of 10%, 5%, and 1%, respectively.

to distort data are likely to be much higher in financial statements than in survey responses, since financial statements affect operational and financing decisions.

Although the possibility of data bias due to unaudited self-reporting can never be totally eliminated, we believe that it is unlikely to be a significant source of bias in this study. The stated purpose of the WBES survey is to evaluate the business environment, not firm performance. Firms were asked few specific questions about their performance and such questions were asked only at the end of the interview. This sequencing reduces the respondents' need to justify their own performance when answering the earlier questions about the business environment. Respondents were asked about a large range of business conditions and government policies. Thus, to the extent that firms need to shift blame for poor performance to outside forces, an unsuccessful firm that is not financially constrained is likely to find other, more immediate excuses for its internal failures.

To assess the importance of financing obstacles, the firms were asked to rate, again on a scale of 1–4, how problematic specific financing issues are for the operation and growth of their business. These are (1) collateral requirements of banks and financial institutions; (2) bank paperwork and bureaucracy; (3) high interest rates; (4) need for special connections with banks and financial institutions; (5) banks lacking money to lend; (6) access to foreign banks; (7) access to nonbank equity; (8) access to export finance; (9) access to financing for leasing equipment; (10) inadequate credit and financial information on customers; and (11) access to long-term loans.

Among the specific financial obstacles to growth, high interest rates stand out with a value of 3.24, which should be a constraint for all firms in all countries. Access to long-term loans, and bank collateral and paperwork requirements, also appear to be among the greater of the reported obstacles to growth.

The survey also included specific questions on the legal system. Businesses were asked if (1) information on laws and regulations was available; (2) if the interpretation of laws and regulations was consistent; and (3) if they were confident that the legal system upheld their contract and property rights in business disputes 3 years ago, and continues to do so now. These answers were rated between 1, fully agree, to 6, fully disagree.

The survey also asked businesses to evaluate whether their country's courts are (1) fair and impartial, (2) quick, (3) affordable, (4) consistent, and (5) enforced decisions. These are rated thus: 1 equals always, 2 equals usually, 3 equals frequently, 4 equals sometimes, 5 equals seldom, and 6 equals never. Finally, businesses were asked to rate the overall quality and efficiency of courts between 1, very good, to 6, very bad.

Looking at these legal obstacles to growth, speed of courts, which has a value of 4.77, seems to be one of the important perceived obstacles. Other important obstacles include the consistency and affordability of the courts. Below we examine whether in fact growth is related to the firms' perceptions of these obstacles.

The final set of questions we investigate relate to the level of corruption that firms must deal with. The questions are (1) whether corruption of bank

Financial and Legal Constraints to Growth 147

officials creates a problem (rated from 1 to 4 as described above); (2) if firms have to make "additional payments" to get things done; (3) if firms generally know what the amount of these "additional payments" are; (4) if services are delivered when the "additional payments" are made as required; and (5) if it is possible to find honest agents to circumvent corrupt ones without recourse to unofficial payments. Other questions include (6) the proportion of revenues paid as bribes (increasing in payment ranked from 1 to 7);[10] (7) the proportion of contract value that must be paid as "unofficial payments" to secure government contracts (increasing in payment ranked from 1 to 6);[11] and (8) the proportion of management's time in dealing with government officials about the application and interpretation of laws and regulations (increasing in time from 1 to 6). Unless specified, answers are ranked from 1 (always) to 6 (never).

Of the specific corruption obstacles reported, the need to make additional payments is the highest at 4.36. The second highest rated obstacle is firms' inability to have recourse to honest officials at 3.58.

One potential problem with using survey data is that enterprise managers may identify several operational problems, only some of which are constraining, while others can be circumvented. For this reason, we examine the extent to which the reported obstacles affect the growth rates of firms. To do this, we obtain benchmark growth rates by controlling for firm and country characteristics. We then assess whether the level of a reported obstacle affects growth relative to this benchmark. However, note that since many firms in our sample are not publicly traded, we do not have firm-level measures of investment opportunities, such as Tobin's Q. We use indicators of firm ownership, industry, market structure, and size as firm-level controls. Since the sample includes firms from manufacturing, services, construction, agriculture, and other industries, we control for industry effects by including industry dummy variables.

We also include dummy variables that identify firms as government-owned or foreign-controlled. Government-owned firms might grow at different rates because their objectives or their exposure to obstacles might differ from those of other firms. For example, they can have advantages in dealing with the regulatory system, and they could be less subject to crime or corruption by financial intermediaries and more exposed to political influences. The growth rate of foreign institutions can also be different because foreign entities might find it more difficult to deal with local judiciary or corruption. However, foreign institutions might be less affected by financing obstacles, since they could have easier access to the international financial system.

The growth rate of firms can also depend on the market structure in which they operate. Therefore, we also include dummy variables to capture whether the firm is an exporting firm, whether it receives subsidies from local and national governments, and the number of competitors it faces in its market.

[10] On the scale 1 equals 0%, 2 equals less than 1%, 3 equals 1–1.9%, 4 equals 2–9.99%, 5 equals 10–12%, 6 equals 13–25%, and 7 equals more than 25%.

[11] On the scale, 1 equals 0%, 2 equals less than 5%, 3 equals 6–10%, 4 equals 11–15%, 5 equals 16–20%, 6 equals more than 20%.

Firm size can be a very important factor in how firm growth is constrained by different factors. Small firms are likely to face tougher obstacles in obtaining finance, accessing legal systems, or dealing with corruption (see, e.g., Schiffer and Weder (2001)). Here, size is a dummy variable that takes the value of 1 for small firms, 2 for medium firms, and 3 for large firms.

Panel B of Table II shows the correlation matrix for the variables in our study. Foreign firms and exporters have higher growth rates. Government-owned firms have significantly lower rates of growth. Also, firms in richer, larger, and faster-growing countries have significantly higher growth rates. As expected, higher financing, legal, and corruption obstacles correlate with lower firm growth rates.

Correlations also show that government-owned firms are subject to higher financing obstacles, but are subject to lower corruption. On the other hand, foreign-controlled firms and exporters face lower financing and corruption obstacles. Financing obstacles seem to be higher for manufacturing firms. Firms in service industries are less affected by all obstacles. To the extent that firms have a greater number of competitors, they seem to face greater financing obstacles and corruption.

All obstacles are significantly lower in richer, larger, and faster-growing countries, but are significantly higher in countries with higher inflation. Firms are also significantly larger in richer, larger, and faster-growing countries. Firm size itself is not correlated with firm growth. However, size is likely to have an indirect effect on firm growth because larger firms face significantly lower financing, legal, and corruption obstacles. All three obstacles are highly correlated with each other. Thus, firms that suffer from one are also likely to suffer from others.

We compute but do not report here the correlations of specific obstacles with summary financing, legal, and corruption obstacles, respectively. Overall, specific obstacles are highly correlated with the summary obstacles and with each other. The correlation between the summary corruption obstacle and the corruption of bank officials is significant and particularly high at 43%.

We next explore the relation between the financing, legal, and corruption obstacles and firm size, controlling for country-level institutional development. To capture institutional development, we use independently computed country-level measures of the size of the financial sector, development of the legal sector, and the level of corruption. Earlier work has shown that the level of financial development affects firm growth (see Demirgüç-Kunt and Maksimovic (1998)). As a measure of financial development, we use *Priv*, which is given by the ratio of domestic banking credit to the private sector divided by GDP. The index *Laworder* serves as our proxy for legal development and is an index of the efficiency of the legal system. It is rated between 1 and 6, with higher values indicating better legal development. Corruption is captured by *Corrupt*. This measure is an indicator of the existence of corruption, rated between 1 and 6, with higher values indicating less corruption.

In Table III, we regress the firm-level survey responses on size dummies and the country-level variables. The three size dummy variables are small, medium,

Financial and Legal Constraints to Growth 149

Table III
Firm-Level Obstacles and Institutional Development

The regression estimated is

$$Firm\ Level\ Obstacle = \alpha + \beta_1 Priv * Small + \beta_2 Priv * Medium + \beta_3 Priv * Large$$
$$+ \beta_4 Laworder * Small + \beta_5 Laworder * Medium + \beta_6 Laworder * Large$$
$$+ \beta_7 Corrupt * Small + \beta_8 Corrupt * Medium + \beta_9 Corrupt * Large$$
$$+ \beta_{10} Small + \beta_{11} Medium + \varepsilon.$$

Firm-Level Obstacles—Financing, Legal, or Corruption—are summary obstacles as indicated in the firm questionnaire. They take values of 1–4, where 1 indicates no obstacle and 4 indicates a major obstacle. *Priv* is domestic bank credit to the private sector divided by GDP. *Laworder* is a national indicator (values between 1 and 6) that takes higher values for legal systems that are more developed. *Corrupt* is a corruption indicator (values between 1 and 6) at the national level that takes higher values in countries where corruption is lower. *Small, Medium,* and *Large* are dummy variables that take the value 1 if a firm is small (or medium or large) and 0 otherwise. Small firms employ 5–50 employees, medium-size firms employ 51–500 employees, and large firms employ more than 500 employees. These size dummies are interacted with *Priv, Laworder,* and *Corrupt.* We estimate all regressions using country random effects. At the foot of the table we report whether the coefficients are significantly different for large and small firms. We obtain firm-level variables from the WBES. Detailed variable definitions and sources are given in Table AII in the Appendix.

	Financing Obstacle		Legal Obstacle		Corruption Obstacle	
Priv	−0.531***		−0.316*		−0.461**	
	(0.190)		(0.194)		(0.235)	
Priv * Small		−0.167		−0.262		−0.624**
		(0.208)		(0.206)		(0.249)
Priv * Medium		−0.746***		−0.369*		−0.451*
		(0.205)		(0.203)		(0.247)
Priv * Large		−0.864***		−0.340		−0.191
		(0.242)		(0.233)		(0.276)
Laworder	−0.032		−0.137***		−0.245***	
	(0.053)		(0.054)		(0.065)	
Laworder * Small		−0.048		−0.146***		−0.225***
		(0.059)		(0.059)		(0.071)
Laworder * Medium		−0.036		−0.127**		−0.257***
		(0.056)		(0.056)		(0.068)
Laworder * Large		0.008		−0.135**		−0.250***
		(0.063)		(0.062)		(0.074)
Corrupt	−0.160***		−0.059		−0.129**	
	(0.052)		(0.053)		(0.065)	
Corrupt * Small		−0.135***		−0.053		−0.082
		(0.057)		(0.057)		(0.069)
Corrupt * Medium		−0.153***		−0.045		−0.143**
		(0.056)		(0.055)		(0.067)
Corrupt * Large		−0.221***		−0.097*		−0.172**
		(0.063)		(0.061)		(0.074)
Small	0.294***	−0.004	−0.036	−0.163	0.240***	−0.034
	(0.052)	(0.202)	(0.048)	(0.187)	(0.051)	(0.198)
Medium	0.229***	0.134	0.015	−0.184	0.147***	0.172
	(0.050)	(0.187)	(0.046)	(0.171)	(0.049)	(0.183)

(continued)

Table III—*Continued*

	Financing Obstacle		Legal Obstacle		Corruption Obstacle	
R^2-within	0.01	0.02	0.00	0.00	0.01	0.01
R^2-between	0.44	0.45	0.37	0.37	0.55	0.54
R^2-overall	0.08	0.08	0.06	0.06	0.13	0.13
Priv(large − small)		−0.700***		−0.080		0.438**
Laworder(large − small)		0.055		0.014		−0.024
Corrupt(large − small)		−0.085*		−0.046		−0.091*
No of firms	3,549	3,549	3,400	3,400	3,406	3,406
No of countries	49	49	49	49	49	49

*, **, *** indicate significance levels of 10%, 5%, and 1%, respectively.

and large. These variables take the value of 1 if the firm is small or medium or large, respectively, and 0 otherwise. We also report specifications in which we interact country-level variables with firm size.

Table III indicates that on average, the firms' perception of the financing and corruption obstacles they face relates to firm size, with smaller firms reporting significantly higher obstacles than large firms. In contrast, smaller firms report lower legal obstacles than do larger firms, but these differences are not significant.

Table III also shows that in countries with more developed financial systems and with less country-level corruption, firms report lower financing obstacles. These effects are more significant and the coefficients are greater in absolute value for the largest firms, particularly for financial development. The indicator of the quality of the legal system does not appear to explain the magnitude of the firm-level financing obstacles. The firm-level legal obstacles are significant and negatively related to the quality of the country's legal system. The corruption obstacles reported by firms in our sample are higher in countries with less-developed financial and legal systems and in countries that are rated as more corrupt. Lack of corruption at the country level is associated with a significant reduction in the level of corruption obstacles reported by larger firms. In contrast, financial development is significantly correlated with lower corruption obstacles reported by the smaller firms.

Table III shows that even after we control for the quality of a country's institutions, firm size is an important determinant of the level of financial and corruption obstacles. However, to determine if firm size really has an impact, we need to investigate both the level of the reported obstacles and how firm growth is affected by these obstacles.

II. Firm Growth and Reported Obstacles

The regressions reported in Table III indicate that firm size and a country's institutional development predict the obstacles that firms report. However, it

Financial and Legal Constraints to Growth 151

does not follow that they also predict the effect of these obstacles on firm growth. A firm's report that an existing economy-wide institutional obstacle constrains its growth might be accurate, but may not take into account the possibility that the obstacle may also benefit it by affecting its rivals. Obstacles might affect large and small firms differently. Table II also indicates that there is a high degree of correlation between variables of interest and other firm- and country-level controls that affect growth. Thus, we clarify the relation between firm-level characteristics and firm growth using multivariate regression.

We regress firms' growth rates on the obstacles they report. We initially introduce financial, legal, and corruption summary obstacles one at a time, and finally all together. In subsequent regressions, we substitute specific obstacles for these summary obstacles and introduce interaction terms. All regressions are estimated using firm-level data across 54 countries and country random effects. The regressions are estimated with controls for country and firm-specific variables discussed in Section II. The country controls are GDP per capita, GDP, country growth, and the inflation rate. Firm-specific controls are the logarithm of the number of competitors the firm has, and indicator variables for ownership of the firm (separate indicators for government- and foreign-owned firms), industry classification (separate indicators for manufacturing and service industries), and indicators for whether the firm is an exporter and whether it receives government subsidies. Specifically, the regression equations we estimate take the form

$$Firm\ Growth = \alpha + \beta_1\ Government + \beta_2\ Foreign + \beta_3\ Exporter$$
$$+ \beta_4\ Subsidized + \beta_5\ No.\ of\ Competitors$$
$$+ \beta_6\ Manufacturing + \beta_7\ Services + \beta_8\ Inflation$$
$$+ \beta_9\ GDP\ per\ capita + \beta_{10}\ GDP$$
$$+ \beta_{11}\ Growth + \beta_{12}\ Obstacle + \varepsilon. \tag{1}$$

To test the hypothesis that an obstacle is related to firm growth, we test whether its coefficient β_{12} is significantly different from zero. We also obtain an estimate of the economic impact of the obstacle at the sample mean by multiplying its coefficient β_{12} by the sample mean of the obstacle. This impact variable measures the total effect of the obstacle on growth, taking into account both the level of the mean reported obstacle and the estimated relation between the reported obstacle and observed growth.

Table IV shows how firm growth is related to the financing, legal, and corruption obstacles reported by firms. When entered individually, all reported obstacles have a negative and significant effect on firm growth, as expected. The impact of the obstacles on firm growth evaluated at the sample mean is negative, and in all cases, substantial.

Column 4 shows that financing and legal obstacles are both significant and negative, but corruption loses its significance in the presence of these two variables. This suggests that the impact of corruption on firm growth is captured

Table IV
Firm Growth: The Impact of Obstacles

The regression estimated is

$$Firm\ Growth = \alpha + \beta_1\ Government + \beta_2\ Foreign + \beta_3\ Exporter + \beta_4\ Subsidized$$
$$+ \beta_5\ No.\ of\ Competitors + \beta_6\ Manufacturing + \beta_7\ Services + \beta_8\ Inflation$$
$$+ \beta_9\ GDP\ per\ capita + \beta_{10}\ GDP + \beta_{11}\ Growth + \beta_{12}\ Financing$$
$$+ \beta_{13}\ Legal + \beta_{14}\ Corruption + \varepsilon.$$

Firm Growth is the percentage change in firm sales over the past 3 years. *Government* and *Foreign* are dummy variables that take the value of 1 if the firm has government or foreign ownership and 0 if not. *Exporter* is a dummy variable that indicates if the firm is an exporting firm. *Subsidized* is also a dummy variable that indicates if the firm receives subsidies from the national or local authorities. *No. of Competitors* is the logarithm of the firm's number of competitors. *Manufacturing* and *Services* are industry dummies. *Inflation* is the log difference of the consumer price index. *GDP per capita* is real GDP per capita in U.S. dollars. *GDP* is the logarithm of GDP in millions of U.S. dollars. *Growth* is the growth rate of GDP. Financing, Legal, and Corruption are summary obstacles as indicated in the firm questionnaire. They take values between 1 and 4, where 1 indicates no obstacle and 4 indicates major obstacle. We estimate all regressions using country random effects. We obtain firm-level variables from the WBES. Detailed variable definitions and sources are given in Table AII in the Appendix.

	(1)	(2)	(3)	(4)
Government	−0.070***	−0.083***	−0.074***	−0.070**
	(0.028)	(0.029)	(0.029)	(0.030)
Foreign	0.034	0.045*	0.045*	0.037
	(0.025)	(0.025)	(0.026)	(0.026)
Exporter	0.103***	0.104***	0.107***	0.105***
	(0.021)	(0.022)	(0.022)	(0.022)
Subsidized	0.001	0.002	0.007	0.007
	(0.026)	(0.027)	(0.027)	(0.027)
No. of competitors	−0.011	−0.016	−0.001	−0.005
	(0.031)	(0.032)	(0.032)	(0.033)
Manufacturing	−0.032	−0.023	−0.032	−0.035
	(0.028)	(0.029)	(0.030)	(0.030)
Services	0.027	0.052*	0.037	0.036
	(0.027)	(0.028)	(0.028)	(0.028)
Inflation	0.002**	0.002*	0.002	0.002
	(0.001)	(0.001)	(0.001)	(0.001)
GDP per capita	0.002	0.001	0.001	0.000
	(0.003)	(0.003)	(0.003)	(0.003)
GDP ($)	0.007	0.012	0.010	0.013
	(0.011)	(0.011)	(0.011)	(0.012)
Growth	0.021***	0.021***	0.020***	0.019***
	(0.007)	(0.007)	(0.008)	(0.008)
Obstacles				
Financing	−0.031***			−0.023***
	(0.009)			(0.009)
Legal		−0.029***		−0.023**
		(0.009)		(0.011)

(continued)

Financial and Legal Constraints to Growth 153

Table IV—*Continued*

	(1)	(2)	(3)	(4)
Corruption			−0.021***	−0.007
			(0.009)	(0.011)
Impact on growth evaluated at sample mean	−0.087***	−0.063***	−0.052***	−0.134***
R^2-with.	0.01	0.01	0.01	0.02
R^2-between	0.28	0.27	0.25	0.26
R^2-overall	0.02	0.03	0.02	0.03
No. of firms	4,204	3,968	3,991	3,800
No. of countries	54	54	54	54

*, **, *** indicate significance levels of 10, 5, and 1%, respectively.

by the financial and legal obstacles. This is reasonable because corruption in the legal and financial systems can be expected to degrade firms' performance.

When we look at the control variables, we see that the growth rates of government-owned firms are lower, and the growth rates of exporters are higher. Foreign firms also appear to grow faster, although this result is only significant at 10% in two specifications. We do not observe significant differences in the growth rates of firms in different industries. The coefficient of inflation is significant and positive in two of the four specifications. A significant inflation effect most likely reflects the fact that firm sales growth is given in nominal terms. The GDP growth rate and firm growth are significant and positively correlated, indicating that firms grow faster in an economy with greater growth opportunities. Most of the explanatory power of the model comes from between-country differences as indicated by the between-R^2 values of 25–28%.

In Table V, we look at how specific financial, legal, and corruption obstacles affect firm growth. We enter each of the specific obstacles in turn into equation (1). Although our regressions include the control variables, for the sake of brevity we do not report these coefficients.

Panel A shows that collateral requirements, bank paperwork and bureaucracy, high interest rates, the need to have special connections with banks, lack of money in the banking system, and access to financing for leasing equipment all have significant constraining effects on firm growth.

We note that although firms in the WBES survey rate the lack of access to long-term loans as an important obstacle, it is not significantly correlated with firm growth, suggesting that firms might be able to substitute short-term financing that is rolled over at regular intervals for long-term loans. Also, because we expect interest rates to constrain all firms, it is reassuring to see that those firms that perceive high interest rates as an important obstacle actually grow more slowly. We also note that some of these factors are likely to be correlated with lack of development of the financial system. Other potential constraints, such as access to foreign banks, access to nonbank equity, access

Table V
Firm Growth: The Impact of Obstacles

The regression estimated is

$$\text{Firm Growth} = \alpha + \beta_1 \text{Government} + \beta_2 \text{Foreign} + \beta_3 \text{Exporter} + \beta_4 \text{Subsidized} + \beta_5 \text{No. of Competitors} + \beta_6 \text{Manufacturing} + \beta_7 \text{Services} + \beta_8 \text{Inflation}$$
$$+ \beta_9 \text{GDP per capita} + \beta_{10} \text{GDP} + \beta_{11} \text{Growth} + \beta_{12} \text{Obstacle} + \varepsilon.$$

Firm Growth is the percentage change in firm sales over the past 3 years. *Government* and *Foreign* are dummy variables that take the value of 1 if the firm has government or foreign ownership and 0 if not. *Exporter* is a dummy variable that indicates if the firm is an exporting firm. *Subsidized* is also a dummy variable that indicates if the firm receives subsidies from the national or local authorities. *No. of Competitors* is the logarithm of the firm's number of competitors. *Manufacturing* and *Services* are industry dummies. *Inflation* is the log difference of the consumer price index. *GPP per capita* is real GDP per capita in U.S. dollars. *GDP* is the logarithm of GDP per capita in U.S. dollars. *Growth* is the growth rate of GDP. Obstacles are financing obstacles in Panel A, legal obstacles in Panel B, and corruption obstacles in Panel C. Financing obstacles range between 1 and 4. Legal obstacles range between 1 and 6 (1 and 4 in the case of the summary obstacle). The range of the corruption indicators is indicated in parentheses after the variable name, with the first number indicating the least constraint. Unless otherwise noted, obstacles take higher values for higher obstacles and they are entered one at a time. We estimate all regressions using country random effects. We obtain firm-level variables from the WBES. Detailed variable definitions and sources are given in Table AII in the Appendix.

Panel A: Financing Obstacles

	Financing Obstacle	Collateral Requirements	Bank Paperwork/ Bureaucracy	High Interest Rates	Need Special Connections with Banks	Banks Lack Money to Lend	Access to Foreign Banks	Access to Nonbank Equity	Access to Export Finance	Access to Financing for Leasing Equipment	Inadequate Credit/ Financial Information on Customers	Access to Long-Term Loans
	−0.031***	−0.027***	−0.028***	−0.032***	−0.023***	−0.029***	−0.009	0.007	−0.009	−0.022**	0.001	−0.010
	(0.009)	(0.008)	(0.008)	(0.010)	(0.009)	(0.008)	(0.008)	(0.009)	(0.009)	(0.009)	(0.008)	(0.008)
R^2-with.	0.01	0.01	0.01	0.01	0.01	0.01	0.01	0.01	0.01	0.01	0.01	0.01
R^2-between	0.28	0.25	0.26	0.26	0.26	0.26	0.24	0.25	0.29	0.26	0.27	0.25
R^2-all	0.02	0.02	0.02	0.02	0.02	0.02	0.02	0.02	0.02	0.02	0.02	0.02
Impact	−0.087***	−0.070***	−0.070***	−0.104***	−0.051***	−0.062***	−0.002	0.001	−0.018	−0.045***	0.001	−0.027
N (firms)	4,204	3,945	4,069	4,103	3,949	3,853	3,482	3,464	3,007	3,524	3,703	3,928
N (country)	54	54	54	54	54	54	54	54	54	54	54	54

Financial and Legal Constraints to Growth   155

Panel B: Legal Obstacles

	Legal Constraint	Availability of Info. on Laws and Regulations	Interpretation of Laws and Regulations Is Consistent	Overall Quality and Efficiency of Courts	Courts Are Fair and Impartial	Courts Are Quick	Courts Are Affordable	Courts Are Consistent	Court Decisions Are Enforced	Confidence in Legal System to Enforce Contract and Property Rights	Confidence in Legal System—3 Years Ago
	−0.029***	0.002	−0.003	−0.003	−0.004	0.005	−0.009	0.002	0.011	−0.005	0.004
	(0.009)	(0.006)	(0.007)	(0.008)	(0.007)	(0.008)	(0.007)	(0.007)	(0.007)	(0.007)	(0.007)
R^2-with.	0.01	0.01	0.01	0.01	0.01	0.01	0.01	0.01	0.01	0.01	0.01
R^2-between	0.27	0.27	0.26	0.27	0.27	0.28	0.30	0.27	0.31	0.28	0.32
R^2-all	0.03	0.02	0.02	0.02	0.02	0.02	0.02	0.02	0.03	0.02	0.02
Impact	−0.063***	0.006	−0.011	−0.014	−0.013	0.026	−0.035	0.007	0.039	−0.015	0.014
N (firms)	3,968	4,202	4,216	3,513	3,924	3,982	3,901	3,909	3,896	4,197	3,926
N(country)	54	54	54	54	54	54	54	54	54	54	54

Panel C: Corruption Obstacles

	Corruption Obstacle (1-4)	Corruption of Bank Officials (1-4)	Firms Have to Make "Additional Payments" to Get Things Done (6-1)	Firms Know in Advance the Amount of "Additional Payments" (6-1)	If "Additional Payments" Are Made, Services Are Delivered as Agreed (1-6)	If One Agent Asks for Payments It Is Possible to Find Others to Get the Correct Treatment without Payment (1-6)	Proportion of Revenues Paid as Bribes—Annual Figure for Each Firm (1-7)	Proportion of Contract Value That Must be Paid as "Payment" to Do Business with the Government (1-6)	Percentage of Senior Management's Time Spent with Government Officials to Understand Laws and Regulations (1-6)
	−0.021***	−0.017*	−0.003	−0.002	−0.012	−0.002	−0.037***	0.004	−0.012*
	(0.009)	(0.010)	(0.006)	(0.008)	(0.009)	(0.006)	(0.008)	(0.007)	(0.007)
R^2-with.	0.01	0.01	0.01	0.01	0.02	0.01	0.03	0.02	0.01
R^2-between	0.25	0.26	0.28	0.19	0.20	0.28	0.16	0.21	0.24
R^2-all	0.02	0.02	0.02	0.02	0.02	0.02	0.03	0.04	0.02
Impact	−0.052***	−0.030*	−0.014	−0.007	0.035	−0.006	0.087***	0.011	−0.027*
N (firms)	3,991	3,566	3,916	2,306	2,266	3,595	2,824	1,734	3,981
N(country)	54	54	54	53	53	53	53	52	54

*, **, *** indicate significance levels of 10%, 5%, and 1%, respectively.

to export finance, or inadequate information on customers are not significantly correlated with firm growth. Tests of the economic impact of the obstacles at the sample means indicate that the estimated coefficients, when significant, are sufficiently large to impact growth rates materially.

Panel B shows a significant and negative relation between the summary legal obstacle and firm growth. None of the specific legal obstacles has a significant coefficient. It appears that firms are able to work around these specific legal obstacles, although they find them annoying. Nevertheless, regressing the summary legal obstacle on the quality of the courts (i.e., their fairness, honesty, quickness, affordability, consistency, enforcement capacity, and confidence in the legal system), we find that these factors can explain 46% of the cross-country variation in the legal obstacle.[12] To further examine the importance of the specific legal obstacles taken together, we compute the predicted summary legal obstacle from this regression and introduce it as an independent variable in the firm growth equation in place of the actual summary legal obstacle. The coefficient of the predicted summary legal obstacle is positive yet insignificant, suggesting that the specific obstacles are at most weakly related to firm growth. This is also true if we run the regressions only for the sample of small firms. If we split the sample based on legal origin, the explanatory power of the specific descriptors is not significantly different in the common law countries compared to the civil law countries.[13]

Thus, although specific obstacles relate to the summary obstacle, they play a minor role in affecting growth. This finding suggests that the usual intuitive descriptors of how a good legal system operates predict survey responses well, but do not capture the effect of the legal system on firm growth.

Panel C of Table V shows that in addition to the summary corruption obstacle, the proportion of revenues paid as bribes has a negative and highly significant coefficient, indicating that it is a good indicator of corruption. Corruption of bank officials and the percentage of senior management's time spent with government officials also reduce firm growth significantly, but only at the 10% level. Again, the need to make payments or the absence of recourse to honest officials are not significant in regressions, despite their high levels as obstacles.

To investigate the relation between growth and reported obstacles for different-size firms, we next introduce firm size as an explanatory variable and interact the size dummies with individual obstacles. This specification posits that a firm might be affected by an obstacle, such as corruption, at three different levels: (1) at the country level, in that the general level of corruption may affect all the firms in the country; (2) at the "firm category" level, in that some firms (in our case different sized firms) might be affected differently; and (3) at the firm-specific level, in that firms have idiosyncratic exposures to corruption, depending on their business or financing needs. The equations are also estimated using random effects. Thus, the influence of the general

---

[12] If we use firm-level data and include random country effects, the between-R^2 is 41%.

[13] We are only able to do this using firm-level observations, since there are not enough degrees of freedom at the country level.

level of corruption in each country on firm growth is captured by the country random effects. The size variable picks up any systematic effects of exposure to corruption by firms of different sizes. The effect of firm-specific exposure to corruption is picked up by interacting the obstacles reported by each firm with a size dummy.

More generally, for each reported obstacle of interest, we regress firm growth on the control variables, firm size, the reported obstacle, and the interaction of the reported obstacle with three size dummies. These three variables, *Small*, *Medium*, and *Large*, take on the value 1 when the firm is small, medium-sized, and large, respectively, and 0 otherwise. The coefficients of interactions of the size dummies with an obstacle may differ because the impact of an obstacle can depend on firm size.

We also compute an economic impact variable for each firm size by multiplying the coefficients of the interacted variables by the mean level of reported obstacle for the subsample of firms of the corresponding firm size. To determine whether an obstacle affects the growth of large and small firms differently, we report and test the significance of the difference in the economic impacts of the obstacle for large and small firms. Thus, our reported impact variable, *Impact*(*L* − *S*), measures the difference between the total effect of the obstacle on large and small firms at their respective population means.

Our impact measure, *Impact*(*L* − *S*), also controls to a certain extent for a potential bias that could arise if some firms misestimate the effect of the obstacles on their growth, and if this misestimate is related to firm size. For example, if small firms systematically do not appreciate the real cost of the reported obstacles, they may, on average, underreport (relative to large firms) the magnitude of the obstacle. In that case, small firms might report, on average, λ times the true obstacle, where $\lambda < 1$. This in turn would bias upward the estimate of the interaction between *Small* and *Obstacle*. However, since the impact measure is defined as the difference of the products of the estimated coefficients and sample means of reported obstacles for large and small firms, it would therefore also not be affected by such scaling.[14]

In Table VI, we investigate whether financial, legal, and corruption obstacles affect firms differently based on their size. Panel A shows that financial obstacles affect firms differently, based on their size. The column titled 'Financial Obstacle' shows that the financing obstacle constrains the smallest firms the most and the largest ones the least. Multiplying the coefficients with the mean level of the summary financial obstacle for each respective subsample shows that the hypothesis that the economic impact of financing obstacles is the same for large and small firms can be rejected at the 10% level.

These differences become even clearer when we look at specific financing obstacles: The largest firms are barely affected. The only obstacle that affects these firms is that caused by high interest rates, which is different from 0 at

---

[14] As shown in the tables below, for almost all the regressions reported below, the conclusions we draw by testing for the differences of the economic impact variables match those drawn by simply testing for the differences in the coefficients.

Table VI
Firm Growth and Individual Obstacles: Large Compared to Small Firms

The regression estimated is

$$Firm\ Growth = \alpha + \beta_1\ Government + \beta_2\ Foreign + \beta_3\ Exporter + \beta_4\ Subsidized + \beta_5\ No.\ of\ Competitors + \beta_6\ Manufacturing + \beta_7\ Services + \beta_8\ Inflation$$
$$+ \beta_9\ GDP\ per\ capita + \beta_{10}\ GDP + \beta_{11}\ Growth + \beta_{12}\ LSize + \beta_{13}\ Obstacle * Small + \beta_{14}\ Obstacle * Medium + \beta_{15}\ Obstacle * Large + \varepsilon.$$

Firm Growth is the percentage change in firm sales over the past 3 years. *Government* and *Foreign* are dummy variables that take the value of 1 if the firm has government or foreign ownership and 0 if not. *Exporter* is a dummy variable that indicates if the firm is an exporting firm. *Subsidized* is also a dummy variable that indicates if the firm receives subsidies from the national or local authorities. *No. of Competitors* is the logarithm of the number of the firm's competitors. *Manufacturing* and *Services* are industry dummies. *Inflation* is the log difference of the consumer price index. *GDP per capita* is real GDP per capita in U.S. dollars. *GDP* is the logarithm of GDP per capita in U.S. dollars. *Growth* is given by the growth rate of GDP. *LSize* is given by logarithm of firm sales. Obstacles are financing obstacles in Panel A, legal obstacles in Panel B, and corruption obstacles in Panel C. Financing obstacles range between 1 and 4. Legal obstacles range between 1 and 6 (1 and 4 in the case of the summary obstacle). The range of the corruption indicators is indicated in parentheses after the variable name, with the first number indicating the least constraint. Unless otherwise noted, obstacles take higher values for higher obstacles and they are entered one at a time. Obstacles are multiplied by a vector of size dummy variables, Small, Medium, and Large. They take the value of 1 if a firm is small (or medium or large) and zero otherwise. Small firms employ 5–50 employees, medium-size firms employ 51–500 employees, and large firms employ more than 500 employees. For brevity only these coefficients ($\beta_{13} - \beta_{15}$) are reported below. *Impact (L − S)* gives the coefficient for large firms multiplied by the mean value of the obstacle for large firms minus the coefficient for small firms multiplied by the mean value of the obstacle for small firms. Its significance is based on a Chi-square test of these differences. We estimate all regressions using country random effects. Detailed variable definitions and sources are given in Table AII in the Appendix.

Panel A: Financing Obstacles

	Financing Obstacle	Collateral Requirements	Bank Paperwork/ Bureaucracy	High Interest Rates	Need Special Connections with Banks	Banks Lack Money to Lend	Access to Foreign Banks	Access to Nonbank Equity	Access to Export Finance	Access to Financing for Leasing Equipment	Inadequate Credit/ Financial Information on Customers	Access to Long-Term Loans
Large	−0.023**	−0.019	−0.012	−0.024**	−0.007	−0.020	−0.002	−0.004	0.005	−0.006	0.012	0.000
	(0.012)	(0.012)	(0.012)	(0.012)	(0.013)	(0.013)	(0.013)	(0.014)	(0.014)	(0.014)	(0.013)	(0.011)
Medium	−0.031***	−0.025***	−0.027***	−0.031***	−0.021**	−0.029***	0.000	0.002	−0.006	−0.023**	−0.001	−0.012
	(0.009)	(0.009)	(0.009)	(0.010)	(0.010)	(0.009)	(0.010)	(0.010)	(0.010)	(0.010)	(0.010)	(0.009)
Small	−0.034***	−0.031***	−0.031***	−0.037***	−0.028***	−0.034***	−0.002	0.000	−0.019*	−0.027***	−0.001	−0.012
	(0.009)	(0.009)	(0.009)	(0.010)	(0.010)	(0.010)	(0.010)	(0.011)	(0.011)	(0.011)	(0.010)	(0.009)
R^2-with.	0.01	0.01	0.01	0.01	0.01	0.01	0.01	0.01	0.01	0.01	0.01	0.01
R^2-between	0.29	0.25	0.26	0.27	0.27	0.28	0.26	0.28	0.30	0.30	0.28	0.27
R^2-all	0.03	0.03	0.03	0.03	0.02	0.03	0.02	0.02	0.03	0.03	0.02	0.02
Impact (L − S)	0.040*	0.038	0.050**	0.043*	0.051**	0.032	0.002	−0.007	0.047*	0.050***	0.028	0.033
N (firms)	4,182	3,926	4,048	4,083	3,928	3,832	3,463	3,444	2,990	3,504	3,682	3,907
N (country)	54	54	54	54	54	54	54	54	54	54	54	54

Panel B: Legal Obstacles

	Legal Obstacle	Availability of Info. on Laws and Regulations	Interpretation of Laws and Regulations Is Consistent	Overall Quality and Efficiency of Courts	Courts Are Fair and Impartial	Courts Are Quick	Courts Are Affordable	Courts Are Consistent	Court Decisions Are Enforced	Confidence in Legal System to Enforce Contract and Property Rights	Confidence in Legal System— 3 Years Ago
Large	−0.013	0.016	0.006	0.012	0.011	0.013	−0.003	0.014	0.024***	0.010	0.017*
	(0.013)	(0.010)	(0.009)	(0.010)	(0.010)	(0.009)	(0.009)	(0.009)	(0.009)	(0.010)	(0.009)
Medium	−0.026***	0.002	−0.005	−0.002	−0.001	0.006	−0.007	0.003	0.010	−0.003	0.006
	(0.010)	(0.007)	(0.007)	(0.008)	(0.008)	(0.008)	(0.007)	(0.007)	(0.007)	(0.008)	(0.008)
Small	−0.040***	−0.002	−0.005	−0.091	−0.010	0.002	−0.013*	−0.004	0.007	−0.010	−0.003
	(0.011)	(0.007)	(0.008)	(0.008)	(0.008)	(0.008)	(0.007)	(0.008)	(0.007)	(0.008)	(0.008)
R^2-with.	0.02	0.01	0.01	0.01	0.01	0.01	0.01	0.01	0.01	0.01	0.01
R^2-between	0.26	0.28	0.27	0.26	0.27	0.29	0.30	0.27	0.31	0.28	0.32
R^2-all	0.03	0.02	0.02	0.02	0.02	0.02	0.02	0.02	0.03	0.02	0.03
Impact (L − S)	0.057**	0.049**	0.038	0.095***	0.078***	0.059**	0.041	0.073***	0.061**	0.063**	0.065**
N (firms)	3,946	4,180	4,295	3,496	3,902	3,960	3,880	3,888	3,874	4,175	3,905
N (country)	54	54	54	54	54	54	54	54	54	54	54

(*continued*)

Table VI—*Continued*

Panel C: Corruption Obstacles

	Corruption Obstacle (1-4)	Corruption of Bank Officials (1-4)	Firms Have to Make "Additional Payments" to Get Things Done (6-1)	Firms Know in Advance the Amount of "Additional Payments" (6-1)	If "Additional Payments" Are Made, Services Are Delivered as Agreed (1-6)	If One Agent Asks for Payments It Is Possible to Find Others to Get the Correct Treatment without Payment (1-6)	Proportion of Revenues Paid as Bribes—Annual Figure for Each Firm (1-7)	Proportion of Contract Value That Must Be Paid as "Payment" to Do Business with the Government (1-6)	Percentage of Senior Management's Time Spent with Government Officials to Understand Laws and Regulations (1-6)
Large	−0.007	−0.007	0.017	0.018	0.004	0.011	−0.013	0.020	−0.003
	(0.012)	(0.016)	(0.011)	(0.014)	(0.014)	(0.009)	(0.015)	(0.014)	(0.011)
Medium	−0.017*	−0.012	−0.001	−0.002	−0.005	−0.001	−0.033***	0.006	−0.014*
	(0.010)	(0.012)	(0.007)	(0.009)	(0.011)	(0.007)	(0.010)	(0.009)	(0.008)
Small	−0.030***	−0.024**	−0.011	−0.009	−0.018*	−0.009	−0.053***	−0.001	−0.017*
	(0.010)	(0.011)	(0.007)	(0.009)	(0.011)	(0.007)	(0.009)	(0.009)	(0.009)
R^2-with.	0.01	0.01	0.01	0.02	0.02	0.01	0.03	0.02	0.01
R^2-between	0.25	0.28	0.28	0.20	0.21	0.29	0.23	0.21	0.26
R^2-all	0.03	0.03	0.03	0.03	0.03	0.03	0.04	0.05	0.02
Impact (L − S)	0.060**	0.034	0.128***	0.084**	0.067*	0.052**	0.117***	0.047	0.029
N (firms)	3,969	3,545	3,896	2,293	2,255	3,581	2,805	1,712	3,963
N (country)	54	54	53	53	53	53	53	52	54

*, **, *** indicate significance levels of 10%, 5%, and 1%, respectively.

the 5% significance level. Largest firms are completely unaffected by collateral requirements, bank bureaucracies, the need for special connections (probably because they already have them), banks' lack of money, or any of the access issues. In contrast, medium-sized firms, and particularly small firms, are significantly and negatively affected by collateral requirements, bank paperwork and bureaucracy, high interest rates, the need for special connections with banks, banks' lack of money to lend, and access to financing for leasing equipment. The smallest firms are also negatively affected by obstacles to gaining access to export finance. The tests for the difference in the economic impact of specific financing obstacles on the largest and smallest firms confirm significant differences for most of the obstacles that significantly affect the growth of small firms. These results provide evidence that financial obstacles have a much greater impact on the operation and growth of small firms than on that of large firms.[15]

Panel B of Table VI shows that the summary legal obstacle leaves large firm growth unaffected, but has a significant, negative impact on the growth rates of medium-sized and especially small firms. The effect on the growth rate of large firms is insignificant, despite the fact that large firms report a higher level of the legal obstacle (Table III).

To evaluate the economic impact of each obstacle for each subsample of firms by size, we multiply the estimated coefficient by the mean reported level of the obstacle. At the subsample means, the predicted effect of the summary legal obstacle on annual firm growth is 2.8% for large firms, whereas it is 5.7% for medium firms and 8.5% for small firms. The difference between the predicted effects on large and small firms is statistically significant.[16] These results indicate that large firms are able to adjust to the inefficiencies of the legal system. However, the same does not seem to be the case for small and medium enterprises, which end up paying for the legal systems' shortcomings in terms of slower growth. Even looking at specific obstacles, which do not capture relevant differences as well as the summary obstacles, there is an indication that large firms may be using legal inefficiencies to their advantage because poor enforcement of court decisions appears to contribute to large firm growth rates. However, looking at the other specific obstacles, we do not see such an effect. For small firms, the affordability of the court system emerges as an obstacle, although the coefficient is significant only at 10%. The coefficients of the other more specific legal obstacles are not significantly different from 0. When we investigate whether this finding might be explained by the nonlinear coding of the responses to the questions on specific features of the legal system by rescaling the responses, the results are unchanged.

---

[15] Firm size itself never has a significant coefficient in the regressions, consistent with simple correlations reported in Table II.

[16] It is interesting to note that the estimates of the difference in the economic impact of specific legal obstacles on large and small firms are generally statistically significant, even in cases where the coefficients of the specific obstacle are not statistically different from zero. That can occur if the coefficients for large and small firms are of different sign or if the subsample means of the obstacle for large and small firms differs sufficiently.

Panel C shows that again, it is the small and medium-sized firms that are negatively affected by corruption. The mean effects on firm growth are 1.6%, 4.1%, and 7.5% for large, medium-sized, and small firms, respectively. The difference between the economic impact of corruption for large and small firms at the subsample mean is statistically significant at the 5% level. None of the corruption obstacles is significant for large firms. The corruption obstacle is negative but significant at 10% for medium-sized firms and negative and highly significant for small firms.

When we look at specific obstacles, we again see that it is the small and medium enterprises that are affected by bribes. Both coefficients are highly significant, although the impact on small firm growth is larger in magnitude. The percentage of a senior manager's time spent with officials to understand regulations reduces the growth rates of both small and medium-sized enterprises, but only at a 10% level of significance. In addition, small firms are significantly and negatively affected by variables that capture the corruption of bank officials and uncertainty that services will be delivered even after bribes are paid. We do not find a significant relation between firms' growth rates and the need to make bribe payments or the absence of recourse to honest officials, despite these variables' high reported ratings as obstacles. The tests of economic impact at the subsample means support the hypothesis that there is a more adverse effect of corruption on small firms than on large firms.

Next, we address the issue of whether obstacles affect firms similarly in all countries, or if their impact depends on the country's level of financial and legal development and corruption. To examine this issue, we focus on our three summary obstacles and introduce into our regressions a term for the interaction of the summary obstacle with a variable proxying for institutional development. The institutional variable is *Priv* when financial obstacles are being analyzed, *Laworder* when the legal obstacle is entered, and *Corrupt* when the corruption obstacle is entered. The coefficient of the interaction term measures whether the financial development of the economy has an effect on the relation between reported financial obstacles and firm growth. Thus, our specification is

$$
\begin{aligned}
Firm\ Growth = {} & \alpha + \beta_1\,Government + \beta_2\,Foreign + \beta_3\,Exporter \\
& + \beta_4\,Subsidized + \beta_5\,No.\ of\ Competitors \\
& + \beta_6\,Manufacturing + \beta_7\,Services + \beta_8\,Inflation \\
& + \beta_9\,GDP\ per\ capita + \beta_{10}\,GDP + \beta_{11}\,Growth \\
& + \beta_{12}\,Institution + \beta_{13}\,Obstacle \\
& + \beta_{14}\,Obstacle * Institution + \varepsilon.
\end{aligned}
\tag{2}
$$

Table VII presents estimates of equation (2) for the summary financing, legal, and corruption obstacles. The results indicate that firms in financially and legally developed countries with lower levels of corruption are less affected by firm-level obstacles. In all three cases, the coefficient of the obstacle remains negative and significant, and the coefficient of the obstacle interacted

Financial and Legal Constraints to Growth   163

Table VII
Firm Growth and Obstacles: Impact of Institutional Development

The regression estimated is

$$Firm\ Growth = \alpha + \beta_1 Government + \beta_2 Foreign + \beta_3 Exporter + \beta_4 Subsidized$$

$$+ \beta_5\ No.\ of\ Competitors + \beta_6\ Manufacturing + \beta_7\ Services + \beta_8\ Inflation$$

$$+ \beta_9\ GDP\ per\ capita + \beta_{10}\ GDP + \beta_{11}\ Growth + \beta_{12}\ Institution$$

$$+ \beta_{13}\ Obstacle + \beta_{14}\ Obstacle * Institution + \varepsilon.$$

Firm Growth is the percentage change in firm sales over the past 3 years. *Government* and *Foreign* are dummy variables that take the value of 1 if the firm has government or foreign ownership and 0 if not. *Exporter* is a dummy variable that indicates if the firm is an exporting firm. *Subsidized* is also a dummy variable that indicates if the firm receives subsidies from the national or local authorities. *No. of Competitors* is the logarithm of the number of the firm's competitors. *Manufacturing* and *Services* are industry dummies. *Inflation* is the log difference of the consumer price index. *GDP per capita* is real GDP per capita in U.S. dollars. *GDP* is the logarithm of GDP in millions of U.S. dollars. *Growth* is given by the growth rate of GDP. Obstacle is either Financing Legal or Corruption obstacle. The institutional variable is *Priv* when Financial constraint is entered, *Laworder* when Legal obstacle is entered, and *Corrupt* when Corruption obstacle is entered. *Priv* is domestic bank credit to the private sector divided by GDP. *Laworder* is a national indicator (values 1–6) that takes higher values for legal systems that are more developed. *Corrupt* (values 1–4) is a corruption indicator at the national level that takes higher values in countries where corruption is lower. Obstacles range between 1 and 4 and take higher values for greater obstacles. They are also interacted with the respective institutional variables. For brevity only these coefficients are reported below. Impact on growth is evaluated at the mean and is given by the product of the interaction term, the sample mean of the respective obstacle and the mean level of the institutional variable. We estimate all regressions using country random effects. Detailed variable definitions and sources are given in Table AII in the Appendix.

	Financing Obstacle	Legal Obstacle	Corruption Obstacle
Fin obstacle	−0.043***		
	(0.013)		
Fin. Obs. × Priv	0.045*		
	(0.029)		
Legal obstacle		−0.085**	
		(0.027)	
Legal Obs. × Laworder		0.014*	
		(0.009)	
Corruption obstacle			−0.084***
			(0.026)
Corruption Obs. × Corrupt			0.020***
			(0.008)
R^2-with.	0.01	0.01	0.01
R^2-between	0.17	0.26	0.36
R^2-all	0.02	0.02	0.03
Impact	0.039*	0.123*	0.155***
No. of firms	3,596	3,923	3,939
No. of countries	50	53	53

*, **, *** indicate significance levels of 10%, 5%, and 1%, respectively.

with the relevant development variable is positive and significantly different from zero.[17] Evaluating the coefficients at different levels of institutional development shows that in developed countries with *Priv* levels of 95% or higher, *Laworder* values of 6 and *Corrupt* values of 4 or higher, the impact of financial, legal, or corruption obstacles on firm growth is not significantly different from 0. In unreported regressions, we estimate equation (2) with each specific obstacle in turn. In separate regressions, we find positive and significant coefficients for the interaction between the level of development and the lack of money in the banking system, a consistent interpretation of laws, the amount of bribes to be paid, and the fraction of the contract value that must be paid to a government to secure the contract. These results also support the hypothesis that in countries where there is less corruption and better-developed financial and legal systems, firm growth is less constrained by the factors we examine.

We next investigate whether the effect of financial and institutional development on growth varies with firm size. For each summary obstacle, we augment our regression equations by interacting the summary obstacle with a measure of institutional development and with the firm-size dummies, *Small, Medium,* and *Large.* This gives us three triple interaction coefficients corresponding to the three triple interactions, *Obstacle * Small * Institution, Obstacle * Medium * Institution,* and *Obstacle * Large * Institution.*

Significance tests of the coefficient of the triple interactions show whether a marginal change in institutional development affects the relation between the summary obstacles and growth for small, medium, and large firms, respectively. We also test whether the marginal effect of a change in the country's financial system affects the sensitivity of the firm's growth to the financing obstacle equally for large and small firms. This difference in impact, *Impact(L − S),* is computed as the coefficient of the triple interaction term for large firms evaluated at the mean level of *Obstacle* for the subsample of large firms minus the coefficient of the triple interaction term for small firms evaluated at the mean level of *Obstacle* for small firms.

Taking into account firm sizes reinforces the results reported in Table VII. Table VIII shows that the relation between financing, legal, and corruption obstacles and the growth of firms of different sizes depends on the institutional setting.

The first column of Table VIII shows that small firms are again the most severely affected by financing obstacles. However, the interaction term of the financing obstacle with *Priv* and the small firm dummy variable has a positive sign and is significant, suggesting that a marginal development in a country's financial system relaxes the financial constraints on small firms.

In column 2 of the table, we see that marginal improvements in legal efficiency translate into a relaxing of legal constraints for small and medium-sized

---

[17] The variables *Priv* and *Laworder* are not significant when entered together with financing and legal obstacles. On the other hand, corruption enters positively and significantly in some specifications, even when entered together with firm-level corruption obstacles. This result indicates that lack of corruption is associated with higher firm growth.

Financial and Legal Constraints to Growth 165

Table VIII
Firm Growth and the Impact of Obstacles: Firm Size and National Differences

The regression estimated is

$$Firm\ Growth = \alpha + \beta_1 Government + \beta_2 Foreign + \beta_3 Exporter + \beta_4 Subsidized + \beta_5 No.\ of\ Comp.$$
$$+ \beta_6 Manuf. + \beta_7 Services + \beta_8 Inflation + \beta_9 Gdp\ per\ capita + \beta_{10} GDP + \beta_{11} Growth$$
$$+ \beta_{12} Institution * Small + \beta_{13} Institution * Medium + \beta_{14} Institution * Large$$
$$+ \beta_{15} LSize + \beta_{16} Obstacle * Small + \beta_{17} Obstacle * Medium + \beta_{18} Obstacle * Large$$
$$+ \beta_{19} Obstacle * Small * Institution + \beta_{20} Obstacle * Medium * Institution$$
$$+ \beta_{21} Obstacle * Large * Institution + \varepsilon.$$

Firm Growth is the percentage change in firm sales over the past 3 years. *Government* and *Foreign* are dummy variables that take the value 1 if the firm has government or foreign ownership and 0 if not. *Exporter* is a dummy variable that indicates if the firm is an exporting firm. *Subsidized* is also a dummy variable that indicates if the firm receives subsidies from the national or local authorities. *No. of Competitors* is the logarithm of the number of the firm's competitors. *Manufacturing* and *Services* are industry dummies. *LSize* is given by logarithm of firm sales. *Inflation* is the log difference of the consumer price index. *GDP per capita* is real GDP per capita in U.S. dollars. *GDP* is the logarithm of GDP in millions of U.S. dollars. *Growth* is the growth rate of GDP. Institution is either *Priv, Laworder,* or *Corrupt. Priv* is domestic bank credit to the private sector divided by GDP. *Laworder* is a national indicator (values between 1 and 6) that takes higher values for legal systems that are more developed. *Corrupt* is a corruption indicator (values between 1 and 6) at the national level that takes higher values in countries where corruption is lower. *Obstacle* is either Financing, Legal, or Corruption. These are summary firm-level obstacles as indicated in the firm questionnaire. They take values between 1 and 4, where 1 indicates no obstacle and 4 indicates a major obstacle. *Small, Medium,* and *Large* are dummy variables. They take the value 1 if a firm is small (or medium or large) and 0 otherwise. Small firms employ 5–50 employees, medium size firms employ 51–500 employees, and large firms employ more than 500 employees. Financing obstacles are interacted with *Priv,* legal obstacles are interacted with *Laworder,* and corruption obstacles are interacted with *Corrupt.* These are also interacted with size dummies. Only these interaction terms are reported for brevity. Impact (L – S) is β_{21} evaluated at mean level of the institutional variable and mean obstacle for large firms minus β_{19} evaluated at mean level of the institutional variable and mean obstacle for small firms. Its significance is based on a Chi-square test of these differences. We estimate all regressions using country random effects. We obtain firm-level variables from the WBES. Detailed variable definitions and sources are given in Table AII in the Appendix.

	(1)	(2)	(3)
Financing Obstacle			
Large	−0.023		
	(0.016)		
Medium	−0.031**		
	(0.014)		
Small	−0.058***		
	(0.014)		
Large × Priv	−0.039		
	(0.051)		
Medium × Priv	0.021		
	(0.038)		
Small × Priv	0.097***		
	(0.039)		

(continued)

Table VIII—*Continued*

	(1)	(2)	(3)
Legal Obstacle			
Large		−0.060	
		(0.046)	
Medium		−0.092**	
		(0.040)	
Small		−0.104***	
		(0.044)	
Large × Laworder		0.009	
		(0.013)	
Medium × Laworder		0.018*	
		(0.010)	
Small × Laworder		0.015*	
		(0.010)	
Corruption Obstacle			
Large			−0.020
			(0.037)
Medium			−0.067**
			(0.028)
Small			−0.117***
			(0.029)
Large × Corrupt			0.002
			(0.013)
Medium × Corrupt			0.018**
			(0.009)
Small × Corrupt			0.026***
			(0.009)
R^2-within	0.02	0.02	0.02
R^2-between	0.34	0.26	0.43
R^2-overall	0.04	0.03	0.04
Impact(L − S)	−0.126***	−0.040	−0.197***
No. of firms	3,579	3,906	3,922
No. of countries	50	53	53

*, **, *** indicate significance levels of 10%, 5%, and 1%, respectively.

firms (albeit significant at the 10% level). The corruption results reported in column 3 indicate that as countries manage to reduce corruption, the constraining effect of corruption on the growth of small and medium-sized firms diminishes. The differential effect of the interaction of *Priv* and of the level of corruption on the growth of large and of small firms is statistically significant, indicating a material difference in the economic impact of these variables on the growth of large and small firms.

To address two possible sources of bias, we perform robustness checks of our specifications. Our estimates will be biased if firms that are not growing because of internal problems systematically shift blame to the legal and financial institutions and report high obstacles. This type of reverse causality problem,

Financial and Legal Constraints to Growth   167

Table IX

Sensitivity Test: IV Estimation and Using Real Firm Growth

The IV regression estimated is

$$Firm\ Growth = \alpha + \beta_1 Government + \beta_2 Foreign + \beta_3 Exporter + \beta_4 Subsidized$$

$$+ \beta_5\ No.\ of\ Competitors + \beta_6 Manufacturing + \beta_7 Services + \beta_8 Inflation$$

$$+ \beta_9\ GDP\ per\ capita + \beta_{10}\ GDP + \beta_{11}\ Growth + \beta_{12}\ Financing$$

$$+ \beta_{13}\ Legal + b_{14}\ Corruption + \varepsilon.$$

Firm Growth is the percentage change in firm sales over the past 3 years. *Government* and *Foreign* are dummy variables that take the value of one if the firm has government or foreign ownership and zero if not. *Exporter* is a dummy variable that indicates if the firm is an exporting firm. *Subsidized* is also a dummy variable that indicates if the firm receives subsidies from the national or local authorities. *No. of Competitors* is the logarithm of the number of the firm's competitors. *Manufacturing* and *Services* are industry dummies. *Inflation* is the log difference of the consumer price index. *GDP per capita* is real GDP per capita values in U.S. dollars. GDP is the logarithm of GDP in millions of U.S. dollars. *Growth* is the growth rate of GDP. Financing, Legal, and Corruption are summary obstacles as indicated in the firm questionnaire. They take values between 1 and 4, where 1 indicates no obstacle and 4 indicates a major obstacle. In Panel A, we estimate all regressions using instrumental variables, where the firm-level obstacles are instrumented by country-level institutional variables (*Priv, Laworder,* and *Corrupt*). In Panel B, obstacles are interacted with size dummies—small, medium, and large—and are instrumented by the three country-level institutional variables interacted by the three size dummies. In this specification we also control for *Size* in the regression. In Panel C, instead of interacting the obstacles with the three size dummies, we interact them with firm size. In Panel D, the dependent variable, *Firm Growth*, is replaced by real firm growth constructed using GDP deflator. Inflation is dropped from the specification. In Panel E, firm growth and obstacles are averaged for different size groups in each country. The averaged firm growth is regressed on averaged obstacles and all macro variables plus an interaction term of the averaged obstacle with a dummy variable that takes the value 1 if the firm is a small or medium firm and 0 otherwise. Each panel also reports Impact—the relevant coefficient evaluated at the mean level of the obstacle, or Impact (L − S), the differential impact on large versus small firms evaluated at the mean level of the obstacle for large and small firms. For brevity we report only the coefficients of the obstacles. Robust standard errors are reported in parentheses. We obtain firm-level variables from the WBES. Detailed variable definitions and sources are given in the Table AII in the Appendix.

	(1)	(2)	(3)
		Panel A	
Financing	−0.575***		
	(0.125)		
Legal		−0.029***	
		(0.009)	
Corruption			−0.021***
			(0.009)
Impact	−1.637***	−0.063***	−0.051***
No. of firms	3539	3390	3396

(continued)

Table IX—*Continued*

	(1)	(2)	(3)
		Panel B	
Financing * large	−0.341***		
	(0.111)		
Financing * medium	−0.448***		
	(0.111)		
Financing * small	−0.790***		
	(0.186)		
Legal * large		0.073	
		(0.065)	
Legal * medium		0.023	
		(0.081)	
Legal * small		−0.104	
		(0.076)	
Corruption * large			−0.156**
			(0.081)
Corruption * medium			−0.207***
			(0.087)
Corruption * small			−0.272***
			(0.084)
Impact (L − S)	1.431***	0.382***	0.314***
No. of firms	3538	3389	3395
		Panel C	
Financing	−0.046***		
	(0.013)		
Financing * size	0.002*		
	(0.001)		
Legal		−0.049***	
		(0.013)	
Legal * size		0.003**	
		(0.001)	
Corruption			−0.036***
			(0.012)
Corruption * size			0.002*
			(0.001)
R^2-within	0.01	0.01	0.01
R^2-between	0.31	0.28	0.27
R^2-overall	0.03	0.03	0.03
Impact (at mean size)	−0.032***	−0.029***	−0.021***
No. of firms	4,183	3,947	3,970

(continued)

if it exists, is likely to be most severe in the case of the summary obstacles.[18] To examine this possibility, we reestimate the specifications in Table IV by using *Priv, Laworder,* and *Corrupt* as the instrumental variables. The coefficients of

---

[18] We are grateful to the referee for pointing this out.

Financial and Legal Constraints to Growth 169

Table IX—*Continued*

	(1)	(2)	(3)
		Panel D	
Financing	−0.030***		
	(0.009)		
Legal		−0.030***	
		(0.009)	
Corruption			−0.021***
			(0.009)
R^2-within	0.01	0.01	0.01
R^2-between	0.28	0.28	0.27
R^2-overall	0.15	0.16	0.14
Impact	−0.085***	−0.065***	−0.051***
No. of firms	4204	3968	3991
No. of countries	54	54	54
		Panel E	
Financing	0.015		
	(0.0364)		
Financing * SME	−0.021**		
	(0.011)		
Legal		0.043	
		(0.038)	
Legal * SME		−0.027**	
		(0.014)	
Corruption			−0.003
			(0.032)
Corruption * SME			−0.024**
			(0.012)
R^2	0.12	0.12	0.12
Impact (L − SME)	0.060***	0.059***	0.058***
No. of observations	162	162	162
No. of countries	54	54	54

*, **, *** indicate significance levels of 10%, 5%, and 1%, respectively.

interest are reported in Panel A of Table IX. The coefficients show that the same variables remain significant at roughly comparable levels of significance.

In Panel B, we estimate the size splits for the three summary indicators using *Priv*, *Laworder*, and *Corrupt* interacted with the three size dummies as instrumental variables. Although the results for financing and corruption obstacles do not change significantly, those for the legal obstacle lose significance.

In Panel C, rather than looking at the differences between the three size groups, we interact the obstacles by firm size given by the logarithm of firm sales. Even when we use this continuous definition of firm size, we see that larger firms are less affected by the three obstacles.

Panel D shows the relation between the obstacles and firms' real growth. In this specification, we drop the rate of inflation variable from the right-hand side. Inspection of Panel D shows that adjusting the dependent variable for inflation does not alter the results.

In Panel E, we examine the robustness of our findings when we average the variables by country for different firm sizes. This procedure provides an alternative and more stringent test of the relation between firm growth and obstacles because it ignores the firm-level heterogeneity across firms in the same country belonging to the same size classification. Because this aggregation procedure reduces the degrees of freedom, in Panel D, we also reduce the number of independent variables and focus on the differences between SMEs and large firms. The results reported in Panel E are consistent with the firm-level results reported in earlier tables. There exist significant differences in the impact of financial, legal, and corruption obstacles on SMEs and large firms.

III. Conclusions

In this paper, we investigate whether the financial, legal, and corruption obstacles that firms report actually affect their growth rates. By making use of a unique survey database, we investigate a rich set of obstacles reported by firms and directly test whether any of these reported obstacles are significantly correlated with firm growth rates. The database also allows us to focus on differences in firm size, since it has good coverage of small and medium-sized enterprises in 54 countries. We investigate if the extent to which the firms are constrained by different obstacles depends on the level of development of the financial and legal systems. We are particularly interested in investigating the previously unexamined national level of corruption and its impact on firm growth.

Our results indicate that the extent to which financial and legal underdevelopment and corruption constrain a firm's growth depends very much on a firm's size. We show that it is the smallest firms that are consistently the most adversely affected by all obstacles.

Taking into account national differences between financial and legal development and corruption, we see that firms that operate in underdeveloped systems with higher levels of corruption are affected by all obstacles to a greater extent than firms operating in countries with less corruption. We also see that a marginal development in the financial and legal system and a reduction in corruption helps relax the constraints for the small and medium-sized firms, which are the most constrained.

All three obstacles—financial, legal, and corruption—do affect firm growth rates adversely. But not all specific obstacles are equally important, and the ones that affect firm growth are not necessarily the ones rated highest by the firms themselves. When we look at individual financing obstacles, we see that difficulties in dealing with banks, such as bank paperwork and bureaucracies, and the need to have special connections with banks, do constrain firm growth. Collateral requirements and certain access issues—such as financing for leasing equipment—also turn out to be significantly constraining. Macroeconomic issues captured by high interest rates and lack of money in the banking system also significantly reduce firm growth rates. Further, these effects remain

Financial and Legal Constraints to Growth   171

significant even after we control for the level of financial development. We are interested to find that another obstacle that is rated very highly by firms, access to long-term loans, does not affect their growth rates significantly. Perhaps, firms find it possible to substitute short-term funding for long-term loans.

Legal and corruption obstacles, particularly the amount of bribes paid, the percentage of senior management's time spent with regulators, and corruption of bank officials, also represent significant constraints on firm growth. However, other obstacles, such as the speed with which the courts work, or the need to make additional payments, both of which are rated very highly by firms as important obstacles, do not affect firm growth significantly. These results suggest that the surveys elicit all kinds of complaints that may appear equally important. However, our methodology allows us to distinguish between obstacles that are merely annoying from those that truly constrain firm performance.

There are two particularly interesting findings. First, corruption of bank officials does indeed affect firm growth, particularly for small firms. This finding provides evidence for the existence of institutional failure, which must be taken into account when modeling the monitoring role of financial institutions in overcoming market failures due to informational asymmetries. Second, while the intuitive descriptors of an efficient legal system are related to the summary obstacle, they are not related to firm growth. This finding suggests that the mechanism by which the legal system affects firm performance is not yet well understood.

There are several policy implications in our results. Development institutions devote a large amount of their resources to SMEs because they believe the development of the SME sector is crucial for economic growth and poverty alleviation and that small entrepreneurs face greater constraints. While this paper does not address the issue of SME impact on economic development, it does provide evidence confirming that indeed, small and medium-sized firms face greater financial, legal, and corruption obstacles compared to large firms, and that the constraining impact of obstacles on firm growth is inversely related to firm size. Our paper also shows that it is the small firms that stand to benefit the most from improvements in financial development and a reduction in corruption.

Appendix

Table AI
Number of Firms in Each Country

	Number of Firms
Albania	85
Argentina	76
Armenia	90
Azerbaijan	66
Belarus	95

(continued)

172   *The Journal of Finance*

Table AI—*Continued*

	Number of Firms
Belize	14
Bolivia	61
Brazil	132
Bulgaria	100
Canada	73
Chile	67
China	69
Colombia	77
Costa Rica	49
Croatia	91
Czech Republic	78
Dominican Republic	73
Ecuador	46
El Salvador	48
Estonia	103
France	55
Germany	59
Guatemala	52
Haiti	42
Honduras	46
Hungary	91
Indonesia	67
Italy	54
Kazakhstan	85
Kyrgizstan	62
Lithuania	66
Malaysia	33
Mexico	35
Moldova	78
Nicaragua	51
Pakistan	55
Panama	47
Peru	65
Philippines	84
Poland	169
Portugal	49
Romania	95
Russia	372
Singapore	72
Slovakia	86
Slovenia	101
Spain	64
Sweden	68
Trinidad & Tobago	59
Turkey	112
Ukraine	165
United Kingdom	53
United States	61
Uruguay	55
Venezuela	54

The data source is WBES.

Financial and Legal Constraints to Growth 173

Table AII
Variables and Sources

Variable	Definition	Original Source
GDP	GDP in current U.S. dollars, average 1995–1999	WDI
GDP per capita	Real per capita GDP, average 1995–1999	WDI
Growth	Growth rate of GDP, average 1995–1999	WDI
Inflation rate	Log difference of Consumer Price Index	IFS, line 64
Priv	$\{(0.5)*[F(t)/P\_e(t) + F(t-1)/P\_e(t-1)]/[GDP(t)/P\_a(t)]$, where F is credit by deposit money banks to the private sector (lines 22d), GDP is line 99b, P_e is end-of period CPI (line 64) and P_a is the average CPI for the year.	IFS
Laworder	Measure of the law and order tradition of a country. It is an average over 1995–1997. It ranges from 6, strong law and order tradition, to 1, weak law and order tradition.	ICRG
Corrupt	Measure of corruption in government. It ranges from 1 to 6 and is an average over 1995–1997. Lower scores indicate that "high government officials are likely to demand special payments" and "illegal payments are generally expected throughout lower levels of government" in the form of "bribes connected with import and export licenses, exchange controls, tax assessment, policy protection, or loans."	ICRG
Firm growth	Estimate of the firm's sales growth over the past 3 years.	WBES
Government	Dummy variable that takes on the value 1 if any government agency or state body has a financial stake in the ownership of the firm, 0 otherwise.	WBES
Foreign	Dummy variable that takes on the value 1 if any foreign company or individual has a financial stake in the ownership of the firm, 0 otherwise.	WBES
Exporter	Dummy variable that takes on the value 1 if firm exports, 0 otherwise.	WBES
Subsidized	Dummy variable that takes on value 1 if firm receives subsidies (including tolerance of tax arrears) from local or national government.	WBES
Manufacturing	Dummy variable that takes on the value 1 if firm is in the manufacturing industry, 0 otherwise.	WBES
Services	Dummy variable that takes on the value 1 if firm is in the service industry, 0 otherwise.	WBES
No. of competitors	Regarding your firm's major product line, how many competitors do you face in your market?	WBES
Firm size dummies	A firm is defined as small if it has between 5 and 50 employees, medium-sized if it has between 51 and 500 employees, and large if it has more than 500 employees.	WBES
Size	Logarithm of firm sales	WBES
Financing obstacle	How problematic is financing for the operation and growth of your business: no obstacle (1), a minor obstacle (2), a moderate obstacle (3), or a major obstacle (4)?	WBES

(continued)

Table AII—*Continued*

Variable	Definition	Original Source
Legal obstacle	How problematic is functioning of the judiciary for the operation and growth of your business: no obstacle (1), a minor obstacle (2), a moderate obstacle (3), or a major obstacle (4)?	WBES
Corruption obstacle	How problematic is corruption for the operation and growth of your business: no obstacle (1), a minor obstacle (2), a moderate obstacle (3), or a major obstacle (4)?	WBES
Collateral requirements	Are collateral requirements of banks/financial institutions no obstacle (1), a minor obstacle (2), a moderate obstacle (3), or a major obstacle (4)?	WBES
Bank paperwork/ bureaucracy	Is bank paperwork/bureaucracy no obstacle (1), a minor obstacle (2), a moderate obstacle (3), or a major obstacle (4)?	WBES
High interest rates	Are high interest rates no obstacle (1), a minor obstacle (2), a moderate obstacle (3), or a major obstacle (4)?	WBES
Need special connections with banks	Is the need of special connections with banks/financial institutions no obstacle (1), a minor obstacle (2), a moderate obstacle (3), or a major obstacle (4)?	WBES
Banks lack money to lend	Is banks' lack of money to lend no obstacle (1), a minor obstacle (2), a moderate obstacle (3), or a major obstacle (4)?	WBES
Access to foreign banks	Is the access to foreign banks no obstacle (1), a minor obstacle (2), a moderate obstacle (3), or a major obstacle (4)?	WBES
Access to nonbank equity	Is the access to nonbank equity/investors/partners no obstacle (1), a minor obstacle (2), a moderate obstacle (3), or a major obstacle (4)?	WBES
Access to export finance	Is the access to specialized export finance no obstacle (1), a minor obstacle (2), a moderate obstacle (3), or a major obstacle (4)?	WBES
Access to financing for leasing equipment	Is the access to lease finance for equipment no obstacle (1), a minor obstacle (2), a moderate obstacle (3), or a major obstacle (4)?	WBES
Inadequate credit/financial information on customers	Is inadequate credit/financial information on customers no obstacle (1), a minor obstacle (2), a moderate obstacle (3), or a major obstacle (4)?	WBES
Access to long-term loans	Is the access to long-term finance no obstacle (1), a minor obstacle (2), a moderate obstacle, (3) or a major obstacle (4)?	WBES
Availability of information on laws and regulations	In general, information on the laws and regulations affecting my firm is easy to obtain: (1) fully agree, (2) agree in most cases, (3) tend to agree, (4) tend to disagree, (5) disagree in most cases, (6) fully disagree.	WBES
Interpretation of laws and regulations are consistent	In general, interpretation of regulations affecting my firm is consistent and predictable: (1) fully agree, (2) agree in most cases, (3) tend to agree, (4) tend to disagree, (5) disagree in most cases, (6) fully disagree.	WBES

(*continued*)

Financial and Legal Constraints to Growth 175

Table AII—*Continued*

Variable	Definition	Original Source
Overall quality and efficiency of courts	Overall quality and efficiency of the judiciary/courts: (1) very good, (2) good, (3) slightly good, (4) slightly bad, (5) bad, (6) very bad.	WBES
Courts are fair and impartial	In resolving business disputes, do you believe your country's courts to be fair and impartial: (1) always, (2) usually, (3) frequently, (4) sometimes, (5) seldom, (6) never.	WBES
Courts are quick	In resolving business disputes, do you believe your country's courts to be quick: (1) always, (2) usually, (3) frequently, (4) sometimes, (5) seldom, (6) never.	WBES
Courts are affordable	In resolving business disputes, do you believe your country's courts to be affordable: (1) always, (2) usually, (3) frequently, (4) sometimes, (5) seldom, (6) never.	WBES
Courts are consistent	In resolving business disputes, do you believe your country's courts to be consistent: (1) always, (2) usually, (3) frequently, (4) sometimes, (5) seldom, (6) never.	WBES
Court decisions are enforced	In resolving business disputes, do you believe your country's courts to enforce decisions: (1) always, (2) usually, (3) frequently, (4) sometimes, (5) seldom, (6) never.	WBES
Confidence in legal system to enforce contract and property rights	I am confident that the legal system will uphold my contract and property rights in business disputes: (1) fully agree, (2) agree in most cases, (3) tend to agree, (4) tend to disagree, (5) disagree in most cases, (6) fully disagree.	WBES
Confidence in legal system— 3 years ago	I am confident that the legal system will uphold my contract and property rights in business disputes: 3 years ago: (1) fully agree, (2) agree in most cases, (3) tend to agree, (4) tend to disagree, (5) disagree in most cases, (6) fully disagree.	WBES
Corruption of bank officials	Is the corruption of bank officials: no obstacle (1), a minor obstacle (2), a moderate obstacle (3), or a major obstacle (4)?	WBES
Firms have to make "additional payments" in advance	It is common for firms in my line of business to have to pay some irregular "additional payments" to get things done: (1) always, (2) mostly, (3) frequently, (4) sometimes, (5) seldom, (6) never.	WBES
Firms know the amount of "additional payments" in advance	Firms in my line of business usually know in advance about how much this "additional payment" is: (1) always, (2) mostly, (3) frequently, (4) sometimes, (5) seldom, (6) never.	WBES
If "additional payments" are made, services are delivered	If a firm pays the required "additional payments," the service is usually also delivered as agreed: (1) always, (2) mostly, (3) frequently, (4) sometimes, (5) seldom, (6) never.	WBES

(continued)

176   *The Journal of Finance*

Table AII—*Continued*

Variable	Definition	Original Source
It is possible to find honest agents to replace corrupt ones	If a government agent acts against the rules, I can usually go to another official or to his superior and get the correct treatment without recourse to unofficial payments: (1) always, (2) mostly, (3) frequently, (4) sometimes, (5) seldom, (6) never.	WBES
Proportion of revenues paid as bribes	On average, what percentage of revenues do firms like yours typically pay per year in unofficial payments to public officials: (1) 0%, (1) less than 1%, (3) 1–1.99%, (4) 2–9.99%, (5) 10–12%, (6) 13–25%, (7) over 25%.	WBES
Proportion of contract value that must be paid for government contracts	When firms in your industry do business with the government, how much of the contract value must they offer in additional or unofficial payments to secure the contract: (1) 0%, (1) up to 5%, (3) 6–10%, (4) 11–15%, (5) 16–20%, (6) over 20%.	WBES
Management's time (%) spent with officials to understand laws and regulations	What percentage of senior management's time per year is spent in dealing with government officials about the application and interpretation of laws and regulations?	WBES

Sources of data: WDI = World Development Indicators; IFS = International Financial Statistics; ICRG = International Country Risk Guide; WBES = World Business Environment Survey.

REFERENCES

Ball, Ray, S. P. Kothari, and Ashok Robin, 2000, The effect of international institutional factors on properties of accounting earnings, *Journal of Accounting and Economics* 29, 1–51.

Beck, Thorsten, Asli Demirgüç-Kunt, and Ross Levine, 2000, A new database on the structure and development of the financial sector, *World Bank Economic Review* 14, 597–605.

Beck, Thorsten, Asli Demirgüç-Kunt, and Vojislav Maksimovic, 2001a, Financing patterns and constraints: The role of institutions, mimeo, World Bank.

Beck, Thorsten, Asli Demirgüç-Kunt, and Vojislav Maksimovic, 2001b, Financial and legal institutions and firm size, mimeo, World Bank.

Beck, Thorsten, Ross Levine, and Norman Loayza, 2000, Finance and the sources of growth, *Journal of Financial Economics* 58, 261–300.

Carlin, Wendy, and Colin Mayer, 2003, Finance, investment, and growth, *Journal of Financial Economics* 69, 191–226.

Clarke, George, Robert Cull, and Maria Soledad Martinez Peria, 2001, Does foreign bank penetration reduce access to credit in developing countries? Evidence from asking borrowers, mimeo, World Bank.

Demirgüç-Kunt, Asli, and Vojislav Maksimovic, 1998, Law, finance, and firm growth, *Journal of Finance* 53, 2107–2137.

Demirgüç-Kunt, Asli, and Vojislav Maksimovic, 1999, Institutions, financial markets and firm debt maturity, *Journal of Financial Economics* 54, 295–336.

Demirgüç-Kunt, Asli, and Vojislav Maksimovic, 2001, Firms as financial intermediaries: Evidence from trade credit data, World Bank Working paper.

Hung, Mingyi, 2001, Accounting standards and value relevance of financial statements: An international analysis, *Journal of Accounting and Economics* 30, 401–420.

Financial and Legal Constraints to Growth 177

Khanna, Tarun, and Krishna Palepu, 2000, Is group affiliation profitable in emerging markets? An analysis of diversified Indian business groups, *Journal of Finance* 55, 867–891.

King, Robert G., and Ross Levine, 1993, Finance and growth: Schumpeter might be right, *Quarterly Journal of Economics* 108, 717–738.

La Porta, Rafael, Florencio Lopez-de-Silanes, Andrei Shleifer, and Robert W. Vishny, 1998, Law and finance, *Journal of Political Economy* 106, 1113–1155.

Levine, Ross, and Sara Zervos, 1998, Stock markets, banks, and economic growth, *American Economic Review* 88, 537–558.

Love, Inessa, 2001, Financial development and financing constraints: International evidence from the structural investment model, World Bank Working paper No. 2694.

Maksimovic, Vojislav, and Gordon Phillips, 2002, Do conglomerate firms allocate resources inefficiently? Evidence from plant-level data, *Journal of Finance* 57, 721–767

Mauro, Paolo, 1996, The effects of corruption on growth, investment and government expenditure, IMF Working paper 96/98.

Rajan, Raghuram G., Henri Servaes, and Luigi Zingales, 2000, The cost of diversity: The diversification discount and inefficient investment, *Journal of Finance* 55, 35–80.

Rajan, Raghuram G., and Luigi Zingales, 1998a, Financial dependence and growth, *American Economic Review* 88, 559–587.

Rajan, Raghuram G., and Luigi Zingales, 1998b, Which capitalism? Lessons from the East Asian crisis, *Journal of Applied Corporate Finance* 11, 40–48.

Scharfstein, David S., and Jeremy C. Stein, 2000, The dark side of internal capital markets: Divisional rent-seeking and inefficient investment, *Journal of Finance* 55, 2537–2564.

Schiffer, Mirjam, and Beatrice Weder, 2001, Firm size and the business environment: Worldwide survey results, IFC Discussion Paper number 43.

World Bank, 2002, SME. World Bank Froup Review of Small Business Activities. Washington, DC: World Bank.

Wurgler, Jeffrey, 2000, Financial markets and the allocation of capital, *Journal of Financial Economics* 58, 187–214.

Available online at www.sciencedirect.com

SCIENCE ⒟ DIRECT°

Journal of Financial Economics 69 (2003) 5–50

ELSEVIER

JOURNAL OF
Financial
ECONOMICS

www.elsevier.com/locate/econbase

The great reversals: the politics of financial development in the twentieth century [✩]

Raghuram G. Rajan*, Luigi Zingales

The University of Chicago Graduate School of Business, 1101 E. 58th St., Chicago, IL 60637, USA

Abstract

The state of development of the financial sector does not change monotonically over time. In particular, by most measures, countries were more financially developed in 1913 than in 1980 and only recently have they surpassed their 1913 levels. To explain these changes, we propose an interest group theory of financial development where incumbents oppose financial development because it breeds competition. The theory predicts that incumbents' opposition will be weaker when an economy allows both cross-border trade and capital flows. This theory can go some way in accounting for the cross-country differences in, and the time-series variation of, financial development.
© 2003 Elsevier Science B.V. All rights reserved.

JEL classification: G100; G180; G200; G380; O160; P000

Keywords: Financial markets; Growth; Politics; Financial development; Reversals; Trade; Capital flows

[✩] This paper is a development of some ideas in a previous working paper entitled "The Politics of Financial Development." We thank the Bradley Foundation, the George J. Stigler Center for the Study of the Economy and the State, the Center for Research in Securities Prices, the Kauffman Foundation, and the World Bank for funding support. Rajan also thanks the National Science Foundation and M.I.T. for research support. Claudio Callegari, Henrik Cronqvist, Shola Fafunso, Isidro Ferrer, Jorg Kukies, Roger Laeven, Jamers Mello, Galina Ovtcharova, Nahid Rahman, Sofia Ramos, Ruy Ribeiro, Amir Sasson, and Elfani Wen provided excellent research assistantship and Arnoud Boot, Pratip Kar, Claus Parum, Kristian Rydqvist, and Elu Von Thadden provided invaluable help. We benefited from comments by Lucian Bebchuk, Stijn Claessens, Peter Hogfeldt, Louis Kaplow, Colin Mayer, Mark Ramseyer, Eric Rasmussen, Mark Roe, Andrei Shleifer, Richard Sylla, and an anonymous referee.
*Corresponding author. Tel.: +1-773-702-4437; fax: +1-773-834-8172.
E-mail address: raghuram.rajan@gsb.uchicago.edu (R.G. Rajan).

doi:10.1016/S0304-405X(03)00125-9

6 *R.G. Rajan, L. Zingales / Journal of Financial Economics 69 (2003) 5–50*

1. Introduction

There is a growing body of evidence indicating that the development of a country's financial sector greatly facilitates its economic growth (e.g., Demirguc-Kunt and Maksimovic, 1998; King and Levine, 1993; Jayaratne and Strahan, 1996; Rajan and Zingales, 1998a). Why then do so many countries still have underdeveloped financial sectors?

The simple answer, and one favored by many economists, is the absence of demand. Certainly demand is a prime driver of financial development, but it cannot be the only explanation. Demand (as proxied for by level of industrialization or economic development) cannot explain why countries at similar levels of economic development differ so much in the level of their financial development. For instance, why was France's stock market much bigger as a fraction of its gross domestic product (GDP) than markets in the United States in 1913, even though the per capita GDP in the United States was not any lower than France's? It is hard to imagine that the demand for financing in the United States at that time was inadequate. At the time, the demand for more, and cheaper, credit was a recurrent theme in political debates in the United States, and it was among the most industrialized countries in the world even then.

An alternative explanation is that there are structural impediments to supply rising to meet demand. Perhaps a country does not have the necessary levels of social capital (Guiso et al., 2000) or "savoir faire" to create a viable financial sector (e.g., Bencivenga and Smith, 1991; Greenwood and Jovanovic, 1990). Or perhaps it has not inherited the right legal, cultural, or political system. In particular, the seminal work of La Porta et al. (1997, 1998) shows that countries with a Common Law origin seem to have better minority investor protection, and furthermore, these countries have more highly developed equity markets. There has been some debate as to the precise channel through which a country's institutional inheritance affects its financial development (e.g., Berglof and Von Thadden, 1999; Coffee, 2000; Holmen and Hogfeldt, 2000; La Porta, et al., 1999a, 1999b; Rajan and Zingales, 1999; Stulz and Williamson, 2001). Some question whether the influence of certain forms of Civil Law heritage can be distinguished from the influence of a Common Law heritage (e.g., Beck et al., 1999). Yet, there is a burgeoning literature suggesting that a country's "structure" matters.

There are other implications, however, of structural theories of financial development. For instance, once a country has overcome the structural impediments, the supply of finance should rise to meet demand. In other words, we should not see measures of financial development waxing and waning independent of demand. Similarly, conditional on demand, the relative position of different countries should not change dramatically over time. If some countries have a system that is pre-disposed towards finance, that pre-disposition should continue to be relatively strong since structural factors are relatively time-invariant.

To test these implications, we collect various indicators of financial development for developed countries over the twentieth century. By most measures, countries were more financially developed in 1913 than in 1980 and only recently have they

R.G. Rajan, L. Zingales / Journal of Financial Economics 69 (2003) 5–50 7

surpassed their 1913 levels. Furthermore, even after controlling for the different levels of industrialization, the pattern across countries is quite different from the 1990s. In 1913, France's stock market capitalization (as a fraction of GDP) was almost twice that of the United States (0.78 vs. 0.39) even though the French Civil Code has never been friendly to investors (La Porta et al., 1998). By 1980, roles had reversed dramatically. France's capitalization was now barely one-fourth the capitalization in the United States (0.09 vs. 0.46). And in 1999, the two countries seem to be converging (1.17 vs. 1.52). More generally, in 1913, the main countries of continental Europe were more developed financially than the United States. What is especially interesting is that indicators of financial development fell in all countries after 1929, reaching their nadir around 1980. Since then, there has been a revival of financial markets.

In fact, in contrast to the findings of La Porta et al. (1997) for the 1990s, we find that countries with Common Law systems were not more financially developed in 1913. There is some indication that these differences had to do with differences in financial infrastructure. Tilly (1992) indicates that corporate share issues in Germany in the beginning of the Twentieth Century were greater than in England. He suggests this is because of the "paucity of information and relatively weak financial controls on the operations of company founders and insiders" (p. 103) in England. The common wisdom today is the reverse, that German corporations are much less transparent than corporations in the United Kingdom, as reflected by their lower scores on accounting standards.

The disruption in demand caused by the Great Depression and World War II are not sufficient to explain the reversal in financial markets. The economies of the hardest-hit countries recovered within a decade or two. Why did it take financial markets until the late 1980s to stage a recovery? Moreover, such a delay was not seen after the World War I.

All this is not to suggest that structural theories are incorrect, but that they are incomplete. A theory with a more variable factor is needed to explain both the time-series variation in financial development as well as the cross-sectional differences. In our view, the strength of political forces in favor of financial development is a major variable factor. The challenge for such a theory is to identify who is opposed to something as economically beneficial as financial development. We believe that incumbents, in the financial sector and in industry, can be hostile to arm's length markets. This is because arm's length financial markets do not respect the value of incumbency and instead can give birth to competition. There are occasions, however, when the incentives, or the ability, of incumbents to oppose development is muted. In particular, we argue that when a country's borders are open to both trade and capital flows, we see the opposition to financial development will be most muted and development will flourish.

Of course, the decision to open to trade and capital flows is also partly political. This raises two questions. First, why do some countries become more open than others, or open up at some times rather than at others—do the incumbents not oppose opening up? And second, how can we provide evidence of a causal link rather than simply a correlation: How can we argue that the link between openness and financial development should be interpreted as one causing the other rather than simply as evidence that incumbents who favor openness also favor financial development?

Let us answer the first question first. Some countries have no choice. Because they are small, or because they are close to other countries, they are likely to have more trade. Therefore, these countries are likely open for reasons that are not political. Also, even if the decision is political, countries' decisions whether to open up are likely strategic complements. If important parts of the world are open, then natural leakages across borders (the gray trade, smuggling, under-invoicing, over-invoicing, etc.) are likely to be high and make it hard for a country to remain closed. Moreover, groups that are in favor of openness (for example, exporters) are likely to gain in prospective profitability and strength relative to those who rely on controls, and they are likely to have more success in pressing for openness (e.g., Becker, 1983). The economic importance of other countries that are open can be thought of as largely exogenous to a country's domestic politics.

These observations suggest ways to test whether openness has a causal effect. First, in examining the link between trade openness and financial development, we instrument trade openness with a measure of natural openness (largely based on a country's distance from its trading partners) developed by Frankel and Romer (1999). We thus focus on the exogenous component of a country's trade. Because distance matters less for capital, we do not have a similar instrument for cross-border capital flows. But precisely because capital is more mobile, the strategic complementarities in cross-border capital flows are likely to be stronger. So we can use world-wide cross-border capital flows over time as an exogenous measure of whether countries are more open to capital flows. International capital mobility is high both in the beginning and towards the end of the twentieth century for most countries. Thus, we test in the cross-section of countries if financial development is positively correlated with the exogenous component of a country's openness to trade (correcting for the demand for finance), both in the beginning of the century and towards the end of the century, and it is.

By contrast, in the intermediate periods (from the 1930s to the 1970s) when cross-border capital flows had dwindled to a trickle for a variety of reasons, we find that trade openness did not have as strong a positive correlation (if at all) with financial development. These findings suggest that it takes the combination of openness in product and financial markets to mute incumbent incentives to oppose financial development. They also suggest a rationale for why indicators of financial development fell between the 1930s and the 1970s. Cross-border flows, especially of capital, were relatively small, so incumbents could oppose financial development without constraints.

We are, of course, not the first to point to the influence of private interests on financial development, though our focus is quite different from previous work. Jensen (1991) argues that legislation motivated by potential targets crimped the market for corporate control even while it was having salutary effects on US industry. Kroszner and Strahan (1999) explain the timing of financial liberalization across states in the United States in the 1970s and 1980s with variables that relate to

R.G. Rajan, L. Zingales / Journal of Financial Economics 69 (2003) 5–50 9

the power of private interest groups. Morck et al. (2000) find that the share prices of heir-controlled Canadian firms fell on news that the Canada–US free-trade agreement would be ratified. One reason they suggest is that the treaty had a provision for greater capital market openness, which would reduce the advantage heir-controlled firms had from access to capital. Bebchuk and Roe (1999) argue that corporate governance regimes will be strongly influenced by the initial positions of owners. Our paper is related to all these in that we also emphasize the role of private interests in retarding financial development, but we differ in that we attempt to find general patterns across countries.

We will postpone a discussion of the other related literature until we present the theoretical reasoning and tests. The rest of the paper is as follows. Section 2 describes how we collect the data and presents measures of financial-sector development in different countries at various points in the twentieth century. Section 3 presents our interest group theory of why some countries develop their financial systems (and others not) and argues why this could explain the reversals in the data. Section 4 tests both the time-series and cross-sectional implications of this theory. Section 5 concludes.

2. Evolution of financial development over the twentieth century

We are faced with two problems in analyzing the historical evolution of financial development over the twentieth century. First, it is difficult to obtain reliable sources for historical information about financial markets. In Appendix A, we describe how we deal with this problem. The second problem is how to measure financial development.

2.1. What do we mean by financial development?

The right measure would capture the ease with which any entrepreneur or company with a sound project can obtain finance, and the confidence with which investors anticipate an adequate return. Presumably, also, a developed financial sector can gauge, subdivide, and spread difficult risks, letting them rest where they can best be borne. Finally, it should do all this at low cost.

In our view, the most important word in the above definition is "any." In a perfect financial system, it will be the quality of the underlying assets or ideas that will determine whether finance is forthcoming, and the identity of the owner (to the extent it is orthogonal to the owner's capability of carrying out the project) will be irrelevant. Because our focus is on how easy it is to raise finance without prior connections or wealth, our measures of financial development will emphasize the availability of arm's length market finance (and if the data were available, the availability of non-relationship-based bank finance).

This choice is not innocuous. In some financial systems, capital is easily available for anyone within a circle of firms and financiers, but it does not percolate outside (e.g., Hellwig, 2000; Rajan and Zingales, 1998b). Most investment opportunities

10   *R.G. Rajan, L. Zingales / Journal of Financial Economics 69 (2003) 5–50*

originate within this closed group, and this group can undertake more daring investment than would be possible in an economy with more widespread access. We would not deem this economy to be financially developed. In a sense, we adopt the Schumpeterian view that a critical role of finance is creative destruction, and this is possible only if there is a constant flow of capital into new firms and out of old firms.

Our definition of development then suggests different ratios of the size of arm's length markets to the size of the economy as our measures of financial development. For example, measures include ratios such as equity market capitalization to GDP, volume of equity issues to gross fixed-capital formation, or number of listed firms to population in millions. While they are no doubt crude proxies, these ratios broadly capture a country's level of financial sophistication and they are standard in the literature. For the sake of comparison, we will also report a measure of the development of the banking sector.

2.2. Various measures of financial development

Let us now describe the various indicators of financial development we use.

2.2.1. Banking sector

We use the ratio of deposits (commercial banks plus savings banks) to GDP as a measure of the development of the banking sector. One shortcoming is that this measure captures only the liability side of banks, ignoring differences in the composition of the banks' assets. Another shortcoming is that this measure cannot indicate if banks operate as a cartel, forming a closed shop to new industrial entrants. Despite this shortcoming, the measure has the virtue that it is available for a long time-series and for a large cross-section of countries. In more recent periods, we have domestic credit from the private sector to GDP, which will be our measure of banking-sector development.

2.2.2. Equity issues

One measure of the importance of equity markets is the fraction of investments that are funded through equity issues. The proxy we use is the ratio of equity issues by domestic corporations to gross fixed capital formation (GFCF) during the year. Ideally, we would have liked to normalize corporate equity issues by the amount of corporate investments, but this datum is not consistently available. In interpreting the results, therefore, it is important to realize that our measure will tend to underestimate the level of financial development of countries where agriculture (which does not enter in corporate investments but does enter in total investments) is more significant. It will also tend to underestimate the level of financial development in the earlier part of the century, when corporate investments were a smaller fraction of total investments.

Another drawback of this measure stems from the well-known cyclicality of equity issues. A disproportionate amount of equity issues are concentrated during boom years (Choe et al., 1993). This can bias cross-country comparisons to the extent stock market booms are not contemporaneous across economies. It also biases the

R.G. Rajan, L. Zingales / Journal of Financial Economics 69 (2003) 5–50 11

time-series comparisons if one of the reference years is a boom year. To minimize the problem, we average issues over a number of years when we have easy access to annual data.

2.2.3. Capitalization

A more stable measure of the importance of the equity market is the total stock market capitalization. A drawback is this measure captures the amount of equity listed, not the amount of equity raised. Thus, the presence of few companies that have greatly appreciated in value can give the impression of an important equity market even when the amount of funds raised in the market is tiny. On the positive side, however, this measure is less cyclical than the previous one and thus is better for making comparisons across countries and across time periods.

In measuring both equity issues and stock market capitalization we restrict ourselves whenever possible to domestic companies. At the beginning of the twentieth century, London and Paris attracted foreign listings. More recently, New York attracts many foreign listings. We are especially interested, however, in how a country's financial and legal institutions help domestic industries raise funds, and as some have argued (e.g., Kennedy, 1989), the financial sector's ability to fund foreigners may not imply an ability to fund domestic firms. Moreover, our focus reduces the possibility of mechanical correlations in our tests. This is why we limit ourselves to domestic companies.

2.2.4. Number of companies listed

A final indicator of the importance of equity markets is the number of publicly traded domestic companies per million of population. This is a measure that is not tainted by fluctuations in stock market valuations and possible mismeasurement of the level of GDP. This also suggests a drawback. It could be too slow-moving a measure to fully capture high frequency changes in the environment. Also, the measure will be affected by the process of consolidation as well as by the fragmentation of the industrial structure. Countries with a more concentrated industrial structure will have fewer, but larger, companies and thus might score low according to this measure. Since concentration will reflect, only in part, limited access to finance, this measure will be a noisy proxy for what we want to capture.

One indicator that is missing from our list is the volume of securities traded. Unfortunately, the way volume is recorded (even today) is quite controversial. The Federation Internationale Bourses Valeurs (FIBV) classifies data on volume traded into two groups: trading system view (TSV) and regulated environment view (REV). The TSV system counts as volume only those transactions which pass through the exchange's trading floor, or which take place on the exchange's trading floor. The REV system includes in volume all the transactions subject to supervision by the market authority, with no distinction between on- and off-market transactions. As the FIBV warns, comparisons are not valid between stock exchanges belonging to different groups, because the numbers differ substantially depending on method used. For example, in Paris, according to the TSV method the volume of equity traded in 1999 was $770,076 million, while the REV method suggests a volume four times greater ($2,892,301 million). Given the magnitude of the difference and the impossibility of obtaining consistent data both across countries and over time, we chose to disregard this indicator.

In sum, any indicator has its own drawbacks. This is the reason why they should be looked at together to get a better sense of the development of a country's financial structure.

2.3. Stylized facts

In Table 1, we report the average value of our four indicators of financial development for the period 1913–1999. The countries in our sample are those for which we could get pre-World War II financial market data. Since the availability of data on financial development has exploded recently, we include all the countries whose data we can get in our tests for the most recent years. For every indicator we report both the average across all available observations and the average for the countries with observations throughout the sample period. In Tables 2–5 we report the value of each indicator for each country. An examination of these tables suggests the following facts.

2.3.1. Financial systems were highly developed in 1913

Regardless of the way we measure, the average level of financial development in 1913 is quite high, comparable to that in 1980 or 1990. The average ratio of deposits to GDP in 1913 is very similar to that in 1980 (see Table 1). The absence of an upward trend reflects the fact that countries depend less on banks and more on financial markets as they develop economically. But the data on the capitalization of the stock market (Tables 1 and 3) suggest that in most countries equity markets were bigger relative to GDP in 1913 than in 1980. Only by the end of the 1990s do they seem to exceed their 1913 level.

Equity issues also an important source of funds for corporate investments than 1980 (and even 1990) for most countries whose data we have (see Tables 1 and 4). This is particularly noteworthy when we recognize that the 1913 figures are biased downwards relative to the 1990 ones, because we normalize by Gross Fixed Capital Formation, and corporate investments represent a much smaller proportion of GFCF in 1913 than in 1990.

Most countries have the same number of listed companies per million people in 1913 as in 1980 (see Tables 1 and 5). In some countries, even with the explosion of financial markets during the late 1990s, the 1913 level has not been surpassed.

While, in general, the richest countries had highly developed financial sectors in 1913, the degree of development does vary widely. The level of economic development explains only 14% of the cross-country variation in the deposit-to-GDP ratio and it is not even statistically significant in explaining the level of equity market capitalization. For example, in 1913 Argentina shows about the same per capita GDP as Germany and France, but its level of deposits is only about two-thirds that of France and Germany. Similarly, our data show that in 1913

R.G. Rajan, L. Zingales / Journal of Financial Economics 69 (2003) 5–50 13

Table 1

Evolution of the different indicators of financial development

Whole sample indicates an average across all the countries we have data for. Constant sample indicates an average across countries for which we have data every year. Deposits to GDP is the ratio of commercial and savings bank deposits to GDP. Stock market cap to GDP is the ratio of the aggregate market value of equity of domestic companies divided by GDP. Number of companies to population is the ratio of number of domestic companies whose equity is publicly traded in a domestic stock exchange to the country's population in millions. Equity issues to GFCF is the ratio of funds raised through public equity offerings (both initial public offerings and seasoned equity issues) by domestic companies to gross fixed capital formation. N is the number of observations. Sources are in the Data Appendix, which is available on request from the authors.

Year	Deposits to GDP			Stock market cap to GDP			No. of companies to population			Equity issues to GFCF		
	Whole	N	Constant sample (N=20)	Whole	N	Constant sample	Whole	N	Constant sample	Whole	N	Constant sample (N=7)
1913	0.38	22	0.40	0.57	22	0.40	28.68	22	24.00	0.12	12	0.13
1929	0.49	21	0.51	0.60	11	0.53	33.80	14	27.75	0.35	15	0.34
1938	0.45	21	0.46	0.58	13	0.57	30.12	13	27.69	0.13	12	0.10
1950	0.33	22	0.34	0.30	14	0.27	38.63	16	23.80	0.06	11	0.03
1960	0.31	22	0.33	0.47	18	0.44	31.85	19	22.38	0.07	16	0.05
1970	0.31	22	0.33	0.49	19	0.42	23.66	19	21.22	0.06	16	0.02
1980	0.34	22	0.35	0.26	22	0.25	26.70	21	23.71	0.03	18	0.03
1990	0.41	21	0.40	0.57	21	0.51	22.18	22	23.21	0.05	20	0.05
1999	0.46	21	0.45	1.02	23	1.08	26.30	22	24.46	0.13	20	0.18

Table 2
Evolution of the ratio of deposits to GDP
Deposits to GDP is the ratio of commercial and savings deposits divided by GDP. Until 1990 the source is
Mitchell (1995). We extrapolate the 1999 data from the 1994 data in Mitchell using the rate of growth of
deposits as reported in *International Financial Statistics* published by the International Monetary Fund.

Country	Year								
	1913	1929	1938	1950	1960	1970	1980	1990	1999
Argentina	0.29	0.36	0.36	0.30	0.22	0.19	0.28	0.07	0.24
Australia	0.37	0.45	0.45	0.69	0.43	0.38	0.29	0.42	0.49
Austria	1.12	0.37	0.33	0.21	0.28	0.31	0.62	0.73	0.70
Belgium	0.68	0.48	0.69	0.44	0.35	0.40	0.39	0.38	0.85
Brazil	0.12	0.16	0.21	0.20	0.15	0.12	0.17		
Canada	0.22	0.13	0.16	0.17	0.13	0.37	0.47	0.49	0.61
Chile	0.16	0.15	0.09	0.10	0.06	0.07	0.07	0.12	0.19
Cuba									
Denmark	0.76	0.46	0.39	0.32	0.27	0.25	0.28	0.55	0.54
Egypt				0.17	0.17	0.14	0.31	0.67	0.51
France	0.42	0.44	0.36	0.24	0.30	0.33	0.45	0.42	0.47
Germany	0.53	0.27	0.25	0.15	0.23	0.29	0.30	0.32	0.35
India	0.04	0.09	0.12	0.08	0.08	0.09	0.08	0.09	0.09
Italy	0.23	0.21	0.31	0.23	0.81	0.54	0.59	0.40	0.28
Japan	0.13	0.22	0.52	0.14	0.21	0.33	0.48	0.51	0.53
Netherlands	0.22	0.32	0.52	0.28	0.28	0.26	0.25	0.73	0.69
Norway	0.65	0.89	0.56	0.52	0.43	0.49	0.30	0.50	0.49
Russia	0.21								
South Africa	0.09	0.09	0.16	0.18	0.18	0.16	0.12	0.16	0.21
Spain	0.07	0.24	0.24	0.33	0.37	0.53	0.44	0.66	0.71
Sweden	0.69	0.69	0.73	0.59	0.54	0.50	0.48	0.40	0.39
Switzerland	0.93	1.08	1.13	0.79	0.78	0.69	0.69	0.54	0.66
UK	0.10	2.88	1.34	0.67	0.32	0.22	0.14	0.33	0.39
US	0.33	0.33	0.44	0.40	0.30	0.25	0.18	0.19	0.17

Argentina's per capita GDP was three times as big as Japan's, but the relative size of
its equity market was only one-third of Japan's.

2.3.2. Countries most advanced in 1913 do not necessarily stay advanced

By our measures, countries that were financially developed in 1913 do not
necessarily continue to be so. In 1913, equity issues appear more important in
France, Belgium, and Russia than in the United States. Thus, by this measure, some
continental European markets seem at least as developed as the US market at that
time. The data on market capitalization in Table 3 confirm this impression. While
the UK had a high capitalization in 1913, Belgium, France, Germany, and Sweden
were all ahead of the United States. Recent studies highlight the distinction between
Civil Law continental European economies and Common Law Anglo-American
economies, but the early data do not confirm this. In fact, this distinction seems to be
a post-World War II phenomenon implying financial markets in Civil Law countries

R.G. Rajan, L. Zingales / Journal of Financial Economics 69 (2003) 5–50   15

Table 3

Evolution of stock market capitalization over GDP

Stock market capitalization to GDP is the ratio of the aggregate market value of equity of domestic companies to GDP. Sources are in the Data Appendix, which is available on request from the authors.

Country	Year								
	1913	1929	1938	1950	1960	1970	1980	1990	1999
Argentina	0.17				0.05	0.03	0.11		0.15
Australia	0.39	0.50	0.91	0.75	0.94	0.76	0.38	0.37	1.13
Austria	0.76					0.09	0.03	0.17	0.17
Belgium	0.99	1.31			0.32	0.23	0.09	0.31	0.82
Brazil	0.25						0.05	0.08	0.45
Canada	0.74		1.00	0.57	1.59	1.75	0.46	1.22	1.22
Chile	0.17				0.12	0.00	0.34	0.50	1.05
Cuba	2.19								
Denmark	0.36	0.17	0.25	0.10	0.14	0.17	0.09	0.67	0.67
Egypt	1.09				0.16		0.01	0.06	0.29
France	0.78		0.19	0.08	0.28	0.16	0.09	0.24	1.17
Germany	0.44	0.35	0.18	0.15	0.35	0.16	0.09	0.20	0.67
India	0.02	0.07	0.07	0.07	0.07	0.06	0.05	0.16	0.46
Italy	0.17	0.23	0.26	0.07	0.42	0.14	0.07	0.13	0.68
Japan	0.49	1.20	1.81	0.05	0.36	0.23	0.33	1.64	0.95
Netherlands	0.56		0.74	0.25	0.67	0.42	0.19	0.50	2.03
Norway	0.16	0.22	0.18	0.21	0.26	0.23	0.54	0.23	0.70
Russia	0.18								0.11
South Africa				0.68	0.91	1.97	1.23	1.33	1.20
Spain							0.17	0.41	0.69
Sweden	0.47	0.41	0.30	0.18	0.24	0.14	0.11	0.39	1.77
Switzerland	0.58					0.50	0.44	1.93	3.23
UK	1.09	1.38	1.14	0.77	1.06	1.63	0.38	0.81	2.25
US	0.39	0.75	0.56	0.33	0.61	0.66	0.46	0.54	1.52

appear to have declined more between 1913 and the early 1990s (though the gap has narrowed since).

Another way of seeing the change in patterns is to compute the correlation between indicators of financial development at different points in time. Using the Spearman rank correlation test, we find a correlation of 0.4 between capitalization to GDP in 1913 and capitalization to GDP in 1999. We reject the hypothesis that the two distributions across countries are independent at the 10% level (21 observations). The cross-country pattern of financial development in 1999 is positively correlated with that in 1913. However, this is not true a decade earlier. The correlation of the 1913 data with 1990 and 1980 data is lower (0.21 in 1990, −0.07 in 1980), and we cannot reject the hypothesis that the distributions are independent.

By way of comparison, consider the cross-country correlation of per-capita GDP measured at two different points in time. Using the Spearman rank correlation test, we find a correlation of 0.55 between per-capita GDP in 1913 and per-capita GDP in 1999 (independence rejected at the 1% level with 22 observations). The correlation of the 1913 data with 1990 and 1980 data is equally high (0.62 for 1990, 0.73 for 1980).

16   *R.G. Rajan, L. Zingales / Journal of Financial Economics 69 (2003) 5–50*

Table 4
Evolution of fraction of gross fixed-capital formation raised via equity
Amount of funds raised through public equity offerings (both initial public offerings and seasoned equity issues) by domestic companies divided by gross fixed capital formation. Sources are in the Data Appendix, which is available on request from the authors.

Country	1913	1929	1938	1950	1960	1970	1980	1990	1999
Argentina					0.01		0.01	0.10	0.02
Australia		0.13		0.19	0.09	0.05	0.05	0.09	0.24
Austria		0.07			0.04	0.07	0.00	0.07	0.03
Belgium	0.23	0.85	0.03		0.09	0.08	0.03	0.01	0.06
Brazil				0.20	0.19	0.19	0.06	0.01	0.07
Canada		1.34	0.02	0.03	0.03	0.01	0.04	0.01	0.07
Chile									
Cuba									
Denmark		0.03	0.01				0.01	0.08	0.09
Egypt									0.31
France	0.14	0.26	0.03	0.02	0.04	0.04	0.06	0.02	0.09
Germany	0.07	0.17	0.06	0.00	0.04	0.02	0.01	0.04	0.06
India						0.00	0.00	0.00	0.08
Italy	0.07	0.26	0.03	0.02	0.08	0.02	0.04	0.04	0.12
Japan	0.08	0.13	0.75		0.15	0.03	0.01	0.02	0.08
Netherlands	0.38	0.61	0.45	0.02	0.02	0.00	0.01	0.10	0.67
Norway		0.05	0.01					0.04	0.06
Russia	0.17								
South Africa						0.33	0.08	0.10	0.14
Spain	0.01	0.33		0.08	0.11	0.07	0.03	0.06	0.10
Sweden	0.08	0.34	0.06	0.01	0.03	0.00	0.00	0.03	0.10
Switzerland	0.03				0.02			0.02	
UK	0.14	0.35	0.09	0.08	0.09	0.01	0.04	0.06	0.09
US	0.04	0.38	0.01	0.04	0.02	0.07	0.04	0.04	0.12

Thus over long periods, the relative ranking of countries according to financial development seems more volatile than ranking according to economic development.

2.3.3. Indicators of financial development fall then rise between 1913 and 1999

The most striking fact that emerges from Table 1 is that indicators of financial development fall considerably and then rise again. It is not easy to define precisely where the indicators start falling, but the data suggest that the turning point is somewhere in the 1930s or 1940s.

It is worth noting that the decline in indicators is not limited to the countries that lost the war, although it is more pronounced for such countries. It is not even seen only in countries involved in the war, since we see it in Sweden, Argentina, and Brazil. Finally, it cannot be attributed to a decline in the standard of living, since during the period (from 1938 to 1950) the average per-capita GDP in 1990 dollars increased from $4,036 to $4,644.

R.G. Rajan, L. Zingales / Journal of Financial Economics 69 (2003) 5–50 17

Table 5
Evolution of number of listed companies per million people
The number of listed companies per million people is the number of domestic companies whose equity is publicly traded in a domestic stock exchange divided by the population in millions. Sources are in the Data Appendix, which is available on request from the authors.

Country	Year								
	1913	1929	1938	1950	1960	1970	1980	1990	1999
Argentina	15.29				26.78	15.58	9.85	5.54	3.63
Australia	61.74	76.92	84.88	122.05	93.72		68.53	63.89	64.91
Austria	38.72	42.62	30.06	16.29	13.34	12.05	8.74	12.57	12.02
Belgium	108.7			55.09	42.60	38.39	22.85	18.50	14.33
Brazil	12.43	9.85	5.17	41.02		4.32	4.06	3.86	3.18
Canada	14.65			66.61	62.43	55.20	50.52	42.99	130.13
Chile	20.62				44.52	38.72	23.78	16.32	19.03
Cuba	12.69								
Denmark	38.22	54.86	85.25	81.28	75.75	52.14	42.54	50.18	44.80
Egypt	16.58	13.44			10.58	1.76		11.01	13.71
France	13.29		24.64	26.20	18.34	15.98	13.99	15.05	
Germany	27.96	19.73	10.91	13.22	11.33	9.07	7.46	6.53	12.74
India	0.82	1.81	2.59	3.13	0.00	0.00	3.11	7.31	6.48
Italy	6.32	6.40	3.11	2.70	2.79	2.46	2.36	3.82	4.54
Japan	7.53	16.65	19.48	9.15	8.35	15.19	14.80	16.76	20.00
Netherlands	65.87	95.48			21.42	15.95	15.12	17.39	15.14
Norway	33.51	41.50	45.98	37.98	37.10	37.90	44.53	44.80	49.62
Russia	2.02								0.81
South Africa				69.05	60.93	51.39	42.48	20.75	15.86
Spain							25.20	10.96	22.25
Sweden	20.64	16.36	14.93	12.83	14.04	13.18	12.39	14.14	31.46
Switzerland	61.53	67.80	55.46	52.47	51.74	58.72	78.03	49.61	34.01
UK	47.06						47.22	29.63	31.11
US	4.75	9.72	9.16	8.94	9.33	11.48	23.11	26.41	28.88

While we cannot also date the recovery in indicators precisely, the turning point lies somewhere in the 1970s or 1980s. Over the 1980s and 1990s, for the countries reporting throughout, the average ratio of deposits to GDP increased by 35%, the average ratio of stock market capitalization to GDP increased four times, as did the fraction of GFCF raised via equity. The number of listed domestic companies shows a more modest increase (30%).

3. An interest group theory of financial development

We now describe a parsimonious theory to explain broad patterns in the data. In essence, our theory suggests why financial development can differ so much between countries at similar levels of economic and industrial development. It also suggests a reason for reversals. No doubt, the specifics of each country will differ and the theory, on occasion, can seem a caricature, but this is the price we have to pay for parsimony.

18   *R.G. Rajan, L. Zingales / Journal of Financial Economics 69 (2003) 5–50*

3.1. The necessity for government intervention

The essential ingredients of a developed financial system include the following: (1) respect for property rights, (2) an accounting and disclosure system that promotes transparency, (3) a legal system that enforces arm's length contracts cheaply, and (4) a regulatory infrastructure that protects consumers, promotes competition, and controls egregious risk-taking.

No doubt, private arrangements could go some way in achieving all this. But the government has the ability to coordinate standards and enforce non-monetary punishments such as jail terms. Such power gives it some advantage in laying out and policing the ducts in which financial plumbing will go. For instance, a number of studies suggest that the mandatory disclosures required by the Securities Act of 1933 did improve the accuracy of pricing of securities (e.g., Simon, 1989). Given that government action is needed for financial development, the focus of our inquiry then shifts to when there is a political will to undertake these actions.

3.2. The political economy of financial development

Financial development is so beneficial that it seems strange that anyone would oppose it. However, financial development is not always win-win. It could pose a threat to some.

Consider, for instance, established large industrial firms in an economy, a group we will call industrial incumbents. In normal times, these incumbents do not require a developed financial system. They can finance new projects out of earnings (as most established firms do) without accessing external capital markets. Even when their business does not generate sufficient cash to fund desired investments, they can use the collateral from existing projects and their prior reputation to borrow. Such borrowing does not require much sophistication from the financial system. Even a primitive system will provide funds willingly against collateral. Because of their privileged access to finance in underdeveloped financial systems, incumbents enjoy a positional rent. Anybody else who starts a promising business has to sell it to the incumbents or get them to fund it. Thus, not only do incumbents enjoy some rents in the markets they operate in, but they also end up appropriating most of the returns from new ventures.

These rents will be impaired by financial development. Better disclosure rules and enforcement in a developed financial market will reduce the relative importance of incumbents' collateral and reputation, while permitting newcomers to enter and compete away profits.

Similar arguments apply to incumbent financiers. While financial development provides them with an opportunity to expand their activities, it also strikes at their very source of comparative advantage. In the absence of good disclosure and proper enforcement, financing is typically relationship-based. The financier uses connections to obtain information to monitor loans, and uses various informal levers of power to cajole repayment. The key, therefore, to the ability to lend is relationships with those who have influence over the firm (managers, other lenders, suppliers, politicians, etc.)

R.G. Rajan, L. Zingales / Journal of Financial Economics 69 (2003) 5–50 19

and the ability to monopolize the provision of finance to a client (either through a monopoly over firm-specific information, or through a friendly cartel amongst financiers). Disclosure and impartial enforcement tend to level the playing field and reduce barriers to an entrance into the financial sector. The incumbent financier's old skills become redundant, while new ones of credit evaluation and risk management become necessary. Financial development not only introduces competition, which destroys the financial institution's rents and relationships (e.g., Petersen and Rajan, 1995), it also destroys the financier's human capital.[1]

In sum, a more efficient financial system facilitates entry, and thus leads to lower profits for incumbent firms and financial institutions. From the perspective of incumbents, the competition-enhancing effects of financial development can offset the other undoubted benefits that financial development brings. Moreover, markets tend to be democratic, and they particularly jeopardize ways of doing business that rely on unequal access. Thus, not only are incumbents likely to benefit less from financial development, they can actually lose. This would imply that as a collective, incumbents have a vested interest in preventing financial development. They may also be small enough (e.g., Olson, 1965; Stigler, 1971) to organize successfully against financial development. In doing so, they will rely on other incumbent groups (such as organized labor). Previous studies show such groups benefit from an economy with limited competition. For example, Salinger (1984) and Rose (1987) provide evidence that unions share in rents from industrial concentration.

Critical to the above arguments is that financial development aids the entrance of new firms, thus enhancing competition. There is some evidence for this. In a comparative study of the textile industry in Mexico and Brazil around the beginning of the twentieth century, Haber (1997) shows that Brazil, following its political revolution, liberalized finance, and saw the textile industry grow faster and become less concentrated than the Mexican textile industry. Porfirio Diaz, the Mexican dictator during this period, was much more a prisoner of incumbent interests. Mexico's financial markets remained underdeveloped during his regime, with the consequence that Mexico's textile industry, while starting out larger and relatively more competitive, had less opportunities for entry, and ended up smaller and more concentrated than Brazil's.

Studies of larger samples of countries support the idea that financial development facilitates the entry of newcomers. Rajan and Zingales (1998a) find that the growth in the number of new establishments is significantly higher in industries dependent on external finance when the economy is financially developed. In a study of trade credit in transitional economies, Johnson et al. (2000) find that an important consequence of an effective legal system is that a firm offers more trade credit to new trading partners. Firms that believe in the effectiveness of the legal system are also more likely to seek out new trading partners.

---

[1] One could also argue for the existence of political incumbents. The relationship between financial development and political incumbency is less clear-cut.

3.3. Financial repression is not the only way to protect incumbent rents

Financial underdevelopment is not the only barrier to newcomers. Incumbents with political influence could restrict or prevent entry into their industry directly through some kind of licensing scheme. There are, however, reasons why some prefer financial underdevelopment to more direct barriers.

First, direct-entry restrictions often require very costly enforcement. Enforcement becomes particularly difficult, if not impossible, when innovation can create substitutes for the product whose market is restricted. Each new threatening innovation has to be identified, categorized, and then banned. Second, the active enforcement of restrictions on entry is very public and, therefore, politically transparent. Citizens are unlikely to remain rationally ignorant when confronted with such blatant opportunism, especially when they face the poor service and extortionate prices of the local monopoly. By contrast, the malign neglect that leads to financial underdevelopment is less noticeable (it goes with the grain to have comatose bureaucrats who do not act rather than have overly active ones) and can be disguised under more noble motives such as protecting citizens from charlatans. Leaving finance underdeveloped is an act of omission with few of the costs entailed by an act of commission such as the use of the apparatus of the state to stamp out entry.

In general, however, we would expect direct entry restrictions and financial underdevelopment to be used as complementary tools. In Fig. 1, we graph the Djankov et al. (2002) measure of the number of procedures in different countries to start a business (a measure of the direct barriers to entry) against the size of equity

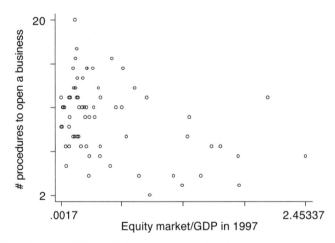

Fig. 1. Regulation of entry and financial development. On the *x*-axis we report a measure of financial development: the ratio of equity market capitalization to GDP in 1997 (average 1996–1998, from the World Bank's World Development Indicators). On the *y*-axis we report a measure of direct regulation of entry. As a measure of direct regulation we use the number of procedures necessary to open a business, as computed by Djankov et al. (2002). As the graph shows there is a clear negative correlation between the two. Countries that regulate entry more tend also to be less financially developed.

R.G. Rajan, L. Zingales / Journal of Financial Economics 69 (2003) 5–50 21

markets relative to GDP in that country. The correlation is significantly negative, and regression estimates (not reported) show that it persists after correcting for the level of GDP. Financial underdevelopment does seem present along with other bureaucratic barriers, and this suggests a common purpose.

3.4. What determines outcomes?

In an industrialized economy, incumbent industrialists and financiers ordinarily would have enough political power, because of their large economic weight and small numbers, to collectively decide the development of the economy's financial sector. In earlier times, the landed gentry could have been more powerful in many developed countries than the "commercial" interests. How their power waned is a matter beyond the scope of this paper (though see Rajan and Zingales (2003) for one account). So financial development will take place only when the country's political structure changes dramatically, or when the incumbents want development to take place.

By creating a fresh power structure, political change can foster anti-incumbent institutions, one of which is financial infrastructure. For example, a number of new mortgage banks and institutions like the Credit Mobilier were supported by the government of Louis Napoleon after its coming to power in 1848. They were meant as a counter to the Bank of France and the Rothschilds who were thought to be sympathetic to the deposed monarchy (e.g., Cameron, 1961). More recently, Weber and Davis (2000) find that a country's transition to a multi-party democracy increases its estimated rate of creation of a stock exchange by 134% during the subsequent 3 years.

If, however, we examine a period of relatively little structural political change, we should see finance develop faster when both financial and industrial incumbents will it to do so and slower when both are against it. When one of these powerful groups is for development and the other is against, predictions are more ambiguous.

Incumbent incentives are powerfully affected by competition, especially that emanating from outside their political borders, which they cannot control. The degree to which a country's borders are open to both the flow of trade and capital is thus likely to matter. Of course, an important question is what causes a country to be open. We will address this shortly. But first let us examine how incumbent incentives can altered by cross-border competition.

3.5. Financial development and openness

Consider a country that is open to trade. While foreign markets bring opportunity, openness also brings foreign competitors to domestic markets. Foreign entry drives down domestic rents. Lower profits means established firms have lower internal cash flow, making them more dependent on external finance. At the same time, outside opportunities (or the need to defend domestic markets against superior foreign technologies) increase the need for incumbents to invest more.

22 *R.G. Rajan, L. Zingales / Journal of Financial Economics 69 (2003) 5–50*

Unfortunately, the need for external finance need not translate into reforms that improve transparency and access in the financial system. In fact, given their greater need for finance, industrial incumbents can press for greater financial repression so that the available finance flows their way. Financial incumbents can also be unwilling to accept the increased competition in the financial sector (from greater transparency and access) in exchange for the additional industrial clientele that reforms generate. It may be far more profitable to support the existing relationships with industrial incumbents and ply them with greater amounts of capital they now need.

Industrial incumbents can also petition the government for loan subsidies in the face of foreign competition, instead of improving the quality of the domestic financial system. Selective government intervention can further reduce the transparency of, and the access to, the financial system. Thus openness to trade flows (i.e., industrial sector openness) alone may not be enough to convince either, or both, dominant interest groups to support financial development.

Consider next the possibility of cross-border capital flows (or financial openness) alone. Free access to international capital markets will allow the largest and best-known domestic firms to tap foreign markets for funds. But in the absence of domestic or foreign competition in product markets, these firms will have little need to access external funds. And given the state of information asymmetries across markets, it is unlikely that small domestic firms are financed directly by foreign investors. If potential domestic entrants are not financed by foreigners, industrial incumbents will still retain an incentive to keep entrants at bay by opposing financial development. The domestic financial sector will see its sizeable profits from providing finance and services to the largest industrial firms diminish as these firms threaten to tap foreign financial markets and institutions. It will face the opposition of domestic industrial incumbents if it tries to liberalize access and improve transparency. So cross-border capital flows alone are unlikely to convince both our interest groups to push for financial development.

It is when both cross-border trade flows and capital flows are unimpeded that industrial and financial incumbents will have convergent incentives to push for financial development. Industrial incumbents, with depleted profits and the need for new investment, will need funds to meet foreign challenges. But with free cross-border capital flows, the government's role in directing credit to incumbents will become more circumscribed. As product markets become more competitive, the risks in, and information requirements for, lending will increase. The potential for large errors from the centralized direction of credit will increase. Moreover, the ability of the government to provide large subsidized loans to favored firms will decrease as mobile capital forces governments to maintain macro-economic prudence. For example, Loriaux (1997), provides a description of the constraints on French intervention in domestic credit in the 1980s. The government's role in the financial sector will diminish.

The healthiest industrial incumbents will tap the now open foreign markets for finance. These firms, able to compete in international markets, may not be much worried, or affected, by domestic entry, and thus may not oppose domestic financial development. While the not-so-healthy industrial incumbents can be the hardest hit by foreign product market competition, there are reasons why they, too, will not oppose financial development and in fact support it. They will need finance. And their existing financiers will be reluctant to lend to them on the old cozy terms. Because of product market competition, these firms will now be much less profitable, while needing much more investment. Moreover, competition in financial markets will make long-term relationships, through which the traditional financier could have hoped to recover investments, more difficult. Both factors would combine to make finance more difficult. Difficulty in financing will lead these firms to push for greater transparency and access so that their own access to finance improves. Unlike the case when the country is only open to capital flows, industrial incumbents now will also push for financial development. The accompanying threat of domestic industrial entry will now seem relatively minor, given the competitive state of product markets.

Moreover, as the domestic financial sector loses some of its best clients, domestic financial institutions will want to seek new clients among the unborn or younger industrial firms that hitherto did not have the relationships to obtain finance. Since these clients will be riskier, and less well known, financial institutions will have no alternative but to press for improved disclosure and better contract enforcement. In turn, this leveling of the playing field will create the conditions for more entry and competition in the financial sector.

An example of such a virtuous circle is provided by Rosenbluth (1989). As the most reputable Japanese exporters escaped their financial system in the 1980s to raise arm's length finance from the Euromarkets, Japanese banks were forced to change their practices. One beneficial outcome is that access to the Japanese corporate bond markets, that hitherto had been tightly controlled by the banks, is now liberalized.

Other influences will kick in over time. As the domestic financial incumbents improve their skills, they will seek to compete abroad. As they look for new clients outside, they will be forced as a quid pro quo to increase access for foreigners and dismantle domestic regulations that give them their privileged competitive positions. For example, the German government banned lead underwriting of Deutschmark bonds by Japanese financial institutions until Japan agreed in 1985 to allow foreign securities firms to act as lead underwriters for Euroyen bonds (e.g., Rosenbluth, 1989). Foreign financial firms that enter the domestic market are another powerful constituency for financial development. Since they are not part of the domestic social and political networks, they would prefer transparent arm's length contracts and enforcement procedures to opaque negotiated arrangements. It is not a coincidence that these are the very requirements of would-be domestic entrepreneurs who are also outsiders to the domestic clubs.

4. A test of the private interest theory of financial development

Direct measures of the political power of interest groups and their ability to influence outcomes are controversial at best. The following example should illustrate the problems. French financial liberalization was kicked off in 1983 by a Socialist government. Socialists do not seem to be an interest group that would push for

24   *R.G. Rajan, L. Zingales / Journal of Financial Economics 69 (2003) 5–50*

liberalization. A more detailed examination of the facts (e.g., Helleiner, 1994) suggests that there was a liberalizing faction in the French Socialist party, led by Prime Minister Pierre Mauroy and Finance Minister Jacques Delors, whose hand was strengthened by France's increased trade integration into the European Community. This faction argued that liberalization was necessary to preserve trade and won the day. How could one ever hope to capture the strength of such factions in a large sample cross-country study without a subjective country-by-country exercise?

Our theory, however, does lead to some indirect, but more objective, tests. According to it, incumbent interests are least able to coordinate to obstruct or reverse financial development when a country is open to both trade and capital flows. When a country is open to neither, they coordinate to keep finance under heel. Matters are unlikely to be much better when a country is open only to capital flows or only to trade. In the former case, incumbent industrial interests can hold back financial development, fearful of the domestic competition that might be financed. In the latter case, both industrial and financial incumbents want to strengthen existing financial relationships to combat the foreign threat. Free access and transparency are likely to get short shrift at such times.

4.1. A test

To test the theory, we need a measure of financial development. The amount of funds raised from arm's length financial markets or the amount of credit offered by competitive banking systems could be measures (albeit crude) of financial development. Unfortunately, we do not know how competitive the banking system is. Instead, we only have measures of the quantity of deposits. The banking system could be concentrated and captive to incumbent interests, dominated by state owned banks, or just plain inefficient. Therefore, we prefer to use the size of the arm's length financial markets as our measure of development. This also accords well with the view that arm's length markets will emerge only when financial infrastructure such as disclosure requirements (e.g., Sylla and Smith, 1995) and investor protection are reasonably developed (e.g., La Porta et al., 1998). Meanwhile banks can exist even when infrastructure is primitive (e.g., Rajan and Zingales, 1998b).

The obvious test would be to regress measures of financial development against measures of openness. But we are immediately faced with another issue. A country's openness to trade and capital flows is also a matter of government policy, liable to influence by different interest groups. A large literature (e.g., Gourevitch, 1986; Rogowski, 1989; O'Rourke and Williamson, 1999) suggests that the decision to open up or close down an economy to trade is a political one, based on the relative strengths of the sectors that stand to gain or lose from openness. This creates a potential problem. A country may open to trade when it sees opportunity, yet is also likely to be a time that financial markets expand. A correlation between trade openness and the size of financial markets can simply reflect a common driving force (opportunity) rather than a causal relationship. In independent work Svaleryd and Vlachos (2002) explore the Granger causality between openness and financial

R.G. Rajan, L. Zingales / Journal of Financial Economics 69 (2003) 5–50   25

development. While they find evidence that openness can cause financial development, they do not find evidence in the opposite direction.

We have a way to deal with this problem when we consider openness to trade as the explanatory variable. For we can instrument trade openness with measures of a country's natural propensity to trade—because of its small size or its proximity to trading partners. If the exogenous component of trade correlates with financial development, we can be more confident that openness indeed causes financial development.

Openness to capital flows is more problematic. First, the extent to which capital flows into a particular country may directly reflect the sophistication of its financial system. Moreover, unlike with trade, no obvious instruments present themselves. The mobility of capital, however, suggests a way out.

The decision to open up to capital flows is likely to be a strategic complement. When the rest of the world is open, it is both more difficult for a country to prevent cross-border capital movement and less attractive for it to do so. It is more difficult to prevent capital movements because the openness of the rest of the world makes it easier for domestic agents to expatriate funds to a safe haven or borrow funds from it, despite domestic controls. These leakages are especially likely for countries that are more open to trade. In open countries, funds can be transferred through underinvoicing or overinvoicing of trade, transfer pricing between units of a multinational, etc. A country can also find controlling capital flows unattractive when others are open. Its domestic financial institutions can find themselves at a comparative disadvantage. For example, a domestic exchange may not be able to provide as much liquidity as exchanges in other countries that are open to capital movements. In fact, competition between New York, London, and Tokyo to become global financial centers was responsible for the rapid demise of capital controls in these countries after the collapse of Bretton Woods (e.g., Helleiner, 1994).

Given all this, for each individual country the decision to allow capital to flow across its borders is strongly influenced by overall global conditions, which can be regarded as exogenous to specific domestic political considerations. And there is considerable variation in the flow of capital across borders during the twentieth century. Consider the mean absolute value of current account over GDP over five-year intervals for a sample of fourteen developed countries as calculated by Taylor (1998) and extended by us until 1999. This indicator suggests international capital mobility remained high only up to 1930s (3.8% before World War I and 3.2% in the 1920s, dropping to 1.6% in the 1930s). Following the Depression and the Bretton Woods agreement, capital movement remained severely curtailed till the 1980s (oscillating around 1.4%). The United States opened up in the mid 1970s, United Kingdom and Japan in 1980, while the countries of Continental Europe only in the late 1980s. As a result, the indicator rose to 2.1% in the 1980s and 2.6% in the 1990s.

In what follows, we will instrument openness to trade to get an exogenous measure, while we will use the variation in global capital flows over time as an exogenous measure of a country's variation in openness to capital flows. Let us now frame the hypothesis. In periods of high capital mobility, countries that conduct a lot of foreign trade are also likely to have well-developed capital markets. Countries that

26　　　　*R.G. Rajan, L. Zingales / Journal of Financial Economics 69 (2003) 5–50*

conduct little trade are unlikely to have developed capital markets (they are open on only one dimension). So

(1) *For any given level of demand for financing, a country's domestic financial development should be positively correlated with trade openness at a time when the world is open to cross-border capital flows.*

Changes in capital mobility over time give us the data to test the other dimension of our theory:

(2) *The positive correlation between a country's trade openness and financial development should be weaker when worldwide cross-border capital flows are low.*

We will need a proxy for the demand for financing. Bairoch (1982) computes an index of industrialization across a group of countries for a number of years. The index number in a year reflects a country's absolute level of industrialization in that year, with England in 1900 set at one hundred. The index is calculated on the basis of data on per-capita consumption of manufactured goods and from the sectoral distribution of labor. The index is computed in two stages, with the data for the UK calculated in the first stage and the relative importance, sector by sector, of other countries calculated in the second stage. There are measurement issues with any index, but this one seems well accepted among economic historians. Bairoch's index is our preferred control for the demand for financing whenever it is available. This is because GDP is a poorer proxy for the demand for financing in earlier years, when much of GDP was generated by agriculture. We will use per-capita GDP when Bairoch's numbers are not available, though sectoral differences between countries at very different levels of development will add noise.

To test the first hypothesis, we examine the correlation between openness and financial development in 1913, the earliest date for which we have data for a sizeable number of countries, and 1996–1998, the last period for which we have data. Capital flows are relatively free in both periods.

4.2. Financial development in 1913

Consider first financial development in 1913, a period of relatively free capital flows and varying degrees of openness to trade. We present summary statistics and pairwise correlations in Table 6 Panels A and B. Equity market capitalization to GDP is positively correlated with Bairoch's index of industrialization (0.58, $p = 0.01$), with openness (0.33, $p = 0.19$), and negatively correlated with tariffs on manufacturing (-0.37, $p = 0.15$). Its correlation with the interaction (between the index of industrialization and openness) is both high and very significant (0.67, $p = 0.002$).

In Table 7, Panel A, the ratio of stock market capitalization to GDP is our measure of financial development. As the estimates in Column (i) show, more industrialized countries have more developed financial markets. More relevant to our hypothesis, more open countries have more developed financial markets, but due to the small number of observations, this effect is not statistically significant at

R.G. Rajan, L. Zingales / Journal of Financial Economics 69 (2003) 5–50 27

Table 6
Summary statistics
Equity market cap./GDP is the equity market capitalization of domestic companies to GDP in 1913. Issues to GDP is the sum of equity and bond issues by domestic firms in 1912 to GDP in 1913. Per Capita Industrialization is the index of industrialization for that country in 1913 as computed by Bairoch (1982). Openness is the sum of exports and imports of goods in 1913 (obtained from the League of Nations Yearbook) divided by GDP in 1913. Tariffs are import duties as a percentage of special total imports (1909–1913) obtained from Bairoch (1989).

	Mean	Standard deviation	Minimum	Maximum	Observations
Panel A. Summary statistics					
Equity market capital/GDP	0.490	0.294	0.02	1.09	18
Issues to GDP in 1912	0.022	0.015	0.002	0.055	17
Per capita industrialization	49.5	37.08	2	126	18
Openness (trade volume/GDP)	0.59	0.51	0.11	2.32	18
Tariffs	13.0	9.5	0.4	37.4	17
Interaction of per capita industrialization and openness	29.1	31.1	0.36	118.67	18

Panel B. Pairwise correlations between variables (significance in parentheses)

	Equity market cap to GDP	Per capita industrialization	Openness (trade volume/GDP)	Tariffs
Per capita industrialization	0.58 (0.01)			
Openness (trade volume/GDP)	0.33 (0.19)	0.01 (0.98)		
Tariffs	−0.37 (0.15)	−0.24 (0.35)	−0.37 (0.15)	
Interaction of per capita industrialization and openness	0.67 (0.00)	0.55 (0.02)	0.69 (0.00)	−0.37 (0.15)

conventional level. Our hypothesis, however, is that for any given level, more openness should lead to more financial development. Therefore, in column (ii) we include the interaction between openness and the index of industrialization, which is our proxy for the demand for finance. The coefficient estimate for the interaction term is highly statistically significant ($p = 0.034$). The magnitude of the effect is also large. A one standard deviation increase in the interaction term increases the ratio of stock market capitalization to GDP by 50% of its standard deviation. Since we have so few observations, we plot the data in Fig. 2 to show the result is not driven by outliers.

We can try to tell the effect of openness (apart from the effect of openness working through demand) by including both the level of openness and the interaction term in Column (iii). It turns out that only the interaction has a positive coefficient estimate, and the explanatory power of the specification in Column (ii) is not enhanced by including openness. The magnitude of the interaction coefficient is higher than in Column (ii) but its standard error also goes up. The problem is that openness and the interaction are highly correlated ($= 0.69$), so it is hard to tell their effects apart with

Table 7

Financial development and openness in 1913

In Panel A the dependent variable is equity market capitalization of domestic companies to GDP in 1913, in Panel B it is the number of listed companies per million of population in 1913, and in Panel C it is the total amount of securities issued to GDP, which is the sum of equity and bond issues by domestic firms in 1912 to GDP. Per Capita Industrialization is the index of industrialization for that country in 1913 as computed by Bairoch (1982). Openness is the sum of exports and imports of goods in 1913 (obtained from the League of Nations Yearbook) divided by GDP in 1913. Tariffs are import duties as a percentage of special total imports (1909–1913) obtained from Bairoch (1989). Coefficient estimates for per capita industrialization, its interaction with openness, and the corresponding standard errors are multiplied by one thousand. Columns (iv)–(v) report instrumental variable estimates, where the instrument for openness is population size. All the regressions include a constant, whose coefficient is not reported. Standard errors are in parentheses. (*) indicates significance at the 10% level, (**) at the 5% level, (***) at the 1% level.

Dependent variable	Equity market capitalization/GDP				
	(i)	(ii)	(iii)	(iv)	(v)
Panel A. Equity market capitalization/GDP					
Per capita industrialization	4.61***	2.42	2.11	1.55	8.77**
	(1.52)	(1.71)	(2.25)	(2.05)	(3.18)
Openness	0.18		−0.04		
	(0.11)		(0.19)		
Interaction of per-capita industrialization and openness		4.76**	5.44	6.62**	
		(2.03)	(3.69)	(3.08)	
Interaction of per-capita industrialization and tariffs					−0.38*
					(0.22)
Adjusted R^2	0.37	0.45	0.42		
Observations	18	18	18	18	17

Panel B. Number of domestic companies listed/million population

Dependent variable	No. of companies/million population				
	(i)	(ii)	(iii)	(iv)	(v)
Per-capita industrialization	215.8	−210.6	−199.5	−252.0*	927.7**
	(133.6)	(116.0)	(152.8)	(137.0)	(442.3)
Openness	38.8***		−1.5		
	(9.6)		(12.7)		
Interaction of per-capita industrialization and openness		924.1***	899.8***	1012.8***	
		(138.1)	(250.8)	(206.0)	
Interaction of per-capita industrialization and tariffs					−60.9**
					(29.9)
Adjusted R^2	0.50	0.74	0.72		
Observations	18	18	18	18	17

Panel C. Total securities issued/GDP

Dependent variable	Securities issued/GDP				
	(i)	(ii)	(iii)	(iv)	(v)
Per-capita industrialization	0.17	0.02	−0.09	−0.02	0.52**
	(0.10)	(0.10)	(0.12)	(0.11)	(0.22)
Openness	0.01		−0.01		
	(0.01)		(0.01)		
Interaction of per-capita industrialization and openness		0.33**	0.56**	0.41**	
		(0.11)	(0.19)	(0.17)	
Interaction of per-capita industrialization and tariffs					−0.03*
					(0.01)
Adjusted R^2	0.14	0.39	0.44		
Observations	17	17	17	17	17

R.G. Rajan, L. Zingales / Journal of Financial Economics 69 (2003) 5–50 29

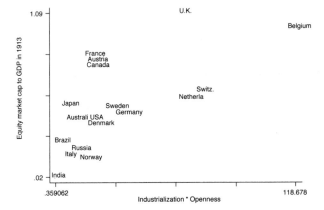

Fig. 2. Market capitalization versus interaction between industrialization and openness. On the *x*-axis we report the product between the level of per capita industrialization of a country and its level of openness. Per capita industrialization is the index of industrialization for that country in 1913 as computed by Bairoch (1982). Openness is the sum of exports and imports of goods in 1913 (obtained from the League of Nations Yearbook) divided by GDP in 1913. On the *y*-axis we report a measure of financial development: the equity market capitalization to GDP ratio in 1923. As the graph shows there is a clear positive correlation between the two, which is not driven by any particular outlier.

so few observations. Since the correct specification could be debated, in what follows we present estimates for both the effect of openness and the effect of the interaction. Our claim is that openness matters, not that we can separate a direct effect of openness from an interaction between openness and our proxy for the demand for finance. Between the two we expect the interaction to be more important, because it is more directly linked to what the theory predicts.

The results thus far indicate that in more open countries, a given demand for finance is correlated with more financial development. Because openness and financial development could be simultaneously determined by some omitted variable, we instrument openness with the size of a country's population in Column (iv). Small countries typically have to be more open since it is difficult to manufacture everything internally (e.g., Katzenstein, 1985). The point estimate of the effect of openness interacted with industrialization increases by 50% and, in spite of an inevitable increase of the standard error, remains statistically significant at the 5% level.

Another concern is that we proxy for openness with the volume of goods traded, and there can be a disguised link between the volume of trade and the volume of financing. One measure of openness that is not directly a measure of volume is the tariff on manufactured goods. We use this as a proxy for the extent of openness in Column (v), and the two-stage least-squares estimate (using the same instrument as in the previous column) is negative and significant.

As discussed before, the ratio of equity market capitalization to GDP is a very imperfect measure of financial development. It is sensitive to fluctuations in relative valuations and to mistakes in the computation of the GDP (national accounts

30		*R.G. Rajan, L. Zingales / Journal of Financial Economics 69 (2003) 5–50*

statistics were widely calculated only after WWII, all previous numbers are estimates computed in recent years). An alternative measure, which is immune to both these criticisms, is the ratio of the number of publicly listed companies to population. In Panel B of Table 7, we re-estimate the specifications in Table 7's Panel with this alternative dependent variable. The correlations are even stronger. Openness has a positive and significant correlation with development even when included alone. When both openness and openness interacted are included, the latter remains statistically significant at the 5% level.

Finally, our measure of financial development captures only the size of the equity market, even though the bond market plays an important role in some of these countries. Unfortunately, we were unable to obtain data for the size of the corporate bond market for the same set of countries. We did obtain data, however, from the 1915 Bulletin of the International Institute of Statistics (IIS) in Vienna on the total issues of public corporate securities (both equity and corporate bonds) by domestic firms in a set of countries in 1912. The IIS sample is slightly different from our 1913 sample (which we have put together from different sources for each country). We have checked that the data in the IIS sample seem accurate by comparing with independent sources, and they do seem to represent net rather than gross issues.

In Panel C of Table 7, we re-estimate the same specifications using total issues to GDP in 1912 as dependent variable. As a denominator we use GDP rather than GFCF to maximize the number of observations available. Here again, the interaction between industrialization and openness has a positive and statistically significant coefficient. A one-standard deviation increase in the interaction term increases the ratio of total issues to GDP by 68% of its standard deviation.

4.3. Financial development in the late 1990s

Regardless of the measure used, openness seems to have facilitated financial development in 1913. The paucity of observations, however, is worrisome. But our hypothesis suggests the results should also be present in recent times, when cross-border capital flows have regained the levels they had reached in the early part of the twentieth century.

In Table 8, we re-estimate the specifications in Table 7 using the largest cross-section of data available today. We obtain data for market capitalization from the World Bank's World Development Indicators, data on the number of domestic listed companies from the Emerging Market Factbook, and data on security issues from Beck et al. (1999). Since Bairoch's index of industrialization is not available, we use instead the log of per-capital GDP in PPP dollar, also from the World Bank's World Development Indicators.

To smooth the effects of the East Asian financial crisis we averaged the dependent variable across three years (1996–1998). As Table 8's Panel A (with dependent variable equity market capitalization to GDP) shows, the results are very similar to those in 1913. Openness has a positive and statistically significant effect on financial development. This is true both if we use openness directly (see Column (i)) and if we

R.G. Rajan, L. Zingales / Journal of Financial Economics 69 (2003) 5–50   31

Table 8

Financial development and openness in the late 1990s

In Panel A the dependent variable is the ratio of equity market capitalization to gross domestic product averaged over 1996 to 1998 from the World Development Indicators (World Bank). In Panel B the dependent variable is the number of domestic companies listed over million inhabitants in 1997 from the Emerging Market Factbook. In Panel C the dependent variable is the sum of equity and long-term private debt issues to GDP averaged over the 1990s from Beck et al. (1999). Log per-capita gross domestic product is the logarithm of the per-capita GDP in PPP dollars as reported in the World Development Indicators. Openness is the average of the sum of exports and imports of goods divided by GDP across 1996–1998 (source: World Bank). In Column (iii) the interaction between logarithm of the per-capita GDP and openness is instrumented by the interaction between logarithm of the per-capita GDP and constructed trade share in Frankel and Romer (1999). All the regressions include a constant, whose coefficient is not reported. The standard errors are in parentheses. (*) indicates significance at the 10% level, (**) at the 5% level, (***) at the 1% level.

	(i)	(ii)	(iii)
Panel A. Equity market capitalization/GDP			
Log per-capita GDP	0.264***	0.243***	0.198***
	(0.044)	(0.046)	(0.063)
Openness	0.214***		
	(0.082)		
Interaction of log per-capita GDP and openness		0.025***	0.048***
		(0.009)	(0.024)
Adjusted R^2	0.34	0.34	
Observations	96	96	82

Panel B. Number of domestic companies listed/million population

	(i)	(ii)	(iii)
Log per-capita GDP	10.96***	8.86**	4.26
	(3.83)	(3.98)	(4.71)
Openness	25.10***		
	(7.11)		
Interaction of log per-capita GDP and openness		2.69***	5.35***
		(0.76)	(1.78)
Adjusted R^2	0.20	0.20	
Observations	91	91	81

Panel C. Security issues/GDP

	(i)	(ii)	(iii)
Log per-capita GDP	0.026***	0.025***	0.018*
	(0.007)	(0.007)	(0.009)
Openness	0.022**		
	(0.011)		
Interaction of log per-capita GDP and openness		0.002*	0.006**
		(0.001)	(0.003)
Adjusted R^2	0.39	0.38	
Observations	34	34	34

interact it with our proxy for the demand for finance, the log of per capital GDP (see Column (ii)). A one-standard deviation increase in the interaction term corresponds to an increase in the ratio of stock market capitalization to GDP by 25% of its standard deviation. In spite of the very high correlation between openness and the interaction between openness and log per-capita income, the larger cross-section allows us to distinguish the two, and it is the interaction that is positively significantly correlated (estimates not reported).

Frankel and Romer (1999) predict bilateral trade between two countries using an expanded version of the gravity model of trade (where trade is a function of the distance between the countries, their size, and whether they have a common border). Their constructed trade share, then, is simply the sum of these fitted values across all possible trading partners and is a good instrument for trade (perhaps better than population) which is all that we have in 1913. When we use this instrument, the estimated coefficient almost doubles (see Column (iii)) and remains statistically significant at the 1% level.

We show these results hold for other measures of financial development. In Panel B the dependent variable is the number of domestic companies listed per million inhabitants in 1997, while in Panel C it is the sum of equity and long-term private debt issues to GDP. To deal with the cyclicality of equity and debt issues, we use an average across all the years during the 1990s that are available in Beck et al. (1999). These panels confirm the finding that financial development is higher for any level of demand when a country is more open.

4.3.1. Robustness

The greater availability of data at the end of 1990s allows us to explore the robustness of our results. La Porta et al. (1997) suggest that a better measure of financial development than market capitalization is the amount of equity held by outsiders. Using this measure of development, openness or openness interacted with GDP per-capita have a positive and statistically significant correlation with equity held by outsiders (estimates not reported). Similarly, a good indicator of the ability to raise external funds, and thus a measure of the development of a financial market, is the quality of the accounting standards, as measured by the Center for International Financial Analysis and Research. This measure is available only for 39 countries, nevertheless openness alone and openness interacted with GDP per-capita are positively and statistically significantly correlated with it (estimates not reported).

One might worry that there is a mechanical link between openness and financial market development. We know that financial liberalization leads to an increase in stock prices (e.g., Henry, 2000) and, thus, at least temporarily to an increase in the ratio of stock market capitalization to GDP, which is one of our measures of financial development. For example, a large trade deficit has to be financed through capital inflows. If domestic government assets are insufficient, and if foreign direct investment is small, the inflows will be reflected in a larger private market for financial assets. Is the link we have found merely the flip side of a trade deficit? We re-estimate the basic specification using the ratio of trade surplus to GDP as a substitute for openness (estimates not reported). Trade surplus does not seem to be correlated with domestic financial development. When we include the interaction of openness with log per-capita GDP, trade surplus loses statistical significance, while the interaction term remains positive and statistically significant.

Another way of getting at this is to look at a form of financing that may not be arm's length (domestic bank credit) and is therefore less likely to be influenced by openness. Openness does not seem to be statistically significantly correlated with the ratio of domestic credit to the private sector to GDP (obtained from Beck et al., 1999). Thus there does not seem to be a mechanical link between openness and financing. Instead the link is to arm's length financing (or we conjecture, if we could measure it, competitive private credit).

4.4. Financial development over time

Our results thus far indicate that both before World War I and in the late 1990s, measures of financial development were higher in countries more open to trade. Of course, many good institutions are associated with more trade. For example, Wei (2000) finds lower corruption in countries that trade more. But our second hypothesis suggests that trade openness is particularly effective when it is accompanied by capital mobility and offers a way of distinguishing our theory from the more general observation that trade is good for institutions. We hypothesize the correlation between trade openness and financial development to be stronger in periods of high international capital mobility than in periods of low mobility.

To begin with, we estimate our basic regression (specification (ii) in Table 7, Panel A) year by year. Unfortunately, we do not have Bairoch's measure of per-capita industrialization over the entire period. Thus, the first seven cross-sections (for the years 1913, 1929, 1938, 1950, 1960, 1970, and 1980) use Bairoch's index as a proxy for demand, while the last two use the logarithm of per capita GDP adjusted for difference in the purchasing power parity (as computed by the World Bank). Consequently, the magnitude of the coefficient before 1980 and after 1981 are not directly comparable.

As Table 9 shows, the interaction between openness and demand for finance has a reliable and statistically significant positive correlation with financial development both at the beginning and at the end of the sample (1913, 1929, and 1997), which correspond to the periods of high international capital mobility. During the period of low capital mobility, the effect is statistically insignificant or even negative when we measure financial development by the ratio of equity market capitalization to GDP.

To formally test whether the effect of openness is smaller during periods of low capital mobility, we pool the different cross-sections. We first report the results for the panel 1913–1980 in Table 10, Column (i), where Bairoch's index is our measure of demand. The specification is the same as Column (iv) of Table 7, with the inclusion of an additional slope term for the years of low capital mobility and year indicators. As an instrument for openness, we use the constructed trade shares

Table 9
Financial development and openness over time
The dependent variable in each regression is a measure of financial development (equity market capital to GDP and number of companies per million inhabitants). The explanatory variables are a constant (coefficient not reported), a measure of industrialization (coefficients not reported), and the interaction between this measure of industrialization and openness (the only coefficient reported). For the period 1913–1980 the measure of industrialization is Bairoch (1982)'s index of industrialization, for the period 1981–1997 it is the logarithm of the per capita GDP in PPP dollars as reported in the World Development Indicators. Coefficient estimates for the interaction of the per capita industrialization index with openness and the corresponding standard errors are multiplied by 1000. Standard errors are in parentheses. Coefficients in bold are statistically different from zero at the 10% level.

Dependent variable	Year									
	1913	1929	1938	1950	1960	1970	1980	1981	1997	
	Coefficient of Interaction Term (Demand = Index of Industrialization)							Coefficient of Interaction Term (Demand = Log Per Capita GDP)		
Equity market capitalization to GDP	**4.76**	7.02	5.53	1.76	−1.90	−1.39	−0.65	0.036	**0.046**	
	(2.03)	(4.94)	(14.25)	(3.19)	(2.85)	(2.28)	(0.89)	(0.05)	**(0.01)**	
Adjusted R^2	0.45	0.13	−0.14	−0.07	−0.14	−0.13	−0.09	0.56	0.46	
N	18	10	12	13	13	16	18	45	45	
Number of Companies per Million	**924.1**	**1741.7**	**1627.5**	552.3	190.6	**128.5**	35.7	**1.78**	**2.71**	
	(138.1)	**(531.6)**	**(675.8)**	(388.5)	(181.9)	**(63.8)**	(68.3)	**(0.72)**	**(0.53)**	
Adjusted R^2	0.74	0.45	0.26	0.00	−0.07	0.17	−0.06	0.21	0.53	
N	18	12	12	15	14	15	18	49	49	

R.G. Rajan, L. Zingales / Journal of Financial Economics 69 (2003) 5–50 35

Table 10
Financial development and variation in capital flows

The dependent variable is the ratio of equity market capitalization to gross domestic product measure in a year. In Column (i), we pool the cross-sections from the following years: 1913, 1929, 1938, 1950, 1960, 1970, and 1980. In Column (ii), we pool the data averaged over 1980–1982 with the data averaged over 1996–1998. In Columns (iii) and (iv) we pool data for 1990 and 1999 with the data used for the estimates in Column (i). All estimates are obtained by instrumental variables, where openness is instrumented by constructed trade share in Frankel and Romer (1999). In the first column the proxy for demand for finance is the index of industrialization for that country in that year as computed by Bairoch (1982) divided by one thousand. In the other columns it is the logarithm of the per-capita GDP. Openness is the ratio of the sum of exports and imports of goods to GDP that year. The indicator for low international capital mobility equals one in the years from 1938–1980 and zero otherwise. The level of capital mobility is the mean absolute level of current account to GDP in 14 countries as computed by Taylor (1998) and extended by us to 1999. All regressions include a calendar year dummy. The standard errors, which are corrected for possible clustering of the residual at a country level, are in parentheses. (*) indicates significance at the 10% level, (**) at the 5% level, (***) at the 1% level.

Sample period:	1913–1980 (i)	1981–1997 (ii)	1913–1999 (iii)	1913–1999 (iv)
Demand for finance	1.201	0.127**	0.143	0.145
	(1.220)	(0.054)	(0.106)	(0.108)
Interaction of demand for finance and openness	6.549***	0.062**	0.037	−0.162
	(0.976)	(0.024)	(0.036)	(0.097)
Interaction of demand for finance and openness *dummy = 1 if period of low international capital mobility	−10.420***	−0.034**	−0.077*	
	(0.222)	(0.015)	(0.040)	
Interaction of demand for finance and openness * level of international capital mobility				6.695**
				(3.038)
Observations	100	90	151	151

computed by Frankel and Romer (1999). While this instrument will be weaker as we go back in time because it is constructed based on country borders in the 1990s, all we care about is that it be correlated with trade and not with financial development. We use population in Table 7 as an instrument because it is available contemporaneously in 1913, but we check that the results hold even when we use the Frankel and Romer instrument. The interaction term is significantly positive, and the additional effect in periods of low capital mobility is significantly negative as predicted.

In Table 10, Column (ii), we report the results for the panel 1981–1997, where the log of per-capita GDP is our measure of demand. The specification is the same as Column (iii) of Table 8, with the inclusion of an additional slope term for the years of low capital mobility. Again, the interaction term is significantly positive, and the additional effect in periods of low capital mobility is significantly negative as predicted.

As discussed earlier, Bairoch's index is probably a better measure of demand for finance in the early years than per-capita industrialization. Since we do not have it

36   *R.G. Rajan, L. Zingales / Journal of Financial Economics 69 (2003) 5–50*

for later years, the only panel we can estimate for all the years is one with log of per-capita GDP as a measure of demand. This is what we report in Column (iii). The interaction effect is positive (though not statistically significant) and it is significantly lower in years of low capital mobility.

Finally, perhaps we should let the data define periods of low and high capital mobility. In Column (iv), instead of multiplying by a dummy indicating periods of low capital mobility, we multiply the interaction by the ratio of cross border flows to GDP in that year (obtained from Taylor, 1998). The coefficient estimates indicate, as predicted, that the interaction is significantly higher in periods of high capital mobility.

We obtain qualitatively similar results to those in Table 10 (not reported) when we use the ratio of number of domestic firms listed to million inhabitants as a measure of financial development or when we use openness rather than openness interacted with demand.

Overall, these results suggest that the positive correlation between openness and financial development re-emerged, and became stronger, in the last two decades of the Twentieth Century, in concert with the increased cross-border capital mobility.

4.5. Summary of results

Overall, the results suggest that financial development is positively correlated with trade openness in periods when cross-border capital flows are high, but less so, or not at all, when cross-border capital flows are low. This is consistent with our theory that incumbents are most able to coordinate opposition to financial development when cross-border capital and trade flows ebb but not when they are vibrant. Of course, other theories could be consistent with our evidence. Nevertheless, when viewed in conjunction with the descriptive histories of financial development in the twentieth century (see below for examples), our theory seems to be an important part of the explanation.

The reversal in financial development in the data is then explained by the diminution of cross-border capital flows that started during the Depression and continued post-World War II until the breakdown of the Bretton Woods agreement. Of course, this raises the question of why most countries collectively shut their borders in the 1930s and 1940s and fully opened up again only recently. While a complete explanation is beyond the scope of this paper, in what follows we try to sketch our main arguments.

4.6. Shutting and re-opening borders

In the 1930s openness fell victim to the Great Depression. The extremely high level of unemployment created by the Great Depression increased the demand for government intervention, which could not take place within the narrow margins of discretion allowed by the Gold Standard. The Gold Standard simply did not allow governments to dislocate their budgets to provide social security and welfare support

R.G. Rajan, L. Zingales / Journal of Financial Economics 69 (2003) 5–50 37

to the needy (e.g., Eichengreen, 1996) even if they wanted to. When the political demand for some form of support became irresistible, country after country abandoned the Gold Standard and devalued its currency. This reaction triggered a round of competitive devaluations between trade partners. To minimize the economic consequences of these competitive devaluations most governments introduced tariffs. Hence, the Great Depression ignited a chain reaction beyond the control of any single country, which almost inevitably led to protectionism. To better understand why this took place in the 1930s, however, we have to analyze the changed political and social conditions after WWI.

4.6.1. The rising political demand for insurance

In the open developed economies in the beginning of the twentieth century, the role of the government was relatively small. Government expenditure as a fraction of GDP was only 12.7% in 1913 for a sample of 17 developed countries, compared to 45.6% in 1996 (e.g., Tanzi and Schuknecht, 2000). Part of the reason for the relatively small role played by the government was that it did not provide insurance to the people to the extent it now does. Only 20% of the labor force in western Europe had some form of pension insurance in 1910, and only 22% had health insurance (vs. 93% and 90% respectively in 1975).

Before World War I, there were a number of reasons why the government played such a small role in social insurance. The prevailing liberal belief in the relentless logic of the market suggested it was unwise for governments to interfere. Intervention, it was thought, would only prolong the pain. The rigidity of the Gold Standard system prevented governments from running large deficits. Last but not least, the poorer sections of society (the workers, the small farmers, and the unemployed) were not organized and had little political voice (e.g., Maier, 1987; Eichengreen, 1996).

World War I and the Great Depression, which followed a decade after, were huge consecutive political and economic shocks, which combined to create an organized demand for insurance and triggered a coordinated response by governments.

Labor was organized by the war. The senseless carnage of a war that left all its main protagonists worse off led many to doubt the caliber and motives of their political leaders and discredited the pre-war free-market consensus. The trenches during the war served as classrooms where the working class absorbed radical ideas. Labor, with its newly found ideas and organization, gave notice even in the 1920s that it would no longer continue unquestioningly to absorb the costs of adjustment to the rigors of the Gold Standard.

The onset of the Depression immensely increased the size of economic adjustments countries would have to undergo to stay on the Gold Standard. Classical liberal economics indicated the cure to falling output was a steep fall in wages. This was simply not acceptable to labor. Faced with increasing resistance from labor, politicians saw little reward in paying a political price to adhere to the Gold Standard. With little thought for the collective consequences, they also started erecting barriers to imports in an attempt to trade their way out of depression. As everyone attempted to beggar their neighbors, trade and capital flows ceased.

Clearly, incumbents were not idle in the policy debates in the 1930s. Equally clearly, many of them welcomed the descent into autarky, for it strengthened their positions. But it would be incorrect to claim that broad policy was shaped primarily, or even largely, by these interests. The Depression had affected too many people for business as usual to prevail. For example, in Sweden, labor and agrarian interests came together in 1932 in what has been termed the "cow trade." Labor accepted higher food prices and price supports in return for stable wages, policies for full employment, and social services. The business interests opposed this coalition at first, but became more accommodating when the party representing labor, the Social Democrats, became stronger in the election of 1936.

Economic policy in the developed democracies was thus broadly a response to the large, across-the-board, adverse shock affecting the uninsured masses. Autarky allowed the governments to implement various insurance schemes that may have been more difficult had the economies been open and the Gold Standard in place. The increase in insurance coverage was significant. Over 56% of the workforce in western Europe was covered by pension insurance by 1935 and 47% had health insurance coverage. Unemployment insurance was introduced for the first time in a number of countries, including the United States, during the Depression.

Incumbents used the protection afforded by autarky to mould policies in their own favor. Thus, Japan, for example, moved from an economy with a flourishing financial market, and a competitive banking system, to an economy with small financial markets and a concentrated banking system. These moves had the support of the government, which felt it could better control resource allocation if funds were channeled largely through the banks. The reversal in openness provided the conditions under which financial markets could be, and indeed were, repressed (see Rajan and Zingales (2003) for a more detailed account).

4.6.2. Why did financial markets take so long to recover?

The disruption to international trade caused by the two wars and the Great Depression was significant. While the average degree of export openness (merchandise exports as a percentage of GDP) was 8.2 in 1913, it was just 5.2 in 1950 (e.g., O'Rourke and Williamson, 1999, p. 30). In contrast to much of the developed world, the United States emerged from World War II with its industries largely intact and highly competitive. Clearly, it had a strong incentive to press for open trade since its markets were likely to expand. Meanwhile, its wartime role as the "Arsenal of Democracy" gave it the political clout to press its agenda. But in return for agreeing to free trade, other developed countries wanted some restrictions on cross-border capital flows.

The rationale was clear. If capital were allowed to flow freely, it would hamper the ability of governments to provide the various kinds of insurance that was increasingly being expected of them by their citizens, especially given the terrible state of post-war government finances. Thus the argument for controlling capital flows and the second-class status accorded to finance in the post-war economic order. As Keynes was one of the architects of the Bretton Woods agreement, which set the stage for the post-war international order. He said (cited in Helleiner, 1994,

p. 164): "Not merely as a feature of the transition but as a permanent arrangement, the plan accords every member government the explicit right to control all capital movements. What used to be heresy is now endorsed as orthodoxy."

This should be contrasted with the general desire of countries after World War I to return to the Gold Standard and thus reduce barriers to capital flow. If openness to trade is, by itself, insufficient to force financial development, then the restrictions on capital movements after WWII can explain why financial markets did not take off even though trade expanded. After all, they recovered rapidly after WWI. Even though the toll taken by the wars was admittedly very different, an important part of the explanation must be that there was no Bretton Woods after World War I endorsing capital controls.

4.6.3. The end of capital controls

The breakdown of the Bretton Woods system (e.g., Eichengreen, 1996, for a lucid exposition of the causes), led to the dismantling of capital controls, and could have been the precipitating factor for financial development across the world. Starting with the Euromarkets, spreading to the United States, and then moving to Europe and Japan, cross-border capital flows went from a trickle to a torrent. Accounts of the process by which this happened suggest that the cross-border flows increased despite, rather than because of, the efforts of domestic interest groups (e.g., Helleiner, 1994). Given the growing volume of trade, it was simply too difficult to control the potential leakage of capital, especially when there were countries abroad where the money could be deposited.

By the end of the 1980s, controls had effectively been removed throughout western Europe, Scandinavia, and Japan. The competition generated by trade and free international capital movements forced a modernization of the financial system and a progressive withdrawal of the State from the economy, through privatization in the industrial and banking sectors. This then would explain the other leg of the reversal. Before we go further, let us take a look at two case studies.

4.7. The case of Japan

Japan, as our data suggest, was making rapid strides to developing a strong financial sector before World War I. Until 1918, there were no restrictions on entry into banking, provided minimum capital requirements were met. There were over 2,000 banks in 1920. The five large Zaibatsu (translated as financial cliques) banks accounted for only 20.5% of the deposits before the war, and there were many small banks. (Aoki et al., 1994; Hoshi and Kashyap, 2001).

As a result of increased competition in the post-World War I years and the Great Tokyo Earthquake in 1923, which caused damage estimated at an incredible 38% of GDP, more and more banks became troubled. This gave the government the excuse to enact regulations promoting mergers in the name of stability. By 1945, there were only 65 banks, and the share of Zaibatsu banks in total deposits had increased to 45.7%. (Aoki et al., 1994).

40   *R.G. Rajan, L. Zingales / Journal of Financial Economics 69 (2003) 5–50*

At the same time as the banking system was becoming more concentrated, the government's control over it was increasing. This became especially pronounced as the government sought to direct funds towards supplying the war against China in 1937. With the Temporary Fund Adjustment Act in 1937 and the Corporate Profits Distribution and Fund Raising Act in 1939, the government, through the Industrial Bank of Japan, assumed control of financing. All security issuances and lending decisions above a certain amount had to be approved by the government, and those that were not related to the war effort were typically not approved. Further Acts simply strengthened the government's control and this culminated in the designated lending system by which each munitions company was designated a major bank which would take care of all its credit needs. By the end of the war, the banking system was not only concentrated, but well and truly under the control of the government.

The accompanying demise of the arm's length financial markets was aided and abetted by the banks. In 1929, 26% of the liability side of large Japanese firm balance sheets consisted of bonds while only 17% was bank debt (see Teranishi, 1994). As bond defaults increased as a result of the earlier crisis and depression, a group of banks together with trust and insurance companies seized on the poor economic conditions to agree in 1931 to make all subsequent bond issues secured in principle. This immediately made it harder for their clients to issue public debt. With the acquiescence of the Ministry of Finance, the agreement was formalized in 1933 through the formation of a Bond Committee. The Committee determined which firms could issue bonds, on what terms, and when. All bonds were required to be collateralized, and banks were to serve as trustees for the collateral in exchange for a substantial fee. Giving banks the responsibility for determining firms' right to access the public bond markets was like giving a fox who resided in a chicken coop the right to determine which chickens could leave. Hoshi and Kashyap (2001) add further support to the claim that this was a cartel by the observation that security houses that were not part of the 1931 agreement started competing fiercely for underwriting business and continued to underwrite unsecured bonds. Thus the market itself did not appear to develop a distaste for unsecured bonds. The obvious outcome was that a flourishing bond market was killed off. By 1936, bonds were down to 14% while bank debt was up to 24% of the liability side. By 1943, 47 percent of liabilities were bank debt while only 6% were bonds.

Japan illustrates yet another point. Entrenched hierarchies have the power to defend themselves. For example, despite their best efforts to break up bank-firm established during the period of militarization, the post-war American occupying forces could not prevent them re-emerging as the Keiretsu or main bank system (e.g., Hoshi and Kashyap (2001), though see Miwa and Ramseyer (2002) who suggest a contrary view that Keiretsus are fiction). Similarly, the Bond Committee, set up ostensibly to improve the quality of bond issuance during the Depression, survived until the 1980s. Even as Japanese industrial firms invaded the rest of the world in the 1970s, their bond markets remained miniscule, and Hitachi, an AA credit, was denied the ability to issue unsecured bonds. It was only in the early 1980s, as Japanese firms decided to borrow abroad in the Euromarkets rather than depend on

R.G. Rajan, L. Zingales / Journal of Financial Economics 69 (2003) 5–50 41

their antiquated financial system that Japanese banks had to loosen their stranglehold. The powers of the bond committee were eventually curtailed, not by a far-seeing government, but by the forces of outside competition.

4.8. Why not the United States?

As with any large sample study, there are exceptions. The United States undertook a variety of market-friendly actions including passing legislation requiring greater disclosure in financial markets, setting up the Securities and Exchange Commission, and passing the Glass Steagall Act, which brought more competition among financial institutions by breaking up the universal banks. Was the United States an exception to the trend at this time?

First, it is possible to overstate the extent to which the legislation was market friendly. The National Recovery Administration, which was set up under the New Deal, sought to fix prices in industry in order to eliminate "ruinous" competition, while Regulation Q attempted to do the same thing in the banking sector. The US government defaulted on the Gold Clause to the detriment of creditors, and the sanctity of contracts (e.g., Kroszner, 1999). Markets and competition were not seriously affected in the long run. This was not for the want of effort by the New Deal politicians. But legislative zeal in the United States was also tempered by checks imposed by the judiciary, a characteristic of Common Law countries (though it was the independent judiciary rather than Common Law that was the source of the check). Roosevelt's primary method of intervention, the National Recovery Administration, was declared unconstitutional by the Supreme Court (Kennedy, 1999, p. 328). When the Supreme Court eventually became more pliant after threats to pack its bench with government supporters, Congress became more nervous about growing executive powers, and growing threats to property, and became the main obstacle to proposed New Deal legislation (Kennedy, 1999, p. 341).

Checks and balances are not sufficient to explain the pro-market legislation. Of course, the legislation was not as pro-market as it is often made out to be. Mahoney (2001) argues that the ostensibly pro-market and pro-competitive Securities Act of 1933 and the Glass Steagall Act, were really protection in disguise for established investment bankers. Various aspects of the Securities Act reduced price competition among investment bankers, while the Glass Steagall Act forced commercial banks out of the underwriting business. Mahoney provides evidence that the Securities Act increased concentration in the underwriting business.

Nevertheless, even if private interests were at work, the United States did not go the way of Japan. In part, the private interests were more fragmented. Investment banks did not see eye to eye with commercial banks, nor did large banks form common cause with small banks. The variety of conflicting private interests and the variety of political support they could count on at both the state and national level, more than any other factor, could have been the reason why outcomes in the United States were not more anti-competitive. There was no way markets could be closed down without hurting some powerful faction in the financial sector.

So this then leaves us with the final question. Why were there so many different groups within the financial sector? Roe (1994) suggests an answer. He claims that there has always been an undercurrent of opposition in the United States to anyone getting overly powerful in the financial sector. Whether it be the setting up of the Federal Reserve to undercut the power of JP Morgan, the Glass Steagall Act to curtail the power of large universal banks, or the refusal of the Federal Reserve to act to save Drexel Burnham, the United States has managed to cut powerful financiers down to size. Perhaps it was its ability to ensure even in normal times that no small group of incumbents ever became really powerful that enabled the United States to pass through crisis relatively unscathed.

4.9. How does structure matter?

Since the work of La Porta et al. (1997, 1998), there has been some debate over why the legal origin of a country appears to matter so much for financial markets. Some suggest it reflects the inherent superiority of Common Law over Civil Law for financial transactions and investor protection. Others argue it matters because it reflects something about a country's culture, religion, or politics (e.g., Acemoglu et al., 2001; Beck et al., 1999; Berglof and Von Thadden, 1999; La Porta et al., 1999; Rajan and Zingales, 1999; Stulz and Williamson, 2001).

Our finding that financial markets in countries with a Civil Law system were not less developed than those in countries with Common Law in 1913 and in 1929 but only after World War II suggests a deeper look at the underlying mechanism for why legal origin seems to matter.

Rajan and Zingales (1999) argue that many complex legal constructs that first emerged in Common Law, such as limited liability, were readily imitated by Civil Law countries. In fact, they argue, when the government has a will, Civil Law countries have a greater ability to translate governmental policy into law because laws emanate from the center rather than evolving through judicial decisions. Private interests therefore have a greater chance of seeing their agenda enacted in a Civil Law country.

One reason is simply that if the governance system is more centralized, it is easier for small private interests to capture it. If, in addition, the legal system is important for validating and enforcing new policy, the Civil Law system is again easier to capture. The focus of influence activity in a Civil Law country only has to be the legislator. By contrast, the judiciary in a Common Law country can restrain a new political climate, and because it is dispersed and subject to local influences, is less easy to capture.

A second reason is that Common Law evolves at the periphery, and innovates around legislative or administrative roadblocks set up by the center. In England, for instance, after the Bubble Act placed constraints on the incorporation of limited liability companies in 1720 (primarily to bolster the position of companies that were already incorporated), Common Law courts continuously evolved their own interpretation of which companies did not contravene the spirit of that law. It was precisely to overcome this ability of the judiciary to defy the will of the center that

R.G. Rajan, L. Zingales / Journal of Financial Economics 69 (2003) 5–50 43

Napoleon introduced the Civil Code as a way to prevail over judges still loyal to the *Ancien Regime.*

In summary, in a Civil Law country, it is easier for a small group representing private interests, such as large incumbent industrialists and financiers to influence the implementation of friendly policies. This need not be all bad. When these private interests are aligned with the national interests, good policy can also be implemented quickly. But when interests are misaligned, matters can become much worse. Empirically, this would suggest that Civil Law countries went further in repressing financial markets when borders closed down (explaining the La Porta et al. findings in the mid-1990s), but have also begun developing them again as borders have opened up again in recent years (explaining the convergence seen in the most recent data). In summary, structure might matter, not so much in directly favoring or disfavoring financial development, but in filtering the impact of interest groups and the forces that affect their incentives.

The data seem to support this view. In Table 11 Columns (i) and (ii) regress the change in the stock market capitalization for a country between 1913 and the breakdown of Bretton Woods (1970) against the changes in its per-capita income in constant dollars and an indicator for Civil Law. Both when we compute change as a change in level and as a change in percentage, the coefficient estimate for the Civil Law indicator is strongly negative, suggesting that stock markets in Civil Law countries did indeed fall by more over the period of the reversal. In Columns (iii) and (iv), the dependent variable is the change in stock market capitalization for a country between the beginning of Bretton Woods's breakdown (1970) and the end of our sample period (1999). In this case, the coefficient estimate for the Civil Law indicator is strongly positive, suggesting that stock markets in Civil Law countries did indeed recover by more in recent times.

While certainly not a test, this evidence suggests that structure may have been found to matter for financial development in recent papers because Civil Law systems can have more exaggerated reactions to changes in private interests. A related finding is that a country's cultural heritage plays the strongest role when the country is shielded from foreign competition and private interests can reign unhindered. Stulz and Williamson (2001) find that the correlation between creditor rights and religion weakens when a country is more open to trade. If we compare systems at a time of transition, we come away with the impression that structure has a strong influence on levels of development even though it has more of an influence on rates of change.

4.10. Related literature

Our view that institutional differences between countries serve to modify the impact of private interests offers a different view of convergence across countries than Coffee (2000). In his view, financial development will take place through changes in practices when a constituency emerges that demands it. Much later, the formal legal system will adapt to reflect these demands. Thus he attributes the convergence to Anglo-Saxon norms of corporate governance practices in continental

44   *R.G. Rajan, L. Zingales / Journal of Financial Economics 69 (2003) 5–50*

Table 11

Openness and legal system over time

In the first two columns the dependent variable is the change in the ratio of equity market capitalization to gross domestic product between 1913 and 1970 (in the first column, it is the absolute change, in the second, the % change). In the next two columns the dependent variable is the change in the ratio of equity market capitalization to gross domestic product between 1970 and 1999 (in the third column, it is the absolute change, in the fourth the % change). In the first two columns the proxy for the change in the demand for finance is the change in the index of industrialization for that country in that year as computed by Bairoch (1982) divided by 1000. In the next two columns the proxy for the change in demand for finance is the change in the logarithm of the per-capita GDP in PPP dollars as reported in the World Development Indicators. The indicator for Civil Law is one in countries with Civil Law and is zero otherwise. All regressions include calendar year indicators. The standard errors, which are corrected for possible clustering of the residual at a country level, are in parentheses. (*) indicates significance at the 10% level, (**) at the 5% level, (***) at the 1% level.

	Change in stock market capitalization/GDP over the 1913–1970 period		Change in stock market capitalization/GDP over the 1970–1999 period	
	Changes in level	Percent change	Changes in level	Percent change
Change in demand for finance	0.655	−2.270**	−0.398	−3.650
	(0.792)	(1.063)	(1.014)	(3.687)
Civil law indicator	−0.745***	−1.551***	0.762*	3.207**
	(0.165)	(0.221)	(0.393)	(1.428)
R^2	0.57	0.77	0.10	0.16
Observations	16	16	18	18

Europe to the privatization in the 1980s, which created a constituency of minority shareholders. We differ primarily in that we attribute a strong role to private interests (not just for, but also against, development) and potentially, a role for structure in modifying the influence of private interests.

Before concluding this section, we must note two other explanations for the reversals. Roe (1999) suggests that corporations in continental Europe became more closely held because of the potential for higher agency costs there as a result of pro-labor legislation passed in the 1920s and 1930s. This diminished the size of public markets. While we do believe that the shrinkage of public equity markets and the passage of pro-labor legislation were coincident in some countries, his theory does not account for the greater government intervention and cartelization witnessed in many countries, or for the demise of corporate bond markets in some.

Pagano and Volpin (2000) develop a model in which entrepreneurs, who have already raised finance, want low investor protection (so as to indulge in private benefits) and get the support of workers by promising them high employment protection. This model of incumbent interests (entrepreneurs who already have finance) is similar to ours. It suggests a different explanation for the correlation Roe finds by saying that incumbent industrialists bribed workers with pro-worker legislation to go along with anti-finance legislation. Our emphasis on openness as a modifying influence is different, and it helps us explain both pro-market and anti-market legislation.

R.G. Rajan, L. Zingales / Journal of Financial Economics 69 (2003) 5–50   45

5. Conclusion

We see four contributions of this work. The first is to show the reversal in financial markets, a finding inconsistent with pure structural theories of financial market development. The second is to add a new fact, which is that trade openness is correlated with financial market development, especially when cross-border capital flows are free. The third is to argue that these findings are consistent with interest group politics being an important factor in financial development across countries. The last is to suggest that a county's institutions might slow or speed-up interest group activities. This might indicate that institutions matter, though the way they matter might primarily be in tempering interest group activities.

If our understanding of the impediments to financial development is correct, then it suggests that the exhortations by international development institutions to countries to develop institutions to aid economic growth are not be enough. It is not that the cognoscenti in developing countries are not aware that the country needs good institutions, it is simply that too many interests will lose out if the institutions are developed (e.g., Olson, 1982). More emphasis needs to be placed on establishing political pre-conditions for institutions.

More thought has to be given then to how interest groups can be reined in. Openness clearly will help. Policies that tend to promote efficient, competitive industries rather than inefficient, rent-seeking ones will also tend to pave the way for institutional development, as will public awareness of the hidden costs of policies that ostensibly promote economic stability. Finally, insurance schemes that will soften the impact of economic adversity on individuals will help ward off an anti-market reaction. How such policies fit together clearly requires more thought and suggests ample scope for further research. In further work, Rajan and Zingales (2003) provide a preliminary effort.

Appendix A. Important notes on data collection

A.1. Historical differences in reporting data

A formidable challenge, specific to the historical nature of our analysis, is the difficulty in obtaining reliable sources for historical information about financial markets. Primary sources are often lost or inaccessible, while secondary sources are contradictory or repeat uncritically the same primary sources. To further complicate our task, the type of information statisticians and governing bodies of stock exchanges were interested in at the beginning of the twentieth century seems quite different from the ones we are interested in today (this seems a topic worthy of a separate study). We discuss some of these differences because they help shed some light on the different perceptions of the nature and role of financial instruments at that time.

A number that is often reported is the total nominal value of securities outstanding in a country. This joins together not only stocks and corporate bonds,

46 *R.G. Rajan, L. Zingales / Journal of Financial Economics 69 (2003) 5–50*

but also Government bonds, making the number difficult to interpret. The clubbing of information on corporate bonds and stocks, which is pervasive even in the United Kingdom, probably the most sophisticated financial market at that time, reflects the similarity of these two instruments at that time. The use of preferred stock paying a fixed dividend was widespread. Also, common stock paid very high dividends, making them more similar to bonds. One consequence of the high dividend payout ratio was that most stocks traded fairly closely to their nominal value. In fact, stock prices in many countries were quoted as a percentage of their nominal value. Thus, even from an investor's point of view, bonds and stocks were perceived as very close substitutes.

A second problem is that the official statistics at the beginning of the twentieth century report the total universe of corporations existing at that time, rather then the subset of those that are publicly traded. To make the numbers more comparable across time, we classify companies as publicly traded only if the firm is quoted during the year. Even with this requirement, we may still have very infrequently traded stock.

A final problem comes from the existence of regional exchanges. At the beginning of the century, not only was trading more fragmented across exchanges, but so was listing. For example, the Banco do Brazil is listed in the Rio Stock Exchange but not in San Paulo. Companies listed only in Osaka represent a considerable portion of the total companies listed in Japan. Most extreme is Germany, probably as a consequence of the delayed political reunification. In 1913 Germany had nine major stock exchanges and Berlin represented only about 50% of the total capitalization.

Data for regional (or secondary) stock exchanges are especially challenging. Since many have disappeared or have been absorbed by the main exchange, they tend not to be well documented. We try, as best as possible, to reconstruct a measure that includes all the major stock exchanges, eliminating double listing. When this is not possible for the date of interest, we compute the ratio of the capitalization of the secondary exchanges to main exchange at the earliest date available and then use this ratio to extrapolate backwards the value of these exchanges. Since the importance of regional exchanges has gone down over time, this procedure clearly biases downwards the estimate of the total stock market capitalization in countries with fragmented stock markets. This should be kept in mind in the analysis.

A.2. Stock market capitalization and number of companies listed

Our starting point was the official publication of the stock exchanges as well as those of the Federation Internationale des Bourses Valeurs (FIBV). These provide extensive information only starting in 1980. Official publications of individual stock exchanges often go back only to WWII. When these are not available, we use information contained in private guides to stock exchanges. Only for Japan and the United States did we find official publications before WWII.

To assess the importance of the equity market in 1913 we rely on two approaches. Whenever possible we secure a copy of a stock exchange handbook in 1913 (or the closest year before 1913). Using the handbook we identify the number of domestic companies listed, the number of shares of each company, and the price per share. We then compute the total stock market capitalization as the sum of the product of price times the number of shares. We were able to do this for Australia, Brazil, Canada, Cuba, Denmark, Germany, Italy, Netherlands, Russia, Sweden, Switzerland, the United Kingdom, and the United States.

A second source was various issues of the Bulletin of the International Institute of Statistics (IIS). Starting in the late nineteenth century, statisticians from all over the world met every year for a conference. This association formed a special group to compute the importance of security markets in different countries. Unfortunately, many of the reports club together stocks and bonds but we do obtain some disaggregate information for some countries.

A.3. Data on equity issues

Data on equity issues are relatively easier to get for the pre-WWII period than for the period immediately after the war. For example, the *League of Nations* statistics include this information, even though it is not contained in more modern publications like the *United Nations Statistics* or the *Financial Statistics of the International Monetary Fund*. This could reflect the greater importance attributed to this information before World War II. When not available from official statistics, we gather this information from financial newspapers of that time such as the *Economist, Commercial and Financial Chronicle, Deutsche Oekonomiste*, etc.

A.4. Data on deposits and national accounts data

Data on deposits, national income, and gross fixed-capital formation come from Mitchell (various issues). Mitchell's data are available until the mid-1990s. We extrapolate this to 1999 for deposits by using the growth rate of deposits from the IMF's International Financial Statistics. For national accounts, we use the data from the NBER website whenever available. Post WWII national accounts data come from the IMF's International Financial Statistics. We indicate whenever data come from a different source. A comprehensive data appendix is available on request.

References

Acemoglu, D., Johnson, S., Robinson, J., 2001. The colonial origins of comparative development: an empirical study. American Economic Review 91, 1369–1401.

Aoki, M., Patrick, H., Sheard, P., 1994. The Japanese main bank system: introductory overview. In: Aoki, M., Patrick, H. (Eds.), The Japanese Main Bank System: Its Relevance for Developing and Transferring Economies. Oxford University Press, New York, pp. 3–50.

Bairoch, P., 1982. International industrialization levels from 1750 to 1980. Journal of European Economic History 11, 269–334.

Bairoch, P., 1989. European trade policy, 1815–1914. In: Mathias, P., Pollard, S. (Eds.), The Cambridge Economic History of Europe, Vol. VIII. Cambridge University Press, Cambridge, England.

Bebchuk, L., Roe, M., 1999. A theory of path dependence in corporate ownership and governance. Stanford Law Review 52, 127–170.

Beck, T., Demirguc-Kunt, A., Levine, R., 1999. A new database on financial development and structure. Unpublished Working Paper 2784. The World Bank, Washington.

Becker, G., 1983. A theory of the competition among pressure groups for political influence. The Quarterly Journal of Economics 98, 371–400.

Bencivenga, V., Smith, B., 1991. Financial intermediation and endogenous growth. Review of Economic Studies 58, 195–209.

Berglof, E., Von Thadden, E.L., 1999. The changing corporate governance paradigm: implications for transition and developing countries. Unpublished working paper. Stockholm School of Economics, Stockholm, Sweden.

Cameron, R., 1961. France and the Economic Development of Europe, 1800–1914. Princeton University Press, Princeton, NJ.

Choe, H., Masulis, R., Nanda, V., 1993. Common stock offerings across the business cycle: theory and evidence. Journal of Empirical Finance 1, 3–31.

Coffee, J., 2000. Convergence and its critics: what are the preconditions to the separation of ownership and control? Unpublished working paper, Columbia University, New York.

Demirguc-Kunt, A., Maksimovic, V., 1998. Law, finance, and firm growth. Journal of Finance 53, 2107–2138.

Djankov, S., La Porta, R., Lopez-de-Silanes, F., Shleifer, A., 2002. The regulation of entry. Quarterly Journal of Economics 117, 1–37.

Eichengreen, B., 1996. Globalizing Capital: A history of the international monetary system. Princeton University Press, Princeton, NJ.

Frankel, J.A., Romer, D., 1999. Does trade cause growth? American Economic Review 89, 379–399.

Gourevitch, P., 1986. Politics in Hard Times: Comparative Responses to International Economic Crises. Cornell University Press, Ithaca, NY.

Greenwood, J., Jovanovic, B., 1990. Financial development, growth, and the distribution of income. Journal of Political Economy 98, 1076–1107.

Guiso, L., Sapienza, P., Zingales, L., 2000. The role of social capital in financial development. Unpublished working paper 7563, NBER, Cambridge, MA.

Haber, S., 1997. Financial markets and industrial development. A comparative study of government regulation, financial innovation, and industrial structure in Brazil and Mexico, 1840–1930. In: Haber, S. (Ed.), How Latin America Fell Behind: Essays on the Economic Histories of Brazil and Mexico. Stanford University Press, Stanford, CA, pp. 1800–1914.

Helleiner, E., 1994. From Bretton Woods to global finance: a world turned upside down. In: Stubbs, R., Underhill, G. (Eds.), Political Economy and the Changing Global Order. Oxford University Press, Toronto, pp. 244.

Hellwig, M., 2000. On the economics and politics of corporate finance and corporate control. In: Vives, X. (Ed.), Corporate Governance: Theoretical and Empirical Perspectives. Cambridge University Press, Cambridge, England, pp. 95–136.

Henry, P.B., 2000. Stock market liberalization, economic reform, and emerging market equity prices. Journal of Finance 55, 529–564.

Holmen, M., Hogfeldt, P., 2000. A law and finance analysis of initial public offerings. Unpublished working paper, University of Chicago.

Hoshi, T., Kashyap, A., 2001. Corporate Finance and Government in Japan. M.I.T. Press, Cambridge, MA.

Jayaratne, J., Strahan, P.E., 1996. The finance-growth nexus: evidence from bank branch deregulation. Quarterly Journal of Economics 111, 639–670.

Jensen, M., 1991. Corporate control and the politics of finance. Continental Bank Journal of Applied Corporate Finance 4, 13–33.

Johnson, S., McMillan, J., Woodruff, C., 2000. Courts and relational contracts. Unpublished working paper, M.I.T, Cambridge, MA.

Katzenstein, P., 1985. Small States in World Markets: Industrial Policy in Europe. Cornell University Press, Ithaca, NY.

Kennedy, D., 1999. Freedom from fear: The American people in depression and war, 1929–1945. In: Oxford History of the United States. Oxford University Press, New York.

Kennedy, W., 1989. Industrial Structure, Capital Markets, and the Origins of British Economic Decline. Cambridge University Press, Cambridge, England.

King, R., Levine, R., 1993. Finance and growth: schumpeter might be right. The Quarterly Journal of Economics 108, 681–737.

Kroszner, R., 1999. Is it better to forgive than to receive? Evidence from the abrogation of gold indexation clauses in long-term debt during the Great Depression, Unpublished working paper. The University of Chicago, Chicago.

Kroszner, R., Strahan, P., 1999. What drives deregulation? Economics and politics of the relaxation of bank branching restrictions. Quarterly Journal of Economics 114, 1437–1467.

La Porta, R., Lopez-de-Silanes, F., Shleifer, A., Vishny, R., 1997. The legal determinants of external finance. Journal of Finance 52, 1131–1150.

La Porta, R., Lopez-de-Silanes, F., Shleifer, A., Vishny, R., 1998. Law and finance. Journal of Political Economy 106, 1113–1155.

La Porta, R., Lopez-de-Silanes, F., Shleifer, A., Vishny, R., 1999a. The quality of government. Journal of Law, Economics, and Organization 15, 222–279.

La Porta, R., Lopez-de-Silanes, F., Shleifer, A., Vishny, R., 1999b. Investor protection: origins, consequences, and reform. Unpublished Working Paper 7428, NBER, Cambridge, MA.

Loriaux, M., 1997. Capital Ungoverned. Cornell University Press, Ithaca, NY.

Mahoney, P. G., 2001. The political economy of the Securities Act of 1933. Journal of Legal Studies 30.

Maier, C., 1987. In Search of Stability. Cambridge University Press, Cambridge, England.

Mitchell, B., 1995. International Historical Statistics. Stockton Press, London.

Miwa, Y., Ramseyer, J.M., 2002. The myth of the main bank: Japan and comparative corporate governance. Law and Social Inquiry 27, 401–424.

Morck, R., Strangeland, D., Yeung, B., 2000. Inherited wealth, corporate control, and economic growth: the canadian disease? In: Morck, R.K. (Ed.), Concentrated Capital Ownership. University of Chicago Press, Chicago.

Olson, M., 1965. The Logic of Collective Action. Harvard University Press, Cambridge, MA.

Olson, M., 1982. The Rise and Decline of Nations: Economic growth, Stagflation, and Social Rigidities. Yale University Press, New Haven.

O'Rourke, K., Williamson, J., 1999. Globalization and History: The Evolution of a Nineteenth Century Atlantic Economy. MIT. Press, Cambridge, MA.

Pagano, M., Volpin, P., 2000. The political economy of corporate governance. Unpublished working paper, Harvard University, Cambridge, MA.

Petersen, M., Rajan, R., 1995. The effect of credit market competition on lending relationships. Quarterly Journal of Economics 110, 407–443.

Rajan, R., Zingales, L., 1998a. Financial dependence and growth. The American Economic Review 88, 559–586.

Rajan, R., Zingales, L., 1998b. Which capitalism? Lessons from the East Asia crisis. Journal of Applied Corporate Finance 11, 40–48.

Rajan, R., Zingales, L., 1999. The politics of financial development. Unpublished working paper, University of Chicago, Chicago.

Rajan, R., Zingales, L., 2003. Saving Capitalism from the Capitalists. Crown Business Division of Random House, New York.

Roe, M., 1994. Strong Managers and Weak Owners: The Political Roots of American Corporate Finance. Princeton University Press, Princeton, NJ.

Roe, M., 1999. Political preconditions to separating ownership from corporate control. Unpublished working paper, Columbia Law School, New York.

50 *R.G. Rajan, L. Zingales / Journal of Financial Economics 69 (2003) 5–50*

Rogowski, R., 1989. Commerce and Coalitions: How Trade Affects Domestic Political Arrangements. Princeton University Press, Princeton, NJ.

Rose, N., 1987. Labor rent sharing and regulation: evidence from the trucking industry. Journal of Political Economy 95, 1146–1178.

Rosenbluth, F., 1989. Financial Politics in Contemporary Japan. Cornell University Press, Ithaca, NY.

Salinger, M., 1984. Tobin's q, unionization, and the concentration-profits relationship. The Rand Journal of Economics 15, 159–170.

Simon, C., 1989. The effect of the 1933 securities act on investor information and the performance of new issues. American Economic Review 79, 295–318.

Stigler, G., 1971. The theory of economic regulation. Bell Journal of Economics and Management Science 2, 3–21.

Stulz, R., Williamson, R., 2001. Culture, openness, and finance. Unpublished Working Paper 8222, NBER, Cambridge, MA.

Svaleryd, H., Vlachos, J., 2002. Market for risk and openness to trade: how are they related? Journal of International Economics 57, 369–395.

Sylla, R., Smith, G., 1995. Information and capital market regulation in Anglo-American finance. In: Bordo, M., Sylla, R. (Eds.), Anglo-American Financial Systems: Institutions and Markets in the Twentieth Century. Irwin Publishers, Burr Ridge, IL.

Tanzi, V., Schuknecht, L., 2000. Public Spending in the twentieth century: a global perspective. Cambridge University Press, Cambridge, England.

Taylor, A., 1998. Argentina and the world capital market: saving, investment, and international capital mobility in the Twentieth Century. Development and Economics 57, 147–184.

Teranishi, J., 1994. Loan syndication in war-time Japan and the origins of the main bank system. In: Aoki, M., Patrick, H. (Eds.), The Japanese Main Bank System: Its Relevance for Developing and Transferring Economies. Oxford University Press, New York.

Tilly, R., 1992. An overview of the role of large German banks up to 1914. In: Cassis, Y. (Ed.), Finance and Financiers in European History 1880–1960. Cambridge University Press, Cambridge, England.

Weber, K., Davis, G., 2000. The global spread of stock exchanges 1980–1998. Unpublished working paper, University of Michigan.

Wei, S., 2000. Natural openness and good government. Unpublished Working Paper 7765, NBER, Cambridge, MA.

Estimating the Value of Political Connections

By Raymond Fisman*

As the Indonesian economy went into a downward spiral in the latter half of 1997, there was much speculation and debate as to the reasons behind the sudden decline. Most explanations gave at least some role to investor panic, which had led to a massive outflow of foreign capital. At the root of this hysteria, however, were concerns that the capital that had flowed into Indonesia and elsewhere in Southeast Asia had not been used for productive investments. Much of this discussion focused on the role of political connections in driving investment. The claim was that in Southeast Asia, political connectedness, rather than fundamentals such as productivity, was the primary determinant of profitability and that this had led to distorted investment decisions. Obviously, the degree to which this type of problem was truly responsible for the Asian collapse depends very much on the extent to which connectedness really was a primary determinant of firm value. In making the argument that this was in fact the case, anecdotes about the business dealings of President Suharto's children were often cited as evidence. Such stories suggest that the value of some firms may have been highly dependent on their political connections. However, investigations in this area have not progressed beyond the level of case study and anecdote. That is, there has been no attempt to estimate the degree to which firms rely on connections for their profitability.

There are numerous difficulties that would

affect any attempt to value political connections, which probably accounts for the paucity of work in this area. In countries where political decision-making is decentralized, simply defining political connectedness is an extremely complicated proposition. For example, in India, analyzing a firm's political associations would require information on its relationships with numerous government decision-making bodies as well as some way of aggregating these connections. Even with a specific measure in mind, collecting the appropriate data would be difficult because business–politics relations is often a taboo topic of conversation and because connections tend to shift considerably over time. Finally, assuming that an appropriate measure were found, it is not clear how one would estimate the *value* of these connections. Simple measures of profitability are unsuitable: in equilibrium, well-connected firms may not earn higher profits, even if they are earning tremendous political rents, because of the resources they may be required to devote to rent-seeking activities. Also, it is plausible that unobservables such as business acumen are correlated with the ability to establish political connections.

By looking at Indonesia, I am able to overcome these problems. Because of Indonesia's highly centralized and stable political structure (until the very end of Suharto's reign), it is possible to construct a credible index of political connectedness. Moreover, my "event study" approach described below allows for a relatively clean measure of the extent to which firms relied on these connections for their profitability.

To infer a measure of the value of connections, I take advantage of a string of rumors about former Indonesian President Suharto's health during his final years in office. I identify a number of episodes during which there were adverse rumors about the state of Suharto's health and compare the returns of firms with differing degrees of political exposure. First, I

* Graduate School of Business, 614 Uris Hall, Columbia University, 3022 Broadway, New York, NY 10027. I thank George Baker, Richard Caves, Gary Chamberlain, Rafael Di Tella, Tarun Khanna, Sendhil Mullainathan, Jan Rivkin, James Schorr, Dr. Sjahrir, Joseph Stern, Peter Timmer, Lou Wells, and seminar participants at Harvard University and the University of California at San Diego for many helpful comments on earlier versions of this paper; two anonymous referees provided thoughtful insights and suggestions. I am also very grateful to the many members of the Indonesian business community who were kind enough to meet with me during my visits to Jakarta. Any remaining errors are my own.

1096   *THE AMERICAN ECONOMIC REVIEW*   SEPTEMBER 2001

show that in every case the returns of shares of politically dependent firms were considerably lower than the returns of less-dependent firms. Furthermore, the magnitude of this differential effect is highly correlated with the net return on the Jakarta Stock Exchange Composite Index (JCI) over the corresponding episode, a relationship that derives from the fact that the return on the JCI is a measure of the severity of the rumor as perceived by investors. Motivated by these initial observations, I run a pooled regression using all of the events, allowing for an interaction between "political dependency" and "event severity." The coefficient on this interaction term is positive and statistically significant, implying that well-connected firms will suffer more, relative to less-connected firms, in reaction to a more serious rumor. My results suggest that a large percentage of a well-connected firm's value may be derived from political connections.

A few earlier papers dealt with related issues, beginning with Anne O. Krueger's (1974) pioneering work, which focused on rent-seeking behavior and efficiency losses resulting from restrictive trade policies. As Krueger herself concedes, however, the proxies she uses for the value of rents are very rough. Moreover, while her paper finds economic rents to be a substantial percentage of total GDP, it deals only with *aggregate* political rents and is therefore unable to say anything directly about the rents obtained by individual firms. A paper in the political science literature (Brian E. Roberts, 1990) looks more directly at the valuation of political connections. It examines the effect of Senator Henry Jackson's (unexpected) death on various constituent interests and on the constituent interests of his successor on the Senate Armed Services Committee. Robert's event study showed that share prices of companies with ties to Senator Jackson declined in reaction to news of his death whereas the prices of companies affiliated with his successor increased. Not surprisingly, the reported effects are quite small—the companies' ties to the two senators presumably reflected only a small fraction of the full value of their aggregate political connections. Thus, although Roberts' paper showed that connections matter, it did not address the larger question that I attempt to answer here: *How much* do connections matter?

The rest of the paper is structured as follows: Section I describes the data that were acquired

for this project. In Section II, I present the paper's basic econometric results and provide an interpretation of the implied effect. Section III looks at some issues of robustness. Finally, conclusions and the implications of the results are given in Section IV.

I. Data

Four separate types of data were acquired for this study: 1) stock market and accounting data for companies traded on the Jakarta Stock Exchange (JSX); 2) data on the group affiliations of all JSX firms; 3) a measure of the political dependence of a subset of these firms; and 4) a series of "events" related to the condition of Suharto's health.

A. *Accounting and Share Price Data*

The accounting data were taken from the *Financial Times'* Extel Financials Database (1997). I used data from 1995 because it is the most recent year with reasonably broad coverage. The accounting variables used include total assets (ASSETS), total debt (DEBT), taxes (TAX), net income (NI), and the international standard industrial classification (ISIC) code of the firm's industry.

For stock price data, I use the *Financial Times'* Extel Securities Database (1997). Unfortunately, there are a few gaps in its coverage of Indonesian firms; to fill in these holes, I used data from Investamatic Database (1998), a financial services data base that is commonly used by Southeast Asian securities firms.

B. *Group Affiliation*[1]

In Indonesia, group affiliations are not publicly reported; they must be inferred by looking at a firm's major shareholders and by examining

[1] Diversified business groups (called *grupos* in Latin America, *chaebol* in Korea, *business houses* in India, and *keiretsu* in Japan) are ubiquitous yet poorly understood organizational forms that dominate the private sectors of many countries. Such groups are comprised of a diverse set of businesses, often initiated by a single family (this is certainly the case in Indonesia), and bound together by equity cross-ownership and common board membership. See Yoshihara Kunio (1988) for a detailed description of groups in Southeast Asia.

the composition of its board and management. Several consulting firms in Jakarta collect and sell this information, which facilitates the collection of these data. My primary source is *Top Companies and Big Groups in Indonesia* (Kompass Indonesia, 1996), which lists the top 200 Indonesian groups along with their affiliated companies. This publication was last revised in 1996 and, as a result, is slightly outdated; for newer firms, the *Indonesian Capital Markets Directory 1997* (Jakarta Stock Exchange, 1997) was used to fill in the blanks. No mention of the Tahija Group was made in either of these primary sources. Firms affiliated with this group were identified by using a list of Tahija-affiliated companies given in a recent *AsiaMoney* article (Matthew Montagu-Pollock, 1995). Finally, all group membership classifications were confirmed by investment analysts in Jakarta in December 1997, which resulted in only slight revisions. There were virtually no changes in the group affiliations of publicly traded companies in the period under study, so there is no need to deal with shifts in ownership.

C. *Political Connectedness*

As a measure of political connections, I use the Suharto Dependency Index (1995) (referred to by the variable *POL* below) developed by the Castle Group, a leading economic consulting firm in Jakarta. Over the past few years, the group has assisted over 150 multinationals with entry and market strategies for Indonesia. Its services include "partner searches" to help foreigners find appropriate local business partners and "customized profiles of Indonesian business groups." Among its more popular products is a *Roadmap of Indonesian Business Groups* (1998), which outlines the relationships among these groups along with information about their holdings and government connections.

The index itself was put together for a seminar given to members of the Jakarta business community in early 1996 and is based on the subjective assessments of a number of top consultants at the Castle Group (including the president, James W. Castle). It consists of a numerical rating of the degree to which each of the 25 largest industrial groups in Indonesia is dependent on political con-

nections for its profitability.[2] The ratings range from one (least dependent) to five (most dependent). Most of these groups have multiple companies listed on the JSX, yielding a total sample of 79 firms.[3] All of the companies affiliated with President Suharto's children (Bimantara and Citra Lamtoro Groups) received a score of five, as did those owned by longtime Suharto allies Bob Hasan (Nusamba Group), Liem Sioe Liong (Salim Group), and Prajogo Pangestu (Barito Pacific Group). At the other extreme, firms owned by the Bakrie brothers and Julius Tahija were given a score of one. For this paper, I subtracted one from the index to facilitate the interpretation of coefficients in regressions involving interaction terms.

Some basic summary statistics of firms, by degree of political dependence, are listed in Table 1. There do not appear to be any systematic differences in size or debt structure across firm type.

D. *Information on Suharto's Health*

During 1995–1997, the Indonesian financial markets were occasionally hit by rumors about Suharto's health. To determine the relevant events, the keywords SUHARTO, HEALTH and INDONESIA, and (STOCK or FINANCIAL) were used in a Lexis-Nexis literature search. This returned 484 stories, most of which referred to one or more of the six episodes outlined in the unpublished Appendix.[4] For nearly all of these episodes, it was possible to

---

[2] Definition from a conversation with James Castle, August 12, 1998.

[3] A number of publicly traded companies are associated with several groups, which raises the issue of how to classify companies with multiple affiliations. In my sample, there were 12 firms for which this problem arose. Of these, only three had multiple "top 25" groups as shareholders. For these three firms, I took a simple arithmetic average of the level of political dependency of the top 25 affiliated groups (in only one of these cases was there a difference of more than one among the rankings of the multiple owners). For the others, each firm was assigned the political dependency of the one top 25 group with which it was affiliated. Because I do not have any measure of dependency for smaller groups, this is my best guess of the firm's overall political dependency. All of the analyses below were repeated excluding firms with multiple affiliations; this affected the results only slightly.

[4] The few articles that did not refer to one of these events were unrelated to Suharto's personal health.

1098   THE AMERICAN ECONOMIC REVIEW   *SEPTEMBER 2001*

TABLE 1—SUMMARY STATISTICS BY DEGREE OF POLITICAL DEPENDENCE AS MEASURED
BY THE SUHARTO DEPENDENCY INDEX

POL	1	2	3	4	5	All firms	Observations
Observations	5	34	10	16	14	79	
	2,145.76	2,228.57	2,206.20	1,634.08	1,765.51	2,033.19	
Assets	(2,843.63)	(3,989.85)	(3,676.99)	(2,561.07)	(2,230.52)	(3,321.59)	76
	707.18	791.32	813.25	397.83	712.57	717.37	
Debt	(702.84)	(1,478.83)	(976.28)	(461.06)	(1,070.83)	(1,186.85)	70
Return on assets							
(net income)/	0.038	0.058	0.043	0.037	0.050	0.050	
(total assets)	(0.031)	(0.058)	(0.023)	(0.032)	(0.029)	(0.044)	76
Tax rate (taxes							
paid)/(pretax	0.23	0.24	0.16	0.22	0.15	0.21	
income)	(0.05)	(0.12)	(0.14)	(0.16)	(0.12)	(0.13)	74

Sources: All data are from the *Financial Times' Extel Database* (1997); Assets and Debt are expressed in millions of 1995 rupiah.

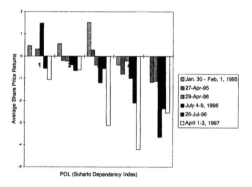

FIGURE 1. EFFECT OF POLITICAL DEPENDENCE ON SHARE PRICE RETURNS

ascertain the date when rumors first hit the Jakarta Exchange—there was generally a specific triggering *event*, which I take as the start of the episode. I assumed that each episode came to an end when it was (1) explicitly put to rest by the revelation of new information or (2) it was reported that analysts had factored the new information about Suharto's health into their pricing of securities.

II. Results

Figure 1 shows the share price returns for the six episodes, with the Suharto Dependency Index on the horizontal axis. The graph strongly suggests that politically dependent firms, on av-

erage, lost more value during these episodes than did less-dependent firms.

To get a sense of the magnitude of the effect of political dependence during each episode, I ran a set of regressions using the following specification:

$$(1) \qquad R_{ie} = \alpha + \rho \cdot POL_i + \varepsilon_{ie}$$

where R_{ie} is the return on the price of security i during episode e, POL_i is the firm's Suharto Dependency Number, and ε_{ie} is the error term.[5] The results of this set of regressions are listed in Table 2; consistent with the raw pattern illustrated in Figure 1, ρ is negative in every instance.

Now, in each episode, investors were reacting to a different piece of news, so we expect the coefficient on POL_i to differ across events. More precisely, a more severe threat to Suharto's health should intensify the effect of political dependence, hence the magnitude of ρ should be increasing with event severity. As a measure of the market's concerns regarding the threat to Suharto's health in each episode, I use

---

[5] All regressions reported in this paper use standard errors that correct for heteroskedasticity. I also ran regressions using an error structure that only allowed for the correlation of ε_{ei}s for each company, i.e., $Cov(\varepsilon_{ei}, \varepsilon_{fj}) \neq 0$ if and only if $i = j$. The regressions were also run using an error structure that allowed for the correlation of ε_{ei}s within each group. These various approaches yielded very similar sets of standard errors.

VOL. 91 NO. 4   *FISMAN: ESTIMATING THE VALUE OF POLITICAL CONNECTIONS*   1099

TABLE 2—EFFECT OF POLITICAL CONNECTIONS ON CHANGES IN SHARE PRICE, SEPARATE ESTIMATION FOR EACH EVENT

	Jan. 30–Feb. 1, 1995	April 27, 1995	April 29, 1996	July 4–9, 1996	July 26, 1996	April 1–3, 1997
POL	−0.58* (0.34)	−0.31 (0.18)	−0.24* (0.15)	−0.95*** (0.27)	−0.57*** (0.22)	−0.90** (0.35)
Constant	1.29 (0.79)	0.21 (0.32)	0.12 (0.46)	0.83 (0.64)	−0.07 (0.41)	0.77 (0.97)
R^2	0.037	0.043	0.025	0.147	0.078	0.075
Observations	70	70	78	79	79	79

Note: Robust standard errors are in parentheses.
 * Significantly different from 0 at the 10-percent level.
 ** Significantly different from 0 at the 5-percent level.
 *** Significantly different from 0 at the 1-percent level.

the return on the Jakarta Stock Exchange Composite Index net of broader Southeast Asian effects[6] [referred to using $NR_e(JCI)$]. The preceding observations suggest that the coefficient on POL should be more negative if the threat to Suharto's health, as proxied by $NR_e(JCI)$, is greater.[7] This turns out to be the case: the correlation between ρ and $NR_e(JCI)$ is 0.98. This implies a specification where observations from all events are pooled together, with an interaction term, $NR_e(JCI) * POL_i$, added to allow the effect of political dependence to vary across events, depending on the event's severity. Thus, I use the following full-sample specification:

TABLE 3—EFFECT OF POLITICAL CONNECTIONS ON CHANGES IN SHARE PRICE

	(1)	(2)
POL	−0.60** (0.11)	−0.19 (0.15)
NR(JCI)	0.25 (0.14)	−0.32 (0.28)
NR(JCI) · POL		0.28* (0.11)
Constant	0.88 (0.27)	0.06 (0.35)
R^2	0.066	0.078
Number of observations	455	455

Note: Robust standard errors are in parentheses.
 * Significantly different from 0 at the 5-percent level.
 ** Significantly different from 0 at the 1-percent level.

$$(2) \quad R(P_{ie}) = \alpha + \rho_1 \cdot POL_i$$
$$+ \rho_2 \cdot NR_e(JCI) + \rho_3$$
$$\cdot [NR_e(JCI) \cdot POL_i] + \varepsilon_{ie}.$$

The results of this regression are listed in Table 3.[8]

If the severity of a rumor affects politically dependent firms more than less-dependent firms, then the coefficient on the interaction term $NR_e(JCI) \cdot POL_i$ should be positive. The estimated coefficient, ρ_3, is statistically significant at 5 percent and is equal to 0.28. Thus, if the overall market declined by 1 percent in reaction to news about Suharto's health, we might expect a firm with $POL = x$ to drop 0.28 percent more than a firm with $POL = x - 1$.

[6] To net out broader Southeast Asia effects, I ran the following "market model" for daily returns during 1994:

$$R_t(JCI) = \alpha + \sum_{m \in M} \beta_m \cdot R_t(m) + \varepsilon_t$$

where $R_t(JCI)$ is the return on the Jakarta Composite on day t, $R_t(m)$ is the return on market index m, and M is the set of ASEAN market indices (including Tokyo's Nikkei 225, Hong Kong's Hang Seng, Singapore's Straits Times, Bangkok's SET, Taiwan's Weighted, Philippines' Composite, Kuala Lumpur's Composite, and Seoul's Composite). This produced a set of coefficients reflecting the degree of correlation between the JCI and other market indices. For each episode e, the *net* return for the JCI is then given by

$$NR_e(JCI) = R_e(JCI) - [\hat{\alpha} + \sum_{m \in M} \beta_m \cdot R_e(m)].$$

[7] It may seem somewhat circular to use $NR_e(JCI)$ as a measure of the severity of the threat to Suharto's health when many of the firms in my sample are constituents of the JCI. Note, however, that $NR_e(JCI)$ is a difference, of which the coefficient on POL is a difference in differences. As Section III, subsection B, illustrates, these two variables need not be correlated.

[8] Regressions were also run using log(ASSETS), log(DEBT), and industry dummies as controls. These additions did not alter the size of significance of the interaction term.

One problem with the events described above is that they cannot be used to infer the full value of connections because the associated rumors only *increased* the probability that Suharto would leave office. To estimate the full value of connections would require an event involving Suharto's sudden and unexpected removal from office. (To the extent that connections were expected to continue to have some value even after Suharto, the shifts in share prices associated with such an event would understate the full value of connections.) However, no such event took place.[9]

In the absence of an actual sudden regime shift, we may be able to infer what the coefficient on *POL* would have been in such an event by using equation (2). During a visit to Jakarta in August 1997, I asked a number of investment bankers how much they thought the Jakarta Composite Index would have dropped if Suharto had died suddenly; 20 percent was the modal response to this question. If this value is taken as the best estimate of investor expectations, then (2) implies that the coefficient on *POL* would have been about 5.8 in the event of a sudden regime shift. This suggests that, in reaction to such an event, the returns for a firm with *POL* = 4 would have been about 23 percentage points lower than the returns for a firm with *POL* = 0. Thus, for plausible parameters, the results suggest that connections were very valuable for well-connected firms (though this calculation involves an inference that is quite far out of sample).

---

[9] Although Suharto was forced from office in May 1998, it is difficult to utilize this event for a number of reasons. Most importantly, there were many confounding events that took place simultaneously, including a drastic devaluation of the Indonesian rupiah, rioting and general political instability, and the implementation of an IMF rescue package. Moreover, by the end of 1997, shares on the Jakarta Stock Exchange were very thinly traded, making it relatively easy for prices to be manipulated. There are also serious difficulties in trying to define an appropriate event window: expectations of a regime shift had begun to form long before Suharto was replaced, so it is difficult to allow for a reasonably short event window. Finally, it is not even clear that Suharto's removal from power was actually accompanied by a regime change, given that he was succeeded by his longtime associate and apparent ally, B. J. Habibie.

Thus, although Suharto's children's companies declined quite drastically over the first few months of 1998, there is no systematic relationship between share price returns and political dependence, perhaps owing to the difficulties described above.

III. Robustness

A. *Thinly Traded Firms*

Whenever the market received adverse information regarding Suharto's health, it declined on average. However, if a company was not traded on that day, it would register no price change, even if it suffered a decline in its underlying value. There are two counteracting biases that may result, and the overall effect depends on their relative strengths. The intuition for a bias toward zero is that, among firms with zero trading volume, no "difference in difference" in returns between different types of firms will be recorded, even if there is such an effect on the underlying values of the securities. This could similarly bias the coefficient on $POL \cdot NR_e(JCI)$ toward zero. The direction of the second source of bias depends on whether connected or unconnected firms are more thinly traded. Suppose that unconnected firms are more likely to have zero trading volume. Then, what is being interpreted as the effect of connectedness may be a manifestation of the general market decline—a smaller decline in unconnected firms is observed simply because they are not being traded. This could also potentially bias the coefficient on the interaction term away from zero if an increase in the size of the rumor decreased the proportion of non-traded well-connected firms relative to non-traded unconnected companies. The data show that the opposite is true so, if anything, a bias toward zero may result.

To further examine the overall bias that these effects may have on the results, I revisited all of the basic models, limiting the sample to the set of firm–event observations where the firm had a positive trading volume during the relevant period. This affected the interaction term in Table 3 only slightly.

B. *Are Politically Dependent Firms More Sensitive to Bad News?*[10]

As noted previously, the JSX consistently declined whenever Suharto's health was

---

[10] This section essentially examines whether politically dependent firms have high betas.

brought into question. If politically dependent firms are more sensitive to bad news of any kind, then they will register larger losses on such days. This could be the source of the "difference in differences" that is being interpreted as the connectedness effect. To examine this possibility, I analyzed share price returns in reaction to other shocks that were more or less unrelated to the longevity of the Suharto regime. The beginning of the Southeast Asian financial crisis in 1997 provides a suitable example. The above analyses were repeated for trading days in the week following August 12, when the rupiah was floated by the Indonesian government. On these days, there was no relationship between share price returns and dependence. Similarly, there was no relationship between returns and political dependence on trading days following those days when the S&P 500 Index lost more than 2 percent.

C. *Appropriateness of the Event Window*

There may be some concern that trading on inside information prior to the onset of the rumors described in the unpublished Appendix could lead to price changes among well-connected firms earlier than my chosen starting day. When regressions were run using *total* returns over an event window expanded to include the two days (or one day) prior to the onset of the actual event, for all events except April 25–27, 1995, there was simply a minor attenuation of the results.

D. *Monotonicity of POL*

I have assumed throughout a linear specification for *POL*. It would be of concern if the relationship between *POL* and R_{ie} were not, at a minimum, monotonic. If this were not the case, it would bring into question the validity of the Castle Index and/or the appropriateness of my analyses. To examine this possibility, I ran the following, which allows *POL* to have a flexible functional form:

$$(3) \quad R_{ie} = \alpha + \sum_{p=2}^{5} \beta_p I_{POL \ge p} + \sum_{e=2}^{6} \gamma_e + \varepsilon_{ie}$$

where

$$I_{POL \ge p} = \begin{cases} 0 & \text{if} \quad POL < p \\ 1 & \text{if} \quad POL \ge p \end{cases}$$

and the γ_es provide event fixed effects.

The coefficients on the indicator variables were uniformly negative, ranging from -0.35 to -0.87. These results are consistent with the use of the Castle Index as a measure of political dependence.

We may go a little further by testing for the equality of the β_ps with the test statistic $F(3, 445) = 0.24$ (3 restrictions, 455 observations, and 10 variables). This implies that the hypothesis of equality of coefficients cannot be rejected at any significance level below 86 percent. Thus, the use of a linear specification on *POL* is also justified.

IV. Conclusion

This paper has concentrated on the valuation of rents for a relatively small subsample of Indonesian firms. However, the 25 groups associated with these firms account for a very large percentage of economic activity in Indonesia, with revenues of more than U.S. $60 billion in 1995 (as a frame of reference, Indonesia's GNP in 1995 was about U.S. $200 billion). Thus, for a very large part of the Indonesian economy, political connections apparently matter a lot.

Although the preceding analysis focused on Indonesia, there is reason to believe that the results apply to many other countries. For example, in Transparency International's frequently cited "Perceived Corruption Ranking (1998)," Indonesia ranks 45th out of the 54 countries surveyed. It was perceived as being less corrupt than, among others, India, Russia, Pakistan, China, Nigeria, and Bangladesh. To the extent that perceived corruption is a reasonable proxy for the prevalence of political rents, the results of this paper suggest that political connections may play an important role in many of the world's largest and most important economies.

REFERENCES

Corruption Perception Index. Berlin: *Transparency International*, 1998.

Extel Financials Database. London: *Financial Times*, 1997.

Extel Securities Database. London: *Financial Times*, 1997.

Investamatic Database. Singapore: *The Investamatic Group*, 1998.

Jakarta Stock Exchange. *Indonesian capital markets directory 1997.* Jakarta: Institute for Economic and Financial Research, 1997.

Kompass Indonesia. *Top companies and big groups in Indonesia.* Jakarta: Kompass Indonesia, 1996.

Krueger, Anne O. "The Political Economy of the Rent-Seeking Society." *American Economic Review*, June 1974, *64*(3), pp. 291–303.

Kunio, Yoshihara. *The rise of ersatz Capitalism in South-East Asia.* Singapore: Oxford University Press, 1988.

Montagu-Pollock, Matthew. "Who's Who in Indonesia." *AsiaMoney*, December 1995, *6*(10), pp. 89–93.

Roadmap of the Indonesian Ecomomy. Jakarta: *The Castle Group*, 1998.

Roberts, Brian E. "A Dead Senator Tells No Lies: Seniority and the Distribution of Federal Benefits." *American Journal of Political Science*, February 1990, *34*(1), pp. 31–58.

Suharto Dependency Index. Jakarta: *The Castle Group*, 1995.

ELSEVIER   Journal of Financial Economics 67 (2003) 351–382

www.elsevier.com/locate/econbase

Cronyism and capital controls: evidence from Malaysia[☆]

Simon Johnson[a,]*, Todd Mitton[b]

[a] *Sloan School of Management, Massachusetts Institute of Technology, Cambridge, MA 02142, USA*
[b] *Marriott School, Brigham Young University, Provo, UT 84602, USA*

Received 24 August 2001; accepted 25 January 2002

Abstract

The onset of the Asian financial crisis in Malaysia reduced the expected value of government subsidies to politically connected firms, accounting for roughly 9% of the estimated $60 billion loss in their market value from July 1997 to August 1998. Firing the Deputy Prime Minister and imposing capital controls in September 1998 primarily benefited firms with strong ties to Prime Minister Mahathir, accounting for roughly 32% of these firms' estimated $5 billion gain in market value during September 1998. The evidence suggests Malaysian capital controls provided a screen behind which favored firms could be supported.
© 2002 Elsevier Science B.V. All rights reserved.

JEL classification: G15; G38; F31

Keywords: Capital controls; Political connections; Financial crises; Institutions

---

[☆]Johnson thanks the MIT Entrepreneurship Center for support. We thank Jim Brau for help with the SDC data. For helpful comments we thank an anonymous referee, Daron Acemoglu, Olivier Blanchard, Jim Brau, Ricardo Caballero, Ray Fisman, Tarun Khanna, Grant McQueen, Randall Morck, Sendhil Mullainathan, Raghuram Rajan, Dani Rodrik, David Scharfstein, Andrei Shleifer, Jeremy Stein, Keith Vorkink, Bernard Yeung, and participants at the MIT Macroeconomics lunch, the NBER conference on the Malaysian Currency Crisis, the NBER corporate finance program spring 2001 meeting, and the Brigham Young University finance seminar. We also thank several Malaysian colleagues for sharing their insights off the record.
  *Corresponding author. Tel.: + 1-617-253-8412; fax: + 1-617-253-2660.
  E-mail address: sjohnson@mit.edu (S. Johnson).

352   *S. Johnson, T. Mitton / Journal of Financial Economics 67 (2003) 351–382*

1. Introduction

Until the late 1970s, capital controls were widely used to prevent the free flow of funds between countries. A cautious relaxation of such controls during the 1980s proved consistent with greater economic integration in Europe and strengthened the case for capital market opening more generally. By the time the IMF and World Bank encouraged a further wave of liberalization for "emerging markets" in the early 1990s, capital controls appeared to be finished as a serious policy tool for relatively open economies (Bhagwati, 1998a). Today, however, capital controls are again being taken seriously. Malaysia reimposed capital controls in September 1998, China and Chile maintain effective capital account restrictions, and there is debate regarding the value of free capital flows in a number of crisis-prone countries, including Korea, Russia, and Turkey. Capital controls have also just begun to be mentioned as a possibility for Japan (Dornbusch, 2001b).

There are two main views on the causes and effects of capital controls. The more established view emphasizes macroeconomics. If a country faces a severe external crisis, particularly one caused by pure panic, and if standard measures have failed, Krugman (1998) argues that imposing capital controls may be an effective way to stabilize the economy. More generally, Bhagwati (1998a, b) and Rodrik (2000) oppose the conventional wisdom that free capital flows help countries benefit from trade liberalization, and argue instead that capital market liberalization invites speculative attacks. The recent performance of Malaysia has been interpreted as demonstrating that capital controls can have positive macroeconomic effects (Kaplan and Rodrik, 2001), although this claim is controversial (Dornbusch, 2001a).

While not denying the importance of macroeconomic issues, the second view puts greater emphasis on institutions (i.e., the rules, practices and organizations that govern an economy). Olson (1982) argues that when societies remain stable, they tend to develop organized interest groups that are rent seeking (e.g., his Proposition 2 on p. 41). He also argues that "on balance, special-interest organizations and collusions reduce efficiency and aggregate income in the societies in which they operate and make political life more divisive" (p. 47). Related ideas are developed in Ekelund and Tollison (1981) and Parente and Prescott (1994). More recently, Morck, Strangeland, and Yeung (2000) argue that Olsonian entrenchment leads to protection for inefficient activities, such as in the form of tariff barriers. Reducing these barriers hurts entrenched firms; for example, established, well-connected firms in Canada (as measured by family inheritance of control) are less efficient and had negative abnormal stock returns when the 1988 Canada-US free trade agreement reduced barriers to foreign capital.

The Morck, Strangeland, and Yeung argument can also be applied to capital controls. If this view is correct, we should expect capital controls to be associated with an increase in cronyism (i.e., the resources available to firms through political favoritism). There are two testable implications at the firm level for a country such as Malaysia. Firms with stronger political connections should (1) suffer more when a macroeconomic shock reduces the government's ability to provide privileges and

S. Johnson, T. Mitton / Journal of Financial Economics 67 (2003) 351–382 353

subsidies and (2) benefit more when the imposition of capital controls allows a higher level of subsidies.

Using data from Malaysia before and after the imposition of capital controls, this paper reports strong support for both hypotheses. In the initial phase of the crisis, from July 1997 to August 1998, roughly 9% of the estimated $60 billion loss in market value for politically connected firms can be attributed to the fall in the expected value of their connections. With the imposition of capital controls in September 1998, about 32% of the estimated $5 billion gain in market value for firms connected to Prime Minister Mahathir can be attributed to the increase in the value of their connections. For connected firms, the value of political connections was approximately 17% of their total market value at the end of September 1998.

Malaysia is an appealing case study for several reasons. Researchers identified important relationships between politicians and firms before capital controls were imposed (Gomez and Jomo, 1997). Politically connected firms could generally differ in unobservable ways relative to unconnected firms, but in the Malaysian data it is possible also to examine variation in performance within the set of politically connected firms. Because the imposition of capital controls in September 1998 coincided with a major political realignment, with Prime Minister Mahathir Mohamad winning and Deputy Prime Minister Anwar Ibrahim losing, any "excess" gain for firms connected to the winner should provide a good measure of cronyism with capital controls.

In this analysis, it is important that whether a firm was affiliated with Mahathir or Anwar is not due to some other unobserved characteristics of the firm. According to the detailed research of Gomez and Jomo (1997), the connection of firms to individual politicians appears to have been based primarily on chance personal histories. Early friendships with rising politicians, such as Mahathir and Anwar, have been an effective way to build firms in Malaysia over the past 20 years. In other words, the personal relationships between individuals in our dataset largely predate associations of these individuals with particular firms and so political connections were not determined by the nature of the firms themselves.

In addition, throughout the Asian financial crisis that began in July 1997, Malaysia maintained a large and liquid stock market, so examining how stock prices varied across firms is a reasonable way to measure the effects of policy changes. Anecdotal evidence suggests that financial markets understood the crisis as a threat to politically favored firms and believed that the imposition of capital controls represented an opportunity for strong politicians to support some firms. The available information also indicates that these expectations have subsequently been met—for example, there have been numerous press reports of government support for well-connected firms after September 1998.

We find that firms' stock price performance in Malaysia is broadly supportive of the view that capital controls create a screen for cronyism. Firms with political connections had worse stock returns in the early phase of the Asian financial crisis, but once capital controls were imposed, these firms did better on average. One way to evaluate the size of this effect is to compare having a political connection with the consequences of having higher leverage when the crisis hit. Malaysian firms with

354 *S. Johnson, T. Mitton / Journal of Financial Economics 67 (2003) 351–382*

more debt suffered larger falls in stock price in the first phase of the crisis (through August 1998). Having political connections had a similar effect (in the sense of inducing a similar fall in stock price) to that of increasing a firm's debt-asset ratio by 50-60 percentage points, e.g., from the median of 23.3% to around 75% (roughly equivalent to a $2\frac{1}{2}$-standard deviation increase in the debt ratio). These results hold when we control for other measurable characteristics of the firms, such as debt, size, and sector. The results also hold when we control for whether a firm has the status of being "Bumiputera," meaning that it is largely owned by Malays and qualifies for some official government support.

Consistent with the view that cronyism increases with capital controls, we find that only firms previously connected to Prime Minister Mahathir experienced a disproportionate increase in stock price in September 1998. The stock market's reaction appears to have been confirmed by subsequent events—over the following year, Anwar-connected firms were either taken over by Mahathir-connected firms or their owners switched allegiance to Mahathir.

The paper closest to our approach is Fisman (2001), who estimates the value of political connections in Indonesia by looking at how stock prices moved when former President Suharto's health was reported to change. Fisman measures the direct effect of health shocks to a dictator, which is presumably quite specific to authoritarian systems, during a period of relative economic stability. The Malaysian experience lets us examine the interaction of cronyism and capital controls in a democracy. In addition, we are able to use variation between firms connected to winning and losing politicians. This helps ensure that political connections rather than some other unobservable characteristics of firms drive our results.

Rajan and Zingales (1998) argue that capital controls are an essential part of the package of policies that allows "relationship-based" capitalism to function. In this system, informal relationships between politicians and banks channel lending towards approved firms, and this is easier to sustain when a country is relatively isolated from international capital flows. If capital controls are relaxed, as in some parts of Asia in the early 1990s, the result may be overborrowing and financial collapse (Rajan and Zingales, 1998).[1] In this context, Rajan and Zingales (2001) suggest that reimposing capital controls may be attractive if it enables politicians to support the financing of particular firms. At the same time, directed lending behind capital controls could create future problems due to bad loans and distorted incentives. Leading proponents of the macroeconomic perspective on capital controls are aware that institutional issues can be important as well. For example, Kaplan and Rodrik (2001) clearly state their concerns that capital controls can distort incentives and undermine future performance in Malaysia. However, their emphasis is on macroeconomic effects (i.e., for all firms) rather than the differential benefits for just some firms.

---

[1] Theoretically, relaxing capital controls can lead to financial distress in at least three ways. First, local financial institutions respond by taking on more risk. Second, local firms borrow directly from international lenders who are either unable to assess risks appropriately or believe that there is an implicit sovereign guarantee. Third, after they lose their monopolies, local banks are less willing to bail out firms that encounter problems, as in Petersen and Rajan (1995).

S. Johnson, T. Mitton / Journal of Financial Economics 67 (2003) 351–382   355

Morck et al. (2000a) also show that while heir-controlled firms initially had lower labor intensity (suggesting superior access to capital for privileged firms), this advantage deteriorated following enactment of the Canada-U.S. free trade agreement. Our results are consistent with their idea that the level of capital mobility affects the degree to which privileged firms can receive favored treatment.

Our paper is part of a growing literature that examines the performance of relatively privileged firms. La Porta et al. (2002) show that well-connected Mexican banks engaged in a considerable amount of irresponsible lending before the 1995 crisis, and this presumably contributed to the severity of the crisis when it came. To our knowledge, no previous papers have tried to measure the combined effects of cronyism and capital controls.

Our work is also related to the recent literature that shows important links between institutions and economic outcomes. Johnson et al. (2000) present evidence that the Asian financial crisis had more severe effects in countries with weaker institutions in general and weaker investor protection in particular (as measured by La Porta et al., 1997, 1998). Mitton (2002) finds firm-level evidence that weaker corporate governance was associated with worse stock price performance in the Asian crisis, and Lemmon and Lins (2003) confirm these results using different definitions of governance and outcomes. More broadly, Morck et al. (2000b) argue that in countries with weak property rights protection, stock price movements are predominantly driven by political shocks.

Section 2 reviews the nature of political connections in Malaysia. Much of this information is taken from Gomez and Jomo (1997), whose research was completed before the Asian financial crisis broke out in July 1997. Section 3 explains our data and methodology in more detail. Section 4 reports descriptive statistics for connected and unconnected firms. Section 5 presents our main results and robustness checks. Section 6 reports the available direct evidence on what happened to firm subsidies after the imposition of capital controls. Section 7 concludes.

2. Political favoritism in Malaysia

Two forms of political favoritism exist in Malaysia today (Gomez and Jomo, 1997). The first is the official status awarded to firms that are run by ethnic Malays. The second consists of much more informal ties that exist between leading politicians and firms that are run by both Malay and Chinese business people.

Although ethnic Malays (known as Bumiputeras, literally "sons of the soil") account for some 60% of the population, business in Malaysia has historically been dominated by ethnic Chinese. With an eye toward correcting this imbalance, and partly in response to ethnic rioting in 1969, the government instituted the New Economic Policy (NEP) in 1970. Since that time, Bumiputeras have been given, among other privileges, priority for government contracts, increased access to capital, opportunities to buy assets that are privatized, and other subsidies. The ruling coalition in Malaysia for the past 30 years has been the Barisan Nasional, which is dominated by the United Malays' National Organisation (UMNO).

Dr. Mahathir Mohamad, president of UMNO and Prime Minister of Malaysia since 1981, has consistently promoted Bumiputera capitalism (Gomez and Jomo, 1997).

The increased state intervention required for implementation of the NEP has opened the door to greater political involvement in the financing of firms in Malaysia. For example, when Mahathir was minister for trade and industry in 1980 he helped set up the Heavy Industries Corporation of Malaysia (known as Hicom). Hicom subsequently invested in the auto industry, steel, and cement. This kind of investment involved the government in picking which private sector firms received access to investment resources (Perkins and Woo, 2000). As the government has more actively handed out favors to firms, businessmen have increasingly used personal connections to influence the allocation of those favors (Gomez and Jomo, 1997). During Mahathir's tenure as Prime Minister, three government officials, along with their associated protégés, concentrated their power to help business in Malaysia. The first is Mahathir himself. The second is Daim Zainuddin, who was finance minister early in Mahathir's term and who was brought back into government in 1998. He has been perhaps the most powerful person in corporate Malaysia and is generally considered to have been consistently close to Mahathir (at least until summer 2001). The third is Anwar Ibrahim, who, before his downfall in September 1998, was second in power to Mahathir and had numerous corporate connections. While Anwar was closely allied with Mahathir before the crisis, in 1998 he came to be regarded as a potential rival. Although other officials in Malaysia may have provided valuable connections for businessmen, Mahathir, Daim, and Anwar have clearly been the most dominant figures. This is illustrated in the Appendix, which lists Malaysian companies and their political connections (based on Gomez and Jomo, 1997) before the Asian financial crisis began in summer 1997.

Note that there is no evidence that the alliances betweem firms and specific politicians were the result of anything other than chance personal relationships. For example, Anwar's connection with Kamaruddin Jaafar, linked to Setron Bhd. at the time of the crisis, dates to their days as schoolmates at the Malay College (Gomez and Jomo, 1997, p. 126). As another example, Daim's relationship with Tajudin Ramli, who came to control Technology Resources Industries in 1990, was forged in the early 1980s before Daim came to power as Mahathir's finance minister (Gomez and Jomo, 1997, pp. 148–149). Before the Asian financial crisis, affiliations to either Anwar or Mahathir were close substitutes, and we have found no evidence that being close to one was preferable to being close to the other. We therefore have no reason to believe that unobserved characteristics of these firms determined their political affiliations. Any systematic differences in the performance of these firms should therefore be due to the changing relative value of their political connections.

3. Data and methodology

In this section we describe our sample of firms, define the crisis period, and describe the variables used and how they were constructed. The sample consists of all Malaysian firms with at least a minimal amount of data in the Worldscope database

S. Johnson, T. Mitton / Journal of Financial Economics 67 (2003) 351–382   357

as of October 1999. Although all firm characteristics are measured on a pre-crisis basis, we use this later version of the Worldscope database because Worldscope has substantially increased the number of firms that it covers over time. (All the firms included in Worldscope prior to the crisis were still included in October 1999, so there is no sample selection bias due to firms dropping out of the data set.) The 424 firms in our sample are representative of the firms listed on the main board of the Kuala Lumpur Stock Exchange. Firms not represented in the sample include smaller unlisted Malaysian firms and multinationals with no local listing.

Fig. 1 shows an index of stock returns of Malaysian firms in Worldscope for 1990 to 1999, measured in dollars and Malaysian ringgit. Lines on the chart delineate the "crisis period" as defined in this paper. The beginning of the crisis period corresponds to the devaluation of the Thai baht on July 2, 1997, a date generally considered to be the starting point of the Asian financial crisis. The end of the crisis period and start of the "rebound period" corresponds to the imposition of capital controls on September 2, 1998 when the stock index began a sustained upward trend.[2]

Other studies have focused on September 1998 as a key date in the Malaysian crisis. Kaplan and Rodrik (2001) explain the nature of Malaysian capital controls in detail, and assess how economic performance differed after September 1998. The most detailed account of Malaysia's economic crisis, Jomo (2001, Chapter 7), also identifies the beginning of September 1998 as the critical turning point.

3.1. Political connections

To identify which firms have political connections with government officials, we rely on the analysis of Gomez and Jomo (1997). Gomez and Jomo (1997) provide a detailed analysis of Malaysian corporations and their political connections prior to the Asian crisis. We code as "politically connected" any firm that Gomez and Jomo (1997) identify as having officers or major shareholders with close relationships with key government officials—primarily Mahathir, Daim, and Anwar. For example, Gomez and Jomo (1997) state that Technology Resources Industries (TRI) is "controlled by Tajudin Ramli, who is closely linked to Daim Zainuddin" (p. 103), so TRI is coded as politically connected, with Daim as the primary connection. As another example, because Gomez and Jomo (1997) state, "The chairman of George Town Holdings was Tunku Abdullah of the Melewar Group, a close friend of Prime Minister Mahathir" (p. 59), George Town Holdings Bhd. is coded as politically connected with its primary connection listed as Mahathir. As a final example, the phrases in Gomez and Jomo (1997) "Setron, one of the first companies linked to Anwar ..."(p. 126) and "... Setron (M) Bhd (in which Kamaruddin Jaafar, probably Anwar's closest confidant, has an interest)" (p. 57) result in Setron (Malaysia) Bhd. being coded as politically connected, with Anwar as the primary connection. We search the entire text of Gomez and Jomo (1997) for all such indications of

---

[2] Capital controls were announced on September 1 and the ringgit-dollar rate was fixed in the early afternoon of September 2, 1998.

358   *S. Johnson, T. Mitton / Journal of Financial Economics 67 (2003) 351–382*

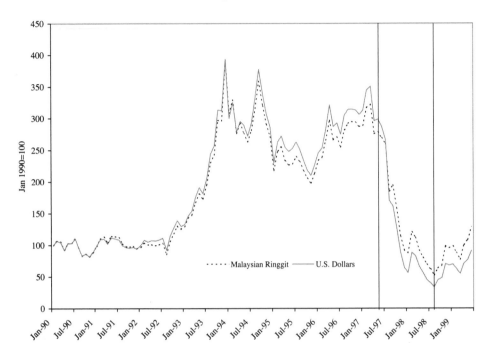

Fig. 1. Index of Malaysian stocks, 1990–1999. The figure shows equal-weighted indexes of stock prices of Malaysian firms in the Worldscope database. Vertical lines delineate the crisis period as defined in the paper.

connections and code them accordingly. The appendix lists each firm identified as connected and the source of the connection.

Using the analysis of Gomez and Jomo (1997) to identify connections has two limitations. First, these authors do not claim to have exhaustively identified every firm with political connections in Malaysia. This limitation is not too troublesome, because they likely focused on the subset of firms with the strongest connections or the subset of the largest firms with connections. The fact that larger firms generally had better stock price performance during the crisis would make it harder for us to find that (larger) connected firms performed worse during the crisis. The second limitation is that, while all connections identified by Gomez and Jomo (1997) are from before the crisis, some are identified from earlier in the 1990s, creating the possibility that a connection could have disappeared prior to the beginning of the crisis.[3] However, given the relative stability of the government over this period, this limitation is also not too worrying. Our "politically connected" dummy variable, then, is set equal to one if the firm has a connection listed in the appendix, and zero otherwise.

---

[3] In the second edition of their book, which was prepared in late 1997 and which appeared in 1998, Gomez and Jomo (1998) updated their list of political connections. We have used this revised list as a robustness check and find that it does not affect any of our main results. However, we prefer to use their pre-crisis list, as this was complete before there was any sign of economic trouble.

S. Johnson, T. Mitton / Journal of Financial Economics 67 (2003) 351–382 359

We use the same source to create an "Anwar connected" dummy variable which is set equal to one for politically connected firms whose connections depended primarily upon Anwar (based on the data presented in the Appendix; 14 firms in total). We code a firm as "Mahathir connected" if the connection in the Appendix is to Mahathir, Daim (Mahathir's consistently close political ally), UMNO (the ruling party controlled by Mahathir), or to another politician. Note that although Anwar was also an important force in UMNO before his downfall, UMNO-connected firms should still benefit from a Mahathir connection after Anwar's downfall because as president of UMNO, Mahathir should have a strong interest in supporting firms linked to UMNO. (Our results are not materially changed if we do not code UMNO-connected firms as Mahathir-connected.) Note that some firms are associated with both camps and that a few firms are politically connected but the precise nature of the connection is not identified.[4]

3.2. Description of other variables

To measure firm performance we use dividend-inclusive monthly stock returns expressed in Malaysian ringgit. We do not calculate abnormal returns using historical betas because data limitations prevent calculation of pre-crisis betas for many of the firms in the sample.[5] Instead, we control for factors that could affect expected returns by including leverage, size, and industry in the regressions.

Firm size is measured as the logarithm of total firm assets. Growth is the one-year growth rate in total assets. As a measure of leverage we use the firm's debt ratio, calculated as the book value of total debt divided by total assets. We include dummy variables for 12 of 13 industries, where industries are defined broadly, similar to the definitions in Campbell (1996), and correspond with the firm's primary SIC code. The book-to-market ratio is defined as the book value per share divided by the stock price. Return on assets is defined as net income (before interest and after taxes) divided by beginning-of-year total assets. Profit margin is defined as net income divided by net sales. The current ratio is defined as current assets divided by current liabilities, and the quick ratio is current assets minus inventory divided by current liabilities. Asset turnover is defined as net sales divided by total assets, and inventory turnover is cost of goods sold divided by inventory. Finally, we assume that short-term debt is anything with maturity of less than a year. All of these variables are constructed using data from Worldscope, and they are measured using the last available information prior to the beginning of the crisis.

As a reasonable proxy for access to international capital markets, we look at where firms' stocks traded and where firms had placed debt before the Asian crisis

---

[4] If a firm is indicated in Gomez and Jomo (1997) as having connections to both Anwar and Mahathir (a total of 5 firms), then it is coded as Mahathir-connected. This seems the best way to identify those firms that a priori we would expect to suffer from Anwar's downfall.

[5] Even requiring a price history of just 24 months, we can calculate betas for only 65% of the firms in our sample. In this subsample, all of our key results are robust to including beta in the regressions.

began in summer 1997.[6] A significant number of Malay firms are traded in countries other than Malaysia, including Singapore (the so-called Central Limit Order Book, CLOB), the US (either a direct listing or an ADR), London, and (in a few cases) Seoul or another foreign exchange. Other firms trade only on the Malaysian market. Of Mahathir-connected firms, 40% trade overseas and 60% trade only in Malaysia. In addition, a search of the Securities Data Corporation database shows that 20 of the firms in our dataset had issued debt on the Eurobond market at some point in the 1990s prior to summer 1997. (A further search shows that none of the firms in our dataset had issued debt in the US) We code a firm as having "foreign capital access" if its stock traded on a foreign exchange or if it had placed debt on the Eurobond market.

To identify whether firms are ethnically favored, we use data from the Kuala Lumpur Stock Exchange *Annual Companies Handbook* (1996–1998). For each firm, the handbook identifies how much of its ownership falls into the following categories: Bumiputera, non-Bumiputera, foreign, or government. The *Handbook* does not provide an exhaustive listing of all firms, so we are able to identify the ethnicity of ownership for only 74% of the firms. To categorize firms as Bumiputera-controlled, we focus on a definition given by the Corporate Affairs Unit of Malaysia's Securities Commission (press release, 8/27/96), which states that a Bumiputera-controlled company is one in which 50% or more of the equity is held by Bumiputera shareholders or institutions.[7] We assume that shareholdings by government agencies contribute toward this percentage. Thus, the "ethnically favored" dummy variable is set equal to one if the Bumiputera shareholdings are above this threshold and zero otherwise.

4. Descriptive statistics

Table 1 reports the basic descriptive data for these firms. The first row reports the number of firms in each category of our sample, breaking it down by politically connected versus unconnected and then by Mahathir-connected versus Anwar-connected. We also look at nonfinancial firms separately.

The second row shows that politically connected firms had significantly worse returns from July 1997 to August 1998, although there was no significant difference between Mahathir- and Anwar-connected firms. The third row shows that politically connected firms had significantly better returns in September 1998, and that Mahathir-connected firms performed much better than Anwar-connected firms. The fourth row shows no significant differences between politically connected and unconnected firms in returns after September 1998. Anwar-connected firms

[6] Lins et al. (2000) and Reese and Weisbach (2002) show that non-US firms that list in the US do so in part to improve their access to equity capital.

[7] A secondary definition from the same source notes that a firm may qualify as "Bumiputera-controlled" if 35% of the equity is held by Bumiputeras and 51% or more of the officers of the firm are Bumiputera. This definition is not useful for our purposes because the ethnicity of officers cannot always be inferred from their names.

S. Johnson, T. Mitton / Journal of Financial Economics 67 (2003) 351–382   361

Table 1
Summary statistics and ratio analysis

The table presents summary statistics of Malaysian firms in the Worldscope database. The numbers reported are simple averages except as noted. Listed *p*-values are from *t*-tests of differences of means, except for last two rows, which are tests of proportions. "Politically connected" refers to a firm with identifiable political connections from Gomez and Jomo (1997). "Ethnically favored" refers to a firm controlled by Bumiputeras (primarily indigenous Malays). "Foreign capital access" means that the firm either had its stock listed on a non-Malaysian exchange or had issued debt on the Eurobond market in the 1990s prior to the start of the crisis. A financial firm is defined as one with primary SIC in the range 6000–6999. Financial figures are based on the last reported financial statements prior to July 1997. Data points are missing for some items, thus the number of observations included for each average may vary.

	All Worldscope firms							Nonfinancial firms only			
	All	Politically connected	Unconnected	(p-value)	Mahathir connected	Anwar connected	(p-value)	All	Politically connected	Unconnected	(p-value)
Number of firms	424	67	357		53	14		312	50	262	
RETURNS											
July 1997 to August 1998	−78.5%	−83.0%	−77.7%	(0.010)	−83.4%	−81.3%	(0.529)	−78.1%	−82.1%	−77.3%	(0.065)
September 1998 to	39.7%	53.2%	37.1%	(0.000)	61.7%	31.3%	(0.021)	38.7%	50.5%	36.1%	(0.007)
October 1998 to September 2000	81.9%	83.5%	81.7%	(0.897)	69.8%	132.2%	(0.036)	81.6%	94.8%	79.1%	(0.348)
SIZE AND GROWTH											
Total assets ($000)	986,606	1,845,217	820,423	(0.012)	1,799,914	2,013,485	(0.816)	599,554	1,299,733	465,535	(0.000)
Total asset growth (1-year)	50.3%	67.3%	46.8%	(0.301)	81.7%	20.3%	(0.376)	42.3%	39.3%	42.9%	(0.834)
PROFITABILITY											
Return on assets	4.0%	−1.2%	4.9%	(0.041)	−3.0%	5.2%	(0.604)	3.7%	−2.7%	4.9%	(0.062)
Profit margin	7.1%	9.7%	6.6%	(0.868)	8.9%	12.3%	(0.681)	1.6%	8.2%	0.3%	(0.746)
LIQUIDITY											
Current ratio	1.77	1.53	1.82	(0.432)	1.52	1.61	(0.846)	1.69	1.54	1.72	(0.516)
Quick ratio	1.26	1.20	1.27	(0.791)	1.27	0.93	(0.423)	1.26	1.21	1.27	(0.807)

Table 1 (continued)

	All Worldscope firms							Nonfinancial firms only			
	All	Politically connected	Unconnected	(p-value)	Mahathir connected	Anwar connected	(p-value)	All	Politically connected	Unconnected	(p-value)
ASSET UTILIZATION											
Asset turnover ratio	0.55	0.47	0.56	(0.147)	0.44	0.55	(0.421)	0.65	0.56	0.66	(0.170)
Inventory turnover ratio	9.43	12.70	8.82	(0.101)	14.79	5.47	(0.195)	9.50	12.71	8.91	(0.116)
LEVERAGE											
Total debt/Total assets (TD/TA)	23.7%	33.7%	21.9%	(0.000)	36.0%	24.6%	(0.298)	26.1%	36.9%	24.0%	(0.000)
Short-term debt/Total debt (STD/TD)	61.8%	57.1%	62.8%	(0.216)	56.8%	58.5%	(0.869)	61.7%	59.3%	62.2%	(0.573)
Increase in TD/TA	2.7%	6.3%	2.0%	(0.062)	8.4%	−70.0%	(0.334)	3.2%	7.7%	2.3%	(0.046)
Increase in STD/TD	−2.2%	−7.7%	−1.1%	(0.088)	−7.6%	−7.9%	(0.975)	−1.9%	−8.9%	−0.5%	(0.062)
OTHER											
Book/market ratio	0.45	0.47	0.45	(0.568)	0.50	0.36	(0.105)	0.42	0.45	0.42	(0.450)
Percent with foreign capital access	29.0%	47.8%	25.5%	(0.000)	47.2%	50.0%	(0.850)	28.2%	50.0%	24.0%	(0.000)
Percent ethnically favored	26.4%	22.6%	27.2%	(0.495)	27.9%	0.0%	(0.058)	26.4%	29.2%	25.8%	(0.642)

S. Johnson, T. Mitton / Journal of Financial Economics 67 (2003) 351–382   363

Table 2
Political connections and pre-crisis firm characteristics
The table reports coefficient estimates from regressions of firm characteristics on a political connections indicator. All Malaysian firms with available data in the Worldscope database are included. Also estimated but not reported is a constant term and industry dummy variables. Profitability is return on assets, defined as net income divided by total assets (expressed in whole percentages). Leverage is defined as total debt over total assets (expressed in whole percentages). Firm size is the log of total assets; growth is the one-year growth rate in total assets. All financial variables are measured at the end of the last full year of financial results before July 1997. "Politically connected" means the firm has an identifiable connection with key government officials from Gomez and Jomo (1997). The number of observations varies in each specification due to missing data on net income and total asset growth. Numbers in brackets are heteroskedasticity-robust t-statistics. Asterisks denote levels of significance: *** means significant at the 1% level, ** is the 5% level, and * is the 10% level.

	Panel A: Profitability			Panel B: Leverage		
	Nonfinancial firms	Nonfinancial firms	All firms	Nonfinancial firms	Nonfinancial firms	All firms
	Dependent variable is pre-crisis return on assets			Dependent variable is pre-crisis debt ratio		
Politically	−11.588	−11.726	−8.960	12.480*	5.100*	4.677**
connected	[−1.02]	[−0.96]	[−0.98]	[1.68]	[1.84]	[2.01]
Firm size	4.801	5.084	3.860	−0.057	1.997	2.758
	[1.29]	[1.32]	[1.22]	[-0.02]	[1.02]	[1.51]
Firm growth		1.442	0.838		1.114	−0.129
		[0.69]	[0.90]		[0.71]	[−0.17]
Profitability					−0.634***	−0.630***
					[−23.10]	[−23.87]
Number of observations	305	270	358	312	270	358
R-squared	0.042	0.045	0.040	0.094	0.572	0.528

outperformed Mahathir-connected firms over this later period, although as we explain below this is probably because most were forced into the Mahathir camp after September 1998.

The fifth row of Table 1 shows that, in terms of total assets, politically connected firms were significantly larger (about twice the size on average) compared with unconnected firms, although asset growth immediately before the crisis was not significantly greater in connected firms (row 6). There is no evidence that Mahathir-connected firms had more assets on average than Anwar-connected firms.

The seventh row of Table 1 suggests that politically connected firms were less profitable than unconnected firms (in terms of return on assets) before the crisis. We further investigate the profitability of firms in Table 2. Panel A of Table 2 shows that once we control for other firm characteristics, there is no evidence that politically connected firms had lower profitability before the crisis.[8] With return on assets (in

_____

[8] Using data through 1995, fewer firms, and a different specification, Samad (n.d.) finds that politically connected firms have higher profitability but no difference in investment behavior.

the last full year of financial results prior to July 1997) as the dependent variable, the dummy variable for being politically connected is consistently insignificant. The separate dummies for Mahathir-connected and Anwar-connected are also not significant in a regression with profitability as the dependent variable (not reported here).

Table 1 reports very little other difference in the operational efficiency of favored and unfavored firms.[9] The ratios for profitability (profit margin in row 8), liquidity (current ratio and quick ratio), and asset utilization (asset turnover ratio and inventory turnover ratio) show no significant differences across the dimensions of political connections (in terms of *t*-tests of the means). The book-to-market ratio is one way to examine whether investors perceive that there is expropriation of assets by managers or controlling shareholders. These ratios are not significantly different for any group of firms before the crisis. Overall, we find no evidence suggesting that favored firms performed differently during the crisis because they were better- or worse-run before the crisis.

4.1. Corporate indebtedness

If politically connected firms had greater leverage prior to the crisis, then this could explain some or all of the performance differences. A firm with higher debt would naturally be expected to perform worse in a crisis both because of the effect of leverage on a firm's covariation with the market and also because the depreciation of the local currency will hurt a firm if any of its debt is denominated in foreign currency. In addition, if the government responds to the crisis by raising interest rates—as in Malaysia early in the crisis—this will raise the cost of servicing corporate debt. The data on leverage in Table 1 shows that firms with political connections had debt–asset ratios some 11 percentage points higher, on average, than unconnected firms prior to the crisis. However, politically connected firms had less short-term debt and while total debt to assets before the crisis was rising faster in politically connected firms, the opposite was true for short-term debt. These differences are only rough measures, however, in that they do not account for differences in industry or other characteristics.

Panel B of Table 2 presents the results of regressions intended to measure the effect of political favoritism on levels of debt more carefully. We estimate the following model:

$$Debt\ ratio = a + b_1(Political\ Connections) + b_2(Size) + b_3(Profitability)$$
$$+ b_4(Growth) + b_5(Industry Dummies) + e, \qquad (1)$$

where the inclusion of size, profitability, and growth follows the lead of Lee, Lee, and Lee (2000).

Panel B of Table 2 confirms that politically connected firms had more debt before the crisis. For nonfinancial firms only, including all control variables, politically

---

[9] In related work, Pomerleano (1998) uses ratio analysis to study the East Asian crisis, but focuses on differences across countries rather than differences among firms within a country.

S. Johnson, T. Mitton / Journal of Financial Economics 67 (2003) 351–382   365

connected firms had debt ratios five percentage points higher (with the coefficient significant at the 10% level). The final column of Panel B shows that the results are similar if all firms are included in the sample.

Panel B of Table 2 shows that controlling for size, profitability, growth, and industry accounts for some, but not all, of the difference in leverage between favored and unfavored firms. Specifically, larger firms had higher debt ratios, as predicted by Titman and Wessels (1988), and more-profitable firms had lower debt ratios, as would be suggested by Myers (1977). Nonfinancial firms with higher growth had higher debt ratios. Only the coefficient on profitability is consistently significant at standard levels, however. Because firms with political connections still had significantly higher debt ratios even after controlling for these other factors, we control for levels of debt in all of our subsequent empirical analysis.

5. Results

This section presents our main results and robustness checks. To assess the impact of political connections on stock price performance during various periods, we estimate the following model:

$$Stock\ Return = a + b_1(Political\ Connection\ Variables)$$
$$+ b_2(Size) + b_3(Debt\ Ratio) + b_4(Industry\ Dummies) + e, \quad (2)$$

where the stock return is measured over the indicated period and the political connection variables change according to the specification.

Olson's argument about the nature of rent seeking suggests two hypotheses for Malaysia:

(1) The stock price of politically connected firms should have fallen more in the early crisis period.
(2) The stock price of politically connected firms should have risen more once capital controls were imposed. Within the set of politically connected firms, the benefits of capital controls should be concentrated in firms that were linked to Mahathir rather than Anwar in September 1998.

We examine the evidence for each of these hypotheses in turn.

5.1. The early crisis: July 1997–August 1998

Table 3 presents the results from these regressions for the period from July 1997 to August 1998. In the first three columns, the politically connected dummy variable is included. For nonfinancial firms, the coefficient on the politically connected dummy is −0.075, indicating that a political connection is associated with a greater stock price decline of 7.5 percentage points, on average, during the crisis period of July 1997 through August 1998. For financial firms, the coefficient is similar, at −0.077. These coefficients are significant at the 1% level of confidence. The control variables

Table 3

Political connections and crisis-period stock returns

The table reports coefficient estimates from regressions of stock returns on political connection variables and control variables over the Asian crisis period of July 1997 to August 1998. All Malaysian firms with available data in the Worldscope database are included. Also estimated but not reported are a constant term and industry dummy variables. "Politically connected" means the firm has an identifiable connection with key government officials from Gomez and Jomo (1997). "Mahathir connected" and "Anwar connected" indicate the source of the political connection as in Gomez and Jomo (1997). Firm size is measured as the log of total assets; the debt ratio is measured as total debt over total assets. Numbers in brackets are heteroskedasticity-robust t-statistics. Asterisks denote levels of significance: *** means significant at the 1% level, ** is the 5% level, and * is the 10% level.

	Political connections			Mahathir and Anwar connections		
	Nonfinancial firms	Financial firms	All firms	Nonfinancial firms	Financial firms	All firms
	Dependent variable is stock return from July 1997 to August 1998					
Politically connected	−0.075***	−0.077***	−0.077***			
	[−2.97]	[−3.42]	[−3.88]			
Mahathir connected				−0.079***	−0.091***	−0.083***
				[−2.78]	[−3.58]	[−3.64]
Anwar connected				−0.059	−0.046	−0.056*
				[−1.61]	[−1.34]	[−2.06]
Firm size	0.074***	0.041*	0.070***	0.074***	0.042*	0.070***
	[5.19]	[1.71]	[5.56]	[5.19]	[1.75]	[5.56]
Debt ratio	−0.0014*	−0.0011	−0.0014**	−0.0014*	−0.0010	−0.0014**
	[−1.87]	[−1.65]	[−2.10]	[−1.85]	[−1.53]	[−2.07]
Number of observations	312	112	424	312	112	424
R-squared	0.269	0.095	0.236	0.269	0.099	0.237

for size and leverage are also significant in these regressions, with larger size being associated with higher returns during the crisis, and higher leverage with lower returns.

In the last three columns, we include separate dummies for connections to Mahathir or Anwar. Both types of politically connected firms had worse stock price performance than did unconnected firms. Among nonfinancial firms, Mahathir-connected firms had a greater decline of 7.9 percentage points, and Anwar-connected firms had a greater decline of 5.9 percentage points. The difference in performance between Mahathir- and Anwar-connected firms is small in this time period.

Note that depending on the precise specification, as many as six of the 12 industry dummies are significant in our "crisis period" regressions. The agricultural sector does relatively well, presumably because the demand for agricultural products is less susceptible to downturns. The other sector dummies that are usually significant are industrial (i.e., manufacturing, which is positive), utilities (also positive), and service firms (also positive). Most important for our analysis, we find that including industry dummies does not weaken the coefficients on the political connection variables.

In the first phase of the financial crisis, therefore, favoritism based on personal relationships had a strongly negative effect on the stock price performance of

S. Johnson, T. Mitton / Journal of Financial Economics 67 (2003) 351–382 367

Malaysian firms. This is broadly consistent with the Rajan and Zingales (1998) view that firms with strong political connections suffer more in a financial crisis, presumably because the expected value of subsidies declines. It is hard to know exactly what the Malaysian government was doing with regard to such subsidies in 1997–1998, but Anwar's policy was to follow tight budget discipline along the lines of a de facto IMF program (although Malaysia did not sign up for official IMF conditionality). There was also a certain amount of political rhetoric regarding the need to reduce cronyism (and various statements from both Anwar and Mahathir about who was or was not a "crony"). Our results indicate that the market interpreted the policies of July 1997 to August 1998 as squeezing politically connected firms.

5.2. The effects of capital controls

If politically connected firms performed poorly during the first phase of the crisis because the connections themselves decreased in value, then the Olson view predicts that connected firms would rebound more than unconnected firms when capital controls were imposed.

In general, it could be difficult to differentiate a rebound based on political connections from a rebound based on operating characteristics of firms. But Malaysian political events allow for a cleaner test. September 1998 marked both the imposition of capital controls and also the downfall of the second-most-powerful political figure in Malaysia, Deputy Prime Minister (and Finance Minister) Anwar. Once considered Mahathir's certain successor, Anwar was fired on September 2, 1998, and then jailed on charges of corruption and sodomy on September 20, 1998. Clearly, over the course of September 1998, these events reduced the value of political connections for firms with strong ties to Anwar. To the extent that politically connected firms enjoyed a rebound in September due to the increased value of their connections, we would not expect the same increase in value to be enjoyed by Anwar-connected firms.

Table 4 presents the results of regressions of stock returns for September 1998 on the same variables as in Table 3. The first three columns present results for the political connections indicator. Politically connected firms as a whole enjoyed a rebound in September 1998. Among nonfinancial firms, a higher return of 8.1 percentage points, not significant at standard levels, can be attributed to political connections. The effect is stronger among financial firms, where connected firms on average had a higher return of 28.5 percentage points, which is significant at the 1% level. For all firms combined, the political connections coefficient shows a higher return of 13.8 percentage points, and is significant at the 5% level.

The final three columns of Table 4 present results for connections broken down between Mahathir and Anwar. Among nonfinancial firms, Mahathir-connected firms on average experienced higher returns of 13.0 percentage points, significant at the 10% level, while Anwar-connected firms on average experienced lower returns of 11.6 percentage points, for a net difference of 24.6 percentage points between Mahathir- and Anwar-connected firms. The effect is even stronger among financial

Table 4
Political connections and stock returns following the imposition of capital controls
The table reports coefficient estimates from regressions of stock returns on political connection variables and control variables for the period September 1998. All Malaysian firms with available data in the Worldscope database are included. Also estimated but not reported are a constant term and industry dummy variables. "Politically connected" means the firm has an identifiable connection with key government officials from Gomez and Jomo (1997). "Mahathir connected" and "Anwar connected" indicate the source of the political connection as in Gomez and Jomo (1997). Firm size is measured as the log of total assets; the debt ratio is measured as total debt over total assets. Numbers in brackets are heteroskedasticity-robust t-statistics. Asterisks denote levels of significance: *** means significant at the 1% level, ** is the 5% level, and * is the 10% level.

	Political connections			Mahathir and Anwar connections		
	Nonfinancial firms	Financial firms	All firms	Nonfinancial firms	Financial firms	All firms
	Dependent variable is stock return for September 1998					
Politically connected	0.081	0.285***	0.138**			
	[1.23]	[2.69]	[2.42]			
Mahathir connected				0.130*	0.403***	0.199***
				[1.76]	[3.02]	[2.98]
Anwar connected				−0.116	0.027	−0.063
				[−1.11]	[0.24]	[−0.81]
Firm size	0.014	−0.038	0.001	0.015	−0.043	0.000
	[0.42]	[−0.50]	[0.04]	[0.43]	[−0.58]	[0.01]
Debt ratio	0.0036***	0.0018	0.0032***	0.0035***	0.0012	0.0031***
	[3.48]	[0.89]	[3.53]	[3.40]	[0.58]	[3.35]
Number of observations	302	111	413	302	111	413
R-squared	0.142	0.115	0.128	0.154	0.153	0.143

firms, where Mahathir-connected firms had higher returns of 40.3 percentage points, significant at the 1% level. Among all firms combined, Mahathir-connected firms on average had higher returns of 19.9 percentage points, significant at the 1% level, while Anwar-connected firms on average had lower returns of 6.3 percentage points. This result suggests that the value of political connections themselves was an important determinant of the fortunes of Malaysian firms during the crisis.

5.3. Variation within connected firms

If capital controls constrain financial flows across borders, we would expect to see smaller gains for connected firms having access to international capital markets compared to connected firms without such access. Table 5 repeats our basic

S. Johnson, T. Mitton / Journal of Financial Economics 67 (2003) 351–382 369

Table 5
Capital controls and the interaction of political connections and foreign capital access

The table reports coefficient estimates from regressions of stock returns on political connection variables interacted with foreign capital access for the periods indicated. All Malaysian firms with available data in the Worldscope database are included. Also estimated but not reported are a constant term and industry dummy variables. "Mahathir connected" and "Anwar connected" indicate the source of the political connection as in Gomez and Jomo (1997). "Foreign capital access" indicates that the firm's stock is traded in a foreign market in addition to Malaysia or the firm has issued debt on the Eurobond market. Firm size is measured as the log of total assets; the debt ratio is measured as total debt over total assets. Numbers in brackets are heteroskedasticity-robust t-statistics. Asterisks denote levels of significance: *** means significant at the 1% level, ** is the 5% level, and * is the 10% level.

	Crisis period: July 1997 to August 1998			Capital controls imposed: September 1998		
	Nonfinancial firms	Financial firms	All firms	Nonfinancial firms	Financial firms	All firms
	Dependent variable is stock return for period indicated					
Mahathir connected*Foreign capital access	−0.068* [−1.75]	−0.082*** [−2.82]	−0.072** [−2.34]	0.122 [1.29]	0.221 [1.42]	0.157* [1.93]
Mahathir connected*No foreign capital access	−0.091*** [−2.80]	−0.097*** [−2.85]	−0.093*** [−3.46]	0.135 [1.32]	0.542*** [3.19]	0.232** [2.51]
Anwar connected*Foreign capital access	−0.120** [−2.46]	−0.121*** [−5.79]	−0.120*** [−3.39]	−0.185 [−1.17]	0.191* [1.93]	−0.074 [−0.58]
Anwar connected*No foreign capital access	0.014 [0.69]	0.007 [0.21]	0.010 [0.50]	−0.031 [−0.27]	−0.103 [−0.71]	−0.054 [−0.59]
Firm size	0.075*** [5.31]	0.043* [1.77]	0.071*** [5.55]	0.017 [0.50]	−0.037 [−0.50]	0.003 [0.08]
Debt ratio	−0.0015* [−1.92]	−0.0010 [−1.30]	−0.0014** [−2.14]	0.0035*** [3.37]	0.0002 [0.11]	0.0031*** [3.33]
Number of observations	312	112	424	302	111	413
R-squared	0.274	0.110	0.243	0.156	0.184	0.144

370 *S. Johnson, T. Mitton / Journal of Financial Economics 67 (2003) 351–382*

regressions, breaking down Mahathir- and Anwar-connected firms according to whether or not they had access to foreign capital.

Column 4 of Table 5 shows that among nonfinancial firms, gains were slightly higher for Mahathir-connected firms without access to foreign capital, with a coefficient of 0.135 compared to 0.122. The difference is more pronounced among Anwar-connected firms, where firms without foreign capital access (coefficient of −0.031) had higher returns than firms with foreign capital access (coefficient of −0.185). Column 5 of Table 5 shows that among financial firms, gains were significantly higher for Mahathir-connected firms without foreign capital access, with a coefficient of 0.542 (significant at the 1% level) compared to 0.221. However, the same pattern does not hold among Anwar-connected firms, where financial firms with foreign capital access performed worse. Column 6 of Table 5 shows that with all firms combined, firms without foreign capital access did somewhat better among both Mahathir- and Anwar-connected firms.

While the evidence is not especially strong, the results from Table 5 are consistent with the idea that capital controls affected Malaysian firms' access to foreign finance. Presumably all Mahathir-connected firms gained some subsidies or access to local capital when capital controls were imposed. But a second effect was that some connected firms also lost their previous access to international capital.

5.4. Economic significance of political connections

Our estimated coefficients indicate that the "political connections" effect is large relative to one of the most important characteristics of firms—their leverage. From Column 3 of Table 3, the coefficient on the debt ratio is −0.0014. Leverage (the debt ratio) is expressed in percentage points, i.e., for a firm with total debt to total assets (TD/TA) of 55%, the variable would be 55.0. An increase in the debt ratio of ten percentage points (e.g., from the median debt ratio of 23.3 to 33.3) would thus correspond to a lower crisis-period return of 1.4 percentage points. The coefficient on the politically connected dummy is −0.077 when we also control for debt, meaning that politically connected firms had a lower crisis-period return of 7.7 percentage points compared to unconnected firms. Put together, this means that having political connections had an effect similar to increasing the debt ratio by 55.0 percentage points (e.g., from the median of 23.3% to around 78%). The standard deviation of TD/TA is 22.5, so having political connections is roughly equivalent to a $2\frac{1}{2}$-standard deviation increase in the debt ratio during the "crisis period."

For September 1998, the magnitude is similar. The coefficient of 0.0032 on the debt-asset ratio (from Column 3 in Table 4) corresponds to a higher return of 0.32 percentage points for each percentage point increase in the debt ratio. So the higher return of 13.8 percentage points for politically connected firms is equivalent to the effect of increasing the debt ratio by 43 percentage points (e.g., from the median debt ratio of 23.3% to 66%). In sum, for both periods, the leverage effect is strong, but the political connections effect is arguably much stronger.

For an alternative measure of economic significance, we use our regression coefficients to estimate the impact of connections on the total market value of firms.

S. Johnson, T. Mitton / Journal of Financial Economics 67 (2003) 351–382 371

We find that during the crisis period, roughly $5.7 billion of the market value lost by connected firms is attributable to their political connections. When capital controls were imposed in September 1998, although market valuations were then on a smaller scale, political connections accounted for an incremental gain of roughly $1.3 billion in market value for connected firms.[10]

As a measure of the size of the effect of political connections in relation to the total variation in returns, we note that in regressions with September 1998 returns, the R-squared of the regression rises incrementally from 0.109 to 0.143 when the political connection variables are added. This suggests that roughly 3.4% of the total variation in returns is explained by differences in political connections. For regressions of returns for the initial crisis period, adding political connection variables increases the R-squared from 0.210 to 0.237, suggesting that 2.7% of the total variation in returns is explained by differences in political connections.

By looking at the outcomes for Anwar- and Mahathir-connected firms separately in September 1998, we can obtain an estimate of the value of political connections as a percentage of total firm value after capital controls were imposed. If we assume that the events of September 1998 destroyed all remaining value of Anwar connections and restored the full value of Mahathir connections, then the loss due to Anwar connections added to the gain due to Mahathir connections should roughly equal the total percentage of firm value attributable to political connections. Our regression coefficients from Column 6 of Table 4 show that Mahathir connections account for a 19.9% increase in firm value in September 1998, while Anwar connections are associated with a 6.3% decrease in firm value. In terms of (higher) valuations at the end of September 1998, these percentages would be about 12% and 5% respectively. Summed together, these estimates suggest that political connections accounted for about 17% of the total market value of connected firms after the events of September 1998. While only a rough estimate, this figure is within the 12–23% range estimated by Fisman (2001) for connected firms in Indonesia.

5.5. Econometric issues

We address several econometric issues to ensure the validity of our results. We use heteroskedasticity-robust standard errors throughout our regression analysis. The significance of our results is not altered if we adjust the standard errors of the coefficients to account for clustering of observations among firms with the same connected entrepreneur. Additionally, multicollinearity does not seem to be a problem in the model, as the average variance inflation factor of the coefficients is about 1.5 with September 1998 returns or crisis-period returns as the dependent variable (with maximum variance inflation factors no greater than 2.8). Also, errors-

---

[10] The estimates of the effects of political connections on market value are based on our estimated regression coefficients, monthly stock prices, and available data on the number of shares outstanding for each firm. Because the number of shares outstanding is not known for every month and is missing for three of the connected firms, the estimated figures are not exact calculations, but reasonable estimates.

372   *S. Johnson, T. Mitton / Journal of Financial Economics 67 (2003) 351–382*

in-variables regressions indicate that our results are not particularly sensitive to measurement error.

Perhaps the most important econometric issue is that errors across firms might not be independent because returns are correlated in calendar time. A lack of pre-crisis stock return data for many of the Malaysian firms in Worldscope prevents us from using some standard methodologies to address this issue. As an alternative approach, we use a diagnostic measure to assess whether correlation of errors across firms appears to be affecting our inferences. We run simulated regressions of the actual return data on a wide variety of randomly generated hypothetical variables. In 10,000 repetitions using September 1998 returns, we find that the coefficients on the hypothetical variables are significant at the 1% level in 1.07% of the repetitions, at the 5% level in 5.27% of the repetitions, and at the 10% level in 9.97% of the repetitions. (The corresponding percentages using crisis-period returns are 0.85%, 4.87%, and 9.61%, respectively.) The lack of spuriously significant coefficients indicates that correlation of the errors is probably not a serious problem in these data.

5.6. Robustness checks

We perform a number of tests in order to check the robustness of the central result that favored firms performed differently during the initial crisis and after the imposition of capital controls compared with unfavored firms. Our results do not appear to be dominated by outliers. All of our key results are robust to truncating the data at the first and 99th percentiles of observations on stock returns, firm size, or debt ratios.

Table 6 provides further robustness checks by adding control variables to our basic regressions. Due to space considerations, we present results for nonfinancial firms only. As discussed in Section 2, some Malaysian firms have advantages because they are officially ethnically favored. Note that the government publicly states its support for Bumiputera businesses and has implied that any direct measures to support firms were primarily designed to help Bumiputeras. For example Prime Minister Mahathir writes, "Recovery must be accompanied by the equitable distribution of the economic pie between *Bumiputeras* and *non-Bumiputeras*. Failure to do so could result in the kind of race riots that broke out in May 1969" (Mahathir, 2000. p. 20). Perkins and Woo (2000) also argue that the government helped Bumiputera firms after the imposition of capital controls. In Panel A of Table 6, we find that whether a firm is officially ethnically favored is not significant and including it does not have a large effect on our political connections coefficients. For crisis-period returns, the coefficient on the Anwar-connected dummy becomes slightly positive. For September 1998 returns, the difference in performance between Mahathir-connected and Anwar-connected firms becomes even more pronounced. These results show that political favoritism, and not simply ethnicity, was the more important factor in determining the fortunes of Malaysian firms during this period.

In Panel B of Table 6 we use the log of net sales as an alternative measure of firm size. The results are essentially unchanged. In other robustness checks (not reported)

Table 6

Robustness checks

The table reports coefficient estimates from regressions of stock returns on political connection variables and control variables during the periods indicated. All nonfinancial Malaysian firms with available data in the Worldscope database are included, except in Panel C where only firms included in International Finance Corporation indexes are included. Also estimated but not reported are a constant term and industry dummy variables. Numbers in brackets are heteroskedasticity-robust t-statistics. Asterisks denote levels of significance: *** means significant at the 1% level, ** is the 5% level, and * is the 10% level. "Ethnically favored" indicates that the firm is controlled by Bumiputera (primarily ethnic Malay) interests. The number of observations is smaller in Panel A because ethnicity is not identifiable for all firms. "Mahathir connected" and "Anwar connected" indicate the source of the political connections of Malaysian firms as in Gomez and Jomo (1997). Firm size is measured as the log of net sales (sales data are missing for 16 firms). The debt ratio is measured as total debt over total assets.

	Panel A: Control for ethnicity		Panel B: Alternative size measure		Panel C: IFC firms only	
	Crisis period: July 1997 to Aug 1998	Capital controls: Sept 1998	Crisis period: July 1997 to Aug 1998	Capital controls: Sept 1998	Crisis period: July 1997 to Aug 1998	Capital controls: Sept 1998
	Nonfinancial firms only (all columns); dependent variable is stock return in period indicated					
Mahathir connected	−0.074** [−2.59]	0.1565* [1.90]	−0.072** [−2.61]	0.1624** [2.19]	−0.073*** [−2.17]	0.1290 [1.10]
Anwar connected	0.014 [0.41]	−0.268** [−2.06]	−0.062* [−1.70]	−0.081 [−0.79]	−0.089* [−1.91]	−0.236 [−1.66]
Ethnically favored	0.022 [1.26]	−0.009 [−0.20]				
Firm size	0.065*** [4.27]	0.031 [0.78]	0.029*** [4.65]	−0.018 [−1.55]	0.101*** [4.67]	−0.060 [−0.95]
Debt ratio	−0.0029*** [−6.81]	0.0037*** [3.02]	−0.0014* [−1.92]	0.0039*** [3.72]	−0.0006 [−0.75]	0.0041** [2.02]
Number of observations	239	232	306	296	116	109
R-squared	0.373	0.174	0.285	0.175	0.383	0.362

we repeat our regressions using a number of other size measures. Our results are robust to including variables for total assets (or sales), total assets (or sales) squared, and total assets (or sales) cubed, as well as the logarithms of all these measures, either separately or in combinations. In short, there is no evidence that size effects are driving our results. Panel C presents the results of regressions with the sample restricted to firms included in the International Finance Corporation (IFC) Global Index. The motivation for using this subsample is to address the concern that some Malaysian stocks in our base sample are not as liquid as others, and thus we could be using some uninformative stock prices. The IFC includes stocks in its Global Index only if they are among the largest and most liquid stocks in the country. In addition, the quality of data reported to Worldscope is often better for IFC Global Index firms. In the IFC Global Index subsample, the coefficients on the Mahathir-connected and Anwar-connected dummies are only slightly different for the crisis period. For the September 1998 period, the coefficient on Mahathir-connected is virtually unchanged; its significance falls, but the sample size is now only 109 firms. The coefficient on Anwar-connected becomes even more strongly negative, falling to -0.236.

In Table 7 we provide further checks on our results by examining the performance of firms in other time periods. In Panel A of Table 7 we regress returns from the year immediately preceding the crisis on our political connection and control variables. Panel A shows that Anwar-connected firms performed relatively well during this period (perhaps due to Anwar's rising influence), but the coefficients on the Mahathir-connected and Anwar-connected dummies are not significant at standard levels. This shows that in contrast to this earlier period, the political connection variables have much greater explanatory power during the crisis and its accompanying political events.

In Panel B of Table 7 we address an alternative interpretation of our results by examining performance in February 1998. The alternative interpretation is that politically connected firms could have done relatively well in September 1998 simply because the market rebounded in that month. Would connected firms have done well in any market recovery irrespective of whether that upturn involved the imposition of capital controls? The data do not support this alternative interpretation. February 1998 was a strong upturn month in the middle of the early crisis period (see Fig. 1). In regressions with stock returns for this month only, the coefficients on the political connection variables are not significantly different from zero, i.e., politically connected firms did not do well just because there was an upturn in the market. We have run similar regressions for returns in November 1998 and April 1999, the two other largest percentage jumps in the index through the end of 2000. In neither case are the political connection variables significant, or even close to being significant. (Results for these months are not reported in the tables to save space; they are available from the authors.) These findings support the hypothesis that in September 1998 the relatively good performance of well-connected firms was due to the political events of that month.

Finally, in Panel C we examine firm performance in the two years following September 1998. Anwar-connected firms did relatively well during this period,

S. Johnson, T. Mitton / Journal of Financial Economics 67 (2003) 351–382 375

Table 7

Political connections and stock returns during other periods

The table reports coefficient estimates from regressions of stock returns on political connection variables for the periods indicated. All Malaysian firms with available data in the Worldscope database are included. Also estimated but not reported are a constant term and industry dummy variables. "Mahathir connected" and "Anwar connected" indicate the source of the political connection as in Gomez and Jomo (1997). Firm size is measured as the log of total assets; the debt ratio is measured as total debt over total assets. Numbers in brackets are heteroskedasticity-robust t-statistics. Asterisks denote levels of significance: *** means significant at the 1% level, ** is the 5% level, and * is the 10% level.

	Panel A: Pre-crisis July 1996 to June 1997		Panel B: Early upturn February 1998		Panel C: Later period Oct 1998 to Sept 2000	
	Nonfinancial firms	All firms	Nonfinancial firms	All firms	Nonfinancial firms	All firms
	Dependent variable is stock return for period indicated					
Mahathir connected	−0.052	−0.075	−0.022	−0.041	0.226	−0.036
	[−0.54]	[−1.08]	[−0.28]	[−0.64]	[1.23]	[−0.23]
Anwar connected	0.577	0.436	0.058	0.013	0.449	0.369
	[1.03]	[1.19]	[0.45]	[0.13]	[1.13]	[1.30]
Firm size	0.037	0.044	−0.028	−0.049	−0.067	0.029
	[0.71]	[0.94]	[−0.76]	[−1.40]	[−0.73]	[0.35]
Debt ratio	−0.0013	−0.0010	−0.0002	0.0000	−0.0017	−0.0023
	[−1.58]	[−1.42]	[−0.23]	[−0.02]	[−0.59]	[−0.93]
Number of observations	277	375	311	422	298	407
R-squared	0.041	0.040	0.013	0.019	0.056	0.053

perhaps because (as discussed below) these firms generally shifted allegiance to Mahathir during this period. But again we see that the political connection variables have no significance during this later period. We test key subperiods of this two-year period and also find no significance of these variables. The crisis and the imposition of capital controls appear to have been unusually powerful political and market events.

6. Support for favored firms after the imposition of capital controls

What did the Malaysian government do once capital controls were imposed? Some general reflationary measures were taken, including cutting interest rates and making credit more readily available to consumers and firms (Kaplan and Rodrik, 2001; Mahathir, 2000, Chapter 8). Mahathir and Daim also encouraged banks to lend more, and announced bailouts for troubled firms (Perkins and Woo, 2000). A new expansionary budget was introduced in October 1998 (Perkins and Woo, 2000).

376   *S. Johnson, T. Mitton / Journal of Financial Economics 67 (2003) 351–382*

There also appear to have been both increased subsidies for some pro-Mahathir firms and punishments for firms that were allied with Anwar. The anecdotal evidence strongly supports the idea that the government used the economy's isolation from short-term capital flows to restore implicit subsidies for some favored firms. The precise distribution of subsidies is hard to measure, as they are usually not reported publicly. However, we can discern the three main forms of these subsidies from high-profile incidents that have been reported in the international media.

First, the state-owned oil company, Petroliam Nasional Bhd. (known as Petronas), has been called upon to provide bailouts to particular distressed firms (Jayasankaran, 1999a). In the most prominent case, Petronas injected cash into the national car company Perusahaan Otomobil Nasional, known as Proton (Restall, 2000a).[11] In mid-1998, Petronas also acquired the shipping assets of the Prime Minister's son, Mahathir Mirzan, who was facing financial difficulties (Lopez, 2001).

Second, a number of companies have received advantageous deals directly from the government. In December 2000, the government bought back the 29% stake held by Tajudin Ramli in Malaysian Air System (MAS), the operator of Malaysian Airlines. The price was reported to be about twice the market price, effectively bailing out Mr. Tajudin while at the same time putting MAS on a firmer financial footing.[12] There has also been serious discussion of the government buying back the assets of two unprofitable privatized light-rail projects in Kuala Lumpur. This would benefit primarily Renong Bhd., controlled by Halim Saad who is reported to be close to the ruling party (Prystay, 2000).

Third, the most significant changes have arguably occurred within the banking system. The government has supervised a process of consolidation, including instructing 58 financial institutions to merge, creating ten "superbanks." The final picture is not yet settled, but it is clear that bankers who were connected to Anwar are likely to do relatively badly and those with connections to Daim will do relatively better (Jayasankaran, 1999b). At the same time, large companies, such as Renong and the Lion group, have been allowed to repeatedly roll over their debts (Dhume et al., 2001).

All three forms of subsidies could benefit minority shareholders, in part because they put the supported firms on a stronger financial basis and reduce the incentives to transfer resources out of the firms (Johnson et al., 2000). In addition, however, the government has permitted companies to carry out actions that might otherwise be considered violations of laws protecting minority shareholders. The most prominent case involves Renong, which is financially distressed but has a "well-connected" chairman (Restall, 2000b). In November 1997, a subsidiary of Renong, United

---

[11] Petronas is not the only government-controlled institution used to save firms. Khazanah Nasional Bhd., the powerful state-owned investment fund, has proved to be an alternative vehicle for providing financial support. For example, in 2000 it purchased shares in Renong's telecom unit (Jayasankaran, 2000).

[12] Mr. Tajudin has a great deal of debt: $263 million personally and 900 million ringgit borrowed by Naluri, the listed company in which Mr. Tajudin owns 44% and which in turn holds the stake in MAS (Asian Wall Street Journal weekly edition, July 31–August 6, 2000). He has had difficulty servicing these loans.

S. Johnson, T. Mitton / Journal of Financial Economics 67 (2003) 351–382 377

Engineers Malaysia, received a waiver of stock market rules, in order to provide a bailout to its parent. The stock market fell sharply on this news, and some observers interpreted this reaction as indicating that the government would have difficulties if it provided further support to favored firms. However, in October 1998 after capital controls were in place, the government took over and paid off some of Renong's debts (Perkins and Woo, 2000).[13] Again in late 2000, United Engineers Malaysia agreed to purchase $1.8 billion of problem assets from Renong. Shareholders have protested these actions.

While it is impossible to measure the size and nature of Malaysian subsidies precisely, the weight of anecdotal evidence supports the notion that well-connected firms received direct and indirect financial support from the government after the imposition of capital controls. This suggests that the market reaction to the imposition of capital controls in September 1998 was correct in anticipating that particular well-connected firms would receive greater subsidies.

In addition, we have investigated the fate of the firms in the Appendix that are listed as affiliated primarily to Anwar. As far as we can ascertain, all of these firms have either been taken over by pro-Mahathir management or the owners have switched allegiance to Mahathir. In many cases there have been asset transfers out of these firms and into firms more closely aligned with Mahathir. Again, it seems that the stock market in September 1998 correctly anticipated what would happen.

6.1. Assessment

Malaysia's macroeconomic performance after the imposition of capital controls was good. Growth was 4.7% in 1999, although there remains a controversy about whether it would have been higher or lower without capital controls (Kaplan and Rodrik, 2001; Dornbusch, 2001a). At the same time, there is clear evidence of some government support for favored firms, both directly and—more commonly— through various forms of indirect subsidies.

Weak institutions in Malaysia mean that the allocation of government favoritism is of first-order importance for firm-level outcomes. As a result, when hit by the initial Asian crisis, favored firms suffered large falls in expected subsidies. The imposition of capital controls, on the other hand, allowed the government to channel greater resources (and provide other advantages) to firms with strong political connections to the Prime Minister. The interaction of shocks and institutions therefore had a large impact on the distribution of outcomes at the firm level.

7. Conclusion

The evidence from Malaysia strongly supports the idea that firms with political connections were expected to lose subsidies in the first phase of the Asian crisis.

---

[13] Halim Saad, chairman of Renong, is quoted as saying "Yes, the government helped. But our creditors will get paid 100% with interest and with no haircuts. What's wrong with that?"(Jayasankaran, 2000).

Table A1

The table lists Malaysian firms in the Worldscope database that have an identifiable connection with high-ranking political figures. The information is compiled from Gomez and Jomo (1997). Under "Primary political connection," Mahathir refers to Mahathir Mohamad, Daim refers to Daim Zainuddin, and Anwar refers to Anwar Ibrahim. "UMNO" refers to the United Malays' National Organisation, an ethnically based political party that dominates the government's ruling coalition.

Company name	Primary connected major shareholder/director	Primary political connection
ADVANCE SYNERGY BHD	Ahmad Sebi Abu Bakar	Daim, Anwar
ANTAH HOLDINGS BHD	Negeri Sembilan royalty	Mahathir
AOKAM PERDANA BHD	Samsudin Abu Hassan	Daim
ARAB MALAYSIAN CORPORATION BHD	Azman Hashim	UMNO
AUSTRAL AMALGAMATED BHD	Samsudin Abu Hassan	Daim
BAN HIN LEE BANK BHD	Quek Leng Chan	Anwar
BANDAR RAYA DEVELOPMENTS BHD	MCA	MCA
BERJAYA GROUP BHD	Vincent Tan Chee Yioun	Daim
BERJAYA SPORTS TOTO BHD	Vincent Tan Chee Yioun	Daim
COLD STORAGE (MALAYSIA) BHD	Basir Ismail, Samsudin Abu Hassan	Daim
CONSTRUCTION AND SUPPLIES HOUSE	Joseph Ambrose Lee, Abdul Mulok Awang Damit	Daim
CYCLE & CARRIAGE BINTANG BHD	Basir Ismail	Daim
DAMANSARA REALTY BHD	Koperasi Usaha Bersatu Bhd	UMNO
DATUK KERAMAT HOLDINGS BHD	Koperasi Usaha Bersatu Bhd	UMNO
DIVERSIFIED RESOURCES BHD	Yahya Ahmad, Nasaruddin Jalil	Anwar, Mahathir
EKRAN BHD	Ting Pek Khiing	Daim, Mahathir, Abdul Taib Mahmud
FABER GROUP BHD	UMNO	UMNO
GADEK (MALAYSIA) BHD	Yahya Ahmad, Nasaruddin Jalil	Anwar, Mahathir
GEORGE TOWN HOLDINGS BHD	Tunku Abdullah	Mahathir
GOLDEN PLUS HOLDINGS BHD	Ishak Ismail, Mohamed Sarit Haji Yusoh	Anwar
GRANITE INDUSTRIES BHD	Samsudin Abu Hassan	Daim
HICOM HOLDINGS BHD	Yahya Ahmad	Anwar, Mahathir
HO HUP CONSTRUCTION COMPANY BHD	Halim Saad	Daim
HONG LEONG BANK BHD	Quek Leng Chan	Anwar
HONG LEONG CREDIT BHD	Quek Leng Chan	Anwar
HONG LEONG INDUSTRIES BHD	Quek Leng Chan	Anwar
HONG LEONG PROPERTIES BHD	Quek Leng Chan	Anwar
HUME INDUSTRIES (MALAYSIA) BHD	Quek Leng Chan	Anwar
IDRIS HYDRAULIC (MALAYSIA) BHD	Ishak Ismail	Anwar
KAMUNTING CORPORATION BHD	T.K. Lim	Daim
KFC HOLDINGS (MALAYSIA) BHD	Ishak Ismail	Anwar
KINTA KELLAS PUBLIC LIMITED CO	Halim Saad	Daim

S. Johnson, T. Mitton / Journal of Financial Economics 67 (2003) 351–382 379

Company	Person(s)	Connection
KRETAM HOLDINGS BHD	UMNO Youth, Wan Azmi Wan Hamzah	Daim
KUMPULAN FIMA BHD	Basir Ismail	Daim
LAND & GENERAL BHD	Wan Azmi Wan Hamzah	Daim
LANDMARKS BHD	Samsudin Abu Hassan	Daim
MAGNUM CORPORATION BHD	T.K. Lim	Daim
MALAKOFF BHD	Malaysian Resources	UMNO
MALAYSIAN AIRLINE SYSTEM BHD	Tajudin Ramli	Daim
MALAYSIAN RESOURCES CORPORATION	UMNO, Wan Azmi Wan Hamzah	Daim, Anwar
METROPLEX BHD	Dick Chan	Unspecified
MULTI-PURPOSE HOLDINGS BHD	T.K. Lim	Daim
MYCOM BHD	Mohd Tamrin Abdul Ghafar	Ghafar Baba
NANYANG PRESS (MALAYA) BHD	Quek Leng Chan	Anwar
NEW STRAITS TIMES PRESS (MALAYSIA)	Unspecified	Anwar
O.Y.L. INDUSTRIES BHD	Quek Leng Chan	Anwar
PACIFIC CHEMICALS BHD	Ting Pek Khiing, Robert Tan	Daim, Mahathir, Abdul Taib Mahmud
PENGKALEN HOLDINGS BHD	Joseph Ambrose Lee, Abdul Mulok Awang Damit	Daim
PRIME UTILITIES BHD	Ahmad Sebi Abu Bakar	Daim, Anwar
PROMET BHD	Ibrahim Mohamed	Mahathir
R.J. REYNOLDS BHD	Wan Azmi Wan Hazmah	Daim
RASHID HUSSAIN BHD	Wan Azmi Wan Hamzah	Daim
RENONG BHD	Halim Saad	Daim
SAPURA TELECOMMUNICATIONS BHD	Shamsuddin bin Abdul Kadir	Mahathir
SETRON (MALAYSIA) BHD	Penang Bumiputera Foundation, Kamaruddin Jaafar	Anwar
SISTEM TELEVISYEN MALAYSIA BHD	UMNO Companies	UMNO
STAR PUBLICATIONS (MALAYSIA) BHD	Vincent Tan Chee Yioun	Daim
TAIPING CONSOLIDATED BHD	Vincent Tan Chee Yioun	Daim
TANJONG PUBLIC LIMITED COMPANY	T. Ananda Krishnan	Mahathir
TECHNOLOGY RESOURCES INDUSTRIES	Tajudin Ramli	Daim
TIME ENGINEERING BHD	Halim Saad	Daim
TONGKAH HOLDINGS BHD	Mokhzani Mahathir	Mahathir
UNIPHOENIX CORPORATION BHD	Ibrahim Mohamed	Mahathir
UNIPHONE TELECOMMUNICATIONS BHD	Shamsuddin bin Abdul Kadir	Mahathir
UNITED ENGINEERS (MALAYSIA) BHD	Halim Saad	Daim
UNITED MERCHANT GROUP BHD	Ahmad Sebi Abu Bakar	Daim, Anwar
UNITED PLANTATIONS BHD	Basir Ismail	Daim
UTUSAN MELAYU (MALAYSIA) BHD	UMNO	UMNO
WEMBLEY INDUSTRIES HOLDINGS BHD	Ishak Ismail	Anwar
YTL CEMENT BHD	Yeoh Tiong Lay	Unspecified
YTL CORPORATION BHD	Yeoh Tiong Lay	Unspecified
YTL POWER INTERNATIONAL BHD	Yeoh Tiong Lay	Unspecified

Conversely, firms connected to the Prime Minister were expected to gain subsidies when capital controls were imposed in September 1998.

The presence of political connections in East Asian economies does not mean that "cronyism" caused the crisis or even that "relationship-based capitalism" was necessarily a suboptimal system for these countries. While politically connected firms were hit harder during the crisis, the evidence presented here does not suggest that this was a punishment for past misdeeds and deficiencies. The evidence suggests rather that the crisis implied that previously favored firms would lose valuable subsidies, and the imposition of capital controls indicated that these subsidies would be restored for some firms.

Our Malaysian results offer empirical evidence that is consistent with the general idea of Blanchard (2000), who argues that macroeconomic dynamics depend on institutional structures: "Institutions also matter for short-run fluctuations, with different mechanisms across countries" (p. 1404). There is growing evidence that institutions matter for long-term growth (e.g., Acemoglu et al., 2001.) A great deal remains to be done, however, to understand precisely how institutions affect short- and medium-term outcomes.

Appendix A. Malaysian firms and their political connections are provided in Table A1.

References

Acemoglu, D., Johnson, S., Robinson, J., 2001. The colonial origins of comparative development: an empirical investigation. American Economic Review 91, 1369–1401.

Annual Companies Handbook, 1996–1998. Kuala Lumpur Stock Exchange, Kuala Lumpur.

Bhagwati, J., 1998a. The capital myth. Foreign Affairs, May.

Bhagwati, J., 1998b. Why free capital mobility may be hazardous to your health: lessons from the latest financial crisis. NBER Conference on Capital Controls, November 7.

Blanchard, O., 2000. What do we know about macroeconomics that Fisher and Wicksell did not? Quarterly Journal of Economics 115, 1375–1410.

Campbell, J., 1996. Understanding risk and return. Journal of Political Economy 104, 298–345.

Dhume, S., Crispin, S., Jayasankaran, S., Larkin, J., 2001. Economic reform—running out of steam. Far Eastern Economic Review, January 18.

Dornbusch, R., 2001a. Malaysia: was it different? NBER working paper 8325.

Dornbusch, R., 2001b. Amazing, but true: Japan is bust. Unpublished working paper, Massachusetts Institute of Technology.

Ekelund, R., Jr., Tollison, R., 1981. Mercantilism as a Rent-Seeking Society: Economic Regulation in Historical Perspective. Texas A&M University Press, College Station, Texas.

Fisman, R., 2001. It's not what you know…estimating the value of political connections. American Economic Review 91, 1095–1102.

Gomez, E.T., Jomo K.S., 1997. Malaysia's Political Economy: Politics, Patronage and Profits, First Edition. Cambridge University Press, Cambridge.

Gomez, E.T., Jomo K.S., 1998. Malaysia's Political Economy: Politics, Patronage and Profits, Second Edition. Cambridge University Press, Cambridge.

Jayasankaran, S., 1999a. Saviour complex. Far Eastern Economic Review. August 12.

Jayasankaran, S., 1999b. Merger by decree. Far Eastern Economic Review. September 9.

Jayasankaran, S., 2000. Entrepreneurs—a question of honour: renong Group chairman Halim Saad wins a postponement of a purchase of shares he is committed to buy; the markets are appalled. Far Eastern Economic Review, December 21.

Johnson, S., Boone, P., Breach, A., Friedman, E., 2000. Corporate governance in the Asian financial crisis, 1997–1998. Journal of Financial Economics 58, 141–186.

Jomo K.S., 2001. Malaysian Eclipse: Economic Crisis and Recovery. Zed Books Ltd, London and New York.

Kaplan, E., Rodrik, D. 2001. Did the Malaysian capital controls work? NBER working paper 8142.

Krugman, P., 1998. Saving Asia: it's time to get radical. Fortune, September 7.

La Porta, R., Lopez-de-Silanes, F., Shleifer, A., Vishny, R., 1997. Legal determinants of external finance. Journal of Finance 52, 1131–1150.

La Porta, R., Lopez-de-Silanes, F., Shleifer, A., Vishny, R., 1998. Law and finance. Journal of Political Economy 106, 1115–1155.

La Porta, R., Lopez-de-Silanes, F., Zamarippa, G., 2002. Related lending. NBER working Paper 8848.

Lee, J.-W., Lee, Y.S., Lee, B.-S., 2000. The determination of corporate debt in Korea. Asian Economic Journal 14 (4).

Lemmon, M., Lins, K., 2003. Ownership structure, corporate governance, and firm value: evidence from the East Asian financial crisis. Journal of Finance, forthcoming.

Lins, K., Strickland, D., Zenner, M., 2000. Do non-U.S. firms issue stock on U.S. equity markets to relax capital constraints? Unpublished working paper. University of Utah.

Lopez, L., 2001. Mokhzani Mahathir exits two firms—Prime Minister's son says he wants to put to rest accusations of nepotism. The Asian Wall Street Journal, April 30.

Mahathir, M., 2000. The Malaysian Currency Crisis: How and Why it Happened. Pelanduk Publications, Selangor Darul Ehsan.

Mitton, T., 2002. A cross-firm analysis of the impact of corporate governance on the East Asian financial crisis. Journal of Financial Economics 64, 215–241.

Morck, R., Strangeland, D., Yeung, B., 2000a. Inherited wealth, corporate control and economic growth: the Canadian disease? In Morck, R. (Ed.), Concentrated Corporate Ownership. NBER and the University of Chicago Press, Cambridge.

Morck, R., Yeung, B., Yu, W., 2000b. The information content of stock markets: why do emerging markets have synchronous stock price movements? Journal of Financial Economics 58, 215–260.

Myers, S., 1977. The determinants of corporate borrowing. Journal of Financial Economics 5, 147–175.

Olson, M., 1982. The Rise and Decline of Nations. Yale University Press, New Haven and London.

Parente, S., Prescott, E., 1994. Barriers to technology adoption and development. Journal of Political Economy 102, 298–321.

Perkins, D.H., Woo, W.T., 2000. Malaysia: adjusting to deep integration with the world economy. In Woo, W.T., Sachs, J., Schwab, K. (Eds.), The Asian Financial Crisis: Lessons for a Resilient Asia. MIT Press, Cambridge, MA, 2000.

Petersen, M., Rajan, R., 1995. The effect of credit market competition on lending relationships. Quarterly Journal of Economics 110, 407–443.

Pomerleano, M., 1998. East Asian crisis and corporate finances: the untold story. Emerging Markets Quarterly 2:4, 14–27.

Prystay, C., 2000. Malaysia reverses course in privatization program—government nationalizes two light-rail projects. The Asian Wall Street Journal, December 27.

Rajan, R., Zingales, L., 1998. Which capitalism? Lessons from the East Asian crisis. Journal of Applied Corporate Finance 11, 40–48.

Rajan, R., Zingales, L., 2001. The great reversals: the politics of financial development in the 20th century. Unpublished working paper, Massachusetts Institute of Technology and University of Chicago.

Reese, W. Jr., Weisbach, M., 2002. Protection of minority shareholder interests, cross-listings in the United States, and subsequent equity offerings. Journal of Financial Economics 66, 65–104.

382   *S. Johnson, T. Mitton / Journal of Financial Economics 67 (2003) 351–382*

Restall, H., 2000a. Malaysia's national car hurts Malaysians. Asian Wall Street Journal weekly edition, August 28–September 3.

Restall, H., 2000b. Reading Malaysia's Rorschach test. Asian Wall Street Journal weekly edition, December 11–17.

Rodrik, D., 2000. Exchange rate regimes and institutional arrangements in the shadow of capital flows. Unpublished working paper, Harvard University.

Samad, M.F.B.A., no date. Performance of politically affiliated businesses in Malaysia: a summary of principal findings. Unpublished working paper, University of Malaya.

Titman, S., Wessels, R., 1988. The determinants of capital structure choice. Journal of Finance 43, 1–19.

Index

Page numbers in *italics* appear in Volume I; those in **bold** appear in Volume II.

Page numbers in *italics* appear in Volume I; those in **bold** appear in Volume II.

Page numbers in *italics* appear in Volume I; those in **bold** appear in Volume II.

Page numbers in *italics* appear in Volume I; those in **bold** appear in Volume II.

Page numbers in *italics* appear in Volume I; those in **bold** appear in Volume II.